LEWIS MUMFORD

LEWIS MUMFORD

Public Intellectual

Thomas P. Hughes
Agatha C. Hughes

New York   Oxford
OXFORD UNIVERSITY PRESS   1990

Oxford University Press

Oxford New York Toronto
Delhi Bombay Calcutta Madras Karachi
Petaling Jaya Singapore Hong Kong Tokyo
Nairobi Dar es Salaam Cape Town
Melbourne Auckland
and associated companies in
Berlin Ibadan

Published by Oxford University Press, Inc.,
200 Madison Avenue, New York, New York 10016

Library of Congress Cataloging-in-Publication Data
Hughes, Thomas P.
Lewis Mumford : public intellectual / Thomas P. Hughes and Agatha C. Hughes.
p. cm.
ISBN 0-19-506173-X
1. Mumford, Lewis, 1895–1990—Views on technology and civilization—Congresses.
2. Technology and civilization—Congresses.
3. Technology—Social aspects—Congresses.
I. Hughes, Agatha C. II. Title.
HM221.M78H84 1990 303.48′3—dc20 89-26510

9 8 7 6 5 4 3 2 1

Printed in the United States of America
on acid-free paper

To Sophia Wittenberg Mumford

Preface

A happy combination of circumstances brought the Lewis Mumford conference to the University of Pennsylvania. The voluminous Mumford Papers are on deposit in the university's Van Pelt Library; Penn has a large and active department of the history of science which emphasizes the history and sociology of modern technology; in 1984 a group of Penn scholars from a wide variety of disciplines established a seminar on Technology and Culture; and the Andrew W. Mellon Foundation through its Program for Assessing and Revitalizing the Social Sciences provided funds for this seminar and the special conference on Mumford that drew scholars from the United States and abroad. The conference generated so much information, so many interesting points of view, and such a variety of imaginative interpretations of the Mumford oeuvre that there was general agreement that the papers should be published.

This volume, however, is not one more set of conference papers. Once the decision to publish was made and the Oxford University Press expressed interest in publication, the essays were subject to formal review. Drawing on these reviews, on what the participants had learned from each other about Mumford at the conference, and on general editorial comment, the authors substantially revised their essays for publication. In addition, the editors have drawn central and unifying themes from the various essays and structured the volume accordingly. As a result, we believe that this volume, along with Donald Miller's recently published biography of Mumford, will stimulate renewed interest in Mumford as arguably America's pre-eminent twentieth-century public intellectual, an author whose books and ideas remain highly relevant to the social and intellectual issues of our day.

The editors appreciate the enthusiastic co-operation of the various authors during the two years that this volume has been in preparation. They also wish to acknowledge the critical role that the members of the Penn seminar on Technology and Culture played in organizing and presenting the conference. Members of the seminar dedicated two of their on-going meetings to Mumford and several provided commentaries at the conference on the papers presented. These were David Brownlee; Margali Larson; David Leatherbarrow; Kathleen Reed; Alfred Rieber; Marsha Siefert; and Frank Trommler.

The conference provided the occasion for several concurrent exhibitions. Dr. Kathleen Reed of Special Collections at the University of Pennsylvania Library organized a rich display of Mumfordiana from the Mumford collection of papers, and Jane Morley of the Department of the History and Sociology of Science organized with the generous co-operation of Monmouth College and Vincent DiMattio an exhibition of Mumford's drawings and paintings. Several televised interviews with Mumford were also shown. These visual encounters along with the Mumford art made the participants feel closer to him and compensated somewhat for the absence of the ailing Mumford who had earlier endorsed the conference. But the presence of Sophia, Lewis's wife, provided an even greater compensation. The participants found conversations with her providing nuances and insights into the creative life she has shared so intimately and for so many years with her husband.

We also wish to acknowledge the support of Dr. Daniel Traister, Assistant Director of the Libraries of Special Collections at Penn, and his staff, especially Ms. Nancy Shawcross who assisted us and other authors in making use of the Mumford Papers. In addition, Edward Lurie, a consultant to the Oxford University Press, has actively furthered the publication of this volume as has Sheldon Meyer, Vice President of the Press. Oxford's Leona Capeless provided wise counsel on matters editorial. Finally, we wish to express our heartfelt gratitude to Jane Morley whose inspired contribution as the executive administrator of the conference contributed immeasurably to its success.

Chestnut Hill, Philadelphia, 1989.   A.C.H. and T.P.H.

As this book goes to press,
we are saddened to learn that Lewis Mumford
died at his home in Leedsville, New York, on 26 January 1990.
He was ninety-four years old.

Contents

Contributors

Casey Blake, Assistant Professor of History at Indiana University, is the author of *Beloved Country: The Cultural Criticism of Randolph Bourne, Van Wyck Brooks, Waldo Frank, and Lewis Mumford* (forthcoming).

Richard Wightman Fox, Associate Professor of History and Humanities at Reed College, is the author of *Reinhold Niebuhr: A Biography* (1986) and *So Far Disordered in Mind: Insanity in California, 1870–1930* (1979); and co-editor of *The Culture of Consumption: Critical Essays in American History, 1880–1980* (1983).

Leo Marx, Keenan Professor of American Cultural History at the Massachusetts Institute of Technology, is the author of *The Machine in the Garden* (1964), and *The Pilot and the Passenger* (1988); and editor, with Susan Danly, of *The Railroad in American Art* (1988).

Everett Mendelsohn, Professor of the History of Science at Harvard University, focuses his work on both the history of the life sciences and the history of the social relations of science. He had an opportunity to work directly with Lewis Mumford, in the 1970s, while they were engaged in helping devise a school curriculum on "People and Technology."

Donald L. Miller, Professor of History and Chairman of the American Civilization Program at Lafayette College, is the author of *Lewis Mumford: A Life* (1989), editor of *The Lewis Mumford Reader* (1986), and co-author of *The Kingdom of Coal* (1985).

Arthur Molella, Chair of the Department of History of Science and Technology at the Smithsonian's National Museum of American History, was an editor of *The Papers of Joseph Henry* and is currently working on the historiography of the history of technology.

Charles Molesworth, Professor of English and Chairperson of the English Department, Queens College, City University of New York, is author, most recently, of *Marianne Moore: A Literary Biography* (1990). He has also published two books of poetry and three books of literary criticism.

Stanislaus von Moos, Professor of the History of Modern Art at the University of Zürich, is the author of *Venturi, Rauch, and Scott Brown: Buildings and Projects* (1987) and *Le Corbusier: Elements of a Synthesis* (1976); and editor of the exhibition catalogue, *L'Esprit Nouveau: Le Corbusier et l'Industrie, 1920–1925* (1987).

Eugene Rochberg-Halton, Associate Professor in the Department of Sociology at the University of Notre Dame, and currently a Visiting Fellow at Yale University, is the author of *Meaning and Modernity* (1986) and co-author of *The Meaning of Things* (1981).

Howard P. Segal, Associate Professor of History and Director of the Technology and Society Project at the University of Maine, is the author of *Technological Utopianism in American Culture* (1985) and co-author of *Technology in America: A Brief History* (1989).

John L. Thomas, George L. Littlefield Professor of American History at Brown University, is the author of *The Liberator: William Lloyd Garrison* (1963), and *Alternative America: Henry George, Edward Bellamy, Henry Demarest Lloyd and the Adversary Tradition* (1983).

Lawrence J. Vale, with a doctorate from Oxford University, where he was a Rhodes scholar, is presently at the Massachusetts Institute of Technology, where he is working on the relations between politics and architecture. He is author of *The Limits of Civil Defence* (1987).

Allen Tullos teaches American studies at Emory University. He is editor of the journal *Southern Changes;* co-producer of the documentary films "Born for Hard Luck," "Being a Joines: A Brushy Mountain Album," and "A Singing Stream"; and author of *Habits of Industry: White Culture and the Transformation of the Carolina Piedmont* (1989).

Robert Westbrook teaches modern American history at the University of Rochester. He is the author of *John Dewey and American Democracy* (1980) as well as many essays on American cultural and intellectual history.

Rosalind Williams, Assistant Professor in the Department of Humanities, Massachusetts Institute of Technology, is the author of *Dream Worlds: Mass Consumption in Late Nineteenth-Century France* (1982) and *Notes on the Underground: An Essay on Technology, Society, and the Imagination* (1990).

Michael Zuckerman, Professor of History at the University of Pennsylvania, author of *Almost Chosen People* (forthcoming), has written recently on such disparate subjects as early American identity, Thomas Jefferson's racism, and the fate of the Constitution in the age of Ollie North.

LEWIS MUMFORD

General Introduction:
Mumford's Modern World

Through Lewis Mumford (1895–1990) we have a unique window on characteristic problems of this technological century and an arresting, sometimes idiosyncratic array of proposed solutions. He sought in a usable past[1] and in utopian visions a critical stance that would allow him to take the measure of modern times. Though an author of books and essays on an astoundingly wide range of subjects and a proposer of solutions to a vast spread of social problems, he never lost sight of his ultimate goal of providing an understanding of life lived in a modern technological, or human-made environment. A few other American intellectuals have faced up to the omnipresence of technology as artifacts and ideas in modern industrial culture, but none has persisted throughout a lifetime in the effort to comprehend the ever-changing interplay of technology and other constituents of modern culture. His remarkable and singular contribution to our understanding of the era in which we live has resulted from this unremitting interest. Books and articles by technological enthusiasts who are notoriously uncritical and by intellectuals who are unrelentingly biased against technology because they consider it destructive of the human spirit and of the social fabric have been commonplace in twentieth-century America. Familiar, too, are the works of intellectuals who, ill-informed about technology, write about social problems without considering the possibility that these are complexly rooted in technological realities. Mumford, on the other hand, is no technological enthusiast but the rare intellectual who recognizes the destructive as well as the constructive nature of modern technology and who tries to foster the spirit and the intellect, to cultivate community, and to nourish the personality. At the same time he becomes ever more aware that these goals have to be pursued in a modern world blessed and cursed by technology. Because of this attitude, a close and loving friend called him a technical intellectual, a person who knew technology yet cherished the life of the mind and the spirit.[2]

Mumford's lifelong commitment to the proposition that technology is the hallmark of modern times originated during his own and the century's formative twenties. Even without a college degree he was able to entrench himself after Word War I as a writer in literary and bohemian New York. He placed a number of articles in the little magazines such as *The Dial, The Freeman, The Nation,* and *The New Republic.* Today the terms "bohemian" and "intellectual" often connote a reaction against technology, but this was not the case before the Great Depression and World War II. In New York such editors of the little magazines as Matthew Josephson, Robert Coady, Jean Heap, and avant-garde artists like Alfred Stieglitz, Charles Sheeler, Charles Demuth, and Georgia O'Keeffe were discovering modern America, and they found it to be a technological culture shaped by prodigious mass-production of goods and conditioned by two centuries of experience as a construction site that had transformed a wilderness into a built environment. Mumford also believed that the modern technology could be the handmaiden of beauty as well as the servant of productivity. He and a few other intellectuals of the 1920s sometimes went so far as to argue that social and psychological redemption would come through the machine.[3] This guarded optimism was never completely extinguished in Mumford—although it became severely eroded. He continued to nourish a lifelong appreciation of technology when it was used as an expression of constructive creativity, and he remained interested in how things worked. In his mid-thirties he spoke of the "fun" of visiting technological museums.[4]

After an early period of youthful technological enthusiasm when he had aspired to be an engineer, and was among the first "lads who monkeyed with radio and . . . was writing articles about apparatus for *Modern Electrics*," Mumford passed through attitudinal phases that anticipated by years, even decades, the mood changes of many other thoughtful Americans who subsequently also reflected on technology and society. These attitudinal changes found expression in his major books that focused on the history and sociology of technology: *Technics and Civilization* (1934) and the two-volume *The Myth of the Machine: I. Technics and Human Development* (1967) and *II. The Pentagon of Power* (1970). Exploring such intellectual and spiritual territory years before it became populated, his attitudes have often proven prophetic of widespread attitudinal shifts among persons generally informed and concerned about the interaction of technology and society. Decades ago he probed, articulated, and took moral positions on the issues and problems, such as technological determinism, with which many intellectuals and the literate public have yet to grapple. Only in the past decade have historians and sociologists of technology and science, for instance, begun a concentrated examination of the interplay of technological determinism and the social—or value—construction of technology.

We can summarize the distinguishing characteristics of each of his attitudinal phases. Initially, he shared in the 1920s the hope of many public figures, opinion makers, and masses of people that technology could, and probably would, usher in an era of material abundance, social harmony, and psychological fulfillment. Theirs was a faith that linked new technology and progress. During these years the American system of mass production seemed to be responding to the American dream of a chicken in every pot and a car in every garage. Even then, however, Mumford qualified his optimism by arguing that technology would fulfill its promise only if there were determined efforts at reform such as one could find in radical programs for regional development and in social democracy.[5]

Then, when he was writing *Technics and Civilization* during the Great Depression, he recognized that this economic and social malaise, along with his reading and reflection during the writing of this history of technology and society, raised doubts in him about his earlier optimism that the technology of a second industrial revolution was moving us into a new and promising world. With this attitudinal shift, he began to question his earlier expectation that the new technology was opening doors we wished to enter; he decided that now the new technology was opening many wrong doors. He felt that we needed revitalized values and institutions in order to redirect technological change and bring new choices. His increased emphasis on values as shapers of technology stemmed in part from his earlier immersion in the literary studies which had resulted in the publication of *The Golden Day* (1926) and *Herman Melville* (1929).

Because of his changing attitudes toward technology, *Technics and Civilization* is bifurcated. The first half, through the chapter "The Neotechnic Phase," is a history of technology from the Middle Ages to the present, enlightened by a number of thematic discourses. This half he structures and gives a Whiggish, or progress, bias by the periodization schema he imposes on the history. This schema organizes the history of technology into three phases: eotechnic (wind and water power and wood materials), paleotechnic (coal, steam, and iron), and neotechnic (electricity and alloys). (Historians more conventionally call the paleotechnic the era of the British Industrial Revolution, and the neotechnic the second industrial revolution.) The next half of the book exhibits a remarkable shift in tone as he eloquently attacks the mechanization and materialism of the paleotechnic era and extols organic growth and values. Besides attacking the surviving forces, institutions, and values of the paleotechnic period, he distances himself from the soft technological determinism implicit in his periodization of history. Years later he wrote that this was at the same time the most original and the most dubious part of the book.[6] As he completed *Technics and Civilization,* he took the position that values and society have often shaped technology and that in the future we must reject a passivity that allows technology to determine the course of history. During the time he was writing *Technics and Civilization* the letters he exchanged with Catherine Bauer, a young woman intensely interested in regional planning— and in Mumford—reveal evidence of an on-going discourse between them about determinism and values. In one letter she questioned the argument that the machine became a condition of our existence before it became an emotive part of it. If one takes this position, how would one explain, she asked, the emotive conditions that led to the acceptance of the machine?[7]

Reviewers at the time tended to concentrate on the portion of the ambivalent book that engaged them. Stuart Chase, author of the popular *Men and Machines* (1929), interpreted Mumford as predicting that technology would bring new freedom. It is puzzling to understand how Chase could write, if he had read the second half of *Technics and Civilization,* that "Mr. Mumford not only accepts the machine, he glories in it." William F. Ogburn, a University of Chicago sociologist, selected the Mumford who describes machines as shaping society—Ogburn's review is titled "The Dictatorship of the Machine." Pursuing a theme he developed elsewhere, Ogburn wanted society to adjust to machine progress. Buckminster Fuller, science and technology enthusiast and inventor, regretted that Mumford did not know more about mathematics and science, but he praised him for providing a comprehensive account of society's growth and dynamism. Herbert Read, an art critic, read *Technics* as a history of the effects the machine had had on civilization. He took exception to Mumford's argument that the introduction of the clock in the fourteenth century shaped history more than the introduction of the steam engine in the eighteenth had done.[8]

The last phase of the Mumfordian intellectual odyssey, his last major attitudinal shift, began at the close of World War II. The loss of his only son Geddes during the war, the dropping of atomic bombs on Hiroshima and Nagasaki, and the onset of the nuclear arms race transformed Mumford into a despairing axiologist, a person clinging to a fading hope that a moral transformation may alter the fateful course of technological development. He speaks of the decade of the Jewish Holocaust and what he calls the nuclear holocaust as one of the worst in human history. Mumford's despair was compounded by his realization that creativity, a human characteristic precious to him, had been perverted. This deep pessimism emerged from the *Myth of the Machine,* which he identified as the fruit of a massive reinterpretation of his views on the history of technology and society, a reinterpretation of *Technics and Civilization.* He intended the new work to be a rewriting of the history of technology "with all the light that linguistics and psychology now throw on it."[9] Contrary to the conventional wisdom of the time, he began to be convinced that technology and science were irrational at their core.[10] Long past was his faith in the soft technological determinism which had led him to believe in the likelihood that our industrial society could move into a neotechnic era characterized by a benign technology that would sustain a new regionalism, one with coherent communities of psychologically fulfilled men and women. No longer was his longing for an organic culture that would displace the mechanical one a minor theme; it became a major theme expressed fortissimo. He stressed that human beings were image- and symbol-makers first, and only later tool-makers; that technology embodied human values, evil and good. On occasion he predicted that industrial society was as fatally doomed as Roman society in the third century had been. Modern society was too sick to realize that it needed a doctor for a mental sickness manifesting "insanity on the widest collective scale."[11] All about him he found those "who are blindly pushing our technology, whipping, indeed flaying that runaway horse, under the impression that they are thereby controlling that dangerous monster."[12] The Mumford of the *Myth of the Machine* is a quite different man from the one who wrote *Technics and Civilization* and saw the probability that the new technology was organic and life support-ing: "One may already say pretty confidently," he said then, "that the refinement, the diminution, and the partial elimination of the machine is a characteristic of the emerging neotechnic economy."[13]

The reviews given *Technics and Human Development,* volume one, in the late 1960s so bitterly disappointed Mumford that he wondered whether he had the courage to proceed with volume two. But, like Ralph Waldo Emer-son's father, he believed, "I still have courage—at least courage enough."[14] Mumford found the front-page review, in the *New York Times Book Review,* of *Technics and Human Development* by Edmund Carpenter, an anthropologist, patronizing and contemptuous.[15] Carpenter wrote that Mumford was "dogmatic, petulant and out of date." Mumford's lament in his book that words like "good" and "bad," "higher" and "lower" were falling into disuse in judging human behavior brought Carpenter to write in his review that "this is just an old man annoyed with his grandchil-dren."[16] Carpenter's main objection to the book lay with its failure to dis-tinguish between the mechanical world of segmentation and sequence, and the electronic world of unity and simultaneity. Carpenter failed to under-stand that Mumford's reference to the megamachine should not have been taken literally as a reference to physical machines; that it was a metaphor for systems of oppressive order and control, characteristics not unknown in a putative electronic world.

Three years later, the long, front-page review by physicist and historian of science Gerald Holton of the second volume, the *Pentagon of Power,* again in the *New York Times Book Review,*[17] also disappointed and angered Mumford. His disappointment must have been heightened by the contrast-ing reactions of Holton and William Shawn, editor of *The New Yorker,* who published a serialized selection from the book and told Mumford, "noth-ing we have done at *The New Yorker* has given me more satisfaction than our publishing "The Megamachine." It is a majestic and awesome work. . . . And it may mark *the* turning point."[18] Holton admired Mum-ford, his friend, as "a marvelously gentle and scholarly man," persuasive and passionately committed to finding the way for humans to live full and spiritually satisfying lives of play, art, sex, friendship, and love in a tech-nological world. Yet Holton's review regrets that, when science and sci-entists were under siege from the counterculture, Mumford in the *Penta-gon of Power* relentlessly attacked scientists, failing to realize that he would find among them many allies in his struggle to loosen the hold of the amoral profit-makers and militarists on the means of production and destruction. Holton also criticizes Mumford not only for his reductionist characterization of science as quantitative and mechanistic—thereby suf-focating the emotional and organic aspects of life—but also for his por-trayal of scientists as compliant members of the military, industrial, and university complex—the most horrendous of the megamachines. Holton predicts that the *Pentagon of Power* will stimulate a two-culture split between Mumford's imagined spheres of the "abstract-mathematical-technical" and the "concrete, the organic, and the human" at a time when persons such as Mumford and many scientists ought instead to close ranks against an anti-intellectual wave and, to quote Holton, "against the technological monstrosities being forced on the nation."

Mumford's change in attitude probably caught Holton and other reviewers familiar with *Technics and Civilization* unawares. In 1934 he had commended scientists for their disinterested search for truth and for their unself-conscious and benign concern for the welfare of humanity; by 1970 he was berating them for their alliance with the military and with capitalism. Their surprise is understandable, for earlier he had idealized nineteenth-century physicists like Michael Faraday and biologists such as Louis Pasteur. His presumption that indifference to power and wealth characterized leading nineteenth- and early twentieth-century scientists, especially biologists, suggests an unexpected naïveté which helped set him up for his post-World War II disillusionment with scientists who involved themselves in the armaments race and worked in profit-driven industrial laboratories.

But in a gesture toward the scientists, Mumford also acknowledges that human beings' marvelous expression of subjective impulses in aesthetic symbols, mechanical systems, and architectural structures has been vastly enhanced by the orderly and co-operative methods of science. He warns, however, that if a balance is not soon established between the subjective (organic and emotive) and the objective (science) that life will be reduced to the level of a computer program and that humans will become passive, machine-conditioned animals. The mechanical—and electronic—systems of production must not be allowed, he argues, to displace the organic world. The forces that drive the spread of technological systems must not override those of organic evolution.[19]

Not only the behavior of scientists in the 1940s disillusioned Mumford, there were other causes for his discontent as well. He attributed the negative reactions to and lack of interest in *Technics and Human Development* to the widening gap between his values and those of society at large. He undoubtedly felt that he and society had been in better tune in the 1920s. The strident tone of the *Pentagon of Power* has been attributed in part to Mumford's disgruntled attitude toward a post-World War II society unable to comprehend and respond to him and his books.[20] He complained that the disintegration of society had reached a point where order, rationality, and purpose—and his books—were ill-regarded.[21]

Even he, however, realized that his despair might be overstated. He decided as he neared the completion of the *Pentagon of Power* that he must not end with a sustained lamentation about society's demoralization, disintegration, and regression, as he had in much of what he had written up to that point. He resolved to offset this impression with an estimate of the effectiveness of positive forces conducive to personal autonomy, to communities situated in organic regions, and to ecological symbiosis. These forces, however, will be overwhelmed, he could not help adding, unless there occurs a dramatic change in values and a displacement of the ideology supporting the power complex. He clung to the slim hope—perhaps compelled by his unwillingness to accept the possibility that destructive, authoritarian technology was unalterably in the saddle—that a conversion in values, well-nigh religious in character, can establish the reign of constructive technological creativity, caring community, and loving personality. Persuaded that existing technology is overwhelmingly destructive of the earth and humans, his only logical recourse was to believe that values could reshape it. If he had continued to hold to his earlier soft determinism, hope would have been extinguished. About this transformation of values he is doubtful,[22] but in his concluding chapters he does suggest the possibility of a great revolution that could displace the mechanical world picture with an organic one.

Generally dispirited, fearful especially of a nuclear holocaust, and exasperated by the failure of those politicians, officers, and scientists presiding over the destructive system of armaments manufacture to attenuate its runaway increase, Mumford, like a physician for the soul, dedicated himself through various media to changing the moral climate, to fostering the spiritual resources that would sustain the benign values that would in turn reshape technology for creative and constructive, not destructive, ends. He realized that his voice would have little effect. Yet, he wrote a friend, hardly any week had passed since that fateful day in August 1946 when the atomic bomb had fallen that he did not actively try to avert that fate. As a result, his energies were given for a decade to lectures and articles about the threat of the nuclear holocaust. He used every literary device at his command from "exhortation to satire, from satire to the jeremiad ('Gentlemen: You are Mad!' [the title of an essay])."[23] As a result, his output— against Mumfordian standards—was meager: only three major books in the twelve years after 1946.

Throughout the decades of his exploring the technology-society relationship when his attitudes shifted, his concept of technology became increasingly complex. During his years in high school and the navy, Mumford seems to have taken the commonplace, hardware view of technology as one of machines, processes, structures, and utensils. When he was writing *Technics and Civilization,* his concept of technology broadened. He began to conceive of technology, which he called "technics" in the German tradition, as more than hardware. He distinguished between *machines,* or specific objects like the printing press or power loom, and *the machine,* a concise reference for an entire technological complex that embraced tools, machines, knowledge, skills, and arts. *The machine* was becoming for him the physical embodiment of the mechanistic means to ends. He was beginning to conceive of technology as problem-solving technique involving order, system, and control, which he referred to in a shorthand fashion as mechanistic. He even began to include institutions in technological problem-solving complexes, or systems, but he preferred to refer to *the machine* rather than to technological systems,[24] thus misleading some critics, as we have noted, into believing that he did not appreciate—though he did—the increasing role of electrical and electronics technology. When he was writing the *Myth of the Machine* he began to refer to *the machine* as the *megamachine,* a system made up of interchangeable parts, inanimate and animate, human, mechanical, and institutional, centrally organized and controlled. Though not explicit enough when he was defining megamachine, Mumford clearly saw that technology was a process of production, not simply the products of the process. He characterized the modern megamachine as a new god which "cannot be approached or argued with, as Moses approached the burning bush or Jonah bargained with God to recall his threat to Nineveh."[25] The essence of technology for the mature Mumford had clearly become orderly, controlled, and systematized production. This belief, because it allowed for the values of order and control to have existed prior to the advent of the megamachine, helped lead him eventually from soft technological determinism to the value determinants, psychological and sociological, of technology. Transcending the various nuances and aspects of technology, machine, and megamachine as he expressed them, his conviction persisted that these activities could not be subsumed under the rubric of economics, a position assigned to technology so often today. In a revealing comment to a friend, he wrote that Marx was concerned about the elimination of profits and the just distribution of goods and services, but that he, Mumford, was more concerned about the wrong goods and services being produced by technology. "The real weakness of the Marx-Engels analysis is that it was too narrowly an analysis of profits rather than products."[26]

At the same time holistic and complex in approach, Mumford sought to understand an interplay more intricate than one simply involving technology and a vaguely defined society. He wanted to fathom a complex involving technology, natural environment, the individual (personality), and society (community). He identified the elements and sometimes analyzed them as if they were entities, but he knew that their intermeshing resulted in a seamless web. In this effort to comprehend interacting, intermeshing complexes, or systems, lies a partial explanation for the sharp criticism that the holistic Mumford often received from academics who were analytical and narrowly specialized. He decided that "there is something in the whole scholarly routine that fosters an antagonism to fresh ideas among the common run of scholars: they turn on an outsider who ventures near them. . . ."[27] The titles of his nearly thirty books reflect his broad interests and his growing tendency to interrelate these. The titles refer to utopias, technics, civilization, culture of cities, faith for living, values for survival, conduct of life, art and technics, and to the transformations of man.[28] The extensive annotated bibliographies in *Technics and Civilization* and the *Myth of the Machine* give evidence of his wide reading in history and the social sciences, mostly in English but occasionally in German. Mumford never defined himself narrowly as a historian, sociologist, urbanist, or cultural and architectural critic, for to do so would have cramped his style, but he partook of some of the defining characteristics of each of these modes of knowing and informing. Russell Jacoby, aware that Mumford with his ranging interests and his broad audience cannot be conventionally labeled, has aptly called him a "public intellectual," a thinker and writer who addresses a literate and general audience about questions and issues undefined or categorized by conventional academic and professional disciplines.[29] Yet as Leo Marx has shown in the opening pages of his essay in this volume, Mumford reached not only a general audience but also the academics with whom he stood in such an ambivalent relationship, for he greatly contributed directly, and through them, to the rise of several new academic fields of study, including the history of technology and American studies.

Mumford was able to address such a broad range of problems and issues, respond to shifting currents of public concern, and at the same time satisfy his persisting interest in technology because he found ways to survive as an independent writer. As such he was free to choose the subjects about which he wrote. He was not constrained by the pressures of employers and institutions. Unlike the modern young academic, he did not have to keep one eye on his tenure-granting colleagues as he chose issues about which to write. The problems he chose did not come down to him through the layers of a bureaucratic structure. To preserve his independence, he turned down numerous editorial and advisory positions and limited his teaching to visiting professorships. There were a number of imaginative, discriminating, and venturesome editors at such book-publishing houses as Boni and Liveright and Harcourt, Brace and at such serious periodicals as *Harper's, Scribner's,* and *The New Yorker,* interested in publishing his work, so that he was not dependent on the editorial policy, even biases, of any of them. Because he, Sophia Mumford, and their two children lived simply, he did not need to write appealingly to a mass public. Supporting a family from his writing, lecturing, and occasional teaching was difficult, however. Not until 1942 could he see sufficient income ahead from royalties and fees for more than a few months at a time. Mumford believed that he and Robert Frost drew close because they knew the insecurity— and integrity—of the independent writer and poet.[30]

Able to range freely in his choice of problems and issues, he did not limit himself to the subject of technology and culture. In time, *Technics and Civilization* and the *Myth of the Machine,* his two major works on technology and culture, may well prove to be his most influential because of our growing realization that technology constructs the parameters of our being; but *The Culture of Cities* (1938) and *The City in History* (1961) may rival them as broad, thought-provoking surveys. These two on cities along with his early book on American architecture, *Sticks and Stones* (1924), and the regular "Sky Line" contributions on architecture published in *The New Yorker* beginning in 1931 established Mumford as the most widely read and arguably the most influential architecture critic of his day. We must not forget the impetus he gave to American literary studies through the publication of *The Golden Day* (1926) and *Herman Melville* (1929). Yet, a broadly interested and cultured intellectual writing about architecture and literature is not rare, while a person of such breadth and depth concerning himself or herself with the place of technology in history and striving to reach a broad literate audience remains rare and, as a result, singularly influential.

Most of Mumford's books remain in print; by 1989 twenty were so listed. An incomplete list of sales also gives evidence that he has been widely read and suggests his influence. By 1989 almost 50,000 paperback copies of *Technics and Civilization*, 11,000 of *Technics and Human Development*, and 11,000 of the *Pentagon of Power*, and, in cloth, 3500 copies of *Technics and Human Development* and 18,000 copies of the *Pentagon of Power* had been sold. (Figures on the number of cloth copies of *Technics and Civilization* are not available.) His most popular book has been *The City in History*, with 31,000 copies in cloth and 100,000 in paperback. The incomplete list of his book sales shows a total of nearly 500,000 since 1938.

Because of the broad-ranging interests and publications of Mumford the public intellectual, the conference at which the following essays were first given had to be broadly conceived. Those invited to present papers were asked to focus on, but not limit themselves to, concepts developed in *Technics and Civilization* and the *Myth of the Machine*. When we discovered that several scholars interested in regionalism and in urban architecture shared an interest in Mumford and placed regionalism and urban architecture in a broad cultural context and that several others interested especially in Mumford's views on values, personality, and community also appreciated his concern with modern technology, we included them in the conference. In retrospect, the broadening of the conference focus seems fortuitous when we recall that in his opening remarks in *Technics and Civilization* Mumford stressed that his original intention in the book was "to deal with the machine, the city, the region, the group, and the personality in a single volume."[31] He decided instead to spread his subjects over several volumes in a series he named "Renewal of Life." It included eventually *Technics and Civilization, The Culture of Cities* (1938), *The Condition of Man* (1944), and *The Conduct of Life* (1951).[32] So one might argue that the conference has caught the essential Mumford with the notable exception of exploring in depth his wide-ranging interest in architecture.

Among paper presenters were those who formally profess American literature, sociology, art history, architectural history, cultural history, intellectual history, American civilization studies, history of science, history of technology, and regional history. Despite their varied disciplinary commitments, the participants in the conference and contributors to this volume realized that they, like Mumford, transcended disciplinary bounds. They found themselves sharing areas of discourse established by the themes running through Mumford's works, the themes associated with his intellectual odyssey and his persistent interest in technology and its various interactions. The tone of the essays, like the conference in which early drafts were first presented, conveys the admiration common among the contributors for Mumford's unswerving dedication to improving the human condition, their respect for his compassion and insights, and their appreciation of the richness and complexity of his mind, even when his reach exceeded his grasp—as it often did. At the same time, these essayists often found contradictions in Mumford's reasoning, rhetoric instead of understanding, scholarship sometimes more derivative than original, repetition of theme and information from book to book, and analogies too clever by half. Yet they felt that the intellectual vistas Mumford unfolded, the synthesis of learning and thought which he created, and the brilliant insights he provided stimulated a memorable conference. We hope that these essays will contribute to similarly stimulating reading, discussion, and reflection.

The essays in this volume have been divided into categories relating to Mumford's attitudinal changes. The first group directs attention to the Mumford who found a pattern in history shaped by technological change and who linked technology and progress. From these essays also emerges his qualifying conviction that progress will follow from technological change only if humans purposefully direct new technology toward desirable social and psychological goals, such as technologically structured regional development. In the next group of essays Mumford's increasing doubts about the benign influences of technology come to the fore as he develops his concepts of the megamachine and the mechanization-organicism dichotomy. These essays are followed by the third group, those exploring Mumford's persistent interest in the possibility that technology socially shaped, especially by appropriate values, can respond to the needs of personality and community. Finally, the two essays in the last section consider Mumford's despair after the tragic misuse of technology in war and his survival of hope despite his despair. We shall briefly, in introductory remarks for each section, draw out from each of the essays the themes which together constitute the odyssey of Lewis Mumford: public intellectual and philosopher of the modern technological age.

These themes display the complexity and even the contradictions in Mumford's attitudes. Yet the strength of his mind and personality manifested itself as he grew older and managed to maintain in a creative tension the diverse attitudes, values, and aspirations that he had held at various times and with varying degrees of conviction throughout his life. He never lost his fascination with invention and discovery despite his anxieties about the fruits of the creative act; his recognition of the influence of tools and machines on the course of history survived despite his growing conviction that mind prevailed over matter; he could sustain a hope for the coming of the neotechnic era despite his awareness that paleotechnic values tended to suffocate the dawn of a new age. He balanced an inclination to withdraw and nurture the personality with a realization that his goals for humanity could be filled only if men and women took action. He nourished a tragic sense of life but never abandoned the hope that miracles might occur and that human beings could find the high road.

PART I

TECHNOLOGY, PROGRESS, AND REGIONALISM

Arthur Molella in the first essay in this section helps us understand why Catherine Bauer, Mumford's close friend and student of regional planning and architecture, called him a "technical" intellectual and why Mumford could appreciate, unlike so many intellectuals today, the creative and constructive side of technological activity. To Mumford, technology was not an inexplicable black box from which streamed goods and services. He was able to peer into the box and appreciate, even intellectually comprehend, its intricate workings. As a youth he had wanted to be an electrical engineer. He tinkered with crystal radios and submitted inventive ideas to *Modern Electrics.* Fortunately for us, he failed math in New York's Stuyvesant High School, so the world lost an engineer but gained a person much rarer, a public intellectual. During World War I he enlisted in the navy and received training in radio, then at the front edge of technological advance. After the war, he delighted in visiting upbeat museums of science and technology and in reading about the progress of invention and how things worked. He was aesthetically pleased by machines, devices, and technical processes, and he shared the fascination for machines widespread in America then. This interest in technical devices and processes endured and informed many of his books and articles even though he later became deeply disturbed by the shaping of society by technology. Molella compares and contrasts Mumford's approach to the history of technology and his appreciation of the creative aspects of things technical with the uncritical enthusiasm of others writing in the period between the two wars about the history of technology.

As we have noted, Mumford deals ambiguously in *Technics and Civilization* with the role of technology in history. Rosalind Williams explores this Mumfordian interpretation in her discussion both of his deterministic scheme for periodizing history and his identification of value-shaped technology. She explains that Mumford derived the periodization in *Technics and Civilization* from Karl Marx, no stranger to determinism, and from Patrick Geddes. In the

1920s Mumford read Marx and was intimately associated with and greatly influenced by the views of Geddes, a Scottish biologist, sociologist, and regional planner whose holistic and organic approach he greatly admired and with whom he regularly corresponded. Mumford's periodization blended Marx's technologically determined stages of history and Geddes's concept of historical stages with names borrowed from anthropology. In *Cities in Evolution* (1915), Geddes substituted *-technic* for *-lithic* in *paleolithic* and *neolithic,* anthropological designations long used for stone-age stages in the evolution of human society. Geddes used paleotechnic to describe the coal, steam, railway, and textile factory era of the early industrial age, especially in Hanoverian and Victorian Britain. By neotechnic, he referred to the electrical power stage of the industrial age that began about mid-nineteenth century and ripened earliest in Germany and the United States around 1870. To these two stages Mumford added the term *"eotechnic"* to characterize the pre-industrial era. As Marx had earlier, Mumford also emphasized that periods of history are identifiable by their predominant energy and materials technology.

Like Mumford, Geddes saw no inconsistency between his periodization with its technological bias and his appreciation of the force of human will as expressed in what he called "life insurgent." Mumford, Williams finds, tried to clarify his seeming ambiguity by arguing that technological determinism often prevailed on a local level, such as the work place, where the physical environment and work process shaped the attitudes and behavior of the worker, but that, on a more general level, values and attitudes shaped the technology and the work place.

In *Technics and Civilization* Mumford also leaned toward geographical determinism in his use of the concept of the valley section. This too was borrowed from Geddes, who thought the valley section the key to understanding human civilization. Geddes graphically portrayed the typical valley section, of which variations could be found throughout the world, as a cross section taken through a geographical region ranging from the high mountains down over plains and lowlands to the sea. The various regions extending from the mountains to the sea—shown from left to right in Geddes's sketches—were populated by fundamental occupational types: miners, foresters or woodsmen, hunters, shepherds, peasants or farmers, and fishermen. Over the centuries these types had taken on geographically determined characteristics which persist today in the makers of the modern world. Mining characteristics appear in modern entrepreneurs who preside over the production of metals;

woodsmen have passed on their characteristics to construction engineers; the hunter spirit manifests itself in the military; nurturant characteristics of shepherds are to be found in the clergy; the frugality of peasants now appears in bankers; and the mobile fisherman has become the merchant-adventurer. Mumford saw the valley section as the site of local technological determinism. Williams finds, however, that Mumford later disclaimed geographical determinism much as he retreated from the technological determinism implicit in the Marx/Geddes periodization.

Despite his inclination toward a soft determinism during the 1920s, he was able, at the same time, to take an activist position in his ventures into the world of policy-making and politics. In articulating a new regionalism, he advocates the purposeful use of neotechnic technology to establish and sustain new regions. In their essays, John Thomas, Allen Tullos, and Howard Segal explain how Mumford equates regionalism with life-enhancing values and with progress toward an ideal community. Mumford finds a precedent to a revitalized community in eighteenth- and nineteenth-century New England and New York state. These regions, he believes, had used economic resources thriftily and intelligently to sustain vital communities with balanced industrial and agrarian activity. For the twentieth century he envisages neotechnic technology, especially electric power, the automobile, the radio, and the telephone, as transforming an industrial society of congested cities into regions with balanced and dispersed communities. Mumford anticipates that after three migrations the fourth will entail a return to the land from megalopolis. The first migration settled the transAppalachian West, the second crowded the industrial cities, and the third heaped people and buildings into the capitalist megalopolis of financial and commercial centers.

Thomas describes how Mumford enriched his regionalist vision through close friendship with Benton MacKaye. A graduate of Harvard College in 1900 who continued his education to receive a masters degree in forestry in 1905, MacKaye is remembered as the creator of the Appalachian Trail. He lived a spartan life and aspired to establish a new social order rooted in America's natural regions. Contacting the young Mumford through mutual friends, MacKaye felt an immediate attraction to him, which Mumford reciprocated. Thomas shares with us the fruits of that friendship and helps us to know Mumford, the activist whose program for change was grounded in his array of intersecting concepts such as stages of history, the valley section, organicism, and life insurgent. Stimulated by MacKaye's broad visions of regionalization, Mumford combined these with the concept of valley section to imagine regions in which, despite their being dispersed throughout the region, the fruits of culture and the products of civilization would be available to everyone.

Segal explains how Mumford conceived of regionalism and decentralization as means of countering the mechanization of life, or the megamachine. In Mumford's mind, regionalism and decentralization were linked with utopianism. *The Story of Utopias* (1922), Mumford's first book, provides a history of utopian thought. He concludes that there were utopias of escape and utopias of reconstruction. Both are idealized projections of the values and technological potential of various societies at particular times. According to Mumford, utopian concepts tell more about the time and place in which they were conceived than about the future. Neither utopias of escape nor of reconstruction can be achieved, but the utopias of reconstruction provide a set of references against which society can evaluate its existing values and technology. Mumford, so persuaded, did not hesitate to draw on his knowledge of utopias to conceptualize a utopian regionalism, not expecting that it would be realized, but using the utopian vision as a measuring rod of progress and as an idealized goal. Segal helps us better understand the Mumford who measured himself and society against standards obvious to the experienced as unrealistic, the Mumford who, for his harsh criticisms in later life was called a Jeremiah. Utopian visions were for him engines of change.

On the other hand, Mumford believed that uncritical utopianism only reinforced the momentum of the megamachine. He foresaw that megamachines could hasten the fulfillment of the hierarchical, even authoritarian, visions of Edward Bellamy and other well-intentioned but myopic nineteenth- and twentieth-century utopians. Their utopias were blueprints—highly ordered projections— requiring the manipulation, systematization, and hierarchical control of political, economic, and social structures, and of people. In these characteristics they resembled, Segal points out, unchanging megamachines without a past or future.

Mumford's views on regionalism, expressed in influential essays, encouraged others throughout the country to pursue regionalist policies, among them Howard Odum of the University of North Carolina at Chapel Hill, who is the subject of Allen Tullos's essay. Odum found Mumford's philosophy of regionalism as set forth in a 1925 regional planning issue of the *Survey Graphic* "an illuminating discussion of the whole problem of regional planning." (Tullos, 117). Odum and the Institute for Research in Social Science which he founded in 1924 took the entire South as a laboratory for regional research and development. Mumford wrote, "thanks to Dr. Howard Odum and his fellow workers, Chapel Hill and the University [of North Carolina] are the home of modern regionalism in America" (Tullos, 111). In fact, however, Odum and his institute abandoned many of the positions that Mumford valued highly. Unlike Mumford the independent writer and public intellectual, Odum depended on the economic and political support of the capitalistic, even paleotechnic, forces that Mumford disdained. Odum, as Tullos points out, did not critically assess the economic and political actors and forces shaping the industralization of the Piedmont region of North Carolina. As a result, co-optation and overcompromise resulted. Mumford's failure to suspect that Odum could not champion "modern regionalism," as Mumford defined it, evidences his repeated failure to realize that it was easier for him, the freelancer, to assume the radical posture and make the provocative remark than for those caged by institutional responsibilities.

Mumford in Historiographical Context

ARTHUR P. MOLELLA

When in the late 1920s Lewis Mumford began his background research for *Technics and Civilization,* he discovered the existence of a rich literature on the history of technology and related subjects. A voracious reader, Mumford devoured hundreds of these books, compiling his findings in an annotated bibliography at the end of *Technics and Civilization.* This bibliography is not only a gift to students of the history of technology but an important guide to the sources of Mumford's thought about the relationship between technology and society. The authors cited by Mumford included historians, economists, political economists, politicians, sociologists, anthropologists, and engineers. Their wide diversity reflected the eclectic mixture of ideas and disciplines that went into the crafting of Mumford's pioneering study of technology in Western civilization.

Not surprisingly, most of Mumford's sources were European, chiefly German, French, and British. As usual, German scholars seemed to lead the way. Of German descent on his mother's side, Mumford was linguistically and intellectually comfortable with their writings. Among the works that Mumford consulted most was Werner Sombart's *Der moderne Kapitalismus,* a work which Mumford described as paralleling *Technics and Civilization* "as the Mississippi might be said to parallel the railway train that occasionally approaches its banks."[1] Although Mumford also admired Karl Marx's *Das Kapital,* he found it overly abstract and much preferred Sombart's Marxian but more concrete approach to understanding the connections between technology and capitalism, a major theme of *Technics and Civilization.*

German scholars also produced definitive compilations. Conrad Matchoss, one of Germany's most famous historians of technology, had produced an exhaustive study of the steam engine, *Die Entwicklung der Dampfmachine* (1908) and a biographical compendium *Männer der Technik* (1925). An "invaluable work" for Mumford was Franz Maria Feldhaus's beautifully illustrated *Ruhmesblätter der Technik* (1926). Ludwig and Theodor Beck produced monumental histories of iron-making and machine-building. These books in turn acquainted Mumford with the textbooks of fifteenth-century German and Italian engineers, who produced the first histories of technology.

Mumford's bibliography also revealed his familiarity with French and British sources for the history of technology and industry. These ranged from the classic *thèâtre des machines* genre of sixteenth- and seventeenth-century mathematicians and engineers, such as Jacques Besson, to the famous *Encyclopédie des sciences, des arts et des métiers,* from which Mumford drew illustrations. Frederic Le Play's *Les Ouvriers européens* (1879) was one of the sociological studies used by Mumford. Of course, the most important sociologist in Mumford's intellectual life was a Scot, Patrick Geddes. Among other British writings, Mumford cited such classics of political economy as Andrew Ure's *The Philosophy of Manufactures* and John Hobson's *The Evolution of Modern Capitalism* (1926), as well as Sidney and Beatrice Webb's studies of British trade-unionism and industrial democracy. Although skeptical of its Victorian moralism, Mumford found valuable information in Samuel Smiles's famous *Lives of the Engineers.*

The European literature, heavily influenced by Marx, defined the terms of the debate on technology and society that formed the core of *Technics and Civilization.* When Mumford's book was published, it stood with the best of the European writings. Yet, Mumford was a thoroughly American intellectual and his approach to the history of technology reflected his American perspective.

It is therefore critically important to understand the American context of Mumford's accomplishment. In comparison with the European contribution, the American literature on the history of technology was in its infancy when Mumford began writing his book. Mumford's bibliography pays special respect to two of his countrymen, A. P. Usher and Thorstein Veblen. The literature was otherwise quite sparse. Yet, interest in the history of technology was quietly growing in 1920s America. Mumford's work was the major but not the only evidence of this new enthusiasm.

By the time *Technics and Civilization* appeared, America had nurtured its own corps of historians of technology, both amateur and professional. Although these new specialists represented a wide range of interests, they tended to fall into four categories, each of which is developed here as a case-study: (1) the museum professional as represented by Carl W. Mitman of the Smithsonian; (2) the amateur enthusiast as represented by Charles Eben Fisher of the Railway and Locomotive Historical Society; (3) the popularizer as represented by Waldemar Kaempffert; (4) the academic scholar as represented by Abbott Payson Usher of the Harvard economics department.

In only a few instances did these people have a direct influence on Mumford. He apparently knew none of them personally and, in general, his approach to the history of technology was quite different from theirs. More important as a context for *Technics and Civilization* were the shared motivations that underlay their writings and Mumford's. If European historians of technology were strongly imbued with Marxist ideology, their American counterparts were far more influenced by a more homespun philosophy centered on the pleasures of technology and invention and their roles in national life.

While Europeans appreciated technology, the love of it was considered essential to the American character. The nation's technological self-image had long been memorialized in such clichés as "Yankee ingenuity." By the 1920s—the peak of the "Machine Age"—technology had become almost a national obsession. No one could avoid the effects of technical change: the steam engine and the locomotive, still vital "paleotechnic" technologies (to use Mumford's expression), had transformed the American landscape. Technical imagery had become the dominant contemporary aesthetic. Margaret Bourke-White's dramatic photographs of gear wheels and other industrial machinery graced art galleries and popular magazines. The machine aesthetic culminated in the widely publicized and controversial *Machine Art* show at the Museum of Modern Art in 1934.[2] Fascination with machines could be seen on many cultural levels—technical and practical, aesthetic, even spiritual.

Historians such as Fisher, Kaempffert, Mitman, and even Usher, the academic scholar, learned about technology not just from books but from field visits and direct experience. Fascinated by mechanical devices and industrial processes, they constantly sought first-hand encounters with technology. They then attempted to fit technological phenomena into a coherent picture of American life, assuming a convergence of technology with traditional values of freedom, happiness, and democracy.

There is no mistaking this fascination with all things technological in Mumford, his dissatisfactions with technological society notwithstanding. In 1922, Mumford wrote to his Scots mentor Patrick Geddes that America was in the throes of a "large technological jump," paced by spectacular developments in radio and aeronautics.[3] Convinced of America's special affinity for the machine, Mumford discovered the roots of authentic American culture in the mechanical arts, shapers of the American mind: "it has given a cast to our manners, it has crept into our philosophy; it has influenced at every turn the development of our culture."[4]

Not surprisingly, the machine loomed as the dominant metaphor and leading actor of *Technics and Civilization*. At the end of his book, drawing upon the compilations of Feldhaus and others cited in his bibliography, Mumford included an extensive list of inventions from the tenth century through 1933, describing it as "an historical framework for the social interpretations of the preceding pages."[5] A high proportion of these inventions were new mechanical devices. Preparing a new edition of his book two decades after its 1934 publication, Mumford recognized the error he had originally made in taking "for my own the machine-limited ideology" and in neglecting such non-mechanical technologies as agriculture and medicine.[6] But that was hindsight; in 1934, the machine had captured his imagination along with the minds of a generation of Americans.

Mumford's interest in technology went back to his youth, when he tinkered with crystal radios and sent ideas for electrical inventions to Hugo Gernsback's *Modern Electrics*.[7] Mumford was then a student at New York's

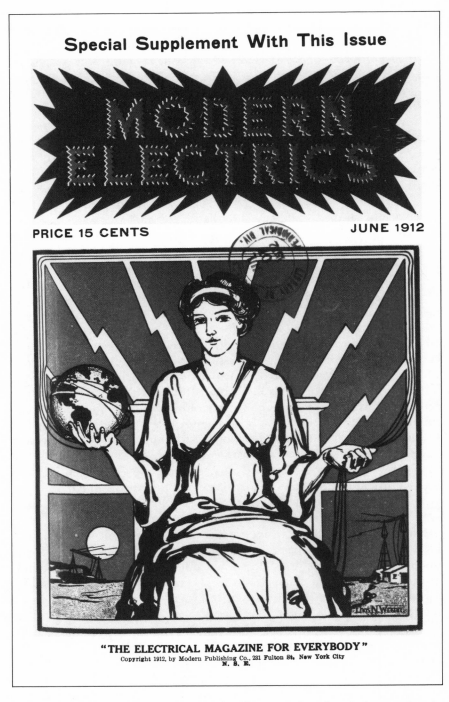

Special Supplement With This Issue

MODERN
ELECTRICS

PRICE 15 CENTS   JUNE 1912

"THE ELECTRICAL MAGAZINE FOR EVERYBODY"
Copyright 1912, by Modern Publishing Co., 231 Fulton St, New York City
M. S. E.

Hugo Gernsback's *Modern Electrics,* the first popular electrical magazine in America.

EXPERIMENTAL DEPARTMENT

This department has been started with the idea to encourage the experimenter to bring out new ideas. Every reader is welcome to contribute to this department, and new ideas will be welcomed by the Editors. WHEN SENDING IN CONTRIBUTIONS IT IS NECESSARY THAT ONLY ONE SIDE OF THE SHEET IS USED. SKETCH MUST INVARIABLY BE ON A SEPARATE SHEET NOT IN THE TEXT. The description must be as short as possible. Good sketches are not required, as our art department will work out rough sketches submitted from contributors. IT IS THEREFORE NOT NECESSARY FOR CONTRIBUTORS TO SPEND MUCH TIME IN SKETCHING VARIOUS IDEAS. When sending contributions enclose return postage if manuscript is to be returned if not used. ALL CONTRIBUTIONS APPEARING IN THIS DEPARTMENT ARE PAID FOR ON PUBLICATION.

FIRST PRIZE, TWO DOLLARS.

Unique Variable Condenser.

WHERE compactness is desired, in portable wireless sets especially, condensers of the rotary or slide plate type, take up twice as much room as they should; while condensers changing their capacity by a switch do not do so gradually enough. In the drawing of the condenser it may be seen that the plates may be nearly any size or shape, depending upon the space to be filled. The stationary plates should be $\frac{3}{8}$ inches apart. The capacity is regulated by turning a thumbscrew. It should be short enough to al-

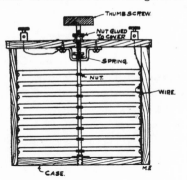

low a leeway only of about 3/16 inches for the movable plates. Battery nuts are soldered to the movable plates, as shown. Holes are, of course, made in the centre of the plates to allow the 8/32 threaded rod to pass through. The top of the rod should not be threaded so as to allow it to slide easily. If the plates are round, the thumb-screw may, of course, be fastened to the rod B directly.

Contributed by

L. C. MUMFORD.

SECOND PRIZE, ONE DOLLAR.

An Audible Detector.

Something new and novel in detectors may be constructed by following the instructions and diagram below.

The detector consists of carborundum

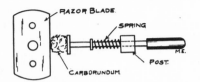

(selected blue crystals), which make contact upon a discarded safety razor blade. When in proper adjustment the detector will respond to signals in close proximity with a clear ringing tone, sufficiently loud to be heard several feet away.

Light contact upon the sharp razor edge, with a strong battery produces best effect. The proper point of contact will best be found by experiment. No tele-

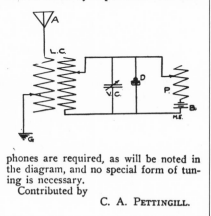

phones are required, as will be noted in the diagram, and no special form of tuning is necessary.

Contributed by

C. A. PETTINGILL.

An electrical contribution by Mumford for the January 1911 issue of *Modern Electrics*.

scientific and technical Stuyvesant High School, founded only a few years before he enrolled in 1909.

A member of the school's drama club, the precocious Mumford co-authored a play in 1911, entitled *Dr. Bilby's Aeroplane,* a delightful farce about an early case of technological espionage in the aviation industry.[8] In the opening scene, a ditty sung by a chorus of Stuyvesant sophomores revealed their school's ethos:

> We are mechanicals,
> Smutty mechanicals.
> We are from Stuyvesant
> As you all may know.
> We know the engine, O.
> We know what makes it go.
> How the deuce did you find that out?
> Gage told us so.

> We are the carpenters,
> Dusty carpenters,
> We are from Stuyvesant
> As you all may know.
> We know the lathe, O.
> We know what makes it go.
> How the deuce did you find that out?
> Ask Merserau.

The names invoked were those of Mumford's shop teachers, whose skills he admired and who stimulated his youthful appetite for technology and the industrial arts.[9] 1911 was something of a crucial year for the young Mumford, according to this succinct autobiographical note: "I decide not to become an engineer; I fail math; my wireless article [*sic*] [for *Modern Electrics*]."[10] Despite his lack of success in technical and scientific subjects, these studies awakened and reinforced a lifelong interest in technics, giving him the technical grounding he needed for *Technics and Civilization.* If Stuyvesant failed to launch Mumford's once-contemplated engineering career, it instilled in him a pedagogical ideal of the "whole man," a rounded individual as at home in the practical arts as in book-learning.

During Mumford's student years, the Stuyvesant curriculum had two tracks: a general, or college preparatory, course and an industrial course.[11] Even the general course, in which Mumford enrolled, required such industry-related subjects as mechanical drawing, joinery, wood turning, pattern making, metal working, and forging. As the ditty in Mumford's play suggested, the students learned not only how to operate the machine but to understand its fundamental principles.

"The purpose of the Stuyvesant High School is to train the hand, the eye, the ear, the brain, the heart, and thus the whole man," according to the *Student's Guide* for 1908. The *Guide* also included among its "wise and foolish sayings" these maxims:

- "Work is our greatest blessing."
- "Without tools [man] is nothing; with tools he is all."
- "Making boards match and surfaces smooth is akin to truth telling."
- "A one-sided education is dangerous. Stuyvesant trains both the hand and mind."[12]

Stuyvesant's pedagogical orientation reflected the general shift in American education from the classical to the modern curriculum, with its new openness to scientific and technological studies. The emphasis on learning-by-doing evoked the ideals of John Dewey, whose notions of technological society both intrigued and disquieted the maturing Mumford.[13] Perhaps first stimulated by his experience at Stuyvesant, Mumford's interest in Dewey was lasting, though his response to Dewey's ideas was ambivalent. It is true that Mumford sharply attacked Dewey's pragmatic philosophy, deeming it complacent, even barbaric, in its affirmation of machine-age values. He criticized Dewey for focusing too narrowly on the material dimension and neglecting essential needs of the mind and spirit, yet praised his attack on traditional philosophy.[14] Although publicly attacking the Columbia professor, Mumford nevertheless privately praised him as a man of "keen, imperturbable mind that cuts through the older philosophies."[15] Still, he warned against accepting Deweyite pragmatism as the last word in philosophy. More impressive to Mumford were the writings of Patrick Geddes. Like Dewey, Geddes addressed the importance of experience in learning, but he dealt more candidly with the religious, emotional, and sexual factors he saw affecting processes of learning and socialization.[16]

Geddes and Mumford—master and disciple—strove to nurture the spirit of the "whole man" by fostering a synthesis of the rational and emotional facets of the human personality. Calling for an end to the traditional dualistic separation of mind and body, spirit and matter, reason and emotion, theory and practice, they counseled indulgence, even celebration of sense experience of the material environment as a vital complement to spirituality.[17]

Such ideals generated a fundamental tension in *Technics and Civilization*. On one hand, the book expressed Mumford's passion for the concrete, for the physicality of life, of which technology was an important aspect. On the other hand, behind these concrete manifestations lay the abstractions that engendered and shaped technology—the social beliefs and the scientific ideas. This tension—more properly, the dialectic—between the material and the spiritual realms accounts for much of the power of *Technics and Civilization* as well as the technological optimism of Mumford's early works. Ultimately, Mumford foresaw a synthesis of matter and spirit, mediated by a higher form of technology, leading to what he and Geddes called the neotechnic phase of civilization.

The Museum Professional

Lewis Mumford had an abiding appreciation of museums as sources of indelible and pleasant educational experiences. In 1932, supported in his research for *Technics and Civilization* by a Guggenheim Fellowship, he toured the great national technical museums in London, Paris, Munich, and Vienna, steeping himself in the material heritage of Western technology. Photographs of artifacts exhibited at these museums, especially Munich's Deutsches Museum, grace the pages of *Technics and Civilization,* not merely as embellishments but as visual explanations of technological devices and processes. Mumford regarded visits to industrial museums as an alternative to "open-air observation in the field" when that opportunity was unavailable and found such visits, in any case, superior to books in imparting the principles and history of industrial practices.[18] The emergence of science and technology museums in the first third of the twentieth century manifested the same Machine Age fascination with technology that infused *Technics and Civilization.* Perhaps it is in such institutions that we can best witness Mumford engaged in an educational process begun years before at Stuyvesant High—working from the sense and study of physical artifacts to insight into the society that produced them.

Europe's industrial museums also attracted American museum men in search of institutional examples. Waldemar Kaempffert, whose philosophy of history and regard for museums closely paralleled Mumford's, hoped to apply exhibit techniques learned at the Deutsches Museum to his own Museum of Science and Industry in Chicago. Another close student of the European museum scene was the Smithsonian Institution's chief curator of technology, Carl W. Mitman, who toured British and Continental museums at the same time Mumford was making his European excursion (though the two men evidently never met).

Industrial museums were then all the rage and Mitman hoped that one day America would establish under the aegis of the Smithsonian its own National Museum of Engineering and Industry, modeled primarily on the Deutsches Museum.[19] The new German science and technology museum, which moved to its current building in 1925, deeply impressed both American visitors. In particular, Mitman regarded the mining exhibit of the Deutsches Museum as "without a doubt the most realistic portrayal of ore, salt and coal mining and ore dressing that could possibly be made."[20] If one could detect the artifice outside the exhibit, "once in the mine nothing exists to prevent one from feeling the underground mining atmosphere." It was the powerful realism of the coal mine exhibit that inspired the comparison in *Technics and Civilization* of the depths of the mineral mine with the dark, inhuman spirit of the Paleotechnic Age, the era of the Industrial Revolution.[21]

Like Mumford, Mitman and other museum professionals of the time fervently believed in the educational mission of technical museums. To the general public, such institutions explained through graphic displays the

Carl W. Mitman (1892–1958) examining patent models at the Smithsonian, c. 1926. Courtesy Smithsonian Institution.

transformations of the material world. At the same time, sectioned artifacts and operating machinery could instruct young engineers in the fundamental principles of technology. Such beliefs provided the principal rationale for a vigorous industrial museum movement in America during the 1920s, which brought into being such institutions as the Museums of the Peaceful Arts in New York, the science and technology branch of the Franklin Institute, and Julius Rosenwald's Museum of Science and Industry in Chicago.[22] Like Mumford, proponents of industrial museums touted the immediacy of technological exhibits, their direct impact on the mind and senses. As the physicist and electrical engineer Michael I. Pupin argued, "Give the youth a chance to be thrilled by the achievements of past generations and do not rely on books alone to produce this thrill. Put them in touch with the things which record those achievements and with the lives of men who made these things."[23]

Mitman considered the historical mode the most effective form of museum instruction and one uniquely suited to the strengths of collections at institutions like the Deutsches Museum and Smithsonian. A mining engineer who was self-taught in history, Mitman developed definitive historical collections of mechanical technology. He also wrote about the history of technology. His studies were narrowly conceived but nevertheless represented a pioneering effort by an American scholar.

Far less critically than Mumford, but in keeping with contemporary attitudes, Mitman invoked "progress" as the directing force of technological evolution. Visiting Europe's museums, he measured the success of their technology presentations by the clarity with which they revealed the essential steps of progressive development. For instance, he regarded the Conservatoire Nationale des Arts et Métiers in Paris as pathetic in the way it crammed historic relics into exhibit cases, making it next to impossible to follow the steps of progressive evolution. He contrasted the ineffective display techniques of the CNAM with the more selective approach taken by the museums in Munich and Vienna, which were "not disposed to visualize progress in fine steps but by more apparent longer strides."[24]

The "longer strides," however, should not be so extended as to obscure the intermediate steps of innovation. Intimate knowledge of the material record convinced Mitman that all innovations, however dramatic, had precedents and that large transformations invariably resulted from the accumulation of many small changes. Technological geniuses existed, of course, but they, too, built upon the work of predecessors. Mitman knew that for every Fulton, there was a Rumsey and a Fitch.[25]

In Mitman's scheme, the Smithsonian's technological exhibits embodied the same Darwinian and Spencerian principles of evolutionary change that underlay the museum's natural history collections. Mitman adopted a "teleological" or "morphological" scheme of organization for technology, arranging the artifacts in parallel "study series," based on the principle that complex machines evolved from simpler machines as complex animals developed from simpler ancestors.[26] Guiding this evolution, Mitman believed, were society's increasingly complex economic requirements, which provided the basic organizing principle for the Smithsonian technological exhibitions in areas such as textiles, food, agriculture, and transport. Similar to the organizational schemes in European museums, Mitman's exhibit plan began with replicas of inclined planes, levers, and other simple machines and gradually progressed to more advanced tools, machines, and vehicles of transportation called into being by the changing economic and commercial needs of America's development as a nation.[27]

Mitman's historical writing expressed the same progressivism. His *catalogue raisonné* of the museum's technological collections, for instance, portrayed the development of American technology as the inevitable product of progressive change.[28] Not surprisingly, Mitman concentrated on engineering practice, virtually ignoring industrial processes and craft forms of technology. In this respect, he differed from Mumford, who used the term "technics" to cover technical practices on all levels. Mitman's bias toward engineering could be seen in his contributions to the *Dictionary of American Biography,* for which he identified more than 325 American technologists. Engineers comprised the vast majority of his sample, which generally excluded craftsmen and artisans, who were probably more numerous than engineers in nineteenth- and early twentieth-century America.[29]

While Mumford shared Mitman's belief in the progressive character of technological change, he denied the inevitability of technology-based social and moral progress. However, Mitman did believe that technology and society progressed hand-in-hand. He seemed entirely oblivious to the "machine debates" and the rising criticism of automation during the period.[30] Interestingly, Mumford voiced no objections to the lack of social criticism in industrial museum displays. On the contrary, he praised industrial museums, apparently considering them outside the debate about technology and values. He was appreciative of the role they played in preserving and displaying the material culture of technology. Informed by books such as *Technics and Civilization,* the public could presumably make its own value-judgments about technological artifacts.

The Amateur Enthusiast

In both America and Europe, newly founded technical museums stimulated a range of amateur historical activities. In 1909, responding to the need of the staff of the Deutsches Museum for historical information, the Verein deutscher Ingenieure put out the first issue of its special annual publication, *Beiträge zur Geschichte der Technik und Industrie,* edited by the pioneering historian of technology, Conrad Matchoss, who played a major role in planning the German science and technology museum.[31] A comparable historical journal published in Vienna by the Osterreichisches Forschungsinstitut was likewise affiliated with the Technical Museum of that city. The first organization devoted exclusively to the history of technology, in particular to industrial archaeology, England's Newcomen Society, founded in 1921, comprised an association of historically concerned engineers. All of these organizations were dedicated to the promotion of technological history, to the preservation of documents and material remains of technology, and to the compilation of biographical information on inventors, engineers, and industrialists.

Many Americans who were affiliated with the Newcomen Society in London soon called for a similar historical organization at home.[32] In 1923, at the centennial celebration of the Delaware and Hudson Railroad, its president, Leonor Loree, an amateur railroad historian, organized an American branch of the Newcomen Society.[33] Encouraging the pursuit of technological history and strongly supportive of the industrial museum movement, the new American society attracted a mixed group of enthusiasts, including engineers among other amateur historians, as well as academic scholars.[34] Loree had serious scholarly intentions; by 1930, however, the American branch separated from its parent society in England, changed its focus, and degenerated into a "chowder society" promoting free enterprise.

Two years before the establishment of the American branch of the Newcomen Society, a group of railroad enthusiasts founded a specialized organization with a more enduring historical tradition. While Lewis Mumford condemned paleotechnic technologies, these enthusiasts hoped to evoke America's glorious age of iron and steam by preserving and honoring its chief symbol, the iron horse. The railroad and the steam engine had been the subjects of America's earliest efforts in technological history. In 1907, Angus Sinclair, a Scottish-American journalist, published *Development of the Locomotive Engine,* a pioneering work for its day. He also founded a modest publishing enterprise in the history of railway engineering.[35] The preservation of railway artifacts, especially locomotives, began in America in the mid-nineteenth century. The preservation effort strengthened with the establishment in 1885 of the Smithsonian Institution's Section of Steam Transportation, predecessor of Mitman's technological department.[36] Although primarily hobbyists, the railway enthusiasts supported the cause of preservation, complementing the work of major museums in this regard.

The Railway and Locomotive Historical Society, founded in 1921, was the first organization in North America to concentrate on the history of the railroad and one of the first to study business or technological history in any form.[37] The society was established by an amateur group led by Charles Eben Fisher (1889–1972), a mechanical engineer and sometime railroad man. He had inherited from his father a passion for early locomotives and an estate sufficient to subsidize full-time pursuit of his historical hobby. Fisher's personal fiefdom, the exclusive society numbered only some fifty enthusiasts by the end of 1921, most of them from New England. The society expanded slowly with the addition of several regional chapters, resulting in more than 500 members by 1940. The membership consisted primarily of enthusiasts who followed different lines of work but were drawn together by their love of railroads. Their goals were to preserve historical documents and other materials, to collect them in a central depository, and to gather "all data possible relative to early locomotives and early railroads so as to know what it is and where it is located."[38] Their underlying motivations represented a common attitude toward technology at the time, one of nostalgia and a desire to preserve what was believed to be good from the past.

In 1927 the society was invited to set up its headquarters at the Baker Library of the (even then historically oriented) Harvard Business School. The library also housed the newly established Business History Society, which dealt tangentially with aspects of technological development.[39] At its headquarters, the R&LHS even established its own small museum, displaying miscellaneous railroad paraphernalia and a large photo collection as well as such documentary ephemera as schedules, stock certificates, and tickets.

In the year of its founding, the society began publication of a semiannual journal, the *Bulletin.* Editor of the journal from its inception until 1970, Fisher favored biographies, corporate histories, narratives of rail journeys, general descriptions of locomotives and trains, and occasional

Charles Eben Fisher (1889–1972). Pen portrait by E. Tone, prepared for the 50th anniversary of the Railroad and Locomotive Historical Society in 1971. Courtesy R&LHS.

tributes, sometimes in poetry, to events, companies, or machines. Fisher himself wrote the same sorts of articles, a very substantial quantity, enough to fill two columns of closely spaced type in a recently published index to the journal. In general, Fisher did not encourage articles dealing with the particulars of technological evolution, evidently preferring to leave such technical issues to qualified engineers writing for trade journals.[40]

One cannot fully appreciate the work of the railroad buff without pondering his devotion to data-gathering. One form of such data featured in virtually every issue of the *Bulletin*—the "roster"—consisted of lists of basic specifications of locomotive and car design, including cylinder bore and stroke, engine weight, and wheel arrangement, as well as such historical facts as date of construction, the builder, rebuilding, renumbering, and eventual disposition of the artifact. To the railway buff, the roster was not only important but the sine qua non of the *Bulletin*. The compilation of such lists clearly entailed much painstaking effort, but what historical purpose were they intended to serve? Printed without commentary, the rosters yield few clues as to the motives of their diligent compilers. Was data-gathering simply an end in itself? Doubtless, for some, that was the case. Possibly they had other goals in mind. At least, there are plausible rationales for this sort of labor: an exhaustive inventory of the types and makers of rolling stock could provide a solid basis for eventually determining the use and diffusion of railroad technology in America.[41] The compilers themselves, however, rarely extended their data in this fashion. Some apparently labored in the faith that future technology historians would put their inventories to use.[42]

Clearly, rosters and other railroad data satisfied nostalgic yearnings. Hobbyists revel in detail for the evocations of the textures of reality. For the railroad buff of Fisher's day, such data could evoke the power and grandeur of the locomotive as well as the economic strength of a powerful industry. The railway buff also summoned the glories of the past through photographic images, the collection of which amounted to a mania in the 1920s and 1930s.[43] The railroad photographs featured in every issue of the *Bulletin* served as two-dimensional surrogates for treasured artifacts, creating and preserving for future generations a sense of physical contact with the object itself. Together, photographs and data compilations kept the past alive for the rail fan. Ironically, this celebration of the railroad coincided with the onset of that industry's long decline in America.

Lewis Mumford apparently had no significant contact with the Railway and Locomotive Historical Society and little in common generally with the rail buff. While curious about the way machines worked, he avoided technical details and never indulged in technological nostalgia. *Technics and Civilization* revealed the darker sides of past technologies and looked rather to the future for salvation. Yet, while Mumford was a far more sophisticated historian than a Charles Eben Fisher, he shared with the amateur historian a basic aesthetic appreciation of machinery in all its forms. Mumford also shared in the awakening interest in the material environment that led to the formation of amateur groups like the Railway and Locomotive Society. Whatever its shortcomings from a scholarly point of view, the R&LHS *Bulletin* reinforced such interests as well as the movement to preserve significant artifacts. In the history of technology as in other fields, amateurs have played an important and continuing role in preserving documentation, providing useful data, and generating public enthusiasm for the pursuit of historical knowledge.

The Popularizer

Popular writers of Mumford's generation contributed to another important stream of technological history. *Technics and Civilization,* itself, straddled the realms of popularization, scholarship, and moral philosophy. The popular literature in the 1920s and 1930s was vast, diverse, and uneven in quality. Many books fell into the superficial and melodramatic "romance-of-invention" category. But the best examples of popular literature contributed useful bits of knowledge to the public's understanding of its technical heritage.

Most of the popular literature focused on inventors and inventions. Typical of the genre were Inez McFee's *Stories of American Inventions* (1921); A. Frederick Collins's *A Bird's Eye View of Inventions* (1926), and *Great Inventions* (1934), edited by Smithsonian Secretary Charles G. Abbot. The flood of books on American inventors fed the established myth of Yankee ingenuity.

Other writers incorporated technology in popular histories of civilization. H. G. Wells's serialized *Outline of History* (1921) commanded a wide American following. Writers in the moralistic tradition of Lewis Mumford included Stuart Chase, author of the popular machine-age critique, *Men and Machines,* and Hendrik Willem Van Loon (1882–1944), science editor for the *Baltimore Sun,* and sometime college professor who addressed history books to both children and adults. Letters he exchanged with Mumford expressed both high mutual regard and a shared vision. Author of *The Story of Mankind* (1921) and *Multiplex Man; or, the Story of Survival Through Invention* (1928) among numerous other works, Van Loon attributed the mounting social problems of the Machine Age not to technology but to mankind's stunted spiritual development. "We are but cave-dwellers going for a joy-ride in a Chevrolet," Van Loon concluded.[44] In *The March of the Iron Men,* among other writings about technology in history, the freelance writer and Scribner editor Roger Burlingame identified the history of America with her achievements in technology.[45]

A prolific contributor to the popular history of science and technology was one of America's first science and technology editors in journalism, Waldemar Kaempffert (1877–1956).[46] Born in New York City, Kaempffert was trained as a patent lawyer but never practiced. Instead, he edited the *Scientific American* (assistant editor, 1897–1911; managing editor, 1912–16), and the *Popular Science Monthly* (1916–21). In 1927, after a stint with a New York engineering firm, he became science editor for the *New York Times,* where he remained for the rest of his career, except for three years (1928–31) as first director of the Chicago Museum of Science and Industry.

Aside from hundreds of articles on science and technology, Kaempffert wrote popular books on the development of the airplane and the radio as well as commentaries on the relationship between technology and society.[47] He also edited a two-volume *Popular History of American Inventions* (1924), his most ambitious work in the history of technology.[48] Cited in the bibliography to *Technics and Civilization,* Kaempffert's book stressed not individual inventions but the organization of large technological systems in power, transportation, and communications. Believing in the ultimate convergence of science and technology, Kaempffert emphasized the increasingly important role taken by science in the evolution of these large-scale enterprises.

This same breadth characterized his editorship of the *Scientific American,* which evolved under his stewardship from its traditional role as inventor's magazine to a scientifically oriented popular magazine dealing with large-scale technologies like dam construction, factory organization, and power systems.

In a 1934 review of *Technics and Civilization* for the *New York Times,* the optimistic Kaempffert played down Mumford's criticisms of paleotechnic

WALDEMAR KAEMPFFERT
PRESENT EDITOR POPULAR SCIENCE MONTHLY

Waldemar Kaempffert (1877–1956), new editor of *Popular Science Monthly*, 1916.

civilization, emphasizing instead the nascent neotechnic phase as confirmation of the "technical ascent of man."[49] Believing that technology rightfully belonged to the people, he focused particular attention on Mumford's assertion that such large neotechnic systems as centralized power, the telegraph, and the telephone facilitated collectivist forms of social organization and militated against individualism.

A professional interest in scientific and technologic education and strong democratic convictions led to Kaempffert's involvement with technology museums. Democracy, he thought, had both enhanced the public role and altered the educational mission of science and industrial museums.[50] Kaempffert saw the position of director of the Chicago Museum of Science and Industry as an opportunity to put these ideas into practice and to seed a new awareness of the individual's potential in the future technologic collective. He was involved in publicizing and planning future exhibits of the new museum, which formally opened in 1933. Looking for examples to follow, he shared with Julius Rosenwald, benefactor and founder of the Chicago museum, a passion for the "live" exhibits of the Deutsches Museum and the showmanship of its founder, Oskar von Miller, who, Kaempffert noted, "knew that a museum should meet the educational needs of the common people. . . ."[51]

In planning his opening exhibitions, Kaempffert followed Miller's example of encouraging direct engagement between visitors and machines. Everything that could move would move in his museum and, as far as possible, exhibits would replicate reality. The idea of live, hands-on, interactive exhibitions has long been part of the conventional wisdom, if a rarely achieved ideal, of museology. But when the Deutsches Museum first introduced such approaches, museums were just emerging from what Kaempffert called their "mausoleum" stage.[52] The new theatrical techniques appealed to an age fascinated with technological processes and attuned to visual and tactile experience. As envisioned by Kaempffert, locomotives "panted" and a simulated mine shaft emitted the smells and sounds of a real coal mine. Interactive devices invited visitor participation in the audible and sensory experiences of the moving apparatus. Kaempffert hoped to make extensive use of the new technology of motion pictures, a "powerful aid in animating a dead collection of implements and apparatus."[53] Minimizing the differences between man and machine, Kaempffert subscribed to Herbert Spencer's notion that "instruments and machines are but extensions of the human organs."[54]

In the Rosenwald museum, Kaempffert planned to tackle social issues, which were virtually ignored in the European science and industrial museums.[55] Great inventors, he believed, manifest an "instinct of contrivance" but nevertheless respond to the economic and social pressures of their times. Conversely, inventors and inventions influence society: typewriters brought women into offices; the Otis elevator made possible the skyscraper. Technological devices also create social problems, albeit almost always unintentionally: the steam engine gave rise to the modern factory and its labor problems; the cotton gin to the importation of slaves "to pick cotton for the greedy gins and textile mills."[56]

Although aware of the social problems inherent in the introduction of some forms of technology, Kaempffert painted a rosy picture of technological society, past, present, and future. As envisioned by him, science, technology, and mankind were progressing together in a cosmic evolution, culminating in technological man's Machine-Age apotheosis. Kaempffert foresaw a museum organized along the lines of this grand evolution, beginning with displays about the origins of the solar system, and progressing through the origins of life, the stages of primitive man, and, finally, of "social man"—the "free agent" in control of nature and "fashioning the machine age."[57]

Kaempffert's utopian vision of the technological future evoked the same images and ideals identified with Mumford's neotechnic phase. Perhaps if the Chicago Museum of Science and Industry had retained Kaempffert as its director it might have popularized other Mumfordian notions as well, especially the social contexts of technology, perhaps even a glimpse of the darker sides of technology. Of contemporary popularizers, Mumford expressed the highest regard for writers such as Kaempffert, H. W. Van Loon, and Stuart Chase, who went beyond mere celebration of inventors and inventions to considerations of the social and moral aspects of technological civilization.

The Academic Historian

Distinguishing him from the popular historian of technology was Mumford's attempt to incorporate the findings of specialized scholarship. The history of technology did not emerge as a formal academic specialty until the late 1950s. However, as early as the 1920s, a handful of revisionist academics, notably Charles Beard and Arthur Schlesinger, began to consider issues of technological change as part of a general reassessment of American history. They shifted their emphasis from traditional political history and its great figures to a more democratic consideration of events impinging on the lives of ordinary citizens. For example, Arthur Schlesinger identified a great number of devices such as the kerosene lamp, the threshing machine, and the modern stove as primary agents in improving our common welfare. He also attempted to demonstrate how the substitution of machines for human labor led to the growth of manufactures and, eventually, to American dominance in production.[58]

Because of their interest in the industrial revolution, economic historians were among the first to pay significant attention to technological factors. But few of them focused on technological processes in their own right. A notable exception was the Harvard economic historian Abbott Payson Usher (1883–1965), arguably America's first scholarly specialist in the history of technology.[59] In *Technics and Civilization,* Mumford singled out Usher's *A History of Mechanical Inventions* (1929) as the "nearest approach" to a comprehensive history of technics in English, admiring it especially for its exhaustive treatment of mechanical implements in antiquity and of the mechanical clock.[60] A pioneering work, Usher's history traced in painstaking detail the evolution of mechanisms from the ancient noria, through the machine tools of mass production, to the vast power systems of the twentieth century.

While Usher's historical sophistication and critical approach distinguished him from the amateur fact-gatherers and even from Mumford, the Harvard historian shared with them basic motivations. Advocating a physical, empiricist approach to history, he was fascinated by the construction and operation of machines and by material evidence in general. He explored industrial sites in his native New England and regularly attended meetings of the American branch of the Newcomen Society, interests which originated partly in his family background—his father was a prominent industrialist—and partly in his Harvard education.[61]

Although a staunch anti-Marxist, Usher, like most other historians of his generation, including Mumford, was heavily influenced by Marxist histor-

Abbott Payson Usher (1883–1965), as a young university instructor, about 1920. Courtesy Eunice Usher Hustvedt and Miriam Usher Chrisman.

ical thought. While Mumford learned much about the relation of technology and capitalism from the Marxist historian Werner Sombart, Usher was most heavily influenced by teachers and colleagues at Harvard, where he spent the major part of his academic career.[62] European-trained colleagues like Edwin Gay and F. W. Taussig introduced Usher to Marxian economic and social historians who stressed the influence of geographic and climatic effects on social relations. Usher, however, rejected what he saw as the deterministic approach of these historians, noting their neglect of technology as society's means of coping with the forces of the physical environment.

At heart a social historian, Usher regarded technology as "the most important fact in the transformation of environment by human activity" and the essential factor in social change.[63] In this respect, Usher went beyond contemporary economic historians, who treated technology as an insignificant factor in economic growth. Technology, Usher believed, gave direction to history by virtue of its cumulative pattern of development and forward-moving dynamic. For analytical purposes, Usher studied technological phenomena in terms of parallel "systems of events," akin to the "study series" developed by Carl Mitman and other Smithsonian curators.

Unlike them, however, Usher explicitly avoided questions about progress toward a better world; he kept his eye on issues of structural change.[64]

Usher's perspective on the history of technology is most easily seen in his analysis of technological novelties. To the question, "how do new things happen," Usher identified two types of response.[65] One, the transcendental, attributed novelties to the rare and inexplicable achievements of great men. A second type of response saw invention as an incremental process, a cumulative development determined by social necessity. Although, like Mumford, Usher favored the social-process school, he criticized W. F. Ogburn, S. C. Gilfillan, and other advocates of this approach for overemphasizing social determinism and minimizing the active role of human beings in the creation of novelties. Their general ignorance of the details of technological change, Usher thought, led them to overestimate the determinative force of social and cultural causes.

Like Mumford, Usher regarded technology not as an impersonal, autonomous process, but as the collective product of many individual human decisions. Usher's belief in the human dimension of technology led him to propose a novel theory of innovation based on the principles of gestalt psychology, newly arrived in America from Germany.[66] Contrary to the usual view, Usher argued, invention is not an essentially rational activity of step-by-step deduction but an intuitive one of pattern-recognition. According to gestalt theorists such as Wolfgang Koehler, all human beings, and even some higher animals, possess an innate ability to grasp technical problems holistically. Usher analyzed technological innovation into a process of four genetically linked stages: (1) the recognition of an incomplete or unsatisfying pattern; (2) the arraying of data pertinent to a solution ("setting the stage"); (3) the sudden insight into a way of completing the pattern; (4) the assimilation and refinement of the solution. The incremental combination of many minor inventions arrived at by this process eventually results in a major technological change. For him, the essence of the gestalt approach to innovation was the implication of a direct, intuitive, emotional, and holistic relationship between human beings and machines unifying, as it were, the realms of the spirit and of matter.

In establishing the terms of the human-machine relationship, Mumford and Usher drew upon common intellectual sources. Inspired by Alfred North Whitehead's philosophical ruminations on the foundations of physics in *Science and the Modern World,* both historians believed that the ongoing revolution in physics portended a major shift in our understanding of technology.[67] Relativity and quantum mechanics underpinned a physical world far different from that envisioned by Galileo, Descartes, Newton, and other mechanical philosophers. The new scientific dispensation stressed the interdependence rather than the independence of phenomena, the holistic integration of the human observer into the physical world, and a substitution of organic for mechanical principles. On the basis of this new cosmic perspective, Mumford and Usher predicted the emergence of a more holistic, human-centered technology. Such ideals underpinned the optimistic "organic mechanism" prophesied in the last two chapters of *Technics and Civilization* as well as Mumford's post-Marxian "basic communism," the social projection of his organicist philosophy.[68]

Conclusion

Reviewers of Mumford's *Technics and Civilization* found it a protean book, extremely difficult to categorize.[69] Was it a philosophical volume, a moral tract, a prophetic work, a historical treatise? Because of its many dimensions, we sometimes forget that the book is a pioneering work in the history of technology, one of the first to analyze the evolution of the machine in the full light of current scholarship and to place that evolution in the cultural context of Western civilization. I have argued that Mumford's interest in the history of technology originated in part in his fascination with machines, a fascination widely shared in that period. His youthful interest in technical devices, technical processes, and industrial practices endured, ultimately informing his masterwork.

This technological enthusiasm gave rise to an early form of the history of technology, the emergence of which was a generational phenomenon. The amateur and professional historians who came of age during and after World War I had witnessed and reacted to the applications of technology to war and the ensuing second industrial wave sweeping in automation, mass production, and revolutionary advances in communication and transportation. Mumford saw the evils as well as benefits of technological advance and challenged the facile linkages between technical and social progress. Yet, that technology *itself* advanced Mumford never challenged. Accepting the conventional wisdom, he saw technology essentially as the product of prior scientific discovery working itself through successive levels of practice, a process of discovery and development that had gone on throughout history. Such beliefs, at least at the writing of *Technics and Civilization,* left him basically receptive to technological advance and optimistic about the future.

Mumford was concerned about the values of a society that had tolerated the inhumanities of capitalism during the Industrial Revolution. But his criticisms of exploitative technologies and materialism never led him to reject the material world. On the contrary, believing in technology and inspired by thinkers such as Dewey and Geddes, he reveled in the physicalities of life, not as ends but as the path to higher wisdom. A visual as well as verbal thinker, he believed in the superiority of empirical knowledge, acquired through direct contact with the material world. This was the basis of his attraction to museums and to the history of technology. For the same reason, Mumford dealt with "technics"—the industrial arts—rather than "technology" as an abstract, rational pursuit.[70] Perhaps the conditions of everyday work and life in his society were less removed from practical and sensate experience than they are today.

What did Mumford have in common with the other early students of technological history discussed in this article? They shared an empiricist ideal and a sense of the aesthetic pleasures of technology. Historians at the new industrial museums envisioned their institutions as showcases of ingenuity delighting the senses as well as the intellect. At the same time, Mumford's enthusiasm for technology was tempered by the influence of thinkers like Patrick Geddes and Thorstein Veblen. Clearly, Mumford offered a more critical and sophisticated perspective on technology than the popularizers and amateur historians of his time. Yet he also learned from them, translating their knowledge into his own terms for his own ends. Of the four men considered here, Kaempffert and Usher had the most direct intellectual relationship with Mumford. Mumford was familiar with their writings and took from them what he needed. Mumford probably had no contact with the Smithsonian's Carl Mitman, but found inspiration in the historic artifacts preserved in his museum and in others. The same preservationist and documentary activities were under way at amateur historical societies like the Railway and Locomotive Historical Society. Though the particularist brand of history they pursued was not to Mumford's taste, it provided the sort of detailed knowledge upon which large-frame histories like Mumford's must rely.

As a man of letters, Mumford moved in a different world from the Mitmans and the Fishers. As a historian of technology, Mumford in fact identified no community as his own. Yet, we should recognize the reinforcement and inspiration provided by other early historians of technology. Individuals like Mitman laid the groundwork for literati and scholars like Mumford. Conversely, the prestige and attention which a man such as Mumford could bring to a new area of study suggest that the seemingly diverse efforts of scholars and amateur enthusiasts provided reinforcement in pursuit of a common goal.

Lewis Mumford as a Historian of Technology in *Technics and Civilization*

ROSALIND WILLIAMS

As Lewis Mumford tells us in a prefatory note to *Technics and Civilization* (1934), that book was originally intended to be a comprehensive study covering not only the machine but also the city, region, group, and personality. He gave this study the working title "Form and Personality," and in the summer of 1930 completed an essay "Machines" that would be its first long chapter. In fact, there are two drafts of the "Machines" chapter: a shorter one (18 pages) dated 27 July, and a longer one (39 pages) dated 22 August. The shorter draft, published in the August issue of *Scribner's Magazine* under the title "The Drama of the Machines," was, in Mumford's own words, "The immediate prelude to *Technics and Civilization*. . . ."[1]

For those of us who know and admire Lewis Mumford primarily as a historian of technology, the 1930 draft chapter on machines is startling in the brevity of its historical discussion. In a brief introduction Mumford announces he intends to discuss both the cultural origins and the cultural prospects of machines, but he has much more to say about their prospects than their origins. For example, in the July manuscript Mumford's discussion of the clock as the crucial invention of modern culture—one of the most admired sections of *Technics and Civilization*—is condensed into half a sentence:

> A new rhythm crept into life; the mechanical readings of the clock supplant the unevenness of endured time, and the dream of mechanically accelerated motion keeps passing through the mind of a Leonardo, a Glanville, and Hooke, a Marquis of Worcester.[2]

In the summer 1930 draft, Mumford's discussion of the origins of the machine takes up only one-third of one chapter, out of a lengthy manuscript that also includes long chapters on buildings, cities, regions, and modern art.[3] Within that chapter the historical discussion is simply a brief prelude to far longer variations on other themes that clearly engage Mumford much more: the concept of machine design, new values implied by

machine design, the relationship between engineering and art, new arts
based on new technologies, social and psychological obstacles in the way
of acceptance of machines, the need for ethical transformation if machines
are to become integral parts of modern culture. Looking at the 1930
acorn, we would never guess that it would grow into a historiographic oak.[4]

Mumford set out to write a critique of the Machine Age, not a history
of the machine. What we know as *Technics and Civilization* is in fact a vastly
expanded preface for that critique. As Mumford revised the preface, it
kept getting longer and longer. He had little problem gathering information about technological history: he had read widely and learned much
from museums and travel. The problem for this accidental historian was
how to structure that information. What would be the organizing concepts, the theoretical assumptions? In this respect Mumford was operating
in something of a void. The discipline of the history of technology was
unformed and still largely at the fact-gathering stage.[5] The one obvious
source of theoretical structure—Marxism—Mumford decisively rejected.
What then would be the structural principles for his work?

The answer to this question rests on two well-known facts: that Mumford
is a moralist and that he is strongly influenced by Patrick Geddes. I want
to show how these facts fit together in the creation of *Technics*, that path-
breaking and still indispensable study of the origins of the machine age. In
particular, I want to show that the historical design of *Technics* has two
major sources: Mumford's own moral consciousness, which led him to view
history as a stage for moral dramas, and his admiration for Geddes, from
whom he borrowed the crucial historical categories of technological phases
and occupational types. As we shall see, in *Technics* these moral structures
and historical concepts merge into a hybrid form of cultural criticism.

History as the Myth of Life Insurgent

In a brief preface to the August 1930 draft chapter on machines, Mumford explained his purpose as a writer:

> During the last three centuries our ways of life have profoundly changed. . . .
> This change manifested itself first as the loss of form: . . . fragmentation, dis-
> order, atomism. . . .
>
> Yet underneath the disorder and the confusion a new civilization has been
> growing. . . . In many departments of art, we seem at last on the brink of
> achieving form: here and there the crystal of a new order has begun to take
> shape. . . . To understand these new potentialities, to further this crystalliza-
> tion, to clarify this change—these are the goals of our present discussion.[6]

Attainment of form, loss of form, renewal of order: as Peter Shaw has commented, this same pattern, this "arc" of synthesis, breakdown, and revival,
is found consistently in Mumford's writings from *The Story of Utopias* to

Interpretations and Forecasts.[7] In *Sticks and Stones* and in *The Golden Day* the pre-existing synthesis was America of the 1830s; in *The Golden Day* the source of breakdown was primarily the Civil War, while in *Sticks and Stones* the "fall" of the early New England village was caused by the same processes of disruption and dissolution that took place over several centuries in Europe.[8] Whatever the particulars of the drama, the primal plot is the same, and the leading role is played by life, or rather Life—not classes, nations, or individuals. History is the stage on which is enacted a primal, ever-repeating moral drama of Life's balance, breakdown, and renewal. Mumford came to denounce the myth of the machine not because myth has no place in historical understanding, but for the opposite reason; myth is the key to historical understanding, and the myth of the machine is a false one which must be displaced by the true myth of Life.

One characteristic of a mythological world-view is the conviction that there is at least potentially a resonance between cosmic and personal events. The primal moral dramas that govern the universe can be replayed in rituals, the smaller dramas of human life. Furthermore, by re-enacting the cosmic dramas, human beings can hope to influence a favorable outcome. Mumford seems to have assumed this mythologizing role when he was writing the "Form and Personality" manuscript. During that period of moral crisis, as he himself called it,[9] Mumford felt he was experiencing the same pattern of breakdown and renewal in his personal life that he discerned in abstract Life.[10]

There were two intertwining causes of Mumford's personal "loss of form." The first was marital and the second professional. From the fall of 1928 to the spring of 1929, Lewis and Sophia Mumford suffered a series of misfortunes: Sophia's miscarriage in November, her subsequent illness, his own, and above all their son Geddes's life-threatening mastoid infections that spring. Physically and emotionally exhausted, by summer the Mumfords entered a period of marital estrangement, which only worsened when in the fall Lewis met Catherine Bauer and eventually began an affair with her.[11]

At the same time, Mumford was restlessly seeking new balance as a writer. With the completion of *The Brown Decades*, his "desk was cleared" of a long cycle of work in American studies, his search for and presentation of a usable past in American culture.[12] In the spring of 1929, even before he had begun preparing *The Brown Decades* for publication, Mumford mentioned in letters that he was "mulling over" and "shaking down into some sort of order" various ideas as to the theme of his next book.[13] For some time he had been contemplating a work on a grander scale, something to do with Western civilization as a whole, with the breakdown of form and crushing of the personality due to industrialization, and the subsequent rediscovery of form and personality in the emerging machine age; but he had little idea where or how to begin such a vast project.[14]

Both as a husband and as writer, then, Mumford felt it was time to redefine himself. In justifying his affair with Bauer, he told himself that he had arrived at a point in life where to continue to follow conventional moral codes would be unbearably constrictive and stifling—as he felt had been the fate of Melville (whose biography Mumford had finished writing in the late summer of 1928), who had failed to "cope with his early erotic promptings or to understand later the effect of his repressions." Instead of wandering "through the bleak waste land of tormented chastity and self-renouncing loyalty,"[15] as Melville had, Mumford felt he had to break free from past habits and received rules, and to endure a period of disequilibrium in order to achieve a new and finer synthesis.

This argument is arrogant and self-serving, but it is also fascinating for what it tells us about Mumford's understanding of his own mission. Like a Romantic poet who assumes a resonance between the inner and the outer landscapes, Mumford assumes a correspondence between the personal and the universal drama. The link between the two is Patrick Geddes's doctrine of life insurgent. On 14 July 1929, Mumford wrote to David Liebovitz that he had been reading Geddes on biology and had found that "his doctrine of Insurgence as a prime quality of all life, life perpetually striving, struggling, overcoming all obstacles, is an excellent medicine in periods of discouragement. . . ." Furthermore—and this is a prime source of Mumford's respect for Geddes—Geddes practices what he preaches. In an appreciation published in *The New Republic* in the fall of 1929, Mumford emphasized that Geddes exemplified his own "doctrine of life: its inception, its development, its struggle, its joyful insurgence."[16] The same language appeared in his August 1930 draft chapter on machines:

> Every form of life [in handwriting Mumford has added "Almost"], as Patrick Geddes shows, exhibits this insurgent reaction upon the world as it is given: in man, the reaction reaches its apex, and manifests itself most completely and objectively in the arts. . . .[17]

The analogy works both ways. By seeing his own personal problems as a microcosmic example of the historical drama, Mumford's sufferings assume a broader significance and purpose: they are necessary to achieve the larger purpose of renewal. And by seeing the problem of historical change as similar to the resolution of a moral drama, Mumford implies that if individuals (such as himself) are able to attain a new equilibrium, renewal might be possible for civilization at large. Like a high priest, he leads a ritualistic re-enactment of the mysterious drama of life's renewal.

By the fall of 1929 he was beginning to see the first glimmers of personal recovery. Thanks in part to encouragement from people like Catherine Bauer, Mumford felt ready to tackle the larger work he had long contemplated.[18] On 22 September he wrote Thomas Beer that "I am already meditating an interim book [which would be *The Brown Decades*] before I take off my shirt and unhitch my pants and start work on another masterpiece."[19] Beginning in April 1930 Mumford began to make random notes titled "form" and "machine,"[20] and by late June 1930 he had sketched out a suggested table of contents for a book on "Form and Personality"—the skeleton that was fleshed out in the draft written in the summer of 1930.[21] By then both Sophia and Catherine had departed separately for Europe, giving Mumford some respite from the tensions in his personal life. Under these circumstances, when he had glimpsed but had not yet regained his own equilibrium, he began writing about the loss and potential recovery of form in Western civilization.

History as Revolutionary Takeover

For Mumford it is a fundamental and unwavering principle that Life, not external mechanisms of any kind, determines historical destiny. In reaction against what he saw as Marxist technological determinism, Mumford proposed that the substructure of history is human life in its creative, artistic, form-giving aspects.[22] As he stated in his preface to the draft chapters on machines, his central concern is to welcome machines into the cultural fold, to show that instead of producing human consciousness they are themselves products of it.[23] The great heap of modern machinery and industry is therefore the external, material, secondary expression of underlying desires and interests that are the primary determinants of history.

The problem is that Mumford hates much of what he sees in that heap. What does the ugliness of modern industry say about the desires and interests that produced it? In particular, how did the human spirit become so perverted as to plunge civilization into the long dark night of what is usually called the Industrial Revolution? This is both a historiographic problem and a moral one, since for Mumford the two adjectives are inseparable. He needs to explain the origin of technological evil. *Technics and Civilization* represents a crucial step in Mumford's lifelong quest to articulate the distinction between "good" machines and "bad" ones, and to explain how both the liberating and the repressive ones have emerged in history.[24] In *Technics* he faces the particular problem of explaining how the desirable values embodied in some machines can be called upon to correct the false values embodied in others.

In the 1930 draft Mumford deals with this problem by narrating a second moral drama which overlies the first. This is "the drama of the machines," to use the title he gave both to his July draft and to the nearly identical article in the August issue of *Scribner's*.[25] After a brief introduction, Mumford begins to narrate the main lines of the drama:

> Five or six centuries before the main body of the army forms, spies have been planted among the nations of Europe. Here and there, in strategic positions, small bodies of scouts and observers appear, preparing the way for the main force: a Roger Bacon, a Leonardo da Vinci, a Paracelsus. But the army of machines could not take possession of modern society until every depart-

ment had been trained; above all, it was necessary to gather a group of creative minds, a general staff, who would see a dozen moves beyond the immediate strategy and would invent a superior tactics. These are the physicists and mathematicians . . . .

Behind the scientific advance-guard came the shock troops, the miners, the woodmen, the soldiers proper, and their inventive leaders. . . . At last the machines are ready. The outposts have been planted, and the army trained. What is the order of the battle, and where does the machine claim its first victory?[26]

After discussing the contribution of the soldier, woodman, and miner, Mumford summarizes the plot:

Once these key inventions were planted, once the medium was established, once the general staff was ready to supply a general system of abstraction, ideas and calculations, the time had come for the machine to take possession of Western Civilization. At last the derivative products of industrialism could spawn and multiply.[27]

This is a plot in more than one sense. Through repeated use of military images Mumford suggests that industrialization is a sort of conspiracy, a takeover by hostile forces within, a revolutionary coup. Even more precisely, he implies a Leninist theory of revolution. The footsoldiers are workers who have been mechanized by the habitual tools and rhythms of their trade (miners, woodmen, and soldiers proper); they are directed by a "general staff," a party of ideologists (physical scientists and the like) "who would see a dozen moves beyond the immediate strategy and would invent a superior tactics."

Mumford therefore uses a local determinism to explain the origin of technological evil. Without renouncing his overarching conviction that technology does not determine consciousness, he argues that in some occupational groups (soldiers, woodmen, miners, physicists, mathematicians) it might. The fundamental myth of history is based on the primacy of spirit over mechanism; the subplot, the "drama of the machines," introduces a limited or local form of technological determinism where that primacy does not obtain. According to Mumford, these two dramas are not inconsistent because Geddes "threw overboard" the notion that life is driven either by external circumstances or by a mysterious internal force of mind. In Geddes's view, Mumford tells us, "Life was active and passive, voluntarist and determinist, outwardly conditioned and inwardly determined; the old alternative was a false one. . . . Life is the harmonization of the inner and the outer."[28]

From "Form and Personality" to "Technics and Civilization"

"October 1930 opened a new period in my life."[29] By then, as Mumford wrote to David Liebovitz, he had his "fighting spirits back." By the time

Catherine Bauer returned from Europe in October, his marriage had not only survived but was even stronger than before. By the spring of 1931 Mumford had completed *The Brown Decades,* so that he was free to devote his full intellectual energies to the "Form and Personality" project. About the same time he began writing art and architecture criticism for *The New Yorker* (efforts that turned into a regular column in 1932), thereby assuring himself a steady if modest source of income.

Most important of all for his "Form and Personality" project, Mumford was asked by Robert M. MacIver of Columbia University, who had been much impressed by the August 1930 *Scribner's* article, to teach a course on technics in the university's extension division. In preparation for that course Mumford "discovered a sizeable literature on technics in German," which made him begin to realize that this topic alone could constitute a book.[30] ". . . in the development of that course the focus changed from America and the modern world to Western civilization and the technical changes that began in the twelfth century of our era."[31]

Mumford again worked on the "Form and Personality" manuscript during the summer of 1931, and by that fall he was working on a third draft. On 13 September 1931 he wrote to his friend James Henderson (of whom we will hear more later):

> I think you will like parts of my new book: . . . it cuts an even wider swathe [than *The Golden Day*]: Machines, Buildings, Cities: Regions, Civilization, a task ambitious enough to sink an even better armored craft than mine. When I finished the Brown Decades last May I was out of breath: now, after a long and devilish job of settling down to work, I have at last got under way and have my second wind: at . . . this present state of the universe, I could finish a dozen new books, one after the other, deliberately, like a swimmer doing the fourth mile of a ten mile race.

As this letter indicates, Mumford was still planning a book that would include nearly everything in the outline he had sketched in the spring of 1930.[32] The spring of 1932, however, was crucial in reorienting the work to focus on machines. Besides his on-going discovery of literature on technics inspired by his Columbia course, Mumford at last took a long-planned,[33] four-month visit to Europe (with financial support from a Guggenheim fellowship) where he discovered books, museums, cities, friends, all of which further redefined the project. ". . . those fruitful months altered the scope and scale of the entire work."[34] By the time he and Sophia steamed back to America, the outlines of *Technics and Civilization* "were already firm enough" so he could sketch out a layout for the illustrations he had gathered.[35] The proposed book still included chapters on regions and cities, however, as well as on machines.[36] Not until the spring of 1933 was Mumford writing a manuscript that is decisively *Technics and Civilization.*[37] In June 1933 he wrote Van Wyck Brooks that the projected book had now become three (one on machines, one on cities, and a third on personality), and that the writing had gone well over the winter and especially in the spring: "all the gray and tangled and incomplete parts of the first draft are gradually disappearing, and what remains seems to my biased but judicious gaze pretty sound: in fact, damned good!"[38]

In understanding how "Form and Personality" became *Technics and Civilization,* the importance of this period in expanding Mumford's sources—in space from America to Europe, and in time back to the Middle Ages—is obvious. As for how this information was organized, however, the most significant event in this period may well have been the death of Patrick Geddes. Mumford had planned to visit Geddes, then living in southern France, on his spring 1932 trip to Europe.

> In my heart, I shrank from this final encounter, knowing how it would in the end only disappoint Geddes and sadden me. Yet I was inwardly unprepared for the announcement of Sir Patrick Geddes's death [on April 17], which appeared in the New York papers just a week before I sailed for Europe.[39]

From their first meeting, their relationship had been tense and often unpleasant. Geddes sorely tried the patience of all his admirers by trying to enlist their aid in what they often considered his misguided projects and by subjecting them to his rambling discourses and even more rambling efforts at writing. For Mumford, however, the tensions were even greater because Geddes had tried to make him not only a disciple but also a son—pathetically proclaiming, only a day after they first met in 1923, that Mumford reminded him of his eldest son Alisdair who had been killed in World War I.

> I put up my guard and never thereafter fully lowered it. . . . The final effect of this encounter was unfortunately to cover over and freeze up some of the natural warmth I felt towards [Geddes].[40]

At every step Mumford resisted falling into a filial role, but Geddes persisted to the end. (One of Geddes's last letters, in response to a fairly harsh one from Mumford, opened, "Dear Mumford—no! Lewis my son!")[41] Upon hearing of Geddes's death, therefore, Mumford must have felt the same kind of mixed sorrow and relief that may come upon the death of a father, especially since he had never really known his biological father. Mumford himself recognized that Geddes's death had a liberating effect:

> Released from the pressure of demands I could not fulfill, I was, at last, not merely to draw freely on those parts of Geddes' life and work that still nourished me and incited me to go further along lines he had often indicated but never followed; but at the same time I could, in a series of essays and introductions, call attention to those parts of his work that my contemporaries seemed most in need of.[42]

Mumford's books before *Technics* are predominantly Brooksian exercises in literary and art criticism; *Technics,* especially in the first half covering the history of technology, is a profoundly Geddesian work. The similarities may not be so evident if we compare Mumford's book with Geddes's best-known book on related topics, *Cities in Evolution*. As a writer, Geddes is as awkward as Mumford is fluent, and those who knew Geddes unanimously agree that his writing did little justice to his ideas. If we compare Geddes's notes with Mumford's, however, similarities of tone and texture are much more striking: they both shift around abstract categories like so many counters (especially in the form of lists of opposites), delight in coining neologisms, and, in playing with words, favor the same key terms (for example, "orientations" and "synthesis" and "escapes"), and above all display the same tone, preachy and self-assured.[43]

More important, though, is the way Mumford uses key concepts from Geddes to structure *Technics*. We have already seen how the concept of life insurgent provides a fundamental plot for the entire book. We shall now look more closely at two other key concepts of Geddes, the valley section and technological phases. As Mumford himself has sarcastically noted, some commentators have "charitably supposed that I have never entertained an original idea that I did not derive from Geddes . . . ."[44] I want to stress how much Mumford transformed even ideas that do clearly derive from Geddes.

In the summer 1930 draft Mumford discussed both the valley section and technological phases—but not in the chapter on machinery. Instead, he presented the valley section at the outset of the chapter on regions, and he located the distinction between paleotechnic and neotechnic phases of industry in the chapter on cities.[45] These are the contexts in which Geddes typically used the concepts. But when Mumford came to focus his writing on machines, he changed the context, so that the valley section and technological phases became crucial categories for organizing, both in time and space, his discussion of technological history. In changing the context, Mumford decisively altered the concepts too, as we shall now see.

From Valley Section to Technological Milieu

In *Technics* Mumford at several points credited Geddes for inventing the terms "paleotechnic" and "neotechnic," but in discussing the valley section he failed to mention that this concept too was derived from Geddes. In fact, though, the valley section played an even more fundamental role in Geddes's world-view. Sketches of it—a wobbly line descending from left to right, showing how mountains gradually decline into plains, lowlands, and eventually the sea—appear repeatedly, even obsessively, in his notes, in every imaginable context. Geddes claimed that the valley section was the key to understanding human civilization; he also used it as the basis for educating his eldest son Alisdair.[46] The origins of Geddes's fixation on the valley section lie in his own childhood. He grew up near Perth in a hillside home opening northward and westward upon a "great landscape . . . that stretched over city and river, plain and minor hills, to noble Highland peaks, clear-cut against the evening sky." With his father he often climbed up the nearby slopes of Kinnoull, a "really glorious hill-top" above the Tay that looked southward down to its "rich alluvial plain." From the rock ridge along the river, father and son could look down into Perth, as if it were "a relief-model in perspective."[47] From childhood, then, the image of the mountains gradually sloping down to the sea was deeply embedded in Geddes's mind.

In the late 1870s Geddes began to transform this image into a general sociological theory. As a student in Paris at that time, he happened to attend a lecture by Edmond Demolins, one of the foremost disciples of the French social scientist Frédéric Le Play (1806–82). Geddes was at once convinced that Le Play's observational method and principles of study were of prime importance to social thought.[48] According to Le Play, the basic categories of social existence are "Lieu, Travail, Famille" (which Geddes translated as "Place, Work, Folk"). Le Play further proposed three primary types of family structure, each evolving from three primary occupations: the patriarchal family from herding, a stock family from fishing, and an unstable family from hunting. Any of the above family types might evolve into a fourth, secondary type based on agriculture, but the secondary type would always have traces of its origins.[49] Le Play above all admired the shepherd's way of life as the fount of spiritual virtue, cultural achievement, and familial strength. In a literal (not a literary) sense, Le Play was a pastoralist.

Geddes was somewhat less inclined toward nostalgia for that particular rural setting, preferring instead to see a more even distribution of virtue among various nature-occupations. Geddes did, however, retain Le Play's insistence that modern urban society is best understood as a derivative of simpler rural life:

> For few discern at all, and hardly any clearly, how this rural world offers us not only the beauties and bounties of nature, but also in its workers and their villages the essentials of our civilisation, the simple origins of our most complex urban and metropolitan institutions, and these easily explained, even to much of their working to this day. . . .
>
> For as we ascend the vale to the mountains, or descend again to the sea, we are for the time freed from our imperial and national cares; for the State, its bureaucrats and lawyers, its politicians and their fluctuating struggles, are for the time forgotten. Of mechanistic industry we see nothing beyond the village smithy, and of business only the convenient little shop . . . . After the fatigues and excitements of the city, we rest amid green peace, and let our tired eyes roam to the far horizon, instead of being near-focussed on task or print—a simple hygiene towards sanity of the mind. . . . [50]

By the 1890s Geddes had expanded and combined Le Play's concept of familial types with his own image of the valley section. According to Geddes, by tracing the valley section from the mountain to the sea, one discerns six fundamental occupations: miner, forester, hunter, shepherd, peasant (or crofter or farmer), and fisherman. These nature-occupations, as he referred to them, are not sequential phases but static types: "all these fundamental occupations we have always with us."[51] The miner is seen in the modern manufacturer of aluminum; the woodman, in the house-builder and finally in all engineers; the hunter becomes the sportsman and "the maker and the leader of war"; [52] the shepherd evolves into pastors, cultural and spiritual leaders, as well as into caravan leaders and "their modern successors, the railway kings"; [53] in the frugal, foresighted peasant lie the origins of the bank and insurance company, as well as of the farmer and politician (when peasants gather to drink and chat, they become polit-ically conscious); and finally the fisherman becomes the merchant-adven-turer, the emigrant, the pirate, and the naval warrior. In all these ways we see "the valley in the town."[54]

In his 1959 appraisal of *Technics* Mumford summarized the valley sec-tion as "an ideal, non-historic scheme worked out by his master Patrick Geddes" which was "a useful device" for the way it "throws some light upon occupational origins" and also for the way these types intermingle in the city. "Unfortunately," Mumford added, the valley section diagram

> . . . was governed by the nineteenth-century usage that gave priority to the external environment and to tangible, observable agents. Such a mode of explanation, attributing war and weaponry to a mere extension of hunting techniques, obscured almost as much as it revealed.[55]

Certainly Mumford pinpointed the basic weaknesses in the valley section theory: its geographical determinism (Geddes preferred the term "geo-graphical control," but the principle is the same),[56] and its ahistorical insis-tence that the complexities of modern civilization can be reduced to sim-ple, eternal rural verities.[57] (For further discussion of Mumford's and Benton MacKaye's uses of valley section concepts, see Thomas, this vol-ume, pp. 67–68, 84–86, 93–97.)

In *Technics,* however, Mumford used the valley section in a more subtle way than Geddes had. As we have already noted, the summer 1930 "Form and Personality" draft explicitly discussed the valley section only in the chapter on regionalism. In the chapter on machines, however, Mumford identified critical occupational types—primarily miners, woodmen, and soldiers—as those forming the "army" that conquered Western civiliza-tion for mechanization. In subsequent drafts, Mumford kept his discussion of these crucial occupations, now identifying them as critical "agents of mechanization" from the "upper end" of the valley section.[58] By the time he wrote *Technics* itself, the conspiratorial drama of the 1930 drafts was considerably muted. Simply by substituting the neutral term "agents" for "army," Mumford softened the hard edges of the drama of the machines. Furthermore, in *Technics* his description of the agents is preceded by a thoughtful discussion of the inner sources of decay that had weakened the

The Valley in the Town: from Geddes's Cities and Towns Exhibition comparing the natural valley section (above) and a street in Edinburgh (below). Courtesy of Patrick Geddes Centre for Planning Studies, University of Edinburgh; and Sofia Leonard.

medieval synthesis and allowed it to become vulnerable to pressures exerted by these occupational types.

Most important, though, Mumford looked more closely at the crucial occupations in order to define with greater precision the relation between internal and external mechanization. In doing so, he left behind Le Play and Geddes's stress on geography alone as a determinant of social character. In describing the animus of the miner, for example, Mumford begins with the physical environment, the "manufactured environment" of the underground, where the miner is cut off from nature and dependent upon artificial means for survival; but then he goes on to describe the business environment, the hit-or-miss, random nature of the miner's work and the "pattern for capitalist exploitation" set by the economic organization of mining.[59] The environment of labor therefore includes not just the landscape but also the temporal rhythm of the work, the tools habitually used, the pattern of rewards, and the structure of management and investment. Mumford concludes that in the occupational environment of the mine, if not in society at large, people tend to become mechanized, to assume false definitions of value, to exploit both landscape and other people, and finally to become brutalized themselves.

As we have already remarked, this analysis suggests that while technology in general might not be autonomous, in local circumstances it might be so,

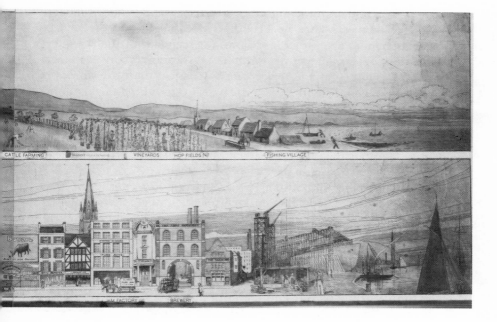

or nearly so. The concept of occupational environment therefore prefigures recent efforts to define relatively autonomous sectors of technological practice—above all, as Mumford himself appreciated, the military sector—that have crucial leverage in altering the direction of technological development in society at large. It also provides a conceptual framework for historians who have espoused a "systems" approach to the study of technologies. Mumford encourages us to see occupations as systems that include bureaucracies, physical environment, labor practices, and business goals. In such a system, the consciousness (or, as Mumford would say, the animus) of the worker is molded by occupational pressures. Here is an opportunity to relate the history of *mentalités* to the history of technology. Here too is an area where historians of technology might fruitfully call upon creative literature for insights into the source of occupational consciousness (as Leo Marx has done, for example, in analyzing the pressures that deform Captain Ahab in *Moby-Dick*).[60]

But the concept of occupational environment can be used without any reference to the ahistorical valley section. Mumford himself does just this in *Technics* when he discusses monastic life as an occupational environment that fostered and institutionalized technologies of time-keeping. Mumford's linkage of the clock and the monastery, of technology and occupation, results in a far more precise and powerful argument than his simple assertion in the 1930 draft that the clock is the crucial invention of modern technology. However, where Le Play or Geddes might have insisted on analyzing the monk, a spiritual leader, as a descendant of the shepherd, Mumford presents his analysis of the monastic vocation before even mentioning the valley section and never tries to connect the two. Moreover, once having outlined the entire section, Mumford pays little further attention to it. Instead of outlining the nature-occupations of the entire valley, he discusses only the miner and the hunter/soldier at any length. He wisely treats the financier, another crucial agent of mechanization, as an independent type rather than as a descendant of the peasant, as Geddes had done.

Indeed, in the hands of both Le Play and Geddes the concept of occupational types seems a willful attempt to evade the category of social class. Geddes, for example, describes the proletariat as a descendant of the peasant, in the form of "stout fellows" who went to the city every six months or year to seek work in the labor market there. "Yet thanks to the stern discipline which his occupation gives in minute economies," especially those compelling the foresighted storage of excess crops, "the peasant is also the source of the banker and the insurance company."[61] To identify both the proletarian and the bank president as descendants of the peasant is, to put it charitably, not especially helpful in understanding contemporary social life. For all his quarrels with Marxism, Mumford appreciated the value of class analysis far more than did Le Play or Geddes—but the inherent danger of occupational analysis, the ever-present risk it presents, is that it will displace rather than complement the category of social class.

Technological Phases

Geddes's notes indicate that the concept of technological phases, like that of the valley section, emerged much earlier and took root more deeply in his thought than his published works show. Only in 1915, in his book *Cities in Evolution,* were the terms put into common circulation, but beginning early in the 1890s Geddes's notes display charts listing characteristics of "paleotechnics" and "neotechnics," as well as experiments with similar terms such as "psychotechnics," "eutechnic," "geotechnic," and "mesotechnic."[62]

Although Geddes continued to use some of these terms, he stressed above all the paleotechnic-neotechnic distinction. The underlying idea is not especially original. By the 1890s the disparity between an old and a new industrial age had impressed many observers, among them Peter Kropotkin, the Russian-born geographer and anarchist living in English exile, who hailed the new technological age in *Fields, Factories and Workshops* (1899).[63] Geddes greatly admired Kropotkin and invited him to lecture at the annual Summer Meetings he organized in Edinburgh in the 1890s. At the same Summer Meetings, Geddes himself regularly taught a course in social evolution in which he stressed the antiquity of man and analyzed the differences between the paleolithic and neolithic stone ages.[64] Evidently in considering these differences he realized they bore an analogy to the two phases of modern industry.[65] In *Cities in Evolution* Geddes explains:

> Recall how as children we first heard of "the Stone Age"; next, how this term has practically disappeared. It was found to confuse what are really two strongly contrasted phases of civilisation, albeit here and there found mingled, in transition; . . . hence we now call these the Old Stone Age and the New, the Paleolithic and the Neolithic. The former phase and type is characterised by rough stone implements, the latter by skilfully chipped or polished ones; the former in common types and mostly for rougher uses, the latter in more varied types and materials, and for finer skills. The first is a rough hunting and warlike civilisation. . . . The latter neolithic folk were of gentler, agricultural type. . . .
> Simply substituting *-technic* for *-lithic*, we may distinguish the earlier and ruder elements of the Industrial Age as Paleotechnic, the newer and still often incipient elements disengaging themselves from these as Neotechnic; while the people belonging to these two dispensations we shall take the liberty of calling Paleotects and Neotects respectively.[66]

Two points should be made about this important passage. First, Geddes drew conclusions about the type of civilization ("rough hunting and warlike" or "gentler, agricultural type") from its surviving artifacts. As Mumford pointed out much later, when he himself came to study the earliest stages of humankind's social and technological evolution, there are all sorts of civilized activities, especially symbolic and aesthetic ones, that have left far less physical evidence in the historical record. To read the character of an entire civilization from its more durable tools is therefore to rely upon biased evidence.[67]

Second, Geddes identified different phases of industry with different types of people, Paleotects and Neotects. In a typical passage in *Cities in Evolution,* Geddes proclaimed that "The paleotechnic mind—whether of Boards of Directors or Worker Unions here matters little—has been too much interested in increasing or in sharing these commercial proceeds, and too little in that of maximising physical efficiency and economy all through."[68] In the same way, he continued, "the present main struggle for existence is not that of fleets and armies, but between the Paleotechnic and Neotechnic order."[69] Thus for Geddes, conventional distinctions of class, race, and nation were relatively unimportant; he substituted for these groups ones defined not by any objective social relations but only by a vague common mindset.

Throughout *Cities in Evolution* Geddes spent considerably more time criticizing the paleotechnic mind and praising the neotechnic one than he did in defining their material bases. In describing paleotechnic industry he remained exceedingly general, saying it was characterized by collieries, the steam engine, "most of our staple manufactures," railways and markets,

"and above all the crowded and monotonous industrial towns to which all
these have given rise."[70] Geddes was even less precise in defining neotechnics, except to say that electrical technologies are foremost among them,
and that wind power is also an example. Mainly he described the paleotechnic and neotechnic phases as urban types—the former being the chaotic, dirty, wasteful city of the iron age, and the later being the unpolluted,
efficient, regional city of the age just dawning.[71]

In his summer 1930 "Form and Personality" draft, Mumford treated
the paleotechnic/neotechnic distinction in much the same spirit, contrast-
ing at length the grimy coal city and the orderly regional city. Unlike Geddes, however, Mumford stressed the technological constraints operative
during the paleotechnic age.[72] In that phase of technology

> One could not plan cities . . . one could only hope to plan out of it: to use
> invention and imagination to get beyond it. So long as coal and steam were
> used in railroads, the yards *had* to be uncovered: so long as local transporta-
> tion was feeble and slow, these yards *had* to push into the heart of the city.
> Better planning awaited a better technology [italics his].[73]

In the dawning age of regional cities, however,

> . . . instead of accepting the limitations of coal industrialism, industry is
> released from its narrow bondage to the railroad track and the coal mine, and
> it can comply with the more imperative demands of living, instead of making
> living conform to its own necessities.[74]

We have already noted one application of local technological determinism in the summer 1930 draft—the argument that the technologies and
practices of certain key occupations tend to "mechanize" those who follow
them. Here is another form of local technological determinism, localized
not in space but in time. Under the conditions of the coal-and-iron age,
Mumford argued, industry *did* "[make] living conform to its necessities."
Fortunately, this was a temporary state that did not apply to neotechnic
industry.[75] Localized occupational determinism explained humankind's
fall into the long paleotechnic night; temporary technological determinism
explained why the renewal of life was so long in coming. In both cases,
Mumford implied, ordinary human beings are not responsible for technological evil.

In *Technics* itself Mumford retained some of his discussion of the technological determinism of the paleotechnic phase, mentioning how the
steam engine "tended toward concentration and bigness" and how it
tended to heap up population in great cities.[76] But in most respects Mumford's discussion of technological phases is quite different from the 1930
draft. Mumford himself succinctly described the major changes in an 8
August 1933 letter to James Henderson:

It was only in the middle of rewriting this second draft that I finally discovered what my thesis was. Roughly, it is this. For the last thousand years there has been a constant technological progress. This has had three phases, and more roughly three time periods: the eotechnic (wind and water and wood complex) from 1000 to 1750: the paleotechnic (coal and iron and steam) from 1700 to 1900: the neotechnic (electricity and the hard alloys and the lighter metals) 1820—? Up to the neotechnic period technological progress consisted in renouncing the organic and substituting the mechanical: this reached its height around 1870. Since then the new trend, visible in technics as well as in philosophy and social life, is the return to the organic by means of the mechanical: a return with a difference, namely, with the whole body of machines and analytical knowledge we have acquired on the way. This last aspect of my thesis was unnoticed by me until the facts thrust themselves into my face.

Three phases, not two; their application to machines in general, not just to cities; and their identification with the organic, the mechanical, and the synthetic respectively—all these changes mean that in *Technics* Mumford largely detached technological phases from the conspiratorial "drama of the machines" and instead incorporated them into the three-part drama of life insurgent. Now each act of that drama has a name: life in balance is the eotechnic; life threatened, the paleotechnic; life insurgent, the neotechnic. Whatever its drawbacks in historical terms (and I shall discuss them soon), in moral terms the identification of this drama with historical periods is, for Mumford, compelling. For him these are not so much technological phases as moral ones. He now has a vocabulary to distinguish "good" machines from "bad" ones, by approving the "organic" or "return-to-the-organic" type while disapproving the purely "mechanical" ones. (As Joseph Duffey has noted, "Mumford employs the organic metaphor as a term of moral judgment.")[77]

In particular, the addition of the third, eotechnic, period makes the moral equilibrium of *Technics* entirely different from the 1930 draft. In the earlier manuscript, the paleotechnic phase had no saving virtues. It resulted from conspiratorial forces, and it was (literally) black while the neotechnic was white. In *Technics,* on the contrary, the paleotechnic period is in some way a necessary interlude, one that expresses significant human traits (even if they became overdeveloped) and that eventually makes possible a higher synthesis, an enriched culture. Moreover, the addition of the eotechnic period means that the neotechnic no longer carries the burden of being the sole repository of all virtue. The eotechnic gives *Technics* a second positive moral pole. A number of critics have found in *Technics,* as well as in other works written about that time, Mumford's neotechnic utopianism: the celebration of a new age of steel and glass, of streamlined toasters and art photography, as if the technical style he admires could be detached from the "pecuniary interests" he despises. They attribute the appeal of this superficial stylistic appeal to Mumford's immaturity; he was still under the spell (these critics argue) of an equally superficial, liberal progressivist ideology that he later outgrew under the pressure of events such as the rise of fascism and the advent of atomic weapons.[78] But in *Technics* there are two utopias: the futuristic *and* the retrospective, the latter being the eotechnic "golden day" of medieval northern Europe to which Mumford pays homage in eloquent and deeply felt passages.[79] As well as looking forward beyond the neotechnic to the geotechnic era as Geddes had,[80] Mumford begins to gaze more steadily the other way, into the more distant past. In subsequent works his gaze became ever more fixed and penetrating, as, in the words of Casey Blake, he "summoned up the past as a standard by which to demystify the present and its claims to progress. . . ."[81]

Does the concept of technological phases have any value for other historians? Mumford thought so. In his 1959 reappraisal of *Technics,* Mumford called its three-part scheme "the most original and yet in some ways the most dubious part of the whole book." In particular he felt that recent nuclear technologies did not fit the pattern because they were far more "mechanical" than "synthetic," adding that

> . . . the whole scheme breaks down as soon as one steps outside the arbitrary thousand-year period and tries to work out a more universal succession of technological phases. . . . The author of *Technics and Civilization* may in fact congratulate himself over the fact that the division he used never effectively caught on; and it broke down in his own mind before it could do any serious damage.[82]

Still, Mumford concluded, his contribution in *Technics,* "still largely neglected," was to define "the nature of a technical phase as consisting of a particular mode of power, particular modes of transportation and communication, and a particular set of metals and other material resources."[83]

This is the issue I wish to address here: not the validity of the particular phases in *Technics,* but the validity of the underlying concept. In order to do so, I need to introduce more formally James Henderson, who has already been mentioned as a correspondent of Mumford's and who was asked by Mumford to comment on the fall 1933 draft of *Technics.* The two first met in April 1920, when they happened to take the same steamer to England. After disembarking they spent some time together in London, where Henderson introduced Mumford to some of his friends. Henderson visited the Mumfords on and off until about 1935.[84] From Mumford's apparently somewhat condescending point of view,[85] Henderson was a useful manuscript reviewer because he was immensely well-read, especially in history and in philosophy, something of a pedant, and a stickler for facts. (For example, it was Henderson who provided Mumford with the statistic that at one time there were 40,000 Benedictine monasteries in medieval Europe.)[86]

What Mumford failed to appreciate—at least judging from his failure to respond to them—was the soundness of Henderson's conceptual critiques.[87] Henderson felt Mumford became carried away by his rhetoric instead of examining more carefully the ideas behind it. Henderson once said of himself, "I get distracted from reading a book by the ideas involved"; [88] Mumford's great fault, in Henderson's view, was to become distracted from thinking by writing. In one letter Henderson cautioned, "Writing is very dangerous to thought especially when you get used to writing and where your statements are taken seriously. . . ."[89]

This is the background to Henderson's response to Mumford's 8 August 1933 letter quoted above, where Mumford excitedly explained his new thesis. In reply Henderson fairly exploded:

> As you express them your theses are too general to be clear . . . . [The organic is hardly the opposite of the mechanical.] You don't mean wood etc. is organic and iron mechanical?! And what would returning to the organic by means of the mechanical mean—it's a way of living of some kind—but you see words like these mean *anything*, and are therefore dangerous—*they* are mechanical—i.e. abstract or rationalistic. . . . [90]

When Mumford asked Henderson to review the fall 1933 draft of *Technics,* Henderson returned it with marginal comments repeatedly criticizing Mumford for relying upon abstractions—the organic, the mechanical, the valley section,[91] the paleotechnic, the neotechnic—without making clear what they meant and for turning them into historical subjects. At another point Henderson simply protested in the margin, "You can't just say this."[92]

Henderson's criticisms were, I think, just, and I also think he was right in suggesting that they arise because Mumford-the-writer tends to take over from Mumford-the-thinker. In *Technics,* Mumford repeatedly borrowed abstractions from Geddes—occupational types and technological phases—which he then reified as historical actors in his own dramatic structures (the drama of life insurgent and the drama of the machines) that so appealed to him as a myth-maker and moralist. Therefore "the eotechnic revolution" can have a goal, the machine can "be" a communist, and so forth. Geddes's terms provided the cast for moral plots, and so the historical stage became populated with pseudo-actors. As a result, in the words of one unfriendly reviewer, Mumford "psychologize[d] causes and . . . moralize[d] effects" and "a mysterious animism" comes to replace analysis.[93]

We have already seen that Geddes too used pseudo-actors such as "the neotechnic mind" or "Paleotects." In fact, many of the historiographic problems noted by Henderson can be traced back to Geddes's original formulation: not only the assumption that mindsets can be historical agents, but also the assumption that the inner spirit of a culture may be read back from its most external technologies, that ugly coal towns incarnate ugly values while cities that look efficient and orderly must express values of efficiency and order. Henderson questioned this assumption when, at the very beginning of the manuscript, he penciled in the questions, "'Form' used synonymous with 'culture'? Explain?"[94] Henderson continued to question Mumford's habit of treating each technological phase as a cultural whole in which spirit and form are always consistent within that phase. When Mumford stated at one point that "the eotechnic revolution was diverted from finding its own goal by a new movement in industrial society," Henderson underlined "its own goal" and added in the margin, "A culture as an abstract entity can be thought of as having a goal from which it is diverted. In reality it creates its own destructive agents."[95]

This last criticism is not entirely fair. Mumford does make room for understanding cultures as dialectic processes when he combines the chronological typology of technological phases with the static typology of the valley section. In this, he is unlike Geddes, who originated both concepts without trying to harmonize them. Mumford describes the eotechnic phase as a cultural unity, in which outer forms faithfully express the inner spirit, but he also describes occupational types within the eotechnic phase (miners, woodmen, and soldiers) who operate according to other goals and values and who therefore act as destructive agents. In much the same way, the paleotechnic phase is subverted from within by occupational types who operate by non-paleotechnic goals and values—above all scientists and some engineers who act according to the values of economy, life-efficiency, and the like.[96] Thus Mumford describes both a dominant culture and occupational subcultures that operate as destructive—or constructive—agents within.

The main problem with Mumford's use of technological phases is not that he ignores the existence of processes that work against the dominant culture, but rather that he too much identifies that dominant culture with its technological forms. If a technological phase were defined (as Mumford does in his 1959 appraisal of *Technics*) as "consisting of a particular mode of power, particular modes of transportation and communication, and a particular set of metals and other material resources," then it becomes something very much like what historians of technology now call a technological style.[97] In that case, Mumford's discussion is helpful in illuminating the historical progression of technological styles. He suggests how these styles might be defined and analyzed in terms of dominant forms and rhythms and materials, and in addition he tries to relate technological systems to systems of sense impressions.

But Mumford goes further and equates styles with values. For example, he looks at the eotechnic era and sees objects he admires, and therefore reads back enlightened values into that epoch. Henderson had to remind Mumford that many of the abuses he attributes in *Technics* to the paleotechnic era had really begun much earlier in the eotechnic phase. Henderson pointed out that wood-and-water technologies were also highly developed not only in northern Europe, where Mumford focused almost exclusively in describing the eotechnic, but also in Mesopotamia, North Africa, southern Italy and France, and Spain. In other words, similar technological styles arose in vastly dissimilar cultures.[98]

Similar distortions arise from Mumford's attempt to read back paleo-technic culture from its industrial artifacts. As Henderson noted, Mumford treats modern history as consisting only of scientists, inventors, and industrialists, as if there had been no Berkeley, Kant, Hegel, Croce, poets, novelists, artists, musicians, and others outside the "mechanical" scope.[99] Finally, in lauding the neotechnic phase, Mumford assumes that since its technological forms look efficient, dynamic, and organic, the values of efficiency, dynamism, and organism must be emerging in the general culture too. Many critics have noted the asymmetry of *Technics:* an entire section explains the "cultural preparation" that eventually generated paleotechnic forms, but neotechnic forms precede, and are themselves supposedly generating, corresponding cultural changes.[100]

Mumford began writing *Technics* as a nineteenth-century-style social prophet whose response to the disintegrating forces of industrialization and democracy was to advocate a return to a more organic culture—that is, to a deeply rooted and coherent set of values that would provide social unity and direction. In the English language, this tradition is exemplified by Matthew Arnold's essay "Culture and Anarchy"; the British tradition as a whole has been analyzed by Raymond Williams in *Culture and Society.* On the Continent, many other thinkers developed similar themes.[101] Seen in this perspective, *Technics* reads as an old-fashioned appeal to culture as a moral agent, as a corrective to the anarchy—which Mumford preferred to call the loss of form—that has descended upon Western civilization with the advent of industrialization.

What is so untraditional, though, is the way Mumford "enlarges the canon of culture"[102] to include technology. A more organic culture? Machines are potentially organic too. Machinery a threat to culture? It is also part of the cultural solution. In Mumford's own words, to see technics as "an integral part of higher civilization" represents "a shift in the whole point of view."[103] This is his fundamental and lasting contribution.

But the contribution carries with it an equally fundamental limitation: the tendency to define culture as a set of artifacts, as objects rather than processes. This weakness ultimately derives from Mumford's determination to refute Marxism by turning it upside down, to treat technological objects as the material expression of substructural cultural values.[104] When he discusses technologies according to this model, Mumford writes as an art critic, a self-appointed arbiter of taste and sensibility; he tells us about streamlined machines and the values of noble austerity and impersonal efficiency that they supposedly incarnate. The result is a consumer-oriented approach to machines, in which they are viewed not as the outcome of social processes but as cultural products. By insisting upon the distinction between the practical and the cultural significance of machines, Mumford ignores the crucial nexus where they meet, in the social conditions of production.

But Mumford ended up writing another book as well, one that embodies another mode of cultural criticism: a utopian mode. These two voices, that of the art critic and that of the utopian, carry on a duet throughout Mumford's entire career. He repeatedly invests a golden day of the past with utopian qualities in order to imagine an ideal society and to criticize the present one. The ideal keeps receding, however, as Mumford moves it back from America of the 1830s (in *The Golden Day* itself) to the eotechnic era in *Technics* until, by the 1960s, he concludes that since the megamachine originated at the very dawn of civilization, an ideal life-centered polytechnics is incompatible with history itself.[105]

The French scholar Miguel Abensour has proposed an important distinction that helps define the nature of Mumford's utopianism. Abensour suggests that before around 1850 a systematic form of utopianism prevailed, and he defines this as utopianism that seeks to build alternative organizational models. Since the mid-nineteenth century, however, there has been a shift toward a heuristic form of utopianism, in which the focus is on the articulation of alternative values. In the systematic mode, a whole society is pictured: in the heuristic mode, new values, feelings, and relationships, with comparatively little attention to institutions. In the memorable phrase of E.P. Thompson, heuristic utopianism seeks "the education of desire."[106]

Abensour's purpose in making this distinction is to argue against the scientific/utopian dichotomy that he feels has caused Marxism to reject important insights, especially those of William Morris. Certainly the category of heuristic utopia permits new appreciation of the contribution of mavericks like Mumford and Morris. Unfortunately, as we have seen, Mumford—unlike Morris—made little effort to do justice to some important insights of Marxism. In particular, Mumford was so critical of what he considered the Marxist project of changing only institutions that he repeatedly proclaimed that a revolution in values must precede political revolution and might even render it unnecessary. Thus Mumford perpetuated an unrealistic dichotomy between institutions and values: the education of desire becomes a largely apolitical project.

There are obvious autobiographical reasons for Mumford's tendency to see values in such aesthetic and individualistic terms. He himself was so disconnected: fatherless, with only a sketchy family, a free-lancer, a bohemian, he fiercely asserted his independence, whether marital or professional, and always felt he existed outside conventional social niches. But let us not in turn be too individualistic in analyzing the sources of Mumford's heuristic utopianism. We must also consider the larger historical context, the water in which not just Mumford but we ourselves swim. Raymond Williams has suggested that systematic utopianism typically arises in extreme social situations, either one of great confidence, "the mood of a rising class, which knows, down to detail, that it can replace the existing order; or that of social despair, the mood of a declining class or fraction of a class, which has to create a new heaven because its Earth is a hell." Williams continues:

The basis of the more open but also the vaguer [heuristic] mode is different from either. It is a society in which change is happening, but primarily under the direction and in the terms of the dominant social order itself. This is always a fertile moment for what is, in effect, an anarchism: positive in its fierce rejection of domination, repression, and manipulation; negative in its willed neglect of structures, of continuity and of material constraints. . . the heuristic mode . . . seems often to be primarily a response to a constrained reformism. . . . The heuristic utopia offers a strength of vision against the prevailing grain; . . . at the same time, [it] has the weakness that it can settle into isolated and in the end sentimental "desire," a mode of living with alienation. . . .[107]

In *Technics and Civilization* Mumford writes not so much as a historian of technology as a retrospective heuristic utopian who connects changes in values with changes in technology. The book he wrote is not the book he set out to write, however, and we can see traces of both in the final manuscript. Mumford sometimes writes as an art critic and sometimes as a utopian, and he feels the tug of the futuristic utopia as well as of the retrospective one. Still, he reached a pivotal point. Although Mumford would never be able to disentangle history-writing from myth-making, historical dramas from moral ones, he came to discern the invisible components of past technologies—the megamachines of the powerful, and the container-based polytechnics of ordinary people—and therefore to disengage cultural criticism from art criticism. As James Henderson wrote in his "final note" on the title page of the 1933 draft of *Technics and Civilization,* "Write the book you discovered you were writing not the one you intended to write."[108]

For their assistance in making accessible the papers of Mumford and Geddes I am deeply indebted to Dr. Katherine Reed, Van Pelt Library, University of Pennsylvania; James McGrath, Archivist at the University of Strathclyde; and Sofia Leonard, Senior Research Fellow at the Patrick Geddes Centre for Planning Studies, University of Edinburgh. Support for research trips to Philadelphia, Glasgow, and Edinburgh was made possible by the Provost's Fund and from the Old Dominion Foundation, both administered through the Department of Humanities, MIT.

Lewis Mumford, Benton MacKaye, and the Regional Vision

JOHN L. THOMAS

I

In May 1925 the International Town, City, Regional Planning and Garden Cities Congress met in the ballroom of the Hotel Pennsylvania at the corner of 32nd Street and Seventh Avenue in New York City. The selection of the site in midtown Manhattan was a fitting symbol of the mood of the dominant American wing of the postwar urban planning movement, confident of success and eager to present the preliminary findings of their already well-publicized report. The "Regional Plan of New York and Its Environs," financed by the Russell Sage Foundation and compiled under the scrutiny of the internationally recognized urban planner, Thomas Adams, would eventually be published in two volumes—*The Graphic Regional Plan* in 1929 and *The Building of the City* two years later—but already the New York group hoped to impress their colleagues from abroad as well as at home with their new model of what Adams called the "city efficient." Adams, who had been appointed General Director of Plans and Surveys three years earlier, was a highly respected veteran of British and Canadian urban planning who brought to the New York project a hard-headed Scotch utilitarianism summarized in his promise, worthy of Bentham himself, "to so direct urban growth in the future that the greatest practicable measure of health, safety, convenience and general welfare will be secured for the inhabitants."[1] For New York City that promise meant, first of all, acceptance of a projected population of twenty-one million by 1965 and of the resultant need for some plan of "recentralization" to secure "the benefits of concentration without congestion." It also spelled more skyscrapers and highways.

The progressive regional planning movement in the United States dated from the turn of the century, and after a brief interruption during the First World War, had acquired renewed momentum by the mid-1920s. Signs of revived interest in managing metropolitan growth could be seen in Philadelphia's new Tri-State District, Chicago's Regional Planning Association, and stirrings in Los Angeles as well as in Thomas Adams's massive planning project for New York City and environs. Progressive planning rested on the twin assumptions of irreversible urban concentration and the urgent need for citizen enlightenment in the hope of fostering "a passion for improvement," as Adams himself explained. Yet improvement frequently deduced to accommodation to rapid growth of the central city and schemes for zoning reform and projects for slum clearance undertaken for reasons of profit as well as philanthropy. Such genuine decentralization as Adams and his planning staff were willing to consider involved make-shift attempts to relieve congestion in the center city by suburbanizing its surrounding areas and linking them to Manhattan with a modernized system of transportation. The vision of New York City as organically linked to a larger regional social and economic context somehow eluded them.

The Adams group's vision of a metropolis renovated along purely pragmatic lines could be read clearly in their Diagrammatic Scheme for Regional Highway Routes, a series of concentric arcs rippling from an inner beltway around the five boroughs out to the periphery running from Bridgeport to Newburgh to Far Hills to Asbury Park. The philosophy underlying their visualization the New York planners stated with disarming candor: admitting that "we cannot overcome the economic forces that make cities as large as New York," they recognized no danger lurking in megalopolis and believed devoutly in their ability "to plan for that which is good and sound and practical." "There is nothing to be gained by conceiving the impossible," Adams warned as though anticipating an attack on his pragmatic achievements.

That assault had already been mounted by the vanguard of a Spenglerian "Barbarian Invasion" from up the Hudson comprised of Lewis Mumford, Benton MacKaye, Clarence Stein, Henry Wright, and a handful of followers recruited from the ranks of the Regional Planning Association of America and presently encamped across the lobby of the Hotel Pennsylvania with their own battle plans and maps. The Regional Planning Association of America had been formed two years earlier at a gathering of friends at Hudson Guild Farm in Mount Olive, New Jersey, in the foothills of the Poconos. The group of some ten or a dozen architects and planners had acquired experience during the war in planning demonstration garden cities modeled on Ebenezer Howard's alternative to the "dinosaur cities" to which Thomas Adams and his metropolitanists had seemingly become captive. Mumford and MacKaye, who headed the regionalist forces, had prepared their own strategic campaign in advance in a special edition for May 1925 of the *Survey Graphic* calling for a "fourth migration" out of the city and into its regional surroundings. They were also ready to denounce the Adams plan as "nothing bolder . . . than an orderly dilution of New York over a fifty mile circle." Even the title of their official report was a misnomer. True regional planning, Mumford scoffed, was not "just a technique" or the concern of a single profession but "a mode of thinking and a method of procedure." To attack the problem as primarily a matter of housing was to begin at the wrong end. The inevitable results of such faulty logic would be an increase in real estate speculation, a massing of outsized Manhattan towers, overcrowding, and impenetrable commercial zones. Adams and his staff, Mumford complained, had surrendered to the very forces that had produced the urban chaos they now sought to remedy. Their plan was being drafted simply to meet the needs and prejudices of America's corporate rulers, and "its aim from the beginning was as much welfare and amenity as could be obtained without altering any of the political or business institutions which have made the city precisely what it is." A genuine regional plan pointed toward

> . . . the reinvigoration and rehabilitation of whole regions so that the products of culture and civilization, instead of being confined to a prosperous minority in the congested centers shall be available to everyone at every point in a region where the physical basis for the cultivated life can be laid down.[2]

To illustrate their alternative proposal the regionalists countered with a "visualization" of their own—a simple map of the entire state of New York divided into three areas: *Plains* stretching up the Hudson and out into the Mohawk Valley and filled with market gardens and orchards, small factories and medium-sized cities; *Plateau* as table-land for dairy and subsistence farming; and *Highlands* with their forest and water reserves. Together these natural features comprised a relief model of the "valley section" defined by the Scotch urban planner Patrick Geddes—a topographical dish rising from regional cities and rich staple-crop bottomlands up the sides to small farms and diversified agriculture through pastoral slopes to wilderness along the rim. With the valley section as his organizing concept, Mumford proposed the regional dispersal of people and their economy in a planned migration out of New York. "For a hundred years in America," he explained, "business has been concentrating financial resources, concentrating factories and urban districts, attempting to create material prosperity by producing goods which could be quickly 'turned over.'" Now a new industrial revolution was in the process of spreading real income by decentralizing industry and propelling people out of the city and into its supporting environs. This dispersal was Mumford's version of the "fourth migration": an exodus from the metropolis.

In fashioning his own indictment of the Adams plan Mumford's new friend MacKaye agreed that the metropolis "brings its own chaos" from which Americans must escape in a "new exploration" of the valley section from the river's mouth back through the flow to the source. Only by surveying the entire configuration from a vantage-point high on the wilderness ridges, MacKaye insisted, could the planner discern the natural framework in which cities like New York must take their subordinate place. In summing up for his colleagues at the convention his charges against the metropolitanists, Mumford began at the other end of the valley section, in the city itself and the need to lift from it "some of the burden of the business overhead and sales-promotion, ground rents in congested districts and so forth."[3] The appearance of the forty-six-year-old MacKaye and of Mumford sixteen years his junior marching at the head of their self-styled "Barbarian Invasion" marked the convergence of careers but also of vantage-points. Their differing perspectives on the city and the region reduced ultimately to Mumford's view of Manhattan from the massive piers of Brooklyn Bridge and MacKaye's outlook from Hunting Hill across the watershed of the Nashua River in Shirley Center, Massachusetts.

II

MacKaye's outlook in 1925, as it had been in childhood over three decades earlier, was Hunting Hill, a rock cropping only 542 feet high but affording a full sweep of the surrounding countryside. To the southeast flowed Mulpus Brook to join the Nashua River. Beyond the ridge and above its hardwoods rose a white spire identifying Shirley Center and the three-cornered green hard by the MacKaye farmhouse. North lay the Whitman River, along its banks the railroad bringing lumber and staples east to Boston and carrying manufactures back to the Berkshires and beyond. From this familiar elevation, which an adolescent MacKaye properly termed a "drumlin," he could watch what he came to define as two types of "flow"—the natural downstream pitch of the water course to Boston Harbor and the Gulf of Maine and the man-made "molten framework of industry" pouring westward along the railroad in finger-like projections up the same rivers back to the source.

MacKaye had come to Shirley Center as a boy of nine in 1888 from the frenzied theatrical world of Broadway, where his father, Steele MacKaye, the well-known actor, playwright, and producer, staged great "dramas" for his audiences on "the meaning of their country."[4] After a chaotic early childhood in a crowded New York apartment, the farmhouse in Shirley Center offered the young MacKaye feelings of continuity and deep contentment. "MacKaye Cottage," as the neighbors always called it, was a small white clapboard house set in the middle of a shaded yard which looked out on hay meadows and hardwood groves. The center of the village was the nearby common, a triangular green dominated by the meetinghouse and belfry which the boy saw as the sun in the center of his universe. Across the river through thick growths of alder ran the Nashua River in a setting which Thoreau had revealed half-a-century earlier.[5]

Mumford once described the mature MacKaye as "a man built to the measure of a Natty Bumppo, or an Emerson, or Uncle Sam without whiskers, with a touch of the Indian, or more likely the Highland Scot in his saturnine features." The man whom Mumford met and befriended in the 1920s was big-boned, hard-muscled, trim and compact with a prominent Roman nose set between high cheekbones beneath overarching brow and high forehead rising to a shock of coarse black hair. MacKaye claimed to have received two quite different educations. "I graduated from Longley's

barnyard in 1893 and from Harvard in 1900," he explained in memorial-
izing his nextdoor neighbor, Melvin Longley, dairyman, surrogate father,
town selectman and state legislator—altogether the embodiment of "a culture and a mode of government." This rural New England culture became
MacKaye's ideal, a way of life still buffered by the woods and fields west of
Concord from metropolitan Boston which was already spilling across nineteenth-century suburban dikes. "The basic geographic unit of organic
human society," MacKaye later argued, "is the single town of definite
physical limits," a way-station between Boston and the wilderness at the
end of the state.

The seventeen-year-old MacKaye entered Harvard in 1896 and quickly
turned to geology and geography as the academic equivalent of a perch on
the top of Hunting Hill. These two fields in the golden years of academic
reform under President Charles Eliot were the domains of Nathaniel
Southgate Shaler, an immensely popular teacher and author of numerous
works on geology and topics of general social interest, and William Morris
Davis. MacKaye vividly remembered his first day in Davis's *Geography A*
which he gave in a packed lecture-hall in the Agassiz Museum. Standing
immobile on the platform, his hands behind him, Morris suddenly produced a six-inch globe, gave it a spin, and held it aloft as he intoned: "Gentlemen, here is the subject of our study—this planet, its lands, waters,
atmosphere, and life; the abode of plant, animal, and man—*the earth as a
habitable globe.*" Shaler and Morris helped focus MacKaye's attention on
the idea of *process,* both natural and conceptual, as a *drama* of man's interaction with nature in a reflexive relationship which their student would
come to call "flow"—the making of patterns on the land through the transit of people and their goods across it.[6]

The idea for a long-distance trail running the length of the Appalachian
chain which MacKaye spent a lifetime realizing came out of early first-hand
contact with wilderness, beginning with hikes with an older brother "when
he a Big Boy and I a little returned home fishless or gameless but having
'bagged' the one thing—a pursuit at nature's sources—that we were really
after." In the summer of 1897 together with three companions he spent
six gruelling weeks backpacking in New Hampshire on the "toughest and
greatest trip" of his life. Here in dense forests or mountainous terrain was
the evening campfire that he would turn into an emblem of wilderness
complete with story-telling and harmonica-playing, at both of which he
excelled. Again six years later in the deep woods above Keene, having graduated from Harvard but still searching for a vocation, he met naturalist
and conservation pioneer Raphael Zon—"friend, philosopher, and patron
saint"—who urged him to find himself by becoming a forester. MacKaye
received a master's degree in forestry from Harvard in 1905, the year in
which the feisty Gifford Pinchot took command of the United States Forest
Service. Admitted to the "Chief's" domain, MacKaye was dispatched to
New Hampshire, where he surveyed and mapped the forest cover of the
White Mountains in relating it to the flow of the rivers of northern New

England in a pioneer report which provided the technical data for establishing the White Mountain National Forest.

In 1913, MacKaye returned to Washington. Woodrow Wilson's Washington in the years before the outbreak of World War I was a clearinghouse for new reform proposals and a collecting-point for bright young bureaucrats and publicists intent on implementing them. Not until two decades later did the city attract similar talent and dedication to reform. If the symbolic center of the New Deal was a plan for economic recovery, the yardstick of progressive Washington was *conservation* initiated and even managed by a partnership between government and big business, but ramifying through a growing public awareness everywhere in the country. MacKaye took a strong hand in drafting a series of legislative proposals for achieving conservationist goals, the first of them a bill, never passed, to develop and control timber, mining, and transportation in Alaska through the establishment of balanced "primary resource communities" planned, like the original models of John Wesley Powell for the Arid Region, as an alternative to the unregulated and destructive practices of the nineteenth century. Three years later a second of MacKaye's proposals—his National Colonization Bill—met a similar fate, and his vision of redeemed land in the Lake States focusing on the small community modeled on his own Shirley Center went glimmering.[7]

Gradually MacKaye began adding a cultural dimension to his conservationist work. Forestry and watersheds concerned people's relations with primal nature. From then on he began to concentrate increasingly on the kind of community life and culture available to Americans on their land, concerns lying beyond questions of water-courses, cut-capacities, and timber-yields, and involving communal activity as well as individual "self-organization."

By 1920 it was clear that progressivism had stalled and that the regulatory and planning machinery of the war state was being dismantled rapidly. "Washington went down like a circus tent," MacKaye recalled. "Everything dropped. That was the beginning of normalcy right there."[8] There would be no conservation program forthcoming from the new Harding administration or from a suddenly laggard Congress. With little concrete to show for his ten-year education in conservation politics, MacKaye retreated to Shirley Center undismayed by the fact that he now had no job and few prospects of finding one. MacKaye was a man of extreme spartan habits who, like Thoreau, had pared his wants to the bone. Now he was free, after a decade of government service, to develop two ideas he had been holding in reserve for some time: a plan for a regional "folkland" of unspoiled nature along the ridges of the Appalachians; and looming behind it "a new social order the keynote of whose productive system shall be service—not profits."

Then suddenly, in 1921, MacKaye was struck by personal tragedy: his wife died. Shattered and depressed, he retreated on the invitation of the kindly Charles Whitaker, editor of the *Journal of the American Institute of*

Architects, to his farm in Mount Olive in northwestern New Jersey to recover. There he made new friends who helped him regain his health and his equilibrium—the architect Clarence Stein, the landscape architect Henry Wright, and, most important, the young cultural critic and publicist Lewis Mumford. These colleagues formed the nucleus of the American Institute of Architects' recently formed Committee on Community Planning. Within two years all of them, together with a dozen or so other activists, would break off and form their own splinter organization, the Regional Planning Association of America. Whitaker promptly introduced MacKaye to his new circle, and in long weekend walks through the countryside or lively evening discussions around the fire they listened as the newcomer expounded his plan for a "folkland," a wilderness trail running the Appalachian ridge from Maine to Georgia. Mumford and his friends quickly realized that here was a man whose "visualizations," as he called them, embraced more than housing and urban planning, city parks, and slum clearance. MacKaye, they soon understood, was proposing to build a conceptual bridge between the conservation movement in which he had been trained and community planning with which they themselves had been almost exclusively concerned. Here, in short, was a highly original exploratory mind equipped with a forceful if somewhat wooden expository style which mixed Yankee colloquialisms and philosophical meditations in equal proportion but whose sense of regional planning as "a single thing" transcended their own.

MacKaye envisioned his trail as a network of interrelated systems—"a thing to grow and be developed apart from our more *commercial* development." He proposed the establishment of a connected series of wilderness "neutral zones" offering all citizens "equal opportunity for real life." In "An Appalachian Trail: A Project in Regional Planning," which appeared in the October 1921 issue of Whitaker's journal, MacKaye also conceived of the trail as a school—a place where "you look *at* in order to look *through,* where you look at a forest in order to perceive its pyramid and food cycle; where you view a landscape in order to perceive its water cycle." For such "visualizing" the vantage-point is all-important, just as his own had been as a young boy on the top of Hunting Hill. "Let us assume the existence of a giant standing high on the skyline along these mountain ridges, his head just scraping the floating clouds. What would he see from this skyline as he strode along its length from north to south?" Beginning at the summit of Mount Washington, MacKaye as explorer-guide in a "new exploration" points his pupils north to survey the heavily forested hunting-ground of the Indian; then west to the Berkshires and the Adirondacks; next to the "crowded east—a chain of smoky bee-hive cities extending from Boston to Washington, home to a third of the nation's population"; and finally south, down to the Southern Appalachians, the primal environment unchanged since the time of Daniel Boone and climaxing on the summit of Mount Mitchell.

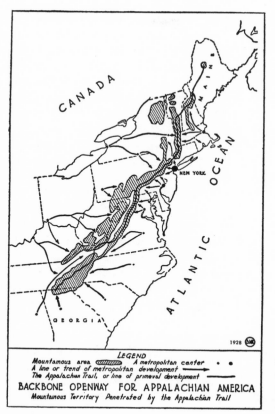

LEGEND

Mountainous area ⬭⬭⬭⬭ A metropolitan center • •
A line or trend of metropolitan development ➤
The Appalachian Trail, or line of primeval development ▬▬

BACKBONE OPENWAY FOR APPALACHIAN AMERICA
Mountainous Territory Penetrated by the Appalachian Trail

Benton MacKaye's Directional Lines: from *The New Exploration,* 1962 edition. His sketch of the Appalachian Trail. Courtesy of the University of Illinois Press.

Here stood revealed a "broad gauged enlightening approach" to the problems presented by industrial and commercial life: a way to preserve "habitability" as a counter to the "grinding-down process of our modern life." Begin, MacKaye advised Mumford and his friends, by building a solid regional base for "a more extensive and systematic development of outdoor community life." Beneath the Appalachian ridge running like a backbone down the Atlantic littoral lay footlands ready for communal farms and recreation camps, the building of which would call forth "the primal instincts of a fighting heroism, of volunteer service, and of working in a common cause." Above these base-camp communities, in MacKaye's "vision," looms the Trail itself, "a path of exploration . . . leading to the physical mysteries of the land and sky inhabited by a primal life dating from the verdant slime on the first pools of water." Just here, he announced, was "something to be dramatized . . . the primal story of Planet Earth—its life, its structure, and its oneness." Then suddenly, as though catching himself before he soared off into mystical realms, he returned to the practical world of the architect and planner. "It is a project in housing and community architecture," he reminded his readers.[9]

MacKaye's vision also proved to him the indispensability of local initiative and popular participation in building the Trail in the spirit of old-time barn-raisings and corn-huskings. He called for government to provide the land and for people to repossess and reclaim it in a new collaboration.

> We should survey and chart our *areas* of highland wilderness as well as cut our *lines* of trail. We should plot the boundaries of our realm. We should find and know what lies within—what forests, actual or potential; what upland range lands; what cabin sites; what vistas to unfold. And on this basis we should visualize a plan of occupation: that is, we should *reveal* the hidden plan of nature to this end.[10]

These were MacKaye's orders to architects and city planners: join forces with conservationists like himself and launch an educative Barbarian Invasion of the metropolis. One of his listeners, first at Whitaker's farmhouse and then at Hudson Guild Farm, the rural retreat of social workers from the West Side, was Mumford who recognized in his new friend with his "eaglelike profile, his black hair, his gift for picturesque epithets and oaths, his campfire stories," the archetypal Yankee—"almost the stage Yankee." Mumford immediately warmed to the lean, laconic MacKaye who seemed a spiritual son of Thoreau, "tart as a wild apple, sweet as a hickory nut," though to more prosaic minds, perhaps, "in Benton's own lingo, 'as wild as a wolf, as crazy as a loon.'"[11]

Mumford had just published his first book, *The Story of Utopias* in which, having surveyed utopian literature from Plato to Bellamy and rejected industrial capitalism and the war state, he called on Americans "to develop an art of regional planning, an art which will relate city and countryside in a new pattern from that which was the blind creation of the industrial and territorial planner." If MacKaye's vantage point was the wilderness view from the top of Mount Washington, Mumford's was the outlook high on the piers of Brooklyn Bridge out across his own New York City, "immense, overpowering, flooded with energy and light."

In the immediate postwar years, however, Mumford's estimate of the possibilities of reconstructing either the city or the nation was not a sanguine one. It was absurd, he had argued in an article for *The Nation* in 1919, to leave corrective measures to the uncertain charitable instincts of those private interests responsible for the problems in the first place.

> The housing problem, the industries problem, the transportation problem, and the land problem cannot be solved one at a time by isolated experts thinking and acting in a civic vacuum. They are mutually interacting elements, and they can be effectively dealt with only by bearing constantly in mind the general situation from which they have been abstracted.[12]

That general context, Mumford was already convinced, was the region itself, visualized from his own urban perspective as well as from Benton MacKaye's mountain-top. Bounding the region, the two men agreed as they began to share ideas and plans, was wilderness at one end of the valley section and the metropolis at the other. Here was the dual focus of the genuine regional planner, one that defined a lifetime challenge for the two new friends.

III

If the young MacKaye graduated from Melvin Longley's barnyard, Lewis Mumford, by his own account, was a child of the city. He was born in Flushing, Queens, in 1895, the illegitimate son of Elvina Conradina Baron Mumford whose marriage years earlier to John Mumford, an Englishman twice her age, was never consummated but whose liaison with the nephew of the well-to-do bachelor for whom she kept house was. The first of the boy's surrogate fathers was his grandfather, Charles Graessel, the retired headwaiter at Delmonico's, now a gentleman of leisure living carefully but well on his "competence," a highly knowledgeable guide to the walking city which was New York at the turn of the century. Lewis accompanied his grandfather on daily jaunts through Central Park to the mansions along Fifth Avenue and back again to stop at the west carriage gate and watch the afternoon procession of broughams and victorias "in a sort of park-wide carousel" that formed the boy's aesthetic background. As he grew older, the journeys became longer—to Canal Street for his grandfather's custom-made shoes and the East Fifties for an occasional box of hand-rolled Cuban cigars. "These excursions," Mumford would recall, "gave me my first impression of the city that lay beyond my neighborhood; and if my grandfather introduced me to a whole variety of strange streets and occupations, he also made me at home in the Metropolitan Museum of Art and the American Museum of Natural History."

The young Mumford's Upper West Side neighborhood was the grid of gray streets running from Central Park West to Riverside Drive that in the 1880s had acquired architectural definition and a class structure of "diagrammatic neatness"—with the working classes confined to cheap tenements along Amsterdam and Columbus Avenues; the costly townhouses of the city's wealthy classes at the extremities facing the Park or the Hudson; and in between the middle classes solidly entrenched in uniform row houses. Mumford's recollection of various uptown interiors was as strong as his sense of the street: dark narrow hallways, their walls lined with lithographs of "The Stolen Kiss" and "Moonlight in Venice," dusty dens stuffed with bric-a-brac and missionary furniture, windows overwhelmed with wooden shutters, roller shades, lace curtains, and velvet drapes. "Visually my domestic memories are mostly bleak and stuffy," an octoge-

Lewis Mumford's Manhattan, from the top of the Palisades: from an early sketch made during his walking tours. "Lewis Mumford Papers," Special Collections, Van Pelt Library, University of Pennsylvania.

narian Mumford recalled, "and I hate to think how depressing the total effect would have been had not Central Park and Riverside Drive always been there to gladden my eyes and beckon my legs to a ramble."[13]

Like the Upper West Side the great city below it had also acquired temporary shape in the 1880s and 1890s as a walking city reachable through wide tree-lined avenues pointing the pedestrian downtown, a scaled city still wearing a Richardsonian air of permanence even as the boy's world was changing irrevocably. The railroad bridge over Hellgate suddenly spanned the East River. Saint John's Cathedral was approaching medium magnificence next door to Columbia. The Flatiron Building now pointed north like the prow of a ship toward new commercial development, and the New York Public Library seemed to the adolescent Mumford both awesome and unnerving. The "colorful, still selective, middle-class world" of uptown, where growing consumerism had not yet prevented New Yorkers from registering a "variety of little changes, little differences," would be gone by 1920—the mature Mumford's lost city—but two decades earlier, when goats still roamed pastures beyond 180th Street and trolleys carried passengers out from dingy tenements to "wide meadows and farms" on route to Belmont Park or Sheepshead Bay, this middle-class lifestyle seemed indestructible. Here was the urban equivalent of Benton Mac-Kaye's "flow" in a metropolis seen in reciprocating motion—the city as regional fact and the core of an intricate ecological complex.

As soon as he was old enough to appropriate a tradition and play the role it assigned, the young Mumford looked to Walt Whitman, whose Manhattan still seemed a "simple, compact, well-join'd scheme" with its solitary observer "disintegrated" yet part of the scheme. Whereas the adolescent Benton MacKaye positioned himself on the crest of Hunting Hill, itself precisely "situated," he noted in his journal, "at the southeast point of a plateau on the North side of Mulpus Brook," a somewhat older Mumford, standing in Brooklyn's Atlantic Avenue neighborhood, stopped to take his urban bearings: "Furman Street has on the West warehouses, refrigerating establishments, the marginal ways and docks: on the East a wall of some twenty feet high under which are occasional saloons, shacks, and hovels, and above which are the gardens and backyards of the old aristocratic district . . . ."[14] MacKaye's visualizations disclosed patterns hidden in nature; Mumford's came as epiphanies like the one on Brooklyn Bridge on a spring day when, with the wind coursing through him, he looked out on what he suddenly recognized as his own city.

Mumford's deepening encounters with New York left a lifelong conviction that the ultimate meaning of the city was *education* as a wholly self-directed process of absorption and reflection. "We must conceive of the city," Mumford would write in 1968 in recalling his own boyhood, "not primarily as a place of business or government but as an essential organ for expressing and actualizing a new personality."[15] His own discovery of a Whitmanic persona was not an accident but a conscious attempt through his city to make connections with the nineteenth century which would figure so prominently in his early excursions into cultural criticism.

Following graduation from Stuyvesant High School on New York's East Side in 1912 Mumford drifted in and out of night classes at City College of New York where there was no required curriculum at the Evening Session, and for the next two years—"the best two years of my college life"—walked often through the deepening twilight up Amsterdam Avenue past the Hebrew Orphan Asylum to the college buildings "in their dark stone masses and white terra cotta quoins and moldings, rising like a collection of crystals above the formless rocks of the hill." But two years of sampling a widening variety of subjects did not qualify him for full-time work in the Day Session, and his formal education—a smoldering rebellion against academic requirements and routine—was cut short by the discovery in 1915 of a lesion on his lung necessitating a withdrawal from college in favor of the seashore in Ogunquit, Maine, where he read Plato and declaimed Whitman, "reciting verses at the top of my voice, or racing along the hard sand for the pure joy of motion."[16]

In his enforced moratorium Mumford made a key intellectual contact which strengthened his preference for amateurism and helped define his career as a generalist. Patrick Geddes, whose writing Mumford stumbled across, was a Scotch biologist-turned-regional planner whose prescription for cities proceeded from a sense of ecological wholeness rooted in his initial discipline. Reading Geddes's *City Development,* his massive report to the Carnegie Dumferline Trust published in 1904, as well as the more recent *Cities in Evolution,* Mumford recognized an organic "three-dimensional" way of conceptualizing the city which provided a focal point for his own scattered impressions.[17] Geddes's survey method which correlated the city with surrounding countryside in the heuristic device of the "valley section" appeared to offer a total clinical picture of the region as the fundamental unit in any future "science of cities."

To teach this new integrated science Geddes had invented a multisyllabic glossary of terms, some of which found their way directly into Mumford's vocabulary—"megalopolis," "conurbation," "geotechnics"—while other undecipherable neologisms—"poliography," "politogenics," "eu-politogenics"—simply attested to the master's delight in coupling and mating sciences. Geddes's most useful intellectual bequest for his American student was a nineteenth-century universalistic history neatly divided into a "paleotechnic" age of mining civilizations based on coal, iron, steam, and capitalist profit, and an emergent "neotechnic" era resting on electricity, improved alloys, increased socialization, and civic efficiency. Geddes's Outlook Tower, his regional "index-museum" at the end of Edinburgh's Royal Mile, that served as the center for the visual exploration of the surrounding valley section, was only one of his innumerable projects for revitalizing the city and the region. Geddes, his young convert realized, had also pioneered with university hostels, urban restoration, mixed housing, folk festivals, educational extension experiments, utopian communities, international expositions—projects taken up not sequentially but simultaneously, and not as a simple instrumentalist "learning by doing" but as a total immersion in an idealist "learning by living."

In 1917 Mumford's draft number came up, and when, despite his brush with tuberculosis, he was pronounced fit for duty he hurried instead to enlist in the navy. Despite an admitted "inner resistance" to routine and the "insistent discipline" imposed by navy regulations, military life toughened him up while access to a life at sea brought him his first sustained contact with New England. Ordered from Newport to Harvard for a course in radio, he spent his first night in Winthrop House which convinced him that he had arrived in heaven. Boston, he discovered, was still the "genuine metropolis in the literal sense of the word: a true 'Mother City,' the attractive nucleus of a whole ring of communities, more nearly country towns than suburbs, which reached out as far as Concord. . . ."[18] Here, approached from the other end of the regional territory, was Benton MacKaye's middle rural ground as it appeared from Beacon Hill and Boston Common, a buffer zone in need of protection and preservation. The wartime Cambridge interlude also introduced him to the architecture of Henry Hobson Richardson—Austin and Seaver Halls and the shingled Stoughton house—and the exciting mixture of housing converging on Harvard Square "from dingy workmen's quarters on Mount Auburn Street to the palatial dwellings of Brattle Street." Across the Charles he strolled along Frederick Law Olmsted's strip of park through the fens and out to the staid suburb of Longwood, gathering impressions of a nineteenth-century New England cultural landscape that would presently acquire precise definition in *The Golden Day.*

Mumford returned in the spring of 1919 to a New York jammed with veterans and a Greenwich Village teeming with young artistic and literary talent. He accounted himself a member of the Younger Generation, "rebellious, defiant of conventions, but not yet wholly disillusioned." He had already made two decisions, more by default than intent. The first was to remain a generalist, ready to undertake any intellectual assignment he fancied and to discover something to say which a literate public would find significant and provocative. His second decision followed from the first: he would support himself by the craft of writing rather than formal university teaching of a single discipline. By the time he returned to New York in search of an editorial position he had committed himself to a journeyman's life of "dabbling here and there, often floundering in water beyond my depth" and constantly subject to the "nagging need" from week to week to cash in quickly on an article or review. Out of these early determinations came a set of lifetime literary habits: maintaining a writing schedule crammed with a variety of assignments; constant oversight of his literary capital and retention of every scrap for reinvestment; and a tendency to reissue, as the market allowed, usually without revising.

In the four years between his return to New York City and his meeting with MacKaye at Hudson Guild Farm, Mumford worked briefly on *The Dial* and wrote for *The Freeman* while contributing an essay on "The City" to Harold Stearns's *Civilization in the United States,* and placing a number of pieces in magazines ranging from *Scientific Monthly* to *The Nation* and *The New Republic.* In the spring of 1920 he sailed to London hoping to make contact with Geddes who in turn sought to enlist him in his planning project for the university in Jerusalem. But a five-month stay at LePlay House in Pimlico persuaded him that intellectual debts to Geddes and his colleagues notwithstanding, he himself was a distinctly American product and that "any further time spent in work extraneous to my own vocation as a writer would be time lost for my essential work." By October 1920 he was back in Greenwich Village bent on the "reconstruction" of postwar American society and an early marriage.[19]

Mumford's first book, *The Story of Utopias,* appeared in 1922. For an advance of $300 he researched, wrote, edited, and saw the book through press in six months, a record he would occasionally approach but never break. In *The Story of Utopias* the interpretive lines lead out of the city and up the valley section through clustered communities along its sides to mountain wilderness against the horizon. The lines sketch a plan for the regional reconstruction of the United States which Mumford would develop, expand, modify, elaborate but never essentially change. Ostensibly a quick survey of utopian literature from Plato to Bellamy, the book finds its conceptual center along that strip of landscape depicted in Patrick Geddes's representation of the valley section. "Geographically speaking,"

Mumford observes in introducing his discussion of Plato's *polis,* "the ideal commonwealth was a city-region; that is, a city was surrounded by enough land to supply the greater part of the food needed by the inhabitants; and placed convenient to the sea." Then Mumford makes the telling comparison that reveals his own present intentions:

> It is a mountainous region, this Greece, and within a short distance from mountain top to sea there was compressed as many different kinds of agricultural and industrial life as one could single out in going down the Hudson Valley from the Adirondack Mountains to New York Harbor. As the basis for his ideal city, whether Plato knew it or not, he had an "ideal" section of land in his mind—what the geographer calls the "valley section."[20]

Mumford's "story" tells of the search for the ultimately good society which lies beyond fictional utopias of "escape" and "reconstruction," beyond such pastoral fantasies as William Morris's *News from Nowhere,* on the one hand, and repressive bureaucracies like Bellamy's *Looking Backward,* on the other. The story is one of declension from Plato's noble Republic through the late medieval artisan democracy, Christianopolis, of Johann Valentin Andreae to Campanella's coercive City in the Sun, to perversions of utopia and the dystopian realities of the Baroque Country House, the grimy industrial Coketown, and its Frankenstein creation, Megalopolis, the organizing center for the modern state. Megalopolis houses the functionaries and bureaucrats who run the National Utopia which is willed into existence as a pure abstraction "without regard to geography, topography, or regional surroundings." Megalopolis, in short, is precisely what the group of planners recently gathered around Thomas Adams had in mind for New York City.

Late in the book Mumford reaches a turning point as his indictment veers from description to prescription with a call for a Regional Survey as the means of entry into the real world of human values. "In looking at the community through the Regional Survey," he insists, "the investigator is dealing with a real thing and not with an arbitrary idolum."[21] Here Mumford's vision of "home, meeting-place, and factory; polity, culture, and art," brought together within the region, merged with MacKaye's "visualization" of an indigenous landscape filled with "hidden potentiality." It was time for the two men to join forces.

IV

The immediate result of the meeting at Hudson Guild Farm was Mumford's and MacKaye's decision to mount an attack on Thomas Adams and the Metropolitanists in a special issue of the *Survey Graphic.* Mumford agreed to undertake the job of editing the various contributions and supplying an interpretive framework. Soon he began to have doubts. "The damned regional planning number," he complained to MacKaye in December, 1924, six months before scheduled publication, "lives up to my worst misgivings." Perhaps the two of them left to their own devices could come up with a "whopping piece," but "for the rest of the crowd the idea is a little unbaked."

> The regional planning idea exists for the present in the negative state of crit-
> icism, criticism of the big city and of "city planning." It is not yet sure enough
> of itself to offer anything positive: or rather, we are not as a group united on
> a positive program; we are, in fact, still fumbling around for it.[22]

Precisely here, he continued, was where MacKaye came in, for neither Clarence Stein nor Henry Wright nor any of the other members of the recently formed Regional Planning Association was able to "visualize" their garden cities "on their social and civic side" in a regional setting. "We must start a regional movement in America before we can have regional planning." Unless and until they broke the habit of considering regional planning as a mere technological exercise, they could not hope to advance the reconstruction of America beyond "what the Russell Sage people are setting out to do."

The answer to the question "What is regionalism?" Mumford had already located in the past; and the recovery of the past, in turn, meant writing history if only as an escape from the present dismal fact "that we live in a spiritual chaos."[23] There were a number of intellectual forces and cultural preferences converging on Mumford as he began to take the measure of American culture in the mid-1920s, predispositions that would combine in a powerful indictment of modernism. There was, first of all, his need to stake out a philosophical middle-ground between John Dewey's instrumentalism and George Santayana's aesthetic idealism—to make "a living synthesis of their philosophies" which would allow him to have the best of both worlds of science and humanism. He confessed to having been helped "enormously" by a reading of Santayana, and insisted that "it's a mistake to consider the pragmatists the sole spokesmen of the American spirit."[24] On the other hand, Dewey's theories of education and the experiments they had engendered held an appeal nearly as strong as that of Geddes's views. Perhaps history could provide the clues to a middle way.

A second determinant in Mumford's rediscovery of history proceeded directly out of first-hand contact with it. While lecturing at Alfred Zimmern's summer institute in Geneva in 1925, he climbed the steep streets of the old city and poked endlessly into its corners. "Age hangs over the stones, the smells are unaltered since the fifteenth century; there are sudden open spaces with trees and fountains; and at the end of dank passageways the blackness heaves abruptly against a garden. . . ."[25] Long ago he had learned how to appropriate a city by walking through it, but now he was acquiring a felt sense of the past and its uses. He knew exactly what he was seeking in history—"a vision to live by again."[26]

Mumford's search for a usable past led him to undertake two books in quick succession—first, *Sticks and Stones: A Study of American Architecture and Civilization* (1924), a thumbnail architectural history of the rise of the modern world out of the collapse of the medieval and its culmination in American building; and scarcely two years later, *The Golden Day* (1926). Both find their center in the culture of nineteenth-century New England which lingers as a counterforce to the pull of the frontier and the depredations of the pioneer. "In the villages of the New World there flickered up the last dying ember of the medieval order."[27] Utopia survives momentarily in New England seaboard towns which nucleate rather than mushroom, and retain their institutions and their identity into the nineteenth century by perpetuating what Benton MacKaye called a form of "Yankee communism." The New Englanders' rough equality and shared spiritual purpose were embodied in the towns they laid out and the homes they built which sealed a tight bargain between men and the earth in severe meetinghouses and stark mills, an absence of decoration and the persistence of the "dynamic qualities of medieval architecture" wholly different from the "prudent regularities" of the Georgian mode that replaced it.[28]

To make his reader see, Mumford conducts a tour of the John Ward House (1684) in Salem, as he would do with countless other buildings and communities in all of his subsequent histories, pointing to the unpainted, weathered oaken masses and taking the measure of their solidity. "Every step that brings one nearer to the house alters the relations of the planes formed by the gable ends. . . ." The Ward House, like the village to which it is fitted, "seems in motion as well as the spectator; and this quality delights the eye."[29] Mumford then leads an excursion out into the village itself, a living core much like Benton MacKaye's Shirley Center with the common as its focal point, a meetinghouse to one side, an adjacent grammar school across the way, and along the converging roads, set at regular intervals, clapboard houses, their dark green shutters visible through the spreading arc of great elms. Here in an infinitely extendable pattern stands MacKaye's "basic geographic unit of organic human society" in "the single town of definite physical limits and integrity." Unlike his friend's insistent Shirley Center, Mumford's townscape is a cultural artifact, a model in the mind signifying community, permanence, and continuity—a benchmark for measuring subsequent backslidings.

The story of the New England village is one of slow decline in the nineteenth century as an industrial revolution destroys the artisanal self-sufficiency of the small town and dissolves the unity of the original community by dangling the promise of unlimited wealth before its pioneering sons. As country village becomes commercial town after the American Revolution, there arrive new invidious distinctions between rich and poor, craftsmen and merchants, "better" and "meaner" sorts. The vaunted Age of the Common Man simply puts its imprimatur on decisions of rich merchants to hire a Samuel McIntire or one of his fellow-practitioners of the vernacular to convert the traditional low-lying New England farmhouse into a "bulky square house with its hipped roof, its classical pilasters, its frequently ill-proportioned cupola, its 'captain's walk' or 'widow's walk.'" Recalling falsely for Americans "a thin and watered Greece," such neo-classical structures marked the victory of the merchant "with his eye for magnitude" over the sturdy yeoman farmer "with his homely interest in the wind and the weather." The transit from outlying hill village to bustling mercantile city can be measured in the piles of conspicuous waste that spread from country manor to city mansion.[30]

Both the vernacular tradition and the neo-classical revival are overrun by the eclecticism of the pioneer, Mumford's nemesis, who makes the first of his many appearances as villain in *Sticks and Stones*. The pioneer is the purveyor of an extractive and exploitative "mining" civilization and appears in two roles: as "land" pioneer following his Manifest Destiny into the abyss; and as "industrial" pioneer propelled by a misplaced faith in material progress. With their partnership these entrepreneurs preside over "a century of disintegration" that is clearly reflected in profit-skimming land deals and jerry-built urban development.[31] Architecture is reduced to a symptom of social and spiritual dislocation and a way of life that becomes "sullen, grim, gauche, unstable." Only the lone Henry Hobson Richardson kept the New England builder tradition alive in shingle-style adaptations of an earlier regional tradition. All else after the Civil War was either a desperate retreat to an imaginary medieval serenity or a masking of the commercial spirit with an imperial façade as architecture abandoned producing towns for spending cities and "came to dwell in the stock exchanges, the banks, the shops, and the clubs of the metropolis."[32]

The decline of American architecture from the original achievements of New England vernacular defined for Mumford the regional planner's present task—establishing contact once more with that cultural totality lost in the moment when the American forest became "an enemy to be conquered" and "the obliteration of the natural landscape became a great national sport."[33] Knitting home, meeting-place, and factory back together again, uniting polity, economy, and art, he was convinced, could only be accomplished in a community "limited in numbers, and in area, and formed, not merely by the agglomeration of people but by their relation to definite social and economic institutions."[34] To express these relations clearly was the aim of the genuine community planner.

In supplying his fellow "Barbarian Invaders" of New York City in 1925 with a philosophy of regionalism and a thumbnail history of architecture and city-planning Mumford anticipated a division of labor with MacKaye. He, as editor and contributor, would provide a historical sketch of three American "migrations" and the imminence of a fourth, while MacKaye, with a bit of editorial prodding and pruning, would describe and map the regional terrain over which these migrations had traveled. Mumford was fully aware of his friend's conceptual strengths as well as stylistic shortcomings, both traceable to his isolation in the family cottage in Shirley Center. In returning to the family homestead, MacKaye had settled into quarters which Mumford once said that "for sheer seediness would make most monastic cells look palatial."[35] MacKaye Cottage was a plain, uninsulated clapboard house, built in 1837, that sat unevenly on its tumbling stone foundation. Since it lacked electricity and running water, all the cooking and household chores were performed with hand pump, coal stove, fireplaces, and kerosene lamps. MacKaye had set up his study in "Sky Parlor," as the family called it, an upstairs room over the kitchen detached from the rest of the house and reached by a narrow stairway. Sky Parlor, with large windows facing north, west, and south, and a smaller one looking east, afforded an interior version of the view from Hunting Hill. Here in a bare workroom whose unpainted walls were lined with bookcases and maps of southern New England, MacKaye retired to do his "digging into the realm of the *living*."

For MacKaye, despite a penchant for dreaming and visualizing, no idea was ever abstract. As a self-defined "hermit," having, like Thoreau, taken a vow of poverty, he was firmly grounded in "the territory around about Shirley Center" and had taken his stance there, and with it a point of view from which to examine the ecological structure of that territory. MacKaye, as Mumford realized, salted and spiced his prose with colloquialisms, folk-language, and regional slang which gave it a conversational directness and earthiness, but he lacked the larger shaping-power of language needed to convey the reality of his vision. On the other hand, as Mumford also sensed, MacKaye's very rootedness in the hill village made him a keen if apprehensive witness to the onrushing metropolitan flood pouring out of Boston into the suburbs and beyond. MacKaye felt an immediacy and an urgency—a need to act quickly—while Mumford as an urbanite still seemed content to educate people as publicist and critic. MacKaye's need for action was fed, not simply by his practical training as a forester, but also by his conviction that the best way, as he explained, to "put across" his plan was "to develop a single idea—to meet the metropolitan challenge by the development of the indigenous environment as a synthetic art." For such a project, as he was frank to admit, he would need his friend's help and advice.

With this unspoken recognition of mutual need and divided responsibilities, the two men undertook their contributions to the special issue of *Survey Graphic* designed by Mumford as an alternative to the emerging Russell Sage plan of Thomas Adams. Mumford intended his essay "The Fourth Migration" as the framing device both for the volume and for his larger history of two Americas: "the America of the settlement" consisting of seventeenth-century communities planted along the Atlantic seaboard and its river valleys; and the "America of the migrations" of which there have been three in the course of two centuries. The first migration cleared the land west of the Alleghenies and opened up half a continent to exploration and exploitation by the "land pioneer" in his covered wagon. Despite its romantic mythology, the first migration is the simple history of "restless men who burned the forests of the Mohawk Valley in order to plant farms, who sifted into the soft glacial deposits of Ohio to cleave their plows through its rich soil; men who grabbed wheat land and skinned it, who grabbed urban sites and 'turned them over'; who staked out railway lines, sometimes strategically . . . sometimes stupidly . . . in a mad scramble to cover the continent." The price of such progress?—"Butchered forest; farms gone to ruin or into a ruinous system of tenantry; villages so sterile that they drive all their ambitious or sensitive young people to the big towns."[36]

This uprooting becomes the second migration—from countryside to factory town—on the iron horse this time rather than the Conestoga wagon: to Cleveland and Columbus in the 1840s, Chicago in the 1850s, and to Milwaukee on the eve of the Civil War. The motive behind this second migration, Mumford argues, was "narrowly industrial," its results a series of "depletions" measured in "homes blocked and crowded by factories; rivers polluted; factories and railroad yards seizing sites that should have been preserved for recreation; inadequate homes thrown together anyhow, for sale anyhow, inhabited anyhow."[37]

The magnet of the metropolis as financial center presently draws Americans out of their small towns and provincial cities in a third migration that begins with the Civil War and culminates in World War I. This time urban concentration exacts as its toll the subjection of industry to finance, advertising, insurance, marketing, and all the other "paper-making" enterprises of consolidated capitalism.[38] Although Mumford was quick to point out that these migrations came in successive if overlapping waves, cumulatively if unintentionally their effect, he insisted, has been to open the way for a fourth migration out of the city as Americans come to realize that the automobile, the airplane, the radio, and the telephone have made concentration of people in mass cities "obsolete" and that twentieth-century technology thus offers "a new opportunity and a new task."[39]

The actual job of engineering the fourth migration MacKaye considered even more urgent than Mumford, and to the application of his friend's general principles he brought a home-grown ecological history of his own. Choosing the word "empire"—a misnomer, Mumford thought—to describe his system of natural and man-made "flows," MacKaye begins his essay "The New Exploration: Charting the Industrial Wilderness" with a search for the "most efficient framework" for containing and managing the movement of resources, goods, people and culture across his home state of Massachusetts from Boston to the Berkshires.[40] Clues lie ready at hand in three types of topography comprising MacKaye's cross-section: the Appalachian barrier at the western end of the state in the Berkshire-Green Mountains chain; the Threshold Plain or the New England Plateau covering three-quarters of the state; and the Seaboard, consisting of the Boston Basin.

The first section of this industrial web is the barrier itself, a "source region with its ample water power and forest growths." Two hundred miles eastward lies the "mouth region," the most densely woven part of the web with its factories, railroads, wharves, and stores serving at once as a mouth ingesting natural resources and as an original source of manufactured goods for the hinterland. In between these two poles lies "a country of fields and woodlots" with a village producerist economy which is more complex than wilderness but less so than the industrial segment in Boston and its environs. Where then, MacKaye asks, do "we of the new exploration" begin our survey? In the Berkshires as the "sphere of origin" and more particularly with Somerset Valley, a miniature "empire" seventeen miles long and eight miles wide comprising the drainage basin of the Upper Deerfield River northwest of Greenfield. The first settlers in Somerset Valley arrived in 1776, and the subsequent history of the region concerns the rise and fall of successive lumber empires that mined the forests and stripped the watershed, only to move on. It is just these ruins left by the timber-mining empire that MacKaye takes as his framework for regional reconstruction. Old railroad grades and rights of way can be remade into good roads for new settlers; abandoned logging camps will serve as refurbished stable communities; timber harvesting will replace the old practice of clear-cutting.

MacKaye's plan for his home region was a conceptual halfway house between his earlier proposals for resource communitarian experiments harking back to nineteenth-century alternatives and an updated version of regional planning aimed at checking the urban outflow and preserving wilderness at the top of the valley section. In his contribution to the *Survey Graphic* issue he encapsulates Mumford's successive migrations and the whole historical process of former explorations. The original explorers, according to MacKaye, charted the wilderness of nature in order to exploit it; the new explorers must chart the wilderness made by people in order to escape it.[41]

Neither of the two friends' hopes for immediate results from their manifesto in the *Survey Graphic* were particularly high, and their skepticism proved warranted. As members of a commission appointed by Governor Alfred E. Smith they joined with other RPAA members to issue *The Regional Report of the New York State Commission on Housing and Regional Planning* published in May 1926. Their report called for a co-ordinated system of rail and motor transportation for the entire Hudson Valley, stringent controls on bulk, height, and use of buildings in Manhattan, a low ceiling on urban property values, and subsidized decentralization of industry, all of which required intervention by state and local government on a monumental scale. Only one thousand copies of their report were published, and most of these mouldered in state archives until they were exhumed fifty years later.

Nor did Thomas Adams's publication in two volumes (1929, 1931) of the "Regional Plan of New York and Its Environs" succeed in attracting much more public attention. Mumford leveled two blasts at it in the pages of *The New Republic* in 1932, accusing Adams of being "willfully obtuse" and dismissing his report as a huge pudding, "indigestible and tasteless." Adams fired back by denouncing Mumford as a hopeless visionary, an apostle of massive economic change that would require "the combined power of the President, Congress and state legislature to bring about."[42] The task of implementing the Adams report fell to the Regional Plan Association, a voluntary clearing-house which could do little more than encourage co-operation among the region's 400 public and private sponsoring organizations. New York City waited until 1937 to establish a modestly financed and empowered planning commission, by which time Robert Moses, another Mumford nemesis, was firmly ensconced in the metropolitan driver's seat. Serious regional planning on a nationwide scale awaited the initiative of a President and Congress confronting a massive collapse of the American economy, catastrophic unemployment, and the appearance of a host of young regional planners. But in 1925, at the beginning of a frenzied financial boom, neither a philosophy of regional reconstruction nor specific schemes for implementing it held any appeal for the politicians.

The significance of the *Survey Graphic* episode and the skirmish with the metropolitanists in 1925 lay elsewhere—in a deepening friendship which lasted until MacKaye's death in 1975, and, of more immediate importance, in sharpening each man's understanding of the meaning of their joint regionalist enterprise and of the resources available for undertaking it. Those resources, spiritual and material, they now knew lay, not in New York City but in New England, and each determined to make use of them. Out of their mutual recognition came two assessments: *The Golden Day* (1926), Mumford's account of the New England renaissance as a legacy for twentieth-century planners; and *The New Exploration* (1929), Mac-Kaye's survey of the available means for putting that inheritance to work.

V

In 1925, driven out of Greenwich Village and then Brooklyn Heights by high rents, Mumford and his wife Sophia moved to Sunnyside Gardens in Long Island City, the RPAA's experimental garden-city project sandwiched in between the railroad tracks and the goat pastures girdling the factory district of this ugly industrial suburb. At first the Mumfords found their surroundings so depressing that they were driven on Sundays to seek respite in the nearest cemetery for a glimpse of nature. "But as this new housing grew under our friends' [Clarence Stein's and Henry Wright's] direction," Mumford recalled, "it created its own environment; and if you knew your way about, you might follow a footpath through a network of rear gardens and green lawns for almost half a mile, with all sorts of charming vistas."[43] Mumford remembered Sunnyside Gardens as a vital community of intellectuals and professionals mixing freely with all classes though not races. For the rest of his life he would associate the garden city experiment on Long Island with the potential for co-operative communal reconstruction of urban life, not as *suburbia* with its single-family isolation and false self-sufficiency, but as *satellite settlement* on the perimeter of the regional city, maintaining an intense and varied participatory culture. Sunnyside convinced Mumford once and for all that "with a little leeway for experiment, the democratic process would still function provided the social unit allowed a mixture of political, religious, and social beliefs—and of occupations, too."[44]

Mumford's uncertain income and modest lifestyle seemed to him opulent compared with MacKaye's "hermit" existence in Shirley Center, where he and his sister Hazel managed a hand-to-mouth existence. He was so poor, MacKaye admitted with wry satisfaction, that on his tax form he listed his chief asset as "not having children." His "cave man" life was intellectually isolated, and his letters to his friend, as he worked in Sky Parlor on the manuscript of *The New Exploration,* were filled with plaintive requests to "send us a wee line sometime" giving the particulars on what "the crowd" was "up to" in his absence.[45] And when Mumford invariably obliged him with a full account of his own life in New York, MacKaye would reply in kind, prefacing his own report with an amiable apology for its length. "There are some souls with whom there is so much in common that a mere pull at their shirt means the unearthing of an avalanche."[46] If Mumford would only agree to come and "do the hermit act" with him, they could have their long "jaw," and "the face of the future earth would be the different for it."

MacKaye combined writing, which came slowly and painfully, with household chores and handyman repairs on "cisterns, roofs, and such" in a heroic effort to keep his cottage livable. He explained his intent to Mumford repeatedly as he groped his way toward an ultimate philosophical statement. "In reading these chapters," he warned Mumford in sending him a batch of manuscript, "you may find them somewhat muddy. Don't fail to tell me if you think so. I have the stuff so firmly in my own head that I am a poor critic of myself (a truism). But I think that I can lighten them, upon revision, and air them out as we can do with soggy hay."[47] There was, in fact, no middle distance in MacKaye's prose written from the perspective of Hunting Hill or Sky Parlor. Ready at hand lay the colloquialisms, the slang and salty sayings that served admirably as the primary vernacular language of the Yankee storyteller who described a spring day in Shirley as "tempestuously glorious" or told of his longing "for a pow-wow with that soul of yours" or admitted going to church now and again "just for the hell of it." This was the straight-faced comic Yankee who insisted on giving "old Lewis" the "latest dope" or admitted to "bellyaching and belching" and then apologized for running off at the mouth in "a long drool." But words to explain the spiritual pull of the primeval wilderness or his need to study the mysteries of nature came only haltingly and with great difficulty. As he struggled to find his expository voice, he found in his friend's writing useful hints. He heard the "voice of an artist" in *The Golden Day,* a copy of which Mumford sent him, and in the words themselves "certainly an urge to the engineer; but Oh, for more of the artist in me to comprehend, and for more of the engineer to carry forth."[48]

Interspersed with inquiries about the Mumfords and reports of domestic routines at MacKaye Cottage in letters explaining "in a few swift words" what "to hell I've been up to," came increasingly detailed accounts of "digging in the realm of the living" as MacKaye began organizing the concepts underlying *The New Exploration.*

> I have carved out a little region in that realm. It consists of the territory around about Shirley Center. This little region embraces the fundamental environments (as I conceive of them) which are necessary for man's full development. These are the primeval, the rural, (the "colonial" in New England), and the urban. The primeval is represented by a little range of mountains— the Wapack Range. The colonial is presented by several little "hill villages," among which is Shirley Center. The urban is represented by Fitchburg (of 40,000), and Boston is near by. Each environment, I point out, should be kept intact, and developed as a basic human resource in itself. But each one is threatened (and the urban already immersed) by a fourth environment (a diseased environment we might call it) called the "metropolitan." And the job of planning a region for play, as I see it, consists in repelling the "invasion" of this metropolitan influence and of developing as assets in themselves, the other three basic environments. This splits itself into three parts: the *preservation* of the primeval; the *restoration* of the colonial; and the salvaging (some day) of the true urban. The immediate tasks seem to the first two just named— the problems of the primeval and the colonial environments.[49]

Mumford responded to these progress reports with an enthusiasm and encouragement that came easily to him. Always there was his ready response to "old Benton's" ideas and plans although such attention competed with an even stronger concern with the present state of his own particular project which he was eager to describe. Now, on reading MacKaye's prospectus, he offered immediate support. "The work that you are doing seems a real crystallization of everything you've been thinking this last six years. Haven't you got the stuff of a book there? As soon as you have it in any sort of shape I'd like to see it; I'll engage to peddle it around this spring, with a high and enthusiastic recommendation."[50]

In a letter of December 1926 offering encouragement to his friend, Mumford reported that his own book, *The Golden Day,* had sold a thousand copies in the first month which "has made my stock rise with the publisher almost as fast as U.S. Steel."[51] *The Golden Day* was intended as a pioneer work in American Civilization and at the same time a piece of regional history unearthing the "cultural motive" he had been seeking for the last six years. Regionalism, Mumford now understood clearly, involved first and foremost the recovery of a specific past.

The creation of an American culture, Mumford announces on the opening page of *The Golden Day,* began with "the unsettlement of Europe," and in the beginning the American Adam was merely "a stripped European" who colonized a continent with other people similarly "incapable of sharing or continuing its past."[52] Mumford traces this European "delocalized man" to the New World where he becomes the "composite American" furnished with a Protestant theology, a capitalistic appetite, and a new abstract politics of possessive individualism. Having emerged from the deep shadows of his ancestral home, the pioneer appears as a silhouette—"a man without a background"—highlighted against the wilderness by his illusions that time is money and opportunity there for the taking. The pioneer's inexorable march across the continent from the seventeenth century through the nineteenth, laying waste to nature as he goes and making the path of progress "smooth as a concrete road," signified the triumph of sheer motion over reflection, of romantic restlessness over steady cultural habit, an incorrigible present-mindedness over values inherited from the past. "The truth is that the life of the pioneer was bare and insufficient: he did not really face Nature, he merely avoided society."[53] The American pioneer could never create a community or establish an identity with the land because he never stopped long enough to reflect on their meaning. Searching for sublimity, he achieved only a self-induced oblivion.

The Golden Day of mid-nineteenth-century America dawned only on those with sense enough to stay at home in New England, where they continued to live "between two worlds" at the precise moment when an inherited social and cultural order fractured. Europe's final disintegration comes in America, but its collapse precipitates a brief but powerful renaissance in the region where its culture was first planted and briefly flourished. "Regionalism" as a cultural motive, for Mumford, was both a *specific time* and a *definite place*, the precise point at which past and present intersect and in so doing inform and determine the future. The regional moment is quite literally a day in the life of a culture. Despite critics who objected to his title as arcane, Mumford knew precisely what he wanted his extended metaphor to say. Emerson is the "morning star" of New England's renaissance, a figure rising on the horizon of a recovered past who portends new cultural achievement. Emerson, more clearly than any of his fellow New Englanders, understood the workings and thus the meaning of history even as he sought to transcend it. It is Emerson's persona even more than his ideas that attracts Mumford, particularly his notion of himself as interpreter or what Benton MacKaye called "visualizer." "The preacher, the farmer, the scholar, the sturdy New England freeholder, yes, and the shrewd Yankee peddler or mechanic were all encompassed by him." But comprehended as promise rather than accomplishment: "what they meant in actual life had fallen away from him: he represented what they stood for in eternity."[54]

What Emerson promises in a dim pre-dawn, Thoreau fulfills at sunrise and Whitman celebrates at high noon. Emerson's thought occasionally abandoned experience and transcended regional realities in its bookishness, "its impatience to assume too quickly an upright position, its too tidy moral housekeeping." Thoreau, on the contrary, showed exactly what the pioneer might have achieved had he honored the surveyor's bounds rather than extending himself in illimitable space. Together Emerson and Thoreau point the way out of a spiritual wilderness to those who seek to be saved from the pioneer's misplaced confidence in "calculating," "reckoning," and "figuring." If Emerson foreshadows, Thoreau bodies forth the "poised and finely balanced personality." Emerson surveys a symbolic New England landscape, but Thoreau inhabits a real one, studying it and learning from it.

> As for his country, he loved the land too well to confuse it with the shifting territorial boundaries of the National State. In this he had that vital regional consciousness which every New Englander shared. What he loved was the landscape, his friends, and his companions in spirit: when the Political State presumed to exercise a brass counterclaim on these loyalties, it might go to the devil.[55]

Noon of the Golden Day arrives with Whitman who gives to American poetry the power of the Veads, the Nackas, the Talmud, and the Old Testament by crystallizing experience and infusing spirituality into everyday life. Following Emerson's example, he absorbs in himself the Quaker, the Puritan, the cosmopolitan, pioneer, and republican, "and what came out in his poems was none of these things; it was a new essence; none of the ordinary labels described it."[56] Whitman visualized—even in the midst of a fratricidal war—a renewed America emerging from the war, a vision quickly demolished by Gilded Age hucksters, yet one leaving a legacy of idealism to be repossessed by a modern world. "What is valid in idealism," Mumford insists, "is the belief in the possibility of re-molding, reforming, recreating cultural life."

Hawthorne, whose art is suffused with the shadows of an autumnal New England afternoon, realized keenly what the pioneer failed to credit—the persistence of evil and thus the inevitability of tragedy. Hawthorne too turned to the past in a spirit which Mumford could only approve: "with a consciousness that remained outwardly Puritan, he projected the figures of his day," animating them with his sense of history. Finally, Melville plunges the Golden Day into dark metaphysical night with his saga of the white whale which "threatens man and calls forth all his heroic power, and in the end defeats him with a final lash of his tail." The early Emersonian promise of endless renewal is baffled and ultimately betrayed by Melville's destructive element. The Golden Day is ended.

The culture of New England's Golden Day rested on a specific political economy of small property—which, as Emerson explained, is "always moral"—and diffused wealth, which ensures respect for the terms dictated by the land, a guaranteed "competence" for industrious farmers and artisans alike, self-government and sturdy independence. This free labor economy, in turn, ensured the survival of necessary cultural traits and personal

values: steadiness of habit and sureness of self, industriousness and invention, the willing embrace of hard work and cultivation of civic spirit. "Manual labor," Emerson reminded Mumford, "is the study of the external
world." And the *social form* revealed by Mumford's own study of that world
was the New England village whose very locus and structure embodied the
values of its builders and sustaining members. For a brief moment, Mumford insists, mid-nineteenth-century New England remained in perfect
equilibrium poised between past and future. Its regional culture was *old*
in its inherited awareness of wholesome tradition but also *new* in its
assumption of the historical mission to make a fresh integration of culture
that would carry America into the modern age.

The accomplishment of the New England renaissance, Mumford concluded, was the work of cultural counter-revolutionaries who at the same
time were precursors of the twentieth-century regionalists, inveighing
against the rapacity of the pioneers in industry and on the frontier who
had destroyed the American land and impoverished the spirit. Their lives
stood for and their work celebrated "an older but more youthful America,
part achieved reality, part hopeful ideal, which we have lost." Their example now calls a postwar generation of Americans to an act of recovery by
acknowledging themselves the spiritual children of those representative
men who "people the landscape with their own shapes" as discoverers of
"a new hemisphere in the geography of the mind."[57]

In *The Golden Day* Mumford succeeded in defining with precision the
regional "cultural motive" he had been seeking. This he did in a series of
linked propositions. "Human culture is a continuous process of choosing,
selecting, nurturing, a process also of cutting down and exterminating
those merely hardy and fecund weeds which have no value except their
own rank life."[58] This process of weeding involves the selective assimilation
of the past, transforming it into new cultural growths. A genuine and vital
culture is tended and managed by a constituent people; and it roots and
flourishes in their locale, for only there are they able to take from their
cultural inheritance needful and life-sustaining elements. When such a culture as that produced by the New England renaissance breaks with the
past, having acquired the essential elements from it, it then becomes *indigenous* to a *place*. In this sense all vital cultures grow in regional soils. Independence comes in a break from tradition but also in the recognition of
what is usable in the past. No previous culture can ever be recovered, nor
would it be desirable to attempt to do so. "But the principal writers of that
time [of the Golden Day] are essential links between our own lives and that
earlier, that *basic America*. In their work, we can see in a *pristine* state the
essential characteristics that still lie *under the surface:* and from their example
we can more readily find our own foundations, and make our own particular point of departure."[59] Whether in the center of Concord village or on
the shoreline of Walden Pond, in the Manse at Salem or on unfathomed
oceans beyond Nantucket, or starting from Paumanok where I was born,
the classical writers of the New England renaissance bore the mark of their
region even as they embarked on their interior explorations which even

now can be repeated. "Culture," Mumford explains finally, ". . . implies the possibilities of repetition."[60] And repetition means renewal.

Mumford sent a copy of *The Golden Day* to MacKaye, who blamed his slowness in reading it on the "cave man" standard of living he had been reduced to in Shirley Center "with wood and water and light and every other primal element to be extracted from its source" with the result that "time for reading is almost nil."[61] Still, he had managed to dip into the book here and there, and marvelled at "your keen powers of expression" which reminded him to get busy and start building his own regionalist structure from indigenous New England materials. Mumford proved a loyal friend, helpful critic, and at times virtual collaborator, urging Mac-Kaye toward ever more concrete formulations of his ideas. Sometimes help came in the form of pointed reminders to use words accurately. Sometimes he made major objections argued at length, as he did in demanding sharper discrimination between hiking trails which were entirely suited to colonial and wilderness environments and costumed masquerades which were not. "It is not merely a digging up of the past, or even a re-living of it," he warned MacKaye, "it is a fresh mode of living." The fate of regionalism in Europe, where it had stalled at the stage of simple cultural recovery, should serve Americans as a warning of the dangers of mere "piety to the past, as if life could or should get stuck in one particular mold and stay there."[62]

MacKaye needed all the editorial help he could get, for he admitted to great difficulty in "getting round" his ideas and putting them "across." *The New Exploration* takes the reader on a New England journey across uneven and occasionally uncertain terrain on a path strewn with stylistic boulders, cluttered with verbal underbrush, and filled with metaphorical potholes. But MacKaye's "war map," as he called it, indicates a clear understanding of his developmentalist enemy and presents a defensive strategy for repelling the metropolitan invaders and saving Thoreau's indigenous world.

The argument of *The New Exploration* is deceptively simple: the old explorers were lone freebooters and adventurers; the new ones are engineers, economists, landscape designers, and—the synthesizer of their findings—the regional planner who serves as a "composite mind." In giving shape to his "visualization," the regional planner discerns three worlds from his mountain height in New England—the indigenous world of the *primeval,* the *rural* world of the hill village, and the *cosmopolitan* world of the big city. Each is a genuine and vital community, and each is now threatened by the spread of a standardized, mass-produced *metropolitan* "slum" oozing out across suburbia. From the top of Mount Monadnock, MacKaye surveys these various environments, the primeval world at his feet, the rural lying in the middle distance, and against the far horizon the city with its cancerous metropolitan growth.[63]

Primeval America of the pre-Columbian epoch still lies within reach of the American imagination, and in places in western and northern New England it is still there to preserve. Monadnock, Aroostook, Katahdin—

"we spell these names and place them on our maps. We cleave to them as symbols. . . . We visualize the *name*. Our job now, in the new exploration, is to visualize the *thing*." To look out across New England is to see remote stands of fir and spruce sliding down into high pastures and rocky upland slopes of hill villages, and rising again to unbroken forest just below the skyline, images reminding modern man of an "indefinite past" imaged in the *campfire*.

The emblematic as well as the functional center of the rural or, in New England, the "Colonial" environment is the village common, serving as a nucleus of the community which is arranged "in all the structural symmetry of a starfish" with its five points representing religion, politics, education, commerce, home:

> There is the church (with its steeple); there is the town hall (with its stately Doric columns); and the little red brick school house; and the general store; and the thirty or so dwelling-houses, these last being placed around the Common and along the radiating roads.

Packed around this structural core of the hill village are fields of corn and hay, sheep and cattle pastures, gardens and woodlots, and at the bottom of the hills in the valley stream, grist mills and saw mills. This rural world is the stage for a vital participatory culture that in following the seasons maintains "a primal natural balance" between outdoors and indoors, daytime and night, summer and winter. The colonial village culture, even in 1929, is no mere exercise in nostalgia or figment of the antiquarian imagination but a living fact with "deeply embedded roots" reaching down into "the indefinite past."[64]

The urban environment—the *cosmopolitan* as distinguished from the bastard *metropolitan*—is no less real or necessary to modern life. The true city is a "village grown up," its various institutions expanded, heightened, intensified. The meetinghouse becomes the cathedral; the town hall a golden-domed State House; the red brick schoolhouse a university; the country store the huge urban mart. In the genuine urban environment the geographical definition of identity and place gives way to new group activities and cultural sectioning into different worlds of drama, music, sport, religion, technology, and statesmanship, each with its own "station."[65]

All three of these structured communities—the primeval, the rural, and the urban—are threatened by a spreading pseudo-environment, a metropolitan massing, and flooding, which has already swamped the center city and now is seeping like back-flowing sewage across suburbia and the surrounding countryside. Ironically, the city itself has become the first victim of the metropolitan flood in which it is now fairly submerged. But the towns and villages in the broad band of rural New England—from river towns along Maine's Kennebec to pastoral enclaves at the mouth of the Connecticut—are beginning to go the way of Goldsmith's Deserted Village. "A rootless, aimless, profoundly disharmonious environment has

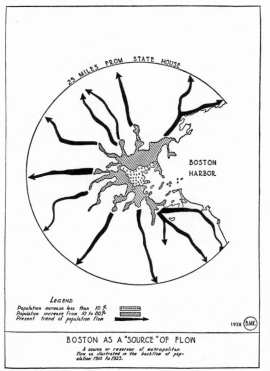

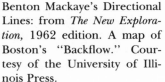

Benton Mackaye's Directional Lines: from *The New Exploration,* 1962 edition. A map of Boston's "Backflow." Courtesy of the University of Illinois Press.

replaced the indigenous one." The ultimate objective of the invading metropolitan developers is wilderness itself—the whole primeval world of the Appalachian chain:

> The invasion would take its start from the central community. Its movements here as elsewhere we may liken to a glacier. It is spreading, unthinking, ruthless. Its substance consists of tenements, bungalows, stores, factories, billboards, filling-stations, eating-stands, and other structures whose individual hideousness and collective haphazardness present that unmistakable environment which we class the "slum." Not the slum of poverty, but the slum of commerce.

When the invading forces finally triumph, New England will have become "a world without a country."[66]

What, then, does the regional planner propose as a strategy for checking, reversing, and hopefully mopping up the metropolitan flow at its source? Since metropolitanism advances along the highways radiating out of the city, it is precisely here on its outskirts that it must be checked by the "intertown (or, as he would presently call it, the "townless highway") banding the city as a major through-route that connects the arteries running out of it but—even more important—serving as a barrier, "dike," or "levee" to hold back the spillage from suburbia. MacKaye's was literally a containment strategy for damming metropolitanism, plugging the "thousand ruptured reservoirs" of suburbia, and turning the flood of people back into the center city where a genuine cosmopolitan culture still survived. Along these "intertown" throughways, MacKaye pointed out on his map, lay wide strips of undeveloped public land to serve as free zones closed to development and reserved for parks. At intervals along these intertowns would cluster *waysides*, as MacKaye somewhat dimly envisioned them, links to the outer framework of the regional city. "This does not mean," he explained a trifle vaguely, "that it would be an urban environment; on the contrary, it would be a rural environment. By no means would it be a suburban environment."[67] Mumford, sensing a certain visual lapse on his friend's part, pointed to "one danger" in the loose concept: "The danger of forming bad little messes of 'towns' on the townless highway itself: hence the planning of certain necessary services on these roads should be an integral part of the project, or they will come in by the backdoor and create the very slum we are trying to prevent." MacKaye acknowledged the justice of Mumford's warning and accepted his suggestion.

The "open ways" and the public land that flank and cut across the intertown highways provide the dikes and levees for holding back the metropolitan flood. At these crucial points the regional planner helps nature recover its primeval territory by planting publicly owned and maintained havens from the developers:

> Mountain crestline and summits (such as the Mt. Holyoke range). Escarpment, or steep slope from a lowland to upland (as the west side of Hoosac Mountain). Canyon, or steep valley along a stream (the Deerfield River). River Bottom, or level valley along a stream (Ipswich River). Swamp (the Great Cedar Swamp and others). Beach (wherever sufficiently unsettled).[68]

In the concluding pages of *The New Exploration*, MacKaye assumes once again the role of "visualizer" and, like Mumford in *The Golden Day*, returns to mid-nineteenth-century New England to place his emblematic environments of campfire, village green, and wayside inside Thoreau's spiritual realm. Each of MacKaye's revealers—naturalist, historian, dramatist, and artist—creates images on paper or canvas, with word or brush, pictures of "the vital forces, rhythms, and aspects" of a vibrant, life-enhancing existence—*a life of living*. The challenge confronting the regional planner is to fuse their several visions "in a medium more vital and real." "It is something," Thoreau wrote in a passage which MacKaye had learned by heart, "to be able to paint a particular picture, or to carve a statue, and so to make a few objects beautiful; but it is far more glorious to carve and paint the very atmosphere and medium through which we look. . . . To affect the quality of the day, that is the highest of arts." Mumford's *The Golden Day* was the work of the transcendental word; MacKaye's visualization in *The*

New Exploration, like Thoreau's original prophecy, was an act of regional spirit. "Environment," he wrote in attempting a summation of his intuited philosophy, "is the influence upon *each* inner mind of the thing shared by *every* inner mind. . . . 'Look *out* and not *in*'—we are told, for when we look *out* we thereby look *in* to our fellow souls on earth. Environment, there-fore, provides a sort of *common mind*—the total life which everyday life must share: it is the least common denominator of our inner selves."[69]

VI

Mumford and MacKaye remained firm friends until the latter's death in 1975, seeing each other only intermittently over the years but keeping up an affectionate if not uninterrupted correspondence in which MacKaye continued to restate his Thoreavian premises and Mumford to report on the many uses to which he put them in his books. *The New Exploration* would be MacKaye's only full-length work, although he continued to labor on a massive manuscript for the rest of his life only to be gently dissuaded by his friend from attempting to publish it. Mumford knew what MacKaye only sensed dimly—that he had had his say, and that his contribution henceforth lay in translating his vision into the engineer's terms which in the 1930s he tried to do by joining the Planning Division of the newly established TVA and writing a series of position papers on preserving the ecology of the Tennessee Valley. His reports, digests of which he for-warded to Mumford, were duly acknowledged and promptly ignored by the bureaucrats. More to his liking was weekend work on sections of the Appalachian Trail and the organizational spadework done with Robert Marshall for the Wilderness Society. After a year's frustration trying to press on his superiors at TVA a preservationist rather than a developmen-tal agenda, MacKaye retreated once more to Shirley Center and the writ-ing of what he hoped would be his magnum opus.

As for Mumford, *The Golden Day* was only one of the first of a growing number of regional reassessments, the most important of which was the 200-page concluding essay in *The Culture of Cities* (1937). With his friend-ship, MacKaye supplied an experiential dimension and a planning tech-nique for the "cultural motive" Mumford had indicated to Patrick Geddes but had not been able fully to define. The New England villages in Mum-ford's early *Sticks and Stones* and *The Golden Day* were symbolic land-scapes—natural images remodeled and refitted to serve as emblems of a vigorous and harmonious late medieval society brought to the New World to flourish briefly and then die. His village spaces were ceremonial settings for the abstract communal dramas he would later stage in his re-creations of the medieval town, the baroque country house, and the mephitic Coke-town. MacKaye, with his simpler and more direct sense of the felt history of the New England town, taught his friend to populate and animate a still vital culture with real people, their routines and ceremonies, and to devise new means of saving it from threatened extinction. Mumford would never lose interest in the city which in the mid-1920s he and his fellow barbarian invaders attacked as the key to a fundamental reorganization of American life. The metropolis would remain for him the center of a vital high culture as well as the commercial command-post of an American empire of paper. But his hopes for a fourth migration as the way to a recovery of traditional Western values remained strong. Increasingly for Mumford it was the region—reaching up the Hudson and embracing his farmhouse in Amenia—that was home to a primary indigenous culture which, with Mac-Kaye as its exemplar, he would define as "healthy," "sane," and "normal." Regionalism, he explained in 1931, did not mean resurrecting a dead way of life or mummifying local customs or canonizing the primitive and the illiterate. Regionalism, correctly perceived, was simply "an effort which recognizes the existence of real groups and social configurations and geographical relationships that are ignored by the abstract culture of the metropolis, and which opposes to the aimless nomadism of the modern commercial enterprise the conception of a stable and settled and balanced and cultivated way of life."

To his friend's conservative cultural philosophy Benton MacKaye added an ecological supplement with his land ethic and concept of a national commons. MacKaye, moreover, put his forester's survey system to work laying out an actual route to Mumford's undiscovered country. In a letter to Van Wyck Brooks in 1934, having completed *Technics and Civilization* and now preparing to embark on *The Culture of Cities*, Mumford explained his own method of thinking and working: "In youth, the sketch: weak in detail, but with the main lines in the right place. In maturity, the main lines get slightly rectified as one alters one's position and takes a wider strip of horizon for background." Yet once the initial lines of argument have been properly aligned, he assured Brooks, "one is justified in filling every inch of canvas. . . ."[70] In helping to draw those directional lines in his friend's early regional sketches Benton MacKaye showed Mumford, in the authenticity of his person as well as in the force of his ideas, the proper alignment.

In the spring of 1968, Mumford and his wife drove out from Cambridge to Shirley Center to visit MacKaye, now nearing ninety. They found him frail and bent, a bit unsteady on his feet, his eyesight failing. Mumford, as was his habit, recorded his impressions of what he sensed would be their last conversation. "By now," he explained in a note in his journal, "Benton is concentrated on two things: his opus and his immediate problems." Cataracts had developed on both eyes. ". . . yet when he wanted to read to us some of the opus, on calculations of population and habitability, he managed by concentration to read it, apparently a word or two at a time." MacKaye appeared to bear his affliction stoically with only a passing comment that it was "a hell of a business not being able to see." He took his guests on a tour of MacKaye Cottage, long vacant, stuffed with dusty bric-a-brac, shabby beyond belief, and then led them to the porch at the rear that looked out over the meadow sloping down to a curtain of woods—

the original view, he boasted, unchanged for over a century and still screening his realm of the living from the commercial development in Shirley Center. Both men knew without having to acknowledge it that this was probably their last meeting. Mumford found himself strangely moved. "We embraced awkwardly; and then we parted, without any overt expression of sentiments; and that, I think, is the way he wanted it to be. . . ." Yet on his return to Cambridge, Mumford confessed to a feeling of profound desolation which memories of a lifetime's public profession of admiration and affection for his friend could not solace. "We were never intimate," he admitted, "in the sense that I had once been with Harry Murray; but I realized that there was much about both our lives that remained to be said, and would never be said."[71]

Mumford's Alternatives to the Megamachine: Critical Utopianism, Regionalism, and Decentralization

HOWARD P. SEGAL

This essay will explore the alternatives to the megamachine that Lewis Mumford has offered in *Technics and Civilization, The Myth of the Machine* (both volumes), and other writings. This essay will not detail Mumford's familiar descriptions and criticisms of the increasingly powerful and deterministic megamachine as it has evolved over time.[1] Instead, after briefly examining Mumford's ambivalence about technology and mankind's future, the essay will focus on his three principal alternatives to it: utopian thought used as social criticism; regional communities and economies; and decentralized living and working arrangements. The essay will argue that far from being separate alternatives, the three are closely related, and that far from being alternatives suggested at varying stages of Mumford's work, they appear throughout it. In addition, the essay will seek to demonstrate that Mumford is a key bridge figure between the Western utopian tradition and the other philosophical and practical proponents of decentralization and regionalism ranging from Patrick Geddes to Howard Odum to E. F. Schumacher.[2]

Ambivalence about Technology and Mankind's Future

Despite Mumford's readily acknowledged growing pessimism about mankind's future from *Technics and Civilization* to *The Myth of the Machine*, he has retained a degree of optimism. Unlike such critics as the French sociologist Jacques Ellul, whose *The Technological Society* (1964) epitomizes pessimism, Mumford has continued to believe that mankind can re-exert control over technology. Where Ellul's writings logically have no purpose beyond provoking despair about the future, Mumford's, even at their most pessimistic, ask readers to try to change contemporary "technological society" (a term ironically popularized by the English mistranslation of Ellul's 1954 original French work, *La Technique*).[3] Mumford never sees technology as wholly autonomous, omnipotent, and so enslaving in the way Ellul does, despite the growth of the megamachine. To Mumford, technology is not a Frankensteinian monster come to life, as it is for Ellul (and many other contemporary social critics). Rather, it remains a human invention that mankind can yet reclaim and redirect. As Mumford says as late as *The Pentagon of Power,* technology has been changed by human beings as much as it has changed them, and, in any event, mankind's principal purpose is not to master technology (or nature) but to improve itself. Indeed, as he insists in that otherwise bleak work, individuals can still refuse to accept the "Power System." They do have a choice.

Consequently, Mumford has disavowed the title "prophet of doom" increasingly ascribed to him following publication of *The Myth of the Machine.* In a letter to historian of technology Melvin Kranzberg following the latter's mixed review of *Technics and Human Development,* Mumford insists that he has never considered himself "a prophet, still less . . . a prophet of doom. On the contrary, the whole effort of my work is to diagnose, at an early stage, the conditions that may, if they are uncorrected, undermine our civilization."[4] This disavowal of prophecy is surely less than convincing, whether Mumford be deemed pessimistic, optimistic, or ambivalent. Ambivalence, in fact, may be the most accurate description of his position on technology and mankind's future. Yet Mumford's implicit endorsement here of the jeremiad as a means of spurring change and so saving mankind from an otherwise inevitable fall relates to his general notion of utopianism, about which more shortly.

Given this overall ambivalence, it is fitting that Mumford has likewise resented being characterized as an outright opponent of modern technology akin to Ellul. He defends himself against such charges, arguing that his works have tried to demonstrate that modern society must accept technology as an integral element, "capable of serving beauty as well as productivity."[5] Although this defense may be true in many respects, Mumford has certainly written about transcending technology and about creating a healthier biological and social environment: "The cycle of the machine is now coming to an end . . . we can no more continue to live in the world of the machine than we could live successfully on the barren surface of the moon."[6]

Critical Utopianism

Mumford is both less ambivalent and more consistent about utopianism than he is about technology: he believes not in the possibility of genuine utopias in the sense of literally perfect societies but rather in the utility of utopias. He allows that, whether as written blueprints or as actual communities, utopias can change existing societies. I call this alternative "critical utopianism." Mumford deems true believers in utopianism of any variety as either naïve regarding human nature or overt/covert authoritarians wishing to force conformity to one ideal. (He cites William Morris's *News from Nowhere* as an exception to the latter generalization.) Mumford also appreciates the danger of stagnation in proposing an unchanging utopian ideal, however attractive it may be in a particular time and place. New and unanticipated social and material conditions require variety. As he aptly puts it and then proves, "Fashions Change in Utopia."[7]

Consequently, and to his credit, he refuses to suggest that the garden city scheme of Ebenezer Howard and others, his own preference, be the sole model for cities, towns, and regions in America, Britain, or elsewhere. Indeed, he is also enthusiastic about small organic communities of the past, like medieval Oxford and Siena, which can still provide models. Mumford's zeal for garden cities was qualified by his visits in the 1950s to the British garden cities or New Towns, so far removed were they from his and Howard's ideals—further evidence of the imperfectibility of societies.[8]

In his autobiographical writings, Mumford confesses to having shared, in his youth, the common optimism of pre-World War I America and Europe: "That the March of Progress would in fact lead to worldwide calamity and catastrophe was something the Age of Confidence never saw as the most remote eventuality."[9] Having long ago abandoned that innocence, he has only scorn for those who persist in such ungrounded beliefs and in turn expect us to join them in their self-destructive folly, that is, their various utopian schemes.

Despite these reservations about genuine utopias, Mumford appreciates the fact that by definition they encompass most if not all aspects of life, from economics to education to leisure. To this extent, they reflect the organic wholeness (if usually not the balance) he advocates for "real world" living. Mumford nevertheless properly reads past utopian efforts as telling us less about the future than about the time and place in which they were written or devised. In a manner akin to German philosopher Ernst Bloch, he sees the unrealized and perhaps unrecognized "potentialities"[10] in societies—and in their past—as constituting their legitimate utopian aspirations. Utopian schemes thereby illuminate these potentials and, ideally, help effect positive changes or at least suggest alternatives to existing plans and directions. For Mumford, then, utopian visions are not ends in themselves but means to improving existing society—just like his own jeremiads. He prefers utopias of reconstruction to utopias of escape. If, as he proclaims repeatedly in his writings, "Life is better [and invariably more interesting] than utopia,"[11] its improvement can nonetheless be spurred through such serious utopian schemes. As he puts it in his first book, "I have . . . no private utopia . . . for life has still too many potentialities to be encompassed by the projects of a single generation, by the hopes and beliefs of a single thinker." Hence "my utopia is actual life, here or anywhere, pushed to the limits of its ideal possibilities."[12]

Mumford recognizes that the gap between prophecy and fulfillment in so many earlier utopian schemes is now closed and that, as others have argued, the danger is that utopias are all too capable of realization.[13] For example, Mumford considers that Edward Bellamy's *Looking Backward* (1888) "has worn better than perhaps any other nineteenth-century utopia. . . . His picture of utopia is very much like that of the United States in the last months of the [First] World War."[14] Far from heralding this fact, Mumford laments it, just as he does such later technological utopian visions as those of limited nuclear war and unlimited space colonies. The real gap in *Looking Backward*, he argues, is the "breach between Bellamy's conception of the good life and the [overly mechanical] structure he erected to shelter it."[15] The same holds for at least some of those more recent visions of the good life.

Equally important, and probably more original, is Mumford's discussion in *The Pentagon of Power* of the role of utopian writings from Bacon's *New Atlantis* on in providing "ideological preparation"[16] and support for the emerging megamachine and so easing its path to dominance. To be sure, Mumford recognizes that few utopian works have had direct concrete influence on any mass movement. Even *Looking Backward*, as I have argued elsewhere, was, despite its enormous sales and popularity, less a major factor in American reform than a reflection of contemporary problems that were addressed more directly by various political and social movements.[17] Mumford argues that indirectly and collectively, these and other utopian writings have had considerable influence. Despite the extreme difficulty of documenting this kind of intellectual power, I would agree. "Utopia," claims Mumford, "is the secret destination of the invisible, all-embracing megamachine. . . . Anyone who has read the literature of utopias during the past two centuries would have had a far better idea of the 'shape of things to come' than a newspaper reader who seduously followed the random reports of events from day to day."[18]

Mumford further argues that, thanks to the domination of the megamachine, it has become increasingly more difficult to conceive of alternatives to the very world anticipated by Bellamy and other nineteenth- and twentieth-century utopians. Simultaneously, it has become ever more necessary to do so, using utopian (and science fiction) writings to anticipate and try to halt "the future." This is imperative since scientists, inventors, and administrators now have advanced facilities that "have inflated their most sinister technological fantasies and given their projectors a freedom from sensible inhibitions hitherto enjoyed only in the form of nocturnal dreams."[19] Once again, Mumford is hardly alone in his insights, and his analyses here lack the intellectual power of those of, say, social critic Herbert Marcuse in *One-Dimensional Man* (1964) and other works.[20] But his understanding of the complex and on-going relationships between utopianism and the megamachine is well-founded.

In this light, Mumford has justified contempt for contemporary self-proclaimed utopians like Buckminster Fuller ("that interminable tape recorder of 'salvation by technology'")[21] and Arthur C. Clarke who ignore history and human nature alike and whose technocratic solutions to fun-

damentally non-technocratic problems are shallow, inadequate, and, ironically, unscientific (if not authoritarian). In addition to criticizing Fuller's
plans for cities under gigantic geodesic domes or on huge floating megastructures as excessively large, impersonal, and dehumanizing, he rejects
proposed space rockets and colonies on similar grounds—but also as
unjustified escapes from terrestrial problems. As early as *Technics and Civilization* he draws parallels between the Egyptian pyramids and early space
rockets as expensive megamachines carrying a selected few to seeming paradise, thanks to the labor of untold thousands. In *The Myth of the Machine*
he extends the analogy by deeming both huge tombs. Reacting to Clarke's
published criticisms of this position, Mumford writes: "What you [Clarke]
call 'life-enhancing' I would characterize as life-cheating or life-defeating—though [yours is] not quite so absurd as Buckminster Fuller's characterization of a space capsule as an ideal environment."[22]

Consequently, Mumford has refused to join the ranks of contemporary
futurists. His correspondence with Edward Cornish of the World Future
Society is revealing: he refuses to be included in a proposed directory of
"individuals active in the futures field" because his concept of the future
is so different from theirs. He correctly claims that where they "conceive
of the future as a separate realm from the past and the present," in his
scheme "past, present, and future form a continuum that is constantly in
process of change." Moreover, "instead of 'predicting the future' I am
concerned with the continuing process of reacting to the future, in order
to take measures to control or arrest forces that threaten the ecological
balance of living organisms, and the mental balance of those who equate
scientific intelligence with godlike power in all terrestrial phenomena."[23]
Hence the significance once again of his half-prophetic jeremiads.

Although Mumford's ideal environment, as indicated, is the garden city,
he has always been equally concerned about improving existing communities of all kinds. As early as *The Story of Utopias* he argues that any future
utopias—or, more realistically, any merely good societies—can and should
use various modern transportation and communications systems to
improve their local communities and to reduce their isolation and parochialism. He contends that if the inhabitants of our would-be utopias or
"Eutopias will conduct their daily affairs in a possibly more limited environment than that of the great metropolitan centers, their mental environment will not be localized or nationalized. For the first time perhaps in
the history of the planet our advance in science and invention has made it
possible for . . . every community to contribute to the spiritual heritage of
the local group. . . ."[24] Yet he displays no less concern for keeping local
cultures intact amidst internal and external changes alike. Even at this
point Mumford recognizes and decries the growing homogeneity of cultures, thanks to the same technological advances that make different cultures accessible in the first place. Technology, he realizes, can be as much
a problem as a solution to problems.

Regionalism

Equally important, as early as *The Story of Utopias,* Mumford argues for regionalism, not as an intellectual abstraction or social imposition but as a welcome fact of life that deserves both recognition and expansion.[25] As in his later, longer writings on regionalism, so here he refuses to specify strict boundaries of size or population (lest regional identity be determined arbitrarily) but instead emphasizes those organic qualities that, more than communications and transportation networks, allegedly hold regions together. Yet even in this initial work he endorses comprehensive and "scientific" regional surveys as practical means of achieving such genuine regionalism. "This common tissue of definite, verifiable, localized knowledge," he claims, "is what all our partisan utopias and reconstruction programs have lacked; and lacking it, have been one-sided and ignorant and abstract—devising paper programs for the reconstruction of a paper world."[26] Although Mumford does not deal explicitly with decentralization until later works, the connection between it and regionalism is already implicit here: regionalism presumes a degree of geographical dispersion from a centralized nation, as does his emphasis on "localized knowledge."

The volumes on American culture that followed *The Story of Utopias* in the 1920s provide examples from the nineteenth century of the kind of integrated and balanced culture that Mumford has sought in his own day through regional planning and other deliberate means. His (romanticized) portraits in those books of New England and New York as once flourishing regions provide interesting comparisons with his later visions of regionalism in twentieth-century America. He argues that the first two hundred years of American coastal development saw economic resources being used "with thrift and intelligence" while "industries and communities were in a state of balance." This produced the "integrated regional life"[27] of New England and New York his earlier books describe. To his credit, however, Mumford engages in limited nostalgia and in his writings of the 1930s and 1940s on regionalism generally looks ahead, not backward. Ironically, though, several reviews of *Technics and Civilization* chided Mumford for his supposedly "utopian" belief in the efficacy of economic and social planning.[28]

Whether or not that criticism is accurate, Mumford *has* veered toward the utopianism he otherwise disavows in his implicit equation of regionalism with organicism and in turn of organicism with the good society. Much of his writing depicts regional networks of organic communities as so superior to any others as to constitute *de facto* utopias. And this applies not only to similarly envisioned future communities but also to actual past ones, especially those of the Middle Ages, when life was supposedly in balance. Although Mumford is not, as noted, overly nostalgic, he does fall into the common trap of the organic/mechanic dichotomy: he separates whole eras and societies into one or the other of these simplistic, biased, ahistorical sociological categories and describes history as a repeated shifting between them.

Moreover, so given is Mumford to those categories that his overall optimism regarding the world's future, as in *The Culture of Cities,* or pessimism, as in *The Pentagon of Power,* is heavily shaped by his prior assessment of whether modern society is becoming more organic (good) or mechanical (bad). As he puts it in the former work, "So long as the machine [i.e., mechanical order] was uppermost, people thought quantitatively in terms of expansion, extension, progress, mechanical multiplication, power. With the organism uppermost we begin to think qualitatively in terms of growth, norms, shapes, inter-relationships, implications, associations, societies. . . . Once established, the vital and social [organic] order must subsume the mechanical one, and dominate it: in practice as well as in thought."[29] In reality, societies of whatever kind usually represent some mixture of the two categories, and organic qualities are not necessarily superior to mechanical qualities, and vice versa. But those kinds of complexities do not engage readers or attract followers as readily as the dichotomy Mumford provides.[30]

Mumford's notion of desirable regionalism thus depends on modern technology but is not, of course, itself technocratic in nature. As he concedes in *The Culture of Cities,* regionalism, like utopianism, is a relative term devoid of meaning until filled in with specific contents—which, for Mumford, include not just geographical and population size and economic base but also environmental quality, cultural opportunities, and other non-quantifiable conditions. Although he advocates no particular scheme, Mumford does favor a balance between agriculture and industry and between open and developed spaces. He rejects the concept of satellite cities, even when composed of garden cities, if it entails a hierarchy rather than an equality of such communities.

Mumfords's correspondence in the late 1930s with agrarian renewal proponent George Weller illuminates his belief in a variety of work and leisure settings. He criticizes Weller for "making the notion of domestic production and partial industrial and agricultural self-sufficiency the only possible pattern for future economic change or for urban planning. . . . [F]ar from denying it," Mumford continues, "I have followed it for three years, at least to the extent of running a garden that keeps us provided with vegetables the better part of the year. . . . But it does not seem to me that this pattern of life is necessarily the only valid one; indeed, my own needs and those of my family are now sending me back to New York again for the winter months. . . . [I]t seems to me that the sort of integration that has been achieved in Radburn and Greenbelt is also worth working for." As Mumford concludes, "you have a far greater bias against collective undertakings than I have against your individualist program. . . . I don't think the apartment is or can be the only type of urban home; but I would not rule it out altogether, as you appear to do—forgetting the existence of bachelors, of childless people, of people who have entered old age, and again of those whose work may temporarily sequester them from active participation in rural industry and rural life."[31]

Decentralization

Mumford's notion of desirable regionalism, whatever its particular manifestations, invariably includes some degree of decentralization. By decentralization he means physically smaller as well as geographically dispersed entities connected to one another in some form of regional network. In *Technics and Civilization* Mumford cites Henry Ford's ongoing "village industry" experiments as representing the kind of decentralization on a regional scale that he favors. These modest-sized but quite modern nineteen automobile plants in impoverished rural communities were generally dismissed as either expensive public-relations ventures or subtle union-busting efforts or both.[32] By contrast, and without ever apologizing for Ford's overall labor policies—or politics—Mumford grasps the importance to technology's future direction of transferring the production and assembly processes of certain automobile parts out of the huge Highland Park and River Rouge facilities, the epitome of industrial centralization, to a growing regional network of such avowedly decentralized plants, none of them more than sixty miles from Ford headquarters in Dearborn.

Indeed, in *The Culture of Cities* Mumford concedes that prior industrial decentralization schemes, usually in the form of conventional branch plants far away from major ones, have invariably been motivated by either the quest for higher profits or union-busting or both. And in that same work he laments the general absence of small-scale, decentralized industries—and, for that matter, of garden cities promoting and sustaining them—from the then emerging Tennessee Valley Authority, the epitome of planned regionalism that drew unqualified praise from so many in its early years. Mumford argues that industrial decentralization can be as efficient and as profitable as traditional centralization. Thus "bigger no longer automatically means better," he writes in *Technics and Civilization,* "flexibility of the power unit, closer adaption of means to ends, nicer timing of operation, are the new marks of efficient industry."[33] Indeed, in a generally favorable review of *Technics and Civilization* the *New York Times* gently criticized Mumford for failing to pursue this further: "There are signs that neotechnic industry will decentralize itself—a possibility that Mr. Mumford does not seem to have considered. With decentralization will go the slums, the diseases of the city, the evils of overcrowding, all that he righteously attacks . . . . And with the possibility of decentralization and a return to the small community comes also the possibility of rational city planning, a subject on which he has written in the past."[34]

Equally important, in both *The Culture of Cities* and *The Pentagon of Power,* Mumford sees decentralization in its very diversity and organic qualities as a practical alternative to the uniformity and conformity of "machine civilization." That the former book waxes lyrical about the liberating qualities of electric power lines, aluminum, radios, automobiles, superhighways, and airplanes—as did so many others in the 1930s—does not quite constitute inconsistency; for Mumford, as noted, writes in that same work of transcending technology and creating a healthier biological and social environment. Consequently, in both works he sees decentralization as a movement looking to the future, not to the past. And in the latter book, published soon after dozens of Third World countries had gained their independence from European powers, he views decentralized revolts before independence as possible rejections of Western technological—not merely political and cultural—domination, though this has rarely been the case.

Mumford is more accurate and more insightful in refusing to equate the spatial decentralization of such (international, not merely regional) schemes as Marshall McLuhan's "global village" and Alvin Toffler's "electronic cottages" with decentralized decision-making and so democracy. He recognizes the likelihood of decisions continuing to be made from the top and, in turn, of forced compliance with them. In addition, Mumford demonstrates that he anticipated McLuhan by thirty years—only to have voiced skepticism even then about the alleged virtues of instantaneous communication insofar as distance of both time and space may be necessary for good judgments and decisions. Moreover, genuine communications may require a common language if not a common culture.[35] In *The Pentagon of Power* Mumford applies these qualifications about modern communications and transportation systems to computers, whose potential for misuse and abuse he readily recognizes. He therefore calls for decentralized decision-making rather than "remote control."[36]

Curiously, Mumford himself has not always practiced decentralized decision-making or democratic planning. Instead, he has often been as guilty of elitism in this respect as those he repeatedly condemns, albeit with more humane and less technocratic motivations than most of them. In a patrician manner he has often decided what is in the best interest of ordinary citizens, whose views are largely missing from his writings. Moreover, Mumford himself has also relied upon an elite of architects, planners, social critics, and even engineers to effect his vision, at least on paper. In this regard, Mumford's 1933 essay "If I Were a Dictator" is revealing. In it he calls for greater regionalism, economic and geographical decentralization, environmental concern, and cultural uplift. He declares: "we must recover the human scale." But he also calls for greater planning, "discipline," and "rehabilitation" from the top down, if only temporarily, in a manner akin to Bellamy's *Looking Backward* and other schemes he elsewhere rejects on those very grounds.[37] Hence one must be cautious about taking too literally his 1937 pronouncement that "planning demands for its success not an authoritarian society but a society in which free thought and voluntary action and experimental effort still play a major part in its existence."[38]

Conclusion

For Mumford, then, decentralization and regionalism are not panaceas and do not provide the royal road to utopia.[39] Nor does Mumford believe in the prospect of any utopia anywhere; instead, he values utopias as means of criticizing, and so trying to change, existing societies. Nevertheless, decentralization, regionalism, and even critical utopianism can offer supposedly practical alternatives to the megamachine, the anti-utopian or dystopian "technological society" that drives Ellul to despair but that Mumford still somehow hopes to eliminate. Mumford's jeremiads, from *The Story of Utopias* on, have obviously failed to accomplish this, as he is painfully aware in recent writings. As he laments in 1975, "It seems to me that, on the basis of rational calculations, derived from what must admittedly be incomplete evidence, if the forces that now dominate us continue on their present path they must lead to collapse of the whole historical fabric, not just this or that great nation or empire."[40] Yet his major works have surely made readers—and sometimes policy-makers—much more sensitive to the need for "human scale"[41] in individual buildings, whole cities, towns, and regions, and even entire nations. His desire for human scale carries over to all of his areas of social concern and integrates them. To this extent his lifelong efforts have hardly been in vain. He is indeed a key bridge figure between the Western utopian tradition and the twentieth century's other philosophical and practical proponents of decentralization and regionalism.

I wish to acknowledge the repeated assistance of Dr. Kathleen Reed, former Curator of Manuscripts, Van Pelt Library, University of Pennsylvania, and of her graduate assistant, Ellen Slack, during my several visits to the Mumford Collection. Their help was invaluable to the preparation of this essay.

The Politics of Regional Development: Lewis Mumford and Howard W. Odum

ALLEN TULLOS

"The re-animation and re-building of regions, as deliberate works of collective art, is the grand task of politics for the opening generation."

Mumford, *The Culture of Cities* (1938)

I

To come to Philadelphia from the American South to discuss, at an international symposium on Lewis Mumford, features of the regionalist movement of the 1920s and 1930s, requires my returning for a moment to the political climate of Alabama and the nation two decades ago. For many of us who were students at the Tuscaloosa campus of the state university as the 1960s turned into the 1970s, contention with American military policy and power was as tangible and personal as our distance from communities of dissent seemed vast. Heartening to hear across that distance came insistent and courageous voices. Among the most compelling was that of Lewis Mumford in *The Pentagon of Power* (1970).

Here was Mumford (in a news magazine photograph shortly after the publication of volume two of *The Myth of the Machine*), physically vigorous in his mid-seventies, tieless, out-of-doors, his vitality complementing his indignation. To some of us in the South—where both history and biblical voice have taught hard lessons—Mumford's interpretations and forecasts spoke prophetically, illuminating the paths over which American power had arrived at such a sorry misapplication as in Vietnam, and down which we were still chasing the delusions of nuclear security. Pessimistic by analysis, optimistic by faith, the evangelical Mumford of *Pentagon of Power* held out the prospect of transformation.

In the following months, reading my way backward through Mumford's writings, I arrived at the 1930s to discover his regionally based critique of the nationalist "power state." Here, clearly, was an organizing principle that depended upon and invigorated both the provincial and the international. Had Mumford in preaching or practicing his regionalism become acquainted with anyone in the South who had shared something of this regional vision? I sent a note in the direction of Amenia. Promptly in return came a hand-written reply. Other replies followed from other inquiries. Eventually there were opportunities to visit Lewis and Sophia Mumford at their farmhouse for conversations and walks among the raspberries.

Throughout the 1970s, Mumford remained enthusiastic about the potential for regionalism even as he surveyed the "disillusion, alienation, dismantlement, and destruction" which he saw at large.[1] Regionalism constituted one necessary dimension of the cultural transformation for which Mumford hoped. But what shape would a renewed regionalism take? In answering, Mumford pointed to the approach and technical practice evident in one of his favorite books at that time—Ian McHarg's *Design with Nature* (1969).[2] Then, for his Southern correspondent and visitor, Mumford turned to one of his first principles—the concept of the usable past.[3]

Mumford suggested that my understanding of the South's regionalists of the 1920s and 1930s begin with his former connections with that section of the country. In 1949, Mumford was visiting lecturer at the North Carolina State College School of Design in Raleigh, the Department of City and Regional Planning at UNC-Chapel Hill, and the Woman's College at Greensboro. At the time, and in a series of essays that were published in 1954 for the *Architectural Record,* he had spoken and written admiringly about the work and the promise of architect Mathew Novicki who taught at the School of Design.[4] In the Polish-born Novicki's best efforts, such as the Arena for the North Carolina State Fair and the designs for buildings in Chandigarh, India, drawn in the late 1940s (just before the architect died in an airplane crash), Mumford saw the promise of an international architecture sensitive to the feeling of regional culture.

During his 1949 stay in North Carolina, Mumford also renewed the acquaintance of the Chapel Hill group of regional sociologists whose work had first caught his notice in the 1920s. "Thanks to Dr. Howard Odum and his fellow workers," Mumford wrote in *The Southern Packet* for April of 1949, "Chapel Hill and the University [of North Carolina] are the home of modern regionalism in America."[5] Even as he praised the Chapel Hill regional sociologists, Mumford was uneasy with the transformation taking place in the Carolina Piedmont. "Almost alone among the industrial areas of the nation," he continued, "North Carolina is still a state in which most of its population is either rural or living in cities of less than a hundred thousand." Industry and agriculture still seemed in balance. Yet, he warned with prophetic accuracy, "In fifty years, if North Carolina does not plan to maintain its present decentralized pattern, Charlotte, Raleigh, and High Point will be indistinguishable from Detroit; and the surrounding countryside will become merely a real-estate speculators' annex to the growing metropolis." In 1949, Mumford wondered whether the region-

The Southern PACKET

A Monthly Review of Southern Books and Ideas

| Volume V | APRIL 1949 | Number 4 |

A Thought *for a Growing South*

By LEWIS MUMFORD

L EWIS MUMFORD, *writer and professor of the Humanities, has been
working with southern students this year
in the fields of architecture, city and
regional planning, and art. As visiting
lecturer at the North Carolina State College School of Design, at the Department
of City and Regional Planning at Chapel
Hill and at Woman's College of the
State University at Greensboro he has
had opportunity to add to his general
knowledge of the South through observation of community growth in North
Carolina.*

*Though he uses this state as his
example, he points out that most of the
South can benefit from similar conditions
in planning for the future.*

*His current writings appear in the
Saturday Review of Literature and the
New Yorker. His interest in higher
education brought him membership on
the Commission on Teacher Education of
The American Council on Education.*

T HE people of North Carolina are
justly proud of their many natural resources, spread out in great
diversity, from seashore to upland. But
one of their most important assets they
seem to have overlooked: their present
pattern of population distribution.

Almost alone among the industrial
areas of the nation, North Carolina is
still a state in which most of its population is either rural or living in cities
of less than a hundred thousand. In
other words, industry and agriculture
are still in balance here. Whether North
Carolina will maintain this balance does
not depend upon uncontrollable forces
of nature: it depends upon whether
people understand the advantages of
such a population pattern and whether
the state uses its powers to maintain it.

alists and the state's citizens would grasp the problems of controlling "profit, prestige, and power" before the agriculture-industry balance was lost. They did not.

Mumford had admired and influenced Odum's Institute for Research in Social Science from a distance. In looking closely at the Chapel Hill regionalists I found much to contrast with the Mumford vision, much to commend, but also much that proved disappointing. As I looked, I also learned of a more critical regionalism in the South, one based in Appalachia and with beginnings that were contemporary with Mumford and Odum. This strain of Appalachian political and cultural regionalism, which continues to thrive in the late twentieth century at Tennessee's Highlander Center, was apparently not known to Mumford, even though it more fully embodied an anti-capitalist politic and a Kropotkin-like stance toward decentralization than did the Institute at Chapel Hill.[6]

II

As he recalled the American regionalist movement in the years prior to World War II, Mumford wrote, "I was one of a larger group that laid the ground for a new approach to urban planning. Odum and his fellow regionalists at Chapel Hill belong to the same company."[7] Today, while the regionalist insights offered by Mumford and other members of the New York-based Regional Planning Association of America retain a valuable, if far from realized potential, the regionalism of University of North Carolina sociologist Odum and his Institute for Research in Social Science has come to represent regionalism's failings and often to justify its neglect. "Who today reads a Howard Odum book?" irreverently asked a Southern historian recently. In considering the regional theory of Howard Odum alongside that of Mumford, I want to suggest that although Odum's regionalism was significantly influenced by Mumford, Odum rejected precisely the Mumford insights that today remain the most resilient and vital. Although nationalistic fervor and the wake of World War II did much to damage the regionalist movement, Odum's regional vision was badly compromised in its formation.

The sociologists of the Institute for Research in Social Science at the University of North Carolina, from the Institute's founding in 1924 until the post-World War II era, were known widely as *the* Southern regionalists. The Chapel Hill group, under the direction of Georgia native Odum, first claimed the name, then sought to draw the boundaries of Southern regionalism. "In using the South as a term for the general living laboratory for regional research and development," wrote Odum's longtime co-worker Katherine Jocher, "there is ample precedent and urge."[8] Columbia University's Sociology Department found its laboratory in New York City; there was the example of the University of Chicago's urban sociologists.

And, antedating these social science outposts was Patrick Geddes's Outlook Tower in Edinburgh.

As a creation of Rockefeller philanthropy and Howard Odum's persuasiveness, the Institute for Research in Social Science was part of a major transformation of the university that coincided with the state's business and industrial emergence, especially in the production of textiles and tobacco. By 1949, political scientist V. O. Key could write of a half-century of "economic oligarchy" in North Carolina.[9] Chapel Hill's fortunes and prospects were thoroughly intertwined with the interests and health of the state's businessmen and manufacturers. In the 1920s the University of North Carolina grew rapidly, adding new departments, doubling its enrollment, providing trained professionals in business, industry, and government. A school of engineering was established, in the words of UNC's historian, "in response to the demand for electrical engineers for the rapidly developing public utilities companies."[10]

Out of this context, the studies of the Institute for Research in Social Science began to appear from the University of North Carolina Press in the mid-1920s with books about cotton tenancy, civics, planning, folk culture, and race relations. Among the best were Rupert Vance's *Human Factors in Cotton Culture* (1929) and *Human Geography of the South* (1932), Guy Johnson's *John Henry* (1929) and *Folk Culture on St. Helena Island* (1930), Odum's *American Epoch* (1930), Arthur Raper's *Preface to Peasantry* (1936), Margaret Jarman Hagood's *Mothers of the South* (1939), and Raper and Ira De A. Reid's *Sharecroppers All* (1941). These were pioneering works of regional discovery and description that remain compelling and important.

The Institute was a comfortable and supportive place to teach and work.[11] Its faculty often undertook collaborative projects. And, unusual for any research organization during this time, a significant number of women figured prominently in Institute projects. The good-spirited longevity of this research community stands, by itself, as an achievement, recalling Mumford's comments about the Regional Planning Association of America: "when friendship and daily intercourse bring people together for a common purpose, the association itself is sufficient reward to those who participate, no matter what the outward success of the enterprise.[12]

Social science of any sort was new to the South of the 1920s and Odum's arrival at the University of North Carolina with doctorate degrees in psychology and sociology from Clark and Columbia universities was enough to raise native suspicions outside the ambiance of Chapel Hill. The willingness of *Social Forces*, the journal Odum founded, to publish essays questioning some of the South's deepest articles of faith stirred moments of protest and outrage from the Ku Klux Klan, from anti-evolutionists, and from the most rabid *laissez-faire* industrialists.[13] The Agrarians of Vanderbilt University scoffed. Donald Davidson, for instance, thought he detected, beneath Odum's thick rhetorical cloak, the shapes of social scientists being slipped into positions of governmental planning authority. By means of a bureaucratic thwarting of democracy, Davidson felt that regionalism would become an instrument of a Leviathan-like State.[14]

Against the reactionaries' railings and the conservatives' fears, the University of North Carolina sociologists established their liberal reputations. "And out of Chapel Hill," observed W. J. Cash, "and all the lesser centers which followed Odum's lead, numbers of young men and women were going out through the schools of the South to hand on and expand the new attitude in ever-widening circles."[15] Outside the South, the Chapel Hill group was encouraged by colleagues in the young profession at Chicago and Yale. H. L. Mencken offered praise and opened the pages of the *American Mercury* to their writings. "Some of the clearest and most enlightened expressions of the regional political philosophy," wrote Mumford in *The Culture of Cities,* "are those that have issued from Professor Howard Odum and his colleagues."[16]

Yet, as Odum developed his regional perspective in this most progressive of Southern universities, he never engaged the critique of political and economic power with which Mumford increasingly examined American society. The resulting regionalism became fatally compromised, unable to generate a trenchant dissent to the capitalist transformation occurring in Odum's own region, the Carolina Piedmont, where an industrial order was rising upon the lives of the displaced sharecroppers and tenant farmers who were flooding an unorganized, low-wage, factory labor pool. When it came to the matters of industrial wages, working conditions, and unionization, manufacturing workers in the Carolina Piedmont, in the 1920s and 1930s as now, sat at the bottom of the list of states.

As for their analysis of the regions's new industrial society, the Chapel Hill regionalists offered nothing so keen as Raper's studies of sharecroppers or Hagood's portraiture of Southern white tenant farm women. Under Odum's guidance, the Institute for Research in Social Science conducted its few industrial studies with a gingerly care for the sensibilities of mill owners and the state's business and political leadership. The history of the Carolina Piedmont's industrialization along with the advocacy of regionalism itself were harmonized with a conflict-free theory of social change and an uncritical allegiance to American nationalism.

Although influenced by Mumford and Geddes, Odum assembled his regionalism eclectically. Significantly missing from the Odum view was Mumford's insistence that the politics of regional development must involve an honest identification and addressing of relations of economic and social power. As Mumford was quick to emphasize, regional industrialization had become "a function of banking and credit. The economies of power, machinery, the natural resources of individual regions, all the elements that contribute to the livelihood of a community," he wrote in 1928, "are perverted, under financial conventions that more or less dominate all minds, into an apparatus estimated almost exclusively in terms of profits and dividends."[17] Odum, prizing harmony, was never so bold. Mumford, never so concerned about Rockefeller grants or university patronage, spoke from a position of greater independence.

III

It was at Clark University in 1908 and 1909, and through Clark's first president, G. Stanley Hall, that the graduate student Odum became aware of Geddes, the Scottish city planner, regionalist, biologist, and intellectual father-figure to Mumford. Geddes and Hall were good friends, exchanging visits and correspondence across the Atlantic for many years.[18] In Edinburgh, between 1892 and 1912, Geddes oversaw the transformation of an old observatory into the "Outlook Tower," a workshop with an eye to the study of an expanding horizon. Beginning with the view of Edinburgh as seen from the top of the Tower, a visitor descended through levels of the building devoted successively to the surrounding region, to Scotland, the British Isles, and the world. Each floor contained books, charts, maps, models, and artifacts of on-going research.

In the summer of 1906 Hall traveled to Edinburgh to visit Geddes. Examining at first-hand the Outlook Tower, he wrote:

> It is a magnificent new idea into which a vast amount of careful intellectual work has been invested. It is so unique and original that the conventional mind would hardly be likely to appreciate it, but every intelligent man and woman deeply interested in science and education will see in the tower a new departure full of untold possibilities.[19]

"This regional Outlook Tower," observed Geddes, "is thus itself a regional product; although its principle is easily adaptable to every region, as that of an encyclopedia may be used anywhere."[20] "Regional Surveys can only yield data for action," wrote Mumford with the Outlook Tower in mind, "when by means of the Laboratory Method, they lead on to Regional Service."[21] Geddes's Outlook Tower, Mumford points out, was an important source for Odum's plan for his own institute.[22] As critical to Odum as the discovery of Geddes was the influence of Hall's vision that the modern research university, established on German principles of graduate study and underwritten by private or state wealth, should shape American society and that university-builders should see themselves as social engineers.[23]

In Chapel Hill in 1925, as Odum was beginning to conceive the regional projects for his newly created Institute, the regional planning issue of the *Survey Graphic* was published. Edited by Mumford and containing essays by Clarence Stein, F. L. Ackerman, Stuart Chase, Benton MacKaye, and Henry Wright, this was the first co-ordinated public expression of the New York-centered Regional Planning Association of America. This issue of the *Survey Graphic* stands among the very first statements of what became, during the following two decades, an outpouring of American regionalist expression.[24] Odum was a regular reader and partisan of the *Survey*, a journal of social documentation and reform. Its editors had applauded his work at Chapel Hill as early as 1921.[25] In 1923, Odum had worked out an arrangement for a "clubbing" of subscriptions that would offer a special rate for the *Survey* and *Social Forces* during the American Country Life Convention.[26]

Writing that the *Survey Graphic's* planning issue presented "an illuminating discussion of the whole problem of regional planning," Odum was especially delighted with Mumford's essay, "Regions—To Live In."[27] For Mumford and the RPAA, regionalism underlay an advocacy of public planning that was seeking to counter the uncontrolled, profit-making urbanization of the Northeast:

> Regional planning [Mumford wrote] asks not how wide an area can be brought under the aegis of the metropolis, but how the population and civic facilities can be distributed so as to promote and stimulate a vivid, creative life throughout a whole region—a region being any geographic area that possesses a certain unity of climate, soil, vegetation, industry and culture.[28]

Excited by Mumford's conception of the relationship of city and region, Odum, who had recently been put in charge of the Henry Holt American Social Science Series, hoped to get Mumford to write a "city" volume. Just then, however, Mumford was too busy for this project, and Odum had to be satisfied with excerpting long sections from "Regions—To Live In" for his own book *Man's Quest for Social Guidance*.[29] According to Mumford, Odum "probably should get the credit as the first—and possibly only—sociologist to recognize the importance of the *Survey Graphic* issue on regional planning.[30]

The *Survey* for the year 1925 also re-acquainted Odum with Geddes. Beginning in February, Geddes contributed six "Talks from the Outlook Tower" which ranged over the fields of regionalism, city planning, folk culture, education, and civics.[31] Mumford wrote the introduction to these "Talks," sounding much like Hall in 1906. "As the Tower embodies a new outlook, a new method, a fresh mode of life," wrote Mumford, "wherever that vision is seen and that mode followed, some new avatar of the Tower must arise."[32]

Years later (in 1944), after submitting Philip Boardman's biography of Geddes to the University of North Carolina Press, Odum acknowledged the influence of the Scot as he had received it through Hall, Mumford, and articles in *The Survey:*

> With reference to the actual influence of Geddes . . . it must be clear that there is no way of measuring it. How much of his influence would come to Chapel Hill, for instance, through Stanley Hall, William James, Percy and Benton MacKaye, Lewis Mumford, Radhakamal Mukerjee, the LePlay School, the *Survey* articles, the Harvard featuring of Geddes' works? It is not possible to evaluate the influence of these as important stimuli in the emerging

research into regional problems of the South and subsequently the Nation. Certainly they were of great importance.[33]

"In some respects," wrote Odum in an essay in *Social Forces* entitled "Patrick Geddes' Heritage to 'The Making of the Future,'" "it may well be said that the new sociological emphasis upon regionalism had its genesis in the Geddes contribution.[34]

Odum mixed the ideas of Geddes and Mumford into the largely undigested amalgam of psychological and social science theories acquired in his graduate study that, in the main, derived from an antiquated, organic, world-view. He was influenced deeply, for example, by William Graham Sumner's concept of "folkways"—a near fatalistic view of the slowness of cultural change, and a view at odds with the dynamics of both Geddes's and Mumford's thought.[35]

Odum's adoption of Sumner's folkways concept and his own development of the idea of "technicways" as "the habits and customs that develop as adjustment to the innovations of science and technology" led to an amorphous and widely inclusive category of "folk" that lacked class and historical definition and to a view of technological development that failed to acknowledge power in society.[36] Technicways were seen to move as if they were natural forces, not the results, as Lewis Mumford would always have it, of contentious human desires, promises, and relations of power played out in particular places.

IV

As he developed his regionalist perspective, Odum was overly anxious to show that American regionalists owed their first allegiance to the national interest. In this desire for harmony he again chose a different tack from Lewis Mumford. Fearful of the nineteenth-century legacy of Southern "sectionalism" with its antagonistic posturings and embittered and tragic consequences, Odum abandoned the use of this term in any but a pejorative sense. "Regionalism," the Agrarian Donald Davidson wrote, as he recognized Odum's tactic, did not have "the taint of war and confusion that hangs about the older words."[37]

In making the distinction between regionalism and sectionalism, Odum argued against Frederick Jackson Turner's prophecy that sectionalism, far from dying, would become more important as America developed.[38] In 1922, the year that Odum founded the journal *Social Forces,* Turner wrote the essay "Sections and Nation" for *The Yale Review.* Said Turner:

We in America are in reality a federation of sections rather than of states. State sovereignty was never influential except as a constitutional shield for the section. We are so large and diversified a nation that it is almost impossible to see the situation except through sectional spectacles. The section either conceives itself as an aggrieved and oppressed minority, suffering from the injustice of the other sections of the nation, or it thinks of its own culture, its economic policies, and well-being as best for all the nation. It thinks, in other words, of the nation in terms of itself.[39]

As an explicit response to Turner, Odum published an essay, "Sectionalism and Its Avoidance," by Edward A. Ross in the 1924 issue of *Social Forces*. Ross agreed that there were long-standing sectional differences in the United States, but he saw forces at work which would "nationalize" and "standardize" everything from clothes and house interiors to thinking and feeling. Such "unifying interests" as Ross found, he celebrated. "As negroes drift North," he wrote, "more northerners are able to get the southern white man's point of view on the race question." The rise of national magazines, mass advertising, motion pictures, and network radio would help ensure "that in our time at least the nationalizing forces have the upperhand of the sectionalizing forces."[40]

In a *Social Forces'* article in 1934, Odum continued to contrast his regionalism with Turner's view, and with the earlier historical forms of "sectionalism." Odum argued that "balance" could be substituted for Turner's inevitable intersectional strife. Under the banner of balance, Odum adapted his regionalism into a nationalistic framework. "In the first place," he said, "regionalism envisages the Nation first, making the national culture and welfare the final arbiter. For whatever else the Southern region may be, it is first of all a major part of the moving inventory of a powerful nation rebuilding its own fortunes and reconstructing its part in the world of nations."[41]

As a contrast to Odum, Mumford and his colleagues in the Regional Planning Association of America were not troubled by the gray ghosts of sectionalism. Mumford points out that:

> Sectionalism . . . is a strictly American term; and it lacks the geographic and historic richness of regionalism: so we never thought of using it. . . . I independently had drawn on the French geographers, like [Paul] Vidal de la Blache and [Jean] Brunhes; and was in touch with Charles Brun, the leader of the French regionalist movement. . . . As early as April 1923, we had called our new association the Regional Planning Association; for [Clarence] Stein had quickly realized that this was an essential part of our new approach.[42]

While Odum's anxiety over sectionalism led him to see the region always "in the perspective of the total national interest," Mumford's regionalism saw nationalism as the ideology of a "war-state" and as "an attempt to make the laws and customs and beliefs of a single region or city do duty for the varied expressions of a multitude of other regions."[43] And while Odum wrote that "to set in motion forces which will turn the Southern potential into national power will constitute the supreme task of the next few generations," it was his colleague, the cultural geographer Rupert Vance, who, in tracing the South's history, put forward the disharmonious term "colonial economy" to express the South's long-dependent status as producer of raw goods or minimally processed finished products.[44]

It was also Vance, whose regionalism stood closer to Mumford's, who pushed Odum to be more straightforward across the whole range of regional theory. In an in-house critique which Vance sent to Odum in 1938, after reading the final draft of the soon-to-be-published *American Regionalism* by Odum and Harry Estill Moore, he asked Odum for a "thesis and a path through the woods" of prose. "I believe," commented Vance, "I must be wanting a more hardboiled view of social conflict. . . . What about class conflict? Is the resolution of Regional views an alternative to an increase of such conflict?"[45]

Odum failed to answer Vance's questions about *American Regionalism*. With the coming of World War II, such questions seemed moot. But if Odum's regionalism fared poorly in the postwar American empire, his institute thrived, entering, in the words of its historians, "into contracts with the Air Force for a series of studies of Soviet industrial capacities and a study of day-and-night populations of Soviet and American 'target cities,' and with the Public Health Service for studies of urbanization in connection with the building of the Savannah River atomic energy plant."[46] University social science research had itself become an industry deeply intertwined with the most irrational forces of the corporate state, the Pentagon of Power as Mumford called it. The alternative, regionalist vision that might have empowered criticism of the "technicways," of the prevailing political economy, and of the increasing military influence upon postwar America were lost in the Institute's attraction to the marketplace of ideas.

PART II

MEGAMACHINE AND ORGANICISM

When he was writing *Technics and Civilization* in the early 1930s, Mumford, as we have noted, was becoming increasingly skeptical of the future that technology would bring unless enlightened and determined persons intervened in the process of technological and social change. His doubt expressed itself in his juxtaposition of the mechanical and the organic: the mechanical he feared; the organic he favored. In several of his books he set forth his concept of the organic growth of forms and structures in counterdistinction to their mechanical development. Mumford and others of his generation, especially in the United States, took from social Darwinism the morphological concept of the organism evolving in the environment. In France, philosopher Henri Bergson, a vitalist, had popularized the concept of creative evolution, and Mumford felt his influence. But Geddes's doctrine of life insurgent, "perpetually striving, struggling, overcoming all obstacles," stimulated Mumford's thinking more directly, as Williams shows in her essay in the previous section. The organic, life-insurgent forces in the world came to mean to Mumford the antithesis of the mechanical. In this view he shared what the philosopher Alfred North Whitehead called the romantic reaction against the mechanical philosophy. Leo Marx in his essay in this section suggests that the version of the organicist-mechanical polarity most like Mumford's can be found in Samuel Taylor Coleridge's notion that organic form is innate and shapes itself from within as it develops. On the other hand, the mechanical is a form impressed from without, one that might not even suit the innate characteristics of that on which it is stamped. As Mumford began to define healthy personality, communities, cities, and regions as essentially organic and even to see the possibility of technology and science becoming organic, organicism became for him a central doctrine that regularly appeared in his writing. Marx reminds us that Van Wyck Brooks, American essayist and literary critic, Mumford's friend and correspondent, observed that Mumford had not *ideas* but one *idea* that he spent his life working out: the contradiction between organicism and mechanism.

Mumford's advocacy of organicism raised the problem, Eugene Rochberg-Halton argues in his essay, of "Mumford's unashamed generalism, his joining together in organic wholes what sociologists and their counterparts in other disciplines have carved into cleanly separated areas of inquiry" (Rochberg-Halton, 127–28). A sociologist, Rochberg-Halton holds that life and evolutionary love are the essence of Mumford's world picture, thus contemporary intellectuals find embarrassing the vision which Mumford so passionately presented. In evoking "emotional depths and cosmic heights," Mumford shattered the dominant "procrustean bed of contemporary rationalism" (Rochberg-Halton, 129). Because he championed organicism and challenged modern mechanistic and rational thought, Mumford becomes for Rochberg-Halton the central social theorist of the twentieth century.

Rochberg-Halton finds Mumford singular because he opposes the prevailing paradigm of sociological thought defined by Karl Marx, Max Weber, and Emile Durkheim, the triumvirate of "classical" sociologists, a paradigm that equates the modern with the rational. Rational materialism forms the "iron cage" of modernity, according to Weber; rational science engenders new gods for modern belief, in the opinion of Durkheim; and the rationally organized machine-mode of production characterizes the modern era, according to Karl Marx. Critical of the modern, they nevertheless believed it to be a culmination of progress. In constrast, Mumford, especially in his later works, Rochberg-Halton believes, found the further development of the modern along a rational trajectory to be not inevitable, holding that the modern, or, specifically, the neotechnic aspects of it, exhibited strong organicist tendencies that opposed the mechanical and the rational. These tendencies, Mumford believed, would have to be determinedly reinforced, for he wanted to displace the iron cage of rationalism with the organic bed from which springs human dreams, imagination, emotional life, free play, and idle curiosity.

He was interested not so much in mechanical production of goods as he was in the self-creation of individuals. He believed that before human beings became *Homo faber,* they had been *Homo symbolicus,* creators of signifying and self-creating symbol. Humans need symbol, ritual words, images, and mores to control and cope with their inner demons even more than they need controls for the terrible forces of the outer world, or nature. In making this assertion, Mumford aligned himself with a few social theorists of like mind, such as Charles Peirce, Victor Turner, and several anthropologists. He and they may, Rochberg-Halton hopes, bring "social theory back to life"—as well as an organic culture.

Ominously obstructing the ripening of the organic, the megamachine, Mumford believes, is the culmination of mechanization. This concept does not appear full-blown in Mumford's writings, Donald Miller tells us in his essay, until the two-volume *Myth of the Machine* (1967, 1970). By then Mumford had witnessed the spread of large and more complex technological systems, especially the military-industrial production complex, as well as the use of once-pure physics to design the bombs that destroyed Hiroshima and Nagasaki. As he wrote the *Myth of the Machine,* the megamachine, another magnetic concept like organicism, became for him a near obsession. He saw megamachines as shaping the course of human history, deadening life insurgent, and likely to bring civilization to a violent end in a nuclear holocaust.

As we have seen, Mumford anticipated his later use of the concept of megamachine as early as *Technics and Civilization* where the word "machine" began to take on new meaning for him. He began to distinguish between *machines,* or specific objects like the printing press or power loom, and *the machine,* a shorthand reference to the entire technological complex that embraced tools, machines, knowledge, skills, and arts. *The machine* became for him the physical embodiment of the mechanistic means to ends, or a technological system. Miller shows in his essay that by the time of the writing of *Technics and Human Development* and *The Pentagon of Power, the machine* had become for Mumford the megamachine, or a system of interchangeable parts, human and physical, centrally organized and controlled, dependent on a priestly or scientific monopoly of knowledge, and ensuring the power, glory, and material well-being of an elite.

Mumford finds that the megamachine originated in Egypt and continues in various guises throughout history. After the Egyptian prototype, as Miller explains, other megamachines continued to appear. Today, the modern bureaucratically administered, military-industrial projects are our contemporary megamachines. In the old megamachines, however, the center of authority lay with the absolute ruler; in the modern megamachine, authority centers in the system itself. A modern equivalent of the megamachine involves nuclear weapons, missiles, computers, and a priesthood of engineers and scientists who oversee the military-industrial complex. Those who control megamachines and those who are regimented by them share the mechanistic, power-centered world-view. The myth of the machine for Mumford, Miller points out, is the widely held but mistaken belief that megamachines are irresistible and ultimately beneficial.

Leo Marx's essay shows how Mumford's concepts of the megamachine and of organism evolved into overarching metaphors which came to dominate and order his critical-polemical, scholarly-historical writing. This "Manichean vision," Marx believes, provided coherence and added drama to the writing, but at the same time partially accounts, Marx decides, for the often tendentious, predictable, and sometimes boring character of Mumford's writing. Having acknowledged Mumford's seminal contributions to the history of technology, architecture, and ideas, Marx faults him for giving the megamachine and the organism, disembodied abstractions and metaphors, the status of historical agencies. (We should note that, in *The Golden Day,* Mumford praises Ralph Waldo Emerson for giving the world of ideas an independent reality.) Specifically, Marx finds questionable Mumford's suggestion in his extensive writing on architecture that buildings are not simply like organisms, they *are* organisms. Marx feels that Mumford thereby transforms a metaphor into an identify. Similarly, a system for organizing people to do work, to build a pyramid is, according to Marx, no more a machine than a building is an organism. In addition, Mumford makes the claim, astonishing to Marx, that the Egyptian megamachine, made "of human parts, provided the prototype, the actual working model, for all later complex machines" (Marx, 177).

We might not be surprised that a person who sees the world as machine—as artifact—would be highly visual in orientation. We would expect this especially if his or her concern about technology was compounded—as it was in the case of Mumford—by an interest in architecture. We might also expect Mumford to employ visual metaphors, or analogies, as freely as verbal ones. Yet, as Stanislaus von Moos shows us in his essay, the illustrations in *Technics and Civilization* not only are not spectacular but they play a subsidiary role in the context of the verbal discourse. Nevertheless, the fifteen pages of illustrations (sixty items) in *Technics and Civilization,* because they are anecdotal, provide another angle of insight into Mumford's attitudes toward technology. The illustrations are grouped in accord with visual analogies, as, for example, those between the frameworks of bridges and the beds of lathes, and those relating the streamlining of both airplanes and locomotives. As we might anticipate, Mumford wants to convey pictorially, in *Technics and Civilization,* several of his major themes. His illustrations pertaining to the paleotechnic convey not only environmental degradation in industrial Pittsburgh but the era's constructive genius as well, in its railways and bridges. Those illustrations linked to the neotechnic characteristically suggest process and dynamism, as in the photos of automation and giant electric power stations. Moos contrasts Mumford's emphasis on the dynamic aspects of modern technology with the architect Le Corbusier's emphasis on its formal, even static, quality. Le Corbusier celebrated modern engineers and technology in his publications of the early 1920s, but he found in automobiles, ocean liners, and airplanes the pure geometric forms that architects and builders had used since the era of classical Greece. Where Mumford would use an angled photograph of an ocean liner to suggest arrival or departure, Le Corbusier would choose an angle that revealed the pure Platonic forms of the liner. By placing a photograph of a modern hydroturbine on the same plate with an x-ray photo of a nautilus, the spiral-chambered sea-shell, Mumford suggests by analogy how neotechnic machinery can—and, he believes, should—be organic in form and function.

Moos compares the visual imagery of Mumford to that of the twentieth-century German architect Erich Mendelsohn, whom, incidentally, Mumford met, found congenial, and with whom he corresponded. Mumford used a photograph of a grain silo from Mendelsohn's photographic essay, *Amerika* (1926). Mendelsohn, who like Mumford sensed that the essence of modern American production technology was flow, perceptively observed that railways from the great wheat fields of America, and ships plying the Great Lakes poured their contents of grain "without interruption" into the gigantic grain elevators. From there the flow continued to the U.S. bread-making factories. Mumford's visual concepts, like Mendelsohns's, imply

> . . . process rather than a set of abstract laws, forces in movement rather than a mechanical end-product that incorporates a principle of design. The theme . . . is visualized industrial process, not mechanics and machinery [Moos, 187].

The Transformation
of Social Theory

EUGENE ROCHBERG-HALTON

Lewis Mumford is world-renowned, yet seldom considered in relation to the sociological tradition. Despite his early connections to Patrick Geddes and Victor Branford (who have also been forgotten), and a brief stint as editor of *The Sociological Review* in 1920, despite his even earlier acquaintance with Thorstein Veblen and John Dewey when all three worked on *The Dial*, he tends not to be considered a sociologist by sociologists. Perhaps this is due, in part, to the professionalizing of sociology and other academic disciplines since the turn of the century, which has resulted in a perceived tradition of "classical" social theory, and an intense socialization of students into the perceived tradition. What in earlier times was known as social philosophy is today considered a speciality within academic sociology, despite the fact that the term "social theory" is widely used across a number of disciplines, including philosophy. Karl Marx, Max Weber, and Emile Durkheim constitute a virtual triumvirate of "classical" social theory, though some would want to include Georg Simmel, George Herbert Mead, Talcott Parsons, and a few others within the "classical" pantheon. No social theorist, as least as far as I have been able to determine, would include Lewis Mumford among the "classics." I have asked sociologists informally over the past few years what they know about Mumford, and their responses indicate that they tend to know him as a writer on cities (and "writer" sometimes carries a pejorative meaning), and some know his architectural and cultural criticism. But the fact that he has written a sizable body of work that could be considered social theory seems to be a well-kept secret these days.

There may be other reasons for Mumford's invisibility in sociology. First may be the matter of his writing style: the fact that Mumford is a master of English prose may disqualify him from serious consideration by purveyors of "sociologese." As one sociologist told me, "Mumford writes in a popular style, not a sociological one." Mumford's use of passionate reason instead of the ideal of dispassionate "value-free" inquiry would also be an obvious cause for disqualification. There is also the problem of Mumford's unashamed generalism, his joining together in organic wholes what soci-

ologists and their counterparts in other disciplines have carved into cleanly
separated areas of inquiry. "His work may be good," as a colleague once
told me, "but is it sociology?"

There is also Mumford's disregard for the perceived classics themselves.
It is not so much that he is ignorant of the "classical" tradition—his work
reveals a working knowledge of German scholars that most Americans
were ignorant of until recently—as that his writings do not have the
"aura" of belief in the perceived tradition that one sees in mainstream
sociology: the attribution to "classical" social theory of a canonical status.

"Classical" is an honorific term used by sociologists both in a vague
sense to mean "old"—and thereby authoritative—and also to signify the
creation myth of sociology, in which a few select authors and their foun-
dational texts form a pantheon of "theorists." That these authors may have
viewed themselves as philosophers, historians, economists, as well as sociologists, but not as "theorists," is not considered. The concept of "classical
social theory" resembles the conditions under which the Mesopotamian
scribes attributed the transmission of divine knowledge to the seven mythic
sages from before the Great Flood. These antediluvian sages were thenceforth regarded as the authors of the scholarly canon of texts.[1]

Talcott Parsons, through his 1937 book, *The Structure of Social Action,*
which claimed a "convergence" in the theories of Weber, Durkheim, and
a few others, was influential in establishing the sociological canon and the
"pure" theorist. He exerted enormous influence over the social sciences
in the 1950s and 1960s, despite an ahistorical, jargon-ridden style of writing which C. Wright Mills derisively termed "grand theory." Parsons
preached the ideology of scientism, "modernization," and a de-humanized
"systems" model of American society and human development. In my
opinion he was representative of the triumph of post World War Two
"Americanism," with its imperial optimism and uncritical technical outlook, and a key symbol of the capitulation of the intellect to the megamachine of modernity. His work could not be more opposed in spirit to that
of Mumford, who is roughly his contemporary. A comparison of these two
prodigious writers would reveal the inner history of the twentieth-century
intellect: Talcott Parsons, the "value-free" sociologist who secretly helped
to bring former Nazi social scientists to the United States after World War
II; Mumford, the advocate of U.S. military intervention against Germany
in the late 1930s, and later the passionate critic of American militarism in
the nuclear era and the Vietnam War. Parsons, who died in 1979, still
wields enormous influence over contemporary theorists despite a lapse in
his hegemony. Lewis Mumford is virtually unknown, perhaps because such
an unquestionably independent thinker can prove an intolerable threat to
what William James so aptly termed "the Ph.D. Octopus."

Finally there is the stuff of Mumford's world-picture itself, with its image
of life and evolutionary love as *axis mundi.* This vision, expressed in varying
ways throughout his work, but always with passionate eloquence, is, I sub-

mit, ultimately embarrassing to the intellectual in general, as presently constituted. For Mumford invokes emotional depths and cosmic heights of the
human creature that utterly shatter the procrustean bed of contemporary
rationalism. Therefore Mumford is wisely avoided by contemporary intellectuals, or whittled down to size.

Mumford, perhaps alone of social theorists, has undercut the fundamental premisses of modernity, and I hope to show why this break and the
alternative he proposes mark him as the central social theorist of the twentieth century.

Modern social theory is usually regarded as founded on responses to the
Enlightenment and the emerging conditions of industrial civilization. As
will become evident later, the concept of life—both in Darwin and Spencer's theories of evolution and the positive and negative reactions they produced—also played a crucial role in the development of social theory
which is too easily overlooked today. Nonetheless, thinkers such as Marx,
Weber, Durkheim, and Simmel were nourished by the legacy of the
Enlightenment and its ideals of freedom, scientific understanding, and
social criticism. These theorists were particularly influenced by the German tradition of Kant and Hegel. But they turned their Enlightenment
foundations toward the new and unsettled conditions of industrial capitalism and its effects on social relations, work, families, individuals, cities,
and particularly on the meaning of modern life. Marx's phrase in *The Communist Manifesto*, "all that is solid melts into air," captures the revolutionary world that capitalism was beginning to bring about, a world in which
not only workers but monarchs too, had much to fear. And his manifesto
with Engels itself acted as an incendiary to the revolution of 1848 which
swept across the nations of Europe like a specter, a revolution Marx hoped
would cause the bourgeoisie to melt into air: "What the bourgeoisie, therefore, produces, above all, is its own grave diggers. Its fall and the victory
of the proletariat are equally inevitable."

The revolution of 1848 failed, but Marx still held out for an inevitable
fall of the bourgeoisie and victory of the proletariat. Although he developed a materialist view of history, in contrast to Hegel's philosophy that
history was the progression of *Geist*—spirit or mind—Marx retained
Hegel's faith in the dialectical advance of history. Marx achieved a concrete, critical theory of human history as rooted in the social practices of
production, yet he did not critically confront the Enlightenment ideal of
inevitable progress.

Max Weber held a more dour view of the modern ethos, a view that
linked the forms of belief and conduct produced by the Reformation with
the rise and dominance of capitalism and its marked rationalism. Capitalism and its brand of "instrumental" or "formal" rationality were not historically inevitable in Weber's form of cultural relativism—other types of
development were also possible. Yet once selected and embodied as the
modern Western ethos, the peculiar rationalism at work in the institutions

of science and technics, economy, and politics formed an "inevitable" internal logic. This system, built on the "mechanical foundations" of rational capitalism, was viewed pessimistically by Weber as producing a "steel-hard casing" of rational materialism, the "iron cage" of modernity, whose legacy would be soul-less specialists and heartless hedonists. And socialism provided no alternative in Weber's eyes, but only a variation on the theme of an ever-enlarging bureaucracy.

One sees the same disturbance and foreboding in Emile Durkheim, who interpreted suicide statistics as revealing patterns of normlessness and norm-breaking individualism. In his search to find the basis of religious and social belief, Durkheim said in his concluding remarks to his *Elementary Forms of the Religious Life* in 1912 that,

> we are going through a stage of transition and moral mediocrity. The great things of the past which filled our fathers with enthusiasm do not excite the same ardour in us, either because they have come into common usage to such an extent that we are unconscious of them, or else because they no longer answer to our actual aspirations; but as yet there is nothing to replace them. . . . In a word, the old gods are growing old or are already dead, and others are not yet born.[2]

Written on the eve of World War I and in the midst of revolutionary modernism, Durkheim's words were indeed prescient. Yet though he questioned the "moral mediocrity" of the modern "stage of transition," he never lost his Enlightenment faith that continuing progress would eventually forge new gods of belief from modern conditions. These gods would most likely arise from science, since Durkheim believed "scientific thought is only a more perfect form of religious thought," both being systems of knowledge. Perhaps the new gods could be formed from the science of sociology, as Durkheim's predecessor Comte, who had coined the term "sociology," had hoped that religion would be refounded on a secular basis: many of my sociological colleagues believe Durkheim himself to be one of these gods, along with Marx and Weber!

One finds then, in these three exemplary figures, theories that attempt to come to terms with industrial conditions through scientific investigation, to criticize or interpret modern life, to reveal its intended and unintended consequences. Yet despite the range and power of their theories, none of these theorists questions the inevitability of the existence of modernity itself.

Let us then consider Lewis Mumford in this context. Throughout his career, Mumford has criticized many aspects of modern culture for being forms of regression rather than truly modern or progressive. His inquiries in a variety of fields share a common concern with the ways that modernity as a whole, instead of providing broader possibilities for expression and development, actually tends toward a more restrictive view and diminution of purpose and scope. Mumford's researches share concerns common to the so-called "classic" sociological tradition. Yet, unlike Marx, Weber, Durkheim, Georg Simmel, or Talcott Parsons, Mumford does not regard the developments of modernity as inevitable, or, to a great extent, as progressive.

Central to Mumford's social theory is a transformed understanding of the concept of life: life considered as a bio-cosmic, transformative, emergent, and purposive process. Central to the development of academic social theory since the early decades of the twentieth-century has been its progressive self-alienation from an organic conception of life. It is Mumford's ascription of purpose to nature, of nature to culture, and of reality to mind, that places him against the grain of twentieth-century thought, and perhaps makes him the "blind spot" of our age of abstraction. It is also these ideas that provide a basis for a transformation of contemporary social theory.

"Classical" Social Theory, Modernity, and Mumford

In his masterwork *Capital,* Marx sets down in relentless detail the paradoxes of industrial capitalism, with its ideals of freedom of competition and individual liberty and its actualities of slave-like working conditions and suppression of competition and workers' rights. His compelling view of the rise of capitalism reveals the radically changed conditions of modern society: the development of mechanized manufacture; the rise of the bourgeois class which displaced traditional ties and personal worth with "the icy water of egotistical calculation"; the need of forcing people into the emergent work conditions of the factories, the diabolical contrast between an ideal of less work through machines and the harsh reality of brutal working conditions for industrialized workers and of loss of work for those displaced by machines. Marx saw clearly how technical innovations in the machines of industry were inseparable from the development of capitalism itself.

Capitalism was a systematic distortion of the practice of production, one which inverted the relationship of the means of work to the ends of work. Instead of "the good life" as the object and aim of work, capitalism made the goal of work to be "the life of goods"—the products of human creation were endowed with an independent life of their own in Marx's view, just as religion projected human experience and suffering on to a make-believe world. In capitalism, as in religion, humans surrendered authority and responsibility for their productions to a human projection which was treated as an alien reality. Hence in his discussion of the place of machines in capitalism Marx says, "In the first place, in the form of machinery, the implements of labour become automatic, things moving and working independent of the workman. They are thenceforth an industrial *perpetuum mobile,* that would go on producing forever, did it not meet with certain natural obstructions in the weak bodies and the strong wills of its human attendants. The automaton, as capital, and because it is capital, is endowed, in the person of the capitalist, with intelligence and will; it is therefore animated by the longing to reduce to a minimum the resistance offered by that repellent yet elastic natural barrier, man."[3]

Marx was a true pioneer in revealing the displacement of the human being by the purely quantitative being of the machine and money—the body and soul of modernity—even if he remained insufficiently critical of the machine in its socialized form. Still, he was a powerful critic of ethereal mind, whether in his critique of Hegel's conception of history or in his account of money's ascendancy in capitalism. Yet his attempt to counter etherealization through a concrete, materialist conception of history was itself a partial manifestation of the other tendency of modernity toward scientific materialism. Though Marx did not fall prey to the severe form of scientific materialism found in utilitarianism, which indeed was a central object of his critique, he nevertheless was not completely free from its influences. He could thoroughly reject the legacy of Descartes's *res cogitans*—ethereal mind—but he retained prejudices favoring *res extensa*— material embodiment per se—that left him insufficiently critical of the machine and insufficiently free from the false dichotomy between thought and things. This gap in Marx's thought, greatly exaggerated and amplified in the positivist form of Marxist-Leninism that assumed control of the Soviet Union, led ironically to a nation relatively inept in the machines of life, though less so in the machines of death, and thoroughly dominated by the bureaucracy of ethereal mind.

Mumford and Marx share an interest in man the self-producing animal, but differ on the question of what counts as production and the place of production in the relative scheme of things. Although acknowledging the profound, if sometimes contradictory, character of Marx's thought, Mumford criticizes him as overly utilitarian and as ignoring other dimensions of human existence that are either non- or extra-productive.

Self-creation becomes, in Mumford's vision, a broader category than self-production. Or one might say, in the language of Charles Peirce, that *abduction,* even more fundamentally than *production,* is essential to the human capacity for self-transformation: the capacity to generate emergent inferences and novel conditions. Abduction was originally introduced by Peirce as a form of logical inference distinct from induction and deduction, thoroughly logical though not limited to conscious rationality, and rooted in a human capacity to make better than chance guesses or hypotheses. In a broad context of human conduct, abduction means not simply to solve problems better, or to meet current needs in an efficient and equitable way, but to create wholly new premises for human existence. Abduction is the bodying forth and incarnation of new ideas in fruitful modes of conduct and is viewed by Peirce, and analogously by Mumford, as rooted in our biocosmic nature. Marx went further than most other social theorists toward a recognition of our socially purposeful nature. But his Enlightenment humanism also prevented him from going still further, as Peirce and Mumford did, toward a biocosmic perspective rooted in the ascription of generality and purpose to nature, and even further again to the ascription of non-practical imagination to nature in general and human nature in particular. We are dream creatures even more fundamentally than rational producers. Mumford and Peirce, in vastly different ways, both echo William Blake's idea that the Poetic Imagination dreamed us into existence.

These ideas are not limited to an overly "aestheticized" conception of society, but extend to the heart of Marx's thought as well: revolution. Revolution is conceived in Mumford and Peirce not only as the lightning-rod of human social change struck by the forces of history, but also as a trans-human fact of nature. In other words, Marx's category of revolution forms one aspect of Mumford's broader category of renewal or transformation.

The human creature is distinguished by critical activity in Marx. Mumford does not so much disagree with Marx as he goes further to show how critical activity is but a portion of extra-critical, extra-rational activity, which includes human social capacities for imagination, dream, ritual communication, and myth-making. One can infer from Mumford's writing that our critical capacities are much more immature than our pre-critical ones: we instinctively purpose myths, and deviate from the myth-making mind at our own peril. Perhaps our most extreme myth, even if wrong, is that we are rationally autonomous beings capable of creating rationally grounded societies. This anti-myth, the myth of modernity, reveals itself to be the myth of the megamachine, the tendency toward self-alienation.

Marx's ingrained scientism helped not only to temper and concretize his Hegelianism, but also caused him to succumb to the same *unvermeidlich* or inevitable view of historical progress that marked Hegel's dialectic. The laws of economic production that marked the stages of history inevitably led to the darkness of capitalism as they would lead inevitably toward goodness and light and socialized society. As Mumford put it, Marx's philosophy "rested on the conception of the continued expansion of the machine, a pushing forward of all those processes that had regimented and enslaved mankind, and yet out of this he expected not only a liberation from the existing dilemmas of society but a final cessation of the struggle. . . . Despite all Marx's rich historical knowledge, his theory ends in non-history: the proletariat, once it has thrown off its shackles, lives happily ever afterward. . . . Historic observation shows that there are many modes of change, other than dialectic opposition: maturation, mimesis, mutual aid are all as effective as the struggle between opposing classes."[4] Although Marx's theory was rooted in the ideas of praxis, process, and development, it projected a finality of communism which seemed to deny these ideas. Communist society was a sort of practical version of Hegel's Absolute, and shared with it the utopian aspect of a world beyond struggle, evil, and human shortcomings. Mumford not only disagrees with Marx's myth, but shows how its reliance on the so-called "inevitable" links it with the very reified power complex it sought to undo. Hence, although Mumford acknowledges Marx as a great social critic and historian, and resonates with many aspects of his critique of capitalism, the machine, and modern life, he departs from Marx's historical materialism and its faith in inevitable and revolutionary progress.

A quite different view of the inverted world of capitalism is given by Max Weber, who stressed the significance of the Protestant Ethic in the development of capitalism. The honest attempt to cleanse a corrupted Christianity was marked by Luther's call to the "calling" *(Beruf)*, the religious significance of one's vocation, which imbued work with a greater sense of the dignity of one's duty to God. Weber shows how Calvinism proceeded much further than Lutheranism in rationalizing work itself, of centralizing it in such a way that other dimensions of human existence, such as emotional life, artistic expression, free play, and idle curiosity were devalued and even repressed. All that could not rationally justify itself within the rationalized asceticism of this ethos became suspect or lost legitimacy. All that could rationally justify itself became paramount: unlimited acquisition, frugality, the quantification of space, time, and personal life, consequently—how should one call it—the disqualification of personal life (meaning both that the non-rational aesthetic qualities of everyday life were either quantified or rejected, and also that personal life was itself predetermined in the great clockwork of predestination).

The paradoxical consequence of this ascetic attempt to purify life was that rationality became ultimate and unlimited, in effect answerable only to itself, and yet based on irrational foundations. Once established, capitalism could dispense with religious motives of spiritual frugality and become transformed into the ethos of unholy hedonism. There arose also the mistaken idea of atomic individuals for whom living relation through community was a mere human artifice and convention, divorced from the nature of things. "Isolatoism" is the word Herman Melville coined to describe this new image of man.

Weber assumed throughout his varied researches a radical and unprecedented uniqueness in modern Western civilization, and here emerges one of the major differences between Weber and Mumford. Where Weber sees the "rationalization" of the West as progressive, if problematic, Mumford interprets the same processes to represent a fatally flawed world view leading ultimately to de-rationalization. What Weber describes as the spirit of capitalism is set by Mumford within a broader concept of the megamachine. Mumford views modernity, with Weber, as an idiosyncratic development, but unlike Weber, he does not see it as unprecedented.

In his earlier works, such as *Technics and Civilization* (1934) and *The Culture of Cities* (1938), Mumford proposed that the roots of modern life are to be found in destabilizing and deurbanizing processes emerging out of late medieval civilization. Although acknowledging the genuine achievements of the modern era, he criticized its inherent destructive potentials, rooted in the rise of centralizing, quantifying, machine-like tendencies in capitalism, baroque political power, the city, and science and technics. In *The Myth of the Machine*, he greatly broadens this critique of modernity, by hypothesizing the megamachine as not solely a product of the modern West, but as rooted in unresolved antagonisms in the emergence of civilization in general.

The modern epoch represents the rebuilding of the ancient megamachine, which was first erected with the advent of civilization. In the earliest river civilizations of Mesopotamia, Egypt, India, and China, there arose new configurations of human relations involving the centralization of power: large-scale military and bureaucratic organizations centered in cities and subject to kings regarded as divine, as in Egypt, or rulers surrounded with the aura of divine power. The transition from village-centered cultures to city-centered civilizations is marked by the gradual emergence of power-minded, mechanically regimented institutions, symbolized, especially in Egypt and Mesopotamia, by the displacement of earthly deities by more rational celestial ones, and personified by the king, who impersonated earthly power and cosmic order. The regimentation of the mass of men by a select elite, who lived in a grandiose style through appropriating the labor of the whole community, signifies the first megamachine in Mumford's perspective, a megamachine whose parts were almost entirely human. In describing the power complexes of early civilization as a megamachine, Mumford uses the term "machine" literally, following the classic formulation of Franz Reuleaux. If a machine be defined, as Mumford says, "as a combination of resistant parts, each specialized in function, operating under human control, to utilize energy and to perform work, then the great labor machine was in every aspect a genuine machine: all the more because its components, though made of human bone, nerve, and muscle, were reduced to their bare mechanical elements and rigidly standardized for the performance of their limited tasks. The taskmaster's lash ensured conformity. Such machines had already been assembled if not invented by kings in the early part of the Pyramid Age, from the end of the fourth Millennium on."[5] (See also Miller essay, this volume.)

Where the original megamachine used mostly human parts, seeking to mold the human to the mechanical, the modern one devoted itself to its own mechanization, progressively replacing human parts with mechanical ones. The cult of the king and the myth of the machine re-emerged in the modern West transformed as the ghost in the mechanical machine: the true spirit of capitalism.

The rise of the mechanical world picture may have helped free the rational mind from irrational constraints, making possible great advances in science and technics, but it falsely conceived an unbridgeable gulf between first causes and final causes, between an objective world mechanism and a subjective, spectral world of values.

Weber assumed this split of "the ghost in the machine," the inherited legacy of Descartes and Kant, as a progressive development, and it pervaded his own thinking on political life and the social sciences. Mumford considers the mechanical world picture as a historical reality, but not as historically necessary for the rise of modern science. In its false materializing of the object and etherealizing of the subject, the mechanical world picture represents a progressive abdication of human autonomy to the automaton. It must ignore generative, incarnating mind in favor of either objective mechanism or subjective, incorporeal spirit. This view leads to either a positivist or a conceptualist theory of science, thereby ignoring the place of living abduction, to return to Peirce's idea, implicitly shared by Mumford.

Although Mumford agrees with Weber's linking of the Calvinist ethic with the machine-like spirit of capitalism, he criticizes Weber's thesis that Protestantism was responsible for the conception and development of the capitalist spirit. From Mumford's perspective, Weber undervalued the prime part played by medieval Catholic culture: "In view of the patent facts of history, this belief is as strange as it is indefensible: for it assumes that modern capitalism did not take form until the sixteenth century; whereas it existed as a mutation at least three centuries earlier and by the fourteenth century it pervaded Italy: a country where Protestantism has never been able to gain a hold. Capitalism was, in fact, the great heresy of the Middle Ages . . . the heresy had been nourished in the very bosom of the church, and almost from the first had the protection of the Papacy. It was not Calvin in the sixteenth century, but Vincent of Beauvais in the thirteenth who first admonished people to work, not just for a living, but for the sake of accumulation, which would lead to the further production of wealth."[6] In other words, Mumford charges Weber with historical shallowness, in not seeing that capitalism grew out of medieval Catholic culture, and not only in opposition to it.

Against Weber's interpretation of the "elective affinities" of ascetic Protestantism with capitalism stands Mumford's discussions of the elective affinities of the Benedictine monastery with the spirit of capitalism and the megamachine. Mumford shows how those distinguishing features of regularity, renunciation of personal autonomy, scrutiny of one's and others' conduct, and especially the performance of daily work as a Christian duty led to a highly rationalized existence. Devotional order proved applicable to generalized economic order: regularized time, record-keeping, exact measurement, and the increasing invention of and reliance on mechanical devices not only helped the soul to prosper, but caused greater economic success. The vow of poverty or, rather, the economic value of a methodically ordered life, produced a great wealth in the Benedictine monasteries, so that, "By the twelfth century the efficient rationalization that had been achieved in the monastery was ready to be transferred to secular occupations. For the Benedictines had proved what the English evangelist, John Wesley, was to point out many centuries later: that Christian thrift, sobriety, and regularity would inevitably lead to worldly success. Most of the habits that Max Weber erroneously treated as the special property of sixteenth-century Calvinist Protestantism were in effective operation in the medieval Cistercian monastery.[7]

In many ways Weber is regarded as the "ideal type" of sociologist by academic sociologists, and in many ways Mumford is Weber's complete antithesis. Weber believed, for example, that professional training of a scholar should be specialistic and should avoid consciously inculcating values; Mumford scorns not only this "value-free" specialism, but the toady professionalism it spawned in universities as well. Weber preserved the rigid neo-Kantian divide between facts and values, claiming that values are relative in their foundations, subjectively chosen, and that one's own values must never interfere with analysis. Mumford denies the split between facts and values, and rejects the idea that values are purely subjective and relative. Values are rooted in their relation to life and social milieu, and objectively tempered through experience. Furthermore, Mumford viewed the "disinterested" model of scholarship and research as an abdication of the responsibility of a scholar or scientist. This is particularly clear in his response to the development of nuclear weapons in which "scientific objectivity" was both a smokescreen for disinterest in the uses and social consequences of the weapons produced and an alibi for continued research funding. Objectivity remains for Mumford a public responsibility, not a means to privatize knowledge through secrecy or specialization.

Weber claims that action has to do with subjectively intended meaning; Mumford views action as fundamentally social and derivatively "subjectively intended." Although Mumford champions the subjective element of human conduct, he does not begin with isolate subjects subjectively "intending" meaning, nor does he see human action exhausted by intentions.

One of the consequences of Weber's neo-Kantian intentionalist perspective is a view of meaning as a human faculty conferred on the chaos of experience. As Weber said: "'Culture' is a finite segment of the meaningless infinity of the world process, a segment on which *human beings* confer meaning and significance."[8] Though Weber saw more deeply into the ever-darkening consequences of modern rationalization than many of his more optimistic contemporaries, he could not see the possibility that the very process of rationalization was itself responsible for conferring meaninglessness on the world process, thereby reducing it to a sensory manifold. That is, he could not see that the Kantian perspective might itself be a product of a faulty and by no means inevitable development of rationalization. That Enlightenment view of the logic of modernity jettisoned those extra-rational, yet reasonable, tempered sources of human intelligence, such as sentiment and imagination, from the institution of scientific understanding. Though Weber is frequently viewed as a "humanistic" sociologist because of his emphasis on an interpretive, *verstehende Soziologie,* his deeply rooted belief in the Kantian world view that so dominated German thought caused him to accept a reified conception of objectivity and science, and a relativist conception of values.

Weber's logic is framed within what I have termed "cultural nominalism."[9] It is a view that says that life's highest purpose is not objectively reasonable. The logic of rationality is to tend increasingly toward an "instrumental rationality" in which purpose is oriented by subjective interest. In moving toward the "instrumental," rationality becomes increasingly not an instrument but a calculating machine, and one in which the user of the "instrument" becomes instrument to the machine's "purpose": single-standard homogeneous system.

Is this the purport of cultural action, biological development, cosmic evolution: to become divested of human qualities in order to assume the requirements of a machine? Or is it rather the outcome of a fundamentally distorted perspective convincingly disproven by anyone with eyes to see by the events of the twentieth century?

Twentieth-century civilization is marked, in my view, by extremism, by tendencies motivated by the very dichotomies of cultural nominalism to achieve pure finality or pure primordiality, pure rationality or pure irrationality (defined as biology, originality, novelty, or charisma), pure objectivity or pure subjectivity. Even those movements of thought that did not claim one side of the dichotomy or the other as the truth tended to define the world as if these aspects of experience were truly dichotomous; as one sees, for example, in the radical splitting of facts and values, in Freud's psychology, in relativism, or, to return to mainstream social theory, in Durkheim.

If Marx's place in the "holy trinity" of canonical social theory is that of "conflict sociologist" of social structure and class and Max Weber's is that of "voluntarist sociologist" of social organization and bureaucratic authority, then Emile Durkheim functions as a "macro" sociologist concerned with how symbolic structures "maintain" the patterns of society and culture, to use the terminology of Talcott Parsons. Of course, each of these theorists was broader than these categories in which they have now been stereotyped by the academy.

Durkheim is probably most noted for his last major work, *The Elementary Forms of the Religious Life*, which was an attempt to find the fundamental structures of society through examination of ethnographies of primitive peoples. Since Durkheim's time the word "primitive" has come to be criticized and qualified—all of the most "primitive" peoples known actually exhibit complex social organization and rich emotional and imaginative lives—but Durkheim believed that the Australian aborigines represented the world's most primitive people.

By turning to Australian aborigines, Durkheim could see social structure in its most pristine primitive state, freed from the "luxuriant growth and accretions" of more developed peoples. He goes on to show how "collective representations," such as "churinga" or symbolic rocks, pieces of wood, and other totemic and ritual objects, function to focalize the "collective conscience" of a people and thereby are the underlying conceptual basis for religion and society. Religion and collective representations are, in effect, the mirror that society holds up to itself. Durkheim claimed that this shows that the basic faculties of knowing are social, as against Kant's individualistic faculty theory of knowledge. He sought to socialize Kant, but nevertheless retained underlying Kantian dichotomies, such as individual versus social or knowledge versus experience. Durkheim was broader than more recent French structuralists in including emotions within collective representations, yet his theory still remains conceptualistic and rationalistic in holding emotions as carriers of social conceptions instead of viewing social conceptions as the surface film of deeper societal, extrarational emotions. In Durkheim's conceptualist theory, collective representations, religious beliefs, and society form a system of knowledge rather than ways of living, just as rituals are but variable and secondary content to an underlying logic rather than enactments of life. Durkheim's theory of collective representations, religious belief, and social structure is virtually ahistorical: the same underlying structure holds, despite a diversity of collective representations, and manifests as either the "mechanical solidarity" of traditional societies in which each member can do the same tasks as others, or in the "organic solidarity" of modern society and economy, in which individuals become progressively and seemingly inevitably differentiated.

It beomes interesting then to contrast Mumford's chapter of *Technics and Human Development* titled with the Australian aboriginal idea, "In the Dreamtime Long Ago." Like Durkheim, Mumford believes the aborigines are "almost as close as we can get in the flesh to early man." Mumford also uses aborigines to reveal underlying connections between them and us, but does not deny that real historical development and transformations have taken place, not reducible to underlying "elementary forms." He also denies the inevitability of progressive differentiation, and uses the terms "organic" and "mechanical" in roughly the opposite sense of Durkheim. Mumford means by "organic" the contextualized relations of parts to whole, which are in many ways more characteristic of traditional peoples and polytechnic civilization. "Mechanical" is the substitution of qualitative uniqueness and multivocal expression by centralization, homogeneity, standardization, and decontextualized differentiation. The worker who turns a screw all day long is not a specialized "organ" in Durkheim's sense, since he or she has been divested of those qualities of purposive spontaneity and growth associated with organic growth. The worker has instead been rendered "mechanical," because deprived of intrinsic connection to the organic context or purposive "whole" of the activity, not to mention the capacity to limit the action or inaugurate other actions. If one knew nothing of organic life and could observe this worker it might be difficult to know which was the screwer and which the screwed.

Mumford implicitly rejects Durkheim's conceptualism when he takes seriously the aboriginal concept of "Alcheringa" or "the dreamtime of long ago." Mumford charges the scientific community with ignoring or underrating valuable evidence, because of the intangible, imaginary nature of dreams. One might say to the human evolutionist, paralleling Mumford's argument, that since "rapid eye movement" or REM sleep is shared by almost all mammals, dreaming is a trans-human phenomenon shared by pre-human life forms, and not solely a human trait. In that case, dreaming would be likely to serve some evolutionary function. Whether a general mammalian development or specific human achievement, perhaps related to the development of human social organization and language, it would be a phenomenon worthy of attention. Yet because of its "inner" and intangible nature it is apparently not counted as significant behavior by evolutionary and social scientists.

In other words, although it is legitimate to discuss world views of the most fantastic natures, the imaging process itself, or what might be termed the autonomic "recombinant mimetics" of the human psyche, is overlooked as a formative influence on human development. Durkheim himself raises interesting questions about dreams in his *Elementary Forms,* but because he was committed to a conceptualist theory of representation he could not allow that dreams might form an intrinsic language of images: that dreams might "stand for" themselves, as sign presentations or icons, as well as "standing for" personal or collective experiences as representations or symbols.

Dreams not only passively symbolize experience but actively create inner experience. Jung, more than Freud, recognized this creative aspect of dreams, but like Freud, succumbed to the one-sided "inwardness" tendency of German thought, and undervalued the "outwardness" and "otherness" that are also irreducible aspects of human experience and human dreaming.

If we consider dreams as "recombinant mimetics," in which time, space, emotions, personalities, familiarities and the exotic, desires and anxieties, assume fantastic juxtapositions through the language of images, it becomes possible to see how dreaming may be as or more potent—and dangerous—than recombinant genetics. If dreaming made possible for pre-speaking proto-humans an expanded sense of time and social relations not limited to immediate experience, as Mumford argues, it may have laid the groundwork for symbolic consciousness. The anxieties produced by dreams and their fantastic and sublime logic could have impelled and even compelled emergent humanity toward interpretation, the simultaneous freedom from instinctive and habituated experience and violent tearing away from the profound envelope of mature truth that instinct provides. Man's inner world, as Mumford says,

> . . . must often have been far more threatening and far less comprehensible than his outer world, as indeed it still is; and his first task was not to shape tools for controlling the environment, but to shape instruments even more powerful and compelling in order to control himself, above all, his unconscious. The invention and perfection of these instruments—rituals, symbols, words, images, standard modes of behavior (mores)—was, I hope to establish,

the principal occupation of early man, more necessary to survival than tool-making, and far more essential to his later development.[10]

Although humanity has become increasingly conscious of itself, it has never stopped dreaming. Nor have its dreams become any less wondrous and terrifying. And as Mumford shows in his discussions of the rise of the megamachine and especially its rebuilding in modernity, there are waking dreams or myths which guide whole epochs, much as our rituals of conscious rationality would deny them. Could it be that the Enlightenment was simply afraid of the dark?

Mumford in Contemporary Context

Lewis Mumford has clearly made a major mark on twentieth-century scholarship. Any one of his original contributions to literary criticism, architectural criticism, American studies, technics, urban history and regional planning, and a number of other areas would in itself be significant. Some have questioned, however, whether Mumford is truly original or merely derivative: a synthesizer of others' ideas. In my view there is no question that Mumford is one of the most original voices of the twentieth-century. It is precisely his great openness to the thought and influence of others that is inseparable from his originality and that contributes to his broadened outlook.

Our time celebrates originality as the unique and absolutely unprecedented, the idiosyncratic. Yet one of the peculiar marks of originality is not so much the radical departure from one's own time, as how original ideas seem so frequently to be expressed by multiple persons at the same time, perhaps as the expression of a *Zeitgeist*. Originality is, in this sense, not antithetical to the social, but the empathic sensing of the social milieu and the generation of new ideas out of it, ideas fitted to yet transcending their time. Mumford's work of the twenties, for example, was part of a rediscovery of literary transcendentalism, which included others such as Waldo Frank, Van Wyck Brooks, Paul Rosenfeld, and D. H. Lawrence. Yet Mumford also contributed to this movement his unique perspective on American culture. Or perhaps one could take the spate of books published on the city around 1961, including Kevin Lynch's *Image of the City,* Gideon Sjoberg's *The Preindustrial City,* Anselm Strauss's *Images of the American City,* Jane Jacobs's *The Death and Life of Great American Cities,* and of course Mumford's majestic *The City in History.* Mumford may have been part of a collective trend of works on the city but, in its historical scope and reconstructive realism, his own work clearly transcends these other efforts.

Another example, one more to the point, is the explosion of interest in symbolism in the 1960s, expressed primarily in anthropology. Key works by Claude Lévi-Strauss, Victor Turner, Clifford Geertz, and others appeared at this time, which radically transformed the face not only of cultural anthropology but of the social sciences generally. Structuralism, semiotics, symbolic anthropology, symbolic interactionism, interpretative or *verstehende* sociology, were some of the major movements that sprang forth from the barren ground of mid-twentieth-century social science and have continued to exert growing interest. Many of these developments had roots going back to the "classical" figures of the turn of the century, but the earlier traditions had been displaced by the combination of Nazism in Europe and ideological scientism in America. The whole question of meaning itself, which had seemed to be in eclipse in the "dead zone" of the middle decades of the twentieth-century, now sprang back with a vengeance. Yet something had happened in the interim, for the dominant feature of the new symbolism in the social sciences and semiotics was and remains a tendency to technicalism, a domination by the techniques and technical jargon of theory-making and symbol interpretation, such as the "infernal culture machine" of Lévi-Strauss's binary structuralism, or, more recently, the anarchistic semiological "fission" advocated by Jacques Derrida's poststructuralism. The question of meaning has become all the rage, but the question of meaningfulness has become all but lost.

Structuralism, descended from Durkheim and linguist Ferdinand de Saussure, and most closely associated with Lévi-Strauss, became a central preoccupation of anthropologists, literary critics, and social theorists in the 1960s and 1970s. It provided a theory of meaning that enabled one to view the hidden sources or codes which structure meaning in everyday life. Structuralism claimed that myths, language, and cultural practices are the mere surface manifestations of "deep structures," codes or conventions. Individual manifestations of speech or conduct are trivial in the structuralist view, only the underlying code, rooted in the notion of the arbitrariness of the sign, is significant. Although it struck the intellectual community as liberating, structuralism was actually a form of intellectual totalitarianism—a "one size fits all" approach to meaning which allowed no deviation from the binary logic of the deep structure. It was too inflexible to do justice to time and place in human affairs, to lived, extralogical experience, to the qualitatively unique, in short, to those features of human experience which are not reducible to the grid of cultural nominalism in its manifestation as French rationalism.

The "logic" of structuralism is that of a binary computer; it cannot encompass the living, inferential metaboly of human thought. For this reason it can be viewed as one of the key manifestations of the megamachine in the twentieth-century, enacting its assigned role to devalue lived, human experience by etherealizing reason as immaterial structure. With structuralism as the dominant theory of meaning in the 1960s, it is no wonder that Mumford's *Technics and Human Development* remained virtually invisible to the anthropological community.

Of the various approaches to meaning developed in the new anthropology of the 1960s, Victor Turner's work stands out as perhaps the closest in spirit to Mumford. Turner's ethnographies of the Ndembu people of south-central Africa are among the richest in all of anthropology, and are distinguished by his ever-present concern with the "incandescent" human shape of meaning. Turner was led through his observation of the Ndembu to an appreciation of the centrality of ritual life and symbols, and attempted to formulate his own theory, drawing from Durkheim, Freud, and Arnold van Gennep. Turner developed a processual approach to meaning, in contrast to the dominant structuralism, and in his work one sees clearly that meaning is no "prepackaged" structure. A specific conflict in a village requiring a ritual resolution may have varied outcomes; a girl being initiated into the matrilineage of women is celebrated in her individuality while simultaneously "grafted" on to the great symbolic *mudyi* milk tree structure. The dramatic enactment of meaning is connected to its bodily sources in Turner's discussions of red, black, and white color symbolism and the related context of blood, excrement, and milk and sperm in ritual life.

In his late work in the 1980s Turner sought to enlarge his "anthropology of experience" by connecting culture with biology through the brain and body. Many cultural anthropologists have dismissed this work as misguided, simply because Turner had broken the taboo against mixing culture and nature. In their embarrassment, I claim, one sees the effete rational intellect, unwilling to confront critically its own extrarational context. Turner's work bears many resonances with Mumford's anthropology, but the intellectual landscape today is dominated by rationalists, such as poststructuralists, who merely vary the totalitarian semiological theory of meaning by moving to its other half: the margins of structure, the fragmentary and chaotic, the "fission" of signs. The anti-rational rationalists claim to have broken with structuralism, but the views of a Derrida or others that society is a "text," preserve the fundamental goal of the etherealization of meaning.

Enter Lewis Mumford with his two-volume *Myth of the Machine*. The first volume, *Technics and Human Development* (1967), published in the midst of the new anthropology, should be seen as a contributing volume to symbolic anthropology and the semiotic turn of the social sciences.

Mumford's *Technics and Human Development* rejects *Homo faber*, man the tool-user, as an adequate standard for understanding the evolution of human beings. This view has dominated physical anthropology, leading, in Mumford's opinion, to an overvaluation of hard physical evidence—bones and stones—and an undervaluation of soft and impermanent physical artifacts, such as wood objects, clothing, hunting nets and baskets, and artistic expressions; and further, to a total ignoring of non-tangible factors such as dreams, ritual, and speech. *Homo faber,* the term popularized by Henri Bergson, is an artifact or by-product of the modern utilitarian age, the machine age which came to view human development as metallically passing from rocks to copper to bronze to iron, and finally to Weber's "steel casing" or "iron cage" of the twentieth century. This externalist view of technics is repeatedly rejected by Mumford as an insufficient explanation

of human genesis and human technics. In its place is *Homo symbolicus,* man
the signifying and self-creating symbol, whose own body forms an infinitely
more sophisticated instrument for the development of technics than hard
functional tools.

The body has recently emerged as a major theme in intellectual life, but
it is for the most part a conceptualized and etherealized body modeled on
the text: the gospel of postmodernism seems to proclaim that "the flesh
was made word, and dwells among us!" In other words, it is not so much
"body language," that is now fashionable, as the body as language. The
rhetoric of the body, the conventionalization of the body, and the symbolism of gender differences can all be significant topics. But when one
notes how little is said about the organic, biological body in these discussions, one begins to suspect that the academic megamachine is continuing
its work of rational etherealization. Such is perhaps more clearly the case
in Paul Ricoeur and Jacques Derrida's calls to view human action and
social life as texts, or in Jürgen Habermas's theory of communicative
action, which says much about rational talkers talking, but very little about
actors acting: felt, perceptive, imaginative, bodily experience does not fit
these theories.

Or consider the systems theorist Niklas Luhmann, who introduced the
idea of *"autopoeisis"* to account for self-generating systems. Here we see
another contemporary avatar of the megamachine. The abstract, lifeless
"systems" theory, because it excludes the living humans who comprise the
social "system" as significant, ignores those natural capacities of life for
self-making and self-generation. Therefore Luhmann can be seen as part
of the age-old dream to give life to the machine, in this case, the machine-
like system.

From this point of view, structuralism, poststructuralism, textualism,
and "communicative rationality" can all be seen as aiding the etherealizing
of the human body in the late twentieth-century. Hence the current interest in the body may have the further undoing of the body as its unacknowledged goal: whether disembodied as conceptualism or reified as mechanistic system, we are still left with the ghost in the machine. Or we can take
Luhmann's concept of *autopoeisis,* like the robot, android, or other automaton fetishes of contemporary popular culture and movies, many of which
involve a transformation of humans into automatons, as signifying the final
capitulation of autonomous life to the golem of modernity.

It is against this stark background that Mumford's organic, purposive,
bio-semiotic body stands, a human body created out of the rich interplay
of ritual action and symbolic communication with biology:

> By means of ritual, I suggest, early man first confronted and overcame his
> own strangeness, identified himself with cosmic events outside the animal
> pale, and allayed the uneasiness created by his huge but still largely unusable
> cerebral capacities. At a much later stage these inchoate impulses would come
> together under the rubric of religion. Actions still "speak louder than words,"

and the movements and gestures of ritual were the earliest foreshadowings of human speech. What could not yet be said in words or shaped in clay or stone, early man first danced or mimed; if he flapped his arms he was a bird: if the group formed a circle and revolved in measured steps they might be the moon. In short, what André Varagnac happily identified as the "technology of the body," expressed in dance and mimetic movements, was both the earliest form of any kind of technical order and the earliest manifestation of expressive and communicable meaning.[11]

By centering on the human body, Mumford develops a much broader semiotic than those conceptualist theories that now form the "leading edge" of social theory, and a much deeper theory of culture—one that roots purposive meaning in biology. His organic world picture also allows him to champion the technics of the body as both the means for our own transformation into humans and the first truly human achievement.

The concern with the conditions of continuing humane social life in the face of the nuclear war golem and the modern cult of anti-life becomes central to Mumford's writings after War War II, and differentiates him from earlier theorists. In my opinion the emergence of the nuclear age posed new and unavoidable problems for social theory which earlier theorists could not foresee and which most theorists have continued to avoid: the preservation, not only of Western civilization, but of human life itself. It is intriguing then, especially given recent discussions of the decline of public intellectuals in America, to consider three unusually sensitive intellectuals who have not avoided this problem. All three came to maturity before the Second World War. They are not usually associated with the academy or with the publicized New York intellectuals of the *Partisan Review,* although all three at times in their careers lived within reach of New York City. These three chose to devote their late work in the 1960s and 1970s to developing "philosophical anthropologies" of the biological and interpretative capacities and limits of the human creature: Mumford, Arthur Koestler, and Suzanne Langer. Mumford's *The Myth of the Machine,* Koestler's *The Ghost in the Machine* and *Janus,* and Langer's three-volume *Mind: An Essay on Human Feeling* mark not only breaks with contemporary ethereal conceptions of human conduct and meaning, and with the machine-like reductionism of Darwinian biology, but also provide an outline for the transformation of social theory. In my opinion these three have engaged the basic questions of the life-threatening nuclear age—even if their answers are not always satisfying.[12]

The Next Phase: Bringing Social Theory Back to Life

The most persistent theme in Mumford's work is the concept of life. Between 1934 and 1951 he published his massive four-volume, twenty-year studies of technics, the city, Western civilization, and human conduct.

By naming this series "the renewal of life," he draws attention to the life-concept as the pivot of all human studies. Mumford enlarged the scope of these studies in his late works, which involved a broadening of his understanding of the life-concept as well, one that required a philosophical anthropology that could do full justice to humankind's bio-symbolic nature.

And it is precisely Mumford's rooting of his ideas in an organic conception of life that sets him apart from the dominant drift of twentieth-century thought. One cannot overestimate how central the life-concept was in the late nineteenth and early twentieth century, exemplified across a range of otherwise diverse thinkers including Herbert Spencer, Friedrich Nietzsche, Wilhelm Dilthey, Henri Bergson, William James, Patrick Geddes, Georg Simmel, John Dewey, and Max Scheler.[13] The concept of the "organic"—organic life, organic architecture, organic art nouveau—seemed to blossom in this time, even as the "cult of anti-life," the mechanical-rational forces of the megamachine, was shifting into high gear. Given the now canonical status of a few key theorists, the centrality of life-philosophies at the turn of the century is too easily overlooked. There is, in addition, an intense anti-naturalism in contemporary intellectual life, so that despite a revival of interest in Nietzsche and Dewey, it is their philosophies of deconstruction and reconstruction which have been stressed, not their concerns with life.

One must point out that the life-concept, as it developed up to about 1930, was often limited as referring to human social life rather than biological life, as in Dilthey; or as signifying a conception of *Homo faber,* as in Bergson; or as in some way bound up in the "fissure" mentality that especially marks German thought, such as the split between life and form in Simmel's philosophy of life or between life and spirit in Scheler's philosophical anthropology. One sees a broader conception in the theory of emergent evolution developed by C. Lloyd Morgan and Samuel Alexander, in Peter Kropotkin's concept of "mutual aid" as a factor in evolution, or in the socialized biology of the pragmatists. Mumford draws from these sources, and takes them yet further toward a trans-historical bio-semiotic social theory.

At the time Mumford outlined his renewal of life series in 1930, the concept of life was on the verge of being perverted by Nazism in Germany, and of being reduced in America to social Darwinism (an active force throughout the previous period) or supplanted by environmental or more sophisticated sociological explanations of human behavior. The one great exception, perhaps, was Dewey, who retained and further refined his organic situationalism. But Dewey and pragmatism as a whole went into eclipse, and when pragmatism partially re-emerged in the figure of George Herbert Mead and the discipline of sociology, it had been divested of its bio-social basis in favor of a one-sided "symbolic interactionism." Even now, despite a widespread renewal of interest in pragmatism, the socialized biology developed by the four major pragmatists remains a dormant secret.

These transitions represent an appropriation of the life-concept by the megamachine away from organic contextuality and dynamic process to those more mechanical ideas of force, will and like-minded submission to authority in the German context, and, in the American context, to capitalistic struggle and maximization in the Chicago school of sociology, and to machine-rooted "systems" theory in the later dominant structural-functionalist school of Talcott Parsons. The net result was either to repress the life-concept, pervert it to ideological dogma, or tranform it to the principles of the inorganic machine.[14]

The life-concept faded in significance in the 1930s as the twentieth century moved into the "dead zone" of rational-mechanical abstraction, which came to dominate all spheres of cultural life. Mumford's growing conception of life needs to be seen against this background. Today one can hardly express an interest in the life-concept without being called a reductionistic sociobiologist, because the leading theories of meaning have come to be radically anti-naturalistic. It is no exaggeration to say that the dominant contemporary theories of meaning have arrived at a view of post-biological man. And in our "post-rational," "post-modern," "post-" culture, post-biological is taken to be a positive achievement, instead of the extreme form of self-alienation that it really is. For these reasons Mumford's life-rooted social theory might be seen as obsolete by those leading theorists who have proudly severed connections between their theories and biological life. But for the same reasons Mumford's social theory forms a profound critique of contemporary theory, and it could very well help bring social theory back to life.

In the first volume of the new journal of reviews of the American Sociological Association, Lewis Coser reviewed *The Pentagon of Power*.[15] His review illustrates the typical inability of the sociological academy to deal with thought that upsets established canon. Instead of seriously confronting Mumford's reconstructive critique of modernity, Coser caricatures him as a prophet of gloom who "hates almost all modern ideas and modern accomplishments without discrimination." Mumford's indictment of the consequences of the "myth of the megamachine" in modernity is indeed broad in scope, but by no means indiscriminate: he is ever the advocate of the broader possibilities inherent, if infrequently realized, in modern life. But his broadened framework calls for a renewal, a fundamental questioning of the entrenched patterns of thought and conduct peculiar to the modern era in particular and to civilization in general. Mumford questions those patterns of thought and conduct that tend to diminish rather than enhance human capacities and possibilities, and that have, to an extent no department of the academy is willing to admit, led to destructive, life-denying, self-annulling consequences. Whether in its reified or etherealized manifestations, the megamachine of modernity tends to treat the human part as the whole human, as though either critical rational intelligence or brute force alone were independently sufficient to direct social life.

The idea that critical rational intelligence as a moving dynamic of social life can by itself bring about the conditions for a free and vital social life is simply insufficient, as is the alternative idea that the blind power and will of *Realpolitik* can by force create the good life. Perhaps the ultimate meaning of modernity has been to develop critical, rational capacities while simultaneously showing how self-destructive and world-destructive they can be when uprooted from the deeper sources of tempered bodily and imaginative intelligence.

When Hegel said, "What is rational is actual and what is actual is rational," he overstated his case. The rational may be actual, but the actual is extra-rational. The great attempt by modernity to equate the rational with the actual in the name of freedom has failed, as those "psychic seismographs" of the twentieth-century, Henry Adams or Mumford, long ago sensed, and as anyone not benumbed by the megamachine or beguiled by its avatars can now see. The Holocaust and the German State which produced it were actual: should we call them rational? The confusion of the actual with the rational has produced massive unfreedom in the world: whether in the guise of the grim face of totalitarianism, left or right, or the great guffaw of Americanism, the cardinal rule seems to be to deny reality in the name of some rational ideology.

Henry Adams and Louis Sullivan saw in the Columbian Exhibition of 1893 the ominous signs of the twentieth century, clothed in electric dynamos and Greek temples. Throughout his work, Lewis Mumford has read these signs, manifest as architecture, cities, technics, personalities, and the very fabric of twentieth-century life. And if we attempt to fathom the present and sense, however darkly, its possible purport, omens abound. Our cities and intellectual life are rife with postmodernism, a movement that claims to break out of modern architecture and its dominant rational box by lopping off the corners or pasting on ornament, or to break out of "logocentrism" in intellectual life by a kind of freewheeling irrationalism or "anti-" or "post-humanism." Aside from the problem that so-called postmodernism simply inverts or varies the premises of modernism rather than creating genuinely new ones, it is also instructive to place the positive valuation of "post-" in postmodernism next to the negative valuation of "post-" in Mumford's discussions of Roderick Seidenberg's term "posthistorical." Instead of transcending history, posthistorical man is deprived of it, whereas postmodern man and woman, whether neo-conservative or neo-anarchist, are deprived not only of living history but also of those positive impulses of modernity. In this perspective, postmodernism becomes the ultimate form of self-alienation, reduced to scavenging an unfelt past or ravaging an unfelt present.

Or let us turn to one of the great mythic rituals of our time, the Olympics. Every four years there opens up a ritual "sacred space" as mortals and the gods touch through the immortal Olympic Flame. The ceremony of the Olympic torch is actually modern, having begun with the 1936 Berlin Olympics and therefore conceivably tainted by the Nazi penchant for pseudo-ancient spectacle. Nevertheless, the lighting of the Olympic Flame with a torch taken from the site of the ancient Games and passed hand-to-hand over great distances has become a powerful symbol of human continuity and transcendence. Yet those of you who saw the opening of the 1984 Los Angeles Olympic Games know that no human hand touched the gods. Instead, an athlete ignited a machine of fire, in the form of the Olympic Rings, which raced upwards to a chimney tower beyond human reach. There the machine of fiery rings automatically brought the Olympic Torch to flame in a literal chain reaction. The sacred flame had already been pimped from coast to coast to anyone who would pay money to run with it, but the capitalization of the sacred was merely a prelude to the mechanization of the sacred: the great flaming metallic chain towered above the human form, the ceremonial performance of Beethoven's ode "To Joy" gave way to the great guffaw of American rock-and-roll entertainment; a Hollywood actor disguised as an American president presided over a thoroughly unspontaneous script of Yahooism. The date, the city, the President, the nation, the ritual symbolism all signify our time as the dynamos did for Henry Adams.

Given the ritual celebration of technical, disembodied automatism in the lighting of the Olympic Fire, is it any wonder that the misbegotten dreams of the *Challenger* space shuttle or Chernobyl should have exploded in our faces soon after? We, who have lost the ability to touch the gods of our fates and to accept the limits of our biological being, give birth to dreams of throwing a "star wars" military machine to the heavens and sacrificing to it human politics, with all its uncertainties. We commodify the human body, separate it from humane relations and its own organic mysteries, and reap AIDS. We race ever-faster in our "inevitable" progress toward ecological disaster. Post-historic man, post-biological genderless person, post-modernity: we are in reality perhaps the first post-humans. To my mind, the world is fast unraveling, and AIDS, Bhopal, Chernobyl, *Challenger* and its defective "O" rings, and the fiery rings of 1984, are but the "opening ceremonies" to the next phase of human self-sacrifice and megamechanical madness.

The canonical social theorists may have differed in their interpretations of modernity, but they did not question the inevitability of its development. These theorists still dominate contemporary discourse, despite the fact that our post-Hiroshima world and its fetishism of nuclear commodities have rendered obsolete the very concept of inevitability. The dominant voices in contemporary social theory have returned to the problem of meaning that so animated the earlier theorists, but in ways that betray domination by the very theoretical techniques that they attribute to society. If the older and now canonical social theory was insufficiently differentiated from the megamachine of modernity it sought to criticize, the newer "grand theory" has become the megamachine itself: contemptuous of organic nature because of overweening pride in a rationalistic conception of culture, ignorant of or indifferent to those qualities and capacities of the human creature and human communities which cannot be fitted into the rational system, and never seriously questioning the whole premisses on which modern civilization and modern social theory are built.

Community is not simply a talk-world, as it is for both Karl Popper and Jürgen Habermas, who have developed theories rooted in rational discourse; nor is it simply a "structurating" coordination of ethereal structures and Isolato "agencies," as it is for Umberto Eco, Pierre Bourdieu, and Anthony Giddens; nor again "subsystem integrations" within the BIG SYSTEM as it was for Parsons and perhaps is again for Niklas Luhmann, Jeffrey Alexander, Richard Münch, and other neo-Parsonians.[16] Community is living social relation incarnate and, as such, involves orders of intelligence and organs of meaning much deeper than all of these varieties of rationalism could allow. And it is precisely in those areas repressed or excluded from meaning by rationalism—in the living, organic, biocosmic tissue of semiosis—that both the organization of communities and members, as well as human transformative possibilities are to be found. The leading theories of our time remain shackled to the modern myth of "the ghost in the machine," to eighteenth- and nineteenth-century modes of thinking clothed in late twentieth-century fashions. Far from being able to confront the self-destroying calamities of our time, they form an intellectual opiate: social theory.

The question confronting contemporary social thought is not simply how to reconstruct "grand theory," as its practitioners seem to think, but rather: how can enchantment and critical reason ever again meet? In Lewis Mumford's two-volume interpretation of *The Myth of the Machine* and earlier works, and in his organic, biocosmic alternative, new foundations are laid which can begin to answer this question.

His work forms a "speculative grammar," to borrow an expression from Duns Scotus, for a new social philosophy and truly non-modern world picture. This new world picture, as I see it in Mumford and in a few others, such as Charles Peirce, rejects rationality's grandiose claim to be equated with actuality or reality. Instead of Hegel's maxim, it holds that the fantastic is involved in the real and that the real is fantastic, and that both are greater than the actual or rational. We live in a fantastic reality, whose purport we can but dimly perceive. Only those beliefs that can most fully capture and convey the wonder of things—of creation, of organic growth and decay, of the drama and tragedy of human existence, of its unending follies, its brutalizations of truth and decency, and of its deepest motivations to participate in and question the incarnate cosmos—only those beliefs are capable of truly motivating and animating a whole culture and civilization. Such beliefs cannot be solely rationally founded, for the rational alone is too meager and rootless to act as inspiration for enduring belief. Such beliefs cannot be arbitrary, for the same reasons. Such beliefs have to be organically rooted in life itself, with its capacity for transformation, growth, and renewal, and in a recontextualized rationality acting as limited organ of a greater reasonableness in all its fullness.

Lewis Mumford has created a body of work in which the human form stands in its wholeness, transilluminated. Although he draws from the guiding ideas of modern social theory, his work fundamentally challenges its premisses and, in so doing, shows the way to a transformation of social theory and the blueprint for a new human epoch.

The Myth of the Machine:
I. Technics and Human Development

DONALD L. MILLER

After completing his master work, *The City in History,* in 1961, Lewis Mumford vowed that he would write no more big books. They took too much out of him. He looked forward to a long period of solitude and reflection, to what he saw as "a harvest time." Instead of reseeding the ground, he would gather in and sort over the late crop on the land "long ago planted," completing a number of projects he had begun earlier in his life. He was then nearly sixty-six years old, and though he felt hale and healthy he began to fear that he was working against time and might leave unfinished the autobiography he thought would be his final book.[1]

While he was working on his autobiography at his home in Amenia, in upstate New York, another project began to claim his attention, a "short" book on technology and culture. The new book would be a revision and update of his pioneering study of the modern machine age, *Technics and Civilization,* the first full-scale study in the English language of the rise of the machine in the modern world and one of the first scholarly studies in any language to emphasize the interplay of technology and the surrounding culture. When he finished it in the mid-1930s, however, Mumford realized that he had side-stepped an immensely important question. He had described the modern age's overvaluation of technology, but he had not sought to locate the origins of this "myth of the machine," the widely held view that technological progress and the expansion of power in its various forms—military, financial, and political—were the chief goals of the human endeavor. This he would seek to do in the book that now began to fill his mind. (For further discussion of *Technics and Civilization,* see Zuckerman, this volume.)

Actually he had already addressed this question in the chapters in *The City in History* dealing with the appearance of the first power systems in the ancient cities of Egypt and Mesopotamia, and this new book, like so many of his previous ones, developed more by a restatement of his answers to an important question than as a reconsideration of his questions. In the first centuries of urban life he had discovered what he believed to be the driving assumptions and aims of all large-scale technology for the past five thousand years, arguing that some of the greatest, if not the most benign, advances in technology have been made by centralized organizations, like the great Egyptian cities of the Pyramid Age, that seek to expand power tremendously in order to achieve control over both human communities and the natural environment. This was his theory of the megamachine; and in an essay he published in 1963, "Authoritarian and Democratic Technics," he emphasized the fundamental antagonism between such big political-military systems and older and smaller systems, based mostly on human skill and animal energy, which were less powerful but more resourceful and resilient. The great megamachines of the United States and the Soviet Union were, in this view, monstrously magnified reincarnations of older, less sophisticated bureaucratic-military models. But where the center of authority in the old system was an actual person, the absolute ruler, in the modern megamachine the center of authority was the system itself. "Unlike Job's God, the new deities cannot be confronted, still less deified."[2]

These were the spinal ideas of the new book Mumford began to sketch out in his mind as he finished the second draft of his autobiography. He had his conclusions; he merely had to find a way of substantiating them.[3] But for this very reason he had a difficult time proceeding. The kind of book he initially had in mind, a swiftly written elaboration of older arguments, a "harvest-time" project, did not really challenge him. But almost as soon as he began concentrated research in the summer of 1963, reading through the multi-volume history of technology edited by Charles J. Singer, E. J. Holmyard, A. R. Hall, and Trevor I. Williams, and re-reading old Egyptian texts, new questions and themes began to fill his head. His amazingly imaginative mind started working in its familiar way, making fresh connections and seeing new combinations, and before he knew it he was off—committed to the kind of big book he had sworn he would never undertake again.[4]

He had a hundred new ideas, but the organizing theme of the book would be a theory he had only sketchily suggested in previous work: that the development of the mind and its greatest creations, language and ritual, were more important to human development than the introduction and utilization of the first primitive tools, that "minding," as he put it, was more important than "making." Man had fashioned himself, Mumford believed, before he fashioned his first sophisticated tools. In this daringly speculative re-reading of human origins, Mumford would try to shift the emphasis from physical survival to cultural and mental development. He had a strong personal reason for doing this, which he revealed in a letter to his old friend Benton MacKaye. If his theory is correct, he told MacKaye, then man still has sufficient resources to alter the direction of modern technology, and is not, as Jacques Ellul argues, a passive victim of technological society. We might call this hypothesis "the primacy of the mind," and to prove it Mumford had to reinterpret the entire history of human development. By the time he was finished with this book "the corpses of a lot of dead ideas will be strewn all over the stage," he predicted to Mac-Kaye, "as in the last scene of Hamlet," and a clearer picture of human-kind's origins will emerge.[5]

The book Mumford completed three years later, *The Myth of the Machine: I. Technics and Human Development,* arose from his sobered view of the age he had lived through. (Mumford in 1970 published a second volume, *The Myth of the Machine: II. The Pentagon of Power.*) It is a search for an answer to what he considered the central question of the century: why had tech-nological progress brought with it such catastrophic wreck and ruin? This is the same question Oswald Spengler had raised in his huge and somber work, *The Decline of the West,* a title that exactly describes Mumford's read-ing of recent history. Mumford was a witness to what he considered the worst twenty years of humankind's history, the age of Hitler and Hiro-shima, and he wanted to explain what had gone wrong. Was the modern association of power and productivity with mass violence and destructive-ness merely coincidental?[6] This was the old Frankenstein problem of man's misuse of his technology, but in this book Mumford puts the problem into the widest possible historical context. The modern "religion" of technol-ogy, he argues, is based upon a gross misconception of human origins and human nature. Furthermore, our modern doctrine of progress, with its association of technological advance with human advance, is merely a "sci-entifically dressed-up justification" for practices the ruling classes had used since the time of the pharaohs to gain and hold power.[7]

This last insight led Mumford's analysis of technology in a new direction. Up to this point he had been principally concerned with the impact of technology upon culture, but in the two volumes of *The Myth of the Machine* he moved to an analysis of the anatomy of technological complexes—of their origins and inner workings as well as their historic consequences. This gave his writing greater weight, breadth, and explanatory power, often, however, at the expense of the prose.

The idea for *The Myth of the Machine* had first come to Mumford in the mid-1950s. In canvassing the history of early technology for a seminar he was giving at MIT, he had been impressed by the ability of the ancient Egyptians to turn out perfect machine work without the aid of complex machines. The colossal stones of the pyramid of Giza are cut to an opti-cian's standard of precision and they were hauled across the blazing desert and placed into position without the aid of a wheeled wagon, pulley, or windlass. This is machine work, yet the Egyptians had no machines. But then it suddenly struck Mumford that the pyramids *had* been built by a machine, one hitherto unrecognized by archaeologists because it was com-posed entirely of human parts, a highly centralized and co-ordinated labor system whose chief assembling agent and prime mover was the deified king. An understanding of the origins, inner workings, and line of descent of this megamachine and the power myth that grew up around it would open the way, Mumford felt sure, to a fresh understanding of the origins of our overmechanized culture and of the fate of modern man. But since the historic record disclosed so little about the megamachine, he would be forced to piece together an argument for its existence from the most fragmentary evidence. To prove this, his boldest and perhaps most original historical hypothesis, he would have to cut into territory even the most radically speculative archaeology had avoided.[8] What he eventually uncovered led to still further questions and to even more challenging conclusions. In observing the building of this book, using as evidence Mumford's own notes and correspondence, we have a wonderful opportunity to watch the way his mind worked, as he leads us back through the centuries in search of the earliest evidence of human behavior.

As always, he worked more like an artist than a historian, and was less concerned with writing so-called objective history than with writing usable history, history that serves as a guide to life. For Mumford, the past had no "objective reality."[9] It was the responsibility of each generation, he had emphasized in his earliest work, to recover and reshape history to its own purposes, to rewrite it in behalf of a better future.

In reconstructing ancient history, Mumford relied heavily on the brilliant archaeological work of V. Gordon Childe. But where Childe emphasizes the part played by inventions like the plow and the military chariot in the emergence of civilization and the first military states, Mumford argues that the critical tools that led to the assembly of the megamachine were inventions of the mind: mathematics and astronomical observation, writing and the written record, and, finally, the religious idea of a universal order derived from observation of the heavens, an idea that gave divine authority to the king.[10] The megamachine emerged when the idea of an absolute cosmic regularity and authority was fused by the king's astronomer-priests with the notion of a human order whose rulers shared in its godlike attributes. By associating the king with the supernatural order of the heavens, the king's priests greatly augmented his political authority. At this juncture the sky gods, particularly Ra, the sun god, became pre-eminent. By the end of the first month of his concentrated research for *Technics and Human Development,* Mumford was convinced that the megamachine was born of this first union of sun worship and political absolutism. He now had an idea, he realized, that would take him two books, not one, to develop, for this idea gave hint of a later relationship between modern science (another form of sky gazing) and political absolutism.

Technics and Human Development is a brilliant but erratically organized book, filled with both flashing genius and repetitious moralizing. Mumford's learning is staggering, and he develops a number of new ideas, but in large sections of the book he is merely pouring new water over old tea leaves. His central argument is often difficult to follow, as he cuts back and forth across immense spans of historic time, drawing risky, sometimes far-fetched analogies, between earlier ages and our own. Readers and reviewers found one argument particularly arresting—and controversial: Mumford's claim that the modern power state is an updated version of the first megamachine. Two devices, he insists, were essential to make both megamachines work: expert scientific knowledge and an elaborate bureaucracy for carrying out orders. In both systems, moreover, scientific knowledge had to remain secret—a priestly monopoly—secret knowledge being the key to all systems of total control. In the ancient city, the king's word was transmitted by a loyal corps of scribes, messengers, stewards, superintendents, and gang bosses—the first primitive bureaucracy. Along with the priests and the army, they formed a level of interlocking power just below the king. They were the brains and nervous system of a power complex that organized scattered populations and put them to work on a scale without precedent.[11]

Mumford saw this "invisible machine" as the archetype and working model for all later complex forms of mechanical organization, though later the emphasis shifted from human operatives to more reliable mechanical parts.[12] The megamachine anticipated the central features of modern production: the interchangeability of parts, the external direction of work, the centralization of scientific and technical knowledge, and the regimentation of the work force. Our modern machine age had its origins, then, not in the Industrial Revolution of the eighteenth century, nor even in the Middle Ages, as Mumford had argued in *Technics and Civilization,* but at the very outset of recorded history, in the organization of a machine composed of men made to endure forced labor at mind-dulling, repetitive tasks in order to ensure the power, glory, and material well-being of a small audacious elite.[13]

The belief that this machine was "absolutely irresistible—and yet ultimately beneficial"—provided one did not oppose it, Mumford calls the myth of the machine. "That magical spell still enthralls both the controllers and the mass victims of the megamachine today."[14] But the great lesson (and this book is packed with admonitory advice) Mumford hoped to drive home to his readers was the role of religion, in this case king-worship, in holding together the first power complex. Once the polarizing force of kingship was weakened, the original megamachine collapsed.[15] This revolt against the grim impositions of kingship occurred, Mumford had first argued in *The Transformations of Man,* between 900 and 600 B.C., "when new voices arose, those of an Amos, a Hesiod, a Lao-tzu deriding the cult of power" and proclaiming values antithetical to those of the power systems. These teachers of righteousness thundered against "gigantic images, imposing buildings, gluttonous feasts, promiscuous sexuality, human sacrifices," and preached withdrawal, fasting, and meditation.[16] The values they, and later prophets like Jesus, Buddha, and Muhammad, fostered eventually broke the magico-religious spell of the megamachine. Their words had the force of a thousand armies. Thus, just as the megamachine had been built on a stronghold of human belief, so, when that belief was withheld, it buckled and fell. Such, at least, was Mumford's highly personalized reading of a long and complex span of human history, an interpretation that surely reveals as much about his mind and moral outlook as it does about the ages he describes. In this view, Thoreau, not Marx, is the more dangerous revolutionary, for Thoreau recognized that disobedience is the first step toward autonomy.

For many centuries after the revolt of the axial religions, the megamachine was confined almost solely to the military. But toward the end of the Middle Ages it began to be reassembled along modern lines. Capitalism, with its emphasis on calculation and record-keeping, the rise of political absolutism, and the introduction of the clock, prepared the way for a new megamachine on a scale that not even Cheops could have thought possible. Only one further thing was needed to polarize the new components of the megamachine: the reappearance of the sun god. In the sixteenth and seventeenth centuries, with Copernicus and Kepler acting as accoucheurs, a new sun god was born.[17] And it is at this breaking point of history that Mumford concludes volume one of *The Myth of the Machine*. Volume two, *The Pentagon of Power*, picks up the story here, describing the rise of the modern megamachine.

When Mumford submitted *Technics and Human Development* for publication he had already written a good part of what would become *The Pentagon of Power*, his most passionate and polemical work. It is an all-out assault on perverted science and the technological state, an indictment so unrelenting, however, that it draws attention away from Mumford's governing purpose: to prove that human nature is biased toward autonomy and against submission to technology in any of its forms. While most reviewers found *The Pentagon of Power* the better of the two books, perhaps because it is a less difficult work and deals with history and events familiar to most readers, *Technics and Human Development* is a more original and important book. It is largely, of course, about the evolution of the megamachine; but there is a subtler and more significant argument in this book, one crucial to understanding everything Mumford ever wrote about technology.

In *Technics and Human Development* Mumford attempts to undercut the idea of *Homo faber*, of man as primarily a tool-making creature, a myth, he contends, that is behind the modern age's total commitment to technology. In overweighting the role of tools and weapons in early human culture, modern social theorists from Thomas Carlyle to Karl Marx to Thorstein Veblen had distorted the actual course of evolution and played directly into the hands of the apologists of the modern megamachine, Mumford asserts. The word "asserts" seems perfectly appropriate here, because, like a priest's assertion of the existence of the Holy Trinity, Mumford's hypothesis is impossible to verify from material evidence. In challenging the myth of the machine he constructs a myth of his own, one closer, he insists, to the facts of human development than modern anthropology has provided thus far.[18]

Reaching back to an argument he had developed in *The Conduct of Life*, published in 1951, Mumford emphasized the role of language in cultural evolution. "But even before language could be invented," he wrote his friend Henry Murray, a psychologist, early in his research, sharing with him some of the new discoveries he planned to bring into the book, "man had to lay a basis for it in the expressive use of his entire body: so if man was anything fundamentally he was a dancing, acting, mimicking, ritual-making animal."[19] Play, not work, had first made us human, an idea Mumford found verification for in Johan Huizinga's *Homo ludens.* (He might also, to his surprise, have found it suggested in Frederick Engels's *The Origin of the Family, Private Property and the State.* Here Engels argues that the appearance of speech was the most important event of prehistory.) In this part of man's development, his dreams and playful fantasies, his magic, rituals, totems and taboos contributed fully as much to his creativity as his primitive tools. From the beginning man was a dream-haunted animal, and the richness of his dreams enabled him to escape from the restrictions of a purely animal existence. The dream, along with the sexual drive, was responsible for our creativity, but it was likewise responsible for much of our destructive behavior.[20]

Primitive man, Mumford argues in the most difficult but intellectually engaging chapter of *Technics and Human Development,* was a dreaming animal, but a deeply disturbed one; and the source of his most irrational fears was his own hyperactive brain. Building on the views of Alfred Russel Wallace, Mumford points out that man's overgrown brain, stimulated by his liberated sexual activities, put him at the mercy of unconscious promptings, some of them destructive and suicidal. Before he could advance, man had to find a way to tame the demons of the psyche. In this task, ritual was crucially important.[21] The performance of ritual—the constant repeating of movements and gestures in the company of others—laid down a pattern of order eventually carried over into language and other expressions of human culture. Where Thorstein Veblen, Mumford's early teacher, regarded ritual as mere waste, a practice that slowed down productivity, Mumford sees it as the key to our humanness.

In the early 1930s, Henry Murray had written to Mumford suggesting a clue to the role of ritual in human development. "I have always been puzzled by the widespread and spontaneous appearance of regular repetitive acts—touching things a certain number of times, counting steps, repeating words, etc.—in children, usually boys. In adults, it appears as a symptom associated with an unconscious sense of guilt. It is related to magic and religious ritual but is more fundamental than any of them. You find it in the infant who wants a story repeated with exactly the same words—it is the most elementary form of mechanization and is in contrast to the whimsies of impulse."[22] In *Technics and Human Development,* Mumford builds on this idea, suggesting that the mechanical order of ritual may have kept early man, literally, from going insane.

Ritual created order and meaning where none had existed, and, later, restored them when they were lost. It allowed man some control over nature and his own irrational promptings.[23] Even some of man's later mechanical proclivities seemed to derive, Mumford wrote Murray while working on *Technics and Human Development,* from his early fondness for repeating the same gestures, and "uttering the same cries long enough to attach some meaning to them."[24] This led Mumford to the interesting argument that mechanization itself had its origin in ritual, ritual being based upon repetition, order, and predictability, an argument that suggests no original separation between art and technics.

Primal satisfaction in repetition thus laid the basis for language as well as ritual. Knowing that he lacked the linguistic qualifications for the job, Mumford nonetheless attempted a hypothetical reconstruction of the birth and development of language, agreeing with Leslie White that the ability to symbolize was the most formidable human achievement, the basis and substance of all human behavior, every advance in human culture, even tool-making, depending upon advances in language and the symbolic arts.[25]

But language, like ritual, had another, health-giving function: it not only opened "the doors of the mind to consciousness but partly closed the cellar door to the unconscious and restricted access of the ghosts and demons of the underworld to the increasingly well-ventilated, lighted chambers of the upper stories." With ritual, language was the chief means of maintaining order in man's outer and inner world.[26]

So while the making of fire and weapons contributed immensely to human development, even more important, from Mumford's perspective, was the slow evolution of the social heritage expressed in ritual, religion, social organization, art, and, above all, language. From the time he dwelled in primitive caves, man possessed an all-purpose tool more important than any other—his overdeveloped brain; and he used this excess mental energy to make himself human and to humanize his world. Man, with his great gift of self-transcendence, had been a controlling figure in cultural evolution, and this leaves the future wide open. Even the megamachine, after all, was largely a product of the mind.[27]

But in Mumford's view, man, the controller, is both a superrational and a deeply irrational being. (It was probably Nazism that demonstrated to him that these traits could exist side by side in the same person, the same nation.) With Freud, Mumford sees the soul as the sphere of an eternal conflict between two forces, one constructive and life-promoting, the other destructive and life-denying. Mumford considered the handling of these ambivalent gifts the supreme human problem.[28] Surely this is why he places such emphasis on personal renewal in his work after 1930. Before man can tame his technology he first has to tame himself, and the first step toward control is the defeat of the demons.

History, humankind's collective memory, can help us to control the demons, Mumford insists in *Technics and Human Development,* his most heavily psychological work. The cultural historian can serve as a kind of midwife to the soul, drawing out the deeper sources of humankind's demonic behavior, knowledge of a problem being essential to its solution.

To break free of the myth of the machine, we would first have to bring it clearly into view and unmask its principal fallacies. But in *Technics and Human Development,* Mumford attempts to do much more than this. He suggests a therapeutic routine to set the patient—civilization—on the path to recovery. He apparently hoped to be minister, as well as midwife, to the soul.

What had kept humankind from going mad in the past? Ritual, along with other stabilizing influences like family, land, and fulfilling work, the so-called village virtues Mumford had been emphasizing in his work since his first confrontation with fascism in the 1930s. As the world became more disordered and irrational, the old stabilizing props and points of support assumed even greater importance. And so did history itself. Escape from the past, escape into an unknown future in the name of progress, is "an excellent prescription," Mumford once remarked, "for sending mankind to the looney bin."[29]

All this helps to explain why Mumford was attracted in old age to Carl Gustav Jung, Freud's disciple and leading rival. In Jung's life and ideas, he found corroboration for his own ideas on the eternal importance of ritual and tradition. While researching *Technics and Human Development,* Mumford read at least twice Jung's autobiographical *Memories, Dreams, Reflections.* At the same time he read Ernest Jones's biography of Freud. Freud and Jung had located the territory where the demons lurked; but Jung, in Mumford's estimation, offered sounder advice for controlling them.[30]

Mumford believed that Jung had made his greatest contribution after he broke from Freud and plunged into a neurosis at midlife. In finding his way back to sanity and stability he taught us something about ourselves. Outwardly, Jung seemed to his patients and readers a poised, balanced figure, a model of perfect control and personal rectitude. Mumford had seen Jung only once, at a lecture Jung gave on a visit to the United States in the 1930s, but the image he left endured. "He gave a quite commonplace lecture, yet he redeemed it by his presence, which seemed that of a shrewd old peasant, his own archetypal Wise Old Man, a man whom one would go to for advice in the barn if not in the clinic." Yet in reading Jung's autobiography Mumford discovered another, more vulnerable man, afflicted in midlife by a severe neurosis. What particularly struck Mumford, however, was not so much Jung's revelation about his illness, but the "ancient therapy" that saved him, a therapy different from the psychoanalytic method he and Freud had been using with their patients. Jung's description of that crisis and cure bears emphasis, for it reveals as much about Mumford as it does about Jung.

Jung writes that at the time he was working on the history of fantasy and dreams he "needed a point of support in 'this world,' I may say that my family and my professional work were that to me. It was most essential for me to have a normal life in the real world as a counterpoise to that strange inner world. My family and my profession remained the base to which I could always return, assuring me that I was an actually existing, ordinary person. The unconscious content could have driven me out of my wits. But my family, and the knowledge: I have a medical diploma from a Swiss university, I must help my patients, I have a wife and five children, I live at 228 Seestrasse in Küsnacht—these were actualities which made demands upon me and proved to me again and again that I really existed, that I was not a blank page whirling about in the winds of the spirit."[31]

Family and work had performed the same function in Freud's life, as Mumford pointed out in a self-revealing essay on Freud and Jung he wrote while working on *Technics and Human Development*. Both physicians were family men; and work was the blood and bones of their lives; Freud maintained this driving discipline through a sixteen-year battle with a horribly painful cancer of the palate, until his death at the age of eighty-three. "As with primitive man, work for them was at once a personal function, an economic necessity, and a compulsive ritual whose daily repetition served, like the prayers of the faithful, to alleviate anxiety: above all, this life-nurturing routine was a means of keeping in check, for a large part of the day . . . the inordinate, crazily destructive impulses that they might have found it impossible to control had they been 'free'; that is open to the demonic incursions of the unconscious."[32] Put more simply, family and work gave them a solid hold on reality; and Mumford might have gone on to say that they had done the same for him, a villager and family man who had taken to heart the timeless admonition of Hesiod: "Whatever be your lot, work is best for you." He must have found Jung's advice on the importance of family and marriage especially reassuring, for Jung had freely experimented in erotic relationships, as Mumford had in the 1930s, although in *Memories, Dreams, Reflections* Jung did not disclose much about his long-standing affair with Antonia Wolff, a psychiatrist and former patient, at the request, reportedly, of surviving family members.[33]

Mumford's reading of Jung's life is a lesson on the perils of fast-paced change. All the points of support that had helped Jung to keep his balance—clear and agreed-upon values, recognizable faces and landmarks, steady vocational duties—Mumford saw threatened in our growth-driven age. But how were we to hold on to these traditional values and supports? Here is where Mumford found Jung more helpful than Freud. Jung saw the unconscious as not merely the "hiding place of the demons but the province of angels and ministers of grace."[34] These archetypes, as Jung called them, were forces of health, unity, and ethical direction, ideas and social practices thousands of years in the making. To try to escape from our past, to ignore these values and experiences, is to mistake forward movement for retreat and rout. "Our cult of progress," Jung wrote, "is in danger of imposing on us even more childish dreams of the future, the harder it presses us to escape from the past."[35] Thus the final task Mumford leaves us in *Technics and Human Development* is to recover the autonomous functions, orderly processes and stabilizing associations we were surrendering to the machine.

Technics and Human Development, then, is an optimistic book, the work of a man who refused to give up hope for mankind. The promise of man, Mumford argues, in this, his most deeply considered book, resides within himself. It is up to him to regain and reassert the freedom and the creative capacities he has too readily surrendered to his machines. Man as interpreter and symbol-maker, as maker of meanings and values, is the image on which Mumford erected his philosophy of history—a theory of human development, not coincidentally, in perfect accord with his own chosen role as a writer and vision-maker. In Mumford's highly personalized reading of history, the word and the symbol, the writer and the artist, truly matter, and the arts take a central place in life.

Mumford's slender yet stubborn faith in the future comes through in a letter he wrote late in his life to his Italian friend Bruno Zevi. "I have not the heart to tell [people] . . . what I actually think about our human prospects," he noted, "unless something approaching a miracle takes place." He then went on to tell Zevi a story he had heard about a famous palmist in Berlin in the 1920s. Writers and artists flocked to this man. He told them things about their character and lives he could have known only by intuition. He also made predictions that turned out to be frighteningly accurate. He prophesied early death, divorces, financial catastrophes. His predictions became so dismal that people hesitated to go back to him. Eventually he became so tortured and dispirited by his own readings that he committed suicide. "I can understand his predicament!" Mumford confided to Zevi, "though I have no intention of committing suicide. For I still believe in miracles."[36]

This faith in miracles is a clue, moreover, to Mumford's evasiveness as a political thinker, for historically those who have looked to awakenings and preached of regeneration have not been very good about advising the faithful on how they are to get to the New Jersualem.[37] Just after he completed *The Myth of the Machine*, Mumford told a friend who had written a book about the impossibility of controlling technology, that "detached (computerized) intelligence" will never triumph over life. "I admit that as a possiblilty. But I suspect man will kick over the traces before this happens." But in his own mind, he had no idea how this might happen, and hence no concrete program for challenging the technocracy.[38] All he was able to offer was faith and hope; these, and the not unuseful example of his own life, and the lives of other principled resisters, "saints and prophets of the new age."[39] Do as I have done! he preached. This is a prescription, however, for the good life, not the good society.

So what was Mumford's view of the future in his last years as a writer? Caution is called for here, for he was subject to extreme mood swings, by turns exuberant and despairing, speaking one moment about the apocalypse, the next about eutopia, the good place. He was the kind of thinker who saw crisis as opportunity, who in the blackest hour of the night looks to the dawn. Realizing all this, he gave, I believe, his truest inner feelings about the future in a letter he wrote to his friend and fellow social critic Roderick Seidenberg in 1969: "I think, in view of all that has happened in the last half century, that it is likely the ship will sink." Not certain, to be sure, but likely.[40]

Still, we must remember that on the sinking whaler in Melville's *Moby-Dick* the last touch is Tashtego's arm nailing a flag to the mast. That is Lewis Mumford, aet. 75. The optimism of his old age is almost a cry of defiance. I will not give in! Mankind will not give in—no matter how impossible the odds! Only in this spirit, he is saying, will we be able to retain our humanity, and, perhaps like Ishmael, live to tell the story.

Lewis Mumford:
Prophet of Organicism

LEO MARX

An age that worships the machine and seeks only those goods that the machine provides, in ever larger amounts, at ever rising profits, actually has lost contact with reality; and in the next moment or the next generation may translate its general denial of life into one last savage gesture of nuclear extermination. Within the context of organic order and human purpose, our whole technology has still potentially a large part to play; but much of the riches of modern technics will remain unusable until organic functions and human purposes, rather than the mechanical process, dominate.

Lewis Mumford, 1962[1]

Lewis Mumford's career in twentieth-century American letters is unlike any other that comes to mind. He published his first book, *The Story of Utopias,* in 1922, and since then—he now is ninety-three—he has brought out some thirty more. His chief subjects have been the history and criticism of architecture, cities, literature, art, and technology. Between 1931 and 1963 he also wrote "The Sky Line" column for *The New Yorker* (an assignment which earned him a reputation as a leading—many would say *the* leading—American critic of architecture and city planning), and all in all he has written more than a thousand occasional essays and reviews during his sixty-five-year career as a writer.

But this display of literary energy, astonishing as it is, does not account for Mumford's uniqueness. Other nonfiction writers have been as industrious, but few if any also have been as original; the fact is that a remarkably large part of Mumford's work was radically innovative. I have in mind his seminal work in American architectural history and criticism: *Sticks and Stones* (1924), *The Brown Decades* (1931); in urban studies and the history of cities: *The Culture of Cities* (1938), *The City in History* (1961); in American literary and cultural history: *The Golden Day,* (1962), *Herman Melville,* (1929); and in the history and criticism of technology: *Technics and Civilization* (1934), *The Myth of the Machine* (2 vols., 1967, 1970). It is hard to think of another twentieth-century American, in or out of the academy, who has written as many books regarded by academic experts as signal contributions to as many—and as diverse a group of—scholarly fields. Except for Edmund Wilson, whose writing may have been as influential but whose interests were not as diverse, not one comes to mind.

Another distinguishing feature of Mumford's career is his outspoken criticism of advanced industrial society. One comes away from Donald Miller's judiciously selected 1986 anthology of Mumford's work with a renewed sense of his persistent, bold if politically uncommitted, icono-clasm, and his increasingly intense alienation from America's dominant institutions, its militarism, and its nationalistic ethos.[2] I say "politically uncommitted" because Mumford, in spite of the obvious affinities between much of his thought and that of the radical left, always has kept clear of left politics. He is opposed to Marxism. In his youth he was a cultural rad-ical, an exponent of avant-garde, stripped-down, functional modernism in the arts, yet from the beginning that commitment was accompanied by his fear that the technological power of the modern state might prove to be uncontrollable. Hiroshima and the onset of the nuclear arms race seemed to him a virtual confirmation of that fear, and everything he has written since has been charged with a mounting, urgent sense of outrage and alarm. Much of that animus has been directed against the intellectual establishment, especially the contributions of American scientists to cor-porate and military power. In view of Mumford's unconcealed disdain for the bland, compartmentalized, morally disengaged kind of scholarship the academy nurtures and rewards—a disdain which on occasion has led him to repudiate empirical rationality itself—it is all the more surprising that he has been awarded just about every prize for which writers of non-fiction are eligible, including the National Book Award, the National Medal for Literature, and the Smithsonian Institution's infrequently awarded Hodg-kins gold medal for innovative work in relating the sciences and the humanities.

How shall we account for this unusual achievement? Part of the answer is that he was born, as Thoreau said of himself, "just in the nick of time." In the 1920s, when Mumford began publishing, circumstances were unu-sually propitious for his kind of unspecialized quasi-scholarly work. The professionalization of learning in the United States was just beginning, and in the areas that interested him most, indeed, the process had scarcely begun. No coherent programs in architectural history or urban studies or city planning, conceived as discrete subjects of university teaching or scholarship, had yet been formulated, and much the same may be said about American literature, American studies, and the history of technol-ogy. Although these subjects already were being explored by some unaffili-ated intellectuals and professors, the difference between their status then and now is immense. By now each has become a full-fledged, independent, academically authorized field of inquiry with its organized cohort of com-mitted specialists working in university degree-granting programs and departments; its own scholarly organization, one or more specialized jour-nals, regular conferences, and a rapidly growing corpus of published scholarship. If we conjure up the huge stockpile of scholarly literature that now has accumulated in any one of these fields—say, the thousands of historical, biographical, and critical works on the nineteenth-century American writers about whom Mumford wrote in *The Golden Day*—it is easy to see why a young scholar starting out today could not hope to match Mumford's achievement.[3] But then of course it is necessary to remember that Mumford's contemporaries were unable to match it either. How did he do it? What intellectual equipment, what viewpoint, enabled him to range so widely and productively in so many fields of inquiry?

I

The place to begin, I think, is with Mumford's special vocation as a writer. From the outset he saw himself as a nineteenth-century man of letters like Carlyle, Emerson, Ruskin, Arnold, or Morris—a writer who addresses general audiences on central issues of public concern. Russell Jacoby recently has argued that Mumford, along with Edmund Wilson, Walter Lippmann, Paul Goodman, and a few others, belonged to a now endangered if not extinct breed of "public intellectuals."[4] They have much more in common with Emerson's idea of an unprofessional "American Scholar" who writes in the common language than with today's academic specialists and their esoteric discourse. Indeed, Mumford always has presented himself as a non- or anti-academic type. He never took a college degree, and save for occasional stints as a visiting lecturer, he never was a regular member of a university faculty.[5] In the 1920s his affinities were with bohemia, not academia, with non-conforming writers and artists like his friends Van Wyck Brooks, Waldo Frank, and Alfred Stieglitz. He had strong aesthetic inclinations, as indicated by a recent University of Pennsylvania exhibition of his charmingly spontaneous drawings and water colors. A large part of his later writing was unacademic in another sense: it consisted of polemics on public policy issues—war and peace (*Men Must Act*, 1931), urban renewal (*The Highway and the City*, 1963), regional planning, disarmament, and environmental protection—and he also wrote a few books in an old-fashioned vein of moral philosophy or general wisdom addressed to Everyman, books like *Faith for Living* (1940), *Values for Survival* (1946), and *The Conduct of Life* (1951).

Mumford's anti-academic stance was not merely temperamental. It was grounded in a principled rejection of the prevailing empirical, scientistic ideology of American universities, with its ideal of detached, context-free, or "objective" knowledge. He routinely condemned the increasingly minute division of intellectual labor to which that orthodox concept of learning gave rise. That animus makes itself felt everywhere in Mumford's writing. Take, for example, his encyclopedia entry about his mentor, Patrick Geddes, the British biologist, city planner, regionalist, and social philosopher, whose work he describes as aiming:

... to break down the sterile isolation and impoverished abstraction of specialized knowledge, so as to be able to move and act freely over the entire range of human experience, even that which lay beyond rigorously scientific description.[6]

Following Geddes, Mumford embraced the opposed conception of the synthesizing "generalist," an intellectual type reminiscent of the unspecialized, unprofessional Emersonian scholar who simply exemplifies democratic "Man" thinking. Here, incidentally, Mumford was anticipating the current neo-Emersonian rejection, by contemporary philosophers like Stanley Cavell, George Kateb, and Richard Rorty, of philosophy as a special, privileged academic discipline or discourse. The generalist, as Mumford describes him, is like a balloonist floating high over the contested intellectual terrain, a writer who aims to bring together "widely separated fields, prudently fenced in by specialists, into a larger common area, visible only from the air." Here is the way he describes the generalist's approach to prehistory:

> Only by forfeiting the detail can the over-all pattern be seen, though once the pattern is visible new details, unseen even by the most thorough and competent field workers . . . may become visible. The generalist's competence lies not in unearthing new evidence but in putting together authentic fragments that are accidentally, or sometimes arbitrarily, separated, because specialists abide too rigorously by a gentleman's agreement not to invade each other's territory.[7]

This is in fact Mumford's characteristic approach to most subjects. The invidious distinction between narrow specialization and wide-ranging, cross-disciplinary generalization is the first principle of his method. His commitment to writing as a generalist accounts for much of the intellectual coherence—the remarkable consistency—of his writing. Unlike many journalistic generalists who write about a wide range of subjects from a neutral, largely undefined viewpoint, however, Mumford is a generalist with strong philosophic convictions. Indeed, I believe that his work is best understood as a sustained vindication of a single view of reality, a comprehensive historical, moral, and metaphysical—one might say cosmological—doctrine which may be called "organicism."

II

The essential presuppositions of Mumford's thinking derive from the counter-Enlightenment, or what Alfred North Whitehead called, in *Science and the Modern World* (1925), "the romantic reaction." Mumford admired Whitehead's influential book. "It's a book of first importance," he wrote to Patrick Geddes, "he has an ingenious solution of the problem of mechanism versus vitalism."[8] Whitehead described the romantic movement as a

late eighteenth-, early nineteenth-century reaction against the version of
scientific materialism known as "the mechanical philosophy"— the view,
he wrote, "which asserts that physcial causation is supreme, and which dis-
joins the physical cause from the final end." The romantic reaction, in
other words, "was a protest on behalf of the organic view of nature, and
also a protest against the exclusion of value from the essence of matter of
fact. . . . The romantic reaction was a protest on behalf of value."[9]

The opposition between the organic and the mechanical, omnipresent
in nineteenth-century thought, dominates Mumford's thinking. Allusions
to this all-encompassing conflict, like the one cited at the beginning of this
essay, recur at crucial junctures of his writing, and they provide it with a
telling coherence and persuasiveness. Mumford derived aspects of this
conception from many of the writers he most admired, among them Emerson, Carlyle, Horatio Greenough, Arnold, Ruskin, Morris, Spengler, and
Geddes. The ultimate source of the doctrine was post-Kantian German idealist philosophy, chiefly as transmitted to Anglo-American culture by Coleridge, Carlyle, and other English writers.[10] In its broadest implications, it
is an all-embracing anti-materialist philosophy that rests at bottom on the
opposition between the concepts of the organism and the machine as alternative models of ultimate reality. Mumford's preference for the organic
comports with the emphasis upon the biological view of life he admired in
Geddes's work; Geddes in turn was influenced by Herbert Spencer and the
widespread post-Darwinian (though not explicitly the social-Darwinist) tendency to apply biological concepts to the study of society and social behavior.[11] The fulcrum of this viewpoint, as applied to the human realm, is a
seemingly straightforward proposition: human beings are organisms,
hence their behavior and their arts are best understood as the outcome of
organic processes.

The version of the mechanical-organicist polarity most pertinent to
Mumford's work, especially his architectural criticism, was Coleridge's
well-known if more limited distinction between two conceptions of aesthetic form:

> No work of true genius dares want its appropriate form, neither indeed is
> there any danger of this. . . . The form is mechanic, when on any given mate-
> rial we impress a pre-determined form, not necessarily arising out of the prop-
> erties of the material;—as when to a mass of wet clay we give whatever shape
> we wish it to retain when hardened. The organic form, on the other hand, is
> innate; it shapes, as it develops, itself from within, and the fullness of its devel-
> opment is one and the same with the perfection of the outward form. Such as
> the life is, such is the form. Nature, the prime genial artist, inexhaustible in
> diverse powers, is equally inexhaustible in forms;—each exterior is the phys-
> iognomy of the being within. . . .[12]

Implicit in Coleridge's statement is the powerful notion that the biological
principles governing the form of organisms also can and, indeed, *should*

govern the form of all human constructions: cities, buildings, works of art and literature.

Mumford's most cogent application of the principles of organic form has been to architecture. By the time he began writing, to be sure, Frank Lloyd Wright already had given prominence to the organicist approach to architecture. Wright's ideas and practices were more or less directly traceable to Louis Sullivan's, and back to the aesthetic ideas of Whitman, Emerson, and Horatio Greenough, who in turn were indebted to Carlyle, Coleridge and their borrowings from the German post-Kantian idealist philosophers (especially Hegel). The two famous mottoes associated with the work of Sullivan and Wright, "form follows function" and "in the nature of the materials," represent a Coleridgian version of functionalist modernism; in their work Mumford found abundant confirmation of the energizing power, the aesthetic and moral unity—a kind of architectural probity—that would issue from the application of the organic principle, properly understood, to the design of buildings.

Mumford's influential essay, "The Case Against 'Modern Architecture'" (1962), illustrates his effective use of the organic/mechanic distinction in the criticism of current trends in building.[13] When architects first made themselves "at home with mechanical processes," the modern movement had been full of promise. But architectural modernism later had disintegrated into a haphazard multitude of sects and mannerisms because, he contends, architects had adopted the prevailing "belief in mechanical progress as an end in itself." The disintegration began with the misconstrual, by Sullivan's successors, of "form follows function," taking it to mean (primarily) "mechanical form and mechanical function." Meanwhile Le Corbusier was giving a central place to the machine, proclaiming its attributes (austerity, economy, and geometric cleanness) to be "almost the sole virtues of the new architecture."

The result, Mumford argues, was a superficial aesthetic "which sought to make the new buildings *look* as if they respected the machine, no matter what the materials or methods of construction." Mies van der Rohe completed the deformation of architectural modernism by designing a kind of building which is less like a machine than a package; he used steel and glass to create a "dry style of machine forms without the contents," buildings which are "elegant monuments of nothingness." Although Mumford concedes that Mies's hollow glass shells possess a crystalline purity of form, they exist in "the Platonic world of his imagination" without any "relation to site, climate, insulation, function, or internal activity."

What modern architects lack, Mumford argues, is a "principle of order" capable of allying architecture to an equally coherent theory of human development. They have

> . . . no philosophy that does justice to organic functions or human purposes, and that attempts to build a more comprehensive order in which the machine, instead of dominating our life and demanding ever heavier sacrifices . . . , will

become a supple instrument for humane design, to be used, modified, or on
occasion rejected at will.

The missing "philosophy" is, of course, Mumford's favored alternative to
the reigning belief in mechanical progress, organicism. Whereas organic
evolution "is cumulative and purposeful," thus linking past, present, and
future, "mechanical progress" exists in a one-dimensional time: the present. To believers in mechanical progress, who assume that human improvement comes about most rapidly when we devote "all our energies to the
expansion of scientific knowledge and to technological inventions," only
the present counts; progress therefore should be "measured by novelty,
constant change, and mechanical difference, not by continuity and human
improvement."

Mumford's timely account of the decline of architectural modernism
exemplifies the persuasiveness, the critical power, of his organicist doctrine. Writing in 1962, he was one of the first to recognize the essential
coldness, sterility, and inhumanity of urban areas dominated by "glass
box" skyscrapers. These buildings are not integrated into the already existing cityscape, nor are they functionally related to the non-economic needs
of the city and its citizens. The power of the organic principle as Mumford's all-purpose intellectual standard is indicated by his successful use of
it here as a frame both for an aesthetic assessment of architectural modernism, and for a historical explanation of the movement's failure.

The buildings are aesthetic failures, Mumford is saying—failures *as*
buildings—because they were not designed according to organic principles. Had the architects been faithful to the functionalist creed, they would
have determined each building's form, and selected the materials out of
which to construct it, in accord with its purpose or function in its relation
to the surrounding environment. This would have resulted in both innovative diversity and a measure of harmony with already existing buildings—with the past. The controlling principle, as with any organic process,
is integration: the integration of the parts guided by a coherent conception
of the whole. But the reigning style of modern architecture, like many
other aspects of modernity analyzed by Mumford, exhibits the supplanting
of organicism, sometimes deliberately, sometimes inadvertently, by the
mechanistic ethos of scientific and technological progress. That mechanistic bias is exhibited in the unadorned, precise, sharp-edged, rectilinear
building style—the architectural embodiment of the machine aesthetic.

But the fate of modern architecture, as Mumford describes it, is merely
one instance of the far-reaching triumph of mechanism in our time. In the
work he has done since the beginning of the Cold War, Mumford has been
increasingly explicit about the conflict between the organic and mechanic
principles as having dominated the history of the West since the Middle
Ages. He regards the medieval city as the last significant, relatively enduring societal embodiment of the organic principle; its street plans tended
"to follow nature's contours," not because of some preconceived goal, but

as the inescapable consequence of "organic planning," a process he defines as moving "... from need to need, from opportunity to opportunity, in a series of adaptations that ... become increasingly coherent and purposeful, so that they generate a complex, final design, hardly less unified than a preformed geometric pattern."[14] Each medieval town developed out of a unique situation, "presented a unique constellation of forces, and produced, in its plan, a unique solution." It grew, as it were, from the inside out, because the decisive determinant was "a consensus ... so complete as to the purposes of town life that the variations in detail only confirm the pattern. That consensus makes it look, when one views a hundred medieval plans in succession, as if there were in fact a conscious theory that guided this town planning."

In Mumford's history of cities, as in his analysis of modern architecture, the controlling theme is a conflict between organic and mechanistic ways of thinking. The medieval spirit of wholeness was kept alive in the greatest fifteenth- and sixteenth-century European cities—cities like Florence and Turin, whose original Roman outlines were still visible; indeed, the post-medieval style (ordinarily called "renaissance," a period label Mumford rejects) remained "so deeply organic," he contends, that it seems "a continuation of its own past." In time, however, this organic mode of urban development was supplanted by one that lent expression to "a new ideological form ... derived from mechanistic physics." The city plans in the new baroque mode, which was closely bound up with the politics of oligarchy and centralized despotism in the new nation-states, resembled the plans of ancient royal cities. Compared with the planners of antiquity, indeed, the planners of baroque cities were "even more ruthless, one-sided, non-cooperative; even more indifferent to the slow, complex interactions, the patient adjustments and modifications, through trial and selection, which mark more organic methods of city development." The baroque style, according to Mumford, arose in tandem with fundamental social changes, among them the shift from a goods economy to a money economy, the development of new military and bureaucratic forms of power and, all in all, the emergence of a whole new way of life:

> The abstractions of money, spatial perspective, and mechanical time provided the enclosing frame of the new life. Experience was progressively reduced to just those elements that were capable of being split off from the whole and measured separately: conventional counters took the place of organisms.[15]

The baroque capitals of Western Europe thus represented "a mechanical order" based "not upon blood or neighborhood or kindred purposes and affections," but upon subjection to a new breed of ruling princes and their new forms of military power.

To Mumford the fate of medieval organicism is a prevision of what is occurring in the late twentieth century. Ours is a society dominated by a latter day version of the mechanistic mentality, an ideology of raw power not unlike that embodied in the great baroque cities of Europe. The triumph of mechanism he discerned in our debased modernist city architecture is most significantly (and fearsomely) embodied in the nuclear-armed nation-state. The "megamachines" he identifies with today's superpowers are the latest socio-political and economic expressions of this mechanistic philosophy. Hence the increasingly hyperbolic character of Mumford's writing during the Cold War.

> In our own time, the mechanical world picture at last reached the state of complete embodiment in a multitude of machines, laboratories, factories, office buildings, rocket-platforms, underground shelters, control centers. But now that the idea has been completely embodied, we can recognize that it had left no place for man. He is reduced to a standardized servo-mechanism: a left-over part from a more organic world.[16]

By the late 1960s he was arguing that to avoid a nuclear holocaust it was urgently necessary to replace the mechanistic ideologies of the "megamachines" with an updated version of the organic philosophy. Our best—probably our only—hope is to get rid of the militarized superpowers and create instead a global network of relatively small-scale, decentralized, varied, regionally integrated communities.

III

So far I have tried to suggest that the remarkable abundance, scope, and coherence—the persuasive power—of Mumford's work is in large measure attributable to its conceptual unity. "Lewis was one of the few men," wrote Van Wyck Brooks, who had "not *ideas* but *an idea,* and was to spend his life working this out."[17] The conflict between organicism and mechanism is that idea. It is the chief ordering principle of his critical-polemical and his scholarly-historical writing, of his moral and aesthetic judgments, and of his explanations of history. Yet it is inappropriate to divide Mumford's work into such distinct genres, for he is a monistic thinker whose scholarly and historical writings are always critical, and whose political, moral, and aesthetic polemics are always informed by a sense of history. In Mumford's work "organic" and "mechanic" are names for warring princples, or belief systems, whose unending struggle has dominated human history at least since the age of pyramid-building.

Granted that this Manichean vision lends an admirable coherence and drama to Mumford's work, the question of its validity—and its effectiveness—necessarily arises. If we credit the vision with much of the remarkable unity of his work, we also must acknowledge that this same totalizing doctrine probably accounts for the disconcertingly tendentious, predictable, hence not infrequently boring aspect of Mumford's writing; at times in fact it makes his *oeuvre* seem like a huge, panoramic morality play in which actors representing key abstractions—especially those indefatigable rivals, Organicism and Mechanism—contend on a world-historical stage. I now want to consider certain defects or distortions which seem to follow from, and may well be inherent in, his universalizing conception of human experience.

If, as I believe, Mumford makes most effective use of his organicist philosophy in his architectural history and criticism, that is in large part due to the greater specificity required by the subject. In writing about architecture he necessarily deals with the creativity of particular people whose ideas issue in tangible, observable artifacts. In praising the builders of medieval or renaissance cities for their seeming adherence to organic principles, however, Mumford neglects an important distinction between them and modern adherents of the doctrine. Unlike Sullivan or Wright, the city-builders of the past were not themselves conscious proponents of organicism as such. In that case Mumford was applying the doctrine retroactively or, as it were, extrinsically, to the work of historical actors who did not expressly adhere to it. For the cultural historian the distinction between the intrinsic and extrinsic roles that ideas play in human affairs is not trivial; it distinguishes between the ideas which actually figure in history—are present to the minds of the actors themselves—and the explanatory ideas retroactively applied to past events. For Sullivan and Wright the organic principle was a conscious article of belief, an aesthetic code to which they deliberately adhered in their work. No comparably explicit doctrine of urban planning was present to the minds of the builders of medieval cities.

This is not to imply that Mumford necessarily is wrong or misleading when he describes the form of medieval cities, or the process by which they were built, as organic. (Nor, for that matter, does he mislead us by applying the concepts of mechanic form and mechanistic ideology to baroque cities.) But it is important to recognize that the concepts of the organic and the mechanic, and of the polarity they constitute, can be applied to historical circumstances with varying degrees of awareness, specificity, literalness, hence verifiability. That is because they are essentially figurative—or metaphoric—concepts. Each gains much of its persuasiveness and credibility from the meanings transferred to particular works by a root metaphor: the organism and the machine.

To illustrate: in architectural discourse the organic principle may be said to imply that the form of a building should be developed, like the growth of a plant or animal, from the inside out; the form will thus seem to be inherent in its nature—the nature of the materials of which it is made—and determined by its function. Thus the whole is more than the sum of its parts.[18] This intuitively compelling doctrine derives its force from an analogy, a transfer of meaning, between, on the one hand, the concept of biological germination and growth, beginning with the seed, and on the other, the designing of the building in question. Ideally, therefore, a building designed in the functionalist spirit of Sullivan and Wright will have its origin in the mind of the architect, where an imaginative conception of the character, needs, and functions of the building's prospective users is joined with the architect's structural thinking as applied to particular materials in order to generate a form ideally suited to that specific set of requirements. In support of this doctrine, Mumford likes to invoke Sullivan: "what the people are within, the buildings express without."[19]

This analogy between the genesis and form of man-made structures and organisms is in my view Mumford's strongest, most persuasive application of the metaphor. He conveys its power and beauty when, for example, he endorses this appraisal of Brooklyn Bridge by Montgomery Schuyler:

> It is an organism of nature. There was no question in the mind of the designer of "good taste" or of appearance. He learned the law that struck its curves, the law that fixed the strength of the relation of its parts, and he applied the law. His work is beautiful, as the work of a ship-builder is unfailingly beautiful in the forms and outlines in which he is only studying "what the water likes" without a thought of beauty.[20]

The analogy between designing the bridge and the growth of an organism is telling because so many of the attributes of each process seem to be interchangeable. Still, when all is said, the engineering or architectural process and its product are only *like* the conception and development of a living organism. It seems odd to have to say so, but a bridge or a building is not a living organism, and there are important differences as well as similarities between the way a man-made structure and, say, an oak tree—to cite a favorite example of Sullivan's and many other romantics—comes into being; there is no architectural equivalent for the fact that the oak tree's form is immutably lodged in, and spontaneously, inevitably, emerges from, the acorn or, if you will, the specific genetic code or DNA, of oak trees. Communities, organizations, cities, and whole societies are even less like actual organisms than buildings, and I suggest that the greater the discrepancy between an organism and the object or experience to which Mumford applies the organic metaphor, the more evident will be the figurative, ahistorical, ideological character of the relationshp in question.

The ahistorical import of the assumptions underlying Mumford's analytic mode becomes obvious, I think, when we look closely at the terms he applies to technology, especially his concepts of "the machine" and, in his later work, "the megamachine." It may seem perverse to charge Mumford, whose extensive knowledge of the history of technology is widely admired, with treating the subject ahistorically. But here I am not questioning the extent or the quality of his learning. My doubts, rather, have to do with his epistemological assumptions or, to be specific, with his tendency to impute historical agency to disembodied abstractions—especially the controlling organic and machine metaphors. It is one thing for a historian to emphasize the role of ideas adhered to by significant social groups, but it is quite another to regard history as driven by unmoored ideas afloat, as it were, above the surface occupied by people and events.

First, however, I want to acknowledge Mumford's illuminating use of the concept of "technics" (rather than "technology") as the umbrella category of tools and utensils that figure in all of recorded human history. The term, borrowed from Geddes, enables him to stress the relatively brief history, hence the distinctiveness, of machine technologies. This is particularly important today, when in popular discourse the word "technology" is assumed to refer almost exclusively to technologies developed in the modern era, since the widespread diffusion of implements driven by various forms of mechanized motive power.

Ever since he wrote *Technics and Civilization*, Mumford has insisted upon the vital importance of a host of ancient, relatively simple technologies (he sometimes refers to them as "domestic" or "democratic")—utensil-making, basket-weaving, dyeing, tanning, brewing, potting, distilling, etc.—and the corresponding uniqueness of modernity's characteristically large-scale (he sometimes calls them "authoritarian"), mechanistic, technological systems. Although Mumford does not make a "feminist" point of the fact, it is noteworthy that these age-old tools and utensils tended to be used by women—or at least when compared with modern machinery, they were much less frequently restricted to use by males. Mumford characterizes these domestic technologies as organic in the almost literal sense that they often were designed to be extensions of the human body. Of the many historical triumphs of mechanism over organicism, the most decisive for Mumford almost certainly was that cluster of changes—the onset of modernity itself—initiated by the invention of the clock; it resulted in the supplanting of "organic time," measured by reference to cyclical processes of nature, by abstract "mechanical" or social time. The mechanical clock, as Mumford describes its advent in his deservedly admired chapter "The Monastery and the Clock," is "the key machine of the modern industrial age."[21]

By the time of *Technics and Civilization* (1934), Mumford also had set up the crucial distinction between *machines,* a word he uses to denote "specific objects like the printing press or the power loom," and *the machine,* a term he would reserve

> . . . as a shorthand reference to the entire technological complex. This will embrace the knowledge and skills and arts derived from industry or implicated in the new technics, and will include various forms of tool, instrument, apparatus and utility as well as machines proper.[22]

In the 1934 work, long before he was to extend and elaborate this concept of "the machine," transforming it into the grandiose idea of "the megamachine," Mumford already exhibits his propensity to treat this technological concept as a virtually autonomous agent of history. The peoples of Western Europe had adopted their whole mode of life, he asserts in the third paragraph of *Technics and Civilization*, "to the pace and the capacities of the machine. How did this happen?" He then rephrases the question, to which the entire book ostensibly is his answer, in this strangely circumlocutious and tendentious question: "How in fact could the machine take possession of European society until that society had, by an inner accommodation, surrendered to the machine?"

If Mumford's attribution of agency to "the machine"—its capacity to "take possession" of society—were merely a rhetorical lapse, convention, or affectation, it hardly would be worth mentioning. But it exemplifies an omnipresent tendency, the nub of his approach to history. This becomes more obvious if we leap ahead to *The Myth of the Machine* (1967–70) and consider the monumental role he attributes to a newly coined abstraction related to "the machine," an entity he variously refers to as the "archetypal machine" or "megamachine." Its invention in ancient Egypt, Mumford contends, was the true source of the modern Machine Age and of our "present over-mechanized culture."[23] Here, incidentally, he repudiates the current consensus of historians which holds that the "industrial revolution" of the eighteenth and nineteenth centuries, a complex process involving socio-economic and political as well as technical changes, gave rise to industrial capitalism, and thus represents the watershed of the modern era. According to Mumford, however, it was the ancient Egyptians who laid the groundwork for the "Machine Age" when they invented the "archetypal machine" some five thousand years ago.

This "extraordinary invention" was not a thing or artifact, it was the system the Egyptians devised for assembling, organizing, and disciplining the manpower they needed to build the great pyramids. This novel mode of organization enabled them to perform "work on a scale never attempted before." As a name for this system, "megamachine" (which Mumford translates as "Big Machine") is apt; it is a clear, understandable, familiar metaphoric extension, just as his original term "the machine" is an extension of "machine" in its literal, physical sense. But Mumford does everything he can to divest "the megamachine" of its metaphoric character. Far from being a poetic or figurative expression, this machine, he writes, was "the earliest working model for all later complex machines." He categorically denies that he is invoking a figurative conception when he refers to the Egyptian system as a megamachine:

> Now to call these collective entities machines is no idle play on words. If a machine be defined . . . as a combination of resistant parts, each specialized in function, operating under human control, to utilize energy and to perform work, then the great labor machine was in every aspect a genuine machine: all the more because its components, though made of human bone, nerve, and muscle, were reduced to their bare mechanical elements and rigidly standardized for the performance of their limited tasks.

This dubious argument deserves close attention because it lays bare Mumford's assumptions about historical agency. Its dubiousness stems from the fact that a system for organizing people to do work, however many attributes it may share with actual machines—with physical objects like power looms or steam engines—can no more *be* a machine than a building can *be* an organism. This is not to deny that his allusion to the workers as "components . . . made of human bone, nerve, and muscle" is a powerful trope—at once paradoxical, hyperbolic, and ironic—directed against any such impersonal, inhumane, totalitarian organization of people as that devised by the Egyptians. One hesitates to diminish Mumford's frightening and all-too-credible vision of humanity imprisoning itself once again in a deadly power system of its own making. Nevertheless, the differences between living, sentient beings and machine components, no matter how enslaved and regimented those people may be, are not trivial. As rhetoric, of course, the efficacy of Mumford's trope depends on our awareness of the gross disparity between people and machine parts: that is in fact what makes the idea of a repressive, atavistic megamachine so appalling. Yet Mumford also wants us to take literally the idea that the "machine" the Egyptians built out of human parts was the prototype, the actual working model, for all later complex machines. Although he reiterates this astonishing claim at several points in the two volumes, he offers little or no historical evidence in its support.

What shall we make of Mumford's curious insistence on the literal, non-figurative character of the megamachine? The answer lies, I think, in his overall rhetorical strategy in *The Myth of the Machine*. After Hiroshima and the intensification of the nuclear arms race he had, as I said earlier, become increasingly alarmed about the potentially catastrophic uses of America's technological power. He no longer could summon the hope he had attached to the latest technologies in the optimistic conclusion of *Technics and Civilization*. At about the time the United States was getting enmeshed in Vietnam, he evidently decided to focus his monumental two-volume survey of Western technology on the impending culmination of the ancient conflict between organic and mechanical technics. If, as he evidently believes, that conflict is the crux of modern history, then America's "pentagon of power"—an updated, nuclear-armed version of the Egyptian pyramid-building system—is its potentially cataclysmic end-product. Hence the importance he retrospectively attaches to the ancient megamachine, with its manifestly totalitarian, death-oriented character, as the precursor of the vast superpower technological systems that dominate global politics in the late twentieth century. "To understand the point of the machine's origin and its line of descent," Mumford writes,

> . . . is to have a fresh insight into both the origins of our present over-mechanized culture and the fate and destiny of modern man. . . . We . . . see . . . that from the outset all the blessings of mechanized production have been undermined by the process of mass destruction which the megamachine made possible.

Mumford's delineation of the metaphoric megamachine as a decisive agent of change exemplifies his commitment to an idealist conception of history very much like Emerson's. In *The Golden Day* (1926), Mumford had cast Emerson, whom he praised for giving "an independent reality to the world of ideas," as the hero of nineteenth-century American culture.[24] And then in the 1960s, after coming under the influence of Carl Jung, he imparted the power of historical agency to a free-floating idea of his own devising: an "archetypal machine composed of human parts."[25] (Jung held that we have access to such archetypal images in the timeless, transcendent, shared realm of the collective unconscious.) But it is one thing retrospectively to name the system the Egyptians used to build the pyramids; it is quite another to argue, as Mumford does, that during the intervening five millennia the idea of such a system, or megamachine, had "an independent reality." Not only does he locate the megamachine in the consciousness of the pyramid-builders, but he would have us believe (without presenting any evidence to indicate how, or whether, it was transmitted from epoch to epoch, mind to mind) that that same concept subsequently was present to the minds of the inventors of all complex forms of machinery.

IV

Mumford's idealist epistemology is the philosophic ground for his visionary organicism. A related theme in *The Myth of the Machine* is his polemic against the excessive emphasis that historians have imparted to technology as a determinant of human development. Mumford rejects the concept of *Homo faber,* arguing that mankind's making of itself—its symbol and language-making—has been far more significant than its capacity to manipulate the external world: its tool-making. Implicit in this argument is the separation of human experience into an inner realm of thought, words, symbols, myths, and dreams, and an outer realm of making, things, bodies, technologies, materials, or, in a word, physicality. As the post-structuralists have made us aware, such polarities invariably have a privileged term. There is no doubt that Mumford comes down on the side of subjectivity as the more creative, distinctive, admirable sphere of human behavior.

For Mumford the most important and attractive aspect of organicism—considered as a world-view, a source of meaning, value, and historical explanation—is the primacy it imparts to relatedness, order, or integration in human affairs. His highest intellectual aim is to arrive at a coherent and comprehensive conception of the whole of life, one that might yield the principles needed to order relations among the parts. The problematic character of this universalized organicist viewpoint becomes most apparent when we shift attention from its aesthetic to its social import. When the norm of organic form is applied to collective or social formations—to institutions, cities, or whole societies—it takes on implications it does not have when it is applied to the creations of gifted individuals—to buildings, poems, paintings, or other artifacts.

In Mumford's admiring account of the unity and coherence of the medieval city, for example, the idea of order takes precedence over justice, freedom, or equality. He is curiously untroubled by the hierarchical character

of the feudal system, or by the mean, unchanging life of drudgery, ignorance, and enforced belief led by much of the peasantry. This complacently conservative medievalism accords with the aloof, patrician tone he
adopts in addressing contemporary problems.[26] His characteristic prescriptions for urban reform are initiated by elites—architects, planners,
artists, intellectuals—and effected from the top down. It almost never
occurs to Mumford that the legitimate discontent and consequent mobilization of the citizenry might be a source of constructive political action.
Anonymous people do not count for much in his view of society. He
belongs to that tradition of secularized, highly individualistic, yet essentially religious moral philosophers like Carlyle, Emerson, and Arnold, who
rely upon persuasion and exhortation, self-culture and self-transformation, rather than organized politics, as the way to effect change and resolve
conflicts.

A conspicuous shortcoming of Mumford's proposals for coping with
contemporary problems is the organicist's preference for holistic solutions. Speaking of the architectural standard for a satisfactory modern city,
for example, he writes: "The architectural embodiment of the modern city
is in fact impossible until biological, social, and personal needs have been
canvassed, until the cultural and educational purposes of the city have
been integrated into a balanced whole."[27] If that is correct, we will have a
very long wait indeed for the modern architecture we want. Here, as often,
Mumford seems to be saying that nothing can be changed until everything
can be changed. His Emersonian prescription for curing the ills of modern
civilization, in *The Conduct of Life* (1951), is that "we must create a new
person, who is at one with nature, and a new concept of nature which does
full justice to the person."

> With the insights and the methods that are now in use, such a deep organic
> transformation in every department of life is inconceivable except by slow
> piecemeal changes. Unfortunately, such changes, even if they ultimately con-
> verged on the same goal, are too partial and too slow to resolve the present
> world crisis. Western civilization needs something more than a drastic recti-
> fication of private capitalism and rapacious profiteering, as the socialists
> believe; something more than the widespread creation of responsible repre-
> sentative governments, cooperating in a world government, as World Feder-
> alists believe; something more than the systematic application of science to
> social affairs, as many psychologists and sociologists believe; something more
> than a re-building of faith and morals, as religious people of every creed have
> long believed. Each of these changes might be helpful in itself, but what is
> even more urgent, is that all changes should take place in an organic inter-
> relationship. The field for transformation is not this or that particular insti-
> tution, but our whole soceiety: that is why only a doctrine of the whole, which
> rests on the dynamic intervention of the human person in every stage of the
> process, will be capable of directing it.[28]

Mumford was led to this desperate hope by the inner logic of his visionary organicism. Indeed, the greatest flaws in his work are attributable,

finally, to the very doctrine that makes it distinctive. It gives his best writing an inspiriting moral force, a principled resistance to large and oppressive systems of power, that puts to shame the timid micro-empiricism that reigns over much of our intellectual life. Yet his commitment to that essentially metaphysical doctrine also accounts for the increasingly apocalyptic tenor of his writing about technology after World War II. He then came to believe that the spirit of mechanism, embodied in a militarized megamachine, was on the verge of total victory in its age-old struggle with organicism. The situation had become so desperate, he now felt, that our only hope was a massive transformation of human consciousness. There is more than a touch of messianism about his insistence that only his own creed, "only a doctrine of the whole," can save humanity from self-destruction. We have learned many things from this courageous writer, but perhaps the most important may be a cautionary message about the dangers of treating large abstractions as autonomous agents of history.

The Visualized Machine Age
Or: Mumford and the European Avant-Garde

STANISLAUS VON MOOS

In memory of Reyner Banham

In a 1929 review of two recent books on architecture, Lewis Mumford, arguably the most literate and verbal among all the commentators of the "Machine Age," wrote: "We do not need verbal outlining so much as we need pictures." He went on, under the impact of the powerful visual demonstrations he found in these two monographs: "The phantasmagoria of the Sunday Graphic Section must be replaced by the coherent views and suggestions offered by an original mind."[1] At any rate, Mumford's own books fall somewhat short of that standard of excellence: they could hardly be more programmatically committed to "verbal outlining." Even when they deal with visual matters, their illustrations—if there are any—are unspectacular and their layouts often dull.[2]

In fact, as is well known, Mumford's articles in *The New Yorker,* which form the backbone of his career as a critic, had no visual support at all (the same holds true for those written for *The Freeman* and *The New Republic*). Speaking of *Technics and Civilization,* the focus of this paper, one would hardly describe it as a picture book, or as a *trattato* in the tradition of Palladio or—to remain in the field of its subject matter—of the *Encyclopédie,* where (at least in part) the illustrations are the *raison d'être* of the text.

In *Technics and Civilization* the pictures, keyed by detailed captions, are concentrated in a somewhat huddled way on fifteen plates scattered throughout the text so as to form a kind of book within the book. At first sight these illustrations seem to play merely a subsidiary role in the context of Mumford's discourse. Yet they reflect "a method of thinking, not abstract and analytical, but concrete and synthetic"; for, as Mumford goes on to say (in the book review previously referred to), "the two processes are complementary."[3]

Mumford's later works such as *The Pentagon of Power* and *The City in History* present similar kinds of juxtaposed verbal and visual messages. In all these books his illustrations offer a visual summary or synthesis of the

Lewis Mumford, "The Brooklyn Bridge," pencil drawing, undated (c. 1915) from *Sketches from Life* (1982).

argument at hand. It may therefore be appropriate to examine these plates as messages in their own right: charged as they are with nothing less than Mumford's iconography of engineering and technology, i.e.—and in the most literal sense—with his view of cultural history at large.

Any one among the fifteen plates of *Technics and Civilization* can be used as an example. For instance, plate IX, where Catherine Bauer's snapshot of Brooklyn Bridge, an old view of the "Galerie des Machines" in Paris, and a close-up of an ocean liner photographed from the pier, together with Maudslay's original screw-cutting lathe of around 1800 document the age of "Paleotechnic Triumphs."[4] Three among these four images belong to the established icons of modernity and, apart from having played an initiatory role in Mumford's early career as a cultural historian,[5] Brooklyn Bridge represents New York and the "Galerie des Machines" represents Paris as the two most important marketplaces of the modern world. Finally, the ocean liner commuting between them suggests the transatlantic exchange of goods, people, and mythologies as one of the critical issues of its history.

Clearly, however, the characteristic "message" of these illustrations emerges not from these modern "icons" alone, but also from the more general issues and concepts of modernity which they enact visually. So the picture of John A. Roebling's bridge is cut in a way that makes the suspension system look even more miraculous than it actually is, while that of the

IX. PALEOTECHNIC TRIUMPHS

1: Maudslay's original screw-cutting lathe: invented about 1800. Perhaps the most original artists of the period were the toolmakers, who translated the old wooden machines into metal, who perfected and standardized the component parts, and who solved some of the other difficult mechanical problems.

(Courtesy of The Director: The Science Museum: London)

2: The Brooklyn Bridge. 1869-1883. Great mass juxtaposed to great delicacy: an adroit solution for a difficult problem. The builders, John A. and Washington Roebling, deserve to be ranked in that great succession of paleotechnic engineers, beginning with Smeaton and Rennie, and including Telford, the Brunels, Samuel Bentham, and Eiffel.

(Courtesy of Catherine Bauer)

3: The Machine Hall at the Paris Exposition of 1889 was one of the finest engineering structures: technically it went beyond any of the existing train-sheds in refinement of design. Created by an architect, Dutert, and an engineer, Contamin, it had perhaps greater significance than the more daring Eiffel Tower done at the same time. Note that the American steel frame skyscraper was a product of the same period.

4: A modern steamship: still essentially paleotechnic in design, but with all the cleanness and strength of the older type of engineering. Like so many other typical paleotechnic products, it was afflicted by giantism. In its inner arrangements, with the luxury and space of the first class contrasting with the cramped quarters and poorer fare of the third class, the big ocean steamship remains a diagrammatic picture of the paleotechnic class struggle.

(Photograph by Ewing Galloway)

Plate IX from Lewis Mumford, *Technics and Civilization* (1934).

bold three-hinged arch of the "Galerie des Machines" of 1889 seems to illustrate above all the enormous scale and the transformation of structural mass into dynamic power lines made possible by the new structural technique.[6] The liner in turn is seen in a perspective view that, while allowing a glance at the streamlined design of its deck, emphasizes arrival or departure as it is experienced from the pier by somebody trying to detect his friend among the cheering crowd on the bridge.

On pages like these the book's message appears concentrated in a nutshell. The possibility that Mumford might have left the choice of illustrations to the improvisation of his editors can evidently be excluded. Even if we would not refer to him as to a great artist, his numerous drawings and watercolors of buildings, landscapes, and people give ample evidence of his "visual" (as opposed to merely moral or intellectual) interest in the environment.[7] Pencil and camera always assisted the typewriter. He seems to have thought with his eyes as much as with his brain.

Mumford versus Le Corbusier

In order to grasp Mumford's personal "style" as a manipulator of images it is enough to compare these plates with those in other books on art and technics, such as those published by Le Corbusier during the 1920s. It is no coincidence that as far as one of the foremost symbols of "Paleotechnics" is concerned—the ocean liner—Mumford chose a photograph by Ewing Galloway and *not*, to give one example, one of the canonic views of the *Aquitania,* the *Flandre* or of *Le Lamorcière* from Le Corbusier's *Vers une architecture*—although he knew that book (and other books by Le Corbusier) well.[8] Referring to what he believes to be "the chief esthetic principle" of the mechanical age, "the principle of economy," Mumford writes:

Le Corbusier has been very ingenious in picking out manifold objects, buried from observation by their very ubiquity, in which this mechanical excellence of form has manifested itself without pretense or fumbling. Take the smoking pipe: it is no longer carved to look like a human head nor does it bear, except among college students, any heraldic emblems: it has become exquisitely anonymous, being nothing more than an apparatus for supplying drafts of smoke to the human mouth from a slow-burning mass of vegetation. Take the ordinary drinking glass in a cheap restaurant: it is no longer cut or cast or engraved with special designs: at most it may have a slight bulge near the top to keep one glass from sticking to another in stacking: it is as clean, as functional, as a high tension insulator. Or take the present watch and its case and compare it with the forms that handicraft ingenuity and taste and association created in the sixteenth or seventeenth centuries. In all the commoner objects of our environment the machine canons are instinctively accepted: even the most sentimental manufacturer of motor cars has not been tempted to paint

Ocean liner from Le Corbusier, *Vers une architecture* (1923).

his coach work to resemble a sedan chair in the style of Watteau, although he may live in a house in which the furniture and decoration are treated in that perverse fashion.[9]

Pipe, drinking glass, watch, and automobile: it is easy to spot the pages in Le Corbusier's *L'Art décoratif d'aujourd'hui* that have inspired this eulogy.[10] Yet if Mumford was so enthusiastic about Le Corbusier's ingenuity in unraveling the icons of our time that are "buried from observation by their very ubiquity," why did he not simply reproduce one of the respective pages from *Vers une architecture, Urbanisme,* or *L'Art décoratif d'aujourd'hui?* The answer is, of course, that his own view of machine culture and machine art differed substantially from Le Corbusier's, and that for a visual mind like his it was imperative to clarify his position on the issue not only in writing but—perhaps even first of all—through the choice of illustrations.

Mumford's comparatively "dynamic"view of the machine seems to have been at the root of his antagonism to Le Corbusier's idealized machine-style (or mechanocentric aesthetic platonism), an antagonism that became increasingly melodramatic over the years. As he himself later put it:

> . . . from the time I read the first edition of his *Vers une architecture,* I knew that we were, by reason of our different temperaments and education, predestined enemies: he with his Cartesian clarity and his Cartesian elegance, but—alas!—with his Baroque insensitiveness to time, change, organic adaptation, functional fitness, ecological complexity. . . .[11]

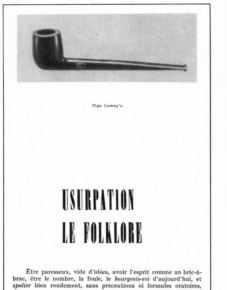

Pipe from Le Corbusier, *L'Art décoratif*   Commercial glasses from Le Corbusier,
d'aujourd'hui (1925).   *L'Art décoratif d'aujourd'hui* (1925).

"Different temperaments, different education"—but also, and first of all, a different "style" in the manipulation of images: If Le Corbusier tends to document the workshop of the modern world in terms of its significant products, Mumford prefers to show it as a stage of human skills and emotions; if Le Corbusier's shows timeless end-products of a Darwinian process of selection, Mumford emphasizes qualities like functional fitness and organic adaptation relative to time and open to change.

Or, to follow Roland Barthes's terminology: in Le Corbusier's case the *objet*—whatever its nature— is generally seized on an anthological level, in Mumford's case on an anecdotal.[12] Whether we prefer to describe the two positions in terms of their underlying didactic aims or in terms of the diverging literary genres at stake, in either case the result is the evidence of two diverging models of dealing visually with the products of industry.

At any rate, the substitution of dynamic for static (Corbusean) images of the "Paleotechnic Triumphs" appears to be a basic thrust of Mumford's visual discourse. When he shows machinery—as on plate X: "Neotechnic Automation"—the focus is not the geometric quality of any single mechanical installation or apparatus, not an alleged absolute and platonic standard submitted to "Eyes That Do Not See."[13] Rather, we get the sense of an endless process, of a continuous flow of mechanical movements linked by crank actions and transmission belts and rolling dangerously

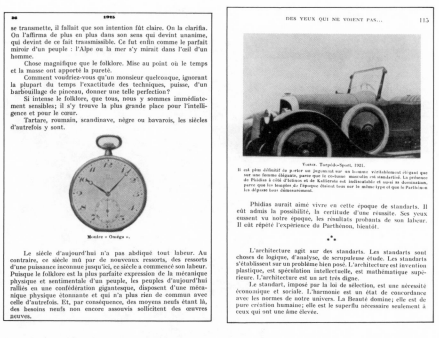

se transmette, il fallait que son intention fût claire. On la clarifia. On l'affirma de plus en plus dans son sens qui devint unanime, qui devint de ce fait transmissible. Ce fut enfin comme le parfait miroir d'un peuple : l'Alpe ou la mer s'y mirait dans l'œil d'un homme.

Chose magnifique que le folklore. Mise au point où le temps et la masse ont apporté la pureté.

Comment voudriez-vous qu'un monsieur quelconque, ignorant la plupart du temps l'exactitude des techniques, puisse, d'un barbouillage de pinceau, donner une telle perfection?

Si intense le folklore, que tous, nous y sommes immédiatement sensibles; il s'y trouve la plus grande place pour l'intelligence et pour le cœur.

Tartare, roumain, scandinave, nègre ou bavarois, les siècles d'autrefois y sont.

Montre « Oméga ».

Le siècle d'aujourd'hui n'a pas abdiqué tout labeur. Au contraire, ce siècle mû par de nouveaux ressorts, des ressorts d'une puissance inconnue jusqu'ici, ce siècle a commencé son labeur. Puisque le folklore est la plus parfaite expression de la mécanique physique et sentimentale d'un peuple, les peuples d'aujourd'hui ralliés en une confédération gigantesque, disposent d'une mécanique physique étonnante et qui n'a plus rien de commun avec celle d'autrefois. Et, par conséquent, des moyens neufs étant là, des besoins neufs non encore assouvis sollicitent des œuvres neuves.

DES YEUX QUI NE VOIENT PAS...   115

Voisin. Torpédo-Sport, 1921.

Il est plus définitif de porter un jugement sur un homme véritablement élégant que sur une femme élégante, parce que le costume masculin est standardisé. La présence de Phidias à côté d'Ictinos et de Kallicrate est indiscutable et aussi sa domination, parce que les temples de l'époque étaient tous sur le même type et que le Parthénon les dépasse tous démesurément.

Phidias aurait aimé vivre en cette époque de standards. Il eût admis la possibilité, la certitude d'une réussite. Ses yeux eussent vu notre époque, les résultats probants de son labeur. Il eût répété l'expérience du Parthénon, bientôt.

×

L'architecture agit sur des standarts. Les standarts sont choses de logique, d'analyse, de scrupuleuse étude. Les standarts s'établissent sur un problème bien posé. L'architecture est invention plastique, est spéculation intellectuelle, est mathématique supérieure. L'architecture est un art très digne.

Le standart, imposé par la loi de sélection, est une nécessité économique et sociale. L'harmonie est un état de concordance avec les normes de notre univers. La Beauté domine; elle est de pure création humaine; elle est le superflu nécessaire seulement à ceux qui ont une âme élevée.

Watch from Le Corbusier, *L'Art décoratif d'aujourd'hui* (1925).

Automobile from Le Corbusier, *Vers une architecture.*

toward us, albeit controlled by a human superivsor.[14] Clearly, that lonely worker, who "lingers on as a machine herd," as Mumford puts it in the caption, is the center of the author's attention. One cannot help thinking of those isolated figures exposed to the sublime power of nature in Caspar David Friedrich's paintings.

If the machine is, as Mumford puts it, "not the mere conquest of nature but her resynthesis," "nature analyzed, regulated, narrowed, controlled by the mind of men,"[15] then the concept of nature that is at stake here implies process rather than a set of abstract laws, forces in movement rather than a mechanical end product that incorporates a principle of design. The theme that interests is visualized industrial process, not mechanics and machinery.

Perhaps the most immediate image that comes to mind—an image that Mumford may have known—is Charles Sheeler's photo-mural entitled "Industry" of 1932 (The Art Institute, Chicago): a triptych made of two vertical pictures flanking a larger center panel. Whereas the side pictures give interior views of the Ford plant in Detroit that show structural and mechanical elements such as wheels, crankshafts, transmission belts, and a stamping press, the center panel consists of a double-exposure montage of various exterior views of the Ford plant dominated by smokestacks and by colossal, diagonally arranged crisscross-conveyors. Industrial architec-

X. NEOTECHNIC AUTOMATISM

1: Modern cotton spinning. During the paleotechnic period the textile industries were the pattern for advanced production, and the term factory was at first applied solely to textile factories. Today the worker has a smaller part than ever to play in them: he lingers on as a machine-herd.

(*Photograph by Ewing Galloway*)

2: The automatic bottle-making machine is not merely a saver of labor but of life, for glass-blowing lays a heavy toll upon its workers. On the other hand, cheap bottles mean greater wastage through carelessness, and the increased demand often tends to cancel out some of the gains of cheap automatic production. (See bottles on Plate XV.)

(*Photograph by Ewing Galloway*)

3: Automatic machine for making screw-caps in the Krausswerke in Saxony. This factory, which has remained in a single family for a century, illustrates the change from the handicraft methods of the old-fashioned smith to the advanced machine methods of the modern engineer.

(*Courtesy of Friedrich Emil Krauss*)

4: Like the stream-lined railroad train, the automatic stoker was invented more than fifty years before it came into general use. The type shown here has done away with a servile form of labor and has led to increased efficiency in fuel utilization. Note the single attendant.

(*Courtesy of the Consolidated Gas Company*)

Plate X from *Technics and Civilization,* ed. 1934, "Neotechnic automation."

Charles Sheeler, "Industry," design for a mural, photo-triptych (1932). Courtesy of The Art Institute, Chicago. Julian Levy Collection, gift of Jean and Julian Levy.

ture is seen here as the theatre of dynamic action, not as a conglomerate of static forms. As Dickran Tashjian has remarked, "Sheeler located the American Dream in the industrial process."[16]

Mumford's Expressionist Bias

Corbusean or not, "structural rationalism" in architecture remained anathema too. Mumford really laid his cards on the table when—as early as 1929—he compared one of the key examples of "rationalism," the church Notre-Dame du Raincy, near Paris (by Auguste and Gustave Perret, 1922) to one of the most exuberant examples of Art Nouveau at the turning point to expressionism:

> Perret's concrete church is as unconvincing for ecclesiastical purposes as a grape arbor: whereas Grundtvig's church in Copenhagen by P. V. Jensen Klint makes one whistle with pleasure, though the construction is massively masonic.[17]

His bias for architectural expressionism as opposed to what he perceived as the mechanocentric idolatry of the early "International Style" is the central theme underlying *Technics and Civilization.* And expressionism remained the permanent focus of his interest in the European avant-garde, so that much later, speaking of Germany in his Preface to the 1971 edition of *The Brown Decades,* Mumford quite naturally mentions Erich Mendelsohn before any other pioneer of the modern movement in Germany:

At that time [i.e. in the 1920s, S.v.M.] Germany, through the Deutscher Werkbund, had established a more continuous modern tradition than either
England, its original home, or France. So even before I visited Germany in
1932 and saw the work of Erich Mendelsohn, Walter Gropius, and Hugo Häring, I was influenced in my own definition of the modern by German ideas
and German examples.[18]

In fact this latter-day view is considerably more balanced than the one we
are able to grasp from *Technics and Civilization.* For while in 1971 Mumford pays tribute to both Mendelsohn *and* Gropius, the Werkbund *and*
Häring, in 1934 neither the Werkbund nor Gropius nor Häring (the
"organic"![19])seems to have been worthy of mention. Nor does Mumford
seem to have come across the writings and the built work of architects and
designers like Peter Behrens, Friedrich Naumann, Hermann Muthesius, or
Mies van der Rohe—to name but the most canonical among the protagonists of the German Werkbund. Nor does he mention, incidentally, Sigfried Giedion's early book on French iron and concrete building.[20] Mys-
teriously enough, none of these men appears in the Bibliography of
Technics and Civilization. The book's copious appendix, a rare gold mine
for any student of German "Philosophie der Technik,"[21] remains absolutely silent on the German roots of the "International Style." Was it that
Mumford was, as Reyner Banham put it, "too remotely placed to have any
real sense of the aesthetic issues involved"?[22]

In any case, the remoteness was cultural, not physical. Mumford visited
Germany in 1932, and after a few weeks of "research and meditation" in
the library of the Deutsches Museum in Munich he made a trip that
brought him close to the birthplaces of modern design in Europe. He
seems, however, to have been most interested in historical architecture and
townscapes *plus* (in part thanks to Catherine Bauer, his friend and travel-
ing companion) the new "Siedlungen" in socialist-run cities like Frankfurt,
Berlin, Vienna, and Amsterdam; at any rate, he took no notice of the artistic and theoretical backgrounds of these developments. The heated
C.I.A.M. debates for and against the "Wohnung für das Existenzmini-
mum" and "Rationelle Bebauungsweisen" escaped him entirely.[23]

From Mendelsohn's *Amerika* to Frank Lloyd Wright

Mumford's most important contact in Germany turns out to have been
Walter Curt Behrendt, an architect and critic who had actually introduced
the American critic to the German public as early as 1952.[24] And then
came Erich Mendelsohn, who had visited America in 1924–25. In Manhattan, he and a group of German friends accompanying him appear to
have had Mumford as Cicerone. As Mumford recalls the episode, in an
unpublished article:

"Stepless Streetcar," from Erich Mendelsohn, *Amerika* (1925).

> My German friends were perhaps more insistent upon the esthetic role of the artist [than their English collegues—S.v.M.]: one of them, perhaps the most dynamic of modern architects, has created a sort of modern baroque in steel and concrete, and he was much more enthusiastic about the esthetic form of some of our stepless streetcars and our subway cars than he was in the buildings themselves.[25]

Needless to say, no architecture of the early 1920s besides Mendelsohn's lends itself to be called "modern baroque in steel and concrete." As far as the "stepless streetcars" go, one cannot help thinking of the photographs of streamlined tramways that Mendelsohn actually published in his monumental scrapbook *Amerika. Bilderbuch eines Architekten* (1925), and it comes as no surprise that one of Mumford's illustrations in *Technics and Civilization* is taken from *Amerika*.[26] The photograph shows the view of a grain elevator, with the following caption:

> Aesthetic effect derived from simplicity, essentiality, repetition of elementary forms: heightened by colossal scale. See Worringer's suggestive essay on Egypt and America.[27]

In fact, Mumford's emphatic claim for "pictures" rather than "verbal outlining" in books had been provoked by Mendelsohn: the full comment on the "phantasmagoria of the Sunday Graphic Section" reads as follows: it must, Mumford argues, be replaced "by the coherent views and suggestions of an original mind like Mendelsohn's."[28] In his hilarious book *Amerika,* Mendelsohn had shown four different grain silos in Buffalo, two

Grain elevator in Chicago, from Erich Mendelsohn, *Amerika* (1925).

Grain elevator in Chicago, from Erich Mendelsohn, *Amerika* (1925).

Grain elevator in Chicago, from Erich Mendelsohn, *Amerika* (1925).

Grain elevator in Chicago, from Erich Mendelsohn, *Amerika* (1925).

in Chicago. Of one among those Chicago grain elevators he reproduced no less than four almost equal views, each on a full page—like stills from a film. His brief comments are rhapsodic and, what is more interesting, they start by focusing on the grain elevator not as an isolated *objet* but as an operating part within what he perceives as the digestive apparatus of America:

> Special railway-wagons from the interior of the continent, ships carrying grain across the Great Lakes pour their content without interruption into the sub-terranean bunkers and mills. Batteries of elevators store the processed out-come into the rows of containers, in Chicago's nutritive harbor.[29]

In other instances, Mendelsohn juxtaposed the "elevator-fortresses" of Buffalo to the "crane-monsters with living gestures," that serve them.[30] For him, these buildings were the visible expression of the "most rational way of production." But what makes them interesting for us is that Mendelsohn uses quite the same kind of functional, organic, anthropomorphic metaphors for these industrial processes that we will find in Mumford.

In contrast, in *Vers une architecture,* we find not even shades of such an interest in the function of this building type. Le Corbusier uses his own selection of silos (partly consisting of "purified" pictures from the *Jahrbuch des deutschen Werkbundes* of 1913) merely to punctuate his Olympian discourse on the futility of architectural "styles" in comparison with the eternal laws of beauty as they are expressed in the great monuments of Rome—and ironically echoed, of course, in modern grain elevators.[31] A large number of sketches for more or less imaginary factories drawn by Mendelsohn from 1914 onward forms the necessary background for his interpretation of American architecture as the spectacle of industrial process. Can Mumford have been familiar with such work? The answer is yes, for samples from these early sketches had been published in the United States at an early date, some even in the monthly *Dial,* where Sophia, Mumford's wife, worked as an editorial assistant.[32] As Bruno Zevi has argued, these buildings for industry were inspired by the machine, although they did not attempt to imitate machinery; "instead, they record the complexity and fervor of the work produced and the materials transformed." In such a way they are certainly closer to Ernst Toller's vision of the smokestacks of a factory in the gleam of early dawn: "armed, alert and threatening,"[33] than to Le Corbusier's purism of form. Almost all of Mendelsohn's sketches give a view from an angled perspective, since this is the most obvious visual representation of an architecture expressive of dynamic industrial process—and it comes as no surprise that Le Corbusier's preference is for the frontal view.

A good example of Mendelsohn's "dynamic" use of architectural form is the interior of the hat factory in Luckenwalde (1921–23) with its roof structure, whose visual function seems to be to echo and to frame the movement of the transmission belts and to celebrate it as a spectacle of modern life. The theatrical quality of this design (the machine being the

Silo à grain.

TROIS RAPPELS
A MESSIEURS LES ARCHITECTES

I

LE VOLUME

Grain elevator from Le Corbusier, *Vers une architecture* (1923).

prima donna and the architecture the orchestra) becomes clear if we hold it next to Gropius's Fagus factory in Alfeld an der Leine of 1911 or the Van Nelle plant in Rotterdam of 1926, where the factory space itself is defined as a neutral box that allows a multitude of processes to go on inside without affecting the architectural envelope.[34]

As far as American architecture is concerned, Mumford's process-oriented images of "automatism" have their most explicit architectural symbol in Frank Lloyd Wright's Johnson Wax administration building in Racine, Wisconsin, but because the building was started two years after Mumford's book was published, it could not possibly have appeared in it. Not unlike Mendelsohn's earlier proposals, and perhaps not wholly uninfluenced by them, Wright's design is both an envelope for and a visual metaphor of the flow of interrelated "organic" operations that make up industrial process. But since what goes on within the building is administration, not production, the imagery is even more detached from the "function" of the architecture than is the case in Mendelsohn's visionary projects. Wright's administration building is the architectural monument to the spirit of *Technics and Civilization*.[35]

"Nature and the Machine": The Spiral . . .

It is not surprising that Mumford's "organic" and "process" obsessions—indeed his "biological" view of technics—should have influenced even his choice of illustrations as such. So in those few instances where Mumford shows isolated pieces of machinery, these machines also incorporate organic—or process-related—messages, like the industrial "landscapes" we have discussed so far. Such is clearly the case on plate XII ("Nature and the Machine"), where we see the section of a modern hydroturbine juxtaposed to a famous X-ray photograph of a nautilus by J. B. Polak (taken from the Dutch avant-garde magazine *Wendingen*—or directly from Moholy-Nagy's Bauhaus book, *Maleri, Fotografie, Film*.[36]).

To quote from Jill Purce's recent book *The Mystic Spiral*, the spiral is

> a continuum whose ends are opposed and yet one; it visualizes the cycles. It contains, with the help of a change in speed, the principles of expansion and contraction and the possibility of simultaneous movement in both directions towards its two end points.[37]

The spiral thus represents a principle of movement, not primarily a form; a movement that both originates from and leads toward the starting point. Modern art on the whole was obsessed with the motif—from Paul Klee and Vladimir Tatlin to Brancusi and Duchamp. That it plays such an important role in the iconography of the Machine Age should therefore not surprise. It is enough to look at the *trattati* by Laszlo Moholy-Nagy, Sigfried Giedion, Frank Lloyd Wright, and Le Corbusier: All these men have been intrigued by the form of the spiral—but in quite different ways.

House of friendship

Erich Mendelsohn, "Industrial Buildings," fantasy project (1917).

Frank Lloyd Wright, Johnson Wax Administration Building, Racine (1936–39). Courtesy of Johnson Wax Company, Racine.

X-ray photograph by J. B. Polak, of a nautilus-shell, from Laszlo Moholy-Nagy, *Malerei, Fotografie, Film.* (1927); reproduced also in *Technics and Civilization* (see fig. 44).

Francesco Borromini, lantern of S. Ivo, Rome (17th century). From Sigfried Giedion, *Space, Time and Architecture.*

Vladimir Tatlin, Monument to the IIIrd International, Moscow (1919) compared with Borromini's S. Ivo. From Sigfried Giedion, *Space, Time and Architecture.*

Moholy described and documented it as one among the fundamental "stereometric and biotechnical elements of sculpture" (*Von Malerei zu Architektur*, 1929);[38] Giedion (*Space, Time and Architecture*, 1941) juxtaposed two archetypal applications of the spiral in architecture: the lantern of Saint Ivo by Borromini in Rome and Tatlin's Monument for the Third International;[39] and Frank Lloyd Wright actually built it (in the Guggenheim Museum, New York, 1947–52).

Le Corbusier, the "Cartesian rigorist," turns out to have been particularly obsessed with the motif. In *Vers une architecture* (1932) he had shown the picture of a low-pressure ventilator cut from an advertisement of the "Société Rateau" next to the famous if ambiguous slogan "Architecture ou révolution."[40] Later he returned to the spiral in his project for a "Museum of Illimited Growth"—a precedent if not an actual source for the Guggenheim Museum. "Expansion" and "simultaneous movement" are the very theme of the project: the spiral-shaped plan suggests the physical process of the "growth" of which the building is a symbol. The museum, Le Corbusier proposes, should be able to grow along its spiral-axis according to the needs of the collection.

Frank Lloyd Wright, Guggenheim Museum, New York (1942–52). Courtesy of the Guggenheim Museum.

Yet Corbu does not turn "organic," of course. The spiral is forced into a rectangular grid conceptually consistent with the "soap box" principle of Modern Architecture so much loathed by Frank Lloyd Wright (and Mumford). It is enough to juxtapose the plan to two well-known sketches by Le Corbusier in order to bring out the key idea of the project: the sketch of a shell and that of a well-known geometric figure that connects the construction of the Golden Section to that of a logarithmic spiral (it is true that, in turn, the plan is based on an Archimedean spiral).[41]

So much for the hydroturbine as mechanical metaphor of the spiral-shaped nautilus shell: the least that can be said is that Mumford was not alone in attributing to the spiral a revelatory role in attempts to associate nature and mechanics.

. . . and the Ball Bearing

The only other piece of machinery isolated in *Technics and Civilization* is a ball bearing. In this case, the source is close at hand: Early in 1934—the year *Technics and Civilization* was published—Philip Johnson showed a piece that had been donated to the Museum of Modern Art by SKF Industries on the cover of his "Machine Age" exhibition.[42] Interestingly, Mumford turned the MOMA image around by 90 degrees, so that it fits in more harmoniously with the spring, glass bottles, and kitchen ladles arranged below on the same page.[43]

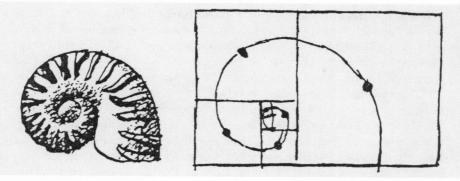

Le Corbusier, sketches illustrating the construction of the logarithmic spiral (n.d., c. 1930).

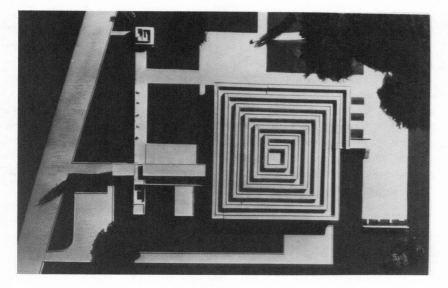

Le Corbusier, "Museum of Illimited Growth" model, seen from above (c. 1931). Photo courtesy of archives Willy Boesiger, Zurich.

But in choosing the ball bearing as a symbol for the "Machine Art" exhibition, Johnson had merely updated an iconography established in New York seven years previously, when the *Little Review* had decided to use a drawing by Fernand Léger that shows the same motif—albeit in abstracted form—on the cover of the catalogue of the "Machine-Age Exposition" of 1927.[44] Although there seems to be an American tradition of using ball bearing and telephone as attributes of industrial power (in portraits of American businessmen[45]) the isolation of the ball bearing for aesthetic purposes is thus an idea imported from the European avant-garde: in fact Léger had celebrated circle and spheres of ball bearings as an archaic symbol in a major painting of 1926, now in the Kunstmuseum in Basle ("Mouvement à billes").

Be that as it may, Léger's is a static vision, not unrelated to the "magic" of elementary geometry cheered by *L'Esprit Nouveau,* and therefore quite antithetical to Mumford's more "organic" view of the machine. We may assume that Mumford—probably unlike Philip Johnson—was more interested in the *function* of ball bearings than in the Philebos-like purity of their mechanical components, and this view is certainly emphasized by the demonumentalized horizontal position in which we find that piece of machinery in *Technics and Civilization.* Since Mumford does not make very explicit his reasons for giving the motif such a key position among the images of modern technics displayed in the book, it is tempting to circumscribe them with the words of Karel Teige, the Czech philosopher, poet, and art critic who wrote, in 1925: "are not ball bearings e.g. a perfect pleasure for the eye?" Teige continues: "The splendour of the glorious modern material, the precision of geometric form—circle and sphere are the most fundamental among all forms, and they flatter our eyes most." Not because of any absolute formal quality, but, as Teige insists, because "they suggest the perfection of their functional performance."[46] In an immediately preceding passage Teige criticizes those artists who use machinery as an aesthetic theme, while, he thinks, it should more appropriately be seen as a lesson to the spirit. He seems to have had in mind the very painting that Léger was to realize the following year.[47]

Modern Art and the "Cultural Assimilation of the Machine"

The fine arts play a secondary role in Mumford's book. Only four among the twenty-four illustrations concerning the twentieth century show individual works by Brancusi, Duchamp-Villon, Léger, and Benton. What puzzles even more—at least what puzzles the art historian—is the great distance from where these works are being looked at and the broad and shallow generalizations proposed as analysis and comment. In fact, Mumford appears to thoroughly enjoy even the most philistine "misunderstandings" of non-figurative modern art. To give one example: the proverbial

"Ball-bearing." Courtesy of Mumford papers, Special Collections, van Pelt Library, University of Pennsylvania.

customs officer's verdict on Braucusi's "Bird" as a plumbing fixture is taken seriously by him as an interpretive key.

An art history obsessed with philological analysis will find no value in such critical perceptions. Yet Mumford's book is not on that sort of art history. In Mumford's scenario, art appears primarily as an illustration of cultural tendencies discovered in industry. Furthermore, it documents the ways of "cultural assimilation of the machine" in different periods of history.

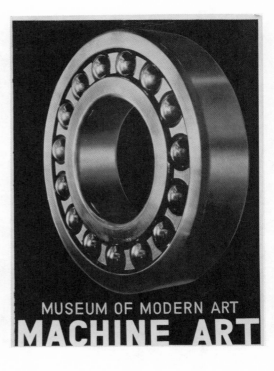

Machine Art cover, exhibition
catalogue, Museum of Modern
Art, New York (1934); cover
design by Josef Albers. Courtesy of Museum of Modern
Art.

So, in the early sections of *Technics and Civilization,* prints and woodcuts
are used to illustrate significant episodes in the history of locomotion,
printing, and the organization of labor from the sixteenth century onward.
Their function is not basically different from that of the photographs used
to illustrate more recent works of mechanics or technology (or older ones
of which no historical renderings were available). They provide documentary evidence.[48]

Occasionally however, specific works of painting and sculpture as well
as illustrations from treatises on art are shown, not because of what they
illustrate but because of the scientific and cultural concepts they embody:
such as the "dawn of naturalism in the twelfth century" in the case of the
relief sculpture at the cathedral at Autun or "the beginning of the Cartesian logic of science" in the case of Dürer's woodcut showing a man drawing a reclining figure with the help of a reticle.[49] In those cases of Gislebertus and Dürer, art is seen as a laboratory of scientific thought from
which the leaps and discoveries that made the modern industrial world
were later to spring.

With this in mind one might expect that Mumford, after all, an early
apologist of avant-garde art in America,[50] would attribute a similar role to
modern art in the context of contemporary culture. Yet his references to
modern art appear in general to be much more cautious. He sees in

XIV. MODERN MACHINE ART

1: Self-aligning ball-bearings. High degree of accuracy and refinement in one of the most essential departments of the machine. The beauty of elementary geometrical shapes. Perfection of finish and adjustment, though already present in fine handicraft, became common—and essential—with machine-craft.

(*Courtesy of the Museum of Modern Art*)

2: Section of spring. Although line and mass are purely utilitarian in origin, the result when isolated has an esthetic interest. The perception of the special qualities of highly finished machine-forms was one of the prime discoveries of Brancusi, and the sculptors in glass and metal, like Moholy-Nagy and Grabo.

(*Courtesy of the Museum of Modern Art*)

3: Glass bottles with caps: typical of modern mass-production. Contrast this simple product of the Owens-Illinois Glass Co. with the extremely complicated machine that makes such mass production possible, shown on Plate XI.

(*Courtesy of the Museum of Modern Art*)

4: Kitchen ladles: another example of serial production, with all the advantages of uniform design and high refinement of finish. But while the machine cannot successfully achieve decoration, handicraft often produced forms as rational as those of the machine. In functional design the two modes overlap. Even in more primitive technics machines like the lathe, drill, and loom conditioned handicraft and in turn eotechnic handicraft furthered the machine.

(*Courtesy of the Museum of Modern Art*)

Plate XIV from *Technics and Civilization*, 1934 edition, "Modern Machine Art."

Machine-Age Exposition Cata-logue, New York (1927). Cover design by Fernand Léger. Courtesy of Museum of Modern Art.

abstract painting and sculpture primarily the reflection of the aesthetic challenge of the machine:

> ... face to face with these new machines and instruments, with their hard surfaces, their rigid volumes, their stark shapes, a fresh kind of perception and pleasure emerges: to interpret this order becomes one of the new tasks of the arts.[51]

He shows works by some among the masters of modern art, but both the layout of his plates and the captions leave no doubt that emphasis is placed not on art in its own right but on the works of technology and engineering that allegedly inspired them. Brancusi, Duchamp-Villon, and Léger thus appear as protagonists of a figurative—more than abstract—kind of "machine art." In the text this hierarchy of interests is confirmed time and again as when Mumford confesses that the "original machines and instruments" which had already inspired the efforts of cubist painting "were often just as stimulating as their equivalents."[52] Did he mean it in the sense Marcel Duchamp had implied when he wrote in 1917 that "the only works of art ever produced by America" were "its sanitary equipment and its bridges"?[53]

Be that as it may—to qualify Duchamp as the leader of the post-impressionist movement who ... "made a collection of cheap, ready-made arti-

Fernand Léger, "Le Mouvement à billes," oil on canvas, 126 x 114 cm (1926). Courtesy of Oeffentliche Kunstsammlung, Basel Kunstmuseum; gift of Raoul la Roche.

II. PERSPECTIVES

1: Dawn of naturalism in the twelfth century.

(*Saint-Lazare d'Autun, France*)

2: Engraving from Dürer's treatise on perspective. Scientific accuracy in representation: co-ordination of size, distance, and movement. Beginning of the cartesian logic of science.

3: Tintoretto's Susanna and the Elders: the complete picture shows a mirror at Susanna's feet: See Chapter II, Section 9, also Chapter III, Section 6.

4: Eighteenth century automaton, or the clockwork Venus: the penultimate step from naturalism to mechanism. The next move is to remove the organic symbol entirely.

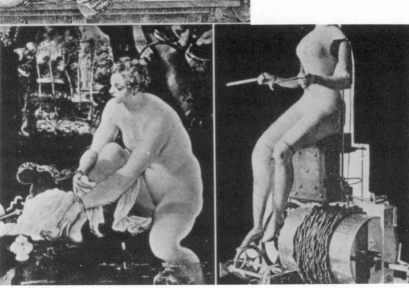

"Perspectives," plate from *Technics and Civilization.*

Marcel Duchamp, "Bicycle Wheel" (1913). Replica after a lost original.

cles, produced by the machine, and called attention to their aesthetic soundness and efficiency"[54] may suit the argument at hand, but the matter is considerably more complex if seen against the aesthetic theories involved; Duchamp, in fact, repeatedly denied that the "ready mades" he had selected corresponded to any standards of aesthetic quality or taste. Of course, we may refuse to take such utterances at face value, as did Thomas B. Hess in a famous article "against" Duchamp:

> He has that interior decorator's eye which spots beautiful items in the dingiest flea-market. When Duchamp sent a commonplace or despicable object to an art exhibition (the hat rack or the urinal), it was an anti-art gesture at modern sculpture, but the additional twist for his fan-club was that the object really is beautiful in itself.[55]

Mumford's appreciation of the sculptor Constantin Brancusi is no less refreshingly simplifying; Brancusi offers, in his view,

> . . . the most complete as well as the most brilliant interpretation of the capacities of the machine. . . . Looking at the bird [Mumford thinks of course of one among Brancusi's most celebrated sculptures, "The Bird" of 1925], one thinks of the shell of a torpedo.[56]

As if he wanted to give this kind of associational art criticism the consecration of popular taste he continues,

> . . . the obtuse United States customs officer who wished to classify Brancusi's sculpture as machinery of plumbing was in fact paying it a compliment. In Brancusi's sculpture the idea of the machine is objectified and assimilated in equivalent works of art.[57]

What a contrast to Mumford's own earlier comments on the works of the same artist! Only a few years before—in an essay on Constantin Brancusi and John Marin published in *The New Republic*—he had insisted on the conceptual, non-figurative qualities of Brancusi's sculpture:

> In Brancusi, intellectual passion is dominant: it is a fine surgical knife that cuts bloodlessly into the innermost form. From the block of marble, from the trunk of riven oak, from a piece of granular stone, he extracts a form—its form—and that plastic medium becomes almost as refined as a concept.[58]

In *Technics and Civilization,* however, Mumford seems content with a modern art that serves, as was the case with the illustrations in the *Encyclopédie* (or with the prints and woodcuts shown earlier in the book), a documentary purpose with regard to the Machine Age. Art is looked at from the distance again; the magnifying glass of the art critic is replaced by the binoculars of the cultural historian.[59]

Mumford's shift from a relatively optimistic to a frankly apocalyptic view of industrial society—his transition from *Technics and Civilization* (1934) to *The Pentagon of Power* (1970)—aggravated his tendency to interpret art on the level of superficial formal analogies with industrial forms. So in *The Pentagon of Power,* he rather unfavorably compares Marcel Duchamp's "Nude Descending a Staircase" of 1912, "one of the most brilliant specimens of cubism" (as Mumford puts it, suggesting a somewhat summary notion of that art movement), to a mildly soft-porno-photograph that does, Mumford feels, "justice to the mobile beauty of woman's body"[60]— whereas Duchamp, we understand, fails to do that.

Another example of this somewhat precocious, if refreshing, strategy of judging art by its formal kinship to images taken from industrial everyday-culture is the alleged "artful nullity" of the typical 1960s art exhibition showing works by an unidentified artist (Morris Louis? Kenneth Noland?) and comparing them with "Computerdom"—and with the Pentagon itself.[61]

Constantin Brancusi, "The Bird" (1925). Courtesy of Museum of Modern Art.

Marcel Duchamp, "Nude Descending a Staircase," Nr. 2 (1912), Courtesy of Philadelphia Museum of Art.

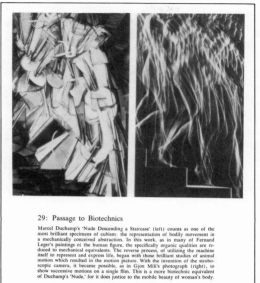

29: Passage to Biotechnics

Marcel Duchamp's 'Nude Descending a Staircase' (left) counts as one of the most brilliant specimens of cubism: the representation of bodily movement in a mechanically conceived abstraction. In this work, as in many of Fernand Leger's paintings of the human figure, the specifically organic qualities are reduced to mechanical equivalents. The reverse process, of utilizing the machine itself to represent and express life, began with those brilliant studies of animal motion which resulted in the motion picture. With the invention of the strobo-scopic camera, it became possible, as in Gjon Mili's photograph (right), to show successive motions on a single film. This is a more biotechnic equivalent of Duchamp's 'Nude,' for it does justice to the mobile beauty of woman's body.

Plate 29 from Lewis Mumford, *The Pentagon of Power* (1970), "Passage to Biotechnics."

Depression Murals

As if to illustrate a new bias in favor of a figurative art capable of carrying messages to a lay audience, Mumford includes, in *Technics and Civilization,* a picture of Thomas Hart Benton's mural at the New School for Social Research in New York showing "steel workers" in the steam and glow of a factory as a "Realization of the dynamic element in modern industry, and the daily heroism which often outvies that of the battlefield."[62] In such a way, turning as it were from the opaque symbolism of Brancusi to the melodramatic pathos of Benton, Mumford pays his tribute to the "American Wave" of the Depression era, even if Benton, described as the "self-proclaimed spokesman for the virtues of America's rural heartland as opposed to the 'decadence' of modern art,"[63] offered a rather anecdotal version of that movement.

Yet in this case Mumford's eye seems to move faster than his mind, for he does not follow up that line in his book. Over such works as Diego Rivera's mural "Portrait of Detroit" in the Detroit Institute of Art (1932–33) or his "Man at the Crossroads" in Rockefeller Center, New York (1933) he passes with silence: works that not only glorified in monumental format the new imagery of industrialized America but placed the social and political issues at stake in an overtly political context. In fact, concerning Rivera's work in Rockefeller Center, which—because it contained a portrait of Lenin—was demolished before its completion,

... mass rallies for and against were held daily, radio discussions filled the air, Sunday pulpits resounded of occasional defense and passionate calumnies.[64]

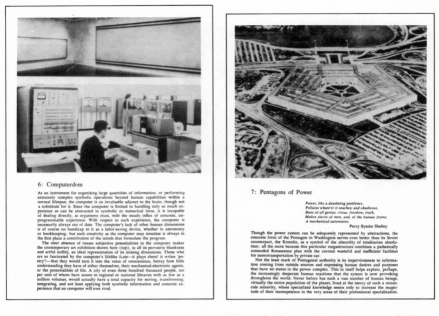

6: Computerdom

As an instrument for organizing large quantities of information, or performing extremely complex symbolic operations beyond human capabilities within a normal lifespan, the computer is an invaluable adjunct to the brain, though not a substitute for it. Since the computer is limited to handling only so much experience as can be abstracted in symbolic or numerical form, it is incapable of dealing directly, as organisms must, with the steady influx of concrete, unprogrammable experience. With respect to such experience, the computer is necessarily always out of date. The computer's lack of other human dimensions is of course no handicap to it as a labor-saving device, whether in astronomy or bookkeeping: but such creativity as the computer may simulate is always in the first place a contribution of the minds that formulate the program.

The utter absence of innate subjective potentialities in the computer makes the contemporary art exhibition shown here (top), in all its pervasive blankness and artful nullity, an ideal representation of its missing dimensions. Those who are so fascinated by the computer's lifelike fêats—it plays chess! it writes 'poetry'!—that they would turn it into the voice of omniscience, betray how little understanding they have of either themselves, their mechanical-electronic agents, or the potentialities of life. A city of even three hundred thousand people, ten per cent of whom have access to regional or national libraries with as few as a million volumes, would actually have a total capacity for storing, transforming, integrating, and not least applying both symbolic information and concrete experience that no computer will ever rival.

7: Pentagons of Power

Power, like a desolating pestilence,
Pollutes whate'er it touches; and obedience,
Bane of all genius, virtue, freedom, truth,
Makes slaves of men, and, of the human frame,
A mechanized automaton.

Percy Bysshe Shelley

Though the power system can be adequately represented by abstractions, the concrete form of the Pentagon in Washington serves even better than its Soviet counterpart, the Kremlin, as a symbol of the absurdity of totalitarian absolutism: all the more because this particular megastructure combines a pathetically outmoded Renascence plan with the current wasteful and inefficient facilities for monotransportation by private car.

Not the least mark of Pentagonal authority is its imperviousness to information coming from outside sources and expressing human desires and preferences that have no status in the power complex. This in itself helps explain, perhaps, the increasingly desperate human reactions that the system is now provoking throughout the world. Never before has such a vast number of human beings, virtually the entire population of the planet, lived at the mercy of such a minuscule minority, whose specialized knowledge seems only to increase the magnitude of their incompetence in the very areas of their professional specialization.

Plate 6 from *The Pentagon of Power* (1970), "Computerdom."

Plate 7 from *The Pentagon of Power* (1970), "Pentagon of Power."

Mumford, of course, knew about all this[65]—but he kept a distance. In the end he preferred the Puritan aestheticism of the Museum of Modern Art to the theatrical visual rhetoric of the "Depression Style." For Mumford, "Machine Art" remains synonymous with the mechanical encyclopedia shown under that title earlier that same year 1934 at the MOMA. The new visual dramatists of "Technics and Civilization," Reginald Marsh, Diego Rivera, David Alfaro Siqueiros, remain totally absent.[66]

Art and Industry in Europe:
Herbert Read and Sigfried Giedion

Mumford, in short, considers modern abstract art a revelatory cultural byproduct of the industrial age, nothing more. Such a detached, cavalier perspective on the battlefields of modernism is unknown among the leading European authors on the subject. In a book, *Art and Industry,* that appeared in 1934—only a few months after Mumford's—the British art historian Herbert Read described the role of modern abstract art in the context of industry:

> It will occupy, in the future, a relationship to industrial design very similar to the relationship pure mathematics bear to the practical sciences.[67]

Read believes that not only industry should find a place among the themes that inspire works of art but that the abstract artist should find a place in industry. For ultimately, according to Read, it is the destiny of abstract art to enter industry as design.[68]

It is no coincidence that this idea so clearly recalls the program of the Bauhaus in Weimar and Dessau, where an active cross-pollination of avant-garde art, handicrafts, and industry formed the basis of the didactic program. In fact, after a long quotation of a paper by Walter Gropius, Read emphasizes that "I have no other desire in this book than to support and propagate the ideals thus expressed by Dr. Gropius."[69]

Even before that date, another art historian who had been a fervent supporter of the Bauhaus idea and a friend of Gropius had started to engage in his campaign toward an appreciation of the "new optic" in art: Sigfried Giedion. The "neue Optik" implies, Giedion argues, in a 1929 paper he gave at the inauguration of an exhibition on contemporary art at the Kunsthaus in Zürich, his home town, the

> . . . urge to abolish the borderlines that in the past used to separate science from science, painting from sculpture, art from technics, and to search for the common fundamental elements that are hidden behind them

and that will ultimately form the "totality" of modern man.[70] Here we find, of course, anticipated in a nutshell, the *raison d'être* of Giedion's later books *Space, Time and Architecture* (1941) and *MechanizationTakes Command* (1948).[71]

Both men, Read and Giedion, speak in defense of contemporary art and both would like to see it recognized as a "key to reality" (as Giedion put it) by engineers and those in charge of industrial design—as well as by society at large. Mumford, as we have seen, does not go quite so far.

Giedion and the "Hasty Reader"

Yet, as if Mumford and Giedion were working side by side in 1929—the year Mumford proclaimed that "we do not need verbal outlining so much as we need pictures"—Giedion wrote, in the preface to a small booklet on housing reform *(Befreites Wohnen):*

> It is quite all right if the author, for once, cannot use words in order to say what he has to say, but is forced to express himself visually. That is—in this case—to use lay-out and comparisons (in a positive sense) for clarification rather than comments. . . . In such a way, the lay-out of images will inevitably appear more concentrated and perhaps for the reader a more sizable survey will result.[72]

A few months previously, Giedion had directly addressed the "hasty reader" in his introductory remark to *Bauen in Frankreich* (1928):

Sigfried Giedion, illustration
in *Befreites Wohnen* (1929).

Wir verkleben unsere Häuser mit „monumentalen" Mauern,
trotzdem neue Konstruktionsmöglichkeiten uns alle Mittel in
die Hand geben, um in unsere Wohn- und Arbeitsräume Licht
und Luft einströmen zu lassen.

> The book was edited and laid out in such a way as to make it possible for the
> *hasty reader* to grasp the course of the evolution from the illustrations, the text
> serves to provide more detailed information, the notes give additional hints.[73]

With Mumford as a backdrop it may be easier to characterize Giedion's
"Handschrift" as a historiographer of the Modern Movement. First, concerning the "graphic style": Mumford works in the classical genre of the
illustrated history book. Perhaps deliberately so, or because he had no
other choice. He does, however, give a visual summary of the text in the
plates, and in doing so he varies themes he had been made familiar with
by Mendelsohn and the Museum of Modern Art.

Giedion transgresses the rule of the history-book genre by adopting an
imagery that unmistakably documents his forming part of the Modern
movement. He sees himself not just as a commentator of that movement
but as a member of it. In other words, with the help of typography, he
visualizes his claim, so emphatically stated in the introductory sentence of
Bauen in Frankreich, that "der Historiker steht in der Zeit, nicht über ihr"

Kurt Schwitters, "Mz. 313, Otto." Collage (1921). Courtesy of Marlborough Fine Art Ltd., London. Photo PCA 8710621.

("the historian stands in his time, not above it").[74] The point of reference, of course, is the Bauhaus, and so the book—which was designed with the help of Moholy—adopts the format of the Bauhaus-Bücher in much the same way as some among the illustrations of *Befreites Wohnen* imitate collages by Kurt Schwitters or handwritten notes from Paul Klee's *Pedagogical Sketchbook*.[75]

Finally, *Mechanization Takes Command* (1948), Giedion's most important book, was, although not explicitly so,[76] his reply to Mumford's *Technics and Civilization*. The subject is anonymous industrial history, mostly American, juxtaposed to (or rather enlighted by) the topical preoccupations of modern art. Again, the style of the book itself appears to have been influenced by techniques practiced by modern art: it resembles a collage made of close-up views of relevant episodes of cultural history juxtaposed to each other in an often more associational than historical way.

Mumford's book is essentially a book *on* modernism, written by a sympathetic but not uncritical observer; Giedion's (closer to *L'Esprit Nouveau*, given its author's activist involvement in the "cause"), represents an authentic document of the modern movement itself. Compared with the surrealist collage-quality and to the (perhaps only partly admitted) fun of *Mechanization Takes Command*, Mumford's *Technics and Civilization* has the moralizing aura of a school book. This time Giedion's models appear to have been above all the American mail-order catalog, *L'Esprit Nouveau* and the "romans illustrés" ("illustrated novels") of the surrealist painter Max Ernst. I have tried elsewhere to show to what degree Giedion's own view of the early development of mechanization was inspired by and in harmony with the ideas and works of artists like Le Corbusier, Fernand Léger, Max Ernst, and Marcel Duchamp.[77]

Technics and Civilization and *Mechanization Takes Command* Compared

In many ways, the works of Mumford and Giedion constitute a curious kind of symmetry. Mumford's interest in German "Philosophie der Technik,"[78] so important in *Technics and Civilization*, is rivaled—or possibly surpassed—by Giedion's European fascination with the "ready mades" of American patent furniture and industrial inventions. On the other hand, some of the most important blank spots in Giedion's books, e.g. his lack of interest in the Arts and Crafts tradition or his idiosyncratic rejection of streamlined design, are more than amply compensated for in Mumford's.

Behind all this we find two different views of art in the context of technological culture. As we can see from a letter sent by Giedion to Mumford in 1948, the two men were quite aware of the gap that separated them: "You point yourself to our different attitude towards contemporary art,"[79] Giedion says, and, concerning this matter (and indeed the topic of this article) he continues:

> Please do not misunderstand me. I am not hovering exclusively around aesthetic problems. I do not regret that I spent three months to note the story of the vacuum cleaner or other two months to give an account of the Yale-lock. But whenever I had to deal with complicated technical methods or the meaning for instance of nineteenth-century interiors, modern art proved a most valuable key to their understanding.

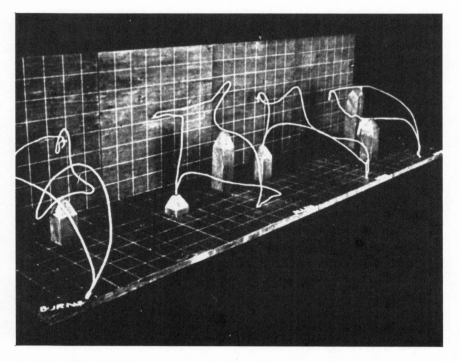

Frank B. Gilbreth, "Movement Translated into Wire Models," illustration from Sig-fried Giedion, *Mechanization Takes Command* (1948).

Many examples from *Mechanization Takes Command* come to mind where works of art are introduced as "eye-openers" for "complicated technical methods" or "the meaning of nineteenth-century interiors" such as when Giedion uses an illustration from Paul Klee's *Pedagogical Sketchbook* in order to explain Frank Gilbreth's motion studies, or Max Ernst's surrealist "romans illustrés" in order to cast an ironic light on the "Reign of the Upholsterer."[80]

Mumford on Giedion and vice versa:
The Problem with Le Corbusier . . .

In order to single out the areas of agreement and those of disagreement between the two men it is enough to consult their writings and, after 1948, their correspondence. Mumford was the first of them to show interest in the other (or at least first to acknowledge his interest publicly): he reviewed *Space, Time and Architecture* in 1941 as "a very exciting piece of work."[81]

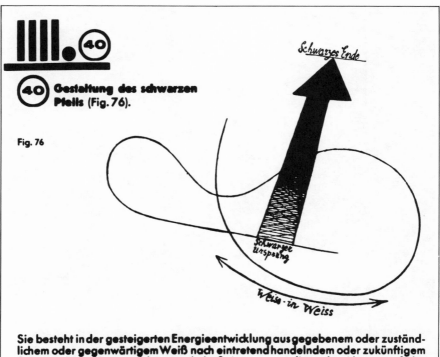

40 Gestaltung des schwarzen Pfeils (Fig. 76).

Fig. 76

Sie besteht in der gesteigerten Energieentwicklung aus gegebenem oder zuständlichem oder gegenwärtigem Weiß nach eintretend handelndem oder zukünftigem Schwarz hin. Warum nicht umgekehrt? Antwort: es liegt der Akzent auf der minoren Besonderheit gegenüber der majoren Allgemeinheit. Letztere wirkt zuständlich, gewohnt, erstere ungewohnt, handelnd. Und der Pfeil fliegt in der Richtung der Handlung.

Bei wohlgeordneter Gliederung in beide Charaktere manifestiert sich die Bewegungsrichtung so zwingend, daß das verfängliche Symbol wegfallen darf.

Das Weißgegebene, das viel- und sattgesehene Weiß, wird als ein Gewohntes vom Auge mit wenig Akklamation aufgenommen; auf das gegensätzlich Besondere der eintretenden Handlung hin aber steigert sich die Lebendigkeit des Blickes bis zum Gipfel oder zum Ende dieser Handlung.

Dieses außerordentliche Anwachsen von Energie (im produktiven Sinne) oder von Energiekost (im rezeptiven Sinne) ist zwingend in bezug auf die Bewegungsrichtung.

Paul Klee, "Gestaltung des Schwarzen Pfeils" ("Design of the Black Arrow"), from *Pädagogisches Skizzenbuch* (1925). The illustration is juxtaposed by Giedion to Gilbreth's wire models in *Mechanization Takes Command* (1948).

On *Mechanization Takes Command* he wrote a few years later, with his characteristic generosity:

> . . .[this book] should cause American architectural scholars again to blush, for their lack of curiosity and zeal has once more forced this European critic to explore a rich store of material that lay at their feet, waiting for a prospector to stub his toe on it. . . . With great pertinacy Giedion has salvaged and appraised some extraordinarily interesting material.[82]

Perhaps it was the pathetic last chapter "Man in Equipoise" that broke the ice. Here Giedion makes his plea in favor of an organic equilibrium between technics and nature, machine and life. Mumford wrote: "From my standpoint, these concluding observations are pure gold."

Furthermore, at about the same time Mumford discovered Giedion as an unexpected ally in his own defense of monumentality and symbolism in architecture. Giedion's famous "9 Points on Monumentality" brought "new winds" to architectural criticism, "winds" that, as Mumford put it, might even invest "old New York." He went on, however, riding his horse against Le Corbusier's machine idolatry once again and finally characterized his Swiss colleague with journalistic irreverence as ". . . the one-time leader of the mechanistic rigorists, [who] has turned into the standard-bearer of monumentality and the symbolic."[83] This irony prompted a rather humorless reaction on Giedion's part. In a letter sent to Philip Johnson (for Johnson had been the one who had forwarded the *corpus delicti* from the *New Yorker* to Zurich), Giedion, apparently alarmed by Mumford's unfriendly tone, spoke up once again in Le Corbusier's defense against what appeared to him an unqualified diatribe against the master's alleged "machine style." Giedion knew what was at stake: nothing less than Le Corbusier's chances as the architect of the United Nations Headquarters, and so he preached that Corbusier's famous phrase "the house is a machine for living in" can be understood only in context and should not be used as a slogan, "as the reactionaries, or Mr. Robert Moses or even the Nazis did. . . ."[84]

. . . and Mendelsohn

Another worm in the bittersweet apple of their friendship was their equally divergent evaluation of Erich Mendelsohn, a matter of concern not only for Giedion but perhaps even more so for his friend Gropius. In a letter to Giedion, Gropius pays his tribute to Mumford's "moral straightness," yet summarizes: "All in all, he is an old-fashioned conservative, and he has no eye for art and architecture." Gropius continues, referring to a recent book review by Mumford on Giedion's *Space, Time and Architecture* : "His comparison of Mendelsohn's doodles with Ronchamp gives him away."[85]

Le Corbusier, Notre-Dame du Haut at Ronchamp, France (1955). South façade, from *Le Corbusier. L'atelier de la recherche patience.*

Mumford's *faux pas* was to have been struck by the formal analogies between Le Corbusier's chapel Notre-Dame du Haut at Ronchamp (1955) on the one hand and Erich Mendelsohn's expressionist sketches of 1915–20 on the other, and to have suggested that the former might owe some of its inspiration to the latter. He was, incidentally, not alone in explaining the neo-archaic "free style" of certain architects in the late 1950s and early 1960s in terms of a revival of architectural expressionism: Just a few years later, in 1965, Nikolaus Pevsner quoted Finsterlin's utopian drawings of 1919 as possible sources for Jörn Utzon's Sydney Opera House.[86]

Yet in the CIAM camp, of which Gropius and Giedion were the surviving veterans (after Le Corbusier's death in 1965), architectural expressionism was taboo and Mendelsohn even more so; therefore Mumford's comparison of Mendelsohn's expressionist fantasies with Ronchamp, one of the icons of the postwar avant-garde, could be perceived by Gropius only as an insult to the Olympian "New Tradition" of modern architecture, as it had been codified by Giedion.

Mendelsohn's name, as one knows, does not appear in Giedion's book. To the degree that *Space, Time and Architecture* was designed as an apologia for Gropius's work and that of the Bauhaus, architectural expressionism inevitably appeared as a mere incident on the fringes of the "New Tradition":

Erich Mendelsohn project sketches for a garden pavilion (1920).

> Faustean outbursts against an inimical world and the cries of outraged humanity cannot create new levels of achievement. They remain transitory facts—however moving they may be—and not constituent ones.

And Giedion continues with a poorly veiled side remark on the work of both Bruno Taut and Erich Mendelsohn:

> The expressionist influence could not perform any service for architecture. Nevertheless it touched almost every German worker in the arts. Men who were later to do grimly serious work in housing developments abandoned themselves to a romantic mysticism, dreamed of fairy castles to stand on the peak of Monte Rosa.

He goes on (knowing that the initiated will inevitably spot Mendelsohn's Einstein tower in Potsdam, 1922, as the victim of the attack): "Others built concrete towers as flaccid as jellyfish."[87]

Technics and "Class Struggle"

Yet the two crucial issues at stake are Mumford's and Giedion's utterly differing sensibilities for the socio-economic interests at work behind the looks of buildings and settlements, past and present, and their respective views of modern art. Needless to say, the two attitudes are complementary. Perspicacity with one eye appears almost fatally to imply shortsightedness in the other. As a historian of architecture and urban design, Mumford never abandoned the focus—and the moral habitus—of the social critic. A medieval or baroque city or an industrial landscape of the nineteenth century is never merely a formal achievement in his eyes, but first of all a mirror of social life and an instrument of class struggle.

Probably Mumford would have approved of the panel that had been prepared in 1935 by Rudolf Steiger, Wilhelm Hess, and Georg Schmidt, three
members of the Swiss CIAM group, showing the historical evolution of the
urban environment as a function of social and economic forces. His own
book, *The City in History,* follows that line. We know that Gropius, in turn,
disapproved of the presentation because of its "materialistic base" which
he thought to be "politically dangerous."[88]

Even the picture of an ocean liner in *Technics and Civilization* offers a
pretext for Mumford to comment on the ubiquitous drama of class struggle. Mumford says (in the caption), after having paid tribute to the liner's
"cleanness and strength":

> In its inner arrangements, with the luxury and space of the first class contrast-
> ing with the cramped quarters . . . of the third class, [it] remains a diagram-
> matic picture of the paleotechnic class struggle.

Vladimir Majakowsky had put it in somewhat cruder terms (in "My Discovery of America," 1925): "The first class vomits where it pleases, the
second upon the third, and the third upon itself."[89]

Class struggle or even a somewhat more than merely occasional and
paternalizing "social concern" is absent from both *Space, Time and Architecture* and *Mechanization Takes Command,* and Mumford did not fail to note
it, as when he wrote (in his review of the former book):

> The weakest part of Giedion's book is his handling of modern city develop-
> ment, particularly his failure to understand the historic significance of the
> future importance of Ebenezer Howard's conception of the garden city.[90]

In fact, where Giedion tends to surrender to his awe for bold technological
innovation and radical planning campaigns, Mumford lets the social historian speak, for example, in the context of baroque urban history. Where
Giedion analyzes the spatial implications of perspective (in *Space, Time and
Architecture*), Mumford focuses on the social costs of technocratic planning
strategies (in *The City in History*). And as far as the modern highway is concerned, Giedion wrote, next to a picture of the Henry Hudson Parkway in
New York:

> Riding up and down the long sweeping grades produces an exhilarating dual
> feeling, one of being connected with the soil and yet of hovering just above
> it, a feeling which is nothing else so much as sliding swiftly on skis through
> untouched snow down the sides of high mountains.[91]

For him, this experience, while recalling the slopes of the Swiss Alps, was
nothing less than the alleged "space-time conception" of modern physics
and of cubism translated into real life: America seen as enacted modernity.
Mumford, in turn, more and more detached from the aesthetic tempta-

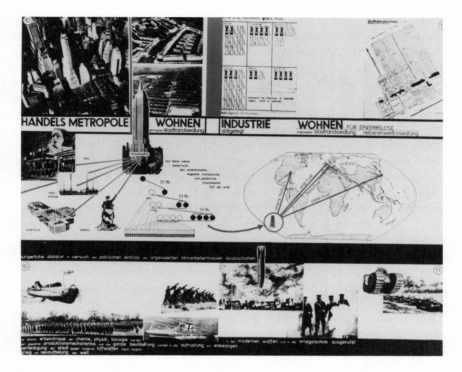

Rudolf Steiger, Wilhelm Hess, Georg Schmidt: Graphic representation of the commercial metropolis. Detail from a panel prepared for the CIAM congress of 1934. Courtesy of Martin Steinmann, *CIAM 1929–39*.

tions of the Machine Age (but perhaps not entirely from those of his own literary habitus), insisted that the exhilarating drive along the highway might end in an ecologic catastrophe.[92]

Cultural History as Manipulation of Images

The symbiosis of words and images in books can follow a wide range of different rules, depending on the kind of message to be conveyed. Among the classical models are the art exhibition, the mail-order catalogue, the illustrated newspaper, or the academic lecture with slides (which is itself a re-interpretation of those older genres). We know not enough about the ways in which the techniques of reproduction and manipulation of images have influenced the didactic practices in art history, if not the art historical discourse as such.[93] The same seems to be true in other fields engaged in the analysis of the visual environment, including, of course, sociology and architectural theory.[94]

Perhaps an analysis of iconographic "styles"[95] in books would have to begin with an analysis of the strategies of comparison preferred by this or that author. The range of possibilities includes "genetic" or "differential" comparisons of very similar objects, as used in art history ever since Heinrich Wölfflin (Giedion's master), as well as "synthetic" comparisons of substantially dissimilar objects.[96] Both Mumford's and Giedion's comparisons (but we should never forget that both show illustrations not for comparative purposes alone) are more often than not about analogies: analogies of form, style, or structure identified in substantially and genetically unrelated objects. The aim, in those cases, is to propose a "synthetic" vision that will embrace both parts of the pair (or all parts of the sequence) and suggest a unifying concept. The more drastically different the two subjects selected for comparison—e.g. an art gallery next to the Pentagon—the more their unexpected similarity will be striking; in other cases—e.g. Brooklyn Bridge juxtaposed to a screw-cutting lathe—the similarity may have merely the effect of ornamental repetition.

Be that as it may, not only the images as such carry distinct messages in Mumford's books (or, for that matter, in Le Corbusier's or Giedion's); the same is true with the ways the images are put together. The sequential litany of images that look alike, despite the fact that they show objects differing in nature and function implies a rhetoric mode that is narrative, not dialectic. Such is frequently the case with Mumford. As a result, the categorical differences—e.g. between works of art and objects of daily use—tend to be neutralized, as when he juxtaposes the nautilus shell and the hydroturbine, and Pier Luigi Nervi's famous stadium in Florence and Duchamp-Villon's "Horse" of 1914; the concrete trusses of Nervi's structure appear to be an ornamental variation of the nautilus shell and its membranes, as they are at the top of the same page (in the book's first version[97]). And Duchamp-Villon's "Horse" is juxtaposed to the hydroturbine in a way that in the end reduces its aesthetic message to a simple mimetic variation on the theme of the turbine.

Mumford is in general eager to juxtapose images that "look alike": whenever possible he combines images that contain striking formal analogies, as when he compares a sail-wagon of 1598 to a foot-driven bicycle of 1817 (plate I, "Anticipations of Speed") or Gislebertus's wonderful Eve, from one of the portals of the cathedral at Autun, with a famous print from Dürer's treatise on perspective (plate II, "Perspectives"). In fact, any among the plates could make the point: Why would Mumford choose the image of a screw-cutting lathe to go along with Brooklyn Bridge if not because it looks, the way it is cut, like a miniature bridge itself? Most striking perhaps: "Neotechnic Automation" placed next to "Airplane Shapes," so that the "Machine Age" itself seems to flow across the page.[98]

In such a way we see at work the social scientist whose science proceeds by classifications based on analogies and similarities found among phenomena that are often distant in time and space. Yet at the same time this social scientist is also a writer and an artist. For the writer, it is achieving

New York, West Side development. Plate from Sigfried Giedion, *Space, Time and Architecture* (1941).

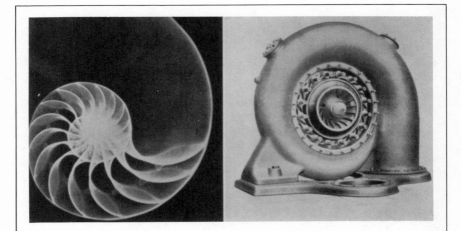

XII. NATURE AND THE MACHINE

1: Roentgen photograph of Nautilus by J. B. Polak. Nature's use of the spiral in construction. The x-ray, like the microscope, reveals a new esthetic world. (*Courtesy of Wendingen*)

2: Section of modern hydro-turbine: spiral form dictated by mechanical necessity. Geometrical forms, simple and complex, are orchestrated in machine design.

3: Grandstand of new stadium in Florence: Pier Luigi Nervi, architect. Engineering in which imagination and necessity are harmoniously composed.

4: R. Duchamp-Villon's interpretation of the organic form of a horse in terms of the machine. (*Courtesy of Walter Pach*)

Place XII from *Technics and Civilization*, "Nature and the Machine."

XI. AIRPLANE SHAPES

1: Modern airplane, designed to decrease wind-resistance and raise lifting power, on lines suggested by study of birds and fish. Since 1920 the development of scientific knowledge and technical design have gone on steadily here; and through the use of new alloys like duralumin both lightness and strength have been achieved. The airplane has set the pace for refined and exact engineering.

(*Photograph by Ewing Galloway*)

2: Perhaps the most radical impulse to correct motor car design came from Glenn Curtiss, the airplane designer, when he ran an ordinary closed car backward and bettered its performance. The best design so far seems to be that of the Dymaxion Car, by Buckminster Fuller and Starling Burgess which has greatly improved speed and comfort without extra horsepower.

(*Photograph by F. S. Lincoln*)

3: The stream-lined train, designed but rejected as early as 1874, now is realized in 1934, thanks to the competition and the lesson of the airplane.

(*Courtesy of the Union Pacific System*)

4: So-called Rail Zeppelin. Experimental and possibly somewhat romantic attempt to adapt to surface transportation the advantages of airplane and dirigible. A still more radical approach to the problem of fast land-transportation is that now under experiment in Soviet Russia, the "sphero-train" invented by a your soviet engineer, M. I. Yarmolchuk. T latter runs on large motorized ball-bearings. The airplane has freed the inventor from the stereotypes of wheel-locomotion.

Plate XI from *Technics and Civilization,* "Airplane Shapes."

the easy, unifying flow of sentences and words that is the problem, and so Mumford's visual discourse too is almost obsessed with finding ways of homogenizing pieces of historical evidence often extremely different in nature and significance. The homogeneity of the motifs and the expressive modes used within pairs of comparison represent Mumford's particular way of "streamlining" historical evidence toward what may be called a visual epic of the machine age.

This "view" of the machine expresses extremely well the deeper concerns of the book as we find them signaled in the titles of its various chapters. More suggestively even than many words, these plates, if put in the more general context of the iconography of the Machine Age, symbolize what Mumford means by "The Esthetic Experience of the Machine" and by "The Dissolution of the 'Machine'"; they display "The Elements of Social Energetics" and anticipate, as it were, Mumford's utopia of a "Dynamic equilibrium."[99]

PART III

VALUES, PERSONALITY, AND COMMUNITY

Beginning with *Technics and Civilization,* Mumford increasingly stressed the influence of values upon technology. His attention to values stemmed in part from the experience of having written earlier about the history of ideas, architecture, and literature. Charles Molesworth, whose essay is first in this section, finds from his reading of *The Story of Utopias* (1922), *Sticks and Stones* (1924), *The Golden Day* (1926), *Herman Melville* (1929), and *The Brown Decades* (1931) that Mumford was an axiologist in his approach to literature and architecture, even before he took this stance toward technology. Molesworth defines an axiologist as a reflective and rational student of the basis, nature, meaning, and practical application of values who seeks, through the study of history, to recover desirable values lost over time. In *Melville,* an exploration of values in a tragic setting, Mumford portrays his protagonist as struggling in a culture with values inimicable to his own. This tension and interplay between the inner person and outer circumstances contribute, Mumford believes, to the reinforcement and formation of values. Melville and other tragic figures have struggled, Mumford concludes, to displace random external powers in the universe by values, order, and art. Yet the struggle between the individual and fate is an uneven and tragic one. So, to mature is to become aware of one's limitations, to become more human, not more powerful. With his highly idealized Judeo-Christian goals and critical stance toward technology, Mumford, too, existed in tension with the values common to his time. There had been other times and places, however, like antebellum New England, when the interplay between the inner man of high ideals and the environment was harmonious and the fruit rich, at the cost, one must assume, of the loss of a sense of tragedy. In *The Golden Day,* his appreciation of the balanced, organic culture of antebellum New England, Mumford finds values, forms, and symbols that need to be reclaimed. Having been emptied of their content during the venal Gilded Age of late nineteenth-century America, they remained latent in the twentieth century and ripe for recovery. For Mumford, the golden days of Ralph Waldo Emerson, Henry Thoreau, Walt Whitman, and Nathaniel Hawthorne provided a vision of a utopia rich with values to be recovered. He takes care, however, to warn that we cannot indiscriminately pillage the past, as Isabella Gardner, a prominent Boston collector of art, did, nor can we ignore the need to transform and adapt past values for our own times, as the Harvard philosopher George Santayana tended to do.

In *Sticks and Stones*, a study of American architecture and civilization, Mumford the historian and axiologist offers a historical survey and an apocalyptic diagnosis of our ills. Always the transdisciplinary generalist looking for connections and analogies, he applies his concept of an inner-outer tension to architecture as well as to the human personality. A good building, he opines, is an envelope, the outer effect of which is rhythmically related to the inner structure. The values, inner necessities, and desires of a society should also shape, and be shaped by, that society's outer, or architectural, environment.

In his essay on Mumford as architectural critic, Lawrence Vale also finds Mumford the axiologist arguing that values shape culture and, furthermore, that architecture is a prime constituent of culture. Mumford sees architecture and technology both as congealed culture and as culture-shaping. Architecture manifests for him the distinctive characteristics of a community located at a particular time in a particular place. Vale uses Mumford's reaction, as revealed in a series of essays on the evolving design for the United Nations headquarters in New York, as a means of sampling his attitude toward values and architecture. Mumford wants the UN buildings to symbolize urban renewal and to point the way to world harmony. He desires the headquarters, wherever located, to be as sacred a space for a secular age as the Vatican City had been for a religious one. When a small area of only seventeen acres, instead of the 1000–3000 acres that he had originally envisaged, was selected in New York and when the American skyscraper form was proposed instead of a transcendent one, he lamented the decisions and interpreted the site and the design as expressions of the values only of Western industrial society, especially of New York, and not expressive of the universal and supranational values that he had envisioned for the United Nations.

In his criticism of the headquarters, Mumford brings to bear the same criteria he did in his evaluations of technology. He asks whether the design is organic and whether it addresses specific human needs. Because the thirty-nine-story building designed to house the UN secretariat was a skyscraper, it failed ipso facto for Mumford, who considers these cathedrals of commerce sterile clichés expressive, at best, of technical virtuosity. Since the secretariat building and the conference and General Assembly buildings that made up the UN headquarters complex are, in his opinion, expressive in their slick modernity of American values, they reinforce the values of nationalism rather than those of universal harmony. In calling for a sacred place comparable in size and siting to Vatican City and as beloved a symbol as the Statue of Liberty, Mumford actually seems to want "to eliminate . . . much of New York" (Vale, 272, 265). Vale believes that Mumford was contradicting his own sensitive concern for the past in wanting to clear the Manhattan site of existing buildings, some slum, but others undoubtedly representative of a viable culture. Mumford's ambiguity also shows on the one hand in his wanting the new headquarters buildings to be a timeless universal symbol and his insistence elsewhere in his writings that architecture should arise organically out of time and place. He also faults Mumford for assuming that others read the same values into the skyscraper as he. For many non-Western delegates, the skyscraper modernity of the UN symbolized in the late 1940s an international culture to which they aspired.

By 1930 Mumford, as we have noted, had identified not only the city, the region, and the machine as his foci of interest, but the personality and the community as well. He spoke truly when he referred to his concern with the human condition. As we would expect, Mumford reflected upon personality and community in a contextual way by situating both in a world increasingly shaped by technology. Casey Blake, following Mumford along this path, considers the stimulation that Mumford's thoughts about personality and community might provide for today's intellectuals who share his earlier concern that both are being eroded and that life insurgent is being suppressed by the imperatives of production embodied in the megamachine. Mumford's views on personality and community varied as he grew older and lived through the Great Depression, war, and the steady growth of large technological systems. Writing books on cultural history and criticism, like *The Golden Day,* enriched his understanding of evolving culture with its forms and symbolic expressions, and deepened his insights into personality and community. Influenced by a circle of cultural critics associated with the journal, *The Seven Arts,* including Van Wyck Brooks, Waldo Frank, and Randolph Bourne, Mumford realized, as Moleworth has also observed, that personality "was the realization of the self in tension—or in dialogue—with its environment" (Blake, 286). For him the environment was material—natural, technological, and architectural—and social (community). Mumford soon found himself in debate with other philosophic minds of his era over the nature of the tension between personality and environment.

His characteristic lack of interest in politics surfaced in this debate. Philosopher John Dewey in his advocacy of political action differed from Mumford, who did not emphasize political action as a way of contributing to positive community and individual development. Mumford depended, Blake reminds us, on the family, the grange, the church, the theater, and the trade union to fashion community. By the time he was finishing *Technics and Civilization,* Mumford believed that neotechnic, as contrasted with paleotechnic, institutions and values could nurture personality and community. Regionalism and organicism made possible by the new technology and science could counter the personality-suppressing megalopolis and the mechanistic aura of the paleotechnic era. Mumford had distanced himself from the political progressives and liberals of the day for, anticipating the French *Annalistes,* he was persuaded that regional and technological developments were the important, deep-running currents of change and that politics was only a surface manifestation. Blake believes that Mumford's writing, whether in the 1920s, 1930s, or the 1970s, retained a particular aversion to accepting responsibilities arising from the recognition that a crisis of culture, personality, and community is a crisis of politics as well.

Mumford's disdain for politics included American political liberalism and especially the pragmatism he associated with it. As early as publication of *The Golden Day,* he had attacked the pragmatism of American psychologist and philosopher William James as well as Dewey's particular utilitarian, instrumentalist version of pragmatism. (In his essay in this volume, Robert Westbrook rejects Mumford's interpretation of Dewey's position as utilitarian.) Mumford argues that the pragmatism undergirding American political liberalism deeply corrupted it. The failure, in Mumford's opinion, of American liberals to foresee and stand against rising fascism in the 1930s could be attributed to the materialism and arid values of pragmatism. Mumford's anti-pragmatism can be associated with his negative view of the era of paleotechnic technology. James's pragmatism was, he felt, an outgrowth of America's Gilded Age when the goods life was confused with the good life, when the eotechnic balance of golden day New England had been destroyed by the great slash of the Civil War, and when industrial exploitation and mammon reigned.

Westbrook in his exploration of the Mumford-Dewey relationship tells us that Mumford accused Dewey of making a pragmatic acquiescence to American society's crude utilitarianism and of propounding it in a writing style as depressing as a subway ride. Dewey's particular brand of pragmatism, Mumford says, bears the marks of its birth amid the shapelessness, the harsh smug utilitarianism of Chicago, the epitome of the paleotechnic city. In a haughty style that must have grated on Dewey, Mumford adds that Dewey's complacent philosophy encourages the values of a George Babbitt, who practiced "so assiduously the mechanistic ritual of American life" and who acted "as if a life spent in the pursuit of . . . [bathroom fixtures and automobile accessories] was a noble and liberal one" (Westbrook, 304). Westbrook, on the other hand, finds Dewey free not only of utilitarianism but also of many of the other corruptions of liberalism which Mumford attributes to him.

Dewey did not deny that he found America shaped by science and technology, and his instrumentalism reflects these influences, but he found Mumford and some other critics simplistic for assuming that he took instruments as ends. Science and technology, as Mumford himself argued in his periods of neotechnic enthusiasm, could be means to the end of the good life and the good society. Dewey believed that science and technology used by a politically active and democratic community could make possible the full realization by each member of his or her individual capacities and powers. Mumford may not have taken Dewey's point, however, because Mumford's conception of political democracy, according to Westbrook, was not profound and tended to an over-appreciation of the role of elites. As their disagreements erupted into public debate, Mumford caricatured Dewey as a technological enthusiast. As early as 1930 he called Dewey and the historian Charles Beard the "New Mechanists" who made a "fetich of the machine." Whatever their differences—and Westbrook believes they were exaggerated by both men—both Mumford and Dewey felt responsibility as public intellectuals to air their differences in a forum where thought led to action and where knowledge was used "as a resource for cultural criticism and social reconstruction" (Westbrook, 321).

Mumford and Dewey in the 1930s were leading non-Marxist, liberal or leftish intellectuals, but Mumford dissociated himself not only from Dewey but others whom he judged to be technological enthusiasts or utilitarians, such as Beard, Thurman Arnold, Adolph

Berle, Bruce Bliven, Stuart Chase, Paul Douglas, Freda Kirchway, Max Lerner, Robert Lynd, Gardiner Means, George Soule, and Rexford Tugwell. This left him a lonely figure among the public intellectuals. Mumford had an uncanny ability—or a distorting bias—that brought him to see in all around him an uncritical commitment to technical rationality and economic efficiency and a lingering paleotechnic cast of mind. Richard Fox is his essay points out that Mumford faults pragmatic liberalism for too lofty an estimate of human nature, too "mechanical" a view of social transactions, and too high an evaluation of the powers of scientific reason.

Taking a tack different from Westbrook's, Fox finds Mumford's rejection of pragmatism, utilitarianism, and liberalism a pivotal contribution, along with those of Joseph Wood Krutch and Walter Lippmann, to the redirection of the American mind away from progressive optimism and liberal utilitarianism toward a sense of tragedy and responsibility in the face of social evil. Krutch, Lippmann, and the mature Mumford realized that there are decided limits to human happiness, neotechnic technology notwithstanding. Experienced and wise, they felt the constraints on the human condition that dampen youthful aspirations. Fox characterizes Mumford before World War II as walking the narrow line between cultural pessimism, or the awareness of evil, as found in his biography *Herman Melville* (1929), and the tempered neotechnic aspirations of *Technics and Civilization.*

Despite this ambivalence, Mumford never questions, as he declared in a book title, that *Men Must Act* (1939), that they must take responsibility in the field of action left open by the soft determinism of a technological world. Through action they must nurture personality and community. Yet, because of his apolitical nature, Mumford feels that the action men and women should take must not be only political. His "action" consists of that of many other intellectuals—a search for understanding, the taking of new attitudes, and the accepting of new values. He believes that the creation of a work of art, including the literary, is the action of the artist; that a work, such as *Melville,* transcends the limits and constraints of an inhospitable social environment and points the way to new attitudes and values. Artists—and Mumford counts himself among them—create the symbols and forms of culture. As he reiterates in numerous essays, culture can be a matrix for action. Even in times of widespread social disintegration, creative men and women can renew art and, therefore, culture. For Mumford, symbols and forms can tranform a formless society, or aggregate of technology, institutions, groups, and individuals, into a holistic community, and a mechanistic technology into an organicist one.

On the role of political action, Mumford's philosophy, Fox informs us, clashed with Reinhold Niebuhr's, as it had earlier with Dewey's. In reviewing *Technics and Civilization,* Niebuhr, a highly influential American theologian and spokesman for the tragic liberals, argued that Mumford's distinction between "the coal and iron period" and the "electricity-and-alloy complex" was adequate history of technology, but that he found wanting Mumford's scheme of periodization with its soft determinism and assumptions about progress. Niebuhr believed that neotechnic technology would not bring the lessening of class divisions or relieve the dehumanizing effects of paleotechnic techology, as Mumford suggests. Science, for which Mumford expressed his admiration in *Technics and Civilization,* would enrich our store of useful symbols, but at the same time, Niebuhr concluded, was liable to destroy essential myths and substitute naïve credulity for a majestic faith. Niebuhr seems to have read the opening sections of *Technics and Civilization* more closely than the less sanguine chapters which followed.

Niebuhr and Mumford grew closer intellectually as each realized he had much to learn from the other about the tragic sense and about responsibility. Niebuhr's *Moral Man and Immoral Society* (1932) served to caution Mumford that even if the individual could transcend circumstances, a community of individuals knit by reason, love, and good will was also needed to act co-operatively and forcibly in a world full of social struggle. Mumford calls Niebuhr's attention to the force of technology, to *the machine,* and to a technological momentum that tends to determine the course of history. He tempers Niebuhr's sense of original sin and consequent evil with a faith that progress can become real, once enlightened men and women of life-fulfilling values that Mumford associates with love, playful and loving sex, art, and creativity begin to use technology as a tool instead of passively accepting it. Each reinforced the other's maturing belief that human history was an arena in which humans must struggle to fulfill their apsirations, not a Whiggish movement driven by new technology or other metahistorical forces toward personal and communal fulfillment. In *Beyond Tragedy* (1937), Niebuhr wrote that "the ultimate problem for Christians was that they were called to act in the world despite the certainty that in acting they would sin" (Fox, 330). Mumford acknowledged in his *Faith for Living* (1940) and *The Condition of Man* (1944) his debt to Niebuhr for this insight.

Inner and Outer:
The Axiology of Lewis Mumford

CHARLES MOLESWORTH

Urbanologist as a term applied to him clearly made Lewis Mumford unhappy, but other labels, such as sociologist, ecologist, architectural historian, generalist, or cultural critic, are also too narrow or too bland to convey accurately the nature of his project. I suggest a term to describe Mumford that I think is both accurate and yet fresh enough to distinguish the special purpose behind most if not all of his writing. Mumford is an axiologist. Axiology, the study of values, comes from a Greek root meaning "worth." Close in sound and also in meaning to axiom and axiomatic, it can therefore serve to alert us to how Mumford was concerned with fundamental values, those beliefs and experiential gists often hidden beneath and inside our most ordinary actions and thoughts. That axiology has not yet become an academic discipline alone makes it attractive as a category for Mumford's work; it also has the requisite air of Greek reflectiveness and rational inquiry that are crucial in all that Mumford accomplished and desired. Mumford is an axiologist rather than a moralist, I argue, because he wants us not only to live better lives but to understand why and how such lives may come to be led. But he is not an axiologist in the narrow sense of a disinterested student of values. He is an axiologist with a clear social purpose: he wants to make available to society a better and fuller set of harmoniously integrated values.

Axiology itself has many aspects, ranging from the familiar to the recondite. In its simplest form it establishes fundamental categories of good and evil, usually by defining values in basic terms. In the Western European tradition this means that good is often equated with love and growth, while evil is seen as privation or destruction. Axiologists also study the ways value is represented in aesthetic and conceptual schemes: for example, good in a moral or spiritual sense is frequently associated with height in spatial terms. Furthermore, the historical transformation of value would be of considerable interest to axiologists. In capitalism, for instance, the labor theory of value obviously offers a fundamental challenge to those earlier, feudalistic theories that posit land or inheritance as chief sources of social or economic value. In terms of rationalistic ethics, axiologists might try to establish values that cut across fields and situations. Ethical systems that identify contractualism as the source of the ethically good will likely establish the value of responsibility and temperance over such virtues as inventiveness or assertiveness. Axiology, then, deals with important issues in such areas as philosophy, aesthetics, economics, and ethics, and it tries to establish the means and measures by which various fields of endeavor and inquiry are able to establish and maintain claims about value. Axiologists might be interested, as well, in an activist sense, with how values could be changed, in both the social and individual realms.

Those who try to change values in society and the individual fall into three rough groupings. The first are those who simply proclaim the immediate need or desirability of new values. At worst these are hucksters, at best moralists-in-advance who must wait for other (often unpredictable) changes that are inextricably tied up with new values to take place. In either case, such moral schemes are often just that, schemes that try to manipulate opinion and behavior. The second group asks for new but long-term changes, and these people realize they must wait to see if history is on their side. Here those who proclaimed the virtues of individual inventiveness and personal interests are good examples, as they doubtlessly won out in the long-range cultural revolution that accompanied the establishment of the capitalist order during the last three and a half centuries in Western Europe. Such reformers can play the role of prophets without honor, and their contributions are buried not in the dusty oblivion of history but, rather, are lost in the delineations of the larger patterns of social development.

The third type of moralist—of whom Mumford is clearly a sterling example—asks that certain important values latent in the society be reclaimed and recharged. While the values are latent, their reclamation is considered urgent. At their worst such people can appear smugly aloof from current conditions, and even at their best they face a difficult challenge. Often the first response to this sort of moral appeal is to argue that if such values are not fully operative, then that is so for a reason, namely, that such values are no longer fully applicable. On the other hand, people may frequently claim that if key values are nevertheless latent, perhaps they are best so, since "bedrock" or "consensus" values often thrive only if they are *not* debated or discussed. Again, in either case the third sort of moral clarion is likely to fall on deaf, or at least preoccupied, ears. This particular situation makes Mumford's career take the course it does, from fully exemplified and historically embedded moral analysis to a more and more directly moral*istic* mode.

In what follows I would like to explore the first five books Mumford wrote, to see what sort of moral, or axiological, analysis and prognosis they contain. I think this will show that his moral vision was grounded in a thorough analysis not only of his own historical moment but of a larger historical framework as he understood it. Mumford found his values exactly where he found the sources of the moral malaise: in American society as it was unfolding in the twentieth century. As both the source of the problem and the source of the answer, America became for him the paradoxical center of his moral search. The social values over which American society has debated, and which activated and agonized its representative men and women, have occupied Mumford throughout his career. As he once said, the existence of human society is a surer fact of experience than the existence of Betelgeuse, and it is with the values of society that Mumford begins his work.

But first I want to offer a brief passage from Mumford's *Works and Days* (1979) as the core to all of his arguments about value. Significantly, the passage is about architecture:

> . . . a building, unlike sculpture, is not so much a plastic mass as an envelope: the outer effect is rhythmically related and in part determined by the inner structure: indeed, the resolution of that double relationship is the very key to a positive work of architecture.[1]

As for buildings, so also for values. The inner dimension of experience is where values are usually located, in some subjective realm of emotive truth or belief. But for Mumford the external, outer world remains equally necessary in formulating, testing, and understanding values. The simple but difficult truth stands behind Mumford's sense that a civilization's architecture is the truest key to its value.[2] But it is also the axiom behind the obverse of this formulation: only if one understands the inner necessities and desires that a civilization or society chooses for itself can its architecture be comprehended. The poised interrelation between inner and outer values became for Mumford the resolving paradox that underlay not only his sense of "positive" architecture but all of his searches for life's central worth.

Mumford begins his search for values simultaneously at the origin of Western thought and in the never-never land of its deepest desire, namely, Plato's ideal republic, the first utopia. But the book is called *The Story of Utopias*,[3] and the plural clearly shows how Mumford was committed in his analysis to historical schemes. History is to ideas as the setting is to architecture, for Mumford, as a good organicist, always understood the inter-definitional quality of objects and fields. By the end of the book Mumford is able to sketch out three features common to the best-known utopias. These are the belief that the land and the incremental values resulting from its development belong to all members of the community. The second is that work is a common, though diverse, function to be shared by all citizens. Third, the human population is (and should be) controllable, in both number and quality; in other words, unlimited growth is irrational and destructive. I believe these are the three necessary beliefs in what I call the tradition of liberal socialism, and they formed the essential part of

Mumford's thought from the early 1920s until his fierce denunciation of the Vietnam War in 1965. *The Story of Utopias* was his first book, but it can also be read as the first chapter in a much longer study.

Mumford's first book is not only remarkably intelligent for so young an author, but it contains the major themes of all his later work as well as subjects and arguments that are if anything even more timely and urgent today than they were sixty-five years ago. The book begins with two key structural moves: it sets out the importance of what Mumford calls the "idolum," the inner world of ideas and beliefs by which we negotiate and understand our experience of ourselves and the external world. Today we call this ideology, and despite the notorious difficulty in defining it, it remains an essential element in all serious analysis. The second move is to divide all utopias into two classes, the utopia of escape and the utopia of reconstruction. This division is useful for Mumford, if only rhetorically, but it's a division that breaks down in the historical schematizing, and as I hope to show, is not fully applied to the later and more urgently argued parts of the book. This breakdown and incomplete application of his terms are, however, themselves further clues to the way Mumford developed as a thinker and axiologist.

Choosing between the utopias of escape and reconstruction, Mumford might well have favored the latter, as much of his later work shows. But the first sort of utopia, related to a desire for escape, might well be related to something like Freud's "pleasure principle." Mumford makes just this point in a letter to Patrick Geddes, in which he also discusses the concept of an inner and an outer world.

> To write a history of these pragmatic Utopias would be to present the historical "world-within" and thus supplement the conventional historian's account of the world-without. Until psychoanalysis claimed the field we did not sufficiently realize the importance of the world-within; or at any rate, we did not see that it had a directive function. . . . So it comes about that a great many of our Utopias are infantile, in that they seek to entrench what Freud called the pleasure principle, and deny the reality-principle. . . .[4]

Here the awareness of the need to take into account the inner world of experience, because of its "directive function," is tied to Mumford's development of his terms, inner and outer. He is trying to synthesize, at the level of explanation, the separated realms of fact and value, of deed and dream, as he calls them in another place, that had been sundered at the earliest stages of the development of the "megamachine." (Earlier in this letter he alluded to the founding of the Royal Society by English scientists and their "dissociation" of science from literature.)

Obviously we can also align, respectively, the utopias of escape and reconstruction with the realms of the aesthetic and the practical. Mumford spoke later of how his work as novelist and playwright was overshadowed and curtailed by his writing as sociologist. This would be another way of saying that he is more interested in the utopia of reconstruction than of escape, as indeed I suggest at the beginning when I put Mumford in the third class of axiologists, those who call on latent values. This, however, is to put too rigid a definition on the aesthetic realm as one of escapist fantasies, and, as we will see, this is not consonant with Mumford's sense of aesthetics. Furthermore, what does not serve in this respective alignment between escape and the aesthetic, and reconstruction and the practical, is that Mumford introduces a third sort of utopia, namely, the utopia of means. This is exemplified by Campanella's and Bacon's utopias and centers on material perfection. Mumford argues that almost all nineteenth-century utopias are of this sort, though he does not discuss the category in any independent way.

I suggest another alignment among the three classes of utopia and certain fundamental historical models by linking the classes to three other terms Mumford introduces into his book: the Country House, Coketown, and Megalopolis myths. Indeed I cannot say clearly why he himself did not make this connection, unless it was due to his fear of over-systematization. In fact, Mumford himself said (in the letter cited above) in 1922 to Patrick Geddes that he was "going to suggest" that each historical period had its own "realized Utopia" (*FK,* 74), though he never explicitly did so. But the alignment seems to me intrinsically part of the book's structure, and in fact offers Mumford—or at least his latter-day audience—a good historical scheme.

Briefly, the alignment looks like this: The utopia of escape finds its degenerate form in the Country House myth, for there the principle motive is creating a place where the problems of the larger community are either ignored or subsumed to what Mumford calls the "passive pleasures" of the rural retreat. The second utopia, that of reconstruction, aligns with the Coketown myth, for here all is subordinated to the needs of production, and the activity of mass manufacture through efficient means is the only idolum. The third alignment, less neat, but still convincing, I believe, is the utopia of means, which becomes distortedly embodied in the myth of Megalopolis. Here Mumford's description of the empire of paper—his imagistically centered version of the rationalized society of Weber's classic description—tallies with the utopia of means and its concern with the perfection of certification, transmission, and accountability in the most narrow bureaucratic sense. Paper, and all its modern analogues in celluloid or computer chips, becomes the ultimate "means" to achieve perfection, as all of reality is eventually turned into tabular records and thus controlled and regulated.[5]

Now Mumford might not have drawn out this alignment of the three utopias and their degraded actualized versions not only because he was against analytic over-systemization but also because he was intent on the final third of his book's argument, where his concern to elucidate his sense of the distorted values of the modern world was paramount. The axiologist, in short, took over from the analyst. But if he had drawn out this alignment, he might have been led to a fuller discussion of just why these utopian schemes fail, and develop instead into rampant and deplorable myths. Mumford is concerned not only to offer an organicist correction to our troubles, but also to provide a historical explanation for them. I think Mumford's first book is weakest where he tries to show how the separation of value from fact originates. In his plea for a world instructed by science and ennobled by the arts, he implicitly admits that their separation is at the root of our problems. For him the separation begins with Aristotle, when the books on natural history are given a standing separate from the more metaphysical books. This, however, puts the division too far back, and makes it seem too much a part of all organized thought. If this were the unique source of the separation, then all observation and theory would be virtually destined to be separated. I would rather agree with those who locate the crucial period of separation in the Kantian and Enlightenment scheme that makes autonomous realms out of science, art, and morality. Here the desire to free these realms from the controlling superstitious habits of mind associated with religion and absolute monarchy has a decidedly positive and beneficial justification, even though eventually it results in the sort of fragmentation and specialization that became one of the main foes of all of Mumford's writings. What Mumford might then have seen, were he to have applied this historical explanation of the origin of specialization, was the paradoxical nature of the development of modern systems of thought, or idola, as he called them. Much modern thought is still lived out under the terms of this paradox, for many acknowledge the need for integrated thought while still mistrusting any totalizing scheme relying on a rigid hierarchical or metaphysical framework.

Mumford came very close to the center of this paradox in his next book, *Sticks and Stones.* The book resembles *The Story of Utopias* in that its first portion is devoted to a historical survey, while its final part offers not only a somewhat apocalyptic diagnosis of our ills, but at least the outline of a transcendent cure for them. The problem comes closest to a paradoxical formulation—or at least a nearly tragically ironic one—when late in the book Mumford offers the following:

> During the last century our situation has changed from that of creators of machinery to that of creatures of the machine system; and it is perhaps time that we contrived new elements which will alter once more the profounder contours of our civilization.[6]

If we could borrow the terms of his contemporary Kenneth Burke, Mumford is saying here that the relation between agent and agency—between man and machine—has been inverted and we are become the agencies of our own machines, now organized into a system that has set its own priorities, its own rules, and its own purposes. *Sticks and Stones,* published only two years after *The Story of Utopias,* can be read as something like an extended last chapter of the earlier book, so close are its arguments and so clearly do both books speak ultimately to the present rather than about the past. And the idea of the "machine system" that stands at the end of both books eventually plays a central role in all of Mumford's writing, as his axiology can easily be read as attempting an antidote to this complex historical development.

The cure for these ills formulated in *Sticks and Stones* resembles that in *The Story of Utopias*. Mumford tries to balance the intuition that inner change must come in advance of outer reconstruction—"Once the necessary conversion in faith and morals has taken place, the other things will come easily . . ." (*SS*, 110)—with the awareness that converting myths into rational knowledge while retaining aesthetic wholeness can be done only with the full force of scientific authority. The last page of *Sticks and Stones* cites as an example the history of Japan's feudal society in its adoption within a hundred years of our modern mechanical gear. Mumford fully appreciates how ironic this example is even as he insists that it offers real force. This ironic, sometimes paradoxical, awareness of the necessary interplay between inner faith and outer forces is both the condition of all of Mumford's writings and his most salient thought.

In *The Golden Day*, his third book, Mumford offers his fullest view of American culture and values. I say this knowing that *Sticks and Stones* covers at least as long a historical stretch, and that *The Brown Decades* was to be written to make up for what had been left out of, or underemphasized in, *The Golden Day*. But the latter shows Mumford at his best because it so aptly balances praise and blame, exhortation and analysis. The centerpiece of the book lies in the chapter that bears the same phrase as the book's title, and the metaphor of the day is further applied to the five central figures of the book. Emerson stands out as the Morning Star, Thoreau the Dawn, Whitman blazes as the High Noon, Hawthorne becomes the Twilight, and Melville the Night. But this center chapter is made fully meaningful by its place in a larger historical scheme that begins with the "unsettled" European culture out of which came the settling of America. Mumford thus sees his five golden American writers as answering the question of what will supplant the abandoned Christian synthesis of the European Middle Ages. But the story is not all exemplary virtue and historical triumph. For the same American culture that was planted here on the shores contained inescapable flaws. Because this culture was "abstract and fragmentary" it foundered in the wilderness and in its later attempts to revitalize itself, turning as it did to an even "bleaker preoccupation with . . . matter, money, and political rights."

By invariably placing American culture against its European background Mumford illustrates not only a key point for all American Studies scholars who succeed him, but he is able to see how the frontier phase of our culture includes important elements of European Romanticism. Indeed, Mumford labels as "one of the most sardonic jests of history" the gap that developed between Romantic hope and pioneer reality in the American frontier. The gap between an inner and an outer reality stands as one of the main negative chords that he repeatedly strikes throughout this book. The main theme of *The Golden Day* may be summed up in the claim, "Life flourishes only in [the]alternating rhythm of dream and deed: when one appears without the other, we can look forward to a shrinkage, a lapse, a devitalization." This belief has its roots in the Romantic theories of artistic and organic unity on which Mumford drew so frequently. This idea is echoed near the end of the book when Mumford writes, "Art in its many forms is a union of imaginative desire, desire sublimated and socialized, with actuality: without this union, desire becomes idiotic, and actualities perhaps even a little more so." Here we can also see unmistakably how Mumford refuted the post-Kantian, formalistic sense of art as existing in an autonomous realm of free play and thoroughly unconnected significa- tion. In his anti-formalist approach to art, as much as in any other single belief, Mumford separates himself from the large majority of his modernist peers in literature and the arts, from the Symbolists to the surrealists to the latest avant-garde experimentalists, for whom such formalist ideas served as the bedrock for their asethetic theories.

Again, if I may schematize his work beyond the author's own intention, I would say that Mumford builds his book around three figures: Emerson, Santayana, and Dewey. This way of seeing the book, of course, dramatizes its function as an introduction to Mumford's contemporary concerns, and his interest in making the America of 1926 and afterward more aware of how best "to conceive a new world." For him, these philosophers were like artists in that they would give us coherent visions, but visions that were also instruments for living. Mumford's high estimate of Emerson, then, is startling if we remember Mumford's immediate historical context, though it is clearly necessary for his argument (and less startling today, of course). And, as we will see, his use of Santayana and Dewey is also imaginatively fresh and shows his extraordinarily adept ability to understand and tap into current thought.

Recalling that the main thesis of the book is that "Life flourishes only in [the] alternating rhythm of dream and deed," we can see Emerson's importance to Mumford. But Mumford must make less of Emerson's dreamy Platonism than is usual, while continuing to stress the Protestant- ism of spirit that lay behind the Concord sage, his "intellectual, or cultural, nakedness." So what we end with is an Emerson who fully appreciated both "physics and dialectic . . . both science and myth." By thus combining an acute awareness of the reality of both the inner and outer worlds, and acknowledging the demands and necessities of each, Emerson is both a poet and a philosopher. "Who was there among Emerson's contemporar- ies in the Nineteenth Century that was gifted with such a complete vision?"[7] The completeness of the vision is based on its ability to compre- hend two different and even contradictory aspects of human experience. The twentieth century offers no single figure that approaches Emerson in terms of complexity of vision. But a synthesis might be possible.

In a letter to Van Wyck Brooks, printed in *Works and Days,* and dated

July 22, 1925, Mumford describes the lecture series he had given at the Summer School of International Studies in Geneva that year, due in large part to Brooks's recommendation. He says that his lecture on philosophy "indicates that something of a synthesis of their [Santayana's and Dewey's] philosophies would, for the first time perhaps, embrace the values of science and humanism." In the book version, however, Mumford does not so explicitly spell out this synthesis, nor does he relate it to the Emerson who sets up the main context of American philosophy. He also says in this letter that he finds "consolingly, that my standards in architecture and literature are one, so that the good life that hovers in the background has, at all events, a unity of exterior and interior." Such a unity becomes partially available for Mumford in both Santayana's and Dewey's philosophies, though something is missing for him from the work of each man.

By the time he reaches his section on Santayana, Mumford has already painted a grim picture of the "pillage of the past," that cultural habit epitomized by Isabella Gardner, who turned her Boston home into a museum devoted to European masterpieces while ignoring indigenous American artists such as Eakins and Ryder. Santayana receives due credit for making reflections on a sense of beauty central to his modern philosophy. But the philosopher, born in Spain and educated at Harvard, was to some extent guilty of his own pillage of the past. For, "unlike Emerson, Mr. Santayana had no roots in his own day and people," and his "vanity and preciousness" Mumford places too closely to the failing of Mrs. Gardner for the reader to miss the connection. Emerson's balanced completeness is lost as Santayana loses contact with the outer world of his experience and retreats into a hermeticism—one that increased after 1926.

As he ends the book, Mumford takes up Dewey and his "instrumentalism," preferring this term to the more tainted "pragmatism." In an earlier chapter Mumford had talked about the Gilded Age as one typified by "pragmatic acquiescence," so the very avoidance of the term "pragmatic" to discuss Dewey shows that Mumford means to leave us with a more balanced, even a positive, assessment. In fact there are few passages in all of Mumford's writing where he tries so hard to be precise in his assessment, mixing in equal measures praise and blame and caution. His main charge against Dewey, that he lacks a transcendent set of values, and that his lack is due to, or at least reflected in, Dewey's impoverished sense of the aesthetic, is answerable in part by Dewey's later work, chiefly, of course, *Art as Experience*. But the charge had genuine force in 1926. We know from a letter he wrote Van Wyck Brooks that Mumford intended in the middle 1920s to write a book about William James and Dewey, and these pregnant paragraphs in *The Golden Day* may well have been the germ of this work. Mumford may also have remembered Brooks's own assessment of pragmatism, in *Letters and Leadership,* where he argued that Dewey and James "were poets, yes, but were not *sufficiently* poets to intensify the conception of human nature they had inherited from our tradition."[8]

Though Mumford does not explicitly set out a synthesis of Santayana and Dewey, perhaps in the knowledge that such an argument might be read as special pleading, he animates the entire book by a sense of value informed by the awareness of the strengths—and weaknesses—of each. In an especially rich passage he speaks about the limitation of both idealists and pragmatists, offering as a corrective to such limits the image of a tree, that favorite of Romantic theorists of the organic:

> We cannot . . . make the ways of other cultures our ways; but by entering into all their life of the spirit, our ways will become more deeply humanized. . . . When we are integrated, we grow like the tree: the solid trunk of the past, and the cambium layer, where life and growth take place, are unified and necessary to each other.[9]

This passage addresses explicitly the problem of those who pillage the past, and by extension shows how cultural values must take place, change, and develop within a historical continuity respectful of both practical needs and imaginative desires. Dewey does better than does Santayana in Mumford's estimation, because Dewey shows how absurd it is to ignore either the high ground of transcendentalism or the rootedness of empiricism, for he is able to "open the way to a more complete kind of activity, in which facts and values, actualities and desires, achieve an active and organic unity."

For Mumford to turn from the end of *The Golden Day* and write at length about Herman Melville, who, after all, represented the night time of that day, seems almost perverse. Surely the novelist was not an apparent example of a synthesis of Dewey and Santayana. He was in the early 1920s generally regarded as a failure, an obscurantist, and, in some quarters, as little more than a madman. Even Van Wyck Brooks, an important influence on Mumford at this time, as several critics have shown,[10] suggested that the last thirty years of the novelist's life were artistically empty. But in *Works and Days*, Mumford drops tantalizing hints as to his rationale. In the late 1920s Mumford found himself engaged by two singular geniuses. Melville and Dante loomed compellingly for Mumford for both were religious men—that is, men who delved into the grounds of ultimate concern, or investigated the roots of value—and both treated directly the problem of evil. Both turned their own personal agony and desire into art, but in so doing represented a comprehensive, more tragic view of life than many subjective or "confessional" writers. And part of this larger representativeness was due to their position at the end of a certain historical period. For Dante stood at the end of the medieval Christian synthesis that had always fascinated Mumford, while Melville flourished just before the Civil War turned America into the model nation for the coming industrial megamachine. Mumford was drawn into a self-identification with Melville for all these reasons, and more.

As early as 4 August 1921, Mumford described himself as an Ishmael, an outsider. In a letter to Sophia Wittenberg (included in *Works and Days*,

86) he sees himself as one who has "specialized in the art of being alive," and who has avoided a restricted existence as either an aesthete or a sociologist. Ishmael was an outsider but also one who had a broader vision. Like Melville himself, Mumford turned his outsider status into an angle of vision that could address both realms, the felt and the observed, the subjective and the empirical. But such an angle of vision and the double focus it entailed provided Mumford with more than a satirist's comfortable point of view. It provided him with a dialectical understanding of how knowledge must itself be a process, one of turning inner visions into outer reality.

This was more than a matter of overcoming illusion or ignorance. It was important for Mumford to make a distinction among various kinds of "untruth," for some of them could be destructive of value while others could provide its very foundation. The interrelationship between inner belief and outer "manifestation" could be far from straightforward, as this passage about Melville's education made clear:

> It is not by dreams that people are defrauded, so much as by misplaced pictures of reality. A dream represents an inner urge and movement; presently it may work through to an objective manifestation; defeated in one place, it attacks in another; and though its final form may be far from the image originally projected, it does not disappoint one like the comparison of an actuality with some previous description.[11]

The disappointment referred to here is Melville's experience of the slums and horrible poverty of Liverpool, as contrasted with his father's descriptions of the city from an earlier period. But the distinction is a crucial one for Mumford, since it involves his notion of the idolum as opposed to self-deception or illusion. This distinction might be traceable back to Nietzsche, a thinker Mumford alludes to often. Nietzsche valued the principle of self-transcendence, while attacking the bad habits of stereotypical and prejudicial thinking. Both schemes of self-transcendence and stereotypes have in common that they often fly in the face of common sense or "realist" thought. It remains a troublesome truism, of course, that one person's myth of self-transcendence is another's deadeningly "traditional" belief. Separating genuinely productive myths from the stereotypes into which they often decay, and further, keeping them separate in a lasting educational scheme, remains a challenge not only to Mumford's thought but to that of all serious thinkers.

When faced with the enormous intellectual challenge this distinction and its perpetuation raise, many people appeal to a criterion of "realism." And Mumford praises Melville because, like all great religious thinkers, Melville was a "realist." But in discussing *Moby-Dick*, Mumford is far ahead of his time by pointing out that it is not a "realistic" novel in the narrow literary sense of belonging to a particular style of representation. For Mumford, "realism" in the narrow literary sense is just one style among many, and if this great novel is not realistic, so much the worse for the realist tradition. No, *Moby-Dick's* realism is that of a vision, not a style. And the chapter on the novel, in which Mumford boldly sets out the meaning of the tale, is at the heart of Mumford's values as well as Melville's. The chapter is hard to paraphrase, but we can see it offers a number of large claims as to the central meaning of the novel and provides the basis for Mumford's claim that it is one of the greatest books of the nineteenth century.

In what is offered as the "plainest interpretation" of the novel, Mumford claims that it shows that "disaster, heroically encountered, is man's true happy ending." But this sense of tragedy is completed only after Mumford discusses a more complex awareness:

> Growth, cultivation, order, art—these are the proper means by which man displaces accident and subdues the vacant external powers in the universe: the way of growth is not to become more powerful but more human. Here is a hard lesson to learn: it is easier to wage war than to conquer in oneself the tendency to be partial, vindictive and unjust: it is easier to demolish one's enemy than to pit oneself against him in intellectual combat which will disclose one's weaknesses and provincialities. . . . Man's defense lies within himself, not within the narrow, isolated ego, which may be overwhelmed, but in that self we share with our fellows and which assures us that . . . good men will remain to carry on the work, to foster and protect the things we have realized as excellent.[12]

This passage combines many thoughts, which we can begin to identify as something like a Romantic sense of tragic humanism, informed by the liberal socialism and *Lebensphilosophie* of George Simmel and others, but its antecedents are less important than its balance and integrity.

But Mumford does not stop there in his explication of Melville's message. He adds more "layers" of meaning, gently allegorizing the novel's fable-like qualities into something even more complex. The next layers of meaning come when Mumford suggests that the whale can symbolize man's unending labor to secure the needs of practical life. This is the whale the sailors seek, while Ahab seeks a spiritual whale. Mumford insists on the paradox that both quests are necessary. And another possible meaning sees the whale as "human purpose in its highest expression." Here the terms of *Lebensphilosophie* come to the fore: "Life, Life purposive, Life formative, Life expressive, is more than the finding of a livelihood." Mumford respects the aesthetic realm in which the novel operates, for he goes on to say that each successive generation will find its own meaning in the whale and the novel's overall shape. But by making these straightforward interpretive arguments about the novel's meaning, Mumford reveals a great deal about his own values.

Mumford turns at the end of the Melville book to a summary of his many insights into this contradictory figure. In doing this he speculates on his own way of dealing with values and visions, and we can say that he even offers something like a deconstructive reading of his own book. He returns to mull over the consequences of his claim that society is as real as a distant star, and that all human experience takes place in what he calls "the environment of life."

> One cannot separate a man from his social environment: a society lives in a man: a man is a creature in society: the inner world is less private and the outer world less public than people habitually and carelessly think. These very words, inner and outer, individual and social, are merely conveniences of thought: there are no actual lines and borders, except practical ones. . . . If the inner world be not a phantasm, it must be united to an outer world that nourishes and supports it, even when it offers oppositions and antinomies.[13]

To say that his terms "inner and outer" are merely "conveniences of thought" is to recognize the inescapably rhetorical foundation of all analysis—this being one of the several lessons that lie behind deconstruction—and moving with this recognition is the beginning of recognizing that neither term is necessarily "privileged" over the other—another one of deconstruction's important lessons. I would not try to enlist Mumford as a deconstructionist, or even a precursor, but I would say that he has given ample evidence of an ability to think through not only the limits of his thought but to question the terms in which he conducts that thought. This is what makes him an axiologist that even a deconstructionist might appreciate, even though he escapes from the final entrapment of skepticism that seems to be an inevitable consequence of this contemporary movement.

This might be the place to mention Mumford as a literary critic. Generalists are denigrated for their efforts in the various "specializations," often in low-grade territorial enmity. But everyone agrees, in theory at least, that to be a good generalist, one must have at least the potential to have been a first-rate specialist in at least some more narrowly defined area. On the basis of his Melville book, Mumford, I am confident, could have been a first-rate literary critic. I cannot judge—at least in a way that would count with experts or specialists—how Mumford's work as a sociologist or architectural critic or city planner would measure up against that of others who work only in those limited disciplines. But the Melville book, though based on material that was limited in availability and scope in 1926, is not only well written, it treats of issues like language and style, literary influence, and authorial psychology in ways that are enviably balanced and informed. Without succumbing to jargon or falling into blandness, Mumford is able to raise and explore all the knotty problems that arise not only with Melville specifically, but that have haunted literary biography in our century. The book makes me think of Edmund Wilson and Lionel Trilling, two acknowledged masters of literary criticism, and I am fairly sure that either of these men would have been proud to have written such a study. Part of Mumford's strength as a critic comes from his respect for the historical context as well as the aesthetic distinctiveness of the work of art.

He made this clear as early as 1920, in a piece on Blake and Turner, republished in *Works and Days,* and he retained this sense of balance throughout his life.

The last of Mumford's books devoted exclusively to American culture, *The Brown Decades,* is relatively thin. I think this is largely due to its being mainly a qualification of certain omissions and imbalances in *The Golden Day,* as well as to its manner of proceeding. Essentially the book is a series of short biographical sketches; it has little of the social and historical contextualizing of the previous books. We could attribute this to its origin as a series of lectures (given at Dartmouth College), though a similar origin did not hamper the structure of *The Golden Day.* But added to the book's reliance on the biographical sketch is the sense that Mumford has had his say. The "usable past" Van Wyck Brooks had called forth as a great cultural need was well on its way to being available. By discovering in Dante and Melville figures of epic scope and great historical moment, Mumford had poised himself on the edge of a different sort of argument, one that would deal less with individual historical figures and more with those large "environmental" forces that contain and transmit and set the limits of our values. For Mumford this environment was the city, not only because of his own personal roots in the metropolis, but because it was pre-eminently the place where human desire and human achievement—the inner and the outer—were most clearly interdefinitional.

There were several other factors contributing to Mumford's decision to deal more with the environment than with individual historical figures. It is surely true that he used the ideas of a New Organicism that he found in the writings of Patrick Geddes and William Branford, which have been traced back to the nineteenth-century Catholic thinker Frederick Le Play.[14] Another commentator has suggested that economic stringency, along with the influence of Geddes in thinking in a global sense, made Mumford take on certain projects.[15] But this explanation leaves out the internal drive, the sense that the study of biography could only yield so much. As important as Mumford felt a biographical subject's sexual life was, he was also in the 1920s increasingly interested in the psychology of Jung. (He even recommended that Brooks see Jung in order to have the doctor treat his melancholia.) The idolum was in some ways close to Jung's "collective subconscious." Mumford's sense that the inner and outer worlds are often overlapping can serve to focus attention on how our fears, desires, and phantasies have a social construction. Added to this was Mumford's sense that art was not simply an autonomous realm but a place where social values were questioned and even virtually altered. And, to repeat an earlier point, Mumford saw from the beginning that social reality—constructed as it was out of a complex of inner and outer orders of experience—was the origin of all experience.

The apparent simplicity of the terms "inner" and "outer" leads many academics to reject Mumford's thought as too generalist, too "undisciplined," too lacking in subtlety. But it is apparent from a close look at his first five books that his use of such terms is both self-critical and flexible. The terms—as "conveniences of thought"—enable him to be both focused and comprehensive, to achieve, in other words, a complex and dialectic balance that appropriately matches the same sort of balance in values that was his sustaining hope for all of society.

Designing Global Harmony: Lewis Mumford and the United Nations Headquarters

LAWRENCE J. VALE

In twenty-nine books and well over a thousand shorter pieces, Lewis Mumford has roamed freely where academic specialists fear to tread. Historian of cities and technology, moral reformer, critic of the arts, he is a master of humanist synthesis. Yet his juxtapositions—whether startling or soothing—often seem fleeting, as if composed through a kaleidoscope. In his effort to spin out the big picture, this self-proclaimed *generalist* often blurs its component parts. One wishes for a stable reference point, some way to tell whether his compelling critiques are illusory or merely elusive.

Mumford's voluminous architectural criticism provides a promising place to seek a firm foundation for his notion of the *organic*. When he writes about architecture, his words are necessarily chosen with reference to a tangible object. In his most extended ruminations on modern architecture, the presence of the building seems to have encouraged his thinking to be similarly concrete. Yet, unfortunately, even concrete is not always structurally sound.

No single building or group of buildings seems to have captivated Mumford as often as the United Nations headquarters in New York (Fig. 1). Between 1946 and 1953 he recorded his hopes and his disappointments in lectures, letters, and a series of "Sky Line" columns in *The New Yorker,* later anthologized.[1] His response to the project commenced even before a site or an architect were chosen, and continued, unabated, throughout the process of design and construction. In criticizing the headquarters, however, Mumford chose an ornery donkey on which to pin the moralist's cautionary tale. And it is here that we may be able to pin down Mumford, as well.

In assessing Mumford's fascination with the design for the United Nations headquarters, I wish to examine the ways he transcends the usual categories of architectural criticism. While writers in the Anglo-American architectural periodicals of the day focused almost exlusively upon matters

Fig. 1. United Nations Headquarters, New York. Courtesy UNPHOTO 165070/ Lois Conner.

of built *form* and technical *function,* Mumford courageously sought to comment not only upon the aesthetics of a building but upon the society that produced it and the culture that gave it meaning. For him, the boundaries of a building went well beyond the edges of its sculpted surfaces. In the case of the United Nations headquarters, these boundaries were especially extended. For Mumford, the UN complex as an *object* was inseparable from his larger hopes for the physical renewal of the whole city and the spiritual renewal of the whole world. As the home for a world organization dedicated to the preservation of peace, Mumford called for it to become a symbol of enduring global harmony.

In this essay, I propose to examine Mumford's critique of the UN headquarters as an example of the way one writer attempts to describe and evaluate the connections between buildings and social ideals. My discussion proceeds in three parts: first, some background on the circumstances of the United Nations design commission: second, an account of Mumford's large agenda of criticism; and finally, an attempt to define the value and limitations of his search for *universal* symbolism in architecture. I argue that Mumford's high-minded insistence upon the correspondence between architectural design and global order detracts from the perspicacity of his less grandly phrased social and cultural judgments.

I. Origins of the United Nations Headquarters

Plans for a postwar United Nations Organization developed while World War II still raged and memories of the failed first attempt at international co-operation remained sharp. The League of Nations had collapsed as an organization, a breakdown seemingly prefigured by the fiasco of the design competition for its headquarters in Geneva. Nine equal first places were awarded by a befuddled jury, and the resultant compromise produced a sprawling starved-classical edifice that was not completed until 1937, twelve years after the initial competition.[2] While there is certainly no obvious or linear connection between the weakness of the building and the weakness of the League of Nations organization, the planning of the United Nations headquarters must be seen in the context of this earlier disaster.

One thing was clear from the outset: the site and the architect for the UN headquarters had to be selected with the greatest possible speed. Less clear was the architectural program that this headquarters should contain. Was this to be a small complex of administrative buildings like those in Geneva, or was this to be the capital of the world? Uncertain about the scope of their enterprise, the members of the UN Headquarters Commission planned for a range of possibilities. In February 1946 the General Assembly voted to house the headquarters in the United States in the vicinity of New York City, and set up a commission to select a series of five alternative sites—ranging from two square miles to forty—in Westchester (New York) and Fairfield (Connecticut) counties. The smallest of these sites was thought sufficient to house all "official buildings" but provided the possibility for only "limited expansion," whereas the forty-square-mile site promised the possibility of a "complete community" of 50,000 persons, and included "allowance for expansion, together with adequate land for separation zones between neighborhoods and for border parks."[3] In selecting these sites, the Commission considered such criteria as usability of the land, property values and land availability, displacement of population and industry, protection of the site from adjacent development, access from New York, interference with public utilities, disruption of existing local government, availability of external facilities, local public opinion, and the probability of metropolitan encirclement.[4] Regarding the last, the commissioners commented that "the encirclement of the headquarters by metropolitan development in the future would make expansion difficult and might affect the amenities of the site."[5] The immediate problem, however, was not urban encirclement but suburban outrage. An annex to the Report lists ten categories of protest of local residents, ranging from anger at domestic dispossession and anxiety about inadequate financial compensation to "unsupported objection to the coming of the U.N."[6]

When the Headquarters Commission was sent off to find its five suburban sites, Lewis Mumford was already setting out his own ideas for the

United Nations headquarters. In a letter to British planner Frederic Osborn of 10 February 1946, Mumford cites his dismay at the "precipitate, amateurish way in which the Site Committee of the UNO has gone about trying to select a site without any clear-cut notion of what they were selecting it for. . . ." Anticipating his lecture before the Royal Institute of British Architects (RIBA) the following July, he adds:

> If the UN holds up the selection of a permanent site long enough, so that my words would not merely whistle down the wind, I might devote my RIBA lecture to a discussion of what such a programme should be and lead up to the suggestion of a world capital conceived on garden city lines.[7]

With Osborn's hearty concurrence about the timeliness of this "grand subject,"[8] Mumford delivered his talk, entitled "A World Centre for the United Nations."[9]

Well aware that his words would not likely be timely enough to "affect the immediate decisions of the United Nations," Mumford nonetheless set out his own account of "the conditions and purposes that should underlie the writing of an adequate programme for the new headquarters of the United Nations."[10] His proposal, he claimed, was put forward "to set in train a fresh discussion, and ultimately to promote further research and reflection as will enable another generation to rectify the errors we are now making."[11] For Mumford, the fundamental error was timidity: "This is no time for small plans, for grudging half-measures, for future projects that will be indistinguishable, in either scale or purpose, from past precedents."[12] In place of the belief, implied by the choice of a site in Westchester County, that "the headquarters of the United Nations may be small, inconspicuous, secluded, designed on the principle of protective colouration,"[13] Mumford set out four proposals for an urban alternative.

First, he told the RIBA, the headquarters should occupy "between 1000 and 3000 acres within an existing world metropolis," to be "created by a large-scale process of slum clearance and replacement, financed wholly by the United Nations." Second, he continued, the United Nations center "should be a legally independent municipality" and be "a balanced urban community . . . capable of growing up to the point where it would hold a population between twenty-five and fifty thousand people in permanent residence." Third, Mumford proposed, the "new world centre" should be a "paragon . . . of the new order we are in the course of building," distinguished by "clarity of design . . . growing unity of treatment . . . studious retention of the human scale . . . resolute avoidance of the pompous and the grandiose . . . insistence on measure and purpose in every element of the design . . ." and a "balance" achieved without being "wholly self-contained." Fourth and finally, he called for a "series of such centres" projected for "all the major continents and sub-continents" as "a means for providing services of an international nature for these regions" and as "a method for demonstrating the essential principle of social relativity, whereby any part of the world may, temporarily, become the centre of its life." Mumford envisioned a minimum of six to seven centers (to "represent every great cultural area"), and suggested that the "central staff" would change centers every five years.[14] Taken together, then, Mumford's vision for the United Nations headquarters is not so much a building complex as it is a way of life. As he puts it, "The city must be cut to the measure of a different kind of man from the powerful, domineering, semi-neurotic types who have left their marks so unmistakably on the great capitals of the past."[15]

As 1946 drew to a close, Mumford's measured man and the United Nations Organization that was supposed to bring him to life were still without a home. Westchester residents successfully resisted efforts to insert the world headquarters into suburbia.[16] With the defeat of this possibility, and the sense that the site offered on the old World's Fair grounds at Flushing Meadow was too small, frustrated UN officials reconsidered offers from many American cities, including Boston, San Francisco, and Philadelphia. When no solution seemed appropriate, the weary site selection committee reluctantly moved toward accepting an offer in Philadelphia. New York chauvinism and New York political power won out at the last minute, however; the machinations of Mayor William O'Dwyer and Robert Moses, the social connections of architect Wallace K. Harrison, the land acquisition of William Zeckendorf, and the $8.5 million check signed by John D. Rockefeller combined to produce an offer of a seventeen-acre site along Manhattan's East River, between 42nd and 48th streets (Fig. 2).[17] Despite nearly a year of careful research on other sites of a completely different character, the new offer was accepted almost instantly; within four days all the papers were signed and the deal ratified by the General Assembly. Soon afterward, an international team of architects—including Le Corbusier and Oscar Niemeyer—was selected and put under the direction of the ubiquitous Harrison. On 1 January 1947, two weeks after the site selection decisions, a disillusioned Mumford wrote his friend Osborn:

> When I wrote my paper on A World Centre for the UN, I little thought it would have such an ironic aftermath as the acceptance of one two-hundreth part of my proposal, in the shape of fifteen acres hastily snatched at the first bid from the philanthropic but peremptory Rockefeller. The way in which the whole decision was arrived at was a caricature of decent public policy, to say nothing of scientific judgement; and even if 3000 acres had been offered, the manner of reaching the conclusion would have been offensive. Unfortunately, I can hardly even plan a campaign to extend the area to be used by the UN, for they have taken a site that is by nature far too hemmed in to exist as an independent unit, in contrast to the vast acres that could have been redeemed in the lower part of Manhattan, in the heel of our stocking-shaped island. Someday the UN will repent of its haste; but I am glad that I shall not live long enough, in all probability, to have the temptation to say: I told you so.[18]

Unwilling to wait for evidence of repentence, Mumford took the offensive.

Fig. 2. UN Headquarters: The Deal. Courtesy *Architectural Forum*, January 1947.

II. The Scope of Mumford's Critique

While other commentators, writing in the major Anglo-American architectural journals, tended to restrict their assessment to aesthetic matters, Mumford's criticism bravely looked beyond such issues and into three other realms. As architectural journalists debated relatively narrow questions of formal composition, Mumford used his critique of the UN headquarters to emphasize the need for: (1) organic design devoted to addressing specific human needs; (2) reformation of urban development in New York City; and (3) world government.

Fig. 3. *Architectural Record* Says: "Sun, Shadow and Silhouette: United Nations Secretariat." Courtesy Architectural Record, May 1950, copyright 1950 by McGraw-Hill, Inc. All rights reserved. Reproduced with the permission of the publisher.

Mumford's Agenda: Organic Design

Faced with the emergence of the United Nations headquarters as a trio of buildings—a skyscraper Secretariat building containing offices, a low-slung General Assembly building, and a river-facing Conference building connecting them—most critics limited their comments to formal issues (Figs. 3–4). In an article entitled, "UN General Assembly Meets a Complex Plan with the 'Visual Poetry' of an Elegant Concave Shape," *Architectural Forum*'s correspondent predictably concluded that "the fascination of the Assembly Building" lies in its "sculptural shape."[19] Two years later, the same journal defended the inconspicuous Conference building as the "visual underpinning" needed to hold up "the mass of the Secretariat," noting that the former is "merely a hyphen" and was therefore "never meant to attract special attention."[20] A writer for the RIBA journal praised the "harmony of proportion" among the "contrasting architectural masses,"[21] a formalist stance echoed in numerous articles with such titles

Fig. 4. *House and Garden*'s Caption Reads, "The United Nations Buildings, Standing Implacably Apart From New York's Jumbled Architecture, Symbolize the Order Its Members Hope to Achieve." Courtesy HOUSE AND GARDEN. Copyright © 1952 (renewed 1980), by The Condé Nast Publications Inc.

as "Sun, Shadow and Silhouette, UN Secretariat"[22] and "UN Builds a Marble Frame for Two Enormous Windows."[23]

By publishing a series of "pictures and drawings," the editors of the June 1949 *Architectural Forum* purported to "give the architectural world its first opportunity to appraise the year's most talked about building, the UN Secretariat."[24] Everything important for judging the building, the editors implied, could be found in these images. Anything apart from questions of form was considered unverifiable: "Whether monumentality belongs to this age, whether work is expedited by the arrangements, whether the beautiful effect is also organic, will be questions of opinion. This preview seeks only to supply the facts."[25]

The UN Secretary-General's 1947 report on the "Permanent Headquarters of the UN" provides a telling index of the primacy given to aesthetic "facts." With no surfeit of modesty, it states that "Every possibly relevant consideration has gone into the final composition presented in this report: landscape, view, plastic organization of architectural masses, functions, working conditions in the interior of the buildings, etc."[26] It was left to Mumford, however, to play out the meaning masked by the unarticulated "et cetera."

In pronouncing the Secretariat building "impeccable but irrelevant,"[27] Mumford called for it to respond to a larger social and cultural agenda:

> The Secretariat should have been planned on the human scale, subordinated in its placement and design to the Assembly Building. The office buildings should have been designed with something more than lip service to economy, to mechanical function, above all, to the actual working needs of their occupants. Instead of having their substance wasted on elaborate mechanical utilities, introduced to counteract the massive errors in general design, the buildings should have been correctly oriented for sun and wind, and surrounded by trees and lawns that would have provided a pleasant microclimate for both winter and summer, with due architectural provision for intervals of recreation and social intercourse that are denied the inmates of the present building.[28]

Mumford's chief complaint was that the Secretariat building failed to function socially because of a misplaced emphasis on technical function, itself poorly executed. In his criticism, Mumford considered the point of view of a whole range of workers, secretaries as well as top officials. He criticized the expense and the social dysfunction of a building that has its north and south walls windowless while presenting a broad glass façade to the heat of the western summer sun, an orientation which, he claimed, rendered the building "functionally often windowless on all four sides."[29] He was especially indignant about the semi-opaque partitions used to separate the centrally placed secretarial typing pools from the window-facing (or at least windowshade-facing) offices on the east and west perimeters. Noting the similarity of these partitions to those used in New York tenements in the 1850s, he remarked: "To see this symbolic substitute for light and air reappearing in a building that prides itself on its aesthetic modernity is like seeing Typhoid Mary pose as a health inspector."[30] In a downtown area where sunlight is precious, he deemed it wasteful that lavatories were placed along the exterior perimeter. Mumford criticized the General Assembly building for its "overwhelming" interior proportions and suggested that it was better designed to service the various media organizations covering the proceedings than it was to serve the delegates themselves.[31] In all the UN buildings, Mumford criticized a lack of "intimate space" in areas both private and public. Such areas, he wrote, were essential in the past, and must be retained: "Diplomacy probably prospered in the 18th century because conversations could be held in recesses behind elaborate hanging."[32] While those who would recall the events of the French Revolution may question just what sort of "hanging" he means, the remark is indicative of Mumford's firm belief that a well-designed physical environment must enhance the possibilities for human interaction. In these ways and others, he judged the failure of the Secretariat against the promise of "an ideal office building." This was an ideal he believed to be attainable, given the ostensible freedom from "the constraints of realty speculation, constricted building lots, and metropolitan overcrowding."[33]

Mumford's Agenda: "Revitalizing" New York

Mumford's judgment of the UN complex is inseparable from his larger desire to "revitalize the whole city" of New York. In his 1946 speech to the RIBA, he made clear his wish that the UN headquarters be a kind of demonstration project: ". . . we must conceive a new kind of world city, more directly designed to embody the good life and to further the processes of international cooperation. And the first place where such a demonstration may take place is, I suggest, in the new centre for the United Nations."[34] In his discussion of the "good life" in the future "world city," however, Mumford was clearer about what must be eliminated than about what should take its place. What he wished to eliminate was much of New York. Three thousand acres "redeemed" from lower Manhattan constitutes an area nearly four times the size of Central Park[35] (Fig. 5).

For Mumford, the largest drawback of the seventeen-acre UN site was the "sordid slum" by which it must be approached.[36] The perception of slum conditions was enhanced by the layout of the buildings: "By placing the tall and narrow Secretariat parallel to the East River, the architects have included in the vista for all who approach the building from the west the jeering, jangling hulk of the plant that ventilates the Queens Midtown Tunnel and the towering chimneys of the Edison works, farther to the south."[37] Moreover, he notes that the great window of the General Assembly looks out on "the sordid industrial wasteland," a vista he compares with "cramped suburban lots where picture windows face their neighbors' garages and clotheslines."[38] Seven years after his RIBA lecture stressed the importance of "the local green belt" for "setting off the old from the new,"[39] Mumford continued to speak in terms of a "world city" that would be somehow set off from the visual clutter of New York. The architects, he wrote in 1953 after the UN complex was completed, "overlooked their unique opportunity to create a group of buildings that would form a city by itself, visually separate from the chaos around it—a sample of the more cooperative world order the U.N. seeks to bring into existence."[40] How it

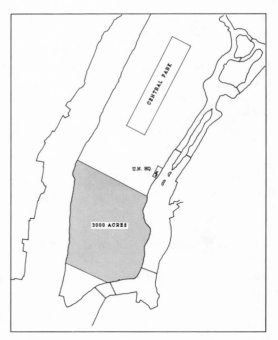

Fig. 5. Effect of Mumford's RIBA Proposal on Manhattan: 3000 Acres "Redeemed." Courtesy Author, with assistance from Conrad Margoles.

is that a new mini city which turns its collective back upon New York may be construed as an example of world cooperation, Mumford did not say.

Mumford's Agenda: World Government

Nonetheless, it is abundantly clear that some hazy notion of world government is at the heart of Mumford's concerns for the UN headquarters. Because he viewed the UN as the nearest thing to such a global political authority, Mumford's architectural critique of the building assumed a radical appreciation of the organization's institutional importance. In a letter to Osborn on 6 March 1947, Mumford defended his belief in a global political order against the doubts of his British colleague:

> What you say about the practical impossibility of world government is true; and in ordinary times I should bow meekly to your judgement. But in the present situation I am tempted to quote the sign that someone saw in one of our military headquarters: the difficult we do immediately; the impossible will take a little longer. I admit that world government will take a little longer; but the nature of our present crisis is such, with respect to the powers of destruction we now command, that if we don't make serious steps toward world government immediately . . . the results will be far more disastrous than the worst mess that premature world government could conjure up.[41]

Though Mumford's response is less than illuminating about the methods for attaining world government, it is indicative of the lingering idealism made manifest in his insistence upon the globally ameliorative effects of United Nations architecture. "Each of us, in his purely national capacity, is only half a man," he said to the RIBA in 1946, "the other half of our-selves is bound up with the whole wide world. The task of building a new world centre is to dramatize this fact and make it visible. We have to create more than an instrument of government: we have to shadow forth a new life."[42] To Mumford's immense disappointment, however, the resultant buildings cast shadows of the same old order.

III. Ideas, Ideals and Forms:
Mumford's Use of Universal Symbolism

Mumford's multi-tiered critique of the UN complex appears coherent to the extent that he was able to insist convincingly on the "organic" inter-connection of socio-political issues with architectural forms and practices. Yet the case for this conjunction requires a considerably closer examina-tion than Mumford provides. While his individual social and cultural observations were consistently acute, his most extreme claim—that archi-tectural order can positively affect world political order—seems both too facile and too grandiose. Mumford had a remarkable ability to explicate the social origins and the cultural meanings of the buildings he observed, but he faltered when he attempted to push his ideas about architectural symbolism to serve his own political agenda of world government.

He was at his most persuasive when demonstrating that the architecture of the United Nations complex was a product of larger social forces and when explicating the ways that architecture may be seen as evidence of a willingness to undertake progressive forms of social change. He got into unacknowledged trouble, however, when he made claims for the ability of architectural design, itself, to exemplify a more perfect global political order. In his insistence that the United Nations complex be nothing less than the "paragon" of the "new world order," he set impossible standards, standards which no building can attain and which Mumford could not con-vincingly explain in terms of architectural form.

In his critique of the UN headquarters, Mumford claimed that its forms did not fit the present and future needs of what he conceived to be a totally new kind of institution, one deemed essential for the survival of the human race. His RIBA lecture was meant not only to challenge the architectural profession to find forms worthy of the lofty ambitions of the UN Charter but also to insist that the challenge is hardly one for architects alone. His subsequent writings dissected the buildings in an attempt to discover the anatomy of their failure. At the heart of Mumford's critique lies the prob-

lem of designing a symbol that is universally understood and shared, a task
far more problematic than he allows.

In his 1941 book, *The South in Architecture,* Mumford set out what he
termed the "two elements in every architecture:"[43]

> One of them is the local, the timebound, that which adapts itself to special
> human capacities and circumstances, that belongs to a particular people and
> a particular soil and a particular set of economic and political institutions. . . .
> The other element is the universal: this element passes over boundaries and
> frontiers; it unites in a common bond people of the most diverse races and
> temperaments; it transcends the local, the limited, the partial.[44]

In his critique of the United Nations headquarters, however, he allowed
his desire for this second element—the universal—to eclipse most aspects
of the local, the limited, or the partial. New York—with its skyscrapers, its
congestion, and its ruthless speculation—was not an element to be incorporated and synthesized, but an obstacle to be overcome.

Mumford's insistence that architecture be viewed as part of a complex
realm of symbolic experience seems clearly influenced by the ideas of philosophers such as Ernst Cassirer and Susanne Langer.[45] Like them, Mumford emphasizes what he calls "the dynamic role of the esthetic symbol, in
revealing man's nature and further modifying it."[46] Within Mumford's
view of this dynamism, however, there remains significant ambiguity. In
partial accord with Cassirer's notion of "symbolic pregnance,"[47] Mumford
sometimes assumes that the UN buildings immediately and concretely convey a non-intuitive meaning. Yet, at the same time, his pointed and prolific
criticism clearly testifies to the need for an interpreter to explicate and
draw out meanings that are not automatically conveyed by the forms of the
buildings themselves. Mumford believed that all buildings are charged with
meaning: he wrote about them to ensure that they were charged with
meanings he could endorse. For the United Nations headquarters, however, the challenge was especially difficult since he needed to assert that its
meanings were universally shared.

Mumford seemed to be on guard against all interpretations that
betrayed nationalist, rather than panhuman, inclinations. This may seem a
paradoxical position for him to take, given that much of the material in his
first five books is devoted to the discovery and explication of a "usable
past" for the United States.[48] Yet, when he came to discuss the United
Nations headquarters, he seemed unwilling to accept the confines of the
region and the nation, realms which in the pre-atomic age he had found
to be congenial. In adopting this larger frame of reference, one in which
architecture must itself take on universal aspirations, Mumford ran the
danger that his sensitivity to "the local, the limited, the partial" could
become obscured. And yet, because he did continue to pay close attention
to the smallest details, it was not the minutiae that he lost. Rather, what
went out of focus was the ground somewhere in the middle. Missing in
Mumford's critique of the United Nations is some recognition of the

importance of factors that lie between the day-to-day organic function of the workplace and the distant promise of world government. In choosing to forget that the United Nations was formed to preserve national sovereignty as well as to preserve world peace, Mumford adopted an overwhelmingly idealized version of the organization. He wished to wipe away feelings of nationalism (and other "tribalisms") with the same ease that would cleanse Manhattan of its slums. In each case, old patterns were to be replaced by new and better ones. Missing in Mumford's heady embrace of wholesale renewal and wholesale world government was, among other things, his earlier sensitivity to place.

America Displaced

In discussing the emergence of a distinctively American architecture during the latter part of the nineteenth century, Mumford invariably rhapsodized about a "deep harmony" with the American soil. In *The Golden Day* (1926), he praised Thoreau's ability to conceive "a form, a habitat, which would retain what was unique in the American contact with the virgin forest, the cultivated soil, and the renewed institutions of the New England town."[49] When he discussed the emergence of a peculiarly *American* architecture in the decades following the Civil War, he championed the "movement toward utilizing the indigenous, the natural, the regional," claiming that this resulted in "the first buildings in the United States that could be properly be called either original or contemporary or consciously wedded to their soil."[50] He lauded such architects as Henry Hobson Richardson, John Wellborn Root, and Frank Lloyd Wright, and he extolled Louis Sullivan as "perhaps the first mind in American architecture that had come to know itself with any fullness in relation to its soil, its period, its civilization. . . ."[51] In these instances, Mumford found evidence of both *soil* and *civilization,* by which he seems to have meant attentiveness to both the *local* and the *universal.* While Mumford celebrated the American soil of the nineteenth century, he was more suspicious about the dirt of the twentieth-century American city.

Mumford's paean to the emergence of an American architecture was ironic in its utter rejection of what is arguably America's most novel contribution—the skyscraper. The skyscraper, for Mumford, was sensitive neither to the local nor the universal, despite Sullivan's contention that it should be a "proud and soaring thing." Sullivan's claim, he wrote, "gives to architecture a spiritual function to perform: whereas, in actuality, height in skyscrapers meant either a desire for centralized administration, a desire to increase ground rents, a desire for advertisement, or all three of these together—and none of these functions determines a 'proud and soaring thing.'"[52] While he did not deny that skyscrapers were an important aspect of American commerce, he found them representative of the increasingly machine-dominated America he wished to alter and transcend.

When Mumford wrote about the development of American cities after 1880, his notion of the *American* became conflated with his notion of the *modern*. Caught up in the possibility of a new formal system, transcendent and universal, he began to lose sight of the distinctively American culture he had struggled to elucidate in his books published between 1922 and 1931. He took special care to champion the ways that American architects had thrown off the alien forms of classical Europe, but was considerably more vague about exactly what was American about the forms that replaced these. In the case of the skyscraper, however, its American character was precisely what Mumford did not like.

Skyscraper Symbolism: The Capitalist Secretariat

The form of the modern skyscraper, for Mumford, was a hegemonic image. It was a form of progress without human purpose, a symbol of greed rather than co-operative unity. He called the Secretariat building a symbol of "the way specious considerations of fashion, profit, prestige, abstract aesthetic form—in a word, 'the package' of commerce—have taken precedence over the need of human beings for good working and living quarters."[53] "As a conscious symbol," he continued, "the Secretariat adds up to zero; as an unconscious symbol, it is a negative quantity, since it symbolizes the worst practices of New York, not the best hopes of the United Nations."[54] Even worse, he wrote, "this skyscraper is an eloquent but unintentional symbol of the general perversion of life values that takes place in a disintegrating civilization."[55]

Mumford's unease about capitalism simultaneously played out many themes: sometimes he seemed to distrust capitalist finance as a basis for a universal order; sometimes his worry seemed to be rooted in the gross global inequalities manifested by the material excesses of capitalist technics. Sometimes he questioned the fundamental premises of capitalism; at other times he seemed concerned only with the perception of capitalist imagery (i.e. the corporate skyscraper) by non-capitalist others. At one level, Mumford clearly found distressing the financial self-interest of the Zeckendorf-Rockefeller land deal,[56] noting that the dubious origin of the United Nations site financing was a matter of rather widespread distrust. "To some of our more difficult brothers overseas, Mr. Rockefeller is Monopoly Capitalism, and the fact that it was he, and not the city of New York or the federal government, who gave this site to the United Nations will not, unfortunately, lessen their suspicions and animosities."[57]

At another point, though, Mumford's displeasure seemed to be rooted in his perception of the building's international image. He termed the Secretariat "a type of building that to distant peoples is a stock emblem of the things they fear and hate—our slick mechanization, our awful power, our patronizing attitude toward lesser breeds who have not acquired the American way of life."[58] For Mumford, this building bespoke the rapacity of the West rather than the equanimity of a future global civilization. Yet this criticism also reveals a certain romanticism on Mumford's part about those from distant lands, whom he viewed as uncorrupted by the inhumanities of the Western city. While Mumford was certainly right to emphasize that the United Nations headquarters was a product of capitalism in its forms as well as its financing, he neglected to point out that it was the delegates themselves—communist and capitalist alike—who wished for an urban New York City site. The perturbation over the imagery of the skyscraper that Mumford attributed to "distant peoples" may be better seen as a projection of his own disquiet. While his point about American condescension toward less technically advanced countries may be valid, this did not stop the elites in such countries from embracing the skyscraper as a symbol of modernity and progress as soon as circumstances permitted. Still, Mumford was correct to emphasize that the architecture of the United Nations headquarters is not neutral; while he may have wished it to portend the pan-human hopes of "the new world centre," its origins were firmly rooted in the speculative practices of 1940s Manhattan.

United Nations Symbolism: Mumford's Alternative

Undaunted by its tainted origins, however, Mumford sought to invest the headquarters architecture with the spirit of a new universal order. He wanted the United Nations headquarters to be an appropriate symbol in at least three related ways. First, he wanted a design that testified to the novelty and distinctiveness of the venture; second, he desired the hierarchy of institutional priorities to be articulated in the hierarchy of architectural forms; and third, he wished the headquarters to be a symbol of the institution's goals.

The Symbolism of Novelty

The first kind of symbolism, for Mumford, must involve visual evidence that the UN headquarters was unlike any other architectural commission that had come before. In his idealization of the potential for world government, however, he tended to lose sight of the ways that the headquarters, while certainly a hybrid, was not so far removed from pre-existing architectural typologies. In his effort to envision the UN as an entirely new architectural phenomenon, he underestimated the extent to which the new institution must inevitably draw upon older models, including the office block, the conference center, the parliament chamber, and the palace. In resisting the connection to past typologies, he emphasized that the institution must assume an unprecedented scale, one appropriate for the center of world government. He complained that, in accepting the Rockefeller offer, UN officials jumped at "the first fleabite of land," thereby indicating "uncertainty" and suggesting the "impermanence" of the institution.[59] Alternatively, Mumford wrote, the United Nations headquarters should be a "real city within a city, dominating its site even more conspicuously than the Vatican City does."[60] In this, he objected, the designers fell far short: ". . . they have failed to create a fresh symbol. . . . Their world city is just a chip off the old block."[61] For Mumford, who wished to chop off many more blocks, this was both insufficient and wrong.

The issue of novel symbolism, however, poses demands beyond the question of scale. The headquarters must be free of the architectural clichés that in the past signaled centers of government. Mumford rejected forms of architectural representation that he saw as stigmatized and outmoded (such as the neoclassical central dome), and he also dismissed modern alternatives that he found lacking in organic expression. In both the traditional and the machine-worshiping modern, Mumford saw only the potential for banality. For the United Nations headquarters adequately to express the global sweep of the institution, it must take on forms which could not easily be copied and trivialized, and these must be forms not exclusively associated with one country or one part of one country. It was for these reasons, too, that he so vehemently objected to the Secretariat skyscraper as the dominant part of the headquarters' architectural composition.

The Symbolism of Architectural Hierarchy

According to Mumford, the dominance of the Secretariat slab over the less visually prominent forms of the General Assembly building and the Conference building constituted a fundamental misrepresentation of what he believed the institution's priorities ought to be. As he put it, this unfortunate juxtaposition "reveals at the start either a complete indifference to symbolism, or a very wry reading of the nature and destiny of the United Nations. With relation to the city itself, a forty-two-story building cannot possibly express dominance: it is just another skyscraper in an urban heap of skyscrapers."[62] In contrast to the office slab, Mumford observed that the Conference building tucked into its base was "almost invisible"[63] and that the Assembly building was the "architectural anticlimax . . . a painful simulacrum, the kind of thing Hollywood might have faked."[64]

Mumford points to two distinct problems here, though he did not distinguish between them. One is the problem of unoriginal representation and the other is the problem of ill-chosen hierarchy. In dismissing the Secretariat as "just another skyscraper" (however elegant in its detailing), Mumford correctly anticipated the way succeeding generations have perceived both the novelty and the hierarchy of the headquarters. We now tend to refer to the headquarters as "the UN Building" and mean the skyscraper part only. We do not speak of it as a complex or an enclave or a district, let alone as a city. Even if it is referred to as a headquarters, the *head* is the slab in the sky, not the flattened bauble on the ground.

Figures 6 and 7 exemplify this same perception of the architectural hierarchy of the United Nations. While it may be that an exceptionally talented

Fig. 6. UN Assembly Speaks From Secretariat. Courtesy *Don Wright*.

Fig. 7. Veto Power of the Bureaucracy?

Fig. 8. Lever House, New York (1951). Courtesy Lever Brothers Company/ Thomas H. Murtaugh.

architect could break the otherwise logical association between the largest structure and the structure that is visually and institutionally most important, this does not seem to have occurred in the case of the UN.[65] In figure 6, a 1982 political cartoon, the artist depicts a General Assembly resolution as emanating not from the Assembly hall (shown fading into the trees in a bottom corner) but from the midpoint of the Secretariat slab. Likewise, in figure 7, a 1983 postage stamp from Iran which condemns the hegemony of the superpower veto in the UN Security Council, the veto power emanates not from the Conference chamber but from the faceless

Fig. 9. Seagram Building, New York (1957). Courtesy *The Seagram Building* 1958. Photographer: Ezra Stoller/ Esto. Courtesy of Joseph E. Seagram & Sons, Inc.

wall of the skyscraper. Significantly, the building is so lacking in anything that would symbolically distinguish this skyscraper from any other that the postal propagandist needs to draw in a large UN logo near the top of the blank north wall.

The UN tower had lost its distinctive stamp almost as soon as it was built. By the late 1950s, other glass and steel Manhattan skyscrapers—designed for corporations such as Lever Bros. and Seagram—emerged as even more elegant than their worldly cousin. A crisp and cultivated style of architecture, intended in one instance to convey the emerging order of global harmony, could also communicate the more immediately universal commodities of clean soap and neat whiskey. In the following years, less carefully detailed glass boxes proliferated to form the corporate canyons that now interlace much of midtown Manhattan. Outdone by both architectural quality and quantity, the design of the UN Secretariat became both marginalized and trivialized, just as Mumford had predicted (Figs. 8–9).

The Symbolism of the Institution's Goals

The first two levels of symbolic association—the need for a *new* symbol
and the need for an appropriate hierarchy—are more clearly articulated
than Mumford's other, related criterion—the need for the headquarters
to symbolize the goals of the institution. At various points in his writings,
Mumford alludes to the purposes of the United Nations but the description never penetrates beyond generalities: he describes such goals as
"order out of chaos," "unity out of diversity," "peace and harmony out
of anarchic belligerence."[66] Yet, in looking only toward the universal,
toward world government, Mumford pursued the goal that is the most distant and the least in focus.

In his attempt to clarify this new order of world peace and world government, he stakes out at least three ways for architectural design to contribute. Good design, for Mumford, could provide the UN personnel and
the larger society with evidence of commitment, with opportunities for
organic flexibility, and with an inspirational base for the organization's
claims of authority.

Architecture as Symbol of Commitment

According to Mumford, architecture provides evidence of commitment
not only through the size and location of the site but also through the
choice of human scale for all that is built upon it. Describing the Secretariat building, he writes:

> A building to house an international personnel devoted to bringing about
> world cooperation and world peace . . . should, by its zealous attention to
> human functions and human needs, itself symbolize the great purposes it
> serves. It should give at least a preliminary glimpse of the new world, the
> world in which human considerations will be uppermost and will set the mold
> for our organizations and institutions. It should be both a visual and an oper-
> ational symbol, and its beauty should arise out of the due fulfillment of all its
> functions, graded in the order of their human importance.[67]

Characteristically, apart from his remarks about the need for daylight and
intimacy, Mumford does not become specific about what he means by commitment to human scale, human needs, or human importance. Nor does
he explain just what an operational symbol might be though, once again,
there is seeming resonance with Cassirer's notion of "symbolic pregnance." What is clear from his comments is that there must be some more
gradual mediation between the smallness of people and the largeness of
buildings, and that he regards the UN headquarters as a logical and essential place for this less alienating hierarchy to develop.

Architecture as Symbol of Flexibility

Mumford's belief in the need for architectural flexibility is an extension of his commitment to human needs. He criticizes the UN headquarters as offering only the image of flexibility, not the substance. Mumford laments the inadequate size of the site and the architects' inability to find forms that permit flexible growth. He notes that, while the 1947 United Nations Headquarters Advisory Commission Report "uses all the right words to describe the architecture," emphasizing "integration, organicism, flexibility, expansion and so on,"[68] the buildings do not live up to the rhetoric. The report describes the UN as a "young and dynamic organization" with "unlimited potentialities for growth and change" and calls for structures to be "planned on so flexible a pattern that their interior areas may be easily and economically rearranged to suit changing needs." "Similarly," the report continues, "while the main building masses will determine the composition and use of the land area, much of the space can be kept free for future needed construction that will be in harmony with the pattern already laid down."[69] But such were the prospects for suburban Westchester County, not for seventeen acres in Manhattan. "In the plans themselves" for the Manhattan site, Mumford concludes, "one too often sees just the opposite—rigidity, confinement, lack of sound provision for growth."[70]

The 1947 report notes that current UN membership stood at fifty-five states but cautions that the buildings should be planned for "a possible membership of at least seventy."[71] Mumford, however, here defends the value of flexibility for just the opposite reason: "It seems not to have occurred to anyone that this constitution [the UN Charter] is amendable, and that the composition of the organization could change, in which case even less seating space might be required." For Mumford, concerned that "the proportions of the [Assembly] hall seem overwhelming," the mis-sizing of the chamber provides one more example of the unfortunate way that "the future is frozen solidly in the form of the present."[72]

If this is an example of the flexibility Mumford seeks, however, it is certainly a curious and revealing one. It implies that he believed that the move toward world government would result either in fewer UN member states or in fewer representatives for existing states. The issue is compounded by his further assertion that it is a "weakness of the charter" that "the smallest state" receives "as many seats as the biggest power."[73] It surely seems paradoxical that Mumford should champion the architectural flexibility to accommodate a diminished membership in an organization he ostensibly seeks to promote, unless he sees the future as bringing a kind of consolidation into a few powerful states. There are no complete answers in his writings, but he certainly implies that national divisions should become increasingly less important. In any case, the subsequent burgeoning of the United Nations membership into more than 150 delegations indicates that

Mumford's eagerness for smaller numbers was something less than prescient.

Architecture as Symbol of Spiritual Authority

What one senses in all this, although Mumford does not say so explicitly, is that the problem of achieving a humane architecture is less a matter of avoiding physical intimidation than it is a need to regain spiritual affinity for large man-made objects in the landscape. Buildings which dwarf humans are not out of place in an age of faith. Mumford's fear is that this faith is gone or, equally troubling, that it has been misappropriated into the unexamined worship of machines. In the skyscraper, the *cathedral of commerce,* Mumford can find no sanctuary.

In seeking architectural forms for an alternative faith, a faith in the renewal of man through world government, Mumford wishes to establish the United Nations headquarters as a modern sacred space. He seems to regard Vatican City as something between a metaphor and a precedent for the realm he envisions, though his new Vatican is surely to be catholic without the capital C. What appeals to Mumford about the Vatican is its legal and spatial separateness from the rest of Rome and the authority of St. Peter's as an architectural symbol. In his RIBA lecture, he calls for "splendid visible symbols to keep our faith alive."[74] For Mumford, it is especially the General Assembly building that must become such a symbol, a structure whose "main effort" must be to "hold the eye and elevate the spirit."[75] He insists further that, if the United Nations "is not to fail us" as an institution, its "authority should be visible."[76]

The central difficulty, which Mumford does not acknowledge, is to find forms that convey both authority and panhuman democractic values. He recognizes that the architectural forms cannot be drawn primarily from the past, but he does not provide a satisfactory alternative: "These buildings should be as beloved a symbol as the Statue of Liberty, as powerful a spectacle as St. Peter's in Rome. Such symbols cannot be created by falling back on clichés, like statues, domes, and skyscraper towers, and they cannot be conceived overnight."[77] And yet, in the only place in any of his writings about the UN complex where he recommends a specific form, he suggests that the architects of the General Assembly building should have made "bold use of a cylindrical or hemispherical form that would have captured the eye or perhaps even captivated it."[78] How such a cylinder or hemisphere could escape the clichés of the skyscraper or the dome he does not explain.

More troublesome still is his assessment of the value of abstraction for conveying the appropriate universal architectural symbolism. After all his talk about the inhumanity of the composition, he admits, curiously enough, to one spatially induced epiphany. From one particular vantage point he is completely entranced:

. . . [F]rom the north, along First Avenue, the two visible buildings (the Conference Building is conspicuously absent) suddenly become a vision of delight, when the steep down curve of the Assembly roof, looking somewhat foreshortened from below, intersects the steep marble slab of the Secretariat to the south. If one could stand permanently at that point, one could forgive all the architectural lapses. Genuine four-dimensional architecture would present a series of such miracles as one moved around from this point and into the buildings, but the UN design, unfortunately, offers only one clean architectural hit. Still, that fine view is worth seeking out, especially on a sunny day with a blue sky, for the pleasures of an abstract composition that is oddly satisfactory as a symbol of the UN itself.[79]

Here Mumford suggests that abstraction, if handled with rigor, can be both powerful and desirable. This kind of gestalt vision, central to Cassirer's and Langer's writing on aesthetic symbolism, appears so powerful, in fact, that Mumford seems startlingly willing to dispense with his whole social and cultural agenda for the building. His desire for even a momentary flash of universal harmony is so great that he forgets his more immediate concerns. He presumably wishes this same kind of transcendent detachment for the UN delegates who, if properly placed and visually coached, should then be able to forget their wars and their factional infighting and grasp the logic of world government.

Unless the architecture manages to induce spiritual uplift in many ways and from many perspectives, however, it is useless because most people will not know how or where to look for it. In his call for a genuine four-dimensional architecture, Mumford seeks the proliferation of architectural miracles, but does not do much to promote the democratization of such symbolism. The jump from perceiving a harmony of forms to the vision of a harmony of nations goes well beyond the conceptual framework of Cassirer or Langer, and is a leap without explanation or the likelihood of much empirical replicability.

Mumford's largely unquestioning call for a universal symbolism disregards the extent to which symbolism depends on ascription. While the UN headquarters may well immediately and concretely convey some component of non-intuitive meaning, this meaning may not necessarily be the same one that Mumford wishes to identify. And, precisely because symbolism is a dynamic force, architectural interpretation may well change over time. The symbolism of the United Nations headquarters cannot simply be treated as part of the architectural commission. As Mumford himself contends, no form is without meaning. What he fails to point out, however, is that this meaning is not always readily apparent or universally shared. Where Mumford roundly rejects the Secretariat building design as an example of the order out of chaos and unity out of diversity, others would see this sleek skyscraper rising out of the cleansed slums as the perfect expression of these ideals. The strength of association between the architectural form of the headquarters and the ideals of the organization will grow only in proportion to the institutional success of the United

Nations. While the symbolism of the corporate skyscraper may indeed invite associations inappropriate to the purposes of the United Nations, different architecture would not necessarily make for better symbolic associations. Though it may be tenable that the delegates might feel a certain uplift because of the beauty and comfort of their surroundings, and may even be stirred by this to recognize the importance of their enterprise, it seems rather farfetched to suggest that the architectural order of the building would cause the participants to adopt a panhuman perspective on issues where this is clearly against their national interests. Nonetheless, this is just what Mumford insists that architecture can and should do.

In his RIBA lecture, he challenged the architects of the future United Nations complex to induce such a universalist ethos through their designs: "He who enters this international city should be forced *by the architecture itself* to drop some of his nationalism, some of his tribalism, at its green barriers, even as the Moslem faithful leave their shoes at the entry of a Mosque" (emphasis added).[80] He called for "the new world centre" to be "a light and a guide to the new order of cultural communion and political understanding."[81] Seven years later, after the disappointing buildings had been constructed, Mumford again suggested that the design of the headquarters should have been able to further the ideals of the organization:

> No one should be able to look at these buildings from afar, or to penetrate their interior, without having his imagination awakened, his conscience touched, his will to peace quickened or reinforced by the design. If the United Nations matures into an organ of effective world government, capable of affectionately commanding men's loyalties throughout the planet, it will be in spite of, not because of, the architecture of its first headquarters.[82]

Mumford's language here admits only two possibilities: good architecture either contributes to world government or hinders it—there is no admission of the possibility that it may be largely irrelevant. While Mumford makes a good case for the value of architecture as providing evidence of commitment, flexibility, and authority, he goes too far when he asks that it actively foster his version of the organization's ideals.

Conclusion: Universal Ideals and Local Realities

The underlying problem with Mumford's universal architectural symbolism is that he wants it to convey, simultaneously, not only what is, but also what ought to be. Equally troubling is Mumford's maintaining that this symbolism is somehow inherent in the architectural object while, at the same time, he demonstrates through the act of writing that much symbolic interpretation relies upon the presence of a critic to draw it out. While it may be that the relative consistency of Mumford's overarching moral stance is his greatest strength, this becomes a weakness when he uses it to gloss over the incongruities of the present.

His vision of world government is at odds with that of the UN Charter, and his vision of a universal architectural symbolism is equally at odds with the human predilection (clearly perceived elsewhere in his writings) for group affiliations of a family, neighborhood, city-wide, regional, or national sort. Mumford's new Vatican, "a group of modern freestanding buildings in harmonious aesthetic relationship,"[83] would be considerably more detached from its urban surroundings than its Roman precursor: his sacred realm is to be "set . . . sufficiently apart from the welter of other buildings."[84] Mumford seems to construct an analogy between this vision of Manhattan redeemed by organic modern architecture from the chaos of its slaughterhouse district and the world rid of its wars by the United Nations.

Yet the analogy falters on both ends; neither modern architecture nor the United Nations seems able to answer the questions that he wants addressed. In viewing slum clearance as the path to urban renewal, he seeks to separate the new from the old in a way that seems incompatible with his call for organic building. His principles for city planning are inconsistent with his principles for architecture. In proposing destruction in the name of organicism, Mumford offers a brutal bulldozer urbanism little better than that of Le Corbusier or Robert Moses, whose urban ideas he so despised. And, for all three urban visionaries, this larger campaign detracts from the smaller victories.

Similarly, in his determination to see the United Nations as the harbinger of world government, Mumford completely ignores its more immediate function as a guarantor, not of world government, but of national sovereignty.[85] His writings make no reference to the UN Charter's pledge to promote the self-determination of peoples still subject to the trusteeship of colonial powers.[86] Like the rest of those who failed to anticipate the rapid tripling of U.N. member states,[87] Mumford does not acknowledge the powerful twin impulses toward pluralism and self-preservation that undergird the Charter. In writing that the UN headquarters should be "public relations for the new world order,"[88] he deliberately blinds himself to the fundamentally conservative nature of the Charter.

Because his dim notion of universal architectural symbolism and his vague vision of global government can be so readily dismissed, Mumford runs the danger that this disregard may also subsume his other, more thoroughly buttressed, observations. This, however, would be unfortunate, as his less grandiose social and cultural insights were prescient in their day and remain compelling still. His ability to articulate social and economic influences upon the form of the capitalist workplace and his skill in identifying cultural meanings attached to such buildings enabled him to bring new and interdisciplinary dimensions to architectural criticism. In so doing, his writings, themselves, have helped to shape our interpretations of the UN headquarters; the power he seemingly wished to invest in the architect is assumed instead by the critic.

Mumford falters when he asks architecture to lead politics in a way that is radically detached from the wishes of politicians. Though it may indeed encourage already latent impulses, architecture itself can never force social change. In a world of power politics, nationalism will never be dropped like shoes at the entry of a mosque. However beautiful the prayer hall, even the Muslim faithful remember to reclaim their footwear when they depart.

In proposing his own ideas about the UN organization and the edifices designed to house it, Mumford searched for a way to counteract the moral degradation and physical destruction he found so rampant in the aftermath of Hitler and Hiroshima. Though his pleas for alternative designs were ignored, he nonetheless continued to chronicle his mounting objections as each successive piece of the Headquarters was completed. Unable to stop it, Mumford the *generalist* was at least able to categorize it and assimilate it into his thinking. The UN Headquarters emerged as another new machine, subject to the same fatal flaws as other forms of misguided technology. For Mumford, then, the failure of the UN complex to exemplify his ideals of organicism was far more than a disappointment about architecture; it was an ominous symbol of global vision gone astray.

The Perils of Personality: Lewis Mumford and Politics After Liberalism

CASEY BLAKE

Mumford as Usable Past

Amid the lively discussions of liberal, communitarian, and radical politics currently taking place among historians and political theorists, Lewis Mumford's name remains strangely absent. The revival of interest in his work among ecologists, urbanists, feminist theorists of housing, and cultural historians has not yet touched those engaged in rethinking and renovating American political culture, even as their debates rehearse many of the themes of Mumford's career. Whether in the form of Richard Rorty's resurgent "pragmatism," the "communitarianism" of Robert Bellah, Alasdair MacIntyre, William Sullivan, and Sheldon Wolin, or the "neo-Marxism" of Richard Bernstein and American followers of Jürgen Habermas, recent efforts at constructing a new, post-liberal opposition return to issues that preoccupied Mumford at the earliest stages of his career, and which form a backdrop to his entire life's work. Chief among the questions that Mumford addressed in the 1920s and 1930s, and which now concern his successors, are those that plumb the cultural crisis of democratic politics: the severing of the bonds of fellowship and community in advanced industrial society; the waning sense of a "public good," and of a vernacular idiom capable of expressing such an ideal in a secular culture; and the antagonism between the instrumental language of statecraft and technique, on the one hand, and the symbolic language of aesthetic experience and moral judgment, on the other. Despite Mumford's renown as an architectural critic and a sociologist of cities and technology, these are the critical issues that undergird virtually every one of his works. As he wrote to Van Wyck Brooks, in the midst of working on the lectures that became *The Golden Day*, "I find, consolingly, that my standards in architecture and literature are one, so that the good life that hovers in the background has, at all events, a unity of interior and exterior."[1]

The mood of skepticism about received liberal dogma and of wary hopefulness about possible alternatives that pervades Mumford's early work links those writings to current attempts to create a post-liberal politics. Like many of his successors, he was shaken by the outcome of a bloody, apparently pointless war overseen by liberals. The result was an uneasiness about the state, and about progressive claims for "scientific" state-sponsored reform, that has since become the dominant mood among chastened liberals and radicals in the 1980s. In reaction, Mumford undertook a project that still remains the central focus of much current political debate. Forsaking the "scientific" claims of progressive thought, which likened the actions of reformers to the technical achievements of the engineer or applied scientist, Mumford sought to ground a democratic politics in the give-and-take of a public conversation, and in the associational ties of a common culture. Such an alternative would not repudiate scientific method, or even many of the fruits of technical innovation, so much as it would return political understanding to its roots in the broader cultural dialogue of which science was only a part. Mumford's "cultural turn" in the 1920s and 1930s, then, anticipates by half a century the current intellectual ferment about the politics of language, culture, and symbolic meaning. It also anticipates the return to a republican idiom of "community" and the "common good" advocated by Robert Bellah and other proponents of a renewal of American politics and culture.

Like Mumford in the 1920s, contemporary advocates of a revitalized public culture condemn what Alasdair MacIntyre calls "the bifurcation of the contemporary world" into two separate spheres, equally indifferent to the claims of public discussion: "a realm of the organizational in which ends are taken to be given and set and are not available for rational scrutiny and a realm of the personal in which judgment and debate are central factors, but in which no rational social resolution of issues is available."[2] Between the dictates of administrative rationality and the "emotivism" of the socially unencumbered self, there exists no middle range of cultural practices to ground public and private behavior in what Mumford called "the good life." When Bellah and his associates demand an understanding of community, in which "the individual self finds its fulfillment in relationship with others in a society organized around public dialogue," they echo Mumford's belief that the crisis of "personality" in the industrial society requires a comprehensive rethinking of American culture and politics.[3] In their search for a politics after liberalism, Bellah, MacIntyre, and other critics of "the bifurcation of the contemporary world" return to a project of personal and public renewal that preoccupied Mumford more than a half-century ago.

This essay aims at making Mumford's early explorations of "the good life" available to the contemporary discussions surrounding the reconstruction of a public culture, and does so in the spirit of Mumford's own understanding of what it means to shape a "usable past." Far from bending the past to fit current ideological imperatives, the "usable past" that Mumford sought in his writings was intended to give a historical dimension to a common culture. History, in his view, was "usable" insofar as it allowed citizens to reflect on the past conditions that shaped their experience, and to grasp the potential for change that lay within themselves and their society. "Establishing its own special relations with its past," Mumford wrote in 1920, "each generation creates anew what lies behind it, as well as what looms in front; and instead of being victimized by those forces which are uppermost at the moment, it gains the ability to select the qualities which it values, and by exercising them it rectifies its own infirmities and weaknesses."[4] Mumford's work may be "usable," then, not as a crutch for one or another position in the current controversy about American politics, but as a way of deepening the historical resonance of that discussion and of taking notes of opportunities missed and of mistakes made in its previous formulations. Above all, I will argue that his work provides a lesson in the ambiguities of "community," a word that reappears throughout Mumford's writings and that has quickly emerged as the cornerstone of all current efforts to transcend the deadlock of American liberalism.

Mumford's work has so much to offer contemporary debates about the recovery of a democratic culture because it directly addresses the need to reconceive of individualism as an ideal of selfhood achieved through participation in a common artistic and civic project. At the center of all of his concerns is his interest in renewing "personality" through a revitalized democratic community life. The personal, in Mumford's work, is never *merely* personal: it always involves questions of politics and culture that transcend the limitations of private life. But this admirable goal of personal and public renewal has taken very different forms at different stages of Mumford's career, as he has alternated between blueprints for utopian, neotechnic organization, and more modest hopes for moral leadership by small groups that have rejected the premises of a modern technological society. In either case, Mumford has been at best tentative, and at worst neglectful, in his treatment of the conflicts—within a polity, or between the individual and the community, or even within the self—involved in overcoming our current cultural predicament. To be faithful to Mumford's project, then, requires going beyond the terms of Mumford's own work; it requires that contemporary communitarianism assess the perils, as well as the promise, of a politics of personality.

Insurgent Personality

In the closing pages of *Technics and Civilization* (1934), Mumford argued that the reaction against "the denial of the organic and the living" in a machine civilization could take one of two forms. The first would involve "the use of mechanical means to return to the primitive," a resurgence of destructive impulses that, left unchecked by any collective moral discipline, would harness the power of new technologies in a final assault on civilized life. Against this prospect of libidinal and mechanical apocalypse, Mumford posed his own vision of personality, community, and a renewed vitalism. The alternative to the cult of power, he explained, "involves the rebuilding of the individual personality and the collective group, and the re-orientation of all forms of thought and social activity toward life."[5]

Of the three constituents of Mumford's vision of cultural renewal, it was the "rebuilding of the individual personality" that had absorbed most of his attention until the publication of *Technics and Civilization.* Throughout the 1920s, Mumford returned again and again to the crisis of personal identity in a corporate industrial society—a theme he inherited from the circle of cultural critics associated with the journal *The Seven Arts* in 1916-17. Like Brooks, Randolph Bourne, Waldo Frank, and Harold Stearns, Mumford believed that a culture of "self-expression" and "personality" was replacing the Victorian culture of "self-reliance" and "character." In this regard, he and his forerunners at *The Seven Arts* were part of a much broader cultural upheaval that centered on the emergence of "personality," which has become a central topic in recent cultural histories of the early twentieth century. The late Warren Susman, Jackson Lears, and other historians have traced the widespread interest in "personality" as a successor to the Emersonian ideal of "character" to the emergence of a therapeutic culture of mass consumption. While nineteenth-century Americans from the middle class extolled self-discipline and training in moral virtues through literary and religious education, advocates of personality equated success with the cultivation of personal charm and the ability to win friends and influence people.[6] In this view, the recurring fascination with "personality," "personal growth," and "self-fulfillment" in the writings of Mumford and his predecessors suggests that theirs is another example of cultural radicalism gone wrong. Once again, the attempt to delineate a counterculture—in this case, what Susman called a "culture of personality"—only fuels the dominant culture's capacity to promote new forms of privatistic, and ultimately conformist, experience as a means of liberation.

Despite the value of this argument as an interpretation of the rhetoric of personality in advertising, popular psychology, and other manifestations of mass culture, it fails to do justice to the search for personality that engaged, first, the *Seven Arts* group and, later, Lewis Mumford.[7] For these critics, the reconstruction of the self required neither therapeutic self-absorption nor the rootless individualism celebrated in the popular notion of self-reliance. Instead, the creation of a full personality involved a reciprocal process of cultural and self-renewal. Mumford and the earlier *Seven Arts* writers sharply distinguished their conception of personality from the therapeutic gospel of affability and charm by insisting that personal growth was possible only within a project of enlarging the domains of civic life and culture, which in turn required the active participation of the individual in his or her community. Personality was the realization of the self in tension—or in dialogue—with its environment, not psychic adjustment to dominant institutions. As Bourne wrote in 1916, "All our idealisms must be those of future social goals in which all can participate, the good life of personality lived in the environment of the Beloved Community."[8]

The radical personalism that Mumford inherited from the *Seven Arts* group dovetailed with the view of organic equilibrium he had learned from his mentor Patrick Geddes. Geddes's vitalistic biology led Mumford to a view of nature as a dynamic interpenetration of dead and living matter, and of human development as a dialectic of subjective consciousness and objective conditions. As he explained in *Technics*, Geddes held that "every form of life . . . is marked not merely by adjustment to the environment, but by insurgence against the environment." It followed then that an organism was "both the victim of fate and the master of destiny: it lives no less by domination than by acceptance." In human life, "this insurgence reaches its apex," because aesthetic experience and historical knowledge allow men and women to glimpse the limitations of their given surroundings and, on occasion, transcend them.[9] Mumford received the same message from both Geddes and the *Seven Arts*. The highest achievements of "personality" were possible only through sustained efforts at shaping the public world and, in so doing, making both that world and oneself more human, more fully "personal."

The need to create the conditions for insurgent personality compelled Mumford to articulate a political position in the 1920s that still resists easy characterization. Despite the publicity surrounding his curt dismissal of "the pragmatic acquiescence" in *The Golden Day* (1926)—and his subsequent debate with John Dewey in *The New Republic*—Mumford was not as far from Dewey's pragmatism as he and others (including Dewey) may have believed. In his arguments for cultural renewal, Mumford was not merely recycling the Romantic critique of utilitarianism, whatever his indebtedness to the English Romantics, from William Blake to William Morris. Nor was Dewey a latter-day positivist, oblivious to the cultural concerns that motivated Mumford. What both men missed in their heated exchanges during the 1920s was their convergence on the importance of symbolic language and communications in providing a cultural foundation for a participatory politics.[10] Mumford's position, like that of Bourne, Brooks, Frank, and Stearns before him, is best seen as a highly subjectivist variant of pragmatism that drew on Romanticism as a corrective to perceived weaknesses in Dewey's thought.

Mumford owed more to Dewey than he usually acknowledged. Like Dewey, he argued that cultural life needed to be grounded in "experience"—the point of convergence between human consciousness and the environment, and the fertile ground of real personal growth. Dewey's philosophy of mind in conscious interaction with society directly paralleled Mumford's own conception of personality developing through experience. Moreover, Mumford shared Dewey's interest in renewing the democratic ideal of a free public sphere based on a shared culture of critical inquiry, which is what both men meant when they spoke of the promise of science or scientific method in re-creating a democratic community life. Finally, Mumford found in pragmatism and in the Romantic critique of capitalism a common veneration of the craftsman as the apogee of realized selfhood. According to Dewey and Morris, craftsmanship transcended the industrial division of theory and practice by giving individuals the fruits of historical experience; it allowed the self to be crafted in interaction with the physical and cultural worlds. The culture of craftsmanship provided a symbolic language and a practice in which personality could engage its environment, without succumbing to its premises.

Mumford did differ with Dewey, and with mainstream pragmatism, in his hostility to the state as an agency of scientific reform and in his insistence that a new politics first required a prolonged attention to aesthetic and moral values. In his earliest essays for *The Dial* after the war, Mumford targeted the state as a threat to culture and values. "Civil life means association," he wrote in 1919, "with the family, the trade union, the grange, the chamber of commerce, the professional institute, the church, the theater, and the forum intermediating between the life of the individual and his life as the member of a political (military) state."[11] Such mediating institutions provided the context for a culture of personality; and as Mumford's thinking developed in the 1920s, he tried to distinguish his "culturist" conception of community from the progressive ideal of state-sponsored social unity. The politics of "culturism" was "rooted in the integrity of the local community," he argued, "in its common *shul*" and other local organs of civic life, not in the nation-state.[12] By 1930, Mumford had become even more resolute in this regard. "As an expression of the will to power, the state is an enemy of culture," he declared.[13] The centralized state had emerged victorious during World War I because bureaucratic means of organization, pioneered in the factory and the corporation, had already loosened the cultural bonds that held together local communities.

Mumford's hostility to the state as an agency of reform was always a submerged element in his debates with Dewey and other progressives over the role of culture in a democratic politics. Fearful that Dewey's work displayed a tendency to overlook the subjective dimensions of experience, Mumford sought to ground a new politics of democratic community in a shared set of aesthetic practices and symbols and in a common understanding of moral values. In Mumford's view, aesthetic experience and values stood at the crossroads of public life and private conduct, creating a cultural "second nature" that would sustain the critical capacities of individuals in search of personality and a revitalized community life. They were the resources needed in the "insurgence" of the human organism against its conditions, and in the rebuilding of regional cultures as alternatives to the nation-state. Like the *Seven Arts* critics, Mumford challenged the pragmatists to broaden their conception of experience to acknowledge the significance of art and values in fostering shared bonds of community and a consciously- informed social practice.

By the mid-1920s, then, Mumford had already arrived at the point of departure for his mature work and at an intellectual position best considered as an aestheticist pragmatism. Convinced of the need to foster personality through a collective project of cultural renewal, Mumford sought alternatives to the bureaucratic structures of authority and association in modern industry and the wartime state. The language of symbolic interaction provided exactly such an alternative, he believed; it deepened the potential for personal experience as it enriched a democratic community life. Much of Mumford's earliest writing on these themes seemed hardly political, but questions of community and cultural democracy were never far from his mind as he began his career as a critic of American architecture, literature, and culture. In the late 1920s and early 1930s, Mumford turned to a more explicitly political formulation of his views on culture, personality, and community, a shift in emphasis that became fully apparent with the publication of *Technics and Civilization* in 1934. With this turn to politics and sociology, he revealed both the potential and the limitations of his "culturism" as a critique of modern culture.

Against Ahab: Mumford's Cultural Ethic

"I have never been a Liberal," Mumford wrote in a 1930 statement of "What I Believe" for *The Forum,* but he added that "if I cannot call myself a revolutionist now, it is not because the current programs for change seem to me to go too far: the reason is rather because they are superficial and do not go far enough."[14] Geddes's organicism had left Mumford ill-disposed toward either classical liberalism or Marxism, with their emphasis on political conflict, competition, and struggles over rights. Instead, Mumford elaborated on the neo-republican and anarchist radicalism of Henry George, Ebenezer Howard, Peter Kropotkin, and Thorstein Veblen, which confirmed his hostility to the nation-state and reinforced Geddes's biological view of community as a healthy organism. Mumford's communitarian politics shared with the radicalism of these turn-of-the-century thinkers a defense of a balanced, organic community of producers against the invasive forces of speculation, monopoly, and war. In this regard, Mumford's politics were more populist than socialist. Following George's lead, Mumford tended to attack finance capitalism as a parasitic force that dissolved mutualistic social bonds and promoted feverish commercial expansion at the expense of any sense of the common good.

The merits of this populist political tradition, in Mumford's eyes, lay in its emphasis on cultural issues and on the importance of local community as a counter to state power—questions ignored by most progressives and socialists. But the very advantages of a populist defense of a producers' commonwealth were also the causes for its most serious limitations as a radical politics of personality and community. These limitations were rarely acknowledged or confronted openly in Mumford's work, even as he tried to adapt this radical tradition to the challenge of interpreting and criticizing an advanced industrial culture. Yet they posed challenges to his own critical project that clearly influenced his thinking in this period. If local communities had in fact been "invaded" and colonized by metropolitan cultures, and their institutions replaced by those of the wartime state and the national market, then the task of self-renewal and cultural reconstruction had to confront questions of power and conflict. Mumford's ideal of a communitarian culture had to come to terms with those institutional arrangements that prevented self-fulfillment and deformed public dialogue. This, in turn, required a project that fortified the critical self— the oppositional self—as an adversary of its surroundings, even as it sought reconciliation with others in a new community. Moreover, it required formulating a culture of opposition that fostered the "organic" values of "wholeness" and "equilibrium" that dominated Mumford's Geddesian political vocabulary, without embracing the undemocratic, "mechanical" unity that had been constructed on the ruins of a civic culture. The challenges facing Mumford as he sought to reconstruct a radical communitarian politics, then, were two-fold: the ideal of the cultural self had to be salvaged from the adjustment of the acculturated self to its surroundings; and the promise of "community" had to be predicated on a realistic appraisal of the threats to its attainment posed by modern social relations.

In his writings from 1929 and 1930, Mumford confronted these challenges by addressing the ethical issues at stake in a communitarian politics of personality. Mumford's biography of Herman Melville, his statement of belief in *The Forum,* and a contemporary polemic against the conservative New Humanism of Irving Babbitt and Paul Elmer More articulated the need for moral reconstruction as the first step toward the renewal of community life. If, as Alan Trachtenberg has argued, Mumford's early politics rested on "a social aesthetics—a grounding of social criticism upon an aesthetic premise"—then so too did his ethics.[15] Mumford looked to the language of symbolic form to provide a successor to prophetic religion as a resource for the critical "personality" and as a common ground for a democratic politics.

Mumford's *Herman Melville* (1929) may be unreliable as biography, but its significance lies in its effort to view Melville's struggle with a hostile culture, and with his own despair, as a usable past for a twentieth-century culture of personality. In Melville's Captain Ahab, Mumford recognized both the Promethean drive of a technological society and the destructive impulses at work in every person's "insurgence" against his or her given state. The very gifts that saved human beings from animal existence beckoned with the promise of limitlessness: of freedom from all inherited restraints and traditions, and of personal reconciliation with an ideal world. The result, the cult of "meaningless force," of the great white whale, drove Ahab to his death and propelled industrial societies to an unending quest for limitless power.[16] It was Melville's accomplishment in his later work—*Clarel* and *Billy Budd*—to find in culture a means of maintaining a tension between his own aspirations to transcendence and acceptance of his limitations. The doubled nature of human life as both creature and creator of its environment made culture the proving-ground for human aspirations and the realm where men and women were compelled to recognize their own mortality. In Mumford's cultural ethics, the creation of forms and symbols provided a stern but not despairing lesson in moral realism. The legacy of culture was, indeed, restraining and, to the Promethean mind, a hindrance to the realization of the human will. Yet only such restraints made possible the transcendence of human limits on terms other than Ahab's: they transmuted the will-to-power into forms, values, and the other durable artifacts of a common culture. "Man's defense lies within himself," Mumford wrote, "not within the narrow, isolated ego, which may be overwhelmed, but in that self which we share with our fellows and which assures us that, whatever happens to our carcasses and hides, good men will remain, so to carry on the work, to foster and protect the things we have recognized as excellent."[17]

By choosing Melville as his source for a personal ethics, as opposed to Emerson or Whitman (the culture heroes of choice for his friends Brooks and Frank), Mumford made clear the importance of a recognition of human limits, of "the tragic sense of life," for his own vision of community. Melville's life and work brought Mumford face to face with the problems of evil, tragedy, and the inescapable sense of loss that plagued Melville as he confronted an indifferent world. Mumford's encounter with Melville left him convinced of the moral shabbiness of American liberalism, and of the need to find a secular equivalent to the insights into human nature once provided by religion. As he argued in 1930, in "What I Believe" and "Towards an Organic Humanism," those committed to renewing democratic community required an ethical middle ground between acquiescence and the pursuit of personal boundlessness that fueled the technological will-to-power. "If a religion be that which gives one a sense of the things that are worth dying for, this community with all life, this sense of a central purpose in oneself, inextricably bound up with the nature of things, even those accidents and brutal mischances that are so hard to assimilate—this faith may be called a religion."[18]

That religion, for Mumford, was a religion of culture, but culture conceived as an inherently dynamic, self-critical, and self-limiting form of human endeavor. Mumford's religion acknowledged that there would always be friction between individuals and their community; far from seeking to erase such conflict, radicals should seek to exploit it as a spur to cultural creativity. "The real problem of life," he wrote, "both for men and societies, is to keep the organism and the environment, the inner world and the outer, the personality and its creative sources, in the state of tension wherein growth and renewal may continually take place."[19] By maintaining personality in a state of tension with its environment, culture could provide individuals with the moral resolve to resist accommodation and the ability to enjoy the fruits of limited victory.

Mumford's moral insights into the connection between the Promethean promise of technology and the cultural crisis of the boundless self became the major theme of his work after World War II. They played a smaller role, however, in *Technics and Civilization*, the first volume of his "Renewal of Life" series. There, as in his other major work of the 1930s, *The Culture of Cities*, Mumford located the origins of modern technology in the collapse of the symbolic universe of medieval Christianity, but he failed to follow up on this observation in his neotechnic program of alternatives. Writing of the seventeenth century, he explained how technology filled a spiritual absence left by the disintegration of Catholic metaphysics. In an "empty, denuded world," bereft of familiar cultural landmarks, "the invention of machines became a duty. By renouncing a large part of his humanity, a man could achieve godhood: he dawned on this second chaos and created the machine in his image: the image of power, but power ripped loose from his flesh and isolated from his humanity."[20] This indictment of the scientific contempt for a value-laden, cultural world might have led Mumford to develop his cultural ethics into a very different alternative to paleotechnic technology from that which emerged in the final chapters of *Technics*. Instead, the promising argument for moral renewal as a foundation for a new culture that had inspired the Melville biography and his 1930 essays now took a back seat to an ambiguous attempt to create personality and community within the context of a technological culture of organicism. "This development of value within the machine complex itself," as Mumford called his portrait of a neotechnic culture, relinquished the tension between personality and its environment that was critical to his cultural religion.[21] By attempting to give a modern, scientific basis to communitarian politics, Mumford had come to substitute technological *Gemeinschaft* for his original vision of a democratic community.

The Camera Eye: Neotechnics and the Objective Personality

Mumford's decision to seek organic values "within the machine complex itself" reflected not only his indebtedness to Geddes's idea of neotechnic synthesis, but his own attempt to overcome the elegiac tone of some of his early work—particularly *The Golden Day*—which had drawn fire from Mumford's friend Waldo Frank, as well as from John Dewey. In a review of *The Golden Day*, Frank complained of the "wistful and vague" nature of the book's conclusion. Mumford was "in love with the gesture, the dream, the childhood faery of our past: yet he rejects the *body*—our present interim of the Machine and of the romanticisms of the Machine—whereby alone this promise from our past may be organized into a living future." Anticipating his own argument for cultural synthesis in *The Re-discovery of*

America (1929), Frank held that "future spiritual action must rise organically from the facts of our hideous present," including the facts of modern industrialism.[22] For Frank, the example of Alfred Stieglitz's life and photography showed that it was possible for an artistic prophet to promote cultural "wholeness" by mastering industrial technology. In correspondence, Mumford assured Frank that he agreed that an organic culture must accept the benefits of "the Machine" in order to transcend its sterilities. This, he explained to Frank, had been the basis of his critical endorsement of architectural Modernism, in which he sought to move beyond the architects of the International Style by reintegrating humanistic values with the efficiency and crisp aesthetics of industrialism.[23] A similar perspective on industrial culture had informed much of his theory of the "fourth migration" for the Regional Planning Association of America during the 1920s, in which electricity, the automobile, and the radio would permit a return to nature by way of modern technology.[24] But it was only in the early 1930s that Mumford elaborated on the cultural implications of such a project by insisting that mechanization and a technical worldview were irreversible gains and the resources for a post-industrial organic synthesis.

By accepting the technical disavowal of religious and aesthetic experience as the first step to a new cultural synthesis, Mumford essentially jettisoned the morally grounded communitarianism of his work from the late 1920s. "In Our Stars: The World Fifty Years From Now," a 1932 sequel to "What I Believe" for *The Forum*, registered the shift in emphasis in Mumford's thinking. Though he mentioned the presence of "humane and well-balanced personalities" populating his 1982 utopia, the overwhelming focus of Mumford's essay was on new techniques and new technologies—buildings built as "bubbles of glass"; "the utilization of the merchant marine for education"; solar energy; scientific agriculture; and "selective mating"—all designed to overhaul the "slums of thought" that needed to be razed along with ghetto neighborhoods. Mumford acknowledged that citizens of this world would have to cultivate "a whole new series of initiatives in the culture of the personality itself," including the "counter-balancing forces" of "communal and personal discipline," in order to prevent their mechanized utopia from becoming "a well-drilled beehive," but even this qualification revealed how much ground had been lost since his *Forum* piece two years earlier.[25] In Mumford's previous formulations of a communitarian politics, it was exactly such "initiatives in the culture of the personality" that took center stage in his analysis, and which dictated both the need to overcome a technocratic civilization and the construction of a more humane alternative. Now, if such initiatives played any significant part in Mumford's work in the mid-1930s, it was as an ambiguous humanistic backdrop to more pressing technical concerns— or worse, as a set of "counter-balancing forces" that checked the excesses of an organicist technology. By 1937, Mumford was fully in step with the progressive consensus on the need to extend "the socialized disciplines of the factory, the laboratory, the accounting office, and the administrative bureau" to the organization of "the community as a whole."[26] Writing in a foreword to a symposium on social planning, Mumford's only real dissent from the technocratic implications of such an approach lay in his insistence that philosophers, teachers, and sociologists join economists and engineers in forming "new human values," and that their plans reflect some wider democratic ferment in culture and values.[27] What had begun as a revolution in art and "values" had come of age in the 1930s as a program to supplement social planning by technicians with cultural planning by humanistic professionals.

Technics and Civilization, published in 1934, caught Mumford in mid-course between his moral communitarianism and his enthusiasm for a post-industrial cultural synthesis.[28] Penetrating insights into the mechanization of thought in the paleotechnic age co-exist in that text with neotechnic proposals that seem only to reproduce such developments on a broader scale. Prescient warnings against the dangers of technological determinism prepare the way for organicist solutions founded on the assumption that "the machine is a communist" which fosters collectivist modes of thought.[29] Morrisite indictments of the capitalist division of labor set the stage for praising the managerial innovations of Frederick Winslow Taylor and Elton Mayo. Despite Mumford's belief that the cult of mechanical power derived from the breaking of cultural restraints on humans' self-destructive impulses, the conclusion of *Technics* celebrates technology for wiping the slate clean of unnecessary cultural clutter and promoting a functionalist aesthetic of "precision, calculation, flawlessness, simplicity, economy."[30] For all the side-glances to the need to cultivate personality, it was the "objective" personality type that Mumford identified as the place where true personal development must begin. "A modulation of emphasis, a matter-of-factness, a reasonableness, a quiet assurance of a neutral realm in which the most obdurate differences can be understood, if not composed, is a mark of the emerging personality."[31] And as befit an objective personality, there now existed an "objective" human environment, which Mumford defended as a site of future cultural renewal. "The concept of a neutral world," Mumford explained, "untouched by man's efforts, indifferent to his activities, obdurate to his wish and supplication, is one of the great triumphs of man's imagination, and in itself represents a fresh human value."[32] In a Hegelian twist, the great white whale of untamed, unacculturated power that haunted Melville returned in *Technics* as the bearer of cultural renewal, community, and personality.

Mumford's confusion about the relation of cultural renewal to modern, "neotechnic," developments in science and industry reflects more than an optimism that later gave way, in the two-volume *Myth of the Machine,* to cultural "pessimism." Nor does such confusion reveal only Mumford's indebtedness to Geddes's chronology of civilization, Frank Lloyd Wright's efforts to reconcile the Ruskin-Morris tradition with a machine aesthetic, and Thorstein Veblen's dichotomy between an atavistic capitalism and "an instinct of workmanship," however much these predecessors contributed to Mumford's thinking. The tensions and contradictions running through *Technics* are indicative, instead, of much deeper problems in the very concepts of personality and community that underlie Mumford's work in this period.

Such problems are evident, above all, in those moments in *Technics* in which Mumford directly addresses the intersection of technology and personality in the neotechnic era. The psychological portraits of such archetypal figures as the hunter and the miner in the early chapters of the book advanced Mumford's claim about the interdependence of technical, cultural, and psychic change, and he was eager to note similar processes at work in his own time. For Mumford, the displacement of the mirror by the camera as the central medium of self-presentation marked a turning-point in human consciousness that accorded with his own theory of an emerging culture of organicism. The invention of the mirror had literally reflected—and, through reflection, reinforced—the emergence of an introspective psychology, Mumford held; the intertwining of bourgeois individualism and its polished image was nowhere more evident than in the work of the seventeenth-century Dutch portrait painters. The psychology of self-reflection depended on a technology of reflection that allowed a Rembrandt or a Hals to peer into his own image in search of something stable in a world in which outer certainties were dissolving. The result was less reassuring than Mumford believed in *Technics:* fascination with the isolated self revealed the self's reliance on the very mirrors used to keep it in focus, and hence prompted Baroque artists to document its fragmentation.

In the twentieth century, however, it was the camera that was busy laying waste to the bourgeois psychology of self-reflection and introspection. Like his contemporaries Bertolt Brecht and Walter Benjamin, Mumford believed that the medium of photography was the harbinger of a new social psychology, in which individuals viewed themselves from all three dimensions—as in a Cubist painting—and perceived the self as a creature of its environment. "The change is from an introspective to a behaviorist psychology, from the fulsome sorrows of Werther to the impassive public mask of an Ernest Hemingway," Mumford wrote. The "constant sense of a public world" that intervenes in Hemingway's fiction and causes its protagonist to imagine "himself as a public character, *being watched,*" testified to the camera's success at opening up the self to public inspection. "The change is significant: not self-examination but self-exposure: not tortured confession but easy open candor: not the proud soul wrapped in his cloak, pacing the lonely beach at midnight, but the matter-of-fact soul, naked, exposed to the sun on the beach at noonday, one of a crowd of naked people."[33] Such an interpenetration of personality and its community was even more evident in the motion picture, which not only promoted a Bergsonian consciousness of time as a constant process of overlapping relations, but also forced upon the audience a relativistic understanding of its own relation to artistic subject matter. "Without any conscious notion of

its destination, the motion picture presents us with a world of interpene-
trating, counter-influencing organisms: and it enables us to think about
that world in a greater degree of concreteness."[34]

Such passages, with their intuitions of the profound psychological implications of technical innovations, are reminders of Mumford's genius as an
interpreter of cultural change, but they also raise serious questions about
his understanding of personality as an interactive form of selfhood and of
community as an organic social group. In his positive view of the photographic self, Mumford approached the very position he had sought to
avoid in his explorations of personality in the 1920s. Hemingway's self-
conscious characters are, in Mumford's description, self-less: they open
themselves up to the camera so as to divest themselves of interiority and
privacy. They exemplify an objective personality type insofar as they are
open to all points of view, and are given neither to internal conflicts nor
to opposition to their culture. Far from fostering an insurgent, transformative personality, Mumford's psychology of the camera reconstitutes the
self as a creature of its environment, lost in the crowd of sunbathers on a
summer holiday. With Brecht and Benjamin, Mumford was oblivious to the
authoritarian and conformist potential of a culture of photographic publicity, in which the camera functions as an instrument of self-surveillance
and as a check against self-absorption. Nor did Mumford consider the possibility that the relativism promoted by the experience of viewing films
might produce, not the "whole," relational self set firmly in its surroundings, but the fragmented psychology of dissonant, incommensurate images
that now pervades post-modernist art. In this regard, the organic community Mumford proposed was one in which there remained little room
for insurgence and few possibilities for the critical function of personality.
As in so many other aspects of his argument in *Technics,* Mumford
embraced a technological solution to the crisis of bourgeois individualism,
which—as much of his own work suggested—required a deeper resolution
at the level of culture, ethics, and politics.

Beyond Mumford: Cultural Renewal as Politics

In a penetrating review of *Technics* for the journal *Christendom,* Reinhold
Niebuhr pointed to two major faults in Mumford's analysis and program
for renewal. Niebuhr held that Mumford's distinction between "the coal
and iron period of civilization and the more recent 'electricity-and-alloy'
complex" was adequate in terms of technology, but added that "Mr. Mumford is writing more than a history of technics."[35] Despite the revival of
organic forms in industrial design, Niebuhr found little reason to believe
that the class divisions and dehumanizing effects of paleotechnic civilization were in any way lessened in an electro-chemical age. More significant,
though, was the book's weakness on religion. "Science did indeed 'widen
the domain of the symbol,'" as Mumford argued, "but unfortunately it

frequently destroyed the permanent myth with the primitive myth and substituted some naive credulity for a majestic faith." Niebuhr recognized a
kindred spirit at work in Mumford's praise for medieval culture and "the
organic aspects of life," but he found baffling his dismissal of myth and
other forms of pre-scientific knowledge.[36] Without a greater sensitivity to
religious culture, *Technics* verged on becoming but one more example of
the "naive" religion of progress.

Niebuhr's critique reflected his own understanding of political and
moral realism. The first element of Niebuhr's criticism, which drew on his
recognition of the inescapability of politcal conflict, found echoes during
the 1930s and 1940s in the reactions to Mumford's work by such secular
leftists as V. F. Calverton, Mike Gold, Meyer Schapiro, Sidney Hook, and
James T. Farrell, all of whom savaged Mumford's "evolutionary" radicalism and his inattention to questions of class and social tensions.[37] These
critics may have retreated to easy Marxist clichés in their attacks, but they
did recognize the aversion to any serious analysis of power relations and
conflict in Mumford's communitarianism. In *Technics*, Mumford's holistic
approach to culture blinded him to the institutional impediments to the
creation of a democratic community life. "Paleotechnic ideals still largely
dominate the industry and the politics of the Western World," Mumford
acknowledged, but the "class struggles" and "national struggles" that he
cited as evidence of such backwardness suggested that such conflicts were
irrelevant to the construction of a new culture.[38] Mumford's hostility to
statist politics translated in *Technics* to an avoidance of any politics—of any
conflict over power, that is—that went beyond humanistic education and
propagation of new neotechnic advances. The danger of Mumford's "culturist" radicalism, then, lay in its confusion of cultural form with political
function. The evidence of holistic symbols in modern culture, and the new
interest among managers and technicians in social science, did not necessarily promise more democratic social relations. In fact, the very opposite
trend may have been at work during the second industrial revolution:
namely, the transference of programs of technical control of production
to the producers themselves.[39] Without the transformation in values
upheld in Mumford's early work, and a corresponding break with industrial power relations, the adoption of a holistic approach to culture would
be more likely to foster an authoritarian system of bureaucratic controls
than it would a democratic politics of community.

Even as Mumford later soured on the promise of "neotechnic" industry,
he still held firm to a communitarian politics that obscured conflicts over
power in modern society. In the 1940s and 1950s, his work took up the
example of the withdrawal of early Christians from Roman civilization as
a model for twentieth-century communitarians in a decadent industrial
culture.[40] That theme of cultural withdrawal remained a dominant motif
in subsequent writings. In 1970, *The Pentagon of Power* endorsed a politics
of retreat that sought "not to capture the citadel of power, but to withdraw
from it and quietly paralyze it." Only such initiatives, Mumford believed,

would "restore power and confident authority to its proper source: the human personality and the small face-to-face community."[41] Whether as neotechnic organicism or as decentralist radicalism, Mumford's communitarianism could never envision a politics of sustained conflict or engagement with the dominant institutions of modern politics. Community could take shape on the margins of power, or come into full bloom under the electric lamps of neotechnic technology, but not in a prolonged contest for power.

Not until the 1940s did Mumford grasp the full implications for his own work of Niebuhr's moral realism, with its insistence on an Augustinian psychology of humans' divided nature. Yet Niebuhr was correct to note a similar sensibility in parts of *Technics*, although these were only echoes of the ethical explorations of personality in Mumford's previous writings. There were certainly points of convergence between Mumford's secular religion of culture, as outlined in *Herman Melville* and his essays from 1930, and Niebuhr's realist appraisal of the inherent conflict between human aspirations and limitations. But Mumford's positive view of culture as a means of confronting that conflict, and of making it a way to enhance lived experience, left him less attentive than Niebuhr to the religious dimensions of a critical ethics. With his faith in symbolic language, Mumford was in the end closer to such cultural prophets as Erich Fromm or Carl Jung than he was to thinkers like Niebuhr or Freud, despite his deepening appreciation in the 1940s of their insights into the fissures within the human psyche.[42] To Niebuhr, faith was a way of allowing individuals to speak truth to culture; it preserved the independent, critical self from the blandishments of a therapeutic ethos. Mumford had argued that his ideal of a common culture was capable of generating its own tensions, and that the realization of personality required the insurgence of the self against culture, even as it forged the self through aesthetic experience. But in *Technics*, Mumford let those tensions slacken: neotechnic community absorbed the self, then remade it in its own image. Instead of deepening the critical stance of his cultural religion, Mumford lashed out at "the rubbish of earlier cultures," including "superstitious forms of religion" that kept the masses "in a state of emotional tutelage to the very forces that were exploiting them."[43]

The tragedy of this dismissal of traditional religious ethics was that Mumford's previous books laid the foundation for a far more compelling alternative to technocratic culture than that outlined in *Technics*. It was not until *The Pentagon of Power* that the full implications of his early treatment of ethics for a critique of technology became apparent. There, Mumford looked to culture as a force for restraining the dual reign of "the automaton and the id," whose interdependence he had first glimpsed through Melville's eyes.[44] Mumford's later work suggests that community must grow out of a moral consensus that recognizes the conflicts within the self, and which adopts an ethic of containment as an alternative to the technological culture of boundlessness.

"In taking an organic model," Mumford wrote in 1970, "one must renounce the paranoid claims and foolish hopes of the Power Complex, and accept finiteness, limitation, incompleteness, uncertainty, and eventual death as necessary attributes of life—and more than this, as the condition for achieving wholeness, autonomy, and creativity."[45] But the muddled notions of wholeness and community in Mumford's *Technics* point to the need for an even more resolute acceptance of finitude than Mumford advocated, one that acknowledges the limitations of personality and community themselves. As responses to the crisis of bourgeois individualism, theories of the "relational" self and of "communities of memory" still beckon with the promise of rootedness, nurturance, and a mutualistic sense of connection with and responsibility toward others.[46] But, as *Technics* demonstrates, the invocation of such values should not be confused with their realization, which may, in fact, require an initial determination to foster strong individuals and a realistic acceptance of conflict. Whatever the virtues of communitarianism as a democratic alternative to liberalism and Marxism, it cannot reject out of hand the emphasis of those traditions on a contested public sphere and their suspicion of claims to organic social unity.[47]

In contrast to contemporary advocates of communitarian democracy, Mumford looked in the 1920s and 1930s to the realm of culture—and particularly to the dynamics of symbolic language—as the source of political renewal. His efforts to restore the rich fabric of aesthetic experience and moral judgment rent by the culture of industrialism make his work of vital importance to contemporary debates about American public culture. According to Mumford, a public culture must be *cultural,* and not narrowly political: it must engage personalities in the creation of cultural form, as well as in the open-air debates of local democracy. A language of public dialogue, in Mumford's view, would have to invigorate art, music, architecture, and craftsmanship, in addition to the terms of political discourse. Here, then, Mumford's communitarianism still has a great deal to teach his successors about the cultural dimensions of civic renewal.

So too does Mumford's own struggle with the slippery implications of community for a new ethics and a new politics. If Mumford's different approaches to the problem of community in the 1920s, 1930s, and after offer anything to contemporary communitarians, it lies in their earnest attempts at reconciling an organicist social ideal with concrete cultural practice. *Technics and Civilization* offers one road to such a reconciliation, *Herman Melville* and *The Pentagon of Power* another. Admiration for Mumford's insights into the predicament of personality in modern culture should not blind us to the shortcomings of many of his own gestures toward a communitarian alternative, in particular his aversion to the political responsibilities of a "culturist" radicalism. The recognition that the crisis of American politics is symptomatic of a profound cultural crisis ought not to foster illusions that culture alone will produce new communities. Likewise, the understanding that the fully consummated self is the cultural self, rooted in communal practices, does not necessarily entail the elimination of boundaries between the self and community. Paradoxically, a recognition of the limits of community may best serve the cause of community; a renewed appreciation of the antagonism between "personality and its creative sources" may hold out the greatest promise of a socially grounded self. Such a view requires a resolve to live with conflicts usually blunted by the mutualistic ethos of community—to maintain that cultural "state of tension," as Mumford put it, "wherein growth and renewal may continually take place."[48]

Lewis Mumford, John Dewey, and the "Pragmatic Acquiescence"

ROBERT WESTBROOK

One of the leading motifs in Lewis Mumford's work in the interwar period was a sharp critique of the "acquiescence" to modern industrial society manifested in the philosophy of American pragmatism, particularly that of John Dewey. This critique began with the sharp attack on William James and Dewey in *The Golden Day* (1926) and culminated in the late 1930s and early 1940s with Mumford's charge that American liberalism had been corrupted by (among other things) its grounding in pragmatism and was, as a consequence, ill-prepared to meet the challenge of fascist barbarism. I would like to offer a revisionist account of this war Mumford waged on Dewey and pragmatism. Unlike most of those who have examined Mumford's criticisms of Dewey, I believe he was often wide of the mark.[1]

Leaning heavily on the criticisms of Dewey's philosophy advanced during World War I by Randolph Bourne (who was a ghostly presence looming over each of the Mumford-Dewey confrontations), Mumford blamed Dewey for depriving modern American liberalism of "values," particularly those values fostered by art and aesthetic experience. Pragmatism, he claimed, had helped transform liberalism into a desiccated, technocratic ideology. Mumford's critique of pragmatism was part of an attack on the ascendancy in modern American liberalism of an ethical thinness that Mumford termed "utilitarianism"—the equation of human happiness with little more than material abundance and a preoccupation with the means to such abundance. This criticism I find powerful and persuasive. It is not Mumford's strictures against liberal utilitarianism and its "belief in the good life as the *goods* life" that I wish to contest, merely his extension of these strictures to Dewey. For Mumford advanced his critique at the very moment that Dewey was shifting his attention as a philosopher to an analysis of the value-laden dimensions of human experience (including art) and articulating a social philosophy decidedly different from what Mumford termed "pragmatic liberalism" and similar, in important respects, to that of Mumford himself.[2]

Mumford has a well-deserved place as a leading critic of the narrowness of the moral vision of the many twentieth-century American liberal intellectuals. But he is less deserving of the pre-eminence he has achieved as a critic of Dewey's philosophy, for he must bear a measure of responsibility for the widespread misconception that Dewey made a signal contribution to the "corruption of liberalism." Perhaps the most unfortunate consequence of Mumford's misreading of Dewey (and Dewey's bitter reaction to it) was that it cut short a potentially fruitful dialogue between two extraordinary public intellectuals who were kindred spirits to a greater degree than either was willing to admit. The stunted Mumford-Dewey dialogue is significant both for the demonstration it affords of the way discourse has often gone awry in American intellectual life and for the riches it makes available to us if, as we continue to wrestle with the issues that troubled Mumford and Dewey, we imagine the conversation that might have been. Historian that I am, I confine myself here primarily to the first demonstration, but I do so with the hope that this might help enable the latter act of imagination.

The Pragmatic Acquiescence

Mumford's initial foray against pragmatism was embedded in the sad tale that he told in *The Golden Day* of the declension of American culture since the mid-nineteenth century. The Civil War, he argued there, had "cut a white gash through the history of the country." On the far side of the conflict lay the advanced "eotechnic" culture of the "Golden Day" of Emerson, Thoreau, Melville, Hawthorne, and Whitman: "the period of an Elizabethan daring on the sea, of a well-balanced adjustment of farm and factory in the East, of a thriving regional culture, operating through the lecture-lyceum and the provincial college; an age in which the American mind had flourished and had begun to find itself." The war had sealed the doom of this culture and had ushered in the reign of industrial exploitation and mammon. In its wake, "all the crude practices of British paleotechnic industry appeared on the new scene without relief or mitigation."[3]

In the Gilded Age, Mumford contended, industrialism ruled the American mind as well as the political economy. The "guts of idealism" went out of late nineteenth-century writers and intellectuals, and they lacked a belief in the "process of remolding, re-forming, re-creating, and so humanizing the rough chaos of existence" (*GD*, 83). Having lost this faith, these intellectuals were paralyzed, and they bowed to the inevitable, idealized the real, and drifted with the prevailing currents of their culture. William James was among the most important of these intellectuals because he named this acquiescence: "he called it pragmatism: and the name stands not merely for his own philosophy, but for something in which that philosophy was deeply if unconsciously entangled, the spirit of a whole age" (*GD*, 92).

James, in Mumford's account, translated the "animus of the pioneer" into philosophical argument by portraying an unfinished universe of boundless possibility and by celebrating the combative instincts and a life of struggle at the expense of a consideration of the ends for which these instincts were marshalled and the struggle waged. In sanctioning "this digging and dogging at the universe," James was doing little more than "warming over again in philosophy the hash of everyday experience in the Gilded Age" (*GD*, 96, 95). He was thus less a creative philosopher than a "reporter," for he offered no *Weltanschauung* that challenged the premises of his culture; in his philosophy one got "an excellent view of America" (*GD*, 95, 93). His new ideas were far less significant and influential than those he took for granted: "protestantism, individualism, and scientific distrust of 'values'" (*GD*, 95). Mumford acknowledged that James's philosophy had been caricatured by many into "a belief in the supremacy of cash-values and practical results" and admitted that "there is an enormous distance between William James and the modern professors who become employees in advertising agencies, or bond salesmen, or publicity experts, without any sense of degradation" (*GD*, 97, 98). Nevertheless, James's thought was "permeated by the smell of the Gilded Age," and Mumford felt that he had to bear a substantial measure of responsibility for the reinforcement his work provided for those whose eye was on the main chance. James, Mumford concluded, "built much worse then he knew" (*GD*, 97, 98).[4]

Though Mumford doubted the value of the substance of James's work, he did admit that it had a "homely elegance" of style, unlike the prose of fellow pragmatist John Dewey, whose writing afforded the reader an experience "as depressing as a subway ride" (*GD*, 130–31). Apart from matters of style, however, Mumford found more to praise in Dewey's "instrumentalist" version of pragmatism than he did in James's philosophy. He applauded, in particular, Dewey's commitment to the co-operative and experimental procedures of science and his efforts to replace a spectatorial "leisure-class notion of thinking" with a conception of creative thought that conjoined ideas and action, ends and means. Dewey had seen that

> action is not opposed to ideas: the means are not one thing, and the final result of attending to them quite another: they are not kitchen maids and parlor guests, connected only by being in the same house. Means which do not lead to significant issues are illiberal and brutal; issues which do not take account of the means necessary to fulfill them are empty and merely "well-meaning" (*GD*, 133).

Critical of speculation with no practical issue and of practice bereft of reflection, Dewey had cleared the ground for an ideal of human activity "in which facts and values, actualities and desires, achieve an active and organic unity" (*GD*, 133).

Nonetheless, despite these promising initiatives, Dewey himself had failed to articulate such an ideal, and therein lay the key to *his* acquiescence to the crude utilitarianism of his culture. Dewey's philosophy, Mumford said, effectively conveyed an appreciation of but half of this desired

organic unity—and not the more essential half. He had succumbed to a
fixation with facts at the expense of values, actualities at the expense of
desires, means at the expense of ends, technique at the expense of moral
imagination, invention at the expense of art, practicality at the expense of
vision. Randolph Bourne had, of course, said much of this nearly a decade
before in attacking Dewey's support for American participation in World
War I, and Mumford acknowledged his debt to Bourne by reproducing
the essentials of this critique. Dewey's thought, Bourne had contended,
was plagued by "an unhappy ambiguity in his doctrine as to just how values
were created," and, as a consequence, the individual attempting to live out
his philosophy "has habitually confused results with product, and been
content with getting somewhere without asking too closely whether it was
the desirable place to get. . . . You must have your vision, and you must
have your technique. The practical effect of Dewey's philosophy has evidently been to develop the sense of the latter at the expense of the former"
(*GD*, 136).[5]

While Bourne had criticized Dewey for caving in to war, Mumford considerably expanded the scope of Dewey's purported acquiescence, rendering him an accomplice to the dominance in American culture of the "utilitarian type of personality" (*GD*, 134). Without "the values that arise out
of vision," Mumford observed, "instrumentalism becomes the mere apotheosis of actualities: it is all dressed up with no place to go" (*GD*, 137). In
taking values for granted and engaging in a "one-sided idealization of
practical contrivances," Dewey had lent a hand to "tendencies which are
already strong and well-established in American life" and underplayed
"things which must still be introduced into our scheme of things if it is to
become thoroughly humane and significant" (*GD*, 137, 136). Dewey's
pragmatism continued to bear the marks of its birth amidst "the shapelessness, the faith in the current go of things, and the general utilitarian
idealism of Chicago," the paleotechnic city *par excellence* of the 1890s. His
complacent philosophy, bred in the "maw of the Middle West," gave the
game away to those like Sinclair Lewis's George Babbitt who practiced "so
assiduously the mechanical ritual of American life" and treated bathroom
fixtures and automobile accessories as ends in themselves "as if a life spent
in the pursuit of these contrivances was a noble and liberal one" (*GD*, 131,
121, 135–36).

Mumford reserved some of his sharpest barbs for Dewey's aesthetics.
Dewey, he said, failed to see anything other than the instrumental value of
art and consequently missed its essence. Dewey did not seem to realize that
inventions and fine art were different: "the invention is good for what it
leads to, whereas a scene in nature, a picture, a poem, a dance, a beautiful
conception of the universe, are good for what they are" (*GD*, 47). Finding
utilitarianism "thoroughly agreeable," Dewey had kind words for Bacon,
Locke, and Bentham, but nothing to say of Shakespeare, Milton, Shelley,
Keats, Wordsworth, and Blake: "a Goodyear and a Morse seem to him as
high in the scale of human development as a Whitman and a Tolstoi." This

was not to say that Dewey was wrong to point out the uses of art, but "the essential criterion of art is that it is good without these specific instrumental results, good as a *mode of life*, good as a beatitude" (*GD*, 47).[6]

If American culture were to see a new golden day, Mumford concluded, the "idola of utilitarianism" to which James and Dewey had acquiesced had to be supplanted by a new idolum, one that recognized, as Emerson and Whitman had, that "in proportion as intelligence was dealing more effectually with the instrumentalities of life, it became more necessary for the imagination to project more complete and satisfying ends" (*GD*, 140–41). Pragmatism had "given depth to the adventure of industrialism" but it "offered no clue as to what made a proper human life outside the mill of practical activity" (*GD*, 100). Man need not accommodate himself pragmatically to external circumstance, for he had the capacity to act creatively, as an artist, to shape the aims and necessities of his world. "Practical intelligence and a prudent adjustment to externalities are useful only in a secondary position: they are but props to straighten the plant when it begins to grow: at the bottom of it all must be a soil and a seed, an inner burgeoning, an eagerness of life" (*GD*, 143). Rescue from the sterility, boredom, and despair of "the sinister world" of modern American culture could come only by means of "the double process of encountering more complete modes of life, and of reformulating a more vital tissue of ideas and symbols to supplant those which have led us into the stereotyped interests and actions which we endeavor in vain to identify with a full human existence" (*GD*, 144).

A Map of Misreading

By 1926 criticisms such as Mumford's were familiar to Dewey. Other literary intellectuals like Bourne, Van Wyck Brooks, Waldo Frank, and Harold Stearns had advanced similar arguments. Philosophers at home and abroad, led by Bertrand Russell, had for over twenty years felt compelled not only to refute pragmatism but to explain its emergence on terrain as philosophically unpromising as the United States. Thus they often moved beyond analysis of what they took to be logical defects of the philosophy to an effort to explain by means of a loose and condemnatory sociology of knowledge how Dewey and others could possibly believe such a peculiar set of ideas to be true.[7]

Dewey had no objections to efforts to explain pragmatism as a variety of Americanism. There was, he said, "something instructive about our spiritual estate in the fact that pragmatism was born upon American soil." The effort to explain the origins of philosophical ideas in terms of the cultures in which philosophers were inextricably embedded was, as far as he was concerned, a quite legitimate undertaking. In the debates in which he was engaged in the early twentieth century, Dewey himself increasingly resorted to supplementing strictly logical arguments with a critical intel-

lectual history and sociology of knowledge designed to explain how particular problems (especially those he saw as pseudo-problems) had developed.
The polemical uses of this sort of argument were by no means foreign to
him either, and he repeatedly charged that absolutist and transcendental
philosophies were the ideological foundation of "class-codes" that had
"done more than brute love of power to establish inequality and injustice
among men."[8]

If Dewey did not object to the rooting of his philosophy in American
life, he did insist that his critics get this connection right, and he was especially incensed by efforts like Mumford's to link pragmatism with the
"obnoxious aspects of American industrialism," which, to his mind, got it
all wrong. He had responded briefly to similar arguments advanced by
Russell, but until his reply to Mumford in 1927 he had ignored the criticism of the young American literary intellectuals.[9]

Dewey's response to his portrait in *The Golden Day* was not as effective
as it might have been. He accused Mumford of perpetuating an accretion
of myths that had gathered around pragmatism and instrumentalism, but
devoted most of his attention to Mumford's shaping of James's thought
into "a pattern which inverts his whole spirit" rather than to a consideration of the criticisms Mumford had made of his own thinking. Near the
end of his reply he briefly acknowledged that it was "a not unreasonable
hypothesis" to suppose that a preoccupation with natural science and the
technology that issued from it and transformed the American landscape
had played a part in the development of his thinking. But, he commented
acerbically, he would have thought that it would be clear to "a mind not
too precommitted" that in calling his philosophy of knowledge "instrumentalism" and in conceiving of science and technology as instruments he
did not intend to substitute instruments for ends. Instruments implied
ends to which they were to be put:

> . . . it would require a mind unusually devoid both of a sense of logic and a
> sense of humor—if there be any difference between them—to try to univer-
> salize instrumentalism, to set up a doctrine of tools which are not tools for
> anything except for more tools. The counterpart of "instrumentalism" is pre-
> cisely that the values by which Mr. Mumford sets such store are the ends for
> the attainment of which natural science and all technologies and industries
> and industriousness are intrinsically, not externally and transcendentally, or
> by way of exhortation, contributory. The essential and immanent criticism of
> existing industrialism and of the dead weight of science is that instruments are
> made into ends, that they are deflected from their intrinsic quality and thereby
> corrupted.

Dewey was not, he said, preoccupied with science and technology for their
own sake but because he was as committed as Mumford to "ideal values
which dignify and give meaning to human life," and was concerned that
science and technology be used as instruments to render valued experi-

ence less "precarious in possession, arbitrary, accidental, and monopolized in distribution."[10]

This response, as Mumford noted in his subsequent reply, missed the force of the criticism he had directed at Dewey's work. Mumford had not contended that Dewey's effort to explore the bearing of science and technology on the pursuit of ideal ends was, in itself, troubling. The difficulty lay in the insufficiency of this inquiry to a "complete philosophic orientation." Dewey had devoted inadequate attention to the ends to which these means should be turned and seemed to believe that ideals would simply come into existence of their own accord and that the critical task was one of devising means to their achievement. This, Mumford said, got things backward:

> . . . we are faced by the fact that knowledge of the necessary technique is common enough to be taken for granted, and that the ability to conceive new forms and channels for life to run in, the ability to think creatively with the artist who says "I will" rather than with the scientist who says "It must" is what is lacking. The desiccation and sterilization of the imaginative life has been quite as important an historic fact as the growth of a sense of casuality, an insight into what Mr. Dewey calls "means-consequences."

Mumford and the other young critics who had criticized pragmatism were not so much rejecting Dewey's philosophy as calling for a more expansive philosophical vision: "we seek for a broader field and a less provincial interpretation of Life and Nature than he has given us."[11]

Dewey had much more to say about the ends of life and hence a considerably broader interpretation of "Life and Nature" to offer than Mumford apparently realized or Dewey let on in his criticisms of *The Golden Day*, but the only place in their exchange where this was at all apparent was in their disagreement about Dewey's interpretation of art, which was also, interestingly enough, the only instance in which Mumford produced any textual evidence for his reading of Dewey's philosophy. *Experience and Nature* (1925), a chapter of which was the basis for Mumford's contention that Dewey had no appreciation for anything other than the "utility" of art, is not the most lucid of Dewey's books, but Mumford's reading of the discussion of art and aesthetic experience in that text as a claim that fine art was merely instrumental was simply blind. As Dewey said, his argument there was clearly that "art which is really fine exhibits experience when it attains completion or a 'final,' consummatory character, and, while it is urged that such art is also contributory, that to which it is held to be auxiliary is 'renewal of spirit,' not, it would seem, a base end, and certainly not a utilitarian one." Dewey's notion of consummatory, aesthetic experience as that of the "immediate enjoyed intrinsic meaning" of an object was, indeed, little different from Mumford's own conception of aesthetic objects as "good for what they are."[12]

Mumford's criticisms of what Dewey had to say about art were misplaced and suggest that he was determined not to find there what he believed to be lacking. He severed Dewey's theory of knowledge and truth—his instrumentalism—from the broader naturalism of which it was a part, and hence missed the central place in his philosophy of non-cognitive experience in general and moral and aesthetic experience in particular. In 1920 Dewey had anticipated Mumford's conclusion to *The Golden Day,* arguing that "surely there is no more significant question before the world than this question of the possibility and method of reconciliation of the attitudes of practical science and contemplative esthetic appreciation. Without the former, man will be the sport and victim of natural forces which he cannot use or control. Without the latter, mankind might become a race of economic monsters, restlessly driving hard bargains with nature and with one another, bored with leisure or capable of putting it to use only in ostentatious display and extravagant dissipation." But such remarks fell on deaf ears, for Mumford was certain that Dewey's philosophy had "no place for art." Dewey's "exertions in trying to open up a wedge for it," he sniffed, "are painful to behold."[13]

The greatest weakness of Mumford's argument that Dewey displayed a lack of concern for the ends of life lay in his failure to consider carefully another aspect of Dewey's thinking without which any portrait of him would be partial and with which any claim that he had acquiesced to industrial capitalism would appear most peculiar: his long-standing commitment to democracy as an ethical ideal of "moral and spiritual association." Mumford did say, correctly, that "above all, Mr. Dewey believes in democracy," but he then went on to identify this belief as the conviction that "what had been produced by the mass of men must somehow be right" (*GD,* 131), which, as Dewey observed, was a travesty of his democratic ideal.[14]

As I noted, Dewey was quite open to an interpretation of pragmatism as an artifact of American culture and, more broadly, to efforts to place the work of philosophers within "the stresses and strains in the community life in which a given form of philosophy arises." Strictly speaking, he argued, philosophy was not "in any sense whatever a form of knowledge." It was rather "a form of desire, of effort at action—a love, namely, of wisdom." Wisdom was not "systematic and proved knowledge of fact and truth, but a conviction about moral values, a sense for the better kind of life to be led." Historically, philosophies "embodied not colorless intellectual readings of reality, but men's most passionate desires and hopes, their basic beliefs about the sort of life to be lived." A philosophy was "an intellectualized wish, an aspiration subjected to rational discriminations and tests, a social hope reduced to a working program of action, a prophecy of the future, but one disciplined by serious thought and knowledge." Because philosophy was wisdom and not knowledge one could speak of American philosophy but not American chemistry; the cultural variation in philosophies reflected "incompatibilities of temperament and expectation. They are different ways of construing life." But to say that a philosophy was "American" was not to say that it was "merely a formulated acquiescence in the immediately predominating traits" of American life, for cultures embodied conflicting elements. Often the values that a philosophy idealized were those opposed to "the ones most in evidence, the most clamorous, the most insistent" and such oppositional values furnished a set of immanent moral possibilities "upon which criticism rests and creative effort springs."[15]

Democracy was the immanent, oppositional American value that Dewey's philosophy idealized; democracy was the name of his social hope, his moral vision, his "intellectualized wish." Though I cannot thoroughly examine Dewey's democratic "idolum" here, little need be said to distinguish it from the utilitarianism Mumford attributed to him. Briefly put, democracy for Dewey was an ethical ideal that called upon men and women to build communities in which the necessary opportunities and resources were available for each of its members to realize fully his or her individual capacities and powers through autonomous participation in the life of the society. This ideal—fully participatory democracy—was that which Dewey's naturalism and instrumentalism were designed to sustain, that which he hoped science and technology (as well as education, politics, and art) would help realize, that which, from the outset of his career, led him to penetrating insights into the obstacles industrial capitalism posed to liberty, equality, and fraternity, and eventually moved him to socialist conclusions. It was this ideal which he rightly believed connected him to the Golden Day of Emerson and Whitman.[16]

Although he hinted in *The Golden Day* and in the subsequent exchange with Dewey that in addition to the utilitarian Dewey he was aware of "another Dewey, still thinking experimentally and freshly, who is reaching out to wider sources of experience," Mumford gave no account of this Dewey. Had he done so, he would have seriously compromised the architecture of *The Golden Day*. This seems to me the best explanation of Mumford's almost willful misreading of Dewey. The book was built around the contention that the happy wedding of fact and value, science and art, tradition and creativity that marked the American Renaissance had come undone in the work of the nation's subsequent writers, and Mumford needed Dewey to stand in as the representative philosopher of half of the sundered unities of the Golden Day (as he needed George Santayana to represent the other half). Hence, he invented a one-eyed Dewey that would fill the bill while at the same time advancing a plea for cultural reconstruction very similar to that Dewey was advocating in the twenties.[17]

Ships in the Night

By the mid-1930s the distance separating the thinking of Mumford and Dewey had closed even farther, and one who simply took their books and articles from this period down from the shelf and read them unaware of the controversy over *The Golden Day* might well imagine the two men to be intellectual brothers-in-arms. They traveled in many of the same circles, wrote for many of the same magazines, and contributed their energies to many of the same causes. In the face of the Depression each had established himself as a leading non-Marxist radical, and both were committed to the construction of a decentralized, planned society and to the proposition that, as Dewey put it, "there is a socialism which is not state socialism."[18]

Invited in 1930 to contribute to a series of essays in which leading American intellectuals told readers "What I Believe," Mumford advanced a decidedly Deweyan philosophy. "Instead of framing our philosophy around an abstract end, and reproaching the universe because it appears indifferent to the particular goal we have erected," he declared, "it would be wiser to begin with the nature of life itself, and to observe at what point one good or another does in fact emerge from it." Values were not subjective window-dressing but were inherent in human experience and exercised "a determining influence over every stage of life and thought." Like Dewey, Mumford defended an ethical naturalism that envisioned the good life as one of ongoing growth in which the self actively sought to construct itself as an increasingly complex whole, an ethics in which self-realization was characterized in aesthetic terms as the harmonizing of various and competing impulses and capacities into "a higher integration of all one's powers in a social personality." Mumford shared Dewey's scorn for the "spatial illusion" of atomistic individualism that failed to recognize that "both physically and spiritually we are members one of another," and he denounced capitalist society for promoting "partial spiritual sterility" in all classes and fostering social relations at odds with the development of a "well-integrated life." As the Depression deepened, both men declared, as Dewey put it in his contribution to the same series, "a faith in the possibilities of human experience and human relationships that will create a vital sense of the solidarity of human interests and inspire action to make that sense a reality."[19]

In 1934, Mumford and Dewey each published a major book reflecting a deep concern for what had in the polemics of 1927 been cast as the exclusive preoccupation of the other. In *Technics and Civilization*, Mumford explored the historical development and future possibilities of the technological instruments of human culture with a thoroughness and imagination that, despite his supposed obsession with such matters, Dewey never came close to matching. The machine, Mumford declared in words that Dewey might easily have uttered, "is a product of human ingenuity and effort: hence to understand the machine is not merely a first step toward re-orienting our civilization: it is also a means toward understanding society and toward knowing ourselves."[20]

Setting himself firmly against technological determinism in the opening pages of his book, Mumford argued that the development of technology had to be placed squarely in the context of culture and the history of the moral imagination, for "men had become mechanical before they perfected complicated machines to express their new bent and interest" (*TC*,

3). Consequently, the problems of modern society were to be attributed not to machines as such but to the "paleotechnic" culture of industrial capitalism and the nation-state—an ethic committed to little more than the accumulation of goods and power—that held both machines and men in its grip. All about him Mumford found "neotechnic" technologies of an emerging "electricity and alloy complex" that might well serve more humane and egalitarian values but were instead perverted by their attachment to the ethos that had generated the earlier "coal and iron complex" of the nineteenth century. "We have merely used our new machines and energies to further processes which were begun under the auspices of capitalist and military enterprise: we have not yet utilized them to conquer these forms of enterprise and subdue them to more vital and humane purposes" (*TC*, 265). This cultural argument was fully in accord with the thinking of Dewey, who had some years earlier remarked with regard to the modern warship that it "could not exist were it not for science: mathematics, mechanics, chemistry, electricity supply the technique of its construction and management. But the aims, the ideals in whose service this marvelous technique is displayed are survivals of a pre-scientific age, that is, of barbarism."[21]

An important difference between Mumford and Dewey in this respect, however, was that, while Dewey went on to argue that the problem that the example of the battleship exposed was that "science has as yet had next to nothing to do with forming the social and moral ideals for the sake of which she is used," Mumford recognized that science had had a great deal to do with the formation of these ideals. It was no accident that the scientific revolution that stripped experience of its qualities in favor of a wholly abstract and quantitative understanding of the natural world went hand in hand with the rise of capitalism, which had worked a similar transformation of conceptions of social life. Dewey idiosyncratically (for his time if not ours) considered science to be, above all, practical reason, and he regarded the abstraction of modern natural science to be a methodological move made in the interest of gaining control over natural processes in order that the life-enhancing, qualitative dimensions of experience might be made more secure. Although he worried deeply over the mistake many had made in converting scientific abstractions into a desiccated metaphysics purporting to describe Reality, he was often blind to the prominent role this worldview had played in shaping the values of modernity. The circuit Dewey envisioned from (precarious) qualitative experience to abstract science to (stable) qualitative experience had shorted out in the middle, and science had been deployed to displace rather than enhance value-laden experience. As a result, as Mumford recognized, science was less an innocent bystander than an accomplice (not always unwitting) in the creation of a world governed by abstract conceptions of labor power and fire power.[22]

As Casey Blake has demonstrated, Mumford was not himself always true to his insights. Eager to prove in *Technics and Civilization* that he was no nostalgic romantic, he occasionally slipped into the very technological determinism and acquiescence to technical rationality against which he warned. Observing that the neo-technic phase in the history of technology owed a great deal to the direct application of the abstract world-view of modern science to invention, he nonetheless went on in the concluding chapters of his book to urge less a reconstruction of these technologies in accord with a more "richly organic" understanding of human personality and society than an accommodation to the values and "objective personality" he found implicit "within the machine complex itself" (*TC*, 55).[23]

At the same time Mumford was both sharpening his critique of modernity and proving not altogether immune to an acquiescence to its blandishments, Dewey published *Art as Experience,* a text in which not Bacon and Locke but Shelley and Browning have the last word, a book leaving no doubts about his appreciation of non-cognitive, non-instrumental, consummatory experience and celebrating art as "experience in its integrity." Aesthetic experience, he declared, was "experience freed from the forces that impede and confuse its development as experience; freed, that is, from factors that subordinate an experience as it is directly had to something beyond itself." It was to art that "the philosopher must go to understand what experience is." Confidently deploying the very standard of judgment by which Mumford had found him most wanting in the twenties, Dewey suggested that what a philosopher had to say about art revealed his capacity "to grasp the nature of experience itself."[24]

Dewey now argued that art was the best guide to the worth of a civilization. "Neither the savage nor the civilized man is what he is by native constitution but by the culture in which he participates," he said, and "the final measure of the quality of that culture is the arts which flourish." Because art was "the means of keeping alive the sense of purposes that outrun evidence and of meanings that transcend indurated habit" it did not merely mirror the life of a culture but served to disclose its unforeseen possibilities. "Imagination is the chief instrument of the good," Dewey concluded in Mumfordian fashion, for art "is a mode of prediction not found in charts and statistics, and it insinuates possibilities of human relations not to be found in rule and precept, admonition and administration."[25]

I do not mean to argue that there were not important differences remaining between Mumford and Dewey in the mid-thirties but only to suggest that Mumford was not always correct about where they lay. In the midst of the crisis of the Great Depression in which the possibility of radically reconstructing American society seemed to many very real, perhaps the most obvious contrast was in their attitudes toward political action. Dewey believed that a popular political movement was an essential means to the sort of democratic socialist society he and Mumford envisioned. Hence he played an important role in the efforts of independent radicals to build a third party in the early 1930s and remained committed to radical electoral politics for the rest of his life. He did not anticipate immediate victory for such a movement, but saw it as an important vehicle for public education as well as an institution that would, as it worked over the long run to secure democratic socialism, prefigure politics "after the revolution" in its own internal structure and practices. Dewey, who might best be thought of as an American guild socialist, was, like Mumford, fearful of the concentrated power of the national state, but he did not see how a fully democratic society could be created without an initial, substantial exercise of state power by radicals. The state, he told his friend Hu-Shih, was "a powerful instrumentality for ends as valuable as they are far-reaching," but the trick was to avoid using this power in such a way that "the instrumentality becomes itself an end." Mumford, on the other hand, eschewed politics of this sort and seems to have believed that a reorientation of American values could take place without it, though he did not indicate how this would occur—the sort of neglect of instrumental considerations that had led Dewey to remark at the end of his critique of *The Golden Day* that "not all who say Ideals, Ideals, shall enter the kingdom of the ideal, but those who know and who respect the roads that conduct to the kingdom."[26]

Mumford and Dewey never debated the strategic merits of political action, for they never came close to conceiving of their differences as anything less than fundamental. The convergences in their work in the early 1930s seem to have made no difference in their attitudes toward one another. Marred by the inadequacies of Mumford's reading of Dewey's work and the insufficiencies of Dewey's response to it, their inconclusive debate over *The Golden Day* generated long-lasting bitterness. A few weeks after he had the last word in the controversy, Mumford delightedly told Van Wyck Brooks that:

> You should hear the howls of Dewey and the Deweyites; [*The Golden Day*] has shattered the Pragmatic Complacence, if it has not established a case against the "acquiescence"! They are so damned smug and obtuse, these pragmatists, and at the first hint that their Idols have feet, if not also posteriors of clay, they break into thinly disguised vituperation.

Years later the "Deweyites" had not forgiven Mumford his transgressions against their idols. Mumford, Wisconsin philosopher Max Otto wrote Dewey in 1940, "gets my goat. His treatment of William James in *The Golden Day* was simply lousy, and his discussion of your philosophy stinks." James T. Farrell advised Dewey that Mumford, Van Wyck Brooks, and Waldo Frank were "god-damned snobs. Maturity to them is shrinking from experience. All of them do not read books in order to understand anything: they read and they write in order to impress people." After their initial encounter, Dewey himself apparently decided that Mumford was someone fruitless for him to engage, and he left it to young friends and allies like Farrell, Sidney Hook, and Meyer Schapiro to uphold the Deweyan position in subsequent polemics against Mumford.[27]

For his part, Mumford continued to misread Dewey through Bourne-colored glasses. Three years after their debate he offered an account of

Dewey's thought even less sympathetic and more misleading than its predecessor. In search of "a modern synthesis" of science and ethics, art and
technology, Mumford set himself against both those he termed the "New
Mechanists," led by Dewey and Charles Beard, who made a "fetich of the
machine" and the "New Humanists," Irving Babbitt and Paul Elmer More,
who made a "fetich of morality." The beliefs and attitudes of the former,
he said, entailed

> . . . the concentration upon the external environment, considered as some-
> thing apart from man's life and destiny, the emphasis upon material progress,
> the belief that expansion of power is equivalent to a deepening of life, the
> view that activity is in itself superior to contemplation and that external
> changes are more important than improvements of thoughts and feelings and
> perceptions, and, finally the notion that control of Nature can be separated
> from the development and expression of the human personality in society.

Dewey and other New Mechanists, Mumford contended, were possessed
of "a deep and persistent bias" that led them to look on "external facts"
as the only abiding reality and hence to see the main problem of life as
"the adjustment of human ideas and needs to these more obdurate
externals."[28]
  This rendering of Dewey's philosophy was plainly wrong. The only relationship Dewey's conception of man's relation to his environment bore to
Mumford's New Mechanism was that of opposition. He had long maintained that the environment, both natural and social, was not something
"external" standing apart from "man's life and destiny" to which he could
only passively accommodate himself but a reality with which man was constantly interacting and which was amenable to reconstruction through purposeful, creative human action. Mumford, like many commentators, may
have misunderstood Dewey's peculiar usage of the term "adjustment."
Throughout his career Dewey clung to a counterintuitive definition of this
term as including "an adaption of the environment to the individual's
needs and ends, rather than vice versa." He reserved the term "accommodation" for "the processes by which the individual assimilates and
reproduces the existing environment with a minimum of reaction against
it or of effort to change it."[29]
  The only thing in this article more notable than Mumford's distortion
of Dewey's perspective was his proposal, as an alternative, of a view that
was thoroughly Deweyan:

> Man's uniqueness consists in the fact that, since the equipoise he seeks
> involves more than his physiological balance, he has created standards and
> ends and purposes of his own which he imposes on nature. Sometimes these
> standards are grotesque and ineffectual, sometimes humane and wise; but
> good or bad, he uses them to modify the conditions of life, to the end that his
> habitat and his institutions, indeed the very direction of his daily activities, are
> altered towards the forms which he himself has conceived. His own balance

cannot be achieved, without altering the natural conditions that environ him. . . . Man himself is part of the conditions under which he lives and is not merely the impotent prisoner of circumstances.

If, as Mumford said, it was Patrick Geddes who had proven that all life forms manifested a degree of this "insurgence" and in man it reached "its apex," Dewey had also argued the point for decades. Mumford's concluding brief for a newer humanism, founded on an awareness that "personality provides . . . the summit of our social achievement," recalled the assertion Dewey had made when he was about the same age that "in one word, democracy means that *personality* is the first and final reality."[30]

The Corruption of Liberalism

This, as far as I know, was the last time in the interwar period that Mumford addressed himself directly to Dewey's philosophy. But that he never revised this sort of reading of Dewey suggests that Mumford considered Dewey to have been a part of the "utilitarian" camp that he continued to assault in the mid-thirties. In *Technics and Civilization* and elsewhere Mumford denounced utilitarianism as the philosophy and "popular working creed" of a capitalist culture of consumption in which spending had become the only source of delight, and the true, the good, and the beautiful were equated with "whatever could be embodied in material goods and profitably sold: whatever made life easier, more comfortable, more secure, physically more pleasant: in a word, better upholstered" (*TC*, 104). Utilitarianism was blind to the fact that, beyond the basic essentials of food, clothing, and shelter, life's "intensities, ecstasies and states of equilibrium cannot be measured mathematically in any relation whatever to the quantity of goods consumed or the quantity of power exercised" (*TC*, 105). Nonetheless, it was this creed, this "disintegration of human values," that had given the modern machine its social goal and its legitimation, ensuring that technics would be used "not to save man from the servitude to ignoble forms of work, but to make more wholly possible the servitude to ignoble standards of consumption" (*TC*, 106).[31]

As total war descended on the world in the late 1930s, Mumford explicitly reconnected utilitarianism and pragmatism in an outpouring of fiery articles and books denouncing liberal acquiescence in the triumphs of fascism. Although Dewey was seldom mentioned by name, this critique drew directly on the language and arguments of his earlier attack on the philosopher and few doubted that Dewey, who opposed American intervention in the war until 1941, was among Mumford's principal targets.[32]

In "The Corruption of Liberalism" (1940), the essay that most firmly established Mumford's standing as a leading "war intellectual," he argued that the record of liberalism in the thirties was one of "shameful evasion and inept retreat." Either bereft of convictions or lacking the courage to defend them, liberals had capitulated to Stalinism by allying themselves in popular front politics with the Communist Party and were now rapidly giving ground to fascism by resorting to "passivist" appeasement and "isolationism" in the face of Hitler's aggression. They had committed themselves to a self-destructive "peace" that entailed the victory of forces fundamentally opposed to the liberal ideals of objective reason, freedom of thought, and human dignity.[33]

The concessions that liberalism had made to barbarism, Mumford argued, were not mere strategic errors but were traceable to "fatal deficiencies that go to the very roots of liberal philosophy" (*CL*, 568). Liberalism was a very mixed doctrine. On the one hand, it was wedded to the "humanist traditions of personal responsibility, personal freedom, and personal expression" that were threatened by fascism (*CL*, 569). On the other hand, the humanism of this "ideal liberalism" had been loosely joined since the eighteenth century to a quite different sort of liberalism, what Mumford termed "pragmatic liberalism," which had left liberals impotent in the face of this threat. Pragmatic liberalism was but a fresh alias for Mumford's old *bête noire*, utilitarianism, and echos of his critique of Dewey in *The Golden Day* sounded through this and many other of Mumford's war essays.

Pragmatic liberalism, he asserted, was "vastly preoccupied with the machinery of life" and "the only type of human character it could understand was the utilitarian one," believing that "the emotional and spiritual life of man needs no other foundation than the rational, utilitarian activities associated with the getting of a living" (*CL*, 569). The pragmatic liberal was color-blind to moral values and had taken "values, feelings, emotions, wishes, purposes, for granted. He assumed either that this world did not exist or that it was relatively unimportant; at all events, if it did exist, it could be safely left to itself without cultivation" (*CL*, 570). Science "would eventually supply all the guidance necessary for human conduct" and the evils of life would be solved by "extending the blessings of the machine" (*CL*, 570). All this rendered pragmatic liberals incapable of understanding the barbarism of Hitler and Stalin and of mustering the courage to resist it with coercive force. "The isolation that is preached by our liberals today," Mumford warned, "means fascism tomorrow" (*CL*, 573).

Although liberal opposition to American intervention in World War II in the late 1930s and early 1940s cannot be so neatly linked to the infection of utilitarianism, there is much to be said for Mumford's impression that this ailment had spread broadly among liberal intellectuals in the 1930s. A significant portion of the non-communist left then was comprised of those I have elsewhere termed "technocratic progressives" who did, for the most part, identify the good life with the goods life and called for the creation of a planned economy directed by experts in the interests of the consumer. This group included Thurman Arnold, Charles Beard, Adolph Berle, Bruce Bliven, Stuart Chase, Paul Douglas, Freda Kirchway, Max Lerner, Robert Lynd, Gardiner Means, George Soule, and Rexford Tugwell, and was bound together, despite differences on the details of theory and policy, by a common commitment to the improvement of the technical rationality of an economy of abundance. For these intellectuals, the good society was that which delivered the greatest amount of high quality goods to the greatest number of people in the most efficient manner possible. They were, as Mumford would have it, utilitarians.[34]

John Dewey, on the other hand, was not a technocratic progressive. He was critical of their anti-democratic conception of economic planning and did not participate in their neo-Veblenian celebration of the engineer (to which Mumford occasionally lent his voice). Dewey was also explicitly critical of the narrow utilitarianism of a social philosophy oriented strictly toward enhancing the efficiency of the production and consumption of material goods. "The ultimate problem of production," he observed, "is the production of human beings":

> To this end, the production of goods is intermediate and auxiliary. It is by this standard that the present system stands condemned. "Security" is a means, and although an indispensable social means, it is not the end. Machinery and technological improvement are means, but again are not the end. Discovery of individual needs and capacities is a means to the end, but only a means. The means have to be implemented by a social-economic system that establishes and uses the means for the production of free human beings associating with one another on terms of equality. Then and then only will these means be an integral part of the end, not frustrated and self-defeating, bringing new evils and generating new problems.[35]

Dewey was free not only of utilitarianism but also of many of the other corruptions Mumford attributed to pragmatic liberalism. He was a relatively early and vigorous opponent of Stalinism (and his record in this regard was far superior to Mumford's), and the charge that he was purblind to values, feelings, emotions, wishes, and purposes was no more accurate in 1940 than it had been in 1926. But Dewey did oppose American intervention in World War II and, in the end, "pragmatic liberalism" was little more than a catch-all term under which Mumford grouped everyone whom he believed had contributed to a "spineless" response to fascism. As Farrell said, the pragmatic liberal became for Mumford "a grouping which includes just about everyone, living or dead, with whom he disagrees."[36]

Dewey's opposition to American participation in the war was not grounded, as Mumford implied, in confidence in the essential goodness of human nature and the power of rational discourse to resolve conflicts of interest with the fascist powers but in deep-seated fears about the consequences of war for democracy in the United States. Dewey had been convinced in the wake of the collapse of liberal hopes at Versailles that Bourne was correct in contending that war was an uncontrollable social force: the "health of the state" and the scourge of democracy. On the eve of World

War II Dewey warned that "it is quite conceivable that after the next war we should have in this country a semi-military, semi-financial autocracy, which would fashion class divisions on this country for untold years. In any case we should have the suppression of all the democratic values for the sake of which we went to war." The war would be "the greatest social catastrophe that could overtake us, the destruction of all the foundations upon which to erect a socialized democracy." As the country drifted toward war it was not the "curse of optimism" but deep pessimism that gripped him, and, for one of the few times in the latter years of his long life, Dewey considered the possibility that he had outlived his usefulness as a social critic: "an epoch has come to an end, I think, but what is beginning is too much for me."[37]

In 1935, Dewey's fears were shared by a fellow contributor to a symposium on "The Second World War": Lewis Mumford. Though Mumford did not agree with Dewey that such fears necessarily entailed an anti-war stance, he did declare his general opposition to war "because of its imbecility, its absence of human purposes, its brutalization of life, its abject failure to achieve reasonable goods, and its futile simplifications of all the conflicts and real issues involved in life in communities." He committed himself to fight the "war animus" in time of peace, and, though he could imagine supporting a war as a lesser evil, he avowed that, in this event, his principal duty as a writer would be to continue this fight and do what he could to prevent the pressures of war from engendering fascism in America. *"By reason of the very technique of fighting and its special behavior patterns—no matter how just and rational the cause seems at the outset,"* Mumford warned, "war is always a losing fight even when it is a just one."[38]

By the end of the 1930s, Mumford was promoting rather than fighting the war animus, convinced that the need to defeat fascism abroad outweighed any temporary damage that might be inflicted by war on democratic values and institutions at home. "We cannot preserve ourselves against this barbarism and worry about the cost of our effort," he said. He admitted that there were dangers in going to war, for the tasks of war were "of their nature brutal and self-deadening ones. . . . The very process of attacking and killing a remorseless enemy inevitably coarsens the human fiber; and the more base that enemy, the more violent his attack, the more terrible to oneself become the consequences of resisting him." Nonetheless, Mumford was confident that any curtailment of democracy at home that the war necessitated would not outlive the conflict, and he was particularly contemptuous of liberals who worried about the effect of war on civil liberties. "Facing a war waged mercilessly by fascism against all his ideals and hopes," he scornfully remarked, "the liberal shows himself more concerned over minor curtailments of private liberties, necessary for an effective defense against fascism, than he is over the far more ghastly prospect of permanent servitude if fascism finally covers the earth." Fascism at home, he contended, was more likely to come about as a result of the economic crisis and psychological security brought on by isolation from a fascist-dominated world order than from armed conflict aimed at preventing the establishment of such barbarism in the rest of the world. Indeed, he argued, the crisis of war against the radical evil of fascism might even engender a "large-scale conversion" of Americans to the moral values necessary for the construction of a more thoroughly democratic and life-enhancing society in the United States.[39]

Dewey remained in the opposition to war, lending his support to left-wing isolationism. He backed the Keep America Out of War Congress organized by Norman Thomas in 1938 and in 1940 headed a committee of intellectuals supporting Thomas's presidential candidacy, a candidacy grounded in little more than opposition to American participation in the war. Dewey's distress and pessimism grew in the defense period in the face of the open acknowledgment by war intellectuals like Mumford that a "totalitarian element" in mobilization for war "will be inescapable," and after Pearl Harbor he devoted his efforts as an activist to preserving civil liberties and combating the widespread mystification of the Soviet alliance.[40]

No doubt, most would agree that Mumford had the better of this argument. Particularly in retrospect, it is clear that the Nazis were barbarians to a degree that even Mumford did not suspect, and American arms were essential to their defeat. Moreover, the American war effort did not create a fascist regime at home. Even without the advantages of hindsight, Mumford's fears of fascism abroad were better placed than Dewey's dread of Thermidor at home. But, though the consequences of the American war effort were worth the costs, there *were* costs and of the sort Dewey feared: unprecedented abuse of civil liberties in the treatment of Japanese-Americans, the ebbing of social reform, the consolidation of the dominant position of large corporations in the political economy, the centralization of state power in the hands of executive elites, and, in general, the constriction of democracy in the United States. In addition, the targeting of civilian populations by all sides in the conflict, which culminated in the dropping of atomic bombs on Hiroshima and Nagasaki, recalls Mumford's remark in 1935 that even just wars may be unjustly fought and Bourne's earlier warnings of the impotence of moral reason in the face of the demiurge of "military necessity."[41]

Ironies abound in this last act of the stormy relationship of Mumford and Dewey. Damned by Mumford in the 1920s with Bourne's words for embracing World War I, Dewey was now condemned by Mumford for accepting the sort of "romantic defeatism that Bourne had preached in 1917." Mumford thus continued to cling to a Bourne-inspired misreading of Dewey's philosophy, while at the same time arguing that Bourne's opposition to Dewey's support for World War I, which had provoked this interpretation, was mistaken and that "perhaps the greatest catastrophe" of the Great War was that many of his generation, including himself for some time, had adopted Bourne's perspective. In the late 1930s and early 1940s, it was Mumford (whom Van Wyck Brooks had invested with the mantle of

Bourne's heir apparent) who, as Dewey once had, waxed eloquent about the possibilities that war afforded for democratic reconstruction at home and abroad, defended the use of war-technique as an efficient ethical means ("a surgeon's knife"), and excoriated "passivist" opponents unduly squeamish about the use of force. At the same time, Dewey emerged from the twilight of idols to echo Bourne's conviction that war was the health of the anti-democratic state.[42]

But this bitter disagreement was no more a clash of fundamentally opposed world-views than that between Dewey and Bourne had been. Although during the war Mumford heightened the emphasis on the "tragic" and "sinful" aspects of human experience that had been subdued in his writing of the 1930s, he was careful to conceive of both tragedy and sin within the framework of the humanism he shared with Dewey, which was not as incompatible with a realism about evil and the limitations on human will as critics like Reinhold Niebuhr contended. Moreover, despite this darkening of his moral vision, Mumford, like Dewey, remained a meliorist, and, in the face of the fascist threat, his conception of democracy became more expansive and drew him closer to Dewey's participatory ideal. Though he never possessed Dewey's common touch and always retained a contempt for the benighted masses, Mumford began during the war to significantly democratize his utopian vision. He continued to bank heavily for "salvation" on "creative people" who were "capable of adapting social forms to social needs as completely as an artist is capable of creating, out of the chaos of experience, a painting, a poem, or a symphony," but he now also stressed the need for a more thoroughly democratic politics in which participation would be "magnified and extended" and called for a social order in which "each citizen, both by thought and action, must spend half his time in public life." Thus this last confrontation between Mumford and Dewey was not, as Mumford argued, a conflict between an "ideal liberal" committed to the values of humanism and a "pragmatic liberal" corrupted by utilitarianism, but rather one grounded in the competing pragmatic judgments of two ideal liberals about the consequences of war for their shared ideals.[43]

Public Philosophy

In recounting the story of the relationship between Mumford and Dewey, I have tried not to indulge too freely the temptation to abandon the confines of their inconclusive debate for independent "shepherding" that would lump together the thinking of these two intellectuals determined in their own time to have few kind words for one another. As Daniel Rodgers has recently said, this sort of lumping by intellectual historians results, too often, in the collection of their subjects into flocks willed by the historian but bearing little relation to the circles of affinity and discord actually produced by those subjects in their own right. I have said enough perhaps to suggest that Dewey and Mumford could well be lumped together as pragmatic naturalists and non-Marxist radicals, but, for the most part, I have acted here less as shepherd than as "interloper," following what Rodgers terms the track of "argument, debate, and (in the active, tension-filled sense of the word) discourse," and, as interlopers often do, I have come upon "a good knock-down disagreement."[44]

There is, however, another affinity between Mumford and Dewey—one less of substantive argument than of cultural role—with which I would like to conclude. Beneath their disagreements lay a common sense of purpose that was unacknowledged if not taken for granted, a conception of their vocation that some have argued has been lost in recent American intellectual life. As I indicated, one of the most important features of Dewey's thinking was that, while ceding the realm of knowledge entirely to science, he, at the same time, left to philosophy what he regarded as the much more important role: the use of knowledge as a resource for cultural criticism and social reconstruction. Cultural criticism, he argued, provided "the basis for projection of values as yet unrealized, values that are to be translated into ends that move men to action. Philosophy thus conceived does not involve a flight and escape to that which is beyond experience. It is concerned with making the most possible out of experience, personal and social. Everyday homely objects and occupations of everyday life are possessed of potentialities that, under the guidance of deliberate and systematic intelligence, will make life fuller, richer, and more unified." Disturbed by the sterility of academic philosophy, Dewey urged philosophers to abandon the claim to knowledge of a higher reality and the consequent pseudoproblems for criticism directed at the public and its problems. Such a public philosophy would be concerned with "the values and ends that known facts and principles should subserve," and this concern would be manifested "in ideas whose claim is to have authority over *action* in effecting realization of the ends and values in question, not to be authoritative in presenting any kind of superior 'reality' and knowledge." Lewis Mumford was as much a public philosopher, in this sense, as John Dewey, and, with powerful jeremiads against the decline of the public intellectual ringing in our ears, we can perhaps be forgiven for losing sight of the meager substantive returns of the debate between these two exemplary instances of this disappearing species in favor of an admiring glance at the fight itself.[45]

In the course of trying to establish a pedigree for themselves, public intellectuals often resort to shepherding suitable ancestors into convenient flocks, and, in a healthy political culture, this is a task that engages the attention of all citizens who will, as Jeffrey Stout has said, "take the many parts of a complicated social and conceptual inheritance and hammer them together to meet the needs of the moment." I suspect it is often the desire of intellectual historians to participate as public intellectuals in this essential project of "moral *bricolage*" that leads them to run the risks of distortion that lie in elucidating common themes in the thinking of subjects ignorant of one another's work or even of subjects who supposed themselves the bitterest of foes. Though I share Rodgers's concerns about the dangers of this sort of thing, I think it is well that historians court them from time to time, for history that confines itself to interloping, and hence to the vision of the actors it studies, borders on antiquarianism. I would regret it if my interloping inhibited the corralling of Mumford and Dewey. Indeed, I must confess to a hope my efforts will persuade a few of our remaining public intellectuals (including shepherd-historians) not simply to read Dewey as Mumford did. That done, let the lumping begin.[46]

Tragedy, Responsibility, and the American Intellectual, 1925–1950

RICHARD WIGHTMAN FOX

I

The intellectual life of the second quarter of this century takes on, in retrospect, a distinctive character. It is not just that one can find certain discrete ideas that many intellectuals pushed to the forefront of their thought. It is also that the fundamental horizon of intellectual life took on a new shape. Intellectuals came in large numbers to share a new set of presuppositions about human nature and society. They came to share a new perspective on the prospects for human action, on the relation of mind and world, on the character of historical development.

This new outlook was a pervasive current that underlay much of the social thinking of these years. One might, with a modicum of poetic license, call it a spirit of the age. It can be described as a dual commitment: to the "tragic" sense of life, and to the exercise of "responsibility" in the face of social evil.

This essay will attempt to elucidate the thinking of Lewis Mumford by putting it in the context of this broad shift in intellectual life. His work was a pivotal part of the reorientation of American thinking, and can be understood only in the light of that larger movement. His own writings deserve more detailed attention than I will give them here. But by concentrating on the wider stream I hope to provide a foundation for finer-grained analyses of his own writings.

Our usual picture of the development of American intellectual life in the first half of the twentieth century runs something like this: Intellectuals were devoted to progressive reform in the first two decades of the century, and in the 1920s they retreated into individual, artistic concerns—often taking flight to Paris, the better to symbolize their withdrawal from society. In the 1930s they once again turned their gaze outwards and embraced socialism and even Communism in large numbers. In the 1940s they backed away from leftism, reaffirmed their allegiance to America, and by the 1950s had made their peace with capitalism by proclaiming the end of ideology and immersing themselves in existential, not social, issues.

Intellectual life, in this common view—a view that exercises a subtle sway over all of us, even specialists in intellectual history—has been a cyclical oscillation between society and self: the pre-World War I years, the Depression, and World War II were allegedly times of social commitment, the 1920s and 1950s times of preoccupation with selfhood. (The cycle continues into the recent past with a social 1960s, a narcissistic 1970s, and a 1980s that is still non-social but much more cynical than the affirmative, if too therapeutically individualistic, 1970s.)

Of course we all do depend upon simplified images of past decades in order to make sense of complex, long-term changes. And there is enough truth in the standard version of cyclical change to make it attractive to many historians—especially to liberals, for whom the rise and fall of liberal reform movements is the essential stuff of history. But the cyclical view is also terribly misleading. I want to offer an alternative, though still simplified, picture that does more justice to the character of American thinking in the first half of the century.

My picture dispenses with the notion of cycles of commitment to self and society. Intellectuals, I suggest, were continuously preoccupied with both self and society throughout those fifty years. I do suggest, however, that a fundamental break occurred in the mid-to-late 1920s. A new insistence on the tragic character of human existence came to mark the writings of a large number of writers, and not only among the conservatives—where one would expect such sentiments. Radicals, too, embraced the tragic perspective earlier associated with Hawthorne, Melville, Twain, and Henry Adams—a perspective submerged in the late nineteenth and early twentieth century by upbeat affirmations about human progress.

The new centrality of the tragic sensibility in the second quarter of the century gave the liberalism and radicalism of the 1930s an entirely different substance and tone from the progressivism of the 1900s and 1910s: it was more attuned to the suffering at the center of human life, more inclined to anticipate disappointment in personal and political affairs. It is true that one can find much "managerial" thinking among liberals such as Thurman Arnold or left-liberals such as Robert Lynd—thinking that is post-progressive in its cynicism about the rationality of the "people" but still not "tragic" since it preaches a new reign of efficiency or justice through rational planning by elites. But managerial rationalism—a sort of liberal or left-liberal Leninism—was not quite as dominant in the thinking of the 1930s as we have assumed. Alongside it, and in some cases intermixed with it, was a new sensitivity to the tragic gap that separated human aspirations from human achievements.

The tragic ethos of much intellectual life in the 1930s links that period much more closely to the years that followed than to the early years of the century. The radicals of the 1930s had much more in common with the moderates of the 1940s than they did with the progressives of the pre-World War I period. In some cases, indeed, the 1930s radicals *were* the 1940s moderates. But even when they were not the same people, their outlooks were fundamentally similar. They could not share the progressive generation's faith in the fundamental goodness of human nature and the generally upward movement of human history. They demarcated their own wizened era by giving new meaning to the term "responsibility"—a term that had also been used, although not with the same frequency, by the progressives.

"Responsibility" became the banner of a chastened generation that had voiced liberal or revolutionary hopes in the 1930s and abandoned those hopes in the 1940s. But in both decades responsibility connoted a simultaneous engagement and retrenchment, a giving of commitment and a holding back, a willingness to act but only within the boundaries set by the tragic necessities of human life.[1]

II

In America the mid-1920s witnessed a marked rekindling of interest in the subject of tragedy and in the philosophical stance that Miguel de Unamuno termed—in his 1912 volume first translated into English in 1921—the "tragic sense of life." Academic writers like Macneile Dixon (*Tragedy*, 1924) and F. L. Lucas (*Tragedy in Relation to Aristotle's Poetics*, 1928) returned to themes neglected since such turn-of-the-century volumes as W. L. Courtney's *The Idea of Tragedy in Ancient and Modern Drama* (1900) and A. C. Bradley's *Shakespearean Tragedy* (1904).[2] But in the 1920s, unlike the 1900s, the scholarly trend was matched by the work of more popular writers such as Walter Lippmann (*A Preface to Morals*, 1929), Joseph Wood Krutch (*The Modern Temper*, 1929), and Lewis Mumford (*Herman Melville*, 1929).

Lippmann, Krutch (the *Nation*'s drama critic), and Mumford all offered somber meditations on the ineradicable limits to human happiness. There was an unbreachable gap between human aspiration and human attainment, a deep-seated dissatisfaction at the center of life. Lippmann took refuge in a Stoic solution: the disciplining of desire permitted the modern person to live in harmony with the world despite the brokenness of existence. Krutch embraced a more thoroughgoing despair: the problem, he thought, ran deeper than Lippmann sensed, and defied solution. Mumford tried to go beyond both Lippmann and Krutch by embracing the Romantic quest for transcendence, but granting that the transcendent could never be reached in living, only evoked in great art.

Mumford's view will emerge in greater relief if we look further at Krutch. In his account, modern human beings were cut off from their own "nature" by the mental processes that had produced the scientific outlook.

The traditional mythologies that had grounded ideals of self-sacrifice, honor, and chivalrous love had been eroded by the acid of critical intelligence. Those mythologies may have been "illusions," he maintained, but they gave life its beauty and meaning. Scientific reason eliminated the drama from human existence. Skeptical and ironic habits of mind undermined the vitality that ensured the survival of the species; they were "intellectual virtues" but "biologic vices." Krutch was placed in the ironic position of arguing that his own book was dysfunctional for the survival of the species. His exercise of critical intelligence furthered the alienation of human beings from their nature.

For Krutch, the final irony of the modern temper was its inability to generate dramatic tragedy of the kind produced by the Elizabethans. Shakespeare and his contemporaries believed in "the greatness of man" and could therefore compose dramatic statements of "triumph over despair." They also believed in human responsibility, in "the ability to sin," which the modern temper had dismissed along with other allegedly prescientific notions. Elizabethan drama was "an affirmation of life" because it was not "intellectual" but "vital"—it sprang from indwelling belief, not ironic detachment. The devotion of the modern world to critical reason destroyed the natural, unforced insight of real tragedy: that human life was majestic despite its unremitting suffering.

Krutch's anti-modern critique paralleled the earlier protests of Dostoevsky and Nietzsche, who scorned the utilitarian doctrines of liberal rationalism. But he lacked their faith that art could still embody a set of values that transcended the mechanical world-view of positivism and empiricism. In Krutch's words, Nietzsche was "the last great tragedian." All he could do in *The Modern Temper* was to document his own eclipse as one who yearned for vitality in the modern wasteland.[3]

For Mumford, Herman Melville was a man of two eras: the product of a vibrant ante-bellum provincial culture, yet a harbinger, in his personal and professional isolation, of a post-bellum cultural desert. The integral, organic world of the ante-bellum "golden day" had produced this new Shakespeare, whose tragic epic *Moby-Dick* reconciled the practical and the theoretical, the scientific and religious, the workaday culture of whaling and the existential despair of man *in extremis*. In the capitalist chaos of the post-bellum era, which respected no regional cultural boundaries and abandoned all sense of form, Melville was silenced.

Yet the model of Melville allowed Mumford to take heart: even in an inhospitable social environment a writer who "clothed his thoughts in poetic vision," who aimed at an "outreaching comprehensiveness of sweep," might create a transcendent work of art. Such a work, in Mumford's Platonic conception, occupied a "durable world of forms"; it possessed an eternal life that artists themselves could not attain. This framework of essence and accident, permanence and impermanence, left a great deal to be desired in its assertion that great art was timeless, and therefore by implication independent of culture and history.

Much more compelling was Mumford's simultaneous perception that the artist was a creator of culture. Even a single work of art was a contribution to the ongoing life of the community. Mumford could rhapsodize too effusively about the power of the single "seed" to squeeze through the cracks of the strongest boulder, but he implicitly offered a telling rebuttal to Krutch. As long as even a single individual spoke the truth about human life, used imagination to probe the gap between ideals and realities, then a vital culture was alive in embryo. Krutch's book refuted itself: the modern temper had not prevented Krutch from creating *The Modern Temper*, an anti-modern text informed by the tragic sense of life.

Artists were creators of culture, and in the process creators of themselves. "The highest product of art," Mumford wrote in *Melville*, "is not a painting, a statue, a book, a pyramid, but a human personality." Cultures and selves grew together. A vibrant community permitted individuals to realize themselves; vital individuals gave life to the community not only through their work, but through their actions as parents and citizens. Melville's greatest failing, for Mumford, was his failing as father: in his solitude he had plumbed the eternal depths and ignored the surfaces of everyday life. "He had brought up fire and lava and ashes, from that deep volcano of his being, but he had never in maturity properly explored the woods and groves and gardens that give men peace and untroubled love."[4]

Mumford's sensitivity to personality—to the interpenetration of the personal and the communal—underlay his thinking from the 1920s on, and gave a distinctive cast to his understanding of tragedy and responsibility. Even as he called in *Melville* for realism about the limits to human achievement, or in the 1930s for "responsibility" in choosing lesser evils (military force) to combat greater evils (fascism), he maintained a view of human community that contained within it the possibility of individual and cultural renewal. He did not suppose that the "personal" and the "political," or the individual and social, were distinct poles, between which people had to tack. For him all human activity was at once personal and cultural, individual and social.

The signal advantage of this standpoint was that in times of political reaction or political apathy, when the path to social progress seemed blocked, there was no need to abandon a progressive vision out of a desire to be "realistic." One could instead stress the cultural transformation that had to underlie any progressive politics, and get to work, even in one's solitude, creating the forms of a new culture. At times, as in *Technics and Civilization* (1934), Mumford was tempted to convert his sensitivity to culture—to the ways in which cultural forms mold everyday life—into a technocratic vision: experts could build planned environments into which ordinary people could fit. But in his best work his commitment to culture produced a perceptive critique of advanced capitalist social relations—including the power and pretensions of professional experts—and a valuable antidote to the narrowly political sensibility of much of the American left.

III

Mumford's biography of Melville showed that a commitment to the tragic sense of life did not necessarily entail, as the cases of Lippmann and Krutch seemed to indicate, a politically conservative stance. And his close friend (at least from the mid-1930s to the late-1940s) Reinhold Niebuhr was also pivotal in linking radicalism with the tragic view. Moreover, he was at the center of the effort to redefine "responsibility" in light of the tragic sense. As much as any other single thinker he elaborated the distinctive position on responsibility that demarcated the radicalism of the 1930s from earlier progressivism—and tied it intimately to the tragic realism of the 1940s.

By the early 1950s, when Niebuhr and Mumford had a disagreement over the issue of nuclear armaments, they stood for the two main positions within the camp of "tragic" liberals: Niebuhr for the larger group of Cold War realists who saw the Soviets as the continuation of the totalitarian threat first mounted by the fascists; Mumford for the smaller group of dissenters who thought tragic realism demanded a renunciation of nuclear stalemate. But even in the 1930s, when they were close allies and dreamed of co-editing a politically radical but culturally traditionalist magazine, one can detect the signs of their later split. Niebuhr believed that in a time of social breakdown and fascist advance, responsibility required jettisoning the old liberal Protestant ideal of "personality." In his view it was too individualist, too roseate, too sentimental, not in accord with harsh realities, large-scale problems, and effective responses. Mumford, by contrast, continued to insist on the centrality of personality in a democratic vision of responsibility.[5]

Niebuhr's *Moral Man and Immoral Society* (1932) shocked the liberal Protestant and democratic socialist community. Niebuhr forthrightly embraced "force" and "coercion" as ethical tools in the social struggle, and went so far as to argue that in some extreme situations the use of force logically implied the use of "violence." For this contention Niebuhr was rebuked, vilified, condemned: former friends attacked him in print as un-Christian and he reciprocated.

But the brouhaha over the use of violence obscured the depth of the transformation that liberal Protestantism was undergoing, most visibly in Niebuhr's own work. It was not just a matter of embracing "realistic" worldly means such as force, coercion, and violence. On a deeper level the issue was not one of means, but of ends. Niebuhr was not just rejecting reason, love, and good will as sufficient tools for the social struggle. He was casting off the long-standing liberal Protestant quest to infuse society with personality. His new, more tempered end was responsibility: the gradual, somber pursuit of a relatively greater degree of justice in society.

For liberal Protestants, as for Mumford, personality was a social as well as an individual reality. Or, more exactly, it was a reality that presupposed a communal context. It demanded self-giving interaction among persons for its realization. For the more effusive of the liberals, human society had an unbounded potential for the realization of personality. So did human history. The future was a realm of indeterminate possibility. There was no guarantee of progress, but there was no structural impediment to a spiral of improvement. The individual capacity for spiritual growth was matched by the social capacity for harmonious fellowship. There was a fundamental fit between individuals, their society, and their history. There were no ineradicable surds in human existence.

Moral Man argued for preserving the liberal goal of the just society (although in the midst of the Great Depression Niebuhr shifted the connotation of "justice": it no longer meant establishing equal access to the means of self-realization—such means as worker control of job structures—but gaining equal access to an adequate standard of living). Yet that goal could only be preserved if the inherited liberal world-view—the view that the social-historical realm was an arena of potential fellowship and harmony—was scrapped.

Niebuhr did not dispose of personality altogether; he just banished it to an ideal realm beyond society. He held on to the view that individuals, unlike groups, could in principle embody the law of love. In practice a rare saint might withdraw from society, escape the confines of self-interest, live out the ideal of self-giving personality. But if one was to live in society and benefit from its social and economic order, one had to participate in a system of power in which group was ranged against group. There was no sacrificial haven, no privileged Christian vantage point within society. Responsible Christians lived in the world, made use of the world's methods, and fought for justice alongside their secular fellows. They did not seek ideal ends, but a new, more just, balance of power.

The critics of *Moral Man* centered their fire on the book's condoning of violence. It was a sign of the times that no one noticed his condoning of a new role for intellectuals, that of propagandists in the social struggle. It was their role to provide the "emotionally potent oversimplifications" that workers needed to pursue justice. The conservative Krutch had longed for the ancient illusions and mythologies that gave life a decent drapery, in Edmund Burke's phrase. Niebuhr converted Krutch's nostalgia into an active quest for new mythologies that could galvanize the workers' movement. *Moral Man* was a key expression of the dominant view on the American left in the 1930s that the course of history would be determined by the most effective propaganda, not the most intelligent argument. The unanswered question was how intellectuals themselves, in giving themselves over to myth-making, would in the end be able to distinguish critical rationality from socially effective story-telling.

Moral Man exhibited a tragic sensibility in its denial that human history was moving toward communal fulfillment. It was an arena not of fulfillment, but of the continuous rebalancing of forces. The earlier generation of progressives, beginning in the 1880s with writers like Edward Bellamy (*Looking Backward*, 1888), defined moral responsibility as the duty to co-operate with history—which was moving in principle toward higher levels of freedom. Bellamy's protagonist Julian West, who arose from a deep sleep to find himself in twenty-first-century Boston, found himself in the care of the proto-progressive Dr. Leete. The good doctor sermonized about the goodness of man and the inevitable movement of history toward liberty and leisure for all. Julian's own responsibility as a good progressive citizen was to entrust himself to the doctor's care. "You are my patient as well as my guest," Dr. Leete told him gently. Julian willingly co-operated with his expert caretaker, who stood for the enlightened managerial elite of modern society.[6]

Niebuhr delivered a telling blow to the progressive faith in history and expertise. Responsible intellectuals did not co-operate with the preordained movement of history, or with the professional authorities who promised to take care of the public interest. They intervened with their myths and illusions to reorder the balance of forces in the interest of the working class. But as the 1930s progressed, Niebuhr came to doubt that the American working class was prepared to respond to well-chosen myths. By 1937, when he published *Beyond Tragedy*, he had worked out a new understanding of Christian responsibility in a fallen world.

Niebuhr now believed that the doctrine of original sin, at which liberals winced, expressed the basic reality of human existence: human beings had the capacity to do good, but they also had an inveterate tendency to aggrandize themselves and do evil. Even Christians remained under the law of sin; piety was no protection against wrongdoing. The ultimate problem for Christians was that they were called to act in the world despite the certainty that in acting they would sin.

Like other thinkers in the 1930s, Niebuhr was voicing his dissatisfaction with merely "social" explanations for human conflict. It was human nature itself, not just class rule or national interests, that produced social disorder and injustice. Like Freud, whose *Civilization and Its Discontents* was published in London in 1930, Niebuhr now asserted that the root problem was human nature itself. With Freud he insisted that the human self was fragmented, unaware of its own depths, bound for disappointment in its search for happiness.

Yet, unlike Freud, Niebuhr insisted on the paradoxical affirmation that for all their limits, evasions, and discontents, human beings were called to act responsibly in the world. They had to act for the good despite the knowledge that they would compromise their efforts to do good by doing evil. The ultimate paradox of the ethical life was that human beings were free moral agents in spite of their sins. Indeed, those who were conscious of their sinfulness were the most truly free, the most capable of responsible action, because they were aware of their limits. They were the most likely to modulate their action, to avoid the temptation to self-righteousness or fanaticism, to remain self-critical even as they acted decisively in the pursuit of justice.

IV

Niebuhr's elaboration of the tragic perspective in the 1930s and 1940s exerted a profound influence on many of his contemporaries, including Mumford (who acknowledged his debt to Niebuhr in such works as *Faith for Living* (1940) and *The Condition of Man* (1944)) and Mumford's and Niebuhr's friend Waldo Frank. Frank was another radical who wrote frequently in the 1930s about the tragic character of life and urged his comrades on the left to transcend "mechanical" reason and embrace an "organic" conception of existence. Frank had become active in the pro-Communist *New Masses* in the late 1920s, but he was an unusual member of the Old Left in his infatuation with organic, Catholic, peasant cultures, which he extolled in *Virgin Spain* (1926) and *America Hispana* (1931). These pre-modern cultures were collectivist by inheritance. Marxists needed to understand that their social solidarity was a product of familial, national, religious traditions, not a function of workplace camaraderie. Frank applied that view to the Soviet Union in *Dawn in Russia* (1932), a paean not to Soviet efficiency—the usual reason for applauding Stalin— but to inherited Russian peasant culture.

Frank, like many other literary intellectuals on the left (Edmund Wilson, Theodore Dreiser, John Dos Passos, Malcolm Cowley, to name a few), decided for a time to support the Communist cause. He took a leading role in organizing the pro-Communist American Writers' Congress in New York in 1935, and joined Mumford, Van Wyck Brooks, James T. Farrell, Lincoln Steffens, Agnes Smedley, and Richard Wright on the National Council of the League of American Writers, the permanent body established by the Congress. For many of them, including Frank, the choice of Communism was not a commitment to scientific materialism, not a reaffirmation of the ability of reason to comprehend the world and gradually change it, but an expression of outrage at human suffering and of a yearning for apocalyptic transformation. It was not the product of a renewed faith in the inevitability of progress, but of a conviction that revolutionary heroism was the only possible response to economic breakdown and class conflict.

Like Kyo Gisors, the hero of André Malraux's *Man's Fate*, they wished to fight for "what in his time was charged with the deepest meaning and the greatest hope." Malraux spoke at a "meeting for Spain" in New York in the late 1930s, and "described the crucifixion of the country in words that wrung our hearts," as Alfred Kazin later recalled in *Starting Out in the Thirties*. "There is much suffering in the world," Malraux said. "But there is one kind of suffering which it is a privilege to endure, the suffering of those who endure because they want to make a world worthy of man. . . . Let each man choose his own way of alleviating this suffering, relieve it he must. That is our responsibility to man's destiny, and perhaps to our own hearts." To conceive of radical action as the alleviation of suffering was to root one's radicalism squarely in the tragic sense of life. To speak of a responsibility both to man's destiny and to one's own heart was to reveal that tragic radicalism encompassed the realms of both self and society.[7]

V

Richard Wright, who actually joined the Communist Party, gave classic expression in his 1940s memoirs, *Black Boy* and *American Hunger*, to the tragic sense that infused 1930s radicalism. He also demonstrated that the commitment to Communism was not simply a choice of society over self but an attempt to put selfhood on a secure foundation. His decision to join the Party after arriving in Chicago in the late 1920s was the product of a long search for a community within which he could develop as a person and writer. His childhood, graphically reconstructed in *Black Boy*, was a time of intense physical and psychological suffering: he turned to literature for relief and sustenance.

His mother's suffering was more painful to him than his own. It "set the emotional tone of life," he wrote. At the age of twelve he had a "somberness of spirit" he never lost, and "a conviction that the meaning of living came only when one was struggling to wring a meaning out of meaningless suffering." He was determined "to drive coldly to the heart of every question and lay it open to the core of suffering I knew I would find there." His insight into the tragedy of life imposed a dual responsibility: to seek the truth about life ("skeptical of everything while seeking everything, tolerant of all and yet critical"), and to offer support to those who struggled with the same feelings ("to sit for hours while others told me of their lives, made me strangely tender and cruel, violent and peaceful.") He offered his "loyalties to the side of men in rebellion," but reserved a primordial loyalty to himself: a devotion to "answers to questions that could help nobody, that could only keep alive in me that enthralling sense of wonder and awe in the face of the drama of human feeling which is hidden by the external drama of life." Moral responsibility contained a political commitment, but it went beyond politics in its lonely devotion to the tragic enterprise of truth-telling.[8]

The Communist Party offered him initially an international community sworn to alleviate human suffering and a concrete outlet for his writing. He conceived his role as that of a teller of stories. He would not create Niebuhrian myths and illusions for the social struggle, but would record the sufferings of the voiceless people from whom he himself had come. Revolution was communication. As the Russian intellectuals of the early twentieth century had given voice to the peasants, so he would allow the Black American masses to speak.

But as he recounts in *American Hunger*, he ran afoul of Party leaders when he put truth-telling above discipline. "The conditions under which I had to work were what baffled them. Writing had to be done in loneliness and Communism had declared war upon human loneliness." Gradually he shifted his social commitment from the Party to the invisible community of writers, past and present, who elucidated the drama of the human spirit. He realized that for him the loneliness, the hunger, of existence was not a problem, but a solution to a problem. His former comrades labeled him an "intellectual" and he knew they were right: he valued questions more than answers, his primary obligation was to the struggle for insight into the human condition. "Politics was not my game, the human heart was my game," though "it was only in the realm of politics that I could see the depths of the human heart."[9]

VI

Like Niebuhr, Wright believed that moral responsibility meant committing oneself to the quest for justice but also holding that commitment under the judgment of a higher truth. Responsibility was a tension between engagement and reticence, action and reserve. Niebuhr's friend and neighbor Lionel Trilling probed the character of that dialectical responsibility in his 1947 novel *The Middle of the Journey*. The book was heavily indebted to his reading of Niebuhr's work, and the product of his reflections on the enthusiasms of the 1930s. On one level it was a rejection of the revolutionary hopes of the 1930s, but on another, deeper level it was an assertion of the "somberness of spirit" in the face of tragedy—a sensibility that tied the moderation of the postwar era to much of the radicalism of the 1930s.

The novel begins with Trilling's protagonist, John Laskell, recovering from scarlet fever. He has had a close brush with death, and as he literally sheds his old skin he realizes that in his former life—that of the liberal housing planner—he had ignored the deepest realities of life. He had been a typical "well-loved child of the middle-class," taught to expect the best from his future development. Everyone had promised him that he would grow and prosper. "This great promise he takes into himself in the form of a pledge" that the future will be "always brighter and more spacious than the present."

If, for Wright, Communism rested on a denial of truth-telling and an evasion of loneliness, for Trilling, middle-class liberal culture rested on a denial of death and an evasion of the present. It was only in sickness that Laskell realized that "there really was no future. He did not mean that *he* had no future. He meant that the future and the present were one—that the present could no longer contrive and manufacture the future by throwing forward, in the form of expectation and hope, the desires of the present moment. It was not that he had 'lost hope,' but only that he did not make a distinction between what he now had and was and what he expected to have and be." Edward Bellamy's hero Julian West had risen from his bed in twenty-first century Boston and been delivered *into* history, placed in a higher stage of historical development. John Laskell rose from his bed and was delivered *from* history, freed of the urge to identify himself with the future.

In rural Connecticut for a summer of recuperation, Laskell meditates on the meaning of moral responsibility with several friends, including Nancy and Arthur Crooms, left-liberals who admire the zeal and commitment of the Communists, and Gifford Maxim, a former underground Communist who has left the Party and embraced Christianity. The Crooms have carried their yearning for social transformation into the postwar world. They still live for the future. When their alcoholic handyman Duck Caldwell fails to appear for work, they excuse him; as a genuine proletarian he has become for them a symbol of the future, their living tie to it. When in a drunken stupor he slaps his young daughter and accidentally kills her, they again absolve him. They explain his actions in environmental terms; he is personally blameless. For the Croomses, common people lack responsibility; educated people have a responsibility to align themselves with history, help build the future in which commoners can finally come into their own.

Gifford Maxim, a character patterned after Whittaker Chambers, shares Laskell's distaste for the Croomses' viewpoint, but has replaced his dogmatic Marxism with an equally dogmatic Christianity. He considers Duck Caldwell "wholly responsible" for his daughter's death. "Wholly. And for eternity, for everlasting. That is what gives him value in my eyes—his eternal, everlasting responsibility. His every act, to me, involves the whole universe. And when it breaks the moral law of the whole universe, I consider that his punishment might be infinite, everlasting. And yet in my system, although there is never-ending responsibility, there is such a thing as mercy." Like Billy Budd in Melville's tale, Duck had committed a crime in a moment of passion, but he must nevertheless be punished in order to uphold the moral law.

Faced with the Croomses' and Maxim's opposing perspectives, Laskell seeks his "middle" ground. "An absolute freedom from responsibility— that much of a child none of us can be. An absolute responsibility—that much of a divine or metaphysical essence none of us is." Human beings are both responsible and conditioned, Laskell insists. Their responsibility lies precisely in their measured "response" to their conditioned fate. Human existence is fenced in, severely constrained, but within its limits people can pursue ends of love, beauty, justice. Laskell's encounter with the ultimate limit of death gives him new appreciation for the good that can be achieved within freely accepted constraints. He admires the Shakespearean sonnet for the same reason that he enjoys fly-fishing: excellence within established limits.

Like Richard Wright, Lionel Trilling considered human existence, in the words of the novel's narrator, "a great sea of misery, actual or to come." Like Reinhold Niebuhr, he regarded human beings as paradoxically determined yet free. All three issued a call for personal responsibility, but dissociated it from a commitment to history or to any Party that claimed to be riding the wave of the future. Through their efforts, and others', the term "responsibility" came in the 1940s to connote a refusal to be swept into social enthusiasms, a mature acceptance of the limits that surround human existence. The responsible self was the self in balance, poised in the middle of the journey: devoted in principle to justice, reticent and discriminating in concrete commitment. The posture of responsibility provided a dominant model for intellectual life in the postwar world.[10]

VII

Niebuhr, Trilling, and Wright, like Mumford, Frank, and Krutch, believed that "pragmatic liberalism" was seriously deficient: it displayed too lofty an estimate of human nature, too "mechanical" a view of the operations of human society, too uncritical a devotion to the powers of scientific reason to grasp reality and shape the course of human events. To combat pragmatic liberalism, all these thinkers called for a deeper sense of the tragic limitations on human achievement, for greater realism in assessing the prospects for social progress. But this broad accord among liberal realists tends to obscure a hidden fissure in their ranks, a fissure that emerged with clarity in the early 1950s when Niebuhr and Mumford split politically and personally, ostensibly over the issue of nuclear armaments.

Mumford and Niebuhr had been in close agreement in the late 1930s and early 1940s over the threat posed by the fascists. They both regarded the defense of bourgeois democracy in Europe as the only hope for preserving Western civilization. Mumford's deep commitment to the ideal of personality gave his interventionist work, *Men Must Act* (1939), its power as propaganda: The bourgeois democratic West, for all its injustices, was qualitatively different from, and superior to, the fascist system because in principle it respected the person. Persons developed themselves in freedom, pursued the path of self-realization; government was subordinate in principle to individuals and their organic communities, within which their growth took place. In a piece written for Niebuhr's *Christianity and Crisis* in 1941, Mumford chastised himself for having fallen under the spell of Randolph Bourne's anti-statism in the 1920s. Only the immediate choice of the lesser evil—the Western democracies—could permit personality to survive.

Niebuhr himself no longer spoke about the self-realization of persons, but in the second volume of *The Nature and Destiny of Man* (1943) and *The Children of Light and the Children of Darkness* (1944) he developed a parallel argument about the superiority of bourgeois democracy: it managed to accommodate the complexities of human nature. Human beings did have the potential to seek justice in community. But since they tended to overstep their bounds whenever given a chance, they had to be restrained. Idealism in the social arena naturally bred fanaticism. The genius of democratic pluralism was its ability to restrain fanaticism while remaining open-ended enough to permit occasional structural reforms. Bourgeois democracy was justified not because it made possible the growth of individuals in community, but because it prevented self-righteous groups from dominating their fellows.

In the late 1940s and early 1950s, while Niebuhr and most other liberal realists continued to defend bourgeois democracy against foreign "barbarism"—this time the barbarism of the Soviets—Mumford took up a dissenting position. He insisted that true realism demanded a hard look at the whole notion of nuclear deterrence. Niebuhr answered for the majority of liberal realists by belittling Mumford's views. In reviewing Mumford's *In the Name of Sanity* (1954), for example, he wrote that "Mr. Mumford's prescription for sanity would seem to be analogous to advising [that] 'You haven't a chance to escape disaster by walking on the edge of the precipice. Your only chance is to fly. I know you haven't any wings, but you must sprout them. The impossible must become possible in an extreme situation.'"[11]

Mumford did leave himself open to caricature. His *New Leader* piece on "Alternatives to the H-Bomb" in 1954 deserved Niebuhr's dismissive retort. "If politics means anything today," Mumford wrote, "it must become the 'art of the *impossible*.'" Americans "must offer the choice, not between fascist domination and capitalist domination by the United States, but between all forms of domination and the true alternative, active world cooperation, with the advanced nations lending their resources, their wealth, and above all their more mature political and technical leadership toward the uplift of the depressed and impoverished masses of mankind." Niebuhr rightly lambasted Mumford for dwelling in the clouds: preaching world government without attending to the obvious obstacles that stood in the way.[12]

The failure of Mumford's political analysis stemmed from his determination to inject an "ideal" perspective into policy debates. His mistake was to imagine that idealism was directly serviceable as policy, rather than as critique of policy. Had he attempted a Bournian critique of power from his "ideal realist" perspective, he would not have been such an easy target for Niebuhr. Rather than assert that Americans could simply choose world government over nuclear stalemate, he might have stepped back and clarified the values that political realists such as Niebuhr were neglecting. In fact that is what he went on to do in *The Myth of the Machine*.

But Mumford's naïve political writing in the early 1950s permitted Niebuhr to rest complacently in his anti-Soviet realism on nuclear and other political questions. Moreover, it permitted him to avoid the deeper issue of the cultural cost of political realism, an issue that Mumford was well equipped to illuminate. The real strength of Mumford's position was his perception that politics rests ultimately on culture, and that even in a time of political stalemate or reaction, cultural renewal may be pursued. Niebuhr was egregiously ignorant of cultural matters; he had no sensitivity to the ways in which the tissue of culture gradually emerges out of the activities of ordinary craftspeople, gifted artists, or attentive parents.

It was Niebuhr's historic role to challenge the pretensions of liberal rationalism and liberal religiosity, both of which dominated the northern Protestant churches in the early twentieth century. But in fighting that battle, in attending to the undoubted "sinfulness" in human nature, he unduly neglected the capacities of human beings to realize themselves in community. When Mumford spoke of the growth of "personality," or John Dewey called for the spread of "science," Niebuhr literally did not know what they were talking about. He thought they were mouthing utopian platitudes, closing their eyes to the barriers to individual or social advance. In fact they were talking about the preconditions for preserving a vital culture and a vital politics.[13]

Mumford's commitment to personality, and to reconciling the ideal of personality with the practice of responsibility, is a perennial feature of his thinking, and one of the most valuable for our time. He may have been too optimistic about the future prospects for human community (at least until the 1960s), but even in his most optimistic formulations he was on the right track. "In time," he wrote in the conclusion of *The Condition of Man* (1944), "we shall create the institutions and the habits of life, the rituals, the laws, the arts, the morals that are essential to the development of the whole personality and the balanced community: the possibilities of progress will become real again once we lose our blind faith in the external improvements of the machine alone."[14] On one level this was a utopian vision. On another level, it was a succinct statement of the individual and collective growth that issues ultimately from small acts of creation, acts that do always lie within our grasp.[15]

PART IV

A PERIL AND A HOPE

World War II shook Mumford's faith for living. Geddes, the only son of Sophia and Lewis, died in action at the age of nineteen in 1944 on Mount Altuzzo during the Italian campaign. His father then wrote *Green Memories: The Story of Geddes Mumford* (1947). The book was, Mumford declared, a composite of his and Sophia's memories of their son. "When love and truth were at odds" in the telling, "I served truth for love's sake," he avowed. He wanted a story to which Geddes would willingly have signed his name.[1] The next year, events in the war also deeply shocked him. He was stunned into days of silence by the news of the dropping of the atom bombs on Hiroshima and Nagasaki.[2] Science and technology had provided the ultimate weapon. In their essays that conclude this volume, Michael Zuckerman and Everett Mendelsohn explore the attitudes and values of an older Mumford disillusioned by the war and the use of the bomb. They consider, especially, his ambivalent evaluation of the post-World War II world as one characterized by both a peril and hope.[3] Zuckerman and Mendelsohn also write of the Mumford who diagnosed the world's parlous situation, despaired at the grim prognosis, but still never completely lost hope that a transformation of values could change the course of scientific and technological development and history. Not only did he believe that such a transformation could occur but, as Mendelsohn stresses, Mumford persuaded himself he could hasten the day of its arrival by playing the role of a diagnostician and a Jeremiah.

Zuckerman believes the two-volume *Myth of the Machine* to be Mumford's "most mature and most audacious work, the ripest and bravest fruition of a lifetime of engagement with the twentieth-century prospect" (Zuckerman, 362). As others of our authors do, he notes the grip that the concept of megamachine had on Mumford when he was writing the *Myth of the Machine* and he also acknowledges that the concept with its implied technological determinism caused Mumford to despair. Yet, Zuckerman is persuaded that the book is essentially optimistic because of Mumford's stress on the themes of mind over matter, of values shaping technology, and his insistence that human beings' construction of meaning has been a greater achievement than their construction of tools. Zuckerman acknowledges Mumford's brooding melancholy, but finds it tempered by the conviction that the deterministic force of the megamachine will prevail only if human beings with supine minds and pliable values become the creatures of megamachines. Zuckerman argues that an older and a less positivistic, a less Aristotelian Mumford sought intellectual succor in a Platonic commitment to the epistemological proposition that values and spiritual forces set the course of history.

Mumford, according to Zuckerman's reading, concentrated his hope for the future on a widespread religious renewal and revolt against the megamachine's materialism, its amoral bureaucratic power, its mechanistic ideology, and its oppressive technological momentum. Dependent as it is on people's acceptance of the myth of its irresistible power, the megamachine, Mumford insists, can be countered only by a religious commitment more powerful than the ideology and veneer of rationality that sustain the megamachine. Mumford had in mind the emotional fervor and moral commitment aroused by the remarkable religious leaders of the first millennium B.C., of Isaiah and Buddha, Confucius and Solon, Socrates and Jesus. From the Zuckerman essay we see that Mumford, in identifying religious teachings and movements as forces that bring about sea changes in history, had moved a long way from the soft determinism implicit in his eotechnic, paleotechnic, and neotechnic periodization in which technological stages followed one another with nearly Marxian predictability.

Zuckerman notes, however, that Mumford found in postwar science a negative influence of such growing proportions that it could snuff out hope for a religious and moral transformation. The designers of atom bombs, the physicists who chose to walk in the corridors of the pentagon of power, had strayed far from the nineteenth-century ideals of pure scientists with their indifference to power and fortune. Subjective inflations, distortions, and perversions helped shape the actions of an increasing number of scientists and their science. Furthermore, he accused scientists of seeking political power. He moderated his attack when he addressed the motives of Enrico Fermi, Leo Szilard, and Harold Urey, elite, morally sensitive scientists who became involved in the making of the bomb. He did not believe that they deliberately sought to establish a new priesthood for the megamachine, a priesthood capable of assuming autocratic authority and wielding satanic power, but that this was the dreadful consequence of their development of atomic physics.

To scientists, generals, admirals, senators, and others who occupied high places at the control center of the megamachine organized to develop the destructive force of nuclear power, Mumford said, in an essay so titled, "Gentlemen, You Are Mad!" In it Mumford writes of them as Melville had of Captain Ahab: that their methods are sane but their ends mad. Their madness would probably lead, the gloomy Mumford prophesies, to the destruction of mankind by atom bombs and other military/industrial means. Yet his despair was not so overwhelming that it prevented him from pursuing the hope that the peril might be averted by a world informed in detail of the grim threat by those who, like him, possess sufficient independence of mind to recognize the arrival of nuclear energy as a curse, and its deployment as a manifestation of megamachine mentality, not as a triumph of science and technology to be celebrated as if it were one sign of material progress.

Mendelsohn examines Mumford's tireless efforts in the *Myth of the Machine*, in his collection of essays *Values for Survival* (1946), in his book *In the Name of Sanity* (1954), and through his articles and lectures to publicize the social and political effects of the nuclear arms race. He places Mumford's writing in the context of the books and articles of others who addressed the perils of the post-bomb world. In a particularly affecting essay that Mendelsohn summarizes, Mumford describes in a March 1946 article published in *Air Affairs* his vision of the course of the nuclear arms race and the aftermath of the Götterdämmerung that would follow if atomic bombs were to be used. Mumford's predictions encompass not only the obvious physical destruction, but the resultant social chaos and lasting psychological damage. Mumford casts his essay as a rational yet eerie set of alternative scenarios of the future of cold war and a third world war. Here we have Mumford the prophet of doom. But the prophet, as Zuckerman has shown, who believes—and hopes—that conversion can give the lie to prophecy.

Mendelsohn also reviews the internecine strife between Mumford and some of his contemporaries in science—internecine because they all believed that they were confronting the peril of the bomb and taking steps to reduce it. Mendelsohn recalls that in 1971 several leading scientists and engineers considered Mumford aligned with those who were part of an anti-intellectual wave. The scientists felt that Mumford's insistence that their method was sterile and destructive because it was objective and analytical, not organic and life-centered, was a retrogression to the ignorance predating the scientific revolution of the seventeenth century. Mumford retaliated by characterizing the scientists' anxiety and alarm before such arguments as his as an effort to avoid the critical self-examination made imperative by the miscarriages of a science and a technics now lodged in the power complex.

Mendelsohn, like Zuckerman, finds the ray of hope, even optimism, in Mumford's dark vision. Mumford himself gives us the clue to unraveling the paradox of a deadly peril that stimulates hope, for he insisted that he and others must diagnose and declare the deadly social symptoms, if there was to be a cure. When René Dubos, a distinguished scientist, presented Mumford with the National Medal for Literature, Dubos described him as both a despairing optimist and an authentic utopian who believed there was the chance that humans could throw off the yoke of technology—if they were thoroughly critical of it. Ironically, Dubos added, those who find nothing to criticize, those who think of themselves as optimists, are fulfilling the gloomy prophecy; not Mumford.

Prophet of Our Discontent:
Lewis Mumford
Confronts the Bomb

EVERETT MENDELSOHN

"Gentlemen, You Are Mad!" was the title of the article in the *Saturday Review of Literature*, 2 March 1946, with which Lewis Mumford opened a campaign against nuclear weapons that he kept active through the remainder of his years of speaking and publishing.

> We are living among madmen. Madmen govern our affairs in the name of order and security. The chief madmen claim the titles of General, Admiral, Senator, scientist, administrator, Secretary of State, even President. And the fatal symptom of their madness is this: they have been carrying through a series of acts which will lead eventually to the destruction of mankind, under the solemn conviction that they are normal, responsible people, living sane lives, and working for reasonable ends. Soberly, day after day, the madmen continue to go through the undeviating motions of madness: motions so stereotyped, so commonplace, that they seem the normal motions of normal men, not the mass compulsions of people bent on total death.[1]

For Mumford there was no possibility of "managing" nuclear weapons, and certainly no justification for integrating them into the military and strategic policies of the United States. His challenge was direct and incisive. There must be a "move toward sanity" which would entail a total reversal of current policy. "Abandon the atomic bomb! Give it up! Stop it now! That is the only order of the day."[2] While others, as we will note below, shared Mumford's fear of nuclear weapons and abhorrence of their use in the war against Japan, few initially demonstrated the hostility toward the nuclear enterprise and the moral revulsion that came to mark Mumford's continued and sharp critique of the bomb, those who built it, those who used it, and those who governed it.

As we examine Lewis Mumford's response to what some hailed at the time as a major achievement of science and technology, I think we can discern two losses that Mumford suffered in the closing days of World War II. One, of course, was the effect of the development and dropping of the atom bomb which, for Mumford, seemed to mark a final reversal of his own hopes for science and technology, hopes which had informed a good number of his earlier assessments of the role of scientific knowledge and "technics" in aiding human progress and adding to human renewal. But I suspect that part of the intensity of Mumford's reaction grew from his second loss: the death in battle of his son Geddes Mumford, sometime around 13 September 1944 on the battlefields of Italy. Geddes, nineteen years old, was seen by his father as an individual of real promise, and perhaps, as indicated by the very name he gave him—Geddes (after Patrick Geddes, Mumford's own teacher and mentor)—an extension and continuation of Mumford's own life, work and values. The loss that the father felt was indicated in the dedication of his first postwar book, *Values for Survival* (1946), to his son Geddes: "Long before his work was done, he was the father, I was the son."[3] In the following year Mumford undertook the painful task of writing a biography, *Green Memories* (1947), of Geddes Mumford.[4]

In the preface to *Values for Survival*, Mumford included the plan for a book which had been proposed by Geddes to his father in a letter written from a base in North Africa shortly before the invasion of Italy. The young soldier, Geddes had said, must be able to look back and examine the question "why he fought."[5] The end of the war would come, he believed, not with the peace treaties, but really only when this question could be answered. Mumford had promised to prepare a book to aid in this task. His understanding of what was involved went to the core of the concerns of fighting a war: "Unconditional surrender will be a mocking symbol of victory unless it leads to the unconditional redemption of man: the victor no less than the vanquished."[6] For Lewis Mumford, this concept of human redemption of a fundamentally religious sort involving value, belief, and commitment became one of the commanding themes of his postwar essays on technology and other human productions. In all of his works of criticism—artistic, literary, historical, technological—Mumford was unafraid of moral dimensions. And indeed, his attitude at many points was informed and forced by moral imperatives.

The carrying out of the first steps of this "redemption of man" seemed to demand a new intensified pace; was it the pledge of a father to the deceased son? In the 1946 book, Mumford reprinted his earlier 1940 essay, "The Reasons for Fighting," which obviously had been written both as an apologia for joining the effort against Nazism, and as a means of injecting specific values for the postwar outcome into the very spirit of war fighting, itself.[7] He outlined demands for a new world order which were to be much more far-reaching than those called for by the victors in World War I. But in his essay of 1940, Mumford noted that we must be more patient than the post-World War I political actors had been. By 1946, however, he had reversed this caution and added an urgent footnote. The atom bomb overruled this judicious council of patience. While there should be no premature discouragement about achieving world order, he urged instead a dogged unwillingness to admit failure. The tone that he set for his postwar efforts was insistent, the pace accelerated, and the mood one of determination.[8]

I am examining in this paper the nature of Lewis Mumford's early response to the use of the atom bomb, his continuing and expanding critique of nuclear weapons, and the social and political implications of this critique. I am interested in the structure of the critique, its elements, its sources, its images, and its foci. I shall also attempt to locate Lewis Mumford's criticisms among those of his contemporaries, comparing attitudes, styles, and politics. There is one other important element that emerged early in Mumford's response to atomic weapons, and then grew in dimension and intensity: his attack on science and technology—practitioners and institutions. Finally, we shall want to evaluate Mumford's campaign.

Lewis Mumford's first public responses to the atomic bomb and its use can be found in several periodicals—both popular and semipopular (including three important contributions to a journal called *Air Affairs*).[9] In addition, he published his collected essays on many occasions, often changing their titles and adding notes. There were also lectures and speeches, including his address to the one hundredth anniversary of the American Association for the Advancement of Science in September 1948.[10] He also added new prefaces to older works as they were being republished, for example, both *Technics and Civilization* and *The Condition of Man*.[11] In 1959, the twenty-fifth anniversary of the publication of *Technics and Civilization* (1934), he took the occasion to look backward and appraise with retrospective criticism his product of a quarter of a century earlier.[12]

His criticism of nuclear weapons was sustained in almost unabated form through the years. The thrust of his argument often remained unchanged, even if he updated it to respond to new events, for example, the Soviet Union's explosion of their first atomic bomb in 1949, and the U.S. decision to build the hydrogen bomb in 1950 and its first test in 1952. In his later papers he imparted a much greater sense of being joined by others in a common criticism, as compared with his earlier essays, where he often seemed alone, the critic outside a movement. It leaves us with the question, of course, of the extent of his political involvements, which seemed slight. There were other movements of opposition to the bomb in the post-World War II period.

If the atom bomb were the early focus of his criticism, Mumford extended the range of his critique over the years to include other elements of technological and human failure. This critique reached its height in *The Pentagon of Power*.[13] The attitude that he displayed earned him the title of "Our Most Distinguished Flagellator," bestowed by Christopher Lehmann-Haupt in his review of *The Pentagon of Power* in the *New York Times* in November, 1970.[14] Although Mumford might have objected to the slightly derogatory tone that Lehmann-Haupt used, he made clear on several occasions, notably in his autobiographical volume *My Works and Days* (1979), that his critical outlook was indeed self-fashioned.[15] As he noted, he had come to see a different world from the one that only slightly discomforted (or even comforted) his contemporaries. "If the forces that now dominate us," he wrote, "continue on the present path, they must lead to collapse of the whole historical fabric." For him, 1945 was the true turning point. He was not satisfied with what others around him were doing, and noted that "only cowardice would allow us to ignore these realities, but because I have dared to face and evaluate them, I have often been dismissed as a 'prophet of doom.'"[16]

In 1972, in an address accepting the National Medal for Literature, Mumford likened himself to the prophet Jonah who, though he had been instructed by God to go to Nineveh to tell the inhabitants of impending doom, had tried to avoid going. But Mumford concluded, "If the truth calls us—this is the lesson of both science and religion—we must obey."[17] He reprinted his talk under the title "Call Me Jonah!"[18] While the Master of Ceremonies on the night of the award, René Dubos, referred to Mumford as "the most outspoken, despairing optimist of our period," he also pronounced him the "most authentic utopian. . . ." "The real prophets of doom," he continued in a vein that surely pleased Mumford, "are not those who criticize technological civilization, but those who accept the domination of the machine."[19] But a later commentator, noting Mumford's three decades of warnings, called him "an indefatigable, scolding voice crying in the wilderness of modern technological civilization, mocking what he sees as its absurdities and deformations, warning us of the apocalyptic fate we will surely suffer if we do not heed his, Lewis Mumford's, prescriptions."[20]

Mumford did not really object to the idea that he was prophesying trouble, but he insisted that he be seen as one who faced the future as an exponent of the "renewal of life." It is more than just doom that he prophesied. He expressed a deep and thorough discontent, both with the new realities and also with current human responses to them. Although he brought his criticisms of technics and of social values to the fullest and sharpest level in his *Pentagon of Power*, it is also worth noting that, in addition, he returned to a measured optimism in this book and some of his later essays of the 1970s. He seemed to be saying, "I am being heard, and perhaps even heeded." But more on Mumford in the 1970s below.

The nature of Lewis Mumford's critique of the atomic bomb was set by his immediate postwar mood. He was pessimistic and fearful. On the title page of his collection of essays *Values for Survival* (1946), he turned once again to John Ruskin (a source from which he gained continuing inspiration) for the very pessimistic lines:

> I could smile when I hear the hopeful exultation of many, at the new reach of worldly science and vigor of worldly effort; as if we were again at the beginning of new days. There is thunder on the horizon, as well as dawn.[21]

The structure of Mumford's critique of atomic weapons and their uses contained several elements. First, he lamented that we could have, and indeed should have, known what to expect since there were earlier prophecies and warnings which went unheeded. Further, he referred often (if briefly) to the history of atomic studies, pointing to Becquerel, the Curies, Rutherford, Soddy, et al. But his use of history is really emblematic, not analytic. The historical figures, the discoverers, flit across his pages in the literary style he used elsewhere, seeming to indicate that he sought legitimacy for the story he had to tell and the points he wanted to make.

He picked up and on many occasions used a particular metaphor. He linked the disintegration of the atom to the disintegration of human societal moral order. On some occasions, the metaphor almost seems to take command. If there is a culprit in his criticisms, it is scientific advance and the scientists who have been its authors. I will return to this issue later, but would note here that Mumford showed a sense of having been betrayed by the very science which at an earlier stage he seemed to give so much credence and credibility. On many occasions he indicated a willingness to dismantle scientific, technological, and industrial structures and procedures if this dismembering would bring us back from the abyss.[22] For Mumford, human life is endowed with a sacredness and every effort must be bent to protect it. He was not afraid to turn to the literary use of fear, fear of the destruction of the human race and all forms of life, as an instrument to attract attention and bring changes in values and policies. In one of his strongest moral criticisms, he pointed out that the victors in World War II, by using the atomic bomb and prior to that the large-scale strategic bombing of civilian targets, were morally as culpable as the defeated enemies. He was quite willing to accept the need for limitations, restraints, and even a moratorium on new invention in order to reverse what he envisaged as the disastrous new path. He identified what we might call technological Malthusianism in which mechanical inventions have been multiplied at a geometric ratio, compared with social skills and moral controls which have grown at only an arithmetic ratio, or, as he suggested, perhaps even regressed.[23] If there is to be a successful future, Mumford noted, it will require the establishment of a new world order. From early in the postwar period he envisaged the United Nations as the instrument for achieving universal law and international restraint. But, at core, he advocated an active human and personal reward of every habit, every action, and every value. Those familiar with Mumford's writings know the manner in which he adopted themes, emblems, and even slogans and repeated them in varied form and contexts on numerous occasions. He insisted that the critical points he raised be heard, and heard again. This is nowhere truer than in the criticisms he made and the proposals he offered concerning atomic weapons and their consequences for the human condition.

The first of Mumford's "prophecies of doom" was written during the autumn of 1946 and published in a new journal, *Air Affairs*, in March 1947 as one of a series of papers examining the implications of atomic energy.[24] Mumford's paper is entitled simply "Social Effects." (He republished it under the title "Assumptions and Predictions" in a collection of essays *In the Name of Sanity*, 1954.) The paper was written before the cold war between the Soviet Union and the United States was fully under way, but it quite clearly anticipated the impending chasm that grew up between the two nations. In tone and content it foreshadowed many of the pessimist visions that became a staple of both his fictional and political prognoses.

Mumford laid out a series of four possible scenarios of a post-bomb world. He adopted "two constants": one, that the atom bomb exists; second, that there will be "a state of chronic non-cooperation between the political powers." He then turned to what he called four assumptions:

Mumford's *first assumption* is that the United States uses its atomic arsenal in pre-emptive strikes before any other nation has the means of retaliation. These occur during the period of the U.S. monopoly on atomic bombs. The intent was to forestall the Soviet Union getting its own bomb. He describes the outcome of this very successful, that is to say very destructive, attack. Thirty-six Soviet cities are destroyed, and many other smaller targets are similarly hit. Twenty-five million people are killed. In a sardonic tone he notes that the newspaper headlines would celebrate this success as "Red menace removed forever!" But the success is by no means complete, and the Soviets, rather than agreeing to unconditional surrender, move their armies to the periphery of Europe and Asia, take over these lands, and summon them to join in battle against a barbarous enemy. In the meantime, the Russian people begin a process of mass migration, with millions mingling with non-Russian populations on the periphery. Back in the United States, all free discussion over the reasons for this new war have been stifled, and when the U.S. administration attempts to raise an army of more than 10,000,000 for an invasion of Europe and Asia, there is deep misapprehension and mistrust. What is seen is that in the place of an inexpensive and quickly won war, there will a be costly and continuous one. As Mumford sums up this first grisly scenario, he notes that too many of the forms of "human cooperation and human understanding" have been destroyed and that "any hope of bringing about peace and order for centuries would be fantastic."[25]

Mumford's *second assumption* is that instead of an immediate war, hostilities are postponed until both the United States and the Soviet Union possess substantial numbers of atomic bombs, although, in this scenario, the U.S. stockpile is significantly larger than that of Russia. During the extended arms race, intrusive national security precautions will have been taken. All the goods of international trade are under continual rigorous inspection; air travel between the continents breaks down; diplomatic relations between the United States and the Soviet Union are terminated, and global tensions and suspicions deeply heightened. Once again, numerous democratic processes in the United States have been renounced. When war finally breaks out, the Soviet Union is able to absorb the United States attack and its losses are less disastrous than those of the United States. U.S. forces in Western Europe are surrounded and killed, and U.S. allies in Europe are massively attacked as a means of cutting off the United States, thereby denying a U.S. base for European operations.

The devastation in the United States is greater than that in the Soviet Union, with some 40,000,000 dead (the figure taken from General Leslie Groves's original estimates; Groves was military commander of the Manhattan Project). Hospital and medical services are unable to care for the casualties, and "mercy deaths" add additional casualties. The war, however, is still not over. The Soviets, from weapons bases hidden in the Ural Mountains, launch a new attack of atomic bombs, and a long-term "war of attrition" and of nerves ensues. With international communication broken down, with the broad destruction of those factories needed to create synthetic substitutes destroyed, the high civilizations disappear, and in their places "island cultures" emerge in distant parts of the world. "There is the deliberate lapse into primeval ways," Mumford wrote, "in some places, machines are attacked and disembowled, and in others they are allowed to fall into complete neglect: in any event, they are treated as symbols of man's decadence, of his will to extinction." Curiosity, invention, and innovation are banned and human life returns to "the repetitive round of tribal society."[26]

Mumford's *third assumption* is that an atomic war does not break out until there is widespread proliferation of nuclear arms to many countries, to at least twenty on various continents. This contributes to the "quota of suspicion, fear, and death." A basis for Mumford's early negative reaction to civilian uses of atomic energy emerges in this scenario in which there is wide-scale production of atomic energy and a marked decrease in the size of the apparatus for the production. He even suggests that, thanks to research of the physicists, elements not previously prone to atomic disintegration will become available for the process (although he does not include the lighter elements, since he was not yet aware of the work on fusion which, by using hydrogen, would create much more powerful bombs). He posits increasing secrecy. This leads ultimately to the classification of all scientific publication and the casting of suspicion even on puzzle magazines and comic books which, it was feared, had been the source of a leak of other secrets. While at one level this secrecy would seem to slow atomic research, the concentration of interest and funds on atomic physics and related fields counteracts this tendency. But in all other areas by this scenario, creativity is slowed, or even reversed. Otherworldly and quack religions grow, and a broad demoralization of young people emerges. As a means of counteracting this, a strong revival of antiquarianism emerges, with the Victorian period being proclaimed humankind's "Golden Age." Secrecy and suspicion give rise to fantasy and deception. The police state grows, the FBI swells to an army, neighbors become distrustful of each other, and there are broad psychotic outbreaks. When a war begins, Mumford supposes that it may occur either by accident or by deliberate intention, with the facts themselves undetermined. Whether it be a single unbalanced person, admirers of Hitler, neo-Hitlarians, or whatever, the effects are devastating, with more than half the world's population killed and, because of the "high order of radioactive saturation, changes take place in the weather and in the balance of vegetable, animal, insect and bacterial life." Even for those who survive, death through starvation or the intake of radioactive contaminants goes on to wipe out three-quarters of the remaining population. In this scenario Mumford sees no "islands of culture surviving." Civilization enters full disintegration and "an age so dark that every other dark age will seem by contrast one of intense illumination." Humans that do survive are almost like animals, with hardly anything left of intelligence or of those other factors that provide human identity. And the damage to the environment is massive, with the transformations in genes causing the emergence of diseases and deformities able to wipe out the remainder of the human species.[27]

In his *fourth assumption*, Mumford posits that no atomic war will break out for at least a century, but that the whole globe remains threatened by it. The violence, destruction, and extermination suggested in his third assumption does not occur in this scenario, albeit the manufacture of atomic weapons continues. Instead, as the threat continues, the central government grows stronger, and in turn more dominated by the military, the scientists, and technicians involved in weapons production and defense. There is an attempt to move cities underground through the building of extensive shelters and new subway systems, though in New York, Mumford notes, because of the rocky nature of the subsoil, underground building is too costly and, therefore, in the atomic age the population of the city dwindles to less than 100,000. Banks, along with insurance companies, are nationalized as attempts to pay the heavy costs of underground building and population redistribution. Needless to say, taxes increase. The development of new weapons, including an "atomic earthquake bomb," challenges the concentration of underground life. The wealthy are able to live in their above-ground houses, but they also purchase from the government standard underground shelters which take the place of the weekend cottage of earlier generations. The rest of the population is assigned to bunks in underground dormitories. Factories, schools, administrative buildings move underground, and a network of underground roads and subways becomes transcontinental. The constitutions of all countries are altered, and rigorous control over all elements of society is put in place. The most talented among the youth are pulled aside for more intensive training in those areas of science and technology deemed necessary for atomic warfare. In turn, other areas of research fall into neglect, and, through the lack of exchange and cross-fertilization, research in the sciences themselves declines. Through full-scale "conditioning," ensured by the centralized control of publication and expression in every form, backed up by constant espionage on conversation, "this state of affairs is characterized as freedom. . . ." With a steady increase in destructiveness of atomic weapons, and no way out to be seen, the future becomes a blank. The psychological disruptions that come with this are "the familiar forms of . . . regressive reactions." Fantasy becomes a major escape; "purposeless sexual promiscuity" becomes common and "narcotic indulgence" is widespread. Most worrying of all, Mumford predicts, "would be the frequent outbreaks of catatonic trance" and resistance to the requirements of normal life. Resistance to this sort of life would grow, and predatory bands would leave their underground workshops and roam the surface. And those troops brought up to control this resistance in some cases become its victims. "Still, no country as yet has made a wholesale atomic attack. Peace reigns, the rigid peace of death." In this fourth assumption, no life has been lost in atomic war, but civilization has begun to disintegrate because of secrecy, isolation, withdrawal, and preoccupation with mere physical survival. In this case, "the social order becomes a prison and existence therein is punishment for life."[28]

Mumford's assessment is pessimistic unless there is a turn toward "world cooperation"; all of the alternatives are disastrous. "The very precautions men may take for safeguarding against atomic warfare may also do away with every sound reason for living." There is only one answer: "Unconditional cooperation on a world scale."[29]

Although there were several other speculative or fictional accounts spelling out some of the implications of the advent of the age of atomic warfare, few, if any, were as uncompromisingly pessimistic as Lewis Mumford's account of the "social effects" of the atomic bomb. By 1946 a number of "informed" fictional accounts of the effects of atomic war were being published.[30] One important account by the physicist Philip Morrison recounted details of the actual effects of the atomic explosion over Hiroshima as he saw them shortly after the bombing. Then, by way of making the implications more accessible, he translated them into comparable effects of an atomic bomb dropped on Manhattan.[31] It must have made a sobering reading! While these accounts alluded to various social effects of atomic warfare, I am aware of no contemporary account that attempted to project the variety of social disruptions that actual warfare or an extended atomic weapons race would bring. Paul Boyer, in his recent study *By the Bomb's Early Light*, notes that "the most exhaustive post-Hiroshima reflections and predictions regarding the bomb's psychological impact were those of . . . Lewis Mumford."[32]

At the time they published Mumford's paper, the editors of *Air Affairs* were clearly nervous, and on the opening page of the article an asterisked footnote called attention to a "comment" by an editorial board member, Henri Bouché, which appeared in the closing pages of the journal.[33] In addition, the editor, in a paragraph-long comment in his note, took issue with Mumford. First, he doubted that a "state of chronic non-cooperation between the political powers" (Mumford's phrase) would really ensue, and instead believed that the "Great Powers" could co-operate, especially once the "facts" were known and considered by peoples of the world. The editor went on to plead for expending energy to seek co-operation. Instead of focusing on "moving immovable government policy," he urged that more attention be paid to educating the uneducated. In the latter case there might emerge a "democratic world ruled by the people's law instead of by government's introverted self-dictates." In retrospect, of course, this plea sounds a note of naïveté, particularly as it was written during the very years that attempts to gain international control of atomic weapons were failing. Assuredly, however, Mumford's prophecies of despair and doom seemed to the editor important to challenge.

In his own "afterword," Henri Bouché noted that upon receiving advance proof of the articles of the journal, he was "particularly impressed by Lewis Mumford's article on the social effects of the atomic bomb."[34] He saw in it the "honest approach of a thoughtful man" to an important issue of the day. But he wondered at the possible danger of publishing an article of this sort. It seemed "sensational and emotional" to accept the assumptions that Mumford made, particularly the idea of a possible preventive war by the United States against the Soviet Union. Perhaps, Bouché speculated, Mumford's statements might be taken out of context and misunderstood. He wondered about another danger as well: whether readers would see the paper as "a romanced and easy mannered fiction" similar to that of Jules Verne and H.G. Wells, and therefore able to be put aside and not taken seriously. But having satisfied himself that this was not the case, he argued, however, that in light of the fact that the Soviet Union, a "powerful and totalitarian State," would almost certainly have the bomb in not many years, would it not be they who would find it easier to launch a preventive atomic attack? Mumford's first assumption, Bouché believed, had to be cast in more general form. Bouché further challenged whether the "devastating effects of such a preventive war" would be common to all the parties. He speculated that it might well be the aggressor who would gain most.

Bouché also felt it necessary to challenge Mumford's fourth assumption—a century or more of a worldwide competitive atomic arms race. He doubted that it would last that long. He thought that "if prepared, the atomic intertribal (international) war will take place," and that the "century of atomic peace" would not be possible. But Bouché was quite willing to accept a theme common to all four of the Mumford assumptions, that is, the gradual loss of freedom. However, he wanted to leave behind a positive afterthought. He found in "the simple fact of technological advance" rather than by any choices that humans themselves have made, that the planet had become unified materially. With this said, the next task, Bouché claimed, is to turn this unity into political institutions and morals, and he hoped that those involved now in "air circles," with a recognition of the necessity of air armaments, would take on the seeking of unity as their "highest duty." Almost as if in reprimand of the prophecy of doom, Bouché looked forward to "constructive discussions and concrete proposals."

One of Lewis Mumford's major themes in his criticism of the development of the atomic bomb and the implications that follow therefrom is that we should have known better, and thereby could have avoided the calamity from which we now suffer. The focal point for Mumford's claim lies in what he identified as the "prophecy" or "observation" of Henry Adams. Just why it is Adams to whom he turns and on whose words he places a very heavy burden is not quite clear to me, for certainly, on the face of it, Adams's words do not seem to have the clarity that Mumford extracted from them.[35] Beginning fairly early in his discussions of the atomic bomb, Mumford identified a letter that Henry Adams wrote to Henry Osbourne Taylor on 17 January 1905 (but published only in 1947), that Mumford claimed to have first read in the 1920s. He pointed to these words:

> The assumption of unity, which was the mark of human thought in the Middle Ages, has yielded very slowly to the proofs of complexity. The stupor of science before radium is proof of it. Yet it is quite sure, according to my score of ratios and curves, that, at the accelerated rate of progression since 1600,

it will not need another century or half century to turn thought upside down. Law, in that case, would disappear as theory or *a priori* principle and give place to force. Morality would become police. Explosives would reach cosmic violence. Disintegration would overcome integration.[36]

Mumford noted Henry Adams's phase rule of history and his prediction that a new phase would emerge in 1917. As validation for Adams's identification of phase change, Mumford pointed to Ernest Rutherford's discovery in 1919 that the degradation of a stable atomic nucleus (nitrogen was the one on which Rutherford was working) would be caused by bombardment of an alpha particle, that is, a proton that is broken off. In Mumford's view, the atom is here split and the beginning of a new phase identified. This idea, Mumford said, is further elaborated in Henry Adams's essay "On the Phase Rule in History." Mumford identified this observation by Adams as "the keenest historic insight," noting that not only would the physical sciences be transformed, but that political and moral changes would accompany it. As Mumford put it: "With the *invention* of the bomb, every item in the prediction was fulfilled except one: the disappearance of law and morality. That took place when the bomb was actually used."[37] For Mumford the prediction and prophecy were there, but nobody paid attention.

In a speech in Berkeley, California, in 1961 (published in the *Virginia Quarterly Review* the following year), Mumford offered a confession and a *mea culpa*.[38] As a way of implicating himself and, by extension, the rest of us in the failure to understand and anticipate the consequences of splitting the atom, he recalled his high school teacher of physics (Stuyvesant High, New York) in 1911 who, during a class session, held up a pencil claiming that "if we could unlock the energy of the atoms within it, enough power would be generated to run the subways of New York." The implied critique is there. Which of us in the years since the discovery of atomic radiation at the turn of the century has not at one time or another been told to think about the power stored in atoms and the potential in being able to harness this power? The warning was given explicitly by Pierre Curie when he received the Nobel Prize in 1903, and by numerous other investigators of the atomic nucleus in the years since.[39] Not to mention, of course, the fictional versions to be found in such scavengers of the sciences as H.G. Wells in his novel written on the eve of World War I, *The World Set Free*.[40]

Mumford's *mea culpa* came when he pointed out that as late as 1934, when he published *Technics and Civilization*, he shrank from dealing with problems attendant on the release of atomic energy, not because of ignorance of the possibility, but, he claimed, out of the cowardly hope that it would not come about. To admit it, he felt, would make it impossible to ignore the demands that the release of atomic energy would impose on all of us. Mumford was concious that he was making a confession of guilt and asked no absolution. In fact, when he wrote the *Pentagon of Power* (1970),

he admitted that perhaps he himself would have worked on the bomb in
the context of an anti-Nazi war and the fear of Germans winning the race
to produce atomic weapons.[41]

As he constructed his critique of the atom bomb, Lewis Mumford displayed the full range and power of the language he could master and the
images he could create. His prose is rich and prophetic, while at other
times strikingly apocalyptic and resigned. Among the postwar commentators and critics of the atom bomb (and there were many), Mumford's tone
and quality stand out. There seems in him, particularly in the earlier years,
a passion and an anger that made the catastrophe of the atom bomb seem
to have a particularly personal quality for him. He was never shy in his
writings about exposing his beliefs: he took special pains to expose his core
values. He intends his writings not to be reasoned political or strategic
arguments so much as expressions wrenched from his soul.

We are not surprised, then, that when Mumford turns to those around
him to see where the faults may lie for the failure of perception of danger,
his criticism is biting and at times disdainful. As indicated in that first article, "Gentlemen, You Are Mad!" Mumford expected little from national
governments and found little good that they had done. There is a certain
mournful tone, however, when he examines the role of his fellow citizens:
"The enemy no longer lies in Berchtesgaden: he has captured the very citadel of our hearts."[42] A poll taken by Elmo Roper for *Fortune* magazine,
and published 8 November 1945, was the source of his despair. Fifty-three
percent of the civilian population, according to the poll, "believe that we
should have used this secret weapon in exactly the way we did." A full
majority of all people, Mumford lamented, of all ages, sex, and geographic
distribution "subscribed to this feeling of satisfaction over the use of the
atomic bomb." As we read his early reflections, we come away with the
sense that he felt almost alone, part of a small minority, deserted by those
who ought to share his judgments. In actuality, of course, there were a
number of other critics, many more modulated in tone who, having criticized the initial use of the bomb, argued from political rather than moral
premises against its further development. He mentioned few of them in
his early essays. Several individuals and groups gained notice in subsequent
years.[43] In "Gentlemen, You Are Mad!" Mumford alluded to warnings fur-
tively sent by some of "the greatest of the madmen, the men who invented
the super-infernal machine itself," who were shocked back into sanity.[44]

As we follow Lewis Mumford's attack on atomic weapons over the years,
it is apparent that he reserved some of his sharpest criticisms for scientists
and engineers—the designers and builders of these new weapons. He
faulted them for failing to heed the prophecies like those of Henry Adams,
claiming that it was these men of knowledge and technique who could have
anticipated the impact of "the bomb" because they had the foreknowledge
to do so. But they failed! He saw scientists as paralyzed by their basic
assumption that science was identified with a "real" world and, therefore,
they felt no need to take into account the human implications of the dis-

coveries being made or to focus on the issues of the use and misuse of the potential achievements. He pointed with some scorn at what he saw as a detached and depersonalized scientific intelligence which boasted of its own neutrality, of its non-concern with issues of morals and responsibility. By way of literary allusion, he called upon Captain Ahab (of Melville's *Moby-Dick*) to testify for the scientist: "All my means are sane: my motives and object mad."[45]

It is almost as though he had been "let down" by a favored friend, for during the 1930s when technique seemed under sharp attack from many quarters, Mumford saw in the aims and goals of science an antidote to despair and a corrective to potentially misguided knowledge.

As he looked back from 1961 and scanned the horizon of scientific work on the bomb, he was scathing in his attack on the scientist and on the project of science itself. "Why were there no martyrs?" he challenged.[46] "Why wasn't there a movement of those who said no and would remove their services from bomb building?" Although he criticized the practitioners of science in his earliest attacks on the atomic bomb, his focus on the role of science and its failures became stronger in subsequent years, moving out from the physicists and engineers directly involved in bomb-building to the whole of the scientific enterprise. Mumford confessed that he had admired the high purposes and the codes of science, and had seen in "disinterested science" a noble ideal, distinct from other selfish endeavors. But he came to feel that scientists, through their work on weapons of mass destruction, had surrendered their freedom and willingly accepted the control of the enterprise by the state. His images are clear. Scientists had been bribed into silence and submission; they had become willing to accept secrecy and to conduct their work not out of the love for truth or for the aid of society, but for the ends of the state. To their claim, "Let truth be pursued though the heavens may fall," Mumford responded bitterly that a claim of this sort was good only if you could be sure that the heavens would not fall. (We are reminded here of the parody of this concept of seeking knowledge independent of its consequences found in Tom Lehrer's lyrics, "Once the rockets go up, I don't care where they come down. That's not my department, said Werner von Braun.") Although Mumford ultimately did give recognition to the existence of a small, and what he considered brave, group of scientists who both opposed the bomb and called for greater concern about the uses of science and its productions (he identified the Society for Social Responsibility in Science), he really never reconciled himself with the scientific community. I must point out that the scientific community, and especially its leaders, saw him as posing a direct challenge to them. For Mumford, the successful making of the bomb by the scientists, and its devastating use in warfare, infinitely complicated what he had designed as a project for the "renewal of life." In this renewal spelling out his prewar explorations, he had high hopes for technology, and he seemed deeply disappointed, almost at a personal level, that it was impossible any longer to hold on to that claim for science and technology.

As he turned to examine what had gone wrong with science, he began to discover problems deep within the history of science itself, connected directly with those who had long been considered heroes of the scientific endeavor. The bifurcation of mind and matter troubled him. Some of the very steps that had been celebrated by seventeenth-century scientists and philosophers and hailed by historians in what was often referred to as the "positivist compromise" he saw as the source of the problems into which science had stumbled. While the Royal Society of London in the draft of their charter could proclaim the normative neutrality of science, and observe that "this society will avoid all discussion of religion, rhetoric, metaphysics, morals and politics," Mumford saw the necessity of consciously restoring values to science and reopening the normative discourse.[47] If a concept of "purpose" had been forced out of the scientific attitude, Mumford claimed the necessity to recognize the part played by *purpose*.[48] He specifically sought to replace the mechanical, the analytical, the instrumental with the organic, the synthetic, and the purposeful.[49] It would indeed be a far different science from that which had grown so strong and seemed to legitimize the separation of fact from value and to separate science from the world. Mumford proposed adopting a moral calculus so that science would be forced to answer the question, "Is it beneficial?" In his view, science alone should not have the autonomy to set its own agenda: instead he quite clearly indicated that he would be willing to limit and restrain and, if necessary, to halt some aspects of scientific activity.[50] It was, of course, this vision of challenge and interference that accounts, in part at least, for the counterattack against Mumford by strong elements within the scientific community.

The *Pentagon of Power*, published in 1970, represented the culmination of Mumford's postwar criticisms of science and technology and presented a lightning rod attracting both praise and sharp attack. Christopher Lehmann-Haupt, reviewing the book for the *New York Times*, 9 November 1970, coined for the occasion what he referred to as a Mumfordian word: "megacritic." This volume, the second of a two-part study entitled *The Myth of the Machine*, finally locates Mumford's criticisms in friendly terrain.[51] This was the era of the anti-Vietnam movement that witnessed the emergence of a sharp rejection of traditional scholarship and a sustained critique of the "neutral knowledge" that had become a hallmark of academic science and scholarship. He compared his "pentagon of power" to the ancient megamachine that he had earlier identified in *Technics and Civilization* (1934) as the source of transformations. Our modern-day megamachine equivalent, with its component parts of nuclear weapons, missiles, computers, and new priesthood of scientists who oversee rocket flight to the lifeless moon, represented "our reenactment of the worship of the dead."

The focal point of Mumford's objections was objective knowledge itself. The Scientific Revolution, which on the one hand had been so successful, had removed from its sphere the scientific observer—human beings were not part of the system.[52] Therefore, Mumford argued, with human subjectivity pushed aside, scientific truths had no more status than superstition. This, of course, is the outlook in other contemporary criticism: for example, from the extreme cultural criticism in Theodore Roszak's *The Making of a Counterculture* and his somewhat later *Where the Wasteland Ends* to the epistemological attacks of the philosopher of science Paul Feyerabend, in his controversial *Against Method*.[53] While his earlier attacks on the atomic bomb gained him celebration in the anti-nuclear weapons movement, Mumford's new volume gained him deep sympathy in the widescale protest movements of the late 1960s and early 1970s. Even further, his major thrust to replace the mechanical with the organic (albeit a theme he had enunciated as early as 1934 in *Technics and Civilization*) put him alongside the newly emergent environmental movement and its criticism of the mechanical and physical ideals that seemed to govern modern industrial society. But Mumford is quite clear that the technological changes occurring between *Technics and Civilization* and *The Myth of the Machine* formed his new outlook: "I have been driven by the wholesale miscarriages of megatechnics, to deal with the collective obsessions and compulsions that have misdirected our energies, and undermined our capacity to live full and spiritually satisfying lives. If the key to the past few centuries has been 'mechanization takes command,' the theme of the present book may be summed up in Colonel John Glenn's words on returning from orbit to earth: 'Let Man Take Over.'"[54]

While some reviewers (e.g. Christopher Lehmann-Haupt) found it surprising that two-thirds of the way through his volume Mumford could become optimistic, I think it is equally arguable that the contemporary politics of 1970 could well make him feel that real change might be in the making. Although there was indeed the deep pessimism of the historical record from Copernicus to his present day, Mumford was not alone in believing that the depth of the new radicalism, which went beyond the anti-war movement to the development of an environmental ethos and a fundamental critique of the scientific way of knowing, might well be the harbinger of basically new attitudes toward nature and humankind.

What seemed to Mumford a natural extension of this critique of the megamachine and the "power complex" was read by those close to the scientific community as an attack on the very core of their practice and their thought. In his commencement address of May 1971, Jerome Wiesner, speaking from the citadel of scientific power, M.I.T., linked Mumford to others whom he saw as threatening the sciences.[55] But the fullest attack on Mumford's book came from Gerald Holton, professor of physics and practitioner of the history of science from Harvard University. In a front-page review in the Sunday *New York Times Book Review* (13 December 1970), Holton was given almost four full pages to explicate and criticize the Mumford vision. Holton was made nervous by elements of Mumford's critique (though there are other parts with which he expressed sympathy) and particularly with his understanding that Mumford believed "there now is needed some religious conversion, a transformation on the large scale that cannot occur by rational thinking and educational indoctrination. The God that will save us will rise in the human soul."[56] While Holton was able to agree easily that "technology is clearly in need of rescue from its chief exploiters," especially industry and the military, he was fundamentally unsympathetic to Mumford's sympathy with the organic world-view and his antipathy to the mechanical outlook. Further, he found Mumford's call for a reorganization of the methodology of science a misunderstanding of the sciences, particularly in regard to Mumford's interest in the issues of autonomy and purpose as seen in living organisms, as opposed to the analytical or isolating style of the sciences. The core of Holton's criticism, as he wrote in the winter of 1970, was his fear that Mumford's book would encourage a two-culture split: "The abstract-mathematical-technical sphere" against "the concrete, the organic, and the human."[57] Underlying Holton's critique was his sense that Mumford would indeed give strength to the "common anti-intellectual wave" that seemed to threaten scientists and the academy alike in the tumultuous days of the close of the sixties.

Needless to say, Mumford was unhappy, and in a rather vitriolic riposte published shortly after the new year (10 January 1971) in the *Times*, he counterattacked, seeing in his former friend an enemy with a real animus against the major themes of the book.[58] Mumford claimed that his work "is not an attack on science, but an attack on the power complex's threat to undermine all human values and purposes, including those of science itself." Mumford wondered out loud at the anxiety and alarm that scientists might feel about the loss of status of the sciences, but concluded that this alarm "is only an attempt to avoid that stern, critical self-examination which every person, every group, and every institution must now undergo if the present miscarriages of science and technics by the power complex are to be rectified."[59] But at a fundamental level Mumford and the scientists were talking past each other. He carried out with religious fervor a campaign to turn around knowledge and technique and break their integration from the megamachine and its threats of war and human degradation. His images, over and over again, are anti-machine and counter-mechanical. It is the organic, the holistic, and the purposeful that hold the promise for human renewal. For most scientists this must have seemed anathema and akin to an alliance with a non-rational, anti-intellectual, and anti-scientific attitude.

But of course Mumford was fundamentally right in his claim that he was not anti-scientific. It is just that the science he so vigorously supported was the one that had been left behind and cast out in the early years of the Scientific Revolution, when values were separated from fact and purpose from the material.

How shall we locate Lewis Mumford among the critics of the atomic bomb? There is one early clue in the review of three books published 7 December 1946 in the *Times Literary Supplement* (London).[60] Mumford's *Program for Survival* is reviewed alongside John Hersey's *Hiroshima* and

Herman Hagedorn's *The Bomb That Fell on America*. There is little doubt that the reviewer saw in Mumford's collection of essays the sharpest moral challenge. As the anonymous author noted, "It is undeniable that the atomic bomb is the enormous and still swelling threat to the world that we know it to be, not because men have discovered how to make it, but because they have reached the stage of moral decay when they can make the decision to use it." It is the moral dimension that the reviewer found so strong in Mumford's writing: "He regards the decision to drop the bomb as almost a Second Fall of Man. It is a conclusion that has much to recommend it."[61]

After awarding encomiums to Mumford, the reviewer found John Hersey's style flat, and he seemed to lament that Hersey "has scrupulously left the facts to speak for themselves, and they have not spoken loudly enough." In retrospect, of course, Mumford's essays have passed into history and disuse while John Hersey's "description" remains a classic of the atomic horror. But to readers then, as now, Mumford's unequivocal moral critique stood out.

There was, of course, what the *New York Times* referred to as "the league of frightened men," that band of scientists who, in the closing days of the war and in the months just after the use of the bomb, joined together in a dual effort to achieve civilian control over atomic development and international control over atomic weapons.[62] While they were a dedicated and highly intelligent group who even enjoyed partial success, the tone of their critique is markedly different from that of Mumford. He wanted to abolish all atomic technology; they were more anxious to see the atom properly guided and controlled. Few matched the passion that Mumford brought to his prose, and none joined in their critique of the bomb a criticism of the sciences themselves. It would be difficult to say that Mumford's campaign against atomic weapons was a unique one in the decade after the bomb was first used, for the literature of, certainly, the early years is filled with rejections of atomic weapons at the moral, the social, the political, and even the strategic levels.[63] In addition, of course, a whole secondary, fictional literature grew up which, in depicting the horrors of atomic war and its aftermath, filled in details far beyond those that Mumford dreamed up in his early scenarios. This fiction served thereby as a continual reminder of what mistakes in judgment might bring or conscious war-fighting efforts might produce.[64]

Although Lewis Mumford was clearly not a full pacifist in his outlook, the nature of his rejection of atomic weapons finds its closest parallels in the writings of such figures as A. J. Muste and Dwight Macdonald, for both of whom pacifism became a fundamental moral stricture.[65] Mumford himself is more accurately characterized as a "nuclear pacifist."

Although George Kennan, the "Dean of U.S. Sovietologists," adopted a fervent tone in his rejection of the bomb, and indeed cast many of his criticisms in the language of strong normative judgment, he was at core a thoughtful political analyst deeply engaged in a study and evaluation of

Soviet power and Soviet intent. He sought continually for policy alternatives, even alongside his own form of nuclear weapons rejectionism.[66]

Lewis Mumford was not alone in the depth of his opposition to the development and use of the atomic bomb. But when we read his words over the years, he remained consistent, unwavering (even repetitive), and never dissuaded from his campaign. In tone and content Mumford has offered a fundamental moral critique not only of machines and their uses, but of the makers and their moral fall. He expressed a disappointment at being let down or abandoned by science and scientists. He expected more, he professed, even though he found in the historical records of science the roots of the very flaws that led to its ultimate misuse. He was prophetic in tone, but also broadly prescriptive: replace the mechanical with the organic, the purposeless with the purposeful; a deep conversion of an almost religious sort will be necessary if humankind is to survive its own making. But he was also largely devoid of politics. He was not an organizer of campaigns or a developer of political platforms. He certainly steered completely clear of the technicians' discussions of the "number, weight and measure" of atomic weapons and the strategists' interests in minimal, stable, or other deterrents. There were limits, therefore, to the frame and the structure of his analysis, limits both tacit and explicit. But, there was no limit at all to his seeking human answers, human in scale and in value, though in the sharpness of his critique and the pessimism of his prophecy Lewis Mumford often seemed bigger than life and impatient with the living.

Faith, Hope, Not Much Charity: The Optimistic Epistemology of Lewis Mumford

MICHAEL ZUCKERMAN

The myth of Mumford is that the polymath of power faltered in his last large books. According to this conventional commentary, his prose grew self-indulgent and overheated, his exposition polemical and under-substantiated. His best arguments were already ingredient in his own earlier work, and now they were tainted by a sour pessimism he had held at bay before: *The City in History* is, on this orthodox account, a darker endeavor than *The Culture of Cities,* and *The Myth of the Machine* a bleaker, more bilious one than *Technics and Civilization.*[1]

Some of the reviews were savage. "There is little here that is really new," said one; *The Pentagon of Power* "does not significantly extend the range of Mumford's social criticism" or even "advance much beyond" views he propounded in his earliest writing on technology. "Rather than being a fitting capstone for his career," said another, *The Myth of the Machine* "has little that is new or useful to offer us"; it is "not so much a summary as a rehash of bits and pieces of his previous work." Its insights "nearly all reproduc[e] thoughts Mumford had already expressed in 1934," said a third. Its argument is "less well documented than it was" in the work of that year, said a fourth.[2]

Those reviews and others as well marked a "gloomy" progression from *Technics and Civilization,* which they took for "a relatively cheerful and optimistic book," to *The Myth of the Machine,* which they conceived as the culmination of Mumford's "evolution toward disillusionment." One of them went so far as to call *The Pentagon of Power* a "doomsday book." And even Donald Miller, Mumford's literary executor, has posited "a profound change in Mumford's social outlook," a "growing disenchantment with modern life and a gathering pessimism," in the years from Mumford's first major works to his last. Miller proclaims *The Myth of the Machine* "a world removed, in temper and tone, from *Technics and Civilization,*" and he holds Mumford's other writings of the 1960s equally the "somber" studies of "a far less sanguine" scholar who had "lost some of his faith in the possibilities of . . . revitalization."[3]

Against all of this conventional wisdom, I mean to argue that neither of the volumes of *The Myth of the Machine—Technics and Human Development* and *The Pentagon of Power*— is derivative in its essential thrust from Mumford's earlier masterwork, *Technics and Civilization,* and that neither is inferior to it in originality or importance. I mean to set forth a conception of *The Myth of the Machine* as Mumford's most mature and most audacious work, the ripest and bravest fruition of a lifetime of engagement with the twentieth-century prospect. And I mean to suggest that this last great statement before the concluding autobiographical essays of the 1970s is not nearly as dismal or despondent as many readers have supposed; that it is, on the contrary, the most intriguingly and compellingly optimistic composition of his career.

If that career defies complete comprehension, it can at least be approached in the epistemological terms in which Mumford himself understood it. As he said in his autobiography, any adequate appraisal of his intellectual outlook would have to "take account of [his] lifelong intercourse with both Plato and Aristotle."[4]

Mumford did oscillate, always, between the philosophical perspectives of the two great ancients. But in his early writings the older Athenian yielded priority to his Peripatetic protégé. In his very first book, *The Story of Utopias,* Mumford focused less on the psyches of the communards than on their social systems, and less on their ideals than on their practices. He did still vacillate. He did insist here on the pragmatic idealism he drew from John Dewey, there on the ecological empiricism he learned from Patrick Geddes. He did set himself now to study "attitudes and beliefs," then to do the "regional surveys" demanded by his Scottish master. He did affirm sometimes an intellectual approach—"our most important task at the present moment is to build castles in the air. . . . it will be easy enough to place foundations under them"—and sometimes a sociological one— "the first step out of the present impasse [is to]return to the real world, and face it, and survey it in its complicated totality," because "our castles-in-air must have their foundations in solid ground."[5]

He was still oscillating for decades afterward. But for all the attenuated idealism of such subsequent early works as *The Golden Day,* he was still, essentially, seeking "foundations in solid ground" to the time of his first great history of technology. In *Technics and Civilization,* he postulated a phasing predicated on technical potentialities and desiderata—eotechnic, paleotechnic, and neotechnic—and he explicated the emergence of each phase from its predecessor in a manner almost Marxian.[6]

After 1945, however, there was a different drift in the direction of his thought and in its epistemological underpinnings, or perhaps simply a turning of the circle. As he addressed the crises he believed beset civilization in the wake of World War II, dreading as he did the future that might follow the age of Hitler and Hiroshima—the worst twenty years in human history, as he thought[7]—he came to doubt the empiricism he had taken from his teachers, Geddes and Thorstein Veblen, and to deepen and clarify his commitment to the primacy of mind in the making of the world. As he found his way to the most daringly original and sweeping syntheses of his entire career, he found his way back to the convictions of his collegiate days, when Plato "took possession" of him for a time. As he surveyed the trajectory of his development, at the completion of *The Myth of the Machine*, he noted that he had begun "as a pragmatist and a positivist" and then moved steadily "closer to . . . platonism."[8]

He had never, of course, categorically discounted the role of mind, or spirit, or will, or values, in his pragmatic and positivist periods. But he had never thought it all the way through, either. Even as he had affirmed the importance of ideas and designs and the imposition of meaning upon experience, he had still conceded much more to an autonomous empirical reality. He had upheld almost unthinkingly, for example, the conventional disjunctions of means and ends and of science and human values which he would dedicate his later works to denying.[9]

Where *Technics and Civilization* had clung to conceptions of technological succession and sociological stages, *The Myth of the Machine* abandons them for a more contingent appreciation of history and a more platonistic conviction of the priority of ideas, ideologies, and spiritual forces in the course of human evolution. Impelled by the urgency he apprehends in our contemporary situation, he reaches beyond the ringing Emersonian rhetoric on which he had always relied, ransacking domains as disparate as archaeology and physiology, experimental psychology and the history of the ancient Middle East, for the data of a new conception of man's destiny.

Where once he had merely gestured, now he specifies. Where earlier he had depended on declamation, now he essays sophisticated elaboration. Where before, at best, he had simply assumed the centrality of mind, now he attempts to account for it.

From the first pages of *Technics and Human Development* to the final pages of *The Pentagon of Power*, his account frames and informs *The Myth of the Machine*. It begins from an arresting assertion of "man's overdeveloped and incessantly active brain" and of the excessive "mental energy" that brain affords, beyond all necessity for "survival at a purely animal level." It insists that that "gift of free neural energy" set the elemental terms of the evolution of human beings, fostering their "exploratory curiosity" and "idle manipulativeness with no thought of ulterior reward" and spurring their creativity for the sheer joy of utilizing their immense resources and expressing their latent potentialities.[10]

Yet the brain, remarkable as it is, remains for Mumford a mere "biological organ." It is sufficient to entail creativity upon men and women as a constitutional function, embedded in their neural structure. It is nonetheless amplified immeasurably upon the advent of mind, "the most radical step in man's evolution." Mind is a "cultural emergent." It "superimposed upon purely electro-chemical changes a durable mode of symbolic organization." It "created a sharable public world of organized sense impressions and supersensible meanings and eventually a coherent domain of significance."[11]

In positing the emergence of man's oversized brain and then of his playful, purposeful mind as the principal drivers of human development, Mumford makes the evolution of *Homo sapiens* hinge far more on plenitude than on the scarcity and parsimony that orthodox accounts assume. In affirming the absence of any specialized adaptation and the presence of an extravagant plasticity as man's evolutionary advantages, Mumford maintains the power of multipotentiality and epitomizes his insistence that humankind be understood as a species that made meaning before—and much better than—it made tools, or, alternatively, that made signs and symbols, out of the special resources of the mind, as its most formative tools.[12]

In this insistence, he assailed all the exponents of materialist conceptions of man, such as the Marxists and the megamechanicians, and more than a few self-styled pyschologists and spiritualists besides. Man, for Mumford, is a "minder" much more than a "maker," a creature of culture and consciousness much more than of artifacts and armaments. From his earliest appearance, as Mumford re-examined the evidence, man had scanned the skies, sacralized ancestral spirits, speculated on death and future existence, and otherwise displayed an awareness that distant, mysterious, and implacable forces might impinge upon his life.[13]

Where materialists, Maslovian as well as Marxist, predicated hierarchies of human needs in which spiritual and aesthetic motives appeared only after more urgent imperatives of survival and amenity had been satisfied, Mumford maintained that an unmistakable consciousness of mystery and concern for artistic effect had marked the human endeavor from the first. As the decisive experiments of Adelbert Ames had demonstrated, cognitive expectancy is indispensable even in the seemingly simplest processes of perception. Men and women always outleap the evidence of their senses, anticipating experience and transcending it. They could no more function now than in the prehistoric past if they did not. And therefore they cannot be comprehended merely as practical problem-solvers or as agile adjusters to environmental demands. They are, on the contrary, creatures who set themselves gratuitous problems. They press beyond present needs, seeking and hypothesizing patterns of significance.[14]

Their very quest for surplus meaning is what defines them, for Mumford, as a species much more appropriately classified *Homo sapiens* than *Homo faber*. In the perspective that pervades *The Myth of the Machine,* the mind is not a late-evolving luxury in the course of human development. It is constitutive of the entire enterprise. Those too committed to technological rationalism to acknowledge this "autonomous original nature" only present symptoms of the disease of megamechanical modernity, not analyses of it. Mumford saves some of his sharpest barbs for such "technological men." He assails them savagely as "ghosts clad in iron," catching exactly as he does the deathly denigration of mind and culture and art which only modern men have dared.[15]

Yet Mumford is too instinctive a dramatist, and his theories themselves too instinct with conflict, to sustain a simple paean to the mind and its priority. The antagonism between the mind and the brain remains. The mental excess which affords man his evolutionary edge over the animals also exposes him to danger. The "immense psychic overflow from man's cerebral reservoir" is the condition of his creativity, but it is also a source of non-adaptive and indeed irrational impulses.[16]

Such irrationality may be as innocuous as that "most peculiar type of inner activity: the dream," for "the dream itself testifies to a more general organic exuberance that can hardly be accounted for on any purely adaptive principle." From the beginning, "man was a dreaming animal." His dreams, born of psychal superfluity, perhaps precipitated his departure from "the restrictions of a purely animal career" and certainly gave him his first hint of an unseen world "veiled from his senses" yet as starkly real as his food or his hand.[17]

Such irrationality may also be far less innocent or intimative. It encompasses "transcendental aspirations and demonic compulsions" alike. It sanctions and even sanctifies the merest of mischiefs and the most monstrous of "destructions and debasements."[18]

Against such capacity for irrational rage and devastation, Mumford posits primitive ritual and the vast cultural apparatus in which it eventuated as ancient people's means of controlling, or at least offsetting, their inordinate unconscious. Only their dogged insistence upon the perpetuation of established ways could curb the creativity and the aggression and sadism that steadily imperiled all possibility of social order. Only the tedium of repetition and the interdiction of innovation could contain the teeming fantasies of their overcomplex brains.[19]

Just as the evolution of language—the expression and transmission of meaning—was "incomparably more important to further human development" than the evolution of weapons, so the elaboration of ceremony was immeasurably more vital than the elaboration of tools. Or, more exactly and more audaciously, technics and language alike flow "from the same common source . . . : the primeval repetitive order of ritual" which early man developed "in self-protection, so as to control the tremendous overcharge of psychal energy that his large brain placed at his disposal."[20]

On this striking supposition, Mumford inverts the Maslovian hierarchy. Men and women invented themselves before they ever invented instruments of merely utilitarian efficacy. In human nature and in human history, the making of meaning had precedence—until our own megamechanical age—over the making of tools. Language and ritual were richly developed even in the most technologically backward societies, and tool-making and tool-using were relatively retarded even in the most technically advanced. Communication and ceremony maintained order—literally held the world together—as technics never could have done.[21]

Ranging over the data of early human development with ingenuity and an unsurpassed erudition, Mumford propounds an unprecedented pre-history and a persuasive ancient history to sustain such arguments. He notes that, in excavations of archaic sites, items of bodily decoration—necklaces and the like—are found alongside people's bones even where tools are not. He observes that, in the first firing of sand into glass, the glass was made into beads rather than more manifestly functional objects. In the earliest smelting of ores into metal in the earliest hearths, the iron was made into rings rather than weapons. And he concludes from such evidence of the fundamentality of ornament that "we are never so sure of the presence of a creature . . . like ourselves as when we find" these signs of his determination to "establish a human identity." From the first, men and women found their crowning concern in the explication of their own purpose and significance. Jewelry was, to them, more important—indeed, more basic—than mechanical or military implements.[22]

Paleolithic peoples also used clay as a medium of animal sculpture thousands of years before they employed it as a material of pottery and in the construction of their housing. They pursued horticulture, with its focus on fine solitary specimens, long before agriculture, with its emphasis on economic yields. In far-flung aspects of their lives, they cultivated artis-tic refinement more than they prized the apparent practicality of produc-tivity. And their preference suggests, to Mumford, that "man began to domesticate himself before he domesticated either plants or animals."[23]

Spiritual and ceremonial preoccupations similarly took precedence over quotidian considerations of survival and material interest. Cattle were har-nessed in ritual processions before they were ever yoked for farm work. Plows were put to the soil in religious rites before they were turned to regular tilling. The massive walls built around the first towns, such as Jer-icho, "performed a magico-religious function before they were found to furnish a decided military advantage."[24]

Sacred stimuli inspired the earliest wheeled vehicles, which were hearses for funerary occasions, not farm wagons or army chariots. Cultic require-ments may even have set the shape of the earliest organized killing, since there is better evidence for human sacrifice than for war in the neolithic community.[25]

And just as Mumford's intrepid re-reading of the archaeological record reveals this extraordinary array of instances in which ideation and the search for significance preceded utility and the desire for material wealth and power, so his reconception of the historical record suggests that every epochal transformation of world civilization—the onset of the neolithic era, the transition to the pyramid cultures, the collapse of that first mega-machine and the reversion to handicraft, and the rise of modern kingship and nationalism—had its essential sources in altered religious sensitivities rather than in technological revolutions.

A "new cultural pattern" overspread the planet six or seven millennia before Christ, forming "the underlayer on which all higher civilizations until now have been based." A normative and "psycho-social" shift constituted the crux of the "profound change" of the third millennium B.C., submerging the village cultures of the neolithic age in the vast agglomerations of centralized power and coercion which took shape in "the hot valleys of the Jordan, the Euphrates, the Tigris, the Nile, and the Indus rivers." A massive "religious transformation" preceded and exceeded the rather modest technological achievements of those cradles of empire. Men and women of Egypt, Persia, and kindred kingdoms subordinated their ancient "gods of vegetation and animal fertility" to the new "gods of the sky." They established an "abstract impersonal order" of standardization and "strict human control" by withdrawing authority from deities who suffered human debilities and investing it in others more implacable who could not "be swayed from their course." They conceded the imperious central powers that commanded the pyramids and comparable monuments by conceiving of their rulers as godlings "lowered down from heaven." Divine kingship—the identification of the person of the king with the impersonal order of the heavens—was from the first "a religious phenomenon, not just an assertion of physical prowess [or] a mere enlargement of venerable ancestral authority." And even into the modern era, it was the transcendental religions, especially Christianity, which conditioned the rise of the capitalist world-system and the nation-state and supplied the twentieth-century megamachine crucial components which widened its province, augmented its efficiency, and enhanced its acceptability to its subjects.[26]

The congruence of these interpretive archaeological and historical accounts with Mumford's epistemological premises is transparent, and the opening they offer for hope for the future, and perhaps even for politics, is almost as evident. Mumford's unremitting onslaught against the American defense establishment and the corporate order which sustains it misled reviewers and subsequent commentators, who supposed *The Myth of the Machine*—and especially its second volume, *The Pentagon of Power*—a bleaker work than its predecessor, *Technics and Civilization*. In fact, *The Myth of the Machine* is markedly more optimistic, and its optimism is ingredient in its enterprise as the optimism of the earlier study never was.

Of course, it should be said at the outset of all consideration of comparative optimisms and pessimisms that neither Mumford's writings nor his sensibility lend themselves to unequivocal conclusions in the matter. In his first works, in the 1920s, when he was treating topics such as utopias and golden days, Mumford still spoke of the "dissipation of Western civilization," the "dismal" outlook for its culture, and the triumph of a machine "servitude" that "paralyzed" the human spirit. In his autobiographical *Sketches from Life*, he describes a "habit of mind" so "mordant" in the 1930s, when he was composing *Technics and Civilization*, that friends routinely sought out his company to compensate their own lack of blackness in disposition. And conversely, in the mid-1960s, at the very moment he was hurling himself into the strident critique of American culture of

The Pentagon of Power, he was hailing, unapologetically, "the New World promise of renewal and responsibility." On the human prospect, Mumford can always be quoted against himself. He was unfailingly ambivalent—now hopeful, now despondent, optimistic in the midst of his most virulent denunciations, pessimistic at his giddiest heights—and it is quite impossible to plot any straight line of development in his sentiments or his presentiments.[27]

Indeed, even if clear conclusions were possible, they might not matter very much. Observing that "much has been made of the gap between optimism and pessimism, and whether a particular writer is a 'prophet of hope' or a 'prophet of doom,'" Langdon Winner has dismissed such distinctions as "in the end . . . vacuous." Winner acknowledges that, in contemporary scholarship, "there exists an almost compulsive need for optimism on this topic." But he goes on to observe, trenchantly, that

> if one notices that an Ellul or Mumford or some other author is pessimistic in his conclusions, that becomes sufficient ground for dismissing anything he or she might be saying. Pessimism, it is argued, leads to inaction, which merely reinforces the status quo. This is somehow different from optimism, which leads to activity within the existing arrangement of things and reinforces the status quo.[28]

Nonetheless, it makes scant sense to see *The Myth of the Machine* as an expression of Mumford's deepening desolation, if only because it could not have been much more melancholic than *Technics and Civilization* already was. In that relatively youthful study, the hopes that Mumford invested in his notorious neotechnic phase were submerged almost as soon as they were floated, in his somber recognition that neotechnic potentials would probably be denied by the power of the paleotechnicians to pervert or prevent the emergence of the new age. The concluding chapters of *Technics and Civilization* plainly prefigure the impasse at which we have now arrived: the paleotechnic world dead, the neotechnic powerless to be born. Those chapters hold out only the palest, frailest Veblenian hope that the intrinsic impulsion of the technological system might somehow speed the dawning of the neotechnic day. But even in 1934, Mumford knew better. The very quietism of his reliance on ineluctable technosocial process admitted as much.

By 1970, Mumford was much more explicit in his acknowledgment that the renovative implications of modern science and technology would not be realized effortlessly or inexorably. *The Pentagon of Power* announced that deliberate and determined action would be necessary for the fulfillment of those redemptive possibilities. Indeed, it declared that "massive measures" would be imperative merely to avert "destruction and extermination."[29]

In this anxiety over the fate of the earth, Mumford did ply a rhetoric resented by readers who found his late works at once more dire and more dour than his earlier writings. *The Pentagon of Power,* especially, has its boding, brooding passages, and its critics were not entirely wrong in marking its melancholy. Mumford had never before been so unrelievedly acerbic in his attack on the world picture of the modern megamechanics. He had never so scathingly assailed their "under-dimensioned" model of man or their complicity in the ascent of the scientized, centralized, militarized capitalism nascent since the seventeenth century and advanced to its apotheosis in America after World War II. He lashed out relentlessly at that megamachine for its hostility to "organic realities and human needs." He denounced again and again its "cult of anti-life" and its readiness to "extirpate" people to make them "conform to the machine." And he traced those characteristics to their theoretical foundations in the earliest envisionings of modern science—in Francis Bacon, René Descartes, and Johannes Kepler—and their "underlying desire to reduce man to a machine, for the purpose of establishing uniform behavior in the army and the factory, or any other potentially disorderly collection of men." The mechanical mode was from the first "an auxiliary . . . to political absolutism," as Hobbes made manifest in his idolization of automatism and control and his pathological fear of a brutish disorder that did not exist in the primitive societies in which he posited it.[30]

Some of Mumford's most telling thrusts point up precisely such delusive dispositions—such "psychotic irrationality"—in the managers of the modern megamachine. Men who style themselves scientists profess to eliminate subjectivity from their operations but end instead by occluding awareness of their "own subjective inflations, distortions, and perversions." Their very ideology of themselves as immaculate aspirants to mastery over nature betrays by that "obsolete military" metaphor their "paranoid fantasy" of "conquest." And the devotion they thereby display to "the existing power system" is made more "pathological" by the "superstitious savagery" of the political and military elites to whom they attach themselves so abjectly.[31]

Over and over again, Mumford poses "the problem towering over all others: how to prevent the human race from being destroyed by its demoralized but reputedly sane leaders." Increasingly, he comes to see another problem "almost as pressing," that those leaders may be little more demoralized than the masses who follow them. Megatechnics touches almost everyone. It offers, "in return for its unquestioning acceptance, the gift of an effortless life," and its "plethora of prefabricated goods" produces, ultimately, an "existential nausea." In the strictest of clinical senses, it provides a repletion without exertion or stress which can be considered only "infantilism or senility," rather like the "organic deterioration" found in laboratory animals under comparable conditions. Just because it sets itself so adamantly against tradition, the megamachine disdains a vast inheritance of ideas and institutions and inflicts an authentic "brain damage" on its subjects. Just because its animus against the past loosens "the binding ties of habit, custom, and moral code," it drives "an increasing portion of the human race . . . out of its mind."[32]

Mumford's deepest indictment of these megamechanical pathologies of presentism and progress brings him back to the epistemological premises with which he began. Man's "overgrown brain," unconstrained by instinct or even by an overriding intelligence for survival, has always been "at the mercy of his unconscious." Man's consequent vulnerability has, historically, been limited only by his culture and its repetition-compulsions. But the "Power Complex" transfers those "stabilizing repetitive processes" from man to the machine, "leaving man himself more exposed than ever to his disordered subjectivity." Precisely by relieving people of their routine obligations, and of the stressful social participation that enabled them to maintain a semblance of psychological balance, the megamachine allows the demonic impulses their archaic dominion and places immeasurably augmented technological resources at their disposal besides. Precisely by pretending a pure rationality, the megatechnicians enhance the destructive promptings of the unconscious.[33]

Some of Mumford's most haunting exposition as well as more than a little of his most venomous rage are given to the pursuit of such ironies. Perhaps the most poignant passages in the book detail the developments by which benevolent men headed, almost unwittingly, the most decisive advances of dehumanization. Francis Bacon sought surcease in scientific collegiality from the fratricidal strife of seventeenth-century politics; he never fully foresaw that his visionary refuge would one day be a positivist prison. Isaac Newton still knew spiritual mysteries and struggled unavailingly with them; he never supposed that his scientific advances—by far the lesser part of his speculative endeavor—would obscure and even obviate such mysteries for men who came after him. Even earlier, others met similar fates. A malign juggernaut began rolling in the Renaissance, and the noblest spirits since have been impotent to impede it. Leonardo da Vinci bent his best efforts to embodying an ampler model of man, but the burgeoning colossus ignored his antipathy and incorporated his technological triumphs. Albert Einstein dedicated a lifetime to the promotion of peace but abetted the engines of war incalculably by a single letter to President Roosevelt. Indeed, almost all the early advocates of nuclear power— Enrico Fermi, Leo Szilard, and Harold Urey as well as Albert Einstein— were themselves "unusually humane and morally sensitive" people. They were "the last scientists one would accuse of seeking to establish a new priesthood capable of assuming autocratic authority and wielding satanic power." Yet just such authority and power were "the dreadful consequences of their effort."[34]

All this melancholy admitted, however, *The Myth of the Machine* remains a rousing work rather than a resigned one. Its vigor and venom belie its ironic bemusement. Its vibrancy belies its anguished bafflement. The very virulence of its impassioned critique and the very energy of its exhortation to renewal and redemption belie the manifest bleakness of its overt message: the engorgement of the megamachine and the closure of the neo-technic opening.

Moreover, Mumford's emphasis on mind, and values, and visions, is much fuller and more focal in *The Myth of the Machine* than it ever was in

Technics and Civilization, and it is in such spheres that Mumford finally finds the sources of solace he can credit. He still implores that the evolutionary studies, such as biology and history, not the timeless ones, such as physics, be taken as exempla of optimal scientific inquiry capable of encompassing wholeness and metamorphosis as well as analytic abstractions of unchanging entities. But he no longer attaches his appeal so substantially to any of the conventional disciplines. He now relies primarily on his own rich elaboration of the growth of the psyche, and he now reserves his most scabrous censure for the ways in which we are complicitous in our own self-diminution and self-denial.

Among many other things, *The Myth of the Machine* is an account of man's advancing abdication of his mind—of his subjectivity and inner integrity—before the pretensions and powers of the machine. It is a nervous narrative of a faith that began as the willed, chosen worship of the sun—of light, in McLuhan's hypnotic, anaesthetic sense—and that became over subsequent centuries less freely offered and more harshly demanded. It is a fiery, fearful interpretation of people's increasing propensity to concede increasing portions of their own vitality and autonomy to the megamachine or, more accurately, to their imagination and creation and construction of that megamachine. And it is a searing summons to men and women to cease such self-abasement and recover "for human use the mechanized and electrified wasteland that is now being constructed, at man's expense and to his permanent loss, for the benefit of the megamachine."[35]

As Mumford grew older, he saw more clearly the futility of counting on mechanism to cure the corruptions of mechanism. As he grew more pessimistic about man's probable fate, he became more resolute in his refusal of his own rational assessment. As he said, "I still believe in miracles." And as he knew, the realm of miracles was the realm of faith and spirit and mind where he situated *The Myth of the Machine,* not the domain of dialectical, developmental automaticity on which he had depended in *Technics and Civilization.*[36]

The contrast between Mumford and the great French student of contemporary technological consciousness, Jacques Ellul, illuminates Mumford's sensibility and strategies in these regards. In his preface to *The Technological Society,* Ellul ponders the possibility of men and women taking thought about their plight and overcoming the essential determinism of "the technological phenomenon." How is this to be done? Ellul confesses that he does not know, but he proceeds to state that the first step "is to arouse the reader to an awareness of technological necessity and what it means. It is a call to the sleeper to awake." Mumford speaks several times in similar accents, but where Ellul calls for recognition and reasoned consciousness, Mumford hopes for widespread religious renewal. Where Ellul, the realist, insists that "there *are* ways out . . . but nobody wants any part of them," Mumford, the platonist, discounts people's declarations of their desires because he believes the breakthrough will not be a rational one anyway. Where Ellul demands "a better basis" for rebellion than "blind acts of unreasonable faith," Mumford welcomes such stirrings of religious revolt.[37]

There is irony in Ellul refusing to countenance what he craves and in Mumford entreating what he does not expect. There is irony upon irony in Ellul, a profoundly faithful Christian, austerely renouncing resistance rooted in faith, and in Mumford, an indifferent believer at best, boldly bidding transformation impelled by religious fervor. But there is also an exquisite aptness in the divergences. In urging any antagonism to *la technique* at all, Ellul violates the assumptions of his own arguments for technological automatism and the technological conditioning of thought. In courting conversions, Mumford follows the flow of his conviction that the source of every profound social shift is spiritual. Having frankly admitted that there is no basis for transformation intrinsic to the megamachine itself—an admission he refused to make in *Technics and Civilization*—Mumford can consistently anticipate alteration from outside the Leviathan.

As if deliberately, Mumford distinguishes himself from Ellul at every opportunity in their essentially concordant analyses, and the distinctions unfailingly disclose Mumford as the more optimistic of the two men. Ellul propounds an irresistibly linear development of modern technique; Mumford establishes a much longer temporal perspective in which history reverses its direction again and again. Ellul argues that technique increasingly obviates individual choice; Mumford insists on the imperative of volition. Ellul defines technique in terms of "the one best way"; Mumford celebrates proliferous plentitude. Ellul regrets the impossibility, under modern conditions, of the community he idealizes; Mumford invested vast energies over several decades in the regional project he revered. And Ellul devotes his brilliance, ultimately, to an intensification of the myth of invincible technology; Mumford sets himself to dispel that myth and demystify the megamachine.[38]

Mumford takes up such tasks so ardently because, on his own platonistic premises, that myth is and always has been the essential support of the megamachine. From its first formulation by Francis Bacon, the modern mechanistic world-view was a faith which outran the empirical evidence and remade the world in its own image. To this very day, despite its massive nuclear arsenals, its monstrous bureaucracies, and its multitudinous corporate consorts, the Pentagon depends in the final analysis on the acquiescence and attachment of the people. On just that account, it is far more vulnerable than its adherents imagine.

Mumford's obsessive assaults on the warfare state's vaunted veneer of scientific rationality are more than just raging rhetoric. They are designed to disclose its reliance on "both the human components and the religious ideology" of its bureaucracy and its military-industrial priesthood. They are intended to deny its pretensions to be above the failings of its individual actors and beyond the ravages of time. Above all, they are meant to enable us to see that our awesome apparatus can no more exempt itself from the vortex of change than any other historical formation.[39]

Like the empires of the Pyramid Age—the original megamachines—the two great power complexes which arose after World War II are structures of centralized exploitation maintained by military rulers with the sanction and support of religion and science. They therefore require the same priestly monopoly of all "higher knowledge" that their predecessors did; they shroud it in the secrecy of security designations and cloister it as classified information.[40]

The managers of the modern megamachines know, as the managers of the ancient ones did, that not even the "mechanized human parts" of the colossi can be "permanently held together without being sustained by a profound magico-religious faith in the system itself." In the era of the pharaohs, megamechanical dynasties collapsed when "the grim impositions" of the rulers "became intolerable"—despite their "superb technological achievements"—and when subjects ceased to concede the "religious exaltation" of divine kingship. Even those most aloof and imperious of Leviathans proved to exist "on a basis of human beliefs, which may crumble, of human decisions, which may prove fallible, and human consent, which, when the magic becomes discredited, may be withheld."[41]

Just as "the basic institutional transformations that preceded the construction of the megamachine were magical and religious," so "the most effective reaction against it drew on the same potent sources." The pharaonic power complexes were "as frail and vulnerable as the theologico-magical conceptions that were essential to their performance." And as then, so now. If and when we come to doubt the worthiness of our institutions and withdraw from them our inner allegiance, they too, maintains Mumford, will collapse. Mind remains primary. Mind—more exactly, mind in history—was ingredient in the emergence of the megamachine and will ultimately be equally ingredient in its demise. Platonism comes full circle to politics.[42]

Of course, it is precisely politics that Mumford's critics contend he cannot confront. Several of them doubt that "the gates of the technocratic prison will open automatically, despite their ancient rusty hinges, as soon as we choose to walk out." They suspect instead "that fundamental change may not come about so easily, that whether the technocratic prison is the work of the human will or not[,] it is unlikely that the gates will open automatically but only when we are prepared to make some difficult political and economic decisions, if even then." They lament in that light Mumford's "political naiveté" and his substitution of prophecy for politics. Conceding his contention that we are on the eve of destruction, they merely maintain that "to escape we are going to have to make some difficult decisions, yet Mumford makes them seem easy—simply matters of life over death, good over evil. . . . He tells us what is wrong, but not how to set it right[,] and leaves us feeling both distressed and impotent." And of course there is something to be said for such critics and such criticisms.[43]

But Mumford is not as obtuse to these issues as his detractors suppose. He is neither so infatuated with his own prophetic voice as to ignore practical constraints nor so enamored of his historical reconfigurations as to imagine that they can be transposed without trouble to another megamachine in another millennium. He does demand that the popular disillusionment that underlaid the revolts that ignited in "seemingly spontaneous combustion" across India, Persia, Palestine, Greece, and Rome, beginning between the ninth and sixth centuries B.C., be taken with supreme seriousness. He does insist that those risings be seen as evidence of the power of widespread refusal of reverence, in fact as well as in the fancies of that fevered moment at the end of the 1960s when *The Myth of the Machine* was taking shape. Yet he is more determined to seek the structure than simply to assert the fact of such successful resistance to the levies of technocracy. He is keen to show that the revolts of that epoch began in the mind every bit as much as the megamachines they helped to overthrow began in the mind. He is much keener to comprehend the conditions and the character of those revolts: the sources of the transformations taught by Amos, Hesiod, Lao-tzu, and other reformers and rebels of that era.[44]

In Mumford's view, the masters of the megamachine have always operated in a state of "anxious tension" even as they promoted the myth of their invincibility. They have always dreaded treason and heresy even as they required "submissive faith and unqualified obedience to the royal will." They have always been obsessed with subversion, and they still are. Their megamachine is "an elephant that fears even the smallest mouse." It tends to a "technological arrogance" that offends even its followers. It is disposed to "misbehaviors of cold intelligence" that provoke reactions of upsurgent vitality and indeed "savage irrationality" among the masses. And simultaneously it is subject to "miscalculations and ignominious breakdowns" that diminish the credibility of its "official caste" and "call into question both their basic assumptions and their ultimate objectives."[45]

These flaws and failings lead to "disintegration and demoralization . . . visible in every culture that the renovated power system has even remotely touched." The beneficiaries of the megamachine themselves show "an increasing unwillingness to keep the system in operation" by their own unstinting efforts. They seek rather to wring from it ever more substantial rewards while "performing ever more reluctantly a minimal amount of work and accepting an equally minimal degree of responsibility." As they are progressively deprived of old skills and autonomies by automation and new modes of centralized control, they display mounting measures of "psychological absenteeism."[46]

A reservoir of commitment does remain, but it tends steadily to depletion, because it is merely a residuum of an "archaic moral culture" to which the megamachine is inherently inimical. In this attrition of traditional moral and social values, instilled under the auspices of "a more lovable, life-sustaining world," power is "stripped of [its] historic clothes." All that is left of man are "two components no longer recognizably human:

the automaton and the id." And the system itself is profoundly imperiled, "for it has no values of its own"—no "appealing moral alternative" of rational distribution or social justice—to supplant those it undermines. It has only its megatechnics, empty at its ethical core of every aim beyond the removal of "all limitations on productivity and power." It has only "its own absolute: the support of the power complex."[47]

At this crisis, according to Mumford, there is only one effective way of "conserving the genuine achievements" of megamechanical technology, and that is "to alter the ideological basis of the whole system." The instances of such alteration which he adduces are those wrought by the remarkable moral mentors of the first millennium B.C. Those men confronted a comparable disaffection from power and material wealth abstracted from communal purpose and significance. Those men gave voice to a popular movement that could no longer accept "assumptions that equated human welfare and the will of the gods with centralized power, military dominance, and increasing economic exploitation." Those men, scattered across Europe, the Middle East, and Asia—Isaiah and Buddha, Confucius and Solon, Socrates and Jesus—saw that the elaboration of a new ideological basis of life "is a human, not a technical, problem," and that it "admits only a human solution." They denounced the myth of the megamachine, asserted "the spirit against the shell," and beckoned believers to a new kingdom of righteousness, co-operation, and humility. They challenged those they inspired to become new men and women. They balked at the virtues and achievements of civilization as much as they condemned its evils. Scorning "all the pomps and vanities of worldly success," they persuaded rather than commanded and taught rather than ruled. Spurning all opportunities to consolidate their authority, they urged their adherents to "return to their own centers and be guided by their hidden lights." Their new vision diverted energy from the service of civilization "more by withdrawal and abstention than by any overt struggle with the ruling classes."[48]

In Mumford's mind, this platonic politics of withdrawal and abstention is as pertinent to our present practice as to our ethical ideals. This rejection of the rewards of large-scale organization and this affirmation of the inner identity against the outer suggest, indeed, a more plausible political program than anything his critics offer at this desperate juncture, and not just because a similar politics of prophecy has prevailed again and again in the past. Mumford means to avoid clashes which cannot be won. He assumes, as the romantic realists do not, that the power complex cannot be conquered by direct confrontation. He knows that such an assault would be a battle fought on the megamachine's terrain by the megamachine's rules, a battle against vastly superior forces. He conjures a rising that does not depend on physical weapons just because such a rising cannot be quelled with physical weapons.

More than that, he entreats avoidance of an overt struggle with the ruling classes because he does not believe such a struggle can be won even if it is won. He is haunted by the emergence of the American megamachine after World War II and by the ways he believes the Nazis transmitted their pathologies, irrationalities, and rigidities to their New World conquerors, who rebuilt and perfected the fascist model of the warfaring state. He cannot shake his agonized conviction that any assault on the megamachine would necessarily be conducted in the very image of the megamachine, with the very instruments of centralized oppression it professed to repudiate.[49]

In just such tortured turns, Mumford keeps faith with his understanding of the contingency of history. At the same time, in the multitudinous continuities which run through his writings from first to last, he keeps faith with himself. *The Myth of the Machine* scouts the far frontiers even as it goes over old ground. It is his most searching reconnaissance of contemporary culture and consciousness, yet it returns to his earliest intellectual attachments—to Plato and the primacy of mind, to regionalism and the centrality of the organic environment, to utopianism and its applications in a tangled, troublous world—and also to his first mature masterwork. It follows *Technics and Civilization* in its determination to demystify the machine, its insistence on history and biology as the most essential of sciences, its awareness of the play of power and money on technology, and its passion for wholeness and its rage against abstraction run amuck. It is a worthy and wonderous capstone of his career not least because, in following that brilliant book, it goes so much further. It achieves a more expansive and vivid development of the psychological, epistemological, and spiritual premises of positions latent but still largely inarticulate in *Technics and Civilization*. It wrestles more conscientiously and convincingly with the revolutionary project implicit in that earlier work.

Almost on every page, *The Myth of the Machine* deepens the despair that was already discernible in *Technics and Civilization*. Mumford does not doubt that ours is a culture drifting ever further from human fullness and vitality, ever closer to death.[50] Yet almost always, he refuses to give in. Though he predicates his entire argument on the power of the mind, he disdains the conclusions to which his intellect impels him. Defiantly he bends his extraordinary erudition to the task of fashioning the only flickering hope he can credit. No one in our time has done better than Mumford in delineating our dilemmas or evoking their urgency. No one has done better at allowing men and women of integrity the faintest faith that we may yet elude our frightening fate.

Notes

General Introduction

1. Mumford used his friend Van Wyck Brooks's expression "usable past," then enriched its meaning. Alan Trachtenberg, "Mumford in the Twenties: The Historian as Artist," *Salmagundi* 49 (Summer 1980): 33.

2. Catherine Bauer to Lewis Mumford, Berlin, 23 July 1932. Lewis Mumford Papers, Special Collections, Van Pelt Library, University of Pennsylvania.

3. Thomas P. Hughes, *American Genesis: A Century of Invention and Technological Enthusiasm, 1870–1970* (New York: Viking Penguin, 1989), 335–38, 355–60.

4. Mumford to Bauer, 31 July 1930, Mumford Papers.

5. His programmatic vision for new technology and a new regionally organized society can be found in the articles he published in the 1920s. See, for example, Mumford, "The Fourth Migration" and "Regions—To Live In," *Survey Graphic* LIV (1925): 130–33, 151–52; and "Regionalism and Irregionalism," *Sociological Review* XIX (1927): 277–88.

6. Donald Miller, *Lewis Mumford: A Life* (New York: Weidenfeld & Nicolson, 1989), 326.

7. Bauer to Mumford, 16 August 1930, Mumford Papers.

8. Stuart Chase, *New York Herald Tribune Books,* 29 April 1934, section vii: 3; William F. Ogburn, *Saturday Review of Literature* X (1934): 657–59; Buckminster Fuller, *The Nation* 138 (1934): 652; and Herbert Read, *Yale Review* 24 (1934): 173–77.

9. Mumford, "Random Notes ["RN"]," 11 September 1963, Mumford Papers.

10. Ibid., 2 July 1967.

11. Mumford to Roderick Seidenberg, 6 August 1956, Mumford Papers.

12. Mumford, "RN," 13 July 1963, Mumford Papers.

13. Mumford, *Technics and Civilization* (New York: Harcourt, Brace, 1934), 258.

14. Mumford, "RN," 27 November 1967.

15. Mumford, "Personalia," 31 May 1968. Mumford so designated a category of memoranda scattered through several files of his papers.

16. Edmund Carpenter, *The New York Times Book Review* [April 1967], 1.

17. 13 December 1970, 1–2, 38–39.

18. Mumford quoting Shawn in Mumford to Hilda L. Lindley, 17 October 1970, Mumford Papers.

19. Mumford, *The Pentagon of Power* (New York: Harcourt Brace Jovanovich, 1964), 393, 420, 430.

20. Miller, *Mumford,* 533.

21. Mumford, "Personalia," 2 June 1968, Mumford Papers.

22. Ibid., 3 February 1969.

23. Mumford to Roderick Seidenberg, 6 August 1956, Mumford Papers.

24. On technological systems, see Thomas P. Hughes, "The Evolution of Large Technological Systems," in *The Social Construction of Technological Systems,* eds. W. E. Bijker, T. P. Hughes, and T. J. Pinch (Cambridge, Mass: MIT Press, 1987), 51–82.

25. Mumford to Roderick Seidenberg, 30 August 1965, Mumford Papers.

26. Mumford to Bauer, 11 September 1932, Mumford Papers.

27. Mumford to Roderick Seidenberg, 30 August 1965, Mumford Papers.

28. For a bibliography of Mumford's books, articles, and other essays, see Elmer S. Newman, *Lewis Mumford: A Bibliography, 1914–1970* (New York: Harcourt Brace Jovanovich, 1971). For an annotated bibliography of books and articles about Mumford and his works, see, *On Lewis Mumford: An Annotated Bibliography,* compiled by Jane Morley (Philadelphia: University of Pennsylvania, Program for Assessing and Revitalizing the Social Sciences, 1985).

29. Russell Jacoby, *The Last Intellectuals: American Culture in the Age of Academe* (New York: Basic Books, 1987), 5.

30. *Sketches from Life: The Autobiography of Lewis Mumford* (Boston: Beacon Press, 1982), 186–91.

31. Mumford, *Technics and Civilization,* v.

32. All published by Harcourt, Brace and Company.

ARTHUR P. MOLELLA: Mumford in Historiographical Context

1. *Technics and Civilization* (New York: Harcourt, Brace, 1934), 470, annotation to the Sombart entry in Bibliography. Other annotations quoted below appear next to the cited item in the Bibliography.

2. Russell Lynes, *Good Old Modern* (New York: Atheneum, 1973), 91–92.

3. 29 March, 1922. Lewis Mumford Papers, Special Collections, Van Pelt Library, University of Pennsylvania. Hereinafter, Mumford Papers.

4. "Invention and the Machine in America," incomplete manuscript, June 1925, box 12, folder 1, Mumford Papers.

5. *Technics and Civilization,* 437.

6. Mumford Papers, box 112, folder 2.

7. Mumford's ideas included an "improved electrolytic detector, *Modern Electrics,* vol. 5, no. 1 (April 1912): 40; a portable receiving outfit, vol. 4, no. 5 (April 1911): 29–30; and the "ultimate crystal set," vol. 4, no. 3 (June 1911): 179.

8. "An original play by Stuyvesant boys." Mumford was president of the Boar's Head society. Mumford Papers, box 66, folder 3.

9. "A New York Adolescence," *New Yorker* 13 (4 December 1937): 89. Mumford to Melvin Kranzberg, 20 December 1969, in the latter's personal files. Parts of the letter were published in Mumford's biography in *Technology and Culture,* vol. 11, no. 2 (April 1970): 205–13.

10. Mumford Papers, box 118, folder 1; box 66, folder 6 has his report cards.

11. *The Student's Guide* (New York: Stuyvesant High School, 1909), in Mumford Papers, box 66, folder 6.

12. Ibid., 25.

13. For Dewey's conception of the role of technology in society, see *Individualism, Old and New* (New York: Minton, Balch & Co., 1930), 29, 30.

14. Gary Bullert, *The Politics of John Dewey* (Buffalo: Prometheus Books, 1983), 82–85, 176–82.

15. Mumford to George Morris, 30 January 1918, Mumford Papers.

16. Mumford to Victor Branford, 3 March 1926, Mumford Papers.

17. Such sentiments abound in the Mumford-Geddes correspondence, Mumford Papers; for example, Mumford to Geddes, 8 September 1920, and see Mumford's *Sketches from Life: The Autobiography of Lewis Mumford: The Early Years* (New York: Dial Press, 1982), 155.

18. *Technics and Civilization*, 447; Mumford to Kranzberg, 20 December 1969, cited note 9.

19. I have treated Mitman's conception of such a national institution in an article, "The Museum that Never Was: Anticipations of the Smithsonian's National Museum of History and Technology," to be published in the proceedings of a conference on "Collections and Culture," Smithsonian Institution and Woodrow Wilson International Center, October 1987. Biographical material on Mitman can be found in Biographical Files, Division of Engineering and Industry, National Museum of American History; personal communication with Mitman's son-in-law, Col. James Newman.

20. Mitman's European diary, 14 May–15 August 1932, from which this and the following quotations are excerpted, is preserved in the Ramsey Room, National Air and Space Museum, Smithsonian Institution.

21. Ibid., 20, 69, 70, 447.

22. For an idea of the breadth of the movement, see Charles R. Richards, *The Industrial Museum* (New York: Macmillan, 1925), and my "Museum that Never Was," cited above, note 19.

23. *The Repertory, Bulletin of the National Museum of Engineering and Industry* (an ephemeral publicity newsletter for Mitman's initiative for a national museum of engineering) 1 (July 1927):3, preserved in R.U. 192, box 253, Smithsonian Institution Archives.

24. Mitman's European Diary.

25. From my interview, 26 June 1987, with Frank Taylor, Mitman's assistant and successor in the technology department.

26. See U.S. National Museum *Annual Report for the Year 1884* (Washington, D.C.: Government Printing Office, 1885), 14–15; and Record Unit 158, box 2, folder 16, pp. 20–21, Curators' Annual Reports, Smithsonian Institution Archives.

27. Inferred from his *Catalogue of the Mechanical Collection in the United States National Museum, Bulletin of the United States National Museum*, no. 119 (Washington, D.C.: Government Printing Office, 1922).

28. Ibid.

29. Mitman's research files for his *DAB* entries are preserved in the Smithsonian Archives and in the biographical files, Division of Engineering and Industry, National Museum of American History, Smithsonian Institution.

30. According to Mitman's assistant Frank Taylor, "I don't believe that any of us had the background or the experience to think in terms of the broad social significance of technologic improvement. We talked about it occasionally—that we would like to do exhibits which would show the impact of the automobile on the society, and we had no idea what that impact was. Then when people who *were* scholars and students, who wrote about man becoming the slave of the machine, we used to pooh-pooh this, you know. We didn't think that man would ever be a slave of a machine." Interview by Pam Henson, 1980, p. 55, Smithsonian Institution Archives.

31. Hans Ude, "Conrad Matchoss, Ein Leben für die Technik und ihre Geschichte," Deutsches Museum, *Abhandlungen und Berichte* 3 (1942): 61.

32. I. N. Lipshitz, "The Study of Technical History," *Mechanical Engineering* 57 (March 1935): 143–47. Summarizing the European developments, Lipshitz urged Americans to establish their own historical organizations.

33. Henry Butler Allen, "Seeing Is Believing," *Proceedings of the Newcomen Society, London, American Branch* (1937), 5.

34. For example, Harvard's Edwin Gay proposed that the Newcomen Society provide dissertation topics for his doctoral students, Gay to C. E. Davies, 29 April, 1927, printed in *Transactions of the Newcomen Society, London, American Branch* (1927); *Proceedings* (first meeting of 1925), 3.

35. (Cambridge, Mass.: M.I.T. Press, 1970), annotated edition prepared by John H. White, Jr.

36. John H. White, Jr., "The Railway Museum: Past, Present, and Future," *Technology and Culture* 14 (October 1973): 599–613.

37. For a concise history of the society, see John H. White, Jr., "On Railroad History and the Railway and Locomotive Historical Society," *The Railroad History Index*, comp. Thomas T. Taber 3d, (Railway and Locomotive Historical Society, 1985).

38. *Bulletin,* no. 1 (Boston: Railway and Locomotive Historical Society, 1921): 6.

39. Charles E. Fisher, "Our Society," *Bulletin,* no. 121 (October 1969): iv–vii. *Business Historical Society, Inc.* (Cambridge, Mass., 1925).

40. For example, for magazines such as *The Railroad Magazine, Railway Age,* and *Railway and Locomotive Engineering.*

41. The journal as well as rosters are still published. I have discussed the core idea of the rosters with current contributors to the journal and current officers of the organization, William L. Withuhn, Robert C. Post, and John H. White, Jr. Withuhn, especially, emphasizes the value of the roster as a source of distilled information on the use and diffusion of the technology.

42. Carl Condit has referred to data-gathering activity of the railroad buff as "ant's-nest labor," but still praised it as the "most nearly unique, most curious, and the most useful to the technological historian," in the belief that urban and transportation historians would use the compilations as sources of illustration and basic quantitative data. "The Literature of the Railroad Buff: A Historian's View," *Railroad History* (successor to the *Bulletin*), no. 142 (Spring 1980): 16, 17, 22.

43. Ibid., 9.

44. *The Story of Inventions: Man, the Miracle Maker* (New York: Garden City Publishing Co., 1928), 138. Van Loon tried to recruit Mumford to write for the *Sun.* See letter of 1 October 1923, to Mumford, in Mumford Papers. Van Loon is cited in *Technics and Civilization,* 472, 475.

45. *Twentieth Century Authors* (New York: H. W. Wilson, 1966).

46. *Dictionary of American Biography* (New York: Charles Scribner's Sons); Obit., *New York Times,* 28 November 1956, p. 35.

47. *The New Art of Flying* (New York: Dodd, Mead, 1911); *The ABC of Radio* (New York: M. H. Ray, 1922); *Invention and Society* (Chicago: American Library Association, 1930); "The War Is Affected by New Inventions," *Review of Reviews* 50 (October 1914): 439–46.

48. (New York and London: Scribner's). A German edition appeared in 1927 (Berlin).

49. "The Machine and Civilization," *New York Times* (Book Review Section), 29 April 1934, p. 17.

50. "Vital Museums of the New Epoch," *New York Times*, 20 March 1932, Sec. 5, p. 12.

51. Ibid.

52. Ibid.

53. Ibid., 12, 22; *From Cave Man to Engineer, The Museum of Science and Industry, Founded by Julius Rosenwald* (Chicago: Museum of Science and Industry, 1933), 12–13: "Ears, eyes, nose, skin—every sense proclaims the coal mine."

54. "Revealing the Technical Ascent of Man in the Rosenwald Industrial Museum," *Scientific Monthly* 28 (June 1929): 485.

55. Ibid., "Revealing the Technical Ascent of Man," 483–84.

56. "The Great Museum of the Machine Age," *New York Times Magazine*, 26 October 1930, p. 16.

57. "Vital Museums of the New Epoch," 22.

58. Arthur Schlesinger, Sr., *Political and Social History of the United States, 1829–1925* (New York: Macmillan, 1932), 79, 280. The book was first published in 1925.

59. *Harvard University Gazette*, 12 March 1966, pp. 155–56; "Memorial," *Technology and Culture* 6 (Fall 1965): 630–32.

60. Ibid., 448.

61. Personal communication from Usher's daughter, Miriam Usher Chrisman.

62. *Technics and Civilization*, 448, 470.

63. *A History of Mechanical Inventions* (New York: McGraw Hill, 1929), 1.

64. *Mechanical Inventions* (Boston: Beacon Press, 1959; paperback of 2d, 1954 rev. ed.), 60.

65. Ibid.

66. *Mechanical Inventions* (1929), chap. 2; more fully in 2d ed., chap. 4.

67. Usher, "The Significance of Modern Empiricism for History and Economics," *The Journal of Economic History* 9 (November 1949): 140, 142–43; *Technics and Civilization*, 368–69. Mumford derived his holistic ideas partly from Patrick Geddes's and J. Arthur Thomson's *Life: Outlines of General Biology*, 2 vols. (New York, London: Harper Brothers, 1931), 1: vii; 2: 1114–15, 1376–83. I have explored the holistic issue in "The First Generation: Usher, Mumford, and Giedion," in Steven Cutcliffe and Robert C. Post, eds., *In Context: History and the History of Technology, Essays in Honor of Melvin Kranzberg*, vol. 1 of *Research in Technology Studies* (Bethlehem, Pennsylvania: Lehigh University Press, 1988).

68. *Technics and Civilization*, 403.

69. For example, the review by Herbert Read, in *Yale Review* 24, new series (Fall 1934): 173.

70. Mumford to Melvin Kranzberg, 15 January 1970, in Kranzberg's personal papers.

ROSALIND WILLIAMS: LM as a Historian of Technology in *Technics and Civilization*

1. Lewis Mumford, "An Appraisal of Lewis Mumford's 'Technics and Civilization' (1934)," *Daedalus* 88 (Summer 1959): 527, commenting on the "The Drama of the Machines," *Scribner's Magazine* 8 (August 1930): 150–63.

The "Form and Personality" draft is found in box 8, folders 3–10, in the Lewis Mumford Papers, Van Pelt Library, University of Pennsylvania. Mumford later added a note to the draft describing it as the first draft of a book that became

Technics and Civilization and *The Culture of Cities,* and stating that it was written in the summer of 1930.

Folder 4 contains the two drafts of the chapter on machines. Mumford wrote a note to himself on the first page of the July version: "OK—but add section (p. 62) on the function and role of machine in independent creative expression." Such a section was in fact added in the longer August draft.

All archival materials referenced here are from the Lewis Mumford Papers, Special Collections, Van Pelt Library, University of Pennsylvania, unless noted otherwise.

2. Box 8, folder 4, 44. In all quotations from Mumford's drafts, obvious typographical errors have been corrected. In the margin Mumford scrawled "Expand," and in the August version the discussion has indeed been expanded into a paragraph: "gestation and growth were supplanted by the mechanical punctuation of the clock. . . . Time became an entity in itself, divorced from the events that were bound up with it and qualified it. . . ." Mumford then mentions how establishing hours and minutes of longitude created similar attitudes toward space (space as an abstract entity, unrelated to historical events, one place as good as another) and concludes, "Wherever this new rhythm became established, industrialism followed quickly" (4–5; page numbers 51–52 crossed out).

3. Discussion of the origins of machines takes up 6 of 18 pages of the July draft chapter, and 13 of the 39 pages in the August version. Mumford had also planned to write chapters on groups and personalities, but in a letter to David Liebovitz (7 October 1930) Mumford writes that he finished only about two-thirds of the first draft he had planned.

4. Mumford himself felt at the time that the summer 1930 "Form and Personality" draft needed less history, not more. He wrote this note to himself on the manuscript (dated 6 July 1930): "What the book now needs is a firmer attitude: more confidence: a less gingerly approach. A little less dwelling on the past: better-knit speculations on the future. More international illustrations. Here is a chance for leadership." Box 8, folder 2.

5. See the paper by Arthur Molella, this volume.

6. Box 8, folder 4, pp. 1–2.

7. Peter Shaw, "Mumford in Retrospect," *Commentary* 56 (September 1973): 72. Eddy Dow, "Lewis Mumford's Passage to India: From the First to the Later Phase," *The South Atlantic Quarterly* 76 (1977): 72, comments on the "astonishing . . . coherence" of Mumford's work. One reason for this coherence is the persistence of this dramatic motif.

8. Joseph Duffey, "Mumford's Quest: The First Decade," *Salmagundi* 49 (Summer 1980): 67.

9. In interpreting this period of breakdown and recovery "Dante's vision of good and evil was of more use to me than Freud's psychoanalytic insights." Mumford, *My Works and Days: A Personal Chronicle* (New York: Harcourt Brace Jovanovich, 1979), 298–99; see also his *Sketches from Life: The Early Years* (New York: Dial Press, 1982), 458–59.

10. Philip West, in "Mumford as Archego," *Salmagundi* 49 (Summer 1980): 112–20, makes a somewhat similar argument that autobiographical concerns form a subtext in Mumford's purportedly historical critiques. Besides being polemical in tone, West's essay seems to ascribe more of his own literary consciousness to Mumford than is warranted. Mumford's consciousness is fundamentally moral rather than literary.

Alan Trachtenberg, in "Mumford in the Twenties: The Historian as Artist," *Salmagundi* 49 (Summer 1980): 28–42, argues that in the 1920s Mumford was trying "to compose history as art" (40). His interpretation and mine converge, except that I would stress that for Mumford "art" is a moral term.

11. Mumford, *Sketches*, 458–61; also *My Works and Days*, 298–301. It is not just in retrospect that the summer of 1930 seemed a dismal period; Mumford's letters written at the time describe it as a time of "the blackest depression" (to Victor Branford, 27 August 1929), as "the most unpleasant summer I can remember since [childhood]" after a "hellish winter" (to Thomas Beer, 22 September 1929), and refer to his trip to Europe that summer as a "fiasco" (to James Henderson, 3 August 1929) when he reached "the lowest depths" (to Victor Branford, 30 October 1929).

12. Dow, "Mumford's Passage to India," 39. Dow points out that in part this redefinition was a matter of necessity; the Great Depression was reaching its bottom, and places Mumford had published before were disappearing (34–37).

13. Mumford to Patrick Geddes (31 March 1929) and to Jerry Lachenbruch (5 April 1929).

14. See Christopher Lasch, "Lewis Mumford and the Myth of the Machine," *Salmagundi* 49 (Summer 1980): 8; also Mumford himself in *Sketches*, 446–49, and in *Works and Days*, 97.

15. Mumford, *Works and Days*, 301

16. Lewis Mumford, "Patrick Geddes, Insurgent," *The New Republic* (30 October 1929), 296.

17. Box 8, folder 4, p. 19 of August draft. See also Mumford's discussion of insurgency in *Technics and Civilization*, 319. As Mumford later explained, "Geddes's essential doctrine was a doctrine of *life:* its inception, its growth, its crises, its insurgence, its self-transcendence." Mumford, "Introduction," in Philip Boardman, *Patrick Geddes: Maker of the Future* (Chapel Hill: University of North Carolina Press, 1944), x.

18. Mumford, *Sketches*, 447, 464.

19. Mumford to Thomas Beer, 22 September 1929.

20. For Mumford's explanation of the importance of these notes, see *Works and Days*, 25.

21. According to the June 1930 plan, the first chapter—called at first "disintegration" and later changed to "ideologies"—would "sketch the disintegration of the arts. It should show the absence of a relevant technique and ideology. . . ." The second chapter is on machines, and the third on symbols; Mumford remarks that these chapters "are fairly clear, except that the symbol needs further development." Chapters 4 and 5, on buildings and cities, are "partly done," and the question is whether to separate or join them, and whether to discuss the city and region together or the city and the landscape. The next chapter on groups "is difficult to focus: how does it relate to Chapter I? What are its interrelations with the other chapters?" The final two chapters on personality and synthesis "are still shadows" (Box 8, folder 2).

22. Mumford later identified his approach with Lévi-Strauss's concept of cultural determinants; see "Technics and the Nature of Man," *Technology and Culture* 7 (Summer 1966): 309. See his comments on his rejection of Marxism in "Appraisal," 528. Christopher Lasch (see note 14) and Casey Blake (the latter in "Lewis Mumford: Values over Technique," *democracy* (Spring 1983): 125–37) have pointed out the intellectual poverty of American Marxism at that time. According

to Blake, in the 1930s and 1940s most American Marxists wrote in a positivistic vein that "dismissed art, religion, and ethics as superstructural irrelevancies—mere fog, mist, and camouflage . . ." (132).

23. In the summer 1930 draft chapters on the machine, Mumford puts the case this way: "The vast material displacements the machine has made in our physical environment are perhaps in the long run less important than its spiritual contribution to our culture." July draft, 43–44, and August draft, 2–3. In the August draft Mumford has penciled in "an esthetic" between "human" and "values."

24. As Joseph Duffey has shown, during the 1920s Mumford repeatedly tried "to get technology into focus," alternating between strident condemnation of ugly modern cities and materialism and, less frequently, praise of an emerging technical aesthetic and value-structure (57). Mumford himself says that in *Technics and Civilization* he at last arrives at a moral resting place, a "balanced judgment" on machines (in his preface to the Dover Press paperback edition of *Sticks and Stones;* quoted by Duffey, 51n). But it was only a temporary resting place, for Mumford continued to redefine the distinction between and varying origins of "good" and "bad" machines, as in his much later distinction between "authoritarian" and "democratic" ones ("Authoritarian and Democratic Technics," *Technology and Culture* 5 (Winter 1964): 1–9).

It should be pointed out that this ambivalence about machines is not a personal problem but a cultural one. According to Mircea Eliade, in his analysis of myths associated with mining and metalworking, " . . . like every sacred object, metal is both dangerous and beneficent. This ambivalent attitude towards smith and metals is fairly universal." Eliade, *The Forge and the Crucible*, 2d ed., trans. Stephen Corrin (Chicago and London: University of Chicago Press, 1978), 96.

25. Mumford later deleted everything but "Machines" in titling the July draft, and he kept this one-word title for the August version.

26. Box 8, folder 4, pp. 44–45 (July draft).

27. Ibid., 47. The August version is generally the same, except that various points have been expanded.

28. Mumford, "Patrick Geddes, Insurgent," 296.

29. Mumford, *Sketches*, 441.

30. Dow, "Mumford's Passage to India," 36.

31. Mumford, "Appraisal," 528.

32. On 17 January 1932, Mumford, writing from Dartmouth College to James Henderson, mentions laying down "my manuscript on Machines and City, or Form and Civilization—or whatever else I choose finally to call the book I was writing last summer and the summer before. . . ."

33. Early in 1930 (the date is uncertain), Mumford was writing to Geddes that he wanted to go to Europe that fall or the following spring "in order to gather a little fresh material from the countries I've not yet visited, and to check up and revivify my old impressions." Also in his 7 October 1930 letter to David Liebovitz, he comments that he wants to go to Europe before finishing his manuscript (evidently referring to "Form and Personality") because "so many of my illustrations and examples come from Europe, and I wish to renew my impressions and see many new things over there. . . ."

34. Mumford, "Acknowledgments," 475.

35. Mumford, *Sketches*, 467.

36. In August 1932, Mumford was trying out different titles for this projected book; in November he was sketching out a trial table of contents which still included chapters on regions and cities as well as on machines. Box 8, folder 2.

37. See box 9; box 11 contains a draft written in the fall of 1933.

38. Mumford to Van Wyck Brooks, 21 June and 30 June 1933.

39. Mumford, "The Disciple's Rebellion," *Encounter* 27 (September 1966): 20. Much of the article is repeated in *Sketches,* 407–8.

Their relationship is also described in Philip Boardman, *The Worlds of Patrick Geddes: Biologist, Town Planner, Re-educator, Peace-warrior* (London: Routledge & Kegan Paul, 1978), 340–42, 370–72. See also Mumford's own description in "Mumford on Geddes," *Architectural Review* 108 (August 1950): 81–87, reprinted in H. T. Moore and K. W. Deutsch, eds., *The Human Prospect* (Carbondale: Southern Illinois University Press, 1965), 99–114.

40. Mumford, "Disciple's Rebellion," 12–13.

41. Mumford, *Sketches,* 407.

42. Mumford, "Disciple's Rebellion," 20. In his Introduction to *The Culture of Cities* (1938) Mumford wrote, "Many disciples slay or betray their masters while they are still alive, perhaps *because* they are still alive. By waiting till Geddes's death before embarking on these systematic works, I perhaps avoided that sad necessity." Quoted in Boardman, *Maker,* 413.

43. Mumford was familiar enough with Geddes's notes, since Geddes was always hoping that Mumford would write up his ideas for him. Mumford gives this accurate description and assessment of them in "Patrick Geddes, Insurgent" (296): "bales of notes, remains as teasing and inscrutable as Leonardo's in their cryptic notations, as comprehensive and pregnant as those we are now recovering from the American philospher, Charles Peirce. Here is his polyphonic notation of thought: no subject broached by itself—an abstract verbal figment—but always with the necessary inter-relations and modifications. Unfortunately, one cannot trace the melody, for that thread was supplied by Geddes's running interpretation; and unlike music, his diagrams do not carry their melodic element with them. As for his books, they are but notes written as it were on the margin of his thinking. Suspicious of hasty results and premature conclusions, his thought has remained suspended in solution: what has been deposited is not always the best part of it."

John P. Reilly, "The Early Social Thought of Patrick Geddes" (Ph.D. diss., Columbia University, 1972; reprint London and Ann Arbor: University Microfilms International, 1980), 90, reminds us that "Geddes' impatience with the written word is perhaps accountable in part by the fact that English was not his native tongue. He was raised in a Gaelic-speaking family and continued to speak with a thick Scottish burr throughout his life. . . . His prose always retained a certain Celtic harshness and his once-removed relationship to English accounts in large part for his recurring wordplay and his propensity for neologisms."

44. Mumford, "Disciple's Rebellion," 20.

45. Box 8, folder 6 for the chapter on cities; box 8, folder 7 for the chapter on regions. In April 1963 Mumford added a note on the title page of the latter chapter to explain that the background it presents was originally done for publication as a pamphlet by RPAA. "When published in *Sociological Review* Branford's introduction of errors and gratuitous interpolations made it impossible to use in that form. Some of it went into *Technics and Civilization* and *Culture of Cities.*"

My discussion here concerns primarily the second and third parts of the historical sections of *Technics* (the "agents of mechanization" and the three phases of technology), while largely neglecting the "cultural preparation" section. Geddes's influence is less pronounced in that opening section. It would be intriguing to learn if Mumford's famous discussion of the clock and the monastery may derive in part from Geddes's analysis of the function of the cloister, which Mumford mentions in

his biography of Geddes which, according to Mumford's notation on the manuscript, was written for *Collier's Encyclopedia* (original manuscript in box 18, folder
25).

Also, Geddes's disciple Victor Branford may be to some degree responsible for
the striking image with which *Technics and Civilization* ends. According to Mumford's obituary article on Branford (*New Republic* 64 (27 August 1930): 43–44),
Branford's "ideal figure for a fine society was that of a symphony orchestra" (44).

46. Patrick Geddes, "The Sixth Talk: The Education of Two Boys," in *Talks
from the Outlook Tower* (which appeared in *Survey* from February to September
1925); quoted in Marshall Stalley, ed., *Patrick Geddes: Spokesman for Man and the
Environment* (New Brunswick: Rutgers University Press, 1972), 365–80. For a
description of the problems Mumford and his *Survey* colleagues had in transcribing
Geddes's six lectures (which were given at the New School for Social Research in
New York during the summer of 1923) for publication, see Stalley's Introduction
(289–93).

Geddes's conviction that the "valley section" should be the basis of childhood
education is also expressed in a similar essay he wrote on the education of his son.
Papers of Sir Patrick Geddes, Section 24.1.331, University Archives, University of
Strathclyde (Glasgow, Scotland).

47. Geddes, "Sixth Talk," *Talks from the Outlook Tower,* in Stalley, ed., 369. Dr.
Sofia Leonard, Senior Research Fellow at the Patrick Geddes Centre for Planning
Studies, Department of Urban Design and Regional Planning, University of Edinburgh, feels that these early experiences were significant in shaping Geddes's lifelong preference for "bird's-eye views" and for relief maps (personal conversation,
8 July 1987). See also the description of these early walks in Boardman, *Maker,* 4–
5.

48. Boardman, *Maker,* 41–42. On Le Play see Michael Z. Brooke, *Le Play: Engineer and Social Scientist* (London: Longmans, 1970); J. R. Pitts, "Frédéric Le Play,"
in D. L. Sills, ed., *International Encyclopedia of the Social Sciences,* 9 (New York: Free
Press, 1968); and Rosalind Williams, "Frédéric Le Play," in Patrick Hutton, ed.,
Historical Dictionary of the Third French Republic, 1 (New York: Greenwood Press,
1968): 535–36.

49. Geddes's description of Le Play's ideas are found in his notes for a sociology course he gave in August 1891 (at the famous Edinburgh Summer Sessions
which he organized). Geddes Papers, Section 3.1.1., Strathclyde University. See
also his manuscript on Le Play in Section 18.1.720.

50. Patrick Geddes and Victor Branford (with corrections by Geddes), "A Contribution of Social Science toward Relationships," n.d., Geddes Papers, Section
3.1.16, Strathclyde University.

51. Geddes, "The Third Talk: The Valley Plan of Civilization," *Talks from the
Outlook Tower,* in Stalley, ed., 333.

52. Ibid., 328.

53. Ibid., 329.

54. Geddes, "The Fourth Talk: The Valley in The Town," *Talks from the Outlook
Tower,* in Stalley, ed., 343. Geddes also expained this idea by saying there are not
one but two valley outlines: that of nature, from snows to the sea, while the second
is that of the modern occupations evident in any city street.

The congruence of the two outlines is strikingly evident in the large drawing of
the valley section Geddes prepared for his Cities and Towns Exhibition: the top
half shows in great detail the natural valley section, running left to right from

mountain to sea, with the six major occupations and their subdivisions portrayed at each point of the section, while below a typical street in Edinburgh is shown, again sloping left to right, with the various shops portrayed below the primitive occupations to which they correspond (the furrier below the hunter, the store selling woolen goods below the shepherd, the baker and corn chandler below the peasant, the bustling modern port below the simple fishing village, and so on). This drawing was called to my attention by Dr. Sofia Leonard (see note 47), who is now cataloguing materials left by Geddes at the Outlook Tower in Edinburgh, including the famous Cities and Town Exhibition.

55. Mumford, "Appraisal," 530. As late as 1958, Mumford was using the valley section in teaching MIT students. MIT lecture notes dated 21 October 1958 show the "Geddes valley section" and note that it shows "division of labor in pre-civilized society, environmental pressure and response." Box 55, folder 1.

56. Personal conversation with Dr. Sofia Leonard, 7 July 1987. Sometimes Geddes takes the principle of geographical control to absurd lengths, as when he used Tennyson's 1833 poem about Lady Clara Vere de Vere as a "specimen" of Le Play's method of studying social origins (which he contrasts with the Darwinist method of studying biological origins). Her pride, which Tennyson considered "aristocratic," Geddes instead traces to her racial and occupational roots. She is a Norman, therefore of "fisher" stock, therefore from a society that requires primogeniture (a ship can have only one captain) and that accords a good deal of freedom to the women left behind. Geddes, text for lecture on Le Play's method (August 1906), Section 2.5.24, Geddes Papers, Strathclyde University. Geddes also refers to this example in "The Fourth Talk: The Valley in the Town," *Talks from the Outlook Tower,* in Stalley, ed., 344.

A very similar example of this approach is contained in a letter to Geddes (dated 25 July 1890) from Edmond Demolins in which the writer mentions a recent holiday at the seaside where he informally studied the local populations and concluded that "all their social organization seemed derived from the marine labor which the large majority of them perform. They are not fishers, but navigators. With our method, only a little time was needed to account for a population; this is one of the marvelous results of science [my translation]." Demolins to Geddes, Section 9.44, Geddes Papers, Strathclyde University.

57. According to Mumford, Geddes was convinced that "Rural thought still deals in these realities; urban thought, particularly metropolitan thought, debauches itself with illusions compared to which the search for perpetual motion is edifying." Mumford, "Patrick Geddes, Insurgent," 296.

58. "It is not until the machine culture becomes dominant, displacing the interests and moral judgments appropriate to the other cultures at the lower end of the valley section, it is not until then that the doctrine of untrammeled power is, practically speaking, unchallenged." Box 9, section 2, 82a.

59. Mumford, *Technics,* 60–77.

60. In *The Machine in the Garden: Technology and the Pastoral Ideal in America* (New York: Oxford University Press, 1964), 297–300, Marx describes how, in *Moby-Dick,* Ishmael attributes some of Captain Ahab's pathology to the conditions of his vocation: "A whaling captain's life, as Ishmael sees it, is peculiarly conducive to illusions of Promethean power. Ahab's vocation endows him with a mastery of what Carlyle had called the 'machinery' of the age—in both senses of the word. As captain he is, of course, master of an intricate piece of machinery in the literal sense. More important, however, is the mechanistic habit of mind. . . ." In Marx's

words, Ishmael concludes that Ahab's "monomania . . . is in some measure a product of the whaling life . . ." (297, 300).

61. Geddes, "The Fourth Talk: The Valley in the Town," *Talks from the Outlook Tower,* in Stalley, ed., 346.

62. Geddes Papers, Section 1.1.6 and 3.11.22, University of Strathclyde.

63. On others who expressed similar ideas see James W. Carey and John J. Quirk, "The Mythos of the Electronic Revolution," *American Scholar* 39 (Spring 1970): 230–34.

64. See notes for these lectures in Geddes Papers, Section 3.1.1., University of Strathclyde.

65. On the origins of the paleotechnic/neotechnic distinction, see Boardman, *Maker,* 374.

66. Geddes, *Cities in Evolution: An Introduction to the Town Planning Movement and to the Study of Civics* (New York: Howard Fertig, 1968 [1915]), 62–64.

67. Mumford, "Technics and the Nature of Man," 304–6.

68. From typescript of *Cities in Evolution,* Geddes Papers, Section 1.1.2, University of Strathclyde, 131.

69. Geddes, *Cities,* 82.

70. Ibid., 64.

71. See ibid., 84–108; also Geddes Papers, Section 3.5.16, University of Strathclyde.

72. Geddes scarcely mentions why the shift from paleotechnics to neotechnics is taking place, except to say that the paleotechnic age is "[dying] away before a better order; since its life, its achievements, were the inevitable preparation for those which replace them" (typescript of *Cities in Evolution,* Geddes Papers, Section 1.1.2, University of Strathclyde, 131). In Geddes's discussion the evils of the paleotechnic era—unemployment, disease, slums, crime—are logical outcomes, not unfortunate side effects. He describes these evils, however, more as results of the commercial mentality of the "paleotects," who short-sightedly focus on the bottom line and who ignore larger, more biologically realistic definitions of efficiency and utility.

73. Box 8, folder 6, p. iii hh.

74. Box 8, folder 6, p. iii jjj.

75. A similar thesis has recently been expressed by Robert Heilbroner, who has suggested that technological determinism may characterize certain stages of history, "specifically that of high capitalism and low socialism—*in which the forces of technical change have been unleashed, but when the agencies for the control or guidance of technology are still rudimentary* [italics in original]." Robert L. Heilbroner, "Do Machines make History," *Technology and Culture* 8 (July 1967): 345.

76. Mumford, *Technics,* 162–63.

77. Duffey, "Mumford's Quest," 66.

78. Blake, "Mumford: Values over Technique," 129–31; Lasch, "Mumford and the Myth of the Machine," 26–27.

79. See, for example, his ode to the eotechnic in *Technics,* 147–48.

80. Boardman, *Worlds,* 308, 440–41.

81. Blake, "Mumford: Values over Technique," 136.

82. Mumford, "Appraisal," 531–32.

83. Ibid., 531.

84. In Mumford's own words, Henderson "had a crush on Sophia that she didn't reciprocate." Several love letters Henderson wrote to Sophia around 1929

and 1930 have been preserved in the files of correspondence in the Lewis Mumford Papers; Mumford's remark on Henderson's crush, dated 6 March 1963, is inserted at the top of the file.

Henderson seems to have led a rather lonely and frustrated life. He never married ("the girls married others," he wrote Sophia in a 1955 letter). He earned his living doing copy-writing and writing for business publications and never got his own more serious writing projects under way. He must have envied and to some extent resented Mumford not only for his wife but also for his writing success. He considered Mumford "proud and haughty...." (Henderson to Mumford, 21 March 1934) and sometimes berated Mumford for being smug and glib (Henderson to Mumford, 3 January 1935).

As Henderson got older he became deaf and felt increasingly isolated, noting in a 1963 letter to Mumford that his "mind is full of things that don't interest people." He re-established contact with the Mumfords around 1955. His last years were spent living with a nephew's family, in the back of their house; the nephew appears to have cared for and appreciated Henderson, who died on 21 September 1969. His last request (according to the nephew) was for a paperback copy of *Technics and Civilization* because he had heard that a new preface corrected an error in the original version: "I certainly hope so, Lewis was much too intelligent to make mistakes like that."

85. In one (undated) letter to Henderson Mumford says how impressed he was with Henderson's writing and tells him "I shall filch at least two good sentences for *Technics!*"

86. Mumford, *Technics*, 13; in a letter of 3 February 1934, Henderson gives the source of the figure, as Mumford had requested.

87. Years later, in 1980, at the top of a long letter of Henderson's covering a wide variety of topics, Mumford wrote the comment, "I wish I had my reply. There was probably more fresh thinking in Henderson's mind than I was able to absorb or make use of—Alas! for my record."

88. Henderson to Mumford, 1963.

89. Henderson to Mumford, 3 January 1935.

90. Henderson to Mumford, 19 August 1933.

91. Henderson commented on the valley section that "[It] is really not even a scientific generalization. It is an abstract picture useful only for exposition by comparison with the complex development of life. If you could treat these as cultures or themes in culture it might be possible to use the idea freely." Box 11, folder 2, p. 73.

92. Box 11, folder 1, p. 43.

93. Meyer Schapiro's review of *The Culture of Cities* (1938), quoted by Peter Shaw in "Mumford in Retrospect," *Commentary* 56 (September 1973): 72. In a similar spirit Duffey says Mumford's writing relies on "metaphysical momentum" (68).

94. Box 11, folder 1, p. 5.

95. Box 11, folder 1, p. 65.

96. Mumford's list of "subversive types" is especially explicit in his incomplete draft "Preface to Action," written in 1931, where he concludes that the real revolutionaries of the day are engineers, educators, planners, economists, scientists, philosophers, and artists who chart regional resources and clarify human needs. "These people are not called revolutionaries, because they are not formed into groups which will focus their knowledge and power for human ends," and because many of them share the attitudes of their class. However, many of them are unwill-

ing servants of capitalism, and "they are ready for a new deal. The cards are in our hands. Let us deal them out." (On 24 March 1934 Mumford added the note, "This was written before Roosevelt made it a popular slogan.") Box 18, folder 3.

97. See Thomas P. Hughes, *Networks of Power: Electrification in Western Society, 1880–1930* (Baltimore and London: Johns Hopkins University Press, 1983), chap. XIV, esp. 405, including note 4; and Eugene S. Ferguson, "The Mind's Eye: Nonverbal Thought in Technology," *Science* 197 (26 August 1977): 827–36.

98. Henderson to Mumford, 21 March 1934. See also Henderson's comments on the manuscript itself: Box 11, folder 3, p. 136, and folder 4, pp. 175, 208.

99. Box 11, chap. 6, p. 62.

100. Casey Blake summarizes the contradiction in this way: "To suggest that the same technology, invented for profit and to further military conquest, would itself spawn a neotechnic order free of those same social forces flew in the face of Mumford's description of the symbiotic growth of a militaristic capitalism and industrial habits and technology" (129).

101. See the discussion of the European as well as the English roots of this tradition in *Raymond Williams: Politics and Letters. Interviews with the New Left Review* (London: Verso, 1981), 113–15. Duffey, "Mumford's Quest," 65, compares Mumford's concept of culture with that of Arnold (see also 61n).

102. Mumford, *Technics*, 324–25.

103. Mumford, "Appraisal," 530.

104. Raymond Williams considers the tendency to view art as object as a consequence of a base-and-superstructure theory of culture. "Now I think the true crisis in cultural theory, in our own time, is between this view of the work of art as object and the alternative view of art as practice." Williams, "Base and Superstructure in Marxist Cultural Theory," in Williams, *Problems in Materialism and Culture* (London: Verso, 1980), 46. (Originally published in *New Left Review* 82 (November–December 1973) and based on a lecture given in Montreal in April 1973.)

105. Mumford, "Technics and the Nature of Man," 311.

106. M.-H. Abensour, "Les Formes de l'Utopie socialiste-communiste" (thèse pour le doctorat d'état en science politique, Paris, 1973); cited by E. P. Thompson, "Romanticism, Moralism and Utopianism: The Case of William Morris," *New Left Review* 99 (September–October 1976): 83.

107. Raymond Williams, "Utopia and Science Fiction," in Williams, *Problems*, 203. (First published in *Science Fiction Studies* 5 (1978), Montreal.)

108. Box 11, folder 1.

JOHN L. THOMAS: LM, Benton MacKaye, and the Regional Vision

1. Thomas Adams et al., *Regional Plan of New York and Its Environs*, 2 vols. (New York: Regional Plan of New York, 1929, 1931) I:131, 408; II: 575–76.

2. Lewis Mumford, "Regions—To Live In," reprinted from *Survey Graphic* 7 (May 1925):151–52 in Carl Sussman, ed., *Planning the Fourth Migration: The Neglected Vision of the Regional Planning Association of America* (Cambridge: MIT Press, 1976), 92–93. For further discussion of Geddes's and Mumford's uses of the valley section, see Williams, this volume, passim.

3. Mumford, "Regions—To Live In," 92.

4. Percy MacKaye, *Epoch: The Life of Steele MacKaye, Genius of the Theatre, in Relation to His Times & Contemporaries* 2 vols. (New York: Boni & Liveright, 1927) 2:319.

5. Ibid., 2: 195–289.

6. Benton MacKaye, "Growth of a New Science," *The Survey* 86 (October 1950):439–452, reprinted in Paul T. Bryant, ed., *From Geography to Geotechnics* (Urbana: University of Illinois Press, 1968), 21–22. For an account of MacKaye's early years see Bryant's *The Quality of the Day: The Achievement of Benton MacKaye* (Ann Arbor: University Microfilms International 1965), passim.

7. See MacKaye's account of his Washington activities in "Growth of a New Science," reprinted in *From Geography to Geotechnics,* 35–38.

8. MacKaye is quoted in an interview with Bryant, *The Quality of the Day,* 118–119.

9. Benton MacKaye, "An Appalachian Trail: A Project in Regional Planning," *Journal of the American Institute of Architects* 9 (October 1921): 3–8.

10. MacKaye's explanation of his "Barbarian Utopia" and the way to achieve it appears in "Outdoor Culture—The Philosophy of Through Trails," *Landscape Architecture* 17 (April 1927):163–71, and is reprinted in Bryant, *From Geography to Geotechnics,* 169–79.

11. Lewis Mumford, *Sketches from Life: The Autobiography of Lewis Mumford* (Boston: Beacon Press, 1982), 340.

12. Mumford's article for *The Nation* published in 1919 is quoted in Sussman, ed., *Planning the Fourth Migration,* 13.

13. For Mumford's account of his origins, early childhood, and family life see *Sketches from Life,* chaps. 2–4. The quotations in this account appear on pp. 62, 16–18, 10.

14. Lewis Mumford, "Urban Notes," *Findings and Keepings: Analects for an Autobiography* (New York: Harcourt Brace Jovanovich, 1975), 25.

15. Mumford is quoted by John Fischer in "Schools for Equal Opportunity," Alvin Toffler, ed., *The Schoolhouse in the City* (New York: Praeger, 1968).

16. For an account of these years see *Sketches from Life,* 100–156, in particular 100–101, 133, 140–41, 151, 156.

17. Sir William Holford cites Mumford in his Foreword to Philip Mairet, *Pioneer of Sociology: The Life and Letters of Patrick Geddes* (London: Lund Humphries, 1957), xi–xii, xvi.

18. For Mumford's account of Cambridge and Boston in 1918, see *Sketches from Life,* 201–10.

19. Ibid., 202, 215, 218, 222, 276.

20. Lewis Mumford, *The Story of Utopias,* Compass edition (New York: Viking, 1950), 33–34. For a full and enlightening discussion of Geddes, Mumford, and the valley section, see Williams, this volume.

21. *Utopias* 280.

22. Lewis Mumford to Benton MacKaye, 18 December 1924, MacKaye Papers, Baker Library, Dartmouth College, Hanover, N.H. Selections from the Mumford-MacKaye correspondence are quoted with the permission of the Baker Library.

23. "Random Notes and Letters," *Findings and Keepings,* 161.

24. "Geneva Adventure," ibid., 94.

25. "Notes on Geneva," ibid., 96.

26. Lewis Mumford to Dorothy Cecilia Loch, 8 December 1925, ibid., 98–99.

27. Lewis Mumford, *Sticks and Stones: A Study of American Architecture and Civilization,* 2nd. rev. ed. (New York: Dover, 1955), 14.

28. Ibid., 28.

29. Ibid., 27.

30. Ibid., 60–61.

31. Ibid., 96.

32. Ibid., 125.

33. Ibid., 201.

34. Ibid., 230.

35. Lewis Mumford, "Introduction," Benton MacKaye, *The New Exploration: A Philosophy of Regional Planning* (New York: Harcourt Brace, 1928), xvi.

36. Lewis Mumford, "The Fourth Migration," in Sussman, *Planning the Fourth Migration,* 57.

37. Ibid., 58.

38. Ibid., 60.

39. Ibid., 62.

40. Benton MacKaye, "The New Exploration: Charting the Industrial Wilderness"; Sussman, *Planning the Fourth Migration,* 98.

41. Ibid., 106–10.

42. The exchange between Mumford and Adams, which originally apeared in *The New Republic,* 15, 22 June, 6 July 1932, is reprinted in Sussman, ibid., 224–67.

43. Mumford, *Sketches from Life,* 411.

44. For Mumford's account of his life in Sunnyside Gardens see ibid., 410–21.

45. Benton MacKaye to Lewis Mumford, 3 December 1926, MacKaye Papers.

46. Ibid.

47. Benton MacKaye to Lewis Mumford, 21 May 1927, MacKaye Papers.

48. Benton MacKaye to Lewis Mumford, 9 March 1927, MacKaye Papers.

49. Benton MacKaye to Lewis Mumford, 3 December 1926, MacKaye Papers.

50. Lewis Mumford to Benton MacKaye, 22 December 1925, MacKaye Papers.

51. Ibid.

52. Lewis Mumford, *The Golden Day: A Study in American Experience and Culture* (New York, Boni and Liveright, 1926), 1. For another discussion of Mumford's concept of the Golden Day, see Molesworth this volume.

53. *Golden Day,* 41.

54. Ibid.

55. Ibid., 41–42, 34, 37.

56. Ibid., 62–63.

57. Ibid., 40–41, 34, 37.

58. Ibid., 89–90.

59. Ibid., 142. Italics added.

60. Ibid., 130.

61. Benton MacKaye to Lewis Mumford, 3 December 1926, MacKaye Papers.

62. Lewis Mumford to Benton MacKaye, 25 July 1927, MacKaye Papers.

63. Benton MacKaye, *The New Exploration,* 50.

64. Ibid., 60–61.

65. Ibid., 63.

66. Ibid., 71–72 ff.

67. MacKaye discusses the controls and their effects on metropolitanism in chap. XII, "Controlling the Metropolitan Invasion," ibid., 168–200.

68. Ibid., 195.

69. Thoreau is quoted in ibid., 212. Mackaye's comment follows directly.

70. Lewis Mumford to Van Wyck Brooks, 30 July 1934; Robert E. Spiller, ed., *The Van Wyck Brooks Lewis Mumford Letters: The Record of a Literary Friendship, 1921–1963* (New York: E. P. Dutton, 1970), 107.

71. Lewis Mumford, "Random Notes and Personalia, 1960s," Lewis Mumford Papers, Special Collections, Van Pelt Library, University of Pennsylvania, Philadelphia. Quoted with permission.

HOWARD P. SEGAL: Mumford's Alternatives to the Megamachine: Critical Utopianism, Regionalism, and Decentralization

1. On the nature of the megamachine in Lewis Mumford's work, see Miller, this volume. See also, Marx's insightful criticisms of Mumford's megamachine as both metaphor and reality in his essay, this volume. Those criticisms do not, however, affect the burden of my essay.

2. Regarding Mumford and Odum see Tullos, this volume.

3. The full title was *La Technique ou l'enjeu du siècle* (Paris: Librairie Armand Colin, 1954); translated literally, it means *Technique: The Stake of This Century*. The reason for the new English title is unclear, but commercial considerations may have been the cause.

4. Mumford to Melvin Kranzberg, 20 April 1968, Mumford Correspondence, Lewis Mumford Papers, Special Collections, Van Pelt Library, University of Pennsylvania. The review appeared in the *Virginia Quarterly Review*.

5. Mumford to Eric Larrabee, 15 September 1957, Mumford Papers. Larrabee was then Editor of *Harper's Magazine*.

6. Mumford, *The Culture of Cities* (1938; reprinted New York: Harcourt Brace Jovanovich, 1970), 492. Meanwhile, in cases where he analyzes the potentially positive aspects of technology—as in *Technics and Civilization*—only to have been overly optimistic in retrospect, he nonetheless congratulates himself in his 1963 new introduction to that work for somehow having anticipated three decades earlier technology's potentially negative aspects. Conversely, however, in his 1959 reappraisal of that same book he laments his retrospectively naïve hopes for transcending technology and, as a partial cause of that regret, his earlier failure to treat atomic power more seriously. See Mumford, "An Appraisal of Lewis Mumford's *Technics and Civilization* (1934)," *Daedalus* 88 (Summer 1959): 532–34.

7. See Mumford, "Fashions Change in Utopia," *New Republic* 47 (16 June 1926): 114–15.

8. Ironically, the model garden city shown in the 1939 film "The City," for which Mumford wrote his narrative, has since been criticized for its sterile, stagnant qualities and for its resemblance to too many modern suburban communities.

9. Mumford, *Findings and Keepings: Analects for an Autobiography* (New York: Harcourt Brace Jovanovich, 1975), 373.

10. Mumford, *The Story of Utopias* (1922; reprinted New York: Viking Compass Books, 1962), new Preface, 7. A good example of Bloch's writing on utopianism is *A Philosophy of the Future*, tr. John Cumming (New York: Herder and Herder, 1970), esp. 84–144.

11. Mumford to Catherine Kraus Bauer, July 1930, reprinted in *Findings and Keepings*, 353. See also his note there regarding his use of this phrase elsewhere.

12. Mumford, *The Story of Utopias*, new Preface, 6, 7.

13. As political theorist George Kateb puts it so well, "There is not, for the most part, skepticism about the capacity of modern technology and natural science to

execute the most vaulting ambitions of utopianism; on the contrary, there is a dread it will" (*Utopia and Its Enemies* (New York: Free Press 1963), 14–15).

14. Mumford, "Bellamy's Accurate Utopia," *New Republic* 68 (26 August 1931): 51. This is a retrospective review of the book, an updating of his treatment of it from *The Story of Utopias*.

15. Mumford, *The Story of Utopias*, 169; the quotation is from the book's original edition.

16. Mumford, *The Myth of the Machine: II. The Pentagon of Power* (New York: Harcourt Brace Jovanovich, 1970), 229.

17. See my *Technological Utopianism in American Culture* (Chicago: University of Chicago Press, 1985), 2–7.

18. Mumford, *The Pentagon of Power*, 212.

19. Ibid., 223.

20. Marcuse's position is summarized in an essay interestingly entitled, "The End of Utopia," in his *Five Lectures: Psychoanalysis, Politics, and Utopia*, tr. Jeremy J. Shapiro and Shierry M. Weber (Boston: Beacon, 1970), 62–82.

21. Mumford, *Findings and Keepings*, 373.

22. Mumford to Arthur C. Clarke, 24 May 1975, Mumford Papers. See Clarke's criticism of Mumford in his *Profiles of the Future: An Inquiry into the Limits of the Possible*, 2d ed. (New York: Harper and Row, 1972), 94–97. Mumford does praise Fuller's "aerodynamic motor car" or dymaxion car in *Technics and Civilization* (1934; reprinted New York: Harcourt, Brace and World, 1963), 446 and illustration #2 between 276–77. But he criticizes Fuller's "completely self-sufficient" dymaxion house as leading to excessive social isolation in his unpublished manuscript, "Form and Personality," Mumford Papers, Box 8, folder 6, IJb. Ironically, Fuller's own mixed review of *Technics and Civilization* in *The Nation* 138 (6 June 1934): 652, criticizes Mumford for not understanding inventors' "inspiration." For an interesting comparison of the two men, see Allan Temko, "Which Guide to the Promised Land: Fuller or Mumford," *Horizon* 10 (Summer 1968): 25–30.

23. Mumford to Edward Cornish, 19 April and 12 July 1976, Mumford Papers.

24. Mumford, *The Story of Utopias*, 306.

25. See Thomas's illumination of this dimension of Mumford's first book in his essay, this volume, 24–25.

26. Mumford, *The Story of Utopias*, 281.

27. Mumford, *The Culture of Cities*, 346.

28. See, for example, the reviews by F. Taylor Ostrander in *The Journal of Political Economy* 43 (June 1935): 419–21, and by David Ramsey in *Partisan Review* 1 (June–July 1934): 56–59.

29. Mumford, *The Culture of Cities*, 303. As he claims in *Technics and Civilization*, "the organic has become visible again even within the mechanical complex," 6.

30. For elaboration on Mumford's use and misuse of organicism, see Marx's essay in this volume. See Werner Stark, *The Fundamental Forms of Social Thought* (London: Routledge and Kegan Paul, 1962), for a comprehensive study of the organic and mechanical conceptions of the social order and of the changing relationship over time between them. On the nostalgia of Mumford and other "urbanologists" of the 1920s and 1930s for smaller American cities prior to the closing of the rural frontier, see Zane L. Miller and Patricia M. Melvin, *The Urbanization of Modern America: A Brief History*, 2d ed. (New York: Harcourt Brace Jovanovich, 1987), 169–70.

31. Mumford to George Weller, 1939 (no specific date given), Mumford Papers.

32. On these experiments, see my "'Little Plants in the Country': Henry Ford's Village Industries and the Beginning of Decentralized Technology in Modern America," in *Prospects: The Annual of American Culture Studies*, ed. Jack Salzman, 13 (New York: Cambridge University Press, 1988), 181–223.

33. Mumford, *Technics and Civilization*, 226.

34. Waldemar Kaempffert, review of *Technics and Civilization*, *New York Times Book Review* (29 April 1934): 17. In this regard see Mumford's later hopes for successful industrial, educational, and demographic decentralization in North Carolina in his "A Thought for a Growing South," *The Southern Packet: A Monthly Review of Southern Books and Ideas* 5 (April 1949): 1–5. I am indebted to Allen Tullos for bringing this article to my attention.

35. Mumford, "Thirty Years Before McLuhan," in *Findings and Keepings*, 328–30; these are excerpts from *Technics and Civilization*. See also his criticisms of McLuhan in *The Pentagon of Power*, 295–97.

36. Mumford, *The Pentagon of Power*, illustration #5 between 180–81.

37. Mumford, "If I Were Dictator," *The Nation* 83 (9 December 1933): 631, 632, 632. The essay was one of a series that publication ran with the same title.

38. Mumford, Foreword, *Planned Society: Yesterday, Today, Tomorrow*, ed. Findlay MacKenzie (New York: Prentice-Hall, 1937), x.

39. On decentralization's varied meanings and applications today, see Langdon Winner, "Decentralization Clarified," in his *The Whale and the Reactor: A Search for Limits in an Age of High Technology* (Chicago: University of Chicago Press, 1986), 85–97. Winner is also properly skeptical of decentralization as a panacea.

40. Mumford, *Findings and Keepings*, 381.

41. Although Mumford, as quoted, uses the term "human scale" at least as early as his 1933 *Nation* essay, see also Kirkpatrick Sale's *Human Scale* (New York: Coward, McCann, and Geoghegan, 1980), which praises Mumford, among others, for advocating and practicing that philosophy.

ALLEN TULLOS: The Politics of Regional Development: LM and Howard W. Odum

1. Lewis Mumford, *The Myth of the Machine: II. The Pentagon of Power*, (New York: Harcourt Brace Jovanovich, 1970), 429.

2. Ian McHarg, *Design with Nature* (Philadelphia: Natural History Press, 1969).

3. See Alan Trachtenberg, "Mumford in the Twenties: The Historian as Artist," *Salmagundi* 49 (1980): 29–34.

4. These essays are collected in Lewis Mumford, *Architecture as a Home for Man*, ed. Jeanne M. Davern (New York: Architectural Record Books, 1975), 63–101.

5. Lewis Mumford, "A Thought for a Growing South," *The Southern Packet* 5 (April 1949): 2.

6. See Anthony P. Dunbar, *Against the Grain: Southern Radicals and Prophets, 1929–1959* (Charlottesville: University Press of Virginia, 1981). And see "Folk, Region, and Society in the Carolina Piedmont," chapter eight in my "The Habits of Industry: A Study of White Culture, Protestant Temperament, and the Emergence of the Carolina Piedmont," (Ph.D. dissertation, Yale University, 1985). "I was a regionalist and still believe in pluralism and decentralization," says Highlander Center co-founder Myles Horton. "I think their [Odum and his colleagues] whole concept of regionalism was to do things very step by stepish, not rock the

boat; bring the whole state along, all the corporations, all the big farmers, all the other black and white people at the bottom, bring them all along. They had the fiction that everybody was in one class." Interview by author with Myles Horton, 13 July 1981, New Market, Tennessee.

7. Correspondence from Lewis Mumford to author, 1 September 1973. Also see the definitions of regionalism in Thomas, this volume.

8. Katherine Jocher, "The Regional Laboratory for Social Research and Planning," *In Search of the Regional Balance of America,* eds. Howard Odum and Katherine Jocher (Chapel Hill: University of North Carolina Press, 1945), 43–44. This volume is a special issue of *Social Forces,* 23 (1945). Among its contents is a list of all Institute publications and manuscripts from 1922 through 1944 (pp. 60–87).

For other views of Odum (b. 1884) and his work, see Howard W. Odum, *An American Epoch: Southern Portraiture in the National Picture* (New York: Henry Holt, 1930); George Brown Tindall, "The Significance of Howard W. Odum to Southern History," *Journal of Southern History* 24 (August 1958): 285–307; Alexander Karanikas, "The Aesthetics of Regionalism," chap. 6 in his *Tillers of a Myth: Southern Agrarians as Social and Literary Critics* (Madison: University of Wisconsin Press. 1966); Harvey A. Kantor, "Howard W. Odum: The Implications of Folk, Planning, and Regionalism," *American Journal of Sociology* 79 (September 1973): 278–295; Wayne Douglas Brazil, "Howard W. Odum, The Building Years, 1884–1930" (Ph.D. dissertation, Harvard University, 1975); Morton Sosna, "The Silent South of Howard Odum," chap. 3 in his *In Search of the Silent South* (New York: Columbia University Press, 1977); chaps. 2–4 of Michael O'Brien's *The Idea of the American South* (Baltimore: Johns Hopkins University Press, 1979); Guy B. and Guion Johnson, *Research in Service to Society* (Chapel Hill: University of North Carolina Press, 1980); chaps. 5 and 10 in Daniel Joseph Singal, *The War Within: From Victorian to Modernist Thought in the South, 1919–1945* (Chapel Hill: University of North Carolina Press, 1982); and Daniel T. Rodgers, "Regionalism and the Burdens of Progress," *Region, Race, and Reconstruction,* eds. J. Morgan Kousser and James McPherson (New York: Oxford University Press, 1982), 3–26. For further discussion of the work of the Institute for Research in Social Science and its relation to the industrialization of the Carolina Piedmont see Tullos, "Folk, Region, and Society in the Carolina Piedmont."

9. V. O. Key, *Southern Politics* (New York: Knopf, 1949), 211.

10. Louis R. Wilson, *The University of North Carolina: The Making of a Modern University* (Chapel Hill: University of North Carolina Press, 1957), 420; Archibald Henderson, *The Campus of the First State University* (Chapel Hill: University of North Carolina Press, 1949), 478.

11. Wayne Douglas Brazil, "Howard W. Odum, The Building Years, 1884–1930," 121–22. Interview with Guy Johnson by Archie Green, Chapel Hill, 15 November 1979, Piedmont Social History Project, Southern Oral History Program Papers, Southern Historical Collection, University of North Carolina at Chapel Hill.

12. Carl Sussman, ed., *Planning the Fourth Migration: The Neglected Vision of the Regional Planning Association of America* (Cambridge: MIT Press, 1976), 22.

13. See Willard B. Gatewood, Jr., "Embattled Scholar: Howard W. Odum and the Fundamentalists, 1925–1927," *Journal of Southern History* 31 (November 1965): 375–392. Johnson and Johnson, *Research in Service to Society,* 38–43.

14. Donald Davidson, *The Attack on Leviathan* (Chapel Hill: University of North Carolina Press, 1938), 52–55, 324–27.

15. W. J. Cash, *The Mind of the South* (New York: Knopf, 1941), 333.

16. Lewis Mumford, *The Culture of Cities* (New York: Harcourt Brace Jovanovich, 1938), 361. Essential to an understanding of Mumford's regional vision are "The Regional Framework of Civilization" and "The Politics of Regional Development," chaps. 5 and 6 of *The Culture of Cities,* 300–401.

17. Lewis Mumford, "The Theory and Practice of Regionalism," *The Sociological Review* 20 (January 1928): 22.

18. Philip Boardman, *Patrick Geddes: Maker of the Future* (Chapel Hill: University of North Carolina Press, 1944), 169, 109, 216–17, 406–7; Lewis Mumford, "The Disciple's Rebellion," *Encounter* 27 (September 1966): 11–21.

19. Boardman, *Patrick Geddes,* 209, 216-17, 169.

20. Charles Zeublin, "The World's First Sociological Laboratory," *The American Journal of Sociology* 4 (March 1899): 577–92. Patrick Geddes, "Talks from the Outlook Tower," *Survey* 53 and 54 (1 February, 1 April, 1 June, 1 July, 1 August, 1 September 1925).

21. Mumford, "Theory and Practice of Regionalism," 30. See the discussion of Geddes, Mumford, and the valley section in Williams, this volume, passim.

22. Mumford to author, 17 February 1977. Not the least of the Scot's contributions was Odum's favorite definition of planning: "the bridging of the distance between science and knowledge and practical problems." See Odum's quoting Geddes in "Patrick Geddes Heritage," 279; Odum's "From Community Studies to Regionalism," in Odum and Jocher, *In Search of the Regional Balance of America,* 3, where Odum uses the expression as his own; and Odum's "The Promise of Regionalism," in Merrill Jensen, ed., *Regionalism in America* (Madison: University of Wisconsin Press, 1951), 405, where Odum again attributes it to Geddes.

23. Howard W. Odum, "G. Stanley Hall," *The Journal of Social Forces* 3 (November 1924): 139, 144–45. Howard W. Odum, "Patrick Geddes' Heritage to 'Making the Future'" *Social Forces* 22 (March 1944):279.

24. *Survey Graphic* 7 (May 1925). Interview with Lewis Mumford by author, 6 May 1977, Amenia, New York.

25. See "Constructive Ventures," a brief article praising Odum's compilation of a citizenship manual for women in *Survey* 47 (October 1921): 118.

26. See Arthur Kellog to Odum, 23 November 1923, in Howard W. Odum Papers.

27. Howard Odum, *Man's Quest for Social Guidance* (New York: Henry Holt, 1927), 515–16.

28. Lewis Mumford, "Regions To Live In," reprinted in Carl Sussman, *Planning the Fourth Migration,* 90.

29. Odum to Moore C. Tussey, 24 February 1926; Tussey to Odum, 5 March 1926; Richard Thornton to Odum, 18 March 1926, all in Odum Papers.

30. Mumford to author, 17 February 1977.

31. Patrick Geddes, "Talk from the Outlook Tower," *Survey* 53 and 54 (1 February, 1 April, 1 June, 1 July, 1 August, 1 September 1925).

32. Mumford, "Who Is Patrick Geddes," *Survey* 53 (February 1925): 524.

33. Letters from Odum to UNC Press Director W. T. Couch, 27 January 1943 and 6 March 1943 in UNC Press "Author's Files" at the Southern Historical Collection, UNC Chapel Hill. Mumford points out that he suggested the UNC Press to Boardman, letter to author, 7 April 1977.

34. Howard Odum, "Patrick Geddes' Heritage to 'The Making of the Future,'" *Social Forces* 22 (March 1944): 275–81.

35. O'Brien, *The Idea of the South,* 36–37. Sumner's *Folkways: A Study of the Socio-*

logical Importance of Usages, Manners, Customs, Mores and Morals first appeared in 1907.

36. Howard W. Odum, "Folk and Regional Conflict as a Field of Sociological Study," Presidential address presented before the American Sociological Society, December 1930, *Publications of the American Sociological Society* 25 (May 1931): 1–17; reprinted in Jocher and Johnson, *Folk, Region and Society,* 239–55. This excerpt comes from 243. Also see Michael O'Brien, *The Idea of the American South,* 64.

37. Donald Davidson, *The Attack on Leviathan* (Chapel Hill: University of North Carolina Press 1938), 41.

38. See Turner's "Is Sectionalism Dying Away," a paper read before the American Sociological Society on 28 December 1907, reprinted in Frederick Jackson Turner, *The Significance of Sections in American History* (New York: Henry Holt, 1932), 287–314.

39. Turner's *Yale Review* essay is also reprinted in *The Significance of the Sections in American History.* This quotation is from pp. 321, 326.

40. Edward A. Ross, "Sectionalism and Its Avoidance," *Social Forces* 2 (May 1924): 484–87.

41. Howard Odum, "Regionalism vs. Sectionalism in the South's Place in the National Economy," *Social Forces* 12 (March 1934): 338–42.

42. Lewis Mumford to author, 17 February 1977. For accounts of the RPAA, see Roy Lubove, *Community Planning in the 1920s: The Contribution of the Regional Planning Association of America* (Pittsburgh: University of Pittsburgh Press, 1963) and Sussman, *Fourth Migration.*

An important statement from the 1930s on European regionalism is Hedwig Hintze's "Regionalism," Vol. 13, *Encyclopedia of the Social Sciences* (New York: Macmillan, 1934): 208–18. Also, Mumford's "The Theory and Practice of Regionalism," *Sociological Review* 20 (April 1928): 131–41.

43. Odum, "From Community Studies to Regionalism," 13; Mumford, *The Culture of Cities,* 349.

44. Odum, "A Southern Promise," Introduction to *Southern Pioneers in Social Interpretation* (Chapel Hill: University of North Carolina Press, 1929), 467–81. In an article for *Social Forces* 8 (December 1929) entitled "The Concept of the Region" (208–28), Vance points to several geographers who influenced his exploration of regionalism, including several familiar to Mumford: Vidal de la Blache, Brunhes, and Patrick Geddes. Vance expresses the hope here that, given time, American cultural geographers can "produce results equal to the best work of the French School." Some of the best of Vance's writing can be found in John Shelton Reed and Daniel Singal, eds., *Regionalism and the South* (Chapel Hill: University of North Carolina Press, 1982).

45. "Memorandum" from Vance to Odum, 21 January 1938. Rupert B. Vance Papers, Southern Historical Collection, University of North Carolina at Chapel Hill. Thanks to Jerrold Hirsch for calling my attention to this item.

46. Johnson and Johnson, *Research in Service to Society,* 121.

EUGENE ROCHBERG-HALTON: The Transformation of Social Theory

1. Francesca Rochberg-Halton, "Canonicity in Cuneiform Texts," *Journal of Cuneiform Studies* 36 (1984): 127–44.

2. Emile Durkheim, *The Elementary Forms of the Religious Life,* translated from the French by Joseph Ward Swain (New York: Free Press, 1915 [1912]), 475.

3. Karl Marx, *Capital,* ed. Frederick Engels (New York: International Publishers, 1967 [1867]), 1:380.

4. Lewis Mumford, *The Condition of Man* (New York: Harcourt, Brace, 1944), 337, 332. Also see *The Myth of the Machine: II. The Pentagon of Power* (New York: Harcourt Brace Jovanovich, 1970), 353.

5. Lewis Mumford, *The Myth of the Machine: I. Technics and Human Development* (New York: Harcourt Brace Jovanovich, 1967), 191.

6. Lewis Mumford, *The Condition of Man,* 159–60.

7. Mumford, *Technics and Human Development,* 272–73.

8. Max Weber, "Objectivity in Social Science and Social Policy," in *The Methodology of the Social Sciences: Max Weber,* translated and edited by Edward A. Shils and Henry A. Finch (New York: Free Press, 1949 [original essay 1904]), 81.

9. Eugene Rochberg-Halton, *Meaning and Modernity: Social Theory in the Pragmatic Attitude* (Chicago: University of Chicago Press, 1986).

10. Mumford, *Technics and Human Development,* 51.

11. Ibid., 62.

12. Arthur Koestler, *The Ghost in the Machine* (Chicago: Henry Regnery, 1967); *Janus: A Summing Up* (New York: Vintage Books, 1978); Susanne K. Langer, *Mind, An Essay on Human Feeling* (Baltimore: Johns Hopkins University Press, 1988 [Abridged edition, original three volumes published 1967, 1972, 1982]).

13. Eugene Rochberg-Halton, "On the Life-Concept in Social Theory," *Comparative Social Research* 11 (1989): 319–342.

14. Eugene Rochberg-Halton, "Life, Literature, and Sociology in Turn-of-the-Century Chicago," in *Consuming Visions: Accumulation and Display of Goods in America, 1880–1920,* ed. S. J. Bronner (New York: W. W. Norton, 1989).

15. Lewis Coser, Review of *The Pentagon of Power* by Lewis Mumford, *Contemporary Sociology* 1 (1972): 38–39.

16. Eugene Rochberg-Halton, "Jürgen Habermas's Theory of Communicative Etherealization," in *Symbolic Interaction,* 12 (1989): 143–63.

DONALD L. MILLER *The Myth of the Machine: I. Technics and Human Development*

1. Lewis Mumford, Random Notes, 30 July 1965 (hereafter cited as RN) Lewis Mumford Papers, Special Collections, Van Pelt Library, University of Pennsylvania (hereafter cited as LM Papers); "S.S. Mauretania," 1961, RN, 9 March 1961, RN, 11 July 1963, all in LM Papers.

2. Mumford, "Authoritarian and Democratic Technics," *Technology and Culture* 5 (Winter 1964):1–8; this paper was Mumford's speech at the Fund for the Republic Tenth Anniversary Convocation held in New York in January 1963.

3. LM-Benton MacKaye, 25 October 1963, Benton MacKaye Collection, Dartmouth College Library, Hanover, N. H.

4. Mumford, RN, 11 Sept. 1963, LM Papers.

5. LM-MacKaye, 31 May 1964, MacKaye Papers.

6. Mumford, *My Works and Days: A Personal Chronicle* (New York: Harcourt Brace Jovanovich, 1976), 475; Mumford, transcript of interview with Edwin Newman on Speaking Freely, WNBC, aired 10 January 1971, copy in LM Papers; *The Myth of the Machine: I. Technics and Human Development* (New York: Harcourt, Brace and World, 1967). Hereafter referred to as *Human Development.*

7. Mumford, "Prologue to Our Time," *The New Yorker,* 10 March 1975, p. 45.

8. Mumford, *Human Development*, 189, 234.

9. Van Wyck Brooks, "On Creating a Usable Past," *The Dial*, 11 April 1918, p. 338.

10. Mumford, notes for "The Myth of the Machine," LM Papers; Mumford, *Works and Days*, 476.

11. Mumford, *Human Development*, 199; Mumford, *Works and Days*, 476.

12. Mumford, *Human Development*, 188.

13. Ibid., 211; Mumford, *The Myth of the Machine: II. The Pentagon of Power* (New York: Harcourt Brace Jovanovich, 1970), 12. Hereafter referred to as *Pentagon*.

14. Mumford, *Human Development*, 224.

15. Ibid., 189, 230.

16. Ibid., 258–60; Mumford, *The Transformations of Man* (New York: Harper & Bros., 1956).

17. Mumford, *Human Development*, 258–60.

18. Ibid., 263, 293–94.

19. LM-Henry Murray, n.d., Henry Murray Papers, Cambridge, Mass.

20. Mumford, *Human Development*, 49–52.

21. Ibid., 49–52, 368–69.

22. Quoted in ibid., 61.

23. Ibid., 65.

24 LM-Murray, 4 August 1963, Henry Murray Papers, Cambridge, Mass.

25. Noam Chomsky provides scholarly verification for this idea that language developed independent of tool-making and was probably more important. In his eagerness to overthrow the so-called Marxian idea of man as a tool-maker, Mumford relied too much on the disciples and popularizers of Marx and Engels. In *The Origin of the Family, Private Property and the State*, Engels, for example, argues that the appearance of speech was the most important event of prehistory. And as Erich Fromm pointed out to Mumford after he read *Human Development*, Marx was influenced by Vico, and for him the concept of work, not the concept of tool-making, which he called the Yankee idea of Benjamin Franklin, was essential. "Actually I think your own position," Fromm remarked to Mumford, "is in no way in contrast to Marx's, but in many ways close to it." (Erich Fromm-LM, 19 January 1971, LM Papers.)

26. See LM., review of Carl G. Jung's *Memories, Dreams, Reflections* (New York: Pantheon) in *The New Yorker* XL (23 May 1964): 155–85; and Mumford, *Human Development*, 1–97.

27. Mumford, *Pentagon*, 9–10, 430.

28. Mumford, *Human Development*, 11.

29. LM, review of *Memories*, 185.

30. Mumford, RN, 26 June 1963, LM Papers.

31. Quoted in Mumford's review of *Memories*, 177–78.

32. LM, review of *Memories*, 178.

33. Ibid.; Mumford, *Human Development*, 259.

34. LM, review of *Memories*, 184.

35. Quoted in ibid., 185.

36. LM-Bruno Zevi, 12 October 1973, LM Papers.

37. See Waldo Frank, "Views on Human Nature," a review of Mumford, *The Conduct of Life*, in *Saturday Review of Literature* 34 (22 September 1951).

38. LM-Roderick Seidenberg, 18 February 1969, LM Papers.

39. LM-Frederic J. Osborn, 31 July 1951, Frederic J. Osborn Mss., Welwyn Garden City, England.

40. LM-Seidenberg, 1969, LM Papers.

LEO MARX: Lewis Mumford: Prophet of Organicism

1. "The Case Against Modern Architecture," in *The Lewis Mumford Reader,* ed. Donald L. Miller (New York: Pantheon, 1986), 82.

2. Ibid.

3. Re-reading *The Golden Day* (Boston: Beacon, 1957) now one realizes that Mumford was more influential than has been generally recognized in shaping the canon of classic American literature that took form around the time of World War II and has now come under attack for its narrowness. Fifteen years before F. O. Matthiessen's *American Renaissance* (New York: Oxford University Press 1941), often cited as the most influential single work in shaping that version of the canon, Mumford had focused upon the same five writers—Emerson, Thoreau, Whitman, Hawthorne, and Melville—singled out by Matthiessen. In his Preface, to be sure, Matthiessen acknowledges that debt to Mumford, but he fails to mention Mumford's prior emphasis on one of his own major themes, namely, the "organic principle" as a decisive moral and aesthetic standard to which many nineteenth-century American artists, artisans, architects, and writers were committed.

4. Jacoby contends that the role of "public intellectual" has been rendered obsolete by the triumph of academic specialization. *The Last Intellectuals: American Culture in the Age of Academe* (New York: Basic Books, 1987).

5. Thomas S. W. Lewis has reviewed Mumford's uneasy relations with the world of professional scholarship in "Mumford and the Academy," *Salmagundi* 49 (1980):99–111.

6. *International Encyclopedia of the Social Sciences,* 2d ed., s.v. "Patrick Geddes."

7. *The Myth of the Machine: I. Technics and Human Development* (New York: Harcourt, Brace & World, 1966), 16–17.

8. Mumford wrote the letter in 1926, the year after the publication of Whitehead's book. *My Works and Days, A Personal Chronicle* (New York: Harcourt Brace Jovanovich, 1979), 113. The "solution" with which he credited Whitehead was to give precedence to the biological, or "organic" properties of the environment over those of "mechanism." He said that Whitehead's book "indicates the important modification of the old physical concepts by biology. . . ." There seems to be a close affinity between this line of thought and the idea of "organismic biology," or "organismalism" (a term coined by the zoologist W. E. Ritter in 1919), which enjoyed a considerable vogue during the 1920s. Although this doctrine is like vitalism in its insistence on a teleological concept of reality, it does not, like vitalism, posit the existence in the organism of some nonphysical but substantial entity. Organismic biology, in short, carries none of the mystical or supernatural implications of vitalism. Morton O. Beckner, "Organismic Biology," *The Encyclopedia of Philosophy,* (New York: Macmillan, 1967), V: 549–51.

9. *Science and the Modern World* (New York: Macmillan, 1925), 111, 138. For a comprehensive theory of romanticism as having at its center "the shift from conceiving the cosmos as a static mechanism to conceiving it as a dynamic organism," see Morse Peckham, "Toward a Theory of Romanticism," *Publications of the Modern Language Association* 66 (1951): 5–23.

10. A version of this opposition which has many close affinities with Mumford's social views (and to which he refers in *The City in History*) is the nineteenth-century German sociologist Ferdinand Tonnies's famous distinction between *Gemeinschaft*

and *Gesellschaft,* between, roughly, community (a relatively small-scale, traditional mode of organization based on "natural will" which "should be understood as a living organism") and society (a larger scale, bureaucratic form of organization based on "rational will" which should be understood "as a mechanical aggregate and artifact"). See Ferdinand Tonnies, *Community & Society,* Charles P. Loomis, ed. and tr. (East Lansing: Michigan State University Press, 1957), 35. There are a number of similar formulations in nineteenth-century social thought, each in essence a binary system more or less homologous with the distinction between organism and machine, or between organic and mechanic form, including Maine's concept of status and contract societies; Spencer's militant and industrial forms; Durkheim's organic and mechanical solidarity; Cooley's primary and secondary groups; Odum's folk and state; and Redfield's folk-urban continuum. For an interesting comparative analysis of these conceptions, see John C. McKinney and Charles P. Loomis, "The Application of Gemeinschaft and Gesellschaft As Related to Other Typologies," ibid., 12–29.

11. For a useful summary of Geddes's biological ideas, see Jill Conway, "Stereotypes of Femininity in a Theory of Sexual Evolution," *Victorian Studies* 14 (1970): 47–62.

12. Donald A. Stauffer, ed., *The Selected Poetry and Prose of Samuel Taylor Coleridge* (New York: Random House, 1951), 432.

13. "The Case Against 'Modern Architecture'" first appeared in *Architectural Record* in 1962, and is reprinted in Miller, *Mumford Reader,* 73–83.

14. "Principles of Medieval Town Planning," in *The City in History* (New York: Harcourt, Brace & World, 1961), 299–305.

15. "The Structure of Baroque Power," ibid., 344–74.

16. *The Myth of the Machine: II. The Pentagon of Power* (New York: Harcourt Brace Jovanovich, 1970), 430.

17. Donald L. Miller, *Lewis Mumford: A Life* (New York: Weidenfield & Nicolson, 1989), 163.

18. One of the chief claims for the superiority of organic systems rests upon their allegedly "holistic" character—the fact that the functioning of the whole organism cannot be understood as the mere sum of the functioning of the parts. No part of a bird can fly. The implication is that in an organic system the whole is everything, the parts nothing, whereas in a mechanical system the whole is nothing more than a collection of parts. But is it clear that the functioning of a complex machine is, in this sense, any less holistic? No part of an airplane can fly either. See Beckner, *op. cit.*

19. Miller, *Mumford Reader,* 65.

20. *The Brown Decades: A Study of the Arts in America, 1865–1895* (New York: Dover Publications, 1971), 46–47.

21. *Technics and Civilization* (New York: Harcourt, Brace, 1934), 12–18.

22. Ibid., 12.

23. *The Myth of the Machine: I. Technics and Human Development,* 189. The quotations on "the megamachine" that follow are drawn from pages 189–211.

24. *The Golden Day: A Study of American Literature and Culture* (Boston: Beacon Press, 1957), 49.

25. *Technics and Human Development,* 11. Donald L. Miller confirms the fact that Mumford was studying Jung in the early 1960s.

26. When applied to social systems, "organic" often takes on the import of "natural," hence an organic society is one that has grown rather than been made; the conservative implications are indicated by its use, in the work of Burke, Carlyle,

Coleridge, and many others, in criticizing revolutionary programs or societies as "artificial," in opposition to the "natural," usually hierarchical and patriarchal, order of things; and this later was extended to the contrasts between primarily agricultural and primarily industrial (or mechanical) social systems. See "Organic," in Raymond Williams, *Keywords: A Vocabulary of Culture and Society* (New York: Oxford University Press, 1976), 189–92.

27. Mumford, "The Modern City," *Forms and Functions of Twentieth-Century Architecture*, ed. Talbot Hamlin (New York, Columbia University Press, 1952), 4: 797.

28. *The Conduct of Life* (New York: Harcourt, Brace, 1951), 223–24. Emphasis added.

STANISLAUS VON MOOS: The Visualized Machine Age

1. Frank Yerbury, *Modern European Buildings*, in *Creative Art*, 4 (May 1929), and Lewis Mumford, "Steel-Chimneys and Beet-Top Cupolas" (review of Erich Mendelsohn, *Russland, Europa, Amerika*), Lewis Mumford Papers, Special Collections, Van Pelt Library, University of Pennsylvania.

During the preparation of this article I was greatly assisted by Jane Morley and Robert Wojtowicz from the University of Pennsylvania, who not only helped me find my way in the Mumford collection at the Van Pelt Library, University of Pennsylvania, but also directed my attention to many relevant sources. Furthermore, I am grateful to Dr. Socratis Georgiadis for his assistance during a visit to the Giedion archives at the Institut für Geschichte und Theorie der Architektur at the ETH, Zürich, and especially to Richard Ingersoll, who has made useful suggestions concerning Mumford as a critic of architecture. Preliminary versions of this paper have been presented at the Lewis Mumford Symposium at the University of Pennsylvania (November 1987) and at the Institute of Fine Arts, New York University (May 1988).

2. There were only fifteen pages with illustrations on glossy paper in the first edition of *Technics and Civilization* (1934); in the later paperback edition (New York and London, 1962) the same number of illustrations is spread over twice the number of pages, so that the individual pictures are larger and the general impression is less cramped.

3. Cf. note 1.

4. All on one page (in the original edition of *Technics and Civilization*), whereas these illustrations are spread over two pages in the later paperback edition (see note 2).

5. In his autobiography, Mumford speaks of "the contrapuntal dynamics of steel and stone that characterized the original Brooklyn Bridge." It was from there, as he recalls, that one night in March 1915, "the world . . . opened before me, challenging me, beckoning me, demanding something of me that it would take more than a lifetime to give. . . ." in *Sketches from Life: The Early Years* (New York, 1982), 334, 130. Mumford's response to Brooklyn Bridge has been discussed by Alan Trachtenberg in *Brooklyn Bridge. Fact and Symbol* (Chicago and London, 1965), 139 and passim.

6. The source of this illustration is Joseph August Lux, *Ingenieur-Aesthetik* (Munich, 1910) (plate vii), a book that Mumford listed in his Bibliography as "one of the early studies" (on engineering-aesthetics).

7. "Long before I responded to buildings as practical or symbolic construc-

tions, I was jotting down my visual impressions of rooftop watertanks, sheetiron cornices, spindly tenement fire escapes—or chance human figures," Mumford wrote in *Sketches from Life: The Early Years* (see note 5), 334. This book contains a large number of drawings and watercolors. It would be interesting to know whether the Mumford archives contain correspondence and other documents relevant for a reconstruction of his actual interest in questions of page-layout and similar matters.

8. Cf. *Vers une architecture* (Paris, 1923), 65–80. In the Bibliography of *Technics and Civilization,* Mumford refers to the book with the following accurate—if slightly idiosyncratic—comment on the architect's significance: "Following the work of Sullivan and Wright and Loos more than a generation later, Le Corbusier re-discovered the machine for himself and is perhaps the chief polemical advocate of machine forms" (p. 462 in the paperback edition).

9. Mumford, *Technics and Civilization,* 1934; quoted after the new edition (New York and Burlingame, 1963), 352.

10. Le Corbusier, *L'Art décoratif d'aujourd'hui* (Paris, 1925), 27, 36, 94, 95 (English translation Cambridge, Mass, 1987). Mumford refers to Le Corbusier's book in the Bibliography of *Technics and Civilization.* Its contents were previously published in the form of articles in the magazine *L'Esprit Nouveau.*

11. Lewis Mumford, "Architecture as a Home for Man," *Architectural Record* (February 1968), 113–16.

12. Roland Barthes, "Image, raison, déraison", in *L'Univers de l'Encyclopédie* (Paris, 1964) (a choice of 130 plates from the *Encyclopédie,* Vol. I, 1964, introduced by Roland Barthes), quoted from *Roland Barthes. Le Texte et l'image,* exhibition catalogue (Paris, 1986), 39–47.

The two concepts of "machine form" epitomized in Le Corbusier's and Mumford's respective visions of the ocean liner had been described by Fritz Schumacher in a book that had just appeared in 1933, at a time when Mumford was completing his manuscript for *Technics and Civilization.* Without alluding to either Le Corbusier (whose books he must have known) or to Mumford (whose book had not yet appeared) Schumacher described the two aspects that make the liner a symbol of modern technology. His comment reads like an attempt to summarize what was to be Mumford's as opposed to Le Corbusier's interest in the steamship, that "most absolute form in which today's technology can be materialized" (Schumacher). The ocean liner embodies, as the architect puts it, "the strongest effects of the machine motivated, thus dynamic possibilities [of technology] and at the same time the strongest effects of its structural, thus static possibilities." Fritz Schumacher, *Schöpferwille und Mechanisierung* (Hamburg, 1933), 22 (my translation). Mumford knew this book and listed it in the Bibliography of *Technics and Civilization.*

13. "Des yeux qui ne voient pas," in *Vers une architecture,* 65–117.

14. That impression of the textile factory as a "romantic landscape" as it were is stronger in the first version of the book, where four images are shown on one page instead of two, cf. note 4.

15. *Technics and Civilization,* 52 (paperback edition).

16. Dickran Tashjian, *William Carlos Williams and the American Scene, 1920–1940* (New York, 1978), 84ff (the quotation is from p. 86). Reyner Banham has remarked that the "spectacular photograph of the River Rouge plant by Charles Sheeler" (that formed the basis of the triptych) appears, unacknowledged, in Laszlo Moholy-Nagy's Bauhaus-Buch, *Von Material zu Architektur* of 1929 (fig. 203 on p. 231; a reprint of Moholy's book appeared in Mainz, 1968). Reyner Banham, *A Concrete Atlantis. U.S. Industrial Building and European Modern Architecture* (Cam-

bridge, Mass., 1986), 164. On Sheeler in general and on his photo-triptych see Bernhard Schulz, "Made in America. Technik und Dingwelt im Präzisionismus," in *America. Traum und Depression, 1920/40*, exhibition catalogue of the Neue Gesellschaft für Bildende Kunst (Berlin, 1980), 72–137; and above all Carol Troyen and Erica E. Hirshler, *Charles Sheeler. Paintings and Drawings*, exhibition catalogue of the Museum of Fine Arts (Boston, 1987), 118–27, as well as Theodore E. Stebbins, Jr., and Norman Keyes, Jr., *Charles Sheeler: The Photographs*, exhibition catalogue of the Museum of Fine Arts (Boston, 1987), 32 and passim.

17. Lewis Mumford, "Steel-Chimneys and Beet-Top Cupolas" (cf. above, note 1).

18. Lewis Mumford, *The Brown Decades* (New York, 1931; ed. 1971), vi.

19. On Häring and his role as a pioneer of "organic" architecture in Germany, see Heinrich Lauterbach and Jürgen Joedicke, *Hugo Häring. Schriften, Entwürfe, Bauten* (Stuttgart/Berne, 1965).

20. Sigfried Giedion, *Bauen in Frankreich. Eisen, Eisenbeton* (Leipzig, 1928). Interestingly, Mumford in his annotated bibliography pays a tribute to Giedion's somewhat younger Swiss colleague, the art historian Joseph Gantner and his booklet *Revision der Kunstgeschichte* (Vienna, 1928).

21. On Friedrich Dessauer's *Philosophie der Technik* (Bonn, 1927), Mumford writes, in one of his interesting short comments on the works listed on the Bibliography: "A book with a high reputation in Germany; but a little given to laboring the obvious" (*Technics and Civilization*, 454). Mumford was, of course, familiar both with Werner Sombart—of whose *Der moderne Kapitalismus* he says that "it parallels the present history of technics as the Mississippi might be said to parallel the railway train that occasionally approaches its banks" (ibid., 470) and with Oswald Spengler, whose *Man and Technics* (New York, 1932) he describes as "a book heavily burdened by a rancid mysticism, tracing back to the weaker sides of Wagner and Nietzsche" (ibid.). To what degree he may have actually worked with these books is of course difficult to evaluate, given Mumford's notorious reluctance to footnote his texts.

22. *A Concrete Atlantis. U.S. Industrial Building and European Modern Architecture*, 230.

23. Later that same year, 1932, the results of Mumford's research were integrated in the famous exhibition on Modern Architecture at the Museum of Modern Art (see *Modern Architecture*, exhibition catalogue, New York: Museum of Modern Art, 1932). On the CIAM (Congrès Internationaux d'Architecture Moderne), see Martin Steinmann ed., *C.I.A.M.-Dokumente, 1928–1939* (Basle, 1979).

Unfortunately, I have not been able to consult the following article by Mumford, "Notes on Germany," in *New Republic* (October 26, 1932), 279–81. The section of Mumford's autobiography concerning the visit to Germany is not yet published. Mumford's travel notes are in the Mumford Papers, (cf. note 1).

24. Behrendt had asked Mumford to write a series of articles on "Amerikanische Baukunst" that were translated and published in *Die Form* from 1925 onward. Fritz Neumeyer recently reproduced Ludwig Mies van der Rohe's reaction to one among these articles (*Die Form*, 1, 1926) in *Mies van der Rohe. Das kunstlose Wort: Gedanken zur Baukunst* (Berlin, n.d. [1986]), 310. Mumford's relation to Behrendt remained close and was even intensified after 1933, when the Nazi takeover had forced Behrendt to leave his country and try to build up a career in the United States.

25. "American Architecture—As Foreigners See It," 4 (unpublished manuscript, probably written in 1926), Mumford Papers. The early encounter of Mendelsohn with Mumford is confirmed by a letter Mendelsohn sent Mumford from

Berlin-Charlottenburg on 8 January 1925 (in English): "After my return to Europe I want to tell you once more what a pleasure it was to me to make your acquaintance and what a joy your 'Stocks and Stones' [sic!] gave me". He is enthusiastic about the book, which he says he read on board during his return trip to Europe, and which appeared to him "like a friend," because it was, in his own words, "so closely related to all the social problems which closely touch our life." In *Erich Mendelsohn. Letters of an Architect,* ed. Oscar Beyer (London and New York, 1967), 75. Equally interesting is a letter Mendelsohn mailed to Mumford together with his book *Amerika,* on Christmas Eve of 1925, in which Mendelsohn expresses his gratitude to Mumford for having referred in friendly terms to his work in the Introduction of the German edition of *Sticks and Stones* (Berlin, 1925).

Mumford himself later gave a slightly later date for his first encounter with Mendelsohn (1927). In his autobiography he credits the German architect for having been among the first to do justice to the architects of the "Chicago School" which had escaped his own attention in his earlier book *Sticks and Stones:* " . . .at our first meeting in 1927 he expressed his enthusiasm to me. By good luck, my chief guide to these buildings was the same architect who had shown them to Mendelsohn, Barry Byrne, who had started his apprenticeship in architecture as an office boy for Frank Lloyd Wright" (*Sketches from Life. The Autobiography of Lewis Mumford,* 1982, p. 429).

26. It may be worth while reporting, in view of what follows, that Gropius himself, who visited the United States some time later (in 1928) was introduced to Mumford with the help of a letter from Mendelsohn. The (undated) letter of introduction is published in *Erich Mendelsohn. Letters of an Architect,* 99.

27. *Technics and Civilization,* plate XIII (caption). Worringer's essay on Egyptian Art (English translation, 1928) is not listed in Mumford's Bibliography. Banham's observation is in *A Concrete Atlantis,* 230.

28. See note 1.

29. Erich Mendelsohn, *Amerika. Bilderbuch eines Architekten* (München, 1925), (my translation).

30. Ibid., 110. Mendelsohn's view of modern engineering as a new "primitivism" that anticipates the forms of a new world may be influenced by Wilhelm Worringer (see above, note 21) or even by Werner Lindner's book *Die Ingenieurbauten* (Berlin, 1923).

31. On the typology and function of American grain elevators see Reyner Banham, *A Concrete Atlantis,* 109–80; on Le Corbusier's interpretation of the theme (and his proverbial modifications of the illustrations from the 1913 *Jahrbuch des Deutschen Werkbundes*) see Thomas P. Hughes, "'Appel aux industriels'" in S. von Moos, ed., *L'Esprit Nouveau. Le Corbusier und die Industrie, 1920–25* (Berlin, 1987), 26–31; and S. R., "Silos," 166f.

32. Cf. Mumford, *Sketches from Life,* 285.

33. Bruno Zevi, *Erich Mendelsohn* (Bologna, 1982; Engl. ed., London, 1985), 22.

34. Bruno Zevi has to be credited for introducing Mendelsohn, together with Antonio Gaudi, as one among the pioneers of an alternative "New Tradition" within the Modern Movement (alternative to the "canonical" one established by Sigfried Giedion, see below): that of "Organic Architecture." Yet his interest in doing so was not, in the end, an alleged machine—symbolism of streamlined forms, but a dynamic concept of function and space. See Bruno Zevi, "Erich Mendelsohn espressionista," in *Pretesti di critica architettonica* (Turin, 1983), 164–227, where he

claims (on p. 206) to have written *Verso un'architettura organica* and *Storia dell'architettura moderna* (1950)—probably his two most influential books—as attempts to correct the lopsided view of modern architecture given by Giedion in *Space, Time and Architecture* (on that latter book, see below). Mumford incidentally is not mentioned in Zevi's otherwise detailed discussion of Mendelsohn's "fortuna critica."

I am grateful to my collegue David Brownlee of the University of Pennsylvania for having insisted, in the discussion of my paper delivered at the Mumford conference of 1987, that "Modern Architecture," contrary to Post-Modernist gossip, represents no monolithical doctrine, but an astonishingly broad spectrum of ideas. This was very much what I have tried to argue here.

35. In this book, Mumford mentions Wright only in passing (347, 370), but he had belonged—together with Erich Mendelsohn!—to Wright's admirers and commentators since the mid-1920s. See H. Allen Brooks, *Writings on Wright. Selected Comment on Frank Lloyd Wright* (Cambridge, Mass., 1981), 126 and passim. On the Johnson Wax administration building see Jonathan Lipman, *Frank Lloyd Wright and the Johnson Wax Buildings* (New York, 1986).

36. Laszlo Moholy-Nagy, *Malerei, Fotografie, Film.* (Munich, 1927), 70; but the photograph appeared in many more avant-garde journals and books of the period.

37. Jill Purce, *The Mystic Spiral* (New York, 1987), 8. I am grateful to Annemarie Bucher, who is currently writing a thesis on the Swiss avant-garde magazine *die spirale*, for having signaled this reference to me.

38. In the context of what he calls "Biotechnik," Moholy refers to the biologist Raoul Francé, probably the most important inspiration for most European avant-garde artists and architects intrigued by the analogies of natural and technical form, specifically so in *Bios* (Passau, 1929), 148. Fritz Neumeyer has recently studied the impact exerted by Francé upon the architect Mies van der Rohe in his *Mies van der Rohe, Das kunstlose Wort* (Berlin, O.J. (1986), 138ff,; Mies owned about forty books by Francé. It is all the more surprising that this author should have escaped Mumford's attention, since he does not appear in his Bibliography.

39. *Space, Time and Architecture* (Cambridge, Mass., 1941, ed. 1974), 118f. Giedion's suggestive use of in general no more than two illustrations per double page may have been in the back of Mumford's (or his publisher's) mind when he decided to change the layout of the plates in the paperback edition of *Technics and Civilization;* cf. above, note 2.

40. *Vers une architecture,* 224. Beatriz Colomina has signaled to me the dual meaning of the word "revolution" in this context: the slogan, she believes, is ambiguous—as far as this ventilator is concerned—because it associates the concept of "revolution" with the mechanical "revolution" of the ventilator in its quasi-spiral-shaped box. Its literal message is of course less obscure; the function of the pathetic alternative "architecture ou révolution?" is to indicate the bourgeoisie's fatal choice: efficient housing policies as remedy against social unrest.

41. For the terminology regarding the spiral as a geometric form, see D'Arcy W. Thompson's classical study, *On Growth and Form* (Cambridge, 1961). The "Museum of Illimited Growth" was first published in *Le Corbusier. Oeuvre compléte 1929–34* (Zürich, ed. 1964), 72f.

Le Corbusier's preoccupation with the spiral and spiral-shaped organisms goes back to his youth. He had been trained to look for the mathematical laws inscribed in the forms of nature since his student days at the Ecole d'Art at his home town

La Chaux-de-Fonds, and he was well aware of Ruskin's drawings that suggest analogies between architecture and nature, cf. (for more information and references) S. von Moos, *Le Corbusier. Elements of a Synthesis* (Cambridge, Mass., 1978), 5ff.

It is interesting that the enigmatic character of the shell as a model (or metaphor) of architecture has been discussed within the Beaux-Arts tradition as well as, for example, by Jean Reynaud, who wrote, in his *Encyclopédie Nouvelle,* vol. I: "On peut, dans un sens profond, comparer les monuments humains à des coquilles formées par des animaux qui y mettent l'empreinte de leur corps et en font leur logis: les méthodes naturelles ne séparent point la description du test de la description des mollusques" (773; quoted after D. van Zanten, *Designing Paris. The Architecture of Duban, Labrouste, Duc and Vaudoyer* (Cambridge, Mass., 1987), 57, 267).

42. Plunged into magical twilight on the cover (that had been designed by Josef Albers), the photograph of the "self-aligning ball bearing" appears again on plate 50. In his Foreword to the exhibition catalogue, Alfred H. Barr, the museum's director, referred to ball bearings as "our classical example" (no pagination). Johnson recently returned to that image of a ball bearing that "suited our thirties ideal of the machine-beauty of form unfalsified by 'artistic' design'"; it now serves as a powerful backdrop for "Deconstructivist Architecture." See Philip Johnson and Mark Wigley, *Deconstructivist Architecture* (catalogue of the Museum of Modern Art), New York, 1988 (Introduction).

For the illustration in *Technics and Civilization,* Mumford was able to use an original print of the photograph reproduced previously in the MOMA catalogue; the print still exists in the Mumford Papers.

43. Again, my description is based on the layout of the first edition; cf. note 2. That there is something wrong with the picture of the ball bearing can be seen even without referring to the MOMA catalogue. As one looks long enough at the picture of that mechanical "crown" (or nimbus) that hovers above the "ballet mécanique" arranged below on the respective plate in *Technics and Civilization,* one cannot help wondering about the black stripe along the left side of the photograph. Of course that stripe should be horizontal, as it shows the edge of the table on which the ball bearings were standing when they were photographed.

44. The exhibition was prepared in collaboration with architects and designers from Brussels, Vienna, Warsaw, and Paris but ultimately shown, to my knowledge, only in New York in a gallery at 119 West 57th Street. Hugh Ferriss wrote the Foreword for the catalogue ("Architecture of this Age"). Alfred H. Barr (in the Foreword to the *Machine Art* exhibition of 1934) refers to the "Machine-Age-Exposition" as to the climax of the "romantic attitude toward the machine" in America: "The Machine-Age Exposition held in New York in 1927 was an important pioneer effort which included fantastic drawings of the city of the future, 'modernistic' skyscrapers, constructivists, robot costumes, theatre settings, and factories, together with some excellent machines and photographs of machinery" (cf. *Machine Art,* no pagination). It is perhaps a measure of Mumford's reservations concerning "modernist" and streamlined design that he did not list that interesting booklet in his Bibliography (whereas he does refer to Philip Johnson's catalogue of 1934).

45. An example is A.L. Cooper's portrait of Alfred P. Sloan, one of the directors of General Motors in Detroit (around 1920). Cf. Werner Oechslin, "Skyscraper und Amerikanismus. Mythos zwischen Europa und Amerika," in *archithese* 20 (1976): 5, and cover.

46. Karel Teige, "Der Konstruktivismus und die Liquidierung der 'Kunst'" (1925), in *Liquidierung der Kunst. Analysen, Manifeste* (Frankfurt a. M., 1968), 53–69; (65 my translation).

47. Mumford's point of view may have been less radical than that of the constructivist theoretician Teige, since in *Technics and Civilization* he does in fact show a painting by Léger (plate XIII, "Esthetic Assimilation," fig. 4). Interestingly, it is an earlier, pre-purist painting of around 1919 that shows no "machinery" and that varies the "industrial" theme on a more conceptual level consistent with Teige's wish to see machinery as a mere "Belehrung des Geistes." Teige condemns not only the mechanistic idolatry of painters like Léger but the "machinist romantics" like Mendelsohn as well, "who don't hesitate to transfer forms derived from aerodynamic calculation to furniture and houses" (cf. note, p. 66).

In order to grasp Mumford's view of the machine and its impact upon art and design more fully, it would be necessary to study his numerous writings on that subject, and in particular his essays on contemporary avant-garde art (to which I am referring below). I want to mention only the most important among the articles that deal explicitly with "the machine": "Machinery and the Modern Style," in *The New Republic* (3 August 1921), 263–65 (reprinted in Lewis Mumford, ed., *Roots of Contemporary American Architecture* (1952; ed. 1972), 196–200); "Architecture and the Machine," *American Mercury* (September 1924), 77–80; "That Monster—The Machine," in *New Masses* (September 1927), 23; "Art in the Machine Age," *Saturday Review of Literature* (8 September 1928), 102–3; "The Drama of the Machines," in *Scribner's Magazine* (August 1930), 150–61, etc.

48. This is true even if the sphere those images depict is not that of mechanics or technology but that of culture at large, including the rituals of sex and luxury cultivated in compensation for the privations of military life, as in the case of Tintoretto's "Susanna and the Elders" (on plate II, fig. 3). Of course, Mumford's evocative discussion of Venus's luxuria as a necessary counterweight to the "abstentions and beastly crudeness of the battlefield" in feudal society (pp. 96ff) goes beyond the iconography and style of Tintoretto's painting. And in the end, looking at the corresponding plate, the reader of the book may be more intrigued by the curious juxtaposition of the Venetian painter's "Susanna" to an eighteenth-century "clockwork Venus" shown immediately below than by the image as such.

49. Plate II, figs. 1 and 2: "Perspectives."

50. The list of avant-garde artists on whom Mumford has written is much too long to be drawn here; it contains Georgia O'Keeffe as well as Matisse, Alfred Stieglitz (on whom he wrote repeatedly, especially in 1929 and 1934) as well as Joan Miró, Salvador Dalì, and Fernand Léger. From November 1932 onward Mumford wrote regularly—at times even weekly —a column entitled "The Art Galleries" in *The New Yorker*, whereas the better known "Sky-Line" series on architecture appeared only at considerable intervals.

51. *Technics and Civilization*, 334.

52. Ibid., 336 (paperback edition).

53. In *The Blind Man*, Nr. 2, May 1917.

54. *Technics and Civilization*, 351.

55. Thomas B. Hess, "J'accuse Marcel Duchamp," in *Art News* (February 1965), 44–45; 52–54; quoted after Joseph Masheck, ed., *Duchamp in Perspective* (Englewood Cliffs, N.J., 1975), 118. In his introduction to this anthology Masheck argues that "With Duchamp the selection process [of the "ready mades"—S.v.M] was evidently not governed by an 'artistic' standard, but instead by a more practical sense of both typicality and careful randomness" (p. 15).

56. Ibid., 336; 337.

57. Ibid., 337. The U.S. Customs Court case involving Edward Steichen, who tried to introduce Brancusi's sculpture (now in the Museum of Modern Art) to the

United States has been documented by Laurie Adams in *Art on Trial. From Whistler to Rothko* (New York, 1976), 35–58.

58. "Brancusi and Marin," *The New Republic* 49 (15 December, 1926): 112f.

59. The question as to what degree the cultural historian's view of modern art—including his sympathy for "common sense" criteria of artistic judgement—may even represent a challenge for a post-modern re-evaluation of the classics of modern art must remain open here. The most recent and by far the most encompassing monograph on Brancusi (Friedrich Teja Bach, *Constantin Brancusi, Metamorphosen plastischer Form* (Cologne, 1987) is a good example for the kind of close-up historiographical and philological analysis of art that tends to exclude any more general cultural issues involved in the process of the reception of works of art by different publics. So Mumford's name does not even appear in Bach's Bibliography (that includes, after all, 800 or so titles). Nor does Bach, of course, comment on the possibility of there being a connection between Brancusi and contemporary techno-culture.

For writers on industrial design in turn, Brancusi appears to have been a household name long ago; see J. Gordon Lippincott, *Design for Business* (Chicago, 1947), especially p. 95; and, more recently, Donald J. Bush, *The Streamlined Decade* (New York, 1975), where the "Bird" appears as a frontispiece, next to the 1934 Airflow Chrysler. For Bush's view of Brancusi and streamline design see pp. 10–14. Interestingly, a connection between Brancusi's biomorphic sculpture and contemporary industrial design had indeed been seen by Herbert Read, *A Concise History of Modern Sculpture* (London, 1964).

60. Lewis Mumford, *The Pentagon of Power* (New York, 1970), plate 29.

61. Ibid., plate 6.

62. Ibid., plate 13, fig. 2.

63. Richard Guy Wilson, "Machine Aesthetics," in Richard Guy Wilson, Dianne H. Pilgrim, and Dickran Tashjian, *The Machine Age in America 1918–1941,* exhibition catalogue of The Brooklyn Museum (New York, 1986), 227.

64. Bertram D. Wolfe, *The Fabulous Life of Diego Rivera* (New York, 1963), 313; quoted after Olav Münzberg and Michael Nungesser, "Die mexikanischen Wandmaler Orozco, Rivera und Siqueiros in den USA," in *Amerika. Traum und Depression, 1920/40,* exhibition catalogue, Neue Gesellschaft für Bildende Kunst, (Berlin, 1981), 378–404; 390 (re-translated from the German by the author).

65. See Lewis Mumford, "The Art Galleries: Early Americans; Ben Shahn and Tom Mooney; Mr. Rivera's Mural," in *The New Yorker* (20 May 1933), 64–66; "The Art Galleries: Rivera and the Workers," in *The New Yorker,* (13 January 1934). Furthermore, Mumford wrote on Orozco in October of the same year, and on "The Three Bentons" in *The New Yorker* (20 April 1935). Finally, cf. the essay "The Treasury's Murals" in *The New Yorker,* (13 January 1937), but a discussion of Mumford's view of these painters is beyond the scope of this paper.

66. In a curious way, Diego Rivera's comments on the "Portrait of Detroit" recall Mumford's view of industry as "dynamic" process and movement. In fact, Rivera says that he had chosen the plastic expression of a "wavelike" movement, as it is to be found in the currents of water, in electric waves, in the layering of the different geological layers beneath the earth's surface and—more generally—in the continuous development of life," *Creative Art,* No. 4 (April 1933): 289–95; quoted after *Amerika. Traum und Depression,* 386f. (re-translated from the German by the author).

Returning to Mumford's plea in favor of a "cultural assimilation of the machine," it has a counterpart in Alfred H. Barr's Foreword to the *Machine Art* catalogue, where Barr uses the concept of the "aesthetic assimilation of the machine" and attributes it to L.P. Jack (an author not listed in the Bibiography of the catalogue or in that of *Technics and Civilization*): "If, to use L.P. Jack's phrase, we are to 'end the divorce' between our industry and our culture we must assimilate the machine aesthetically as well as economically. Not only must we bind Frankenstein—but we must make him beautiful."

67. Herbert Read, *Art and Industry* (London, 1934; ed. New York, 1953), 40.

68. According to D. Thistlewood, Read's book was, in the early stages of its preparation, to be "primarily a defense of the abstract artist . . . whose researches into pure form were crucial to both the aesthetic and commercial well being of the community" (D. Thistlewood, *Herbert Read: Formlessness and Form* (London, 1984), 108. On the history of *Art and Industry*, see Robin Kinross's comprehensive study: "Herbert Read's *Art and Industry*: A History," in *Journal of Design History* (1988), 1: 35–50. Kinross does not discuss the possibility of an impact made by Mumford's book on Read's (or vice versa), but Christopher Green remembers that Read spoke with great respect of Mumford's book that had appeared only a few months before his own (oral communication, summer 1988).

69. H. Read, *Art and Industry*, 44; see also R. Kinross, "Herbert Read's *Art and Industry* . . . ," 37. The literature on the Bauhaus cannot be listed here extensively; the most complete documentation is still to be found in Hans Maria Wingler, *Das Bauhaus. Weimar, Dessau, Berlin, 1919–1933 und die Nachfolge in Chicago seit 1937* (Cologne, 1975).

70. On Sigfried Giedion's life and works, see below, note 71. The inauguration speech "Die Funktion der heutigen Malerei" (1929) has recently been reprinted by Dorothee Huber, ed., *Sigfried Giedion. Wege in die Oeffentlichkeit* (Zürich, 1988), 49.

71. Giedion's biography is of course not at stake here. A few dates may thus suffice. Born in 1888 as a Swiss, he studied mechanical engineering in Vienna and later the History of Art under Heinrich Wölfflin in Munich. His doctoral thesis "Late Baroque and Romantic Classicism" (*Spätbarocker und romantischer Klassizismus*, Munich, 1922), although never translated into English, had a profound impact on subsequent studies on European neoclassicism—as becomes clear from reading the Introduction to H.R. Hitchcock's *Architecture, 19th and 20th Centuries* (Harmondsworth, 1958).

In 1923 he saw the Bauhaus exhibition in Weimar and began a friendship with both Walter Gropius and Laszlo Moholy-Nagy that proved to be decisive for his later career. He met Le Corbusier in 1925 and saw the "Pavillon de l'Esprit Nouveau" at the International Exhibition of Arts and Crafts in Paris. Then, encouraged by Le Corbusier, he started to document and study (as critic, historian, and photographer) what he believed to be the roots of modern architecture in France (*Bauen in Frankreich. Eisen, Eisenbeton*, 1928). That same year he acted as one of the founders and from then on as the General Secretary of the International Congresses of Modern Architecture (CIAM), a function he performed with eloquence and efficiency until 1956.

In 1938 he was invited to give the Charles Eliot Norton lectures at Harvard University. The result was Giedion's best-known work, and in a sense the CIAM-authorized view of modern architectural history: *Space, Time and Architecture* (1941). He died in 1968.

For general information on Giedion and an (almost) complete bibliography of his writings cf. P. Hofer and U. Stucky (eds.), *Hommage à Giedion. Profile seiner Persönlichkeit* (Basel and Stuttgart, 1971); and Sokratis Georgiadis, *Sigfried Giedion. Eine intellektuelle Biographie* (Zürich, 1989).

72. My translation. The original version reads as follows: "Es ist ganz gut, wenn der Autor einmal nicht zu "Wort" kommen kann und gezwungen ist, sich auf optische Art auszudrücken. Also in diesem Fall: mehr durch Anordnung und Gegenüber stellungen (im positiven Sinn) klarzumachen, als durch Erläuterungen. Auch das knappe Format, die Einordnung in eine grosse Serie kann heilsam wirken. Der Autor wird dadurch genötigt, den zu Verfügung stehenden Raum möglichst auszunützen. Daraus ergibt sich zwangsläufig eine grössere Konzentration der Bildanordnung und für den Leser vielleicht eine eindringlichere Uebersicht." *Befreites Wohnen*, 4.

73. My translation. The original version reads as follows: "Das Buch wurde nach Möglichkeit so abgefasst und angeordnet, dass der e i l i g e L e s e r den Gang der Entwicklung aus den beschrifteten Abbildungen ersehen kann, der Text soll die nähere Begründung liefern, die Bemerkungen geben die weiteren Hinweise." *Bauen in Frankreich. Eisen, Eisenbeton.*

74. Ibid., 1.

75. The iconography and graphic style of Giedion's early books are the subject of a paper I gave at a recent Giedion conference at the ETH in Zurich (February 1989, in print).

76. Curiously enough, Mumford's name does not appear in the index of Giedion's book.

77. S. von Moos, "Die zweite Entdeckung Amerikas. Zur Vorgeschichte von 'Mechanization Takes Command,'" in S. Giedion, *Die Herrschaft der Mechanisierung* (Frankfurt a. M., 1982), 781–816 (postface); partly reprinted as "Giedion e il suo tempo" in *RASSEGNA* 25 *(Sigfried Giedion: un progetto storico; 1986)*, 6–17 with English version.

78. This is the title of a book by Friedrich Dessauer (Bonn, 1927) that seems to have had a certain impact upon Mumford's thought. Dessauer, among other things, blames capitalist economy for having misdirected or distorted the logic of technical and industrial progress; he insists that the "sins of economy" should not be attributed to technics: "Die Weihe der Technik kommt vom Schöpfer, nicht vom Mammon," p. 117. Unfortunately, given Mumford's reluctance to footnote his text, it is difficult to determine to what degree his thought was actually dependent on such sources.

79. Letter dated 24 March 1948, Mumford Papers. I shall return at another occasion to the specific context of this correspondence.

80. S. Giedion, *Mechanization Takes Command*, 105 (Paul Klee and Frank Gilbreth) as well as 330f., 362f., and 386f. (Max Ernst and 19th-century furniture). Giedion and Mumford met at least twice in the years following. The Mumford collection contains some eight letters and postcards sent by Giedion to Mumford between 1940 and 1965; it may be worthwhile to quote the following phrase from a letter dated 12 July 1948: "Finally, when I read your comments with the title 'Man Takes Command' I had almost to laugh, because Le Corbusier, whom you treat so harshly, had just written (to) me the same words in a private letter. . . ." Le Corbusier's letter of 21 May 1948 is reproduced in *Hommage à Giedion* (cf. above, note 71), 50f.

81. "The Skyline: The Architecture of Power," *The New Yorker* (7 June 1941), 58–60.

82. "The Skyline: Manhattan Inside Out," in *The New Yorker* (15 May 1948), 84. It was Gropius who had brought this passage to Giedion's attention; the Giedion archive preserves the according page from *The New Yorker* with the necessary markings and a characteristic note in the margin: "Cheerioh! Pius."

83. Quoted (and re-translated from the Italian) after Bruno Zevi, *Storia dell'architettura moderna,* 348; the source is presumably "Skyline: Status Quo," in *The New Yorker,* (11 October 1947).

84. Not suprisingly, Giedion cannot share Mumford's enthusiasm for the Bay Style expressed in *The New Yorker:* "I do not think that the problem lies in a differentiation between a Bay Region Style—which is to be found on the Lake of Zurich as well as on the Golden Gate, and which unobtrusive architecture kills in Switzerland for instance all genuine inventiveness in domestic building—and an International Style." A copy of this letter to Philip Johnson, dated 27 January 1948, is preserved in the Mumford Papers. On the battle over the UN Headquarters in New York, see Vale's essay, this volume.

85. Letter, dated 6 April 1965 in the Giedion-archive at the Institut für Geschichte und Theorie der Architektur, ETH Zürich.

86. Nikolaus Pevsner, "Modern Architecture and the Return of Historicism," *RIBA Journal* (April 1961), 230–40. For the "canonical" (or CIAM) view of the Sydney Opera House see, however, S. Giedion, *Space, Time and Architecture* (5th printing, 1974), 668–95; needless to say—in view of what follows below—the term "expressionism" does not appear in this appraisal of the Danish architect.

87. Sigfried Giedion, *Space, Time and Architecture* (1974), 486.

88. See Martin Steinmann ed., *CIAM Dokumente 1928–1939* (Basle and Stuttgart, 1979), 170f. and Appendix.

89. Vladimir Majakowsky, *Meine Entdeckung Amerikas* (Zürich, 1960), 12 (translated from the German).

90. Lewis Mumford, "The Sky Line: The Architecture of Power," *The New Yorker* (7 June 1941).

91. S. Giedion, *Space, Time and Architecture,* 825.

92. Most explicitly so of course in "The Highway and the City," written in 1958 and reprinted in *The Highway and the City* (London, 1964), 176–89. Mumford's apocalyptic view of "the over expansion of motor and air transportation" as "organized destruction" of the environment is visualized with the help of the alarming comparison of the intersection of the Pasadena and Hollywood Freeways with a monumental junkyard in *The Pentagon of Power,* plate 22.

It is from here and from Mumford's pathetic diatribes against "Industrial pollution and commercial fallout" on the following page that an author like Peter Blake took off (cf. *God's Own Junkyard,* New York, 1964). Since that time, a new wave of aesthetic appreciation of the industrial environment, albeit on quite different social and aesthetic premises, has reconquered American architectural thought (cf. Robert Venturi, Denise Scott Brown, and Steven Izenour, *Learning from Las Vegas,* Cambridge, Mass., 1972ff.)—but that again is a different story.

93. The modes and styles of manipulating images in architectural and art historical publications have not yet been studied systematically. The most acute study on one crucial aspect of the problem—the logic of visual comparison—is by Felix Thürlemann, "Famose Gegenklänge. Der Diskurs der Abbildungen im Almanach 'Der Blaue Reiter,'" in *Der Blaue Reiter,* exhibition catalogue (Kunstmuseum Berne, 1987), 210–22. See also the earlier essay by Andreas Haus, "Fotografische Polemik und Propaganda um das "neue bauen" der 20er Jahre," in *Marburger Jahrbuch für Kunstwissenschaft,* Bd. 20, pp. 90–105. Some suggestive ideas on this problem are to be found in Andreas Hauser, "Grundbegriffliches zu Wölfflin's 'Kunstgeschichtlichen Grundbegriffen,' " in *Schweizerisches Institut für Kunstwissenschaft, Jahrbuch 1984–1986,* 39–55, wherein Wölfflin's classical technique of stylistic comparison is juxtaposed to the principle of montage in film.

A classic on the rules governing didactic uses of imagery is Roland Barthes's analysis of the *Encyclopédie* and its illustrations (cf. note 12).

94. Concerning Le Corbusier's techniques of manipulating visual information, cf. Beatriz Colomina, "Le Corbusier and Photography," in *assemblage* 4: 6–23 (first printed in S. von Moos, ed., *L'Esprit Nouveau. Le Corbusier und die Industrie 1920–25*, exhibition catalogue (Berlin and Zurich, 1987), 32–43.

95. I quite like the paradoxical combination of the terms "iconography" and "style" that are often believed to be mutually exclusive.

96. This typology of the strategies of comparisons has been introduced by F. Thürlemann; cf. above, note 93.

97. Plate XII, "Nature and the Machine," *Technics*; cf. above, note 3.

98. Plate IX, "Paleothechnic Triumphs" (see above!) and plate X, "Neotechnic Automation" next to plate XI, "Airplane Shapes," *Technics*.

99. Concerning Mumford's "organicist" (as opposed to "mechanistic") concept of the machine, see Leo Marx's essay, this volume. Probably Mumford's "dynamic" view of machinery has a lot to do with his "using the body to understand technology", as Carolyn Marvin argued in an as yet unpublished paper delivered at the 1987 Mumford conference.

CHARLES MOLESWORTH: Inner and Outer: The Axiology of Lewis Mumford

1. Lewis Mumford, *Works and Days: A Personal Chronicle* (New York: Harcourt Brace, 1979), 214.

2. See the essay by Lawrence Vale, this volume.

3. Lewis Mumford, *The Story of Utopias* (New York: Boni and Liveright, 1922).

4. Lewis Mumford, *Findings and Keepings: Analects for an Autobiography* (New York: Harcourt, Brace, 1975), 75.

5. See the essay by Howard Segal, this volume.

6. Lewis Mumford, *Sticks and Stones: A Study of American Architecture and Civilization* (New York: Dover, 1955), 92.

7. Lewis Mumford, *The Golden Day* (New York: Dover, 1968), 50.

8. Van Wyck Brooks, *Three Essays on America* (New York: Dutton, 1934), 171.

9. *The Golden Day*, 117.

10. Eddy Dow, "Van Wyck Brooks and Lewis Mumford: A Confluence in the Twenties," *American Literature,* 45 (November 1979): 407–422.

11. Lewis Mumford, *Herman Melville* (New York: Harcourt, Brace, 1929), 33.

12. Ibid., 186–87.

13. Ibid., 346.

14. Joseph Duffey, "Mumford's Quest: The First Decade," *Salmagundi* 49 (1980): 43–68.

15. Eddy Dow, "Lewis Mumford's Passage to India: From the First to the Later Phase," *South Atlantic Quarterly* 76 (1977): 31–43.

LAWRENCE J. VALE: Designing Global Harmony: LM and The UN Headquarters

1. Six of the *New Yorker* pieces are included in *From the Ground Up* (New York: Harcourt, Brace, 1956).

2. The story of the League of Nations competition is told, with illustrations of many of the entries, in John Ritter, "World Parliament: The League of Nations Competition," *Architectural Review* 136 (July 1964): 17–24. For formal analysis of the Le Corbusier entry, see Colin Rowe and Robert Slutsky, "Transparency: Literal and Phenomenal," in Rowe, *The Mathematics of the Ideal Villa and Other Essays* (Cambridge: MIT Press, 1976); and Kenneth Frampton. "The Humanist Versus the Utilitarian Ideal,"*Architectural Design* 38, (1968): 134–36.

3. "Report of the Headquarters Commission to the Second Part of the First Session of the General Assembly of the United Nations" (Lake Success, N.Y.: United Nations, October 1946), 7–11.

4. Ibid., 4–5.

5. Ibid., 5.

6. Ibid., Annex 8, p. 79.

7. Michael Hughes, ed.,*The Letters of Lewis Mumford and Frederic J. Osborn: A Transatlantic Dialogue, 1938–70* (New York: Praeger, 1972), 117–18.

8. Ibid., Osborn letter of 19 February 1946, p. 120.

9. "A World Centre for the United Nations: A Lecture by Lewis Mumford [Hon. A.] at the R.I.B.A. on Friday, 12 July 1946," *Journal of the Royal Institute of British Architects* 53 (August 1946): 427–34. Though the fullest account of Mumford's proposal appears here, the germ of his position on the UN Headquarters is first presented in an editorial in an American architectural publication ("Stop and Think," *Progressive Architecture/Pencil Points* 27 (April 1946): 109). This is written as a response to editor Kenneth Reid's proposal for an international competition, published in the March issue. The August 1946 issue of *Progressive Architecture* also contains a shortened and altered version of the RIBA lecture.

10. Ibid., 428.

11. Ibid.

12. Ibid., 429.

13. Ibid.

14. Ibid., 430–31.

15. Ibid., 430.

16. A few years later, though, they did accept the IBM headquarters; but that is another story.

17. See Robert Caro, *The Power Broker: Robert Moses and the Fall of New York* (New York: Vintage, 1975), 771–74; and "U.N. Takes Manhattan. General Assembly Will Meet in One of World's Most Sought-Out Spots," *Architectural Forum* 86 (January 1947): 11–12.

18. Hughes, ed., *Mumford-Osborn Letters*, 144.

19. "UN General Assembly Meets a Complex Plan Problem with the 'Visual Poetry' of an Elegant Concave Shape," *Architectural Forum* 92 (May 1950): 97.

20. "UN Completes the Link, Conference Building Cleans Up Manhattan's Waterfront, Gives Secretariat a Base To Stand On," *Architectural Forum* 96 (April 1952): 105, 110.

21. Edward Passmere, "The New Headquarters of the UN," *RIBA Journal* 57 (July 1950): 348.

22. *Architectural Record* 107 (May 1950): 120–23.

23. *Architectural Forum* 90 (June 1949): 81–85.

24. "UN Builds a Marble Frame for Two Enormous Windows," 81.

25. Ibid.

26. *Report to the General Assembly of the United Nations by the Secretary-General on*

the Permanent Headquarters of the UN (Lake Success, N.Y.: United Nations, July 1947), 8.

27. "Magic with Mirrors," in *From the Ground Up,* 44.

28. "Symbol and Function in Architecture," in *Art and Technics* (New York: Columbia University Press, 1952), 131.

29. "A Disoriented Symbol," in *From the Ground Up,* 48.

30. Ibid., 49–50.

31. "United Nations Assembly," in *From the Ground Up,* 59. Though Mumford does not dwell on the issue of the effect of mass media on architectural design, the UN building could provide an excellent case study for this as perhaps the world's first "television building."

32. "Workshop Invisible," in *From the Ground Up,* 68.

33. "Symbol and Function in Architecture," 129.

34. "A World Centre for the United Nations," 430.

35. Ibid., 430.

36. "UN Model and Model UN," in *From the Ground Up,* 24.

37. "A Disoriented Symbol," 45–46.

38. "United Nations Assembly," 56.

39. "A World Centre for the United Nations," 431.

40. "Workshop Invisible," 64.

41. Hughes, ed., *Mumford-Osborn Letters,* 149.

42. "A World Centre for the United Nations," 428.

43. "The Basis of Universalism," from *The South in Architecture,* included in Mumford, ed., *Roots of Contemporary American Architecture,* (New York: Dover, 1972; original edition, 1952), 369.

44. Ibid.

45. While Mumford never cites either Cassirer or Langer in any of his writings about the UN Headquarters, he does mention them (along with George Mead and W.M. Urban) in his 1951 lecture "Art and the Symbol," included in *Art and Technics,* 22.

46. Ibid.

47. Ernst Cassirer, *The Philosophy of Symbolic Forms,* 3 vols., trans. R. Manheim (New Haven: Yale University Press, 1957), 3: 191–204.

48. "Usable past" is an evocative phrase coined by Mumford's friend Van Wyck Brooks.

49. Mumford, *The Golden Day* (New York: Boni and Liveright, 1926), 119.

50. "A Backward Glance," in Mumford, ed., *Roots of Contemporary American Architecture,* 13.

51. Mumford, *The Brown Decades: A Study of the Arts in America, 1865–1895* (New York: Dover, 1955; originally published, 1931), 143.

52. Ibid., 153.

53. "Magic with Mirrors," 43.

54. Ibid., 43–44.

55. "Symbol and Function in Architecture," 130.

56. Both Zeckendorf and Rockefeller owned much other Manhattan real estate near the 17 acres given (with the careful stipulation of special tax benefits) by Rockefeller; both men had much to gain from the increase in property values that would inevitably follow from the slum clearance and rebuilding of the United Nations site, as well as from the prestige of the new tenant.

57. "UN Model and Model UN," 25.

58. "United Nations Assembly," 60–61.

59. Mumford, "UN Model and Model UN," 22.

60. Ibid.

61. "Buildings as Symbols," in *From the Ground Up,* 31.

62. "Symbol and Function in Architecture," 129.

63. "Workshop Invisible," 65.

64. "United Nations Assembly," 53.

65. Mumford's view of the architectural hierarchy was not without challenge, however. An article in *Architectural Forum* noted that, though the General Assembly "is the lowest of the major buildings in the UN group," it is the "climax": "eyes are drawn instantly to it by its central position, by the solidity of its unbroken stone walls—and above all by the powerful contrast with the surrounding rectilinear buildings of its sweeping curves." Two years later, the same journal tried to pull rank on Mumford by citing a superior source: "Corbu himself helped set the exterior shape of the Assembly knowing that its sweeping curves would give the smaller building the power of bringing the whole group to a climax (a piece of sophistication that escaped critic Lewis Mumford, who demanded more importance for the Assembly through the primitive device of simply making it bigger [*sic*])," 92 (May 1950): 97; and 97 (October 1952): 141.

66. "United Nations Assembly," 60.

67. "A Disoriented Symbol," 51–52.

68. "Buildings as Symbols," 34–35.

69. *Report on the Permanent Headquarters,* 38.

70. "Buildings as Symbols," 35.

71. *Report on the Permanent Headquarters,* 18.

72. "United Nations Assembly," 59.

73. Ibid.

74. "A World Centre for the United Nations," 432.

75. "Symbol and Function in Architecture," 131.

76. "UN Model and Model UN," 22.

77. "Buildings as Symbols," 35.

78. "United Nations Assembly," 60.

79. Ibid., 57.

80. "A World Centre for the United Nations," 432.

81. Ibid.

82. "United Nations Assembly," 61.

83. "Workshop Invisible," 65.

84. "UN Model and Model UN," 22.

85. *Charter of the United Nations,* Chapter I, Article 2, Section 1.

86. Ibid., Chapter XI, Article 73 and Chapter XII, Article 76.

87. There were 51 original member states in 1945; 100 by the end of 1960; and 159 as of 1989. (Source: *Basic Facts About the United Nations* (New York: United Nations, 1983), 125; and John J. Metzler, "The United Nations—Where the World Meets," *Boston Sunday Globe,* 8 January 1989.)

88. "Buildings as Symbols," 35.

CASEY BLAKE: The Perils of Personality: LM and Politics After Liberalism

1. Lewis Mumford to Van Wyck Brooks, 22 July 1925, in *The Van Wyck Brooks–Lewis Mumford Letters: The Record of a Literary Friendship, 1921–1963,* ed. Robert E. Spiller (New York: E.P. Dutton, 1970), 30.

2. Alasdair MacIntyre, *After Virtue: A Study in Moral Theory,* 2nd ed. (Notre Dame, Ind.: University of Notre Dame Press, 1984), 34.

3. Robert Bellah, et al., *Habits of the Heart: Individualism and Commitment in American Life* (Berkeley: University of California Press, 1985), 218.

4. Lewis Mumford, "The Emergence of a Past," *The New Republic* 45 (25 November 1925): 19.

5. Lewis Mumford, *Technics and Civilization* (New York: Harcourt, Brace & World, 1962), 433.

6. See Warren Susman, "'Personality' and the Making of Twentieth-Century Culture," in Susman, *Culture as History: The Transformation of American Society in the Twentieth Century* (New York: Pantheon, 1984), 271–85; and T.J. Jackson Lears, "From Salvation to Self-Realization: Advertising and the Therapeutic Roots of the Consumer Culture, 1880–1930," in *The Culture of Consumption: Critical Essays in American History 1880–1980,* eds. Richard Wightman Fox and T.J. Jackson Lears (New York: Pantheon, 1983), 1–38.

7. For a fuller discussion of this issue, see Casey Blake, *Beloved Community: The Cultural Criticism of Randolph Bourne, Van Wyck Brooks, Waldo Frank, and Lewis Mumford* (forthcoming, University of North Carolina Press), and "The Young Intellectuals and the Culture of Personality," *American Literary History* (Fall 1989): 510–34.

8. Randolph Bourne, "Trans-national America," in *The Radical Will: Randolph Bourne Selected Writings, 1911–1918,* ed. Olaf Hansen (New York: Urizen, 1977), 264.

9. Mumford, *Technics,* 319.

10. See, for example, Dewey's argument in *The Public and its Problems* (1927) that "communication can alone create a great community," an idea fully compatible with Mumford's position in the 1920s. "Our Babel is not one of tongues but of the signs and symbols without which shared experience is impossible." John Dewey, *The Public and Its Problems* (Chicago: Swallow Press, 1954), 142. See also Robert Westbrook, this volume, which notes the convergence of Mumford's and Dewey's thinking in the 1920s and 1930s.

11. Lewis Mumford, "Patriotism and Its Consequences," *The Dial* 66 (19 April 1919): 406.

12. Lewis Mumford, "A Search for the True Community," in *The Menorah Treasury: Harvest of Half a Century,* ed. Leo W. Schwartz (Philadelphia: Jewish Publication Society of America, 1964), 863.

13. Lewis Mumford, "What I Believe," *The Forum* 84 (November 1930): 264.

14. Ibid., 263.

15. Alan Trachtenberg, "Mumford in the Twenties: The Historian as Artist," *Salmagundi* 49 (Summer 1980): 34.

16. Lewis Mumford, *Herman Melville* (New York: The Literary Guild, 1929), 185.

17. Ibid., 186–87.

18. Mumford, "What I Believe," 268.

19. Lewis Mumford, "Towards an Organic Humanism," in *The Critique of Humanism: A Symposium,* ed. C. Hartley Grattan (New York: Brewer and Warren, 1930), 358–59.

20. Lewis Mumford, *Technics,* 51.

21. Ibid., 55.

22. Waldo Frank, "Dusk and Dawn," in Frank, *In the American Jungle (1925–1936)* (New York: Farrar & Rinehart, 1937), 177.

23. See Lewis Mumford to Waldo Frank, 13 March 1927, Waldo Frank Papers, Special Collections, Van Pelt Library, University of Pennsylvania. See also Mumford's letter to Alfred Stieglitz, 20 July 1933, Alfred Stieglitz Papers, Beinecke Library, Yale University, in which Mumford makes a similar case for reconstructing an organic culture within the confines of modern technology and explicitly cites Stieglitz, among others, as one of the pioneers of such a culture.

24. See Carl Sussman, ed., *Planning the Fourth Migration: The Neglected Vision of the Regional Planning Association of America* (Cambridge: MIT Press, 1976).

25. Lewis Mumford, "In Our Stars: The World Fifty Years from Now," *The Forum* 88 (December 1932): 341, 342.

26. Lewis Mumford, Foreword to *Planned Society Yesterday, Today, Tomorrow: A Symposium by Thirty-five Economists, Sociologists, and Statesmen*, ed. Findlay Mac-Kenzie (New York: Prentice-Hall, 1937), v.

27. Ibid., ix.

28. I have addressed the shortcomings of *Technics* in an earlier essay, "Lewis Mumford: Values Over Technique," *democracy* 3 (Spring 1983): 125–37.

29. Mumford, *Technics*, 354.

30. Ibid., 351.

31. Ibid., 362.

32. Ibid., 361.

33. Ibid., 243–44.

34. Ibid., 343.

35. Reinhold Niebuhr, "Our Machine Made Culture," *Christendom* 1 (Autumn 1935): 187.

36. Ibid., 189.

37. See Mumford's exchange with V.F. Calverton, "A Challenge to American Intellectuals," *Modern Quarterly* 5 (Winter 1930–31):407–21; Mike Gold to Lewis Mumford, n.d. [1934], Lewis Mumford Papers, Special Collections, Van Pelt Library, University of Pennsylvania; Meyer Schapiro, "Looking Forward to Looking Backward," *Partisan Review* 5 (July 1938): 12–24; Sidney Hook, "Metaphysics, War, and Intellectuals," *Menorah Journal* 28 (August 1940): 327–37; and James T. Farrell, "The Faith of Lewis Mumford," in Farrell, *The League of Frightened Philistines and Other Papers* (New York: Vanguard Press, 1945), 106–31.

38. Mumford, *Technics*, 213.

39. See David F. Nobel, *America by Design: Science, Technology, and the Rise of Corporate Capitalism* (New York: Knopf, 1979).

40. For one example for this argument, see Lewis Mumford, *The Conduct of Life* (New York: Harcourt, Brace, 1951), 244–92. Note that MacIntyre also calls on the example of the early Christians in the closing lines of *After Virtue*, 263: "What matters at this stage is the construction of local forms of community within which civility and the intellectual and moral life can be sustained through the new dark ages which are already upon us. . . . We are waiting not for a Godot, but for another— doubtless very different—St. Benedict."

41. Lewis Mumford, *The Myth of the Machine: II. The Pentagon of Power* (New York: Harcourt Brace Jovanovich, 1970), 408.

42. See Richard Wightman Fox, this volume, for further discussion of the differences between Mumford and Niebuhr.

43. Mumford, *Technics*, 408–9.

44. Mumford, *Pentagon*, 350.

45. Ibid., 394–95.

46. For examples of contemporary appeals to replace individualism with a "rela-

tional self," see Bellah, et al., *Habits of the Heart;* MacIntyre, *After Virtue;* Carol Gilligan, *In a Different Voice: Psychological Theory and Women's Development* (Cambridge: Harvard University Press, 1982); and Thomas C. Heller, et al., *Reconstructing Individualism: Autonomy, Individuality, and the Self in Western Thought* (Stanford: Stanford University Press, 1986).

47. In this regard, see Jane J. Mansbridge, *Beyond Adversary Democracy,* rev. ed. (Chicago: University of Chicago Press, 1983), and Jeffrey Stout, "Liberal Society and the Language of Morals," *Soundings* 69 (Spring–Summer 1986): 32–59, both of which question whether communitarian democracy adequately resolves the deadlock of an "adversarial" politics.

48. Mumford, "Towards an Organic Humanism," 359.

WESTBROOK: LM, John Dewey, and the "Pragmatic Acquiescence"

1. Two recent incisive overviews of Mumford's career sympathetic to his criticism of Dewey's pragmatism are Christopher Lasch, "Lewis Mumford and the Myth of the Machine," *Salmagundi* 49 (1980): 4–28; and Casey Blake, "Lewis Mumford: Values Over Technique," *democracy* 3 (Spring 1983): 125–37. My essay draws on on-going conversations with Christopher Lasch and Casey Blake on these matters, and, unconvinced though they may be by my argument, I am indebted to them both. I am grateful as well to Richard Fox, Agatha and Thomas Hughes, and Stewart Weaver for comments on an earlier draft of this essay.

2. Lewis Mumford, *Technics and Civilization* (New York: Harcourt, Brace, 1934), 105.

3. Lewis Mumford, *The Golden Day,* 3d ed. (New York: Dover, 1968), 79. All subsequent references to this book are to this edition and will be cited in parentheses in the text *(GD).* Since Rosalind Williams's essay in this volume describes in detail Mumford's analysis of the "eotechnic," "paleotechnic," and "neo-technic" phases of technological development, I will not rehearse them.

4. I lack the space to consider critically Mumford's treatment of James. I find it less misleading than his criticism of Dewey; insofar as the issue is "acquiescence" to industrial capitalism, James was a mugwump, Dewey a radical. It is precisely those features of James's pragmatism to which Dewey most objected (above all, his use of philosophy "to seek peace rather than understanding" *(GD,* 94)) that lent themselves to Mumford's criticisms. (See Dewey's essay, "What Pragmatism Means by Practical" (1908), *The Middle Works of John Dewey* (Carbondale: Southern Illinois University Press, 1976–83), 4:98–115.)) It does seem to me that Mumford's argument about James was marked by an internal contradiction. He wavered between placing the burden of James's acquiescence on his celebration of the restless striving of the Protestant pioneer or on his therapeutic, "anesthetic" longing for "a comfortable resting place." I have emphasized the former line of argument here because it leads most directly into Mumford's criticisms of Dewey. It is perhaps worth noting Mumford's admiration for the third of the major pragmatists, Charles Peirce (see *GD,* 98 and "Toward the Publication of Peirce's Works," *The New Republic* (31 December 1930), 195).

5. For Mumford's estimate of Bourne's significance see "The Image of Randolph Bourne," *The New Republic* (24 September 1930), 151–52. Bourne's critique, it should be noted, was directed principally at the "younger intelligentsia trained up in the pragmatic dispensation," and when it came to Dewey himself was filled

with qualifications, most of which did not appear in Mumford's appropriation of his arguments. Bourne gave Dewey credit for calling for "a more attentive formulation of war-purposes and ideas" (if not for answering this call particularly well himself) as well as for combining vision and technique in his prewar thinking, though "even in him" there seemed to be "a flagging of values under the influence of the war" ("Twilight of Idols," *The Radical Will: Randolph Bourne Selected Writings, 1911–1918,* ed. Olaf Hansen, (New York: Urizen, 1977), 345). Most of Bourne's war essays amount to a Deweyan criticism of Dewey for a failure during the war to measure up to his own standards of imagination and judgment. From this perspective, it was not instrumentalism but Dewey that had come up short. *This* critique was extremely powerful and I believe Dewey would have found it unanswerable, which may explain why he never addressed it directly and instead did what he could behind the scenes with the editor of *The Dial* to deprive Bourne of an audience by excluding him from the pages of one of the few magazines willing to publish his political essays. See my *John Dewey and American Democracy* (Ithaca: Cornell University Press, forthcoming), chap. 7.

6. For a further instance of Mumford's criticism of Deweyan aesthetics see "Metaphysics and Art," *The New Republic* (18 December 1929), 117–18.

7. See Bourne, "Twilight of Idols"; Van Wyck Brooks, *Letters and Leadership* (1918) in Brooks, *Three Essays on America* (New York, E.P. Dutton, 1970), 169–73; Waldo Frank, "The Man Who Made Us What We Are," *The New Yorker* 2 (22 May 1926): 15–16; Harold Stearns, *Liberalism in America* (New York: Boni and Liveright, 1919), chap. 8; Bertrand Russell, "Pragmatism" (1909) in Russell, *Philosophical Essays* (New York: Simon and Schuster, 1966), 110–11, and "As a European Radical Sees It," *Freeman* 4 (1922): 608–10; William Caldwell, *Pragmatism and Idealism* (London: Adam and Charles Black, 1913), 172–73. Much of what follows in this section draws on my *John Dewey and American Democracy.*

8. Dewey, "Pragmatic America" (1922), *Middle Works* 13:307; "Intelligence and Morals" (1908), ibid., 4:48–49; "The Problem of Truth" (1911), ibid., 6:52–53.

9. In response to Russell, Dewey remarked that to treat pragmatism as the "intellectual equivalent of commercialism" was "of that order of interpretation that would say that English neo-realism is a reflection of the aristocratic snobbery of the English; the tendency of French thought to dualism an expression of an alleged Gallic disposition to keep a mistress in addition to a wife; and the idealism of Germany a manifestation of an ability to elevate beer and sausage into a higher synthesis with the spiritual values of Beethoven and Wagner" ("Pragmatic America," 307). As this suggests, Dewey's writing was quite often *not* as depressing as a subway ride.

10. Dewey, "Pragmatic Acquiescence" (1927), *The Later Works of John Dewey* (Carbondale: Southern Illinois University Press, 1981–), 3:147, 150–51. This reply originally appeared in *The New Republic* (5 January 1927), 186–89.

11. Mumford, "The Pragmatic Acquiescence: A Reply," *The New Republic* (19 January 1927), 250–51.

12. Dewey, "Pragmatic Acquiescence," 146; *Experience and Nature* (1925), *Later Works,* 1:271, 274.

13. *Reconstruction in Philosophy* (1920), *Middle Works,* 12:152; Mumford to Victor Branford, 3 March 1926, Lewis Mumford Papers, Special Collections, Van Pelt Library, University of Pennsylvania. I am grateful to Casey Blake for bringing this letter to my attention.

14. Dewey, "The Ethics of Democracy" (1888), *The Early Works of John Dewey* (Carbondale: Southern Illinois University Press, 1967–72), 1:240. Cf. Bourne: "[Dewey] has seen the implicatons of democracy more clearly than anybody else in the great would-be democratic society about him" ("John Dewey's Philosophy" (1915), *Radical Will*, 332).

15. Dewey, *Reconstruction in Philosophy* (2nd ed., 1948), *Middle Works*, 12:256; "Philosophy and Democracy" (1918), ibid., 11:43–44; "Pragmatic Acquiescence," 147.

16. For Dewey's own estimate of the "Golden Day" see "Emerson—the Philosopher of Democracy" (1903), *Middle Works*, 3:184–92. Since Mumford used the term "utilitarianism" to refer to a way of thinking related to but cruder than the moral philosophy of Bentham, Mill, and their successors, I will not consider here the critique of this philosophical tradition that was a feature of Dewey's ethics from the 1890s onward. Suffice it to say that Dewey was not a "utilitarian" in this more specialized sense either. See, for example, Dewey and James Tufts, *Ethics* (1908), *Middle Works*, 5:241–77.

17. Mumford, "Pragmatic Acquiescence: A Reply," 251; *Golden Day*, 139. On the key place of Dewey and Santayana in the structure of the argument of *The Golden Day*, see Charles Molesworth's essay on Mumford's "axiology," this volume. Mumford's notion of "two Deweys" underestimated the continuities in Dewey's thinking, but it has some merit insofar as it was not until after World War I that Dewey began to explore fully the non-cognitive dimensions of experience (including aesthetic experience). These were, as a presupposition, essential to the theory of knowledge that was his principal concern in the early twentieth century but were not analyzed very thoroughly in that period. Thus, much of Dewey's later work was, in effect, directed toward clearing up what Bourne termed the "unhappy ambiguity in his doctrine as to just how values were created." Hence it is most surprising that Mumford could repeat Bourne's charge after having read *Experience and Nature* and sustain the indictment after the publication of *Art as Experience*. For a good example of the "two Deweys" argument see Joseph Featherstone, "Reconsideration: John Dewey," *The New Republic* (8 July 1972), 27–32. Mumford's failure to describe adequately the democratic vision that was at the heart of Dewey's ethics may have stemmed not only from an awareness that this would muddy his argument by granting Dewey a measure of moral imagination but also from Mumford's wariness of the expansive democratic sensibilities of figures like Dewey and Whitman. In the 1920s, Mumford's own conception of democracy appears to have been thin, amounting to little more than the circulation of elites. "A democracy," he wrote, "is a society in which chiefs, people, intellectuals, and emotionals are sorted out in every generation, upon the basis of worth and ability, and in which there is free passage from group to group, without respect to birth, status, or financial condition" ("Science and Sanctity," *Commonweal* 4 (9 June 1926): 127).

18. Dewey, "I Believe," in Clifton Fadiman, ed., *I Believe* (New York: Simon and Schuster, 1939), 351–52.

19. Mumford, "What I Believe," in Albert Einstein, et al., *Living Philosophies* (New York: Simon and Schuster, 1931), 205–19; Dewey, "What I Believe" (1930), *Later Works*, 5:273–74. The two testimonies originally appeared in the *Forum* in November and March 1930.

20. *Technics and Civilization*, 6. Subsequent references to this book will be cited in parentheses in the text *(TC)*.

21. Dewey, "Science as Subject-Matter and as Method" (1910), *Middle Works*, 6:78.

22. Ibid.

23. See Casey Blake, this volume.

24. Dewey, *Art as Experience* (1934), *Later Works,* 10:278. As he was beginning his preparation for the William James Lectures at Harvard that were to form the basis of *Art as Experience,* Dewey wrote Sidney Hook that "I still feel the desire to get into a field I haven't treated systematically, and art and aesthetics has come to me. One reason is the criticism for neglecting them and the consummatory generally" (Dewey to Hook, 10 March 1930, Sidney Hook Papers, Morris Library, Southern Illinois University). It seems to me there is every reason to believe Dewey numbered Mumford prominently among such critics.

25. *Art as Experience,* 347, 350.

26. Dewey to Hu-Shih, 27 October 1939, Dewey Papers, Morris Library, Southern Illinois University; Dewey, "Pragmatic Acquiescence," 151.

27. Lewis Mumford to Van Wyck Brooks, 21 February 1927 in Robert Spiller, ed., *The Van Wyck Brooks-Lewis Mumford Letters* (New York, Dutton, 1970), 45; Max Otto to John Dewey, 7 September 1940, Max Otto Papers, State Historical Society of Wisconsin, Madison; James T. Farrell to John Dewey, 31 March 1941, Dewey Papers; Farrell, "The Faith of Lewis Mumford," *Southern Review,* 6 (1940/41): 417–38; Sidney Hook, "Metaphysics, War, and the Intellectuals," *Menorah Journal,* 28 (1940): 326–37; Meyer Schapiro, "Looking Forward to Looking Backward," *Partisan Review* 5 (July 1938): 12–24. Decades later, Mumford apparently admitted to one interviewer that, in the wake of their confrontation, he stopped reading Dewey carefully. See David R. Conrad, *Education for Transformation: Implications in Lewis Mumford's Ecohumanism* (Palm Springs, Cal.: ETC, 1976), 174. Mumford sent Dewey a copy of *Technics and Civilization,* but, as far as I know, Dewey never indicated what he thought of the book (*John Dewey's Personal and Professional Library: A Checklist,* comp. Jo Ann Boydston (Carbondale: Southern Illinois University Press, 1982), 73).

28. "A Modern Synthesis," *Saturday Review of Literature* 6 (12 April 1930, 10 May 1930): 1028, 920.

29. For a convenient discussion of Dewey's use of the terms "accommodation" and "adjustment" see his "Contributions to *A Cyclopedia of Education*" (1911), *Middle Works,* 6:359–61, 364–66.

30. Mumford, "A Modern Synthesis," 921–22, 1029; Dewey, "Ethics of Democracy," 244. Mumford's essay met with sharp objections in letters to the editor of *The Saturday Review* from two Deweyans, James Farrell and Joseph Ratner (*The Saturday Review* 6 (12 July 1930): 1194).

31. See also *The Culture of Cities* (New York: Harcourt, Brace, 1938), 152–57. In his introduction to a new edition of *The Golden Day* in 1957 Mumford gave no indication that he had changed his mind about Dewey's acquiescence to utilitarianism. He remarked that "for some of us who had been brought up in an increasingly arid mechanical civilization, committed to a pragmatic instrumentalism if not to a purposeless materialism, the youth and freshness of the Golden Day were like citrus fruits to a crew suffering from scurvy" (*GD,* xviii).

32. Waldo Frank, one of Mumford's comrade-in-arms in this campaign, did explicitly blame Dewey for liberal acquiescence to fascism. See "Our Guilt in Fascism," *The New Republic* (6 May 1940), 603–8.

33. Mumford, "The Corruption of Liberalism," *The New Republic* (29 April 1940), 568. Subsequent references to this article will be cited in parentheses in the text *(CL).* For an extended version of the argument of this essay see Mumford, *Faith for Living* (New York: Harcourt, Brace, 1940), 44–126.

34. See my "Tribune of the Technostructure: The Popular Economics of Stuart Chase," *American Quarterly* 32 (1980): 387–408.

35. Dewey, "The Economic Basis of the New Society" (1939) in Joseph Ratner, ed., *Intelligence in the Modern World: John Dewey's Philosophy* (New York: Random House, 1939), 430. Cf. Mumford: "Material organization, then, is no substitute for moral order. The final test of an economic system is not the tons of iron, the tanks of oil, or the miles of textiles it produces: the final test lies in its ultimate products—the sort of men and women it nurtures, and the order and beauty and sanity of their communites. Divorced from a system of moral and esthetic values, the most powerful industrial organization or political state completely lacks human validity" (*Faith for Living*, 146).

36. Farrell, "Faith of Lewis Mumford," 432. Mumford recognized the difficulties his late arrival as an anti-Stalinist created for him. He told Brooks in 1939 that "I reproach myself for having remained so long indifferent to the fate of Communism in Russia and so silent about the villainies of its dictatorship: the period of suspended judgement lasted too long, and the suspense has now proved almost a noose around our own necks." A few months later he revealed that "I feel deeply my own guilt during the past twenty years, when, despite my extreme skepticism of the totalitarian tyranny that was being built up in Russia, I said nothing and did nothing to counteract it" (Mumford to Brooks, 3 November 1939, 10 February 1940, *Brooks-Mumford Letters*, 167, 181). He may also have regretted his cheerful estimate of the future of Germany in the early 1930s and his discounting of the "childishness and insanity" of the Nazis ("Notes on Germany," *The New Republic* (26 October 1932), 279–81.).

37. Dewey, "No Matter What Happens—Stay Out," *Common Sense* 8 (March 1939): 11; Dewey to Max Otto, 7 July 1941, Max Otto Papers. See also *Freedom and Culture* (New York: Capricorn Books, 1939), 174–75. For Dewey's clear-eyed assessment of Nazism see his new introduction to the second edition of *German Philosophy and Politics:* "The One-World of Hitler's National Socialism" (1942), *Middle Works*, 8:421–46.

38. "The Second World War," *Modern Monthly* 9 (1935): 203–4.

39. Mumford, *Faith for Living*, 307, 232, 106, 57, 191; Mumford, *Men Must Act* (New York: Harcourt, Brace, 1939), 159.

40. Bernard K. Johnpoll, *Pacifist's Progress: Norman Thomas and the Decline of American Socialism* (Chicago: Quadrangle Books, 1970), chap. 7; Charles Howlett, *Troubled Philosopher: John Dewey and the Struggle for World Peace* (Port Washington, N.Y.: Kennikat Press, 1977), chaps. 9–10; Mumford, *Faith for Living*, 194. Dewey was joined on the Thomas committee by Van Wyck Brooks, and Brooks's anti-war stance led to a temporary breach in his friendship with Mumford. See Mumford to Brooks, 1 February 1940, and Brooks to Mumford, 7 February 1940, *Brooks-Mumford Letters*, 177–80.

41. For a consideration of the radical isolationist argument attuned to its insights as well as its substantial defects, see Frank A. Warren, *An Alternative Vision: The Socialist Party in the 1930's* (Bloomington: Indiana University Press, 1974), chap. 9. Mumford, it should be said, later emerged as a leading student of the moral disasters of the "Good War." See especially "The Morals of Extermination," *Atlantic* 204 (October 1959): 38–44.

42. Mumford, "The Aftermath of Utopianism" (1941) in Mumford, *Values for Survival* (New York: Harcourt, Brace, 1946), 63.

43. *Faith for Living*, 300, 295. On Mumford's place among a number of interwar intellectuals who adopted a tragic perspective see Richard Fox, this volume.

Wilfred McClay has recently questioned the depth of Mumford's committment to a tragic sense of life and argued he never shook a deep-seated progressivism ("Lewis Mumford: From the Belly of the Whale," *American Scholar* 57 (1988): 111–18). Sidney Hook reports that, when asked about the assertion that his philosophy failed to come to terms with the darker side of human nature, Dewey responded: "Do I have to believe that every man is born a sonofabitch even before he acts like one, and regardless of why and how he becomes one?" (Hook, *Out of Step: An Unquiet Life in the 20th Century* (New York: Harper and Row, 1987)). For a solid argument for the compatibility of tragedy and pragmatism see Hook's "Pragmatism and the Tragic Sense of Life" in his *Pragmatism and the Tragic Sense of Life* (New York: Basic Books, 1974), 3–25.

44. Daniel Rodgers, "Of Shepherds and Interlopers," *Intellectual History Newsletter* 9 (April 1987): 51–52.

45. Dewey, "The Determination of Ultimate Values or Aims Through Antecedent or a Priori Speculation or Through Pragmatic or Empirical Inquiry" in National Society for the Study of Education, *Thirty-seventh Yearbook* (Bloomington, Ill.: Public School Publishing Co., 1938), 472, 474. See also "Philosophy and Democracy" and *Experience and Nature*, chap. 10. On the decline of the public intellectual see Thomas Bender, *New York Intellect* (New York: Knopf, 1987) and Russell Jacoby, *The Last Intellectuals* (New York: Basic Books, 1987).

46. Jeffrey Stout, "Liberal Society and the Language of Morals," *Soundings* 69 (1986): 56.

RICHARD WIGHTMAN FOX: Tragedy, Responsibility, and the American Intellectual, 1925–1950

1. My analysis of the tragic character of 1930s radicalism complements Warren Susman's view that it was as conservative as it was radical. He notes that intellectuals and others in the 1930s nostalgically invoked the category of the "people." The concept of the people took on new life precisely because so many Americans sensed that their collective existence was breaking down. Susman, "The Thirties," in his *Culture as History* (New York: Pantheon Books, 1984).

2. On the academic study of tragedy, see Richard B. Sewell, *The Vision of Tragedy*, 2nd rev. ed. (New Haven: Yale University Press, 1980), 175–76. Unamuno's *The Tragic Sense of Life* (New York: Dover, 1954; London, 1921) interprets the tragic sense as a "furious hunger for being" that meets inevitable dissatisfaction in its life-long confrontation with the fact of death. I follow Sewell (who follows Reinhold Niebuhr) in viewing the tragic sense more broadly as a tragic "vision": a vision of "the nature and destiny of man that begins with the ineluctable fact of human suffering." See Sewell, 177.

3. Quotations are from Joseph Wood Krutch, *The Modern Temper* (New York: Harcourt, Brace, 1956 (New York, 1929)), 13, 29, 84, 92, 94–95.

4. Quotations are from Lewis Mumford, *Herman Melville* (New York: Harcourt, Brace, 1929), 107, 151, 272, 279, 362. Mumford's meditation on *Moby-Dick*'s "outreaching comprehensiveness of scope"—a phrase of Melville's—is a striking statement of his own Promethean vision of treating human experience in its wholeness, of his determination to follow Melville in (as Melville put it) "writing of this Leviathan," including in his net "the whole circle of the sciences . . . all the revolving panoramas of empire on earth and throughout the whole universe, not excluding its suburbs. Such, and so magnifying, is the virtue of a large and liberal

theme! We expand to its bulk. To produce a mighty volume you must choose a mighty theme" (151).

5. The following discussion of Niebuhr draws freely on my *Reinhold Niebuhr: A Biography* (New York: Pantheon 1985).

6. Edward Bellamy, *Looking Backward* (New York: New American Library, 1960 (1888)), 64.

7. Alfred Kazin, *Starting Out in the Thirties* (New York: Vintage Books, 1980 (1965)), 20, 106, 158. Compare the simultaneous "conservative" position of T.S. Eliot in *The Family Reunion* (1939): "To rest in our own suffering is evasion of suffering. We must learn to suffer more." (Quoted by Sewell, *Vision of Tragedy*, 180.)

8. Quotations are from Richard Wright, *Black Boy* (New York: Harper and Row, 1966, 1945), 111–12.

9. Richard Wright, *American Hunger* (New York: Harper and Row, 1977), 123. *American Hunger*, like *Black Boy*, was written in 1943–44.

10. Quotations are from Lionel Trilling, *The Middle of the Journey* (New York: Scribners, 1975), 34, 139, 299–301.

11. Reinhold Niebuhr, review of *In the Name of Sanity*, in *New York Times Book Review*, 26 September 1954, p. 31.

12. Lewis Mumford, "Alternatives to the H-Bomb," *New Leader*, 28 June 1954, pp. 7, 9; Reinhold Niebuhr, "A Century of Total War," *New Leader*, 2 August 1954, pp. 12–14. See also Niebuhr, "Editorial Notes," *Christianity and Crisis*, 19 April 1954, pp. 2–3, a response to Mumford's *New York Times* plea (following the detonation of two hydrogen bombs in March 1954) to "cease further experiments, lest our self-induced fears further upset our mental balance." Mumford went so far as to write that even the "worst alternative" to the present policy of developing the hydrogen bomb—"submission to communism—" "would still be far wiser than the destruction of civilization." Niebuhr dismissed Mumford's "hysterical reaction," observing that "Mr. Mumford does not really understand that it is not possible for an individual, and even less for a group, to choose a certain and present evil in preference to what is imagined to be a worse future one" (Mumford quoted by Niebuhr, 2).

13. The work of my co-contributors Casey Blake and Robert Westbrook on Mumford and Dewey has taught me much about both thinkers. My grateful thanks to them for their intellectual sustenance over many years.

14. Lewis Mumford, *The Condition of Man* (New York: Harcourt, Brace, 1944), 423. The conclusion to this volume is echoed a quarter-century later in the final paragraphs of *The Pentagon of Power* (New York: Harcourt, Brace, 1970), 433–35.

15. An earlier version of this essay was read to a joint colloquium of American and Hungarian historians at Princeton University, and received very helpful criticism from those present, especially Michael Rogin and David Hollinger. In its current form it benefited from the critical comments of Marsha Siefert and other participants at the Mumford conference that laid the foundation for this book.

INTRODUCTION TO PART IV

1. Mumford, *Green Memories: The Story of Geddes Mumford* (New York: Harcourt, Brace, 1947), 5.

2. Authors' interview with Mumford, January 1985.

3. Alice Kimball Smith, *A Peril and a Hope: The Scientists' Movement in America: 1945–47* (Chicago: University of Chicago Press, 1965).

EVERETT MENDELSOHN: Prophet of Our Discontent: LM Confronts the Bomb

1. *Saturday Review of Literature* (2 March 1946), 5.
2. Ibid., 6.
3. *Values for Survival,* (New York: Harcourt, Brace, 1946), v.
4. *Green Memories,* (New York: Harcourt, Brace, 1947).
5. *Values for Survival,* vii.
6. Ibid., viii.
7. "The Reasons for Fighting," *Values for Survival,* 45–60.
8. Ibid., fn. p. 52.
9. "Social Effects," *Air Affairs,* 1 (1947): 370–82; "Atom Bomb: 'Miracle' or Catastrophe," ibid., 2 (1948): 326–45; "Alternatives to Catastrophe," ibid., 3 (1950): 350–63.
10. "Technics and the Future of Western Civilization," in Lewis Mumford, *In the Name of Sanity* (New York: Harcourt, Brace, 1954), 34–62.
11. *Technics and Civilization* (New York: Harcourt Brace, 1934); *The Condition of Man* (Harcourt, Brace, 1944).
12. "An Appraisal of Lewis Mumford's 'Technics and Civilization'" (1934), *Daedalus* (Summer, 1959), 327–36.
13. *The Myth of the Machine: II. The Pentagon of Power,* (New York: Harcourt Brace Jovanovich, 1970).
14. Christopher Lehmann-Haupt, "Books of the Times, Lewis Mumford: Megacritic," *New York Times* (9 November 1970).
15. *My Works and Days: A Personal Chronicle* (New York: Harcourt Brace Jovanovich, 1979), 16.
16. Ibid.
17. "Lewis Mumford Receives 1972 National Medal," *Publisher's Weekly* 203 (1 January 1973): 32–33.
18. "Call Me Jonah!" *My Works and Days,* 527–31.
19. *Publisher's Weekly,* 33.
20. Wilfred M. McClay, "Lewis Mumford From the Belly of the Whale," *American Scholar* (Winter 1988), iii.
21. *Values for Survival,* title page.
22. See, for example, his claim: *"This means that there is no part of our modern world that we must not be ready to scrap, if the need to scrap it is the price of mankind's safety and continued development,"* from "Program for Survival," *Values for Survival,* 80.
23. Ibid., 103.
24. "Social Effects," *Air Affairs* 1 (1947): 370–82; reprinted in *In the Name of Sanity* (New York: Harcourt, Brace, 1954), 10–33, with the new title, "Assumptions and Prediction."
25. "Social Effects," 372.
26. Ibid., 374.
27. Ibid., 376.
28. Ibid., 381.

29. Ibid., 382.

30. See the recent study and "catalogue" by Paul Brians, *Nuclear Holocausts: Atomic War in Fiction, 1895–1984* (Kent, Ohio: Kent State University Press, 1987).

31. Philip Morrison, "If the Bomb Gets Out of Hand," in *One World or None*, eds. Dexter Masters and Katherine Way (New York: McGraw-Hill, 1946), 1–6.

32. Paul Boyer, *By the Bomb's Early Light* (New York: Pantheon, 1985), 284.

33. "Social Effects," 370.

34. Henri Bouché, "Comment," *Air Affairs.* 1 (1947): 416–18.

35. Lewis Mumford had been deeply impressed by Henry Adams from early in his own career and especially interested in Adam's approach to historical interpretation. See L.M.'s bibliographic note in *Technics and Civilization* (1934) citing Adam's *The Degradation of the Democratic Dogma* (1919), "Adams's attempt to adapt the Phase Rule to social phenomena, though unsound, resulted in a very interesting prediction for the final phase, which corresponds, in effect, to our neotechnic one" (448).

36. The full citation is given in *Pentagon of Power* (1970), 232. A slightly shortened version had been used in 1946 to open his essay, "Program for Survival," in *Values for Survival* (1946), 78.

37. Ibid., 78–79.

38. "Apology to Henry Adams," *Virginia Quarterly Review* 38 (1962): 196–217.

39. Pierre Curie's words are striking: "It is conceivable that radium in criminal hands may become very dangerous, and here one may ask whether it is advantageous for man to uncover natural secrets, whether he is ready to profit from it or whether this knowledge will not be detrimental to him." A full survey of other early warnings is found in Spencer R. Weart, *Nuclear Fear. A History of Images,* (Cambridge: Harvard University Press, 1988).

40. H.G. Wells, *The World Set Free* (London: Macmillan, 1914).

41. *Pentagon of Power,* 256.

42. "Program for Survival," 101.

43. A full study of the early movement by scientists is Alice Kimball Smith, *A Peril and a Hope,* (Chicago: University of Chicago Press, 1965).

44. "Gentlemen: You Are Mad!" 5.

45. *Interpretations and Forecasts: 1922–1972, Studies in Literature, History, Biography, Technics, and Contemporary Society,* (New York: Harcourt Brace Jovanovich, 1973), 380.

46. "Apology to Henry Adams," 213. There actually was one prominent physicist who withdrew after the defeat of Germany. Joseph Rotblat, who later became deeply involved in the Pugwash movement, left the atomic bomb project as a matter of conscience. His departure, however, went largely unnoticed.

47. For an introduction to his literature, see Everett Mendelsohn, "The Social Construction of Scientific Knowledge," in *The Social Production of Scientific Knowledge,* ed. Everett Mendelsohn, Peter Weingart, and Richard Whitley (Dordrecht: Reidel, 1977), 3–26.

48. The reintegration of values in science became a theme for a number of critical studies of modern science. See, for example, Morris Berman, *The Reenchantment of the World,* (Ithaca: Cornell University Press, 1981); Everett Mendelsohn, "A Human Reconstruction of Science," *Boston University Journal* 21 (Spring 1973): 42–52.

49. Mumford probes this approach fully in *The Pentagon of Power.*

50. The concept of limitation entered Mumford's work as early as "Program for Survival" (1946), 80–81, 101–7.

51. *The Myth of the Machine: I. Technics and Human Development* (New York: Harcourt, Brace and World, 1967).

52. See "Program for Survival," 82–83. Compare Mumford's claim with that made by Frances Yates in her fascinating study *Giordano Bruno and the Hermetic Tradition* (Chicago: University of Chicago Press, 1964, Vintage edition, 1969):

> Hence, may it not be supposed, when mechanics and mathematics took over from animism and magic, it was this internalisation, this intimate connection of the *mens* with the world, which had to be avoided at all costs. And hence, it may be suggested, through the necessity for this strong reaction, the mistake arose of allowing the problem of mind to fall so completely out of step and so far behind the problem of matter in the external world and how it works [455].

53. Theodore Roszak, *The Making of a Counter Culture* (New York: Doubleday, 1969); *Where the Wasteland Ends* (New York: Doubleday, 1972); Paul Feyerabend, *Against Method, Outline of an Anarchist Theory of Knowledge* (London: New Left Books, 1975).

54. *Pentagon of Power,* Preface.

55. Wiesner linked together what he perceived to be the negative criticism of science of Lewis Mumford, Herbert Marcuse, and myself! He had in mind an address I had recently given at the Radcliffe Institute and subsequently published as "A Human Reconstruction of Science," *Boston University Journal* 21 (Spring 1973): 42–52.

56. *New York Times,* (13 December 1970), Section 7: 1, 2, 38, 39. The *Times* used as a head for the review: "Science as a monstrosity, scientists as monsters—a view not bought."

57. Ibid., 39.

58. "Letters," *New York Times,* Book Review, 10 January 1971, 36, 37.

59. Ibid., 37.

60. *Times Literary Supplement* (London), 7 December 1946, 605, "The Second Fall of Man."

61. Ibid.

62. Alice Kimball Smith, *A Peril and a Hope.*

63. See Paul Boyer, *By the Bomb's Early Light,* who charts many of the responses; also see the much earlier and often overlooked study by Erwin N. Hiebert, *The Impact of Atomic Energy. A History of Responses by Government, Scientists and Religious Groups* (Newton, Kan.: Faith and Life Press, 1961).

64. A survey of this literature is found in Paul Brian's *Nuclear Holocausts;* David Dowling, *Fictions of Nuclear Disaster* (Iowa City: University of Iowa Press, 1987); and Spencer Weart, *Nuclear Fear.*

65. For a brief introduction, see Paul Boyer, *By the Bomb's Early Light,* 181f, 192f, 219–21, 233–37.

66. George F. Kennan, *Russia, the Atom and the West* (New York: Harper, 1958); and Barton Gellman, *Contending with Kennan. Toward a Philosophy of American Power* (New York: Praeger, 1984).

MICHAEL ZUCKERMAN: Faith, Hope, and Not Much Charity: The Optimistic Epistemology of LM

1. Donald Miller, ed., *The Lewis Mumford Reader* (New York: Pantheon, 1986), 102, 160–61, 300.

2. Ronald Weber, "Mumford But Not Vintage," *Review of Politics* 34 (1972): 107; Victor Ferkiss, "The Megamachine Reconstituted," *Commonweal* 93 (1970–71): 499; William McNeill, "A Novel Vision of Mankind's History," *Virginia Quarterly Review* 47 (1971): 299; Robert Multhauf, review of *The Myth of the Machine: II. The Pentagon of Power,* in *Technology and Culture* 13 (1972): 299.

3. Multhauf, review, 295, 296; Hiram Caton, "The Machine Profaned," *National Review* 23 (1971): 41; Miller, ed., *Mumford Reader,* 300, 301, 102, 160–61.

4. Lewis Mumford, *Sketches from Life: The Autobiography of Lewis Mumford: The Early Years* (Boston: Beacon Press, 1982), 142–43.

5. Lewis Mumford, *The Story of Utopias* (New York: Boni and Liveright, 1922), 298, 279–81, 307, 281. (For a very different view of Mumford's relation to Dewey, see Westbrook essay, this volume; for a view closer to Mumford's own autobiographical account, see Molesworth essay, this volume, 249–50. On Mumford and Geddes, see Williams essay, this volume, 46, 48, 50–65.)

6. For a treatment of the technological phases of the earlier formulation that does not emphasize dialectical automaticity, see Williams essay, this volume, 56–62.

7. Miller, ed., *Mumford Reader,* 301.

8. Mumford, *Sketches,* 142; Lewis Mumford, *The Myth of the Machine: II. The Pentagon of Power* (New York: Harcourt Brace Jovanovich, 1970), 444 (hereafter cited as *TPoP*).

9. Mumford, *Utopias,* 171–72. (For an alternative view of Mumford as abidingly, at bottom, an "axiologist" and a thinker consistently concerned to deny dichotomies of means and ends, facts and values, inner and outer realities, see Molesworth essay, this volume, passim.)

10. Lewis Mumford, *The Myth of the Machine: I. Technics and Human Development* (New York: Harcourt, Brace & World, 1967), 7, 36, 8 (hereafter cited as *T&HD*).

11. *T&HD,* 27, 39, 26, 27.

12. Ibid., 40, 6–7, 43.

13. Ibid., 4, 95, 20–21.

14. Ibid., 43–44.

15. Ibid., 9, 4, 22. (For further discussion of *Homo sapiens* and *Homo faber,* see Miller essay, this volume, 157–58, and passim.)

16. *T&HD,* 48, 49, 50.

17. Ibid., 48, 50, 49, 54.

18. Ibid., 11, 50–51; see also, e.g., 10, 204.

19. Ibid., 50–51, 57, 63.

20. Ibid., 8, 9.

21. Ibid., 63, 66–67.

22. Ibid., 111, 150, 111; see also, 151, 252, 253.

23. Ibid., 123, 136, 132, 123. For Mumford's critique of claims that earliest *Homo sapiens* was a hunter, and his alternative affirmation of the primacy from the first of the body, of the female, and especially of wits rather than weapons, see 99–101. For his argument that, even in mechanization, humans mechanized themselves before they mechanized their tools or other amplifications of their power, see 168.

24. Ibid., 153, 216.

25. Ibid., 153, 150. See also 71, 120, 146–47, 218, 254.

26. Ibid., 136, 163–64, 167, 173, 175, 263. (For the role of religion in the

megamachine, and for a fuller treatment of the megamachine more generally, see Miller essay, this volume, 153–57.

27. *T&HD*, 218, 217, 286, 361, 290.

28. Langdon Winner, *Autonomous Technology: Technics-out-of-Control as a Theme in Political Thought* (Cambridge: MIT Press, 1977), 152–53.

29. *TPoP*, 80.

30. Ibid., 92–3, 91, 94, 84, 100–101.

31. Ibid., 187, 292, 260–61; see also 186, 224, 290, 319–20, 336.

32. Ibid., 253, 338, 340–41, 399, 368; see also 210–12, 298, 358.

33. Ibid., 368–70; see also 378.

34. Ibid., 255.

35. Ibid., 76; see also 75, 78, 92–93, 98, 191, 210–11, 224–28, 243, 276, 279.

36. Miller, ed., *Mumford Reader*, 302.

37. Jacques Ellul, *The Technological Society*, trans. John Wilkinson (New York: Knopf, 1964), xxxii–xxxiii, xvii–xviii.

38. Ibid., 79–81, 55, 207–8, 215, 263–65, 301–3; Mumford, *T&HD*, 224.

39. *T&HD*, 199.

40. Ibid., 189, 190, 199.

41. Ibid., 229, 230, 190, 230.

42. Ibid., 231, 190.

43. Weber, "Mumford But Not Vintage," 108; Ferkiss, "The Megamachine Reconstituted," 499–500.

44. *T&HD*, 258.

45. Ibid., 190; *TPoP*, 246, 303, 313, 312.

46. *TPoP*, 344, 347, 348.

47. Ibid., 351, 350, 352, 348, 351, 352.

48. Ibid., 352; *T&HD*, 258, 259, 260, 261.

49. *TPoP*, 250–51, 360–67, 408.

50. For an assessment more fully attentive to that bleak drift, see Mendelsohn essay, this volume, passim.

Index

Page numbers in *italics* refer to illustrations.